Second Edition

Principles of DATABASE SYSTEMS

JEFFREY D. ULLMAN
Stanford University

COMPUTER SCIENCE PRESS

Computer Science Press, Inc.
1803 Research Boulevard
Rockville, Maryland 20850

5 6 7 8 9 10 11 12 Printing   Year 89 88 87 86 85

Cover concept by Jeffrey D. Ullman

Cover artist Ruth Ramminger

Library of Congress Cataloging in Publication Data

Ullman, Jeffrey D., 1942–
   Principles of database systems.

   (Computer software engineering series)
   Bibliography: p.
   Includes index.
   1. Data base management. I. Title. II. Title:
Database systems. III. Series.
QA76.9.D3U44   1983   001.64   82-2510
US ISBN 0-914894-36-6   AACR2
UK ISBN 0-273-085948

PREFACE TO THE FIRST EDITION

It is evident that a course in database systems now plays a central role in the undergraduate and graduate programs in computer science. However, unlike the more traditional and better established systems areas, like compilers and operating systems, where a good mix of principles and practice was established many years ago, the subject matter in database systems has been largely descriptive.

This book is developed from notes I used in a course at Princeton that attempted to bring database systems into the mainstream of computer science. The course was taught to a mix of seniors and first-year graduate students. In it, I tried to relate database ideas to concepts from other areas, such as programming languages, algorithms, and data structures. A substantial amount of descriptive material was included, since students, being used to conventional programming languages, may find query languages rather unusual. The data structures relevant to databases are also somewhat different from the kinds of structures used in conventional programming, since the large scale of a database makes practical many structures that would be only of theoretical interest otherwise.

However, I added to the mix of topics the relevant theory that is now available. The principal concepts that have been found useful are concerned with relations and with concurrency. I have devoted a large portion of the book to a description of relations, their algebra and calculus, and to the query languages that have been designed using these concepts. Also included is an explanation of how the theory of relational databases can be used to design good systems, and a description of the optimization of queries in relation-based query languages. A chapter is also devoted to the recently developed protocols for guaranteeing consistency in databases that are operated on by many processes concurrently.

Exercises

Each chapter includes exercises to test basic concepts and, in some cases, to extend the ideas of the chapter. The most difficult exercises are marked with a double star, while problems of intermediate difficulty have a single star.

Acknowledgments

I am grateful for the comments and suggestions I received from Al Aho, Brenda Baker, Peter deJong, Ron Fagin, Vassos Hadzilacos, Zvi Kedem, Hank Korth, and Joseph Spinden. The initial draft of this manuscript was ably typed by Gerree Pecht. Her efforts and the support facilities at Princeton University are appreciated.

J. D. U.

PREFACE TO THE SECOND EDITION

The appearance of a large number of interesting and important developments in the database field prodded me to make a substantial revision of the book. The general direction of changes is towards more prominence for the relational model and systems based on that model. I have therefore simplified the material on the hierarchical and network models; however, I brought it up to the front of the book, so there will be some slight tendency for that material to be covered in a course of limited scope, as it should be. The other major changes to the book are the following.

1. The material on optimization has been expanded, by including a discussion of the System R approach to optimization, tableau-based methods, and optimization in the distributed environment.

2. There is a discussion of universal relation systems, which are relational database systems that support a user view that looks like a single relation.

3. Concurrency control by "optimistic," or timestamp-based methods has been introduced.

4. Distributed systems are covered, both for optimization issues and concurrency control.

5. A discussion of data structures for range queries appears.

6. There is an introduction to generalized dependencies and their inference.

Mapping the Old Edition to the New

Those familiar with the first edition will notice that some material has been moved around. A brief guide for finding the transplanted material follows.

Material from the old Chapters 1 and 2 is still there, along with some additional material. The old Chapter 3 has been split up. Introductory material from there now appears in Chapter 1, while some material on the network model (Section 3.2) has been combined with the old Chapter 7 to form the new Chapter 3. Section 3.3 on the hierarchical model has been combined with some of the material from the old Chapter 8 to form the new Chapter 4. Some of the IMS-specific material from Chapter 8 has been removed.

Chapter 4, on the relational model, has been divided into Chapters 5 and 6. Chapter 5 now contains relational algebra and calculus, and all the material on physical organization for relational systems. The query langauges themselves are described in Chapter 6. The old Section 3.4, comparing the various models, now appears in Chapter 5. The old chapters 5, 6, 9, and 10 have been renumbered 7, 8, 10, and 11, and some new material added.

About the Cover

It's a "data baste," get it? No? Uh, well, the chef has this bulb baster, see, and $\cdots$, aw, forget it.

More Acknowledgements

The following people made comments on the first edition or made suggestions that were helpful in the preparation of the second edition: Dan Blosser, Martin Brooks, Mary Feay, Shel Finkelstein, Kevin Karplus, Arthur Keller, Keith Lantz, Dave Maier, Dan Newman, Mohammed Olumi, Shuky Sagiv, Charles Shub, and Joe Skudlarek. Their thoughts are much appreciated.

The second edition was prepared using Don Knuth's TEX typesetting system. I would also like to thank Luis Trabb-Pardo for invaluable assistance debugging my attempts to use the system.

J. D. U.

TABLE OF CONTENTS

1

INTRODUCTION TO DATABASE
SYSTEM CONCEPTS

In this chapter we consider the principal functions of a database management system. We introduce basic concepts such as the different levels of abstraction present in such a system and the kinds of languages used to deal with the system. We then discuss a "real world" model against which to measure the capability of database systems to represent and manipulate realistic data. This model, called the "entity-relationship" model, is discussed in Section 1.3. Then, we briefly introduce three "data models," the relational, network, and hierarchical models. These are abstractions of the real world similar to the entity-relationship model, but they are more closely tuned to the needs of database system designers to deal with efficiency issues than the entity-relationship model is. Thus, it is the latter three models, rather than the entity-relationship model, that most frequently are used in database systems.

1.1 AN OVERVIEW OF A DATABASE SYSTEM

Let us consider an enterprise, such as an airline, that has a large amount of data kept for long periods of time in a computer. This data might include information about passengers, flights, aircraft, and personnel, for example. Typical relationships that might be represented include bookings (which passengers have seats on which flights?) flight crews (who is to be the pilot, copilot, etc., on which flights?), and service records (when and by whom was each aircraft last serviced?).

Data, such as the above, that is stored more-or-less permanently in a computer we term a *database*. The software that allows one or many persons to use and/or modify this data is a *database management system* (DBMS). A major role of the DBMS is to allow the user to deal with the data in abstract terms, rather than as the computer stores the data. In this sense, the DBMS acts as an interpreter for a high-level programming language, ideally allowing the user to specify what must be done, with little or no attention on the user's part to the detailed algorithms or data representation used by the system.

However, in the case of a DBMS, there may be far less relationship between the data as seen by the user and as stored in the computer, than between, say, arrays as defined in a typical programming language and the representation of those arrays in memory.

The database management system is one of the most complex varieties of software in existence. One way to get a feel for the different aspects of a DBMS is to consider the various kinds of users of such a system and the ways they interact with the system and with each other.

The Programmer/User and His Interaction with the System

Thinking again in terms of the airline database, the assistant operations manager has had some training as a programmer, and if he wants to find out what planes are being repaired and where they are located, he might formulate his query in a *query language* or *data manipulation language* (DML), and it might come out something like

> PRINT Plane, Location
> WHERE Status= "broken"

Figure 1.1 shows what happens to such a query; it is represented by the query Q_1. First it is handled by a query processor, which is like a compiler for the query, although the output of this "compiler" is not machine language but rather a sequence of commands that are passed to other parts of the database management system. The query processor needs to know about the structure of the database, and we have shown it in Fig. 1.1 accessing information called the "database description." This information is needed so terms like "Plane" or "Status" can be interpreted in the context of the particular database system. Optimization of the query may also be attempted at this stage, since the speed with which the query can be answered may depend on the choices made by the query processor as to the sequence of steps to be taken by the system. We discuss optimization of queries in Chapter 8.

Many database systems are "ad hoc," in the sense that the software represented by the rectangles in Fig. 1.1 are written for the purpose of the database at hand only. In that case, the information about the database may be built into the query processor itself. Other database systems are built from commercial products; the various pieces of software shown in Fig. 1.1 are supplied by a vendor who has written them to deal with any, or almost any, database his customers may want. In that case, the tables referred to as a database description are essential, since the general-purpose query processor can have no built-in knowledge of the particular database. The description of the database is written in a specialized language called a *data definition language* or DDL, and is compiled into tables that are used by the rest of the DBMS.

The processed query is passed to a collection of routines that we shall term

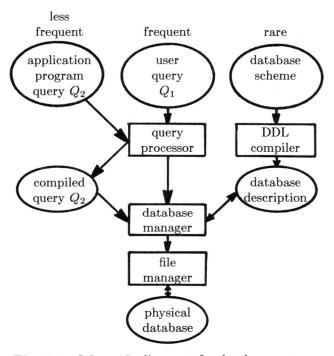

Fig. 1.1. Schematic diagram of a database system.

the *database manager*. One role of the database manager is to translate the query into terms that the file manager can understand, that is, into operations on files, rather than on the more abstract data structures of the database description. The *file manager* may be the general-purpose file system provided by the underlying operating system, or it may be a specialized file system that knows about the particular ways in which the data of the database is stored. The translation of the query into operations on files may be less than trivial, since the database could be represented by complex file structures such as are discussed in Chapter 2; the purpose of these structures is to make access and manipulation of the database as rapid as possible.

The database manager is frequently given several other tasks to perform, such as the following.

1. *Security.* Not every user should have access to all the data. For example, if personnel records are kept, only key personnel with the right and need to know salaries should be able to access this data. The user has presumably identified himself by password to the database manager, and it knows, perhaps from tables included with the database description, that this person is entitled to access data about salaries. We shall discuss the security

aspect of a DBMS in Chapter 10.

2.   *Integrity.* Certain kinds of *consistency constraints,* (i.e., required properties of the data) can be checked by the DBMS, if it is told to do so. It is useful to have such checks made whenever a user gives a command in the data manipulation language to insert, delete, or change some data. Easiest to check are properties of values, such as the requirement that the number of passengers booked on a flight does not exceed the capacity of the aircraft. Somewhat harder to check are structural requirements involving equalities and inequalities of values, without reference to the values themselves (e.g., two aircraft may not be assigned to the same flight). Chapter 7 covers some aspects of structural integrity; Chapter 10 discusses integrity in general.

3.   *Synchronization.* Often many users are running programs that access the database at the same time. The DBMS should provide protection against inconsistencies that result from two approximately simultaneous operations on a data item. For example, suppose that at about the same time, two reservation clerks issue requests to reserve a seat on flight 999. Each request results in the execution of a program that might examine the number of seats available (say one seat is left), subtracts one, and stores the resulting number of seats in the database. If the DBMS does not sequence these two transactions (the two invocations of the reservation program) properly, two passengers might wind up sitting in the same seat. We shall investigate measures for assuring proper synchronization in Chapter 11. Chapter 12 covers some of the more complex problems that occur when the database is not only accessed concurrently by several processes, but the processes and data may be distributed over several machines in widely separated locations.

The Naive User

While the assistant operations manager may have some programming ability, his boss, the operations manager may choose not to develop such a capability. He would rather type a single command like

  RUN REPAIRS

and have the information printed out for him.

 Similarly, the reservations clerk will sit at a terminal and type a command such as BOOK. The program invoked would engage in a dialog with the clerk, asking him for information in a fixed order, e.g. "enter name of passenger," and "enter desired flight number." Obtaining the requisite information from the clerk, the program interrogates the database to determine if space is available and, if so, modifies the database to reflect the reservation; if not, the program so informs the clerk.

The Applications Programmer

Programs such as REPAIRS or BOOK that are stored permanently and are available to users are called *applications programs*. Their creation is the responsibility of the *applications programmer*, a professional who writes and maintains programs written in the data manipulation language. The path taken by such a program is shown in Fig. 1.1 as the query Q_2. This program is written once, or perhaps a few times as needs change. It is compiled by the query processor and stored in the file system. The stored, compiled version can be invoked by commands, and it need not go through the compilation and optimization processes again (unless the database description has changed since the last time it was used).

The Database Administrator

We have shown in Fig. 1.1 a path labeled "rare" in which the database description itself is changed. That is, the data definition language program that describes the database is modified and recompiled into a new description that replaces the old. This operation is indeed an infrequent but important one, and a high-level person, generally called a *database administrator*, is granted responsibility for matters that deal with the database as a whole, while individual queries and manipulations of the database are handled by the applications programmers and users. Some of the responsibilities of the database administrator or his staff are the following.

1. The creation of the original description of the database structure and the way that structure is reflected by the files of the physical database.
2. The granting to the various users of authorization to access the database or parts of it.
3. Modification of the database description or its relationship to the physical organization of the database, should experience indicate that another organization would prove more efficient.
4. Making backup copies of the database and repairing damage to the database due to hardware or software failures or misuse.

1.2 BASIC DATABASE SYSTEM TERMINOLOGY

In this section we shall elaborate upon the concepts introduced in the previous section and develop them more precisely. There are several kinds of distinctions we must make when talking about a database system. We shall begin by discussing three levels of abstraction used in describing databases. We shall also emphasize the scheme/instance dichotomy, that is, the distinction between plans for a thing and the thing itself. Finally, we shall discuss the two different kinds of languages used in a database system, those for data definition and those for data manipulation.

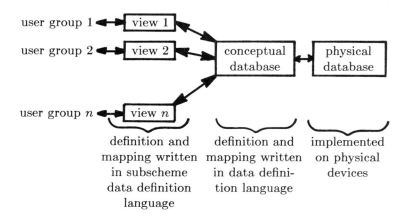

Fig. 1.2. Levels of abstraction in a database system.

Levels of Abstraction in a DBMS

It should be obvious that between the computer, dealing with bits, and the ultimate user dealing with abstractions such as flights or assignment of personnel to aircraft, there will be many levels of abstraction. A fairly standard viewpoint regarding levels of abstraction is shown in Fig. 1.2. There we see a single database, which may be one of many databases using the same DBMS software, at three different levels of abstraction. It should be emphasized that only the physical database actually exists.

The physical database resides permanently on secondary storage devices, such as disks and tapes. We may view the physical database itself at several levels of abstraction, ranging from that of records and files in a programming language such as Pascal, through the level of logical records, as supported by the operating system underlying the DBMS, down to the level of bits and physical addresses on storage devices. In this book we shall concentrate on the level of files and simple data structures. Chapter 2 will discuss the principal data structures used to implement a physical database, while Chapters 3, 4, and 5 point out the special data structures suitable for certain kinds of database systems.

The *conceptual database* is an abstraction of the real world pertinent to an enterprise. It is roughly at the level of passengers, flights, and so on, which we have discussed in connection with the enterprise of an airline. A DBMS provides a data definition language to specify the conceptual scheme and, most likely, some of the details regarding the implementation of the conceptual scheme by the physical scheme. The data definition language is a high-level language, enabling one to describe the conceptual database in terms of a "data model." An example of a suitable data model is the directed graph (the *network model* in the jargon), where nodes represent sets of similar entities (e.g., all passengers, or all flights) and arcs represent associations (e.g., the assignment of aircraft to flights). Section 1.4 discusses the three major data models, network, relational, and hierarchical, in overview, while Chapters 3–5 discuss them in detail.

A *view* or *subscheme* is an abstract model of a portion of the conceptual database. Many, but not all, database management systems provide a facility for declaring views, called a *subscheme data definition language* and a facility for expressing queries and operations on the views, which would be called a *subscheme data manipulation language*.

As an example of the utility of views, an airline may provide a computerized reservation service, consisting of data and a collection of programs that deal with flights and passengers. These programs, and the people who use them, do not need to know about personnel files or the assignment of pilots to flights. The dispatcher may need to know about flights, aircraft, and aspects of the personnel files (e.g., which pilots are qualified to fly a 747), but does not need to know about personnel salaries or the passengers booked on a flight. Thus, there may be one view of the database for the reservations department and another for the dispatcher's office.

In a sense, a view is just a small conceptual database, and it is at the same level of abstraction as the conceptual database. However, there are senses in which a view can be "more abstract" than a conceptual database, as the data dealt with by a view may be constructable from the conceptual database but not actually present in that database.

For a canonical example, the personnel department may have a view that includes each employee's age. However, it is unlikely that ages would be found in the conceptual database, as ages would have to be changed each day for some of the employees. Rather, it is more likely that the conceptual database would include the employee's date of birth. When a user program, which believed it was dealing with a view that held age information, requested from the database a value for an employee's age, the DBMS would translate this request into "current date minus date of birth," which makes sense to the conceptual database, and the calculation would be performed on the corresponding data taken from the physical database.

Example 1.1: Let us illustrate the difference between physical, conceptual, and view levels of abstraction by an analogy from the programming languages world. In particular, we shall talk about arrays. On the conceptual level, we might use an ordinary declaration such as

integer array $A[1..n; 1..m]$

while on the physical level we might see the array A as stored in a block of consecutive storage locations, with $A[i, j]$ in location $a_0 + 4(m(i - 1) + j - 1)$. A view of the array A might be formed by declaring a function $f(i)$ to be the

sum from $j = 1$ to m of $A[i,j]$. In this view, we not only see A in a related
but different form, as a function rather than an array, but we have obscured
some of the information, since we can only see the sums of rows, rather than
the rows themselves. $\square$

Let us remark that the physical level of the database is clearly marked in
our original picture, Fig. 1.1. The conceptual and view levels were not made
explicit in that figure. They are embodied in the "database description," which
is really a description of the conceptual database, of the relationship between
the conceptual and physical databases, of any views that may be defined, and
of the relationship between the views and the conceptual database. The query
processor accepts queries that are about a view (if the system uses views) or
about the conceptual database itself, and translates them into sequences of
commands that make sense to the physical database.

Schemes and Instances

In addition to the gradations in levels of abstraction implied by Fig. 1.2, there
is another, orthogonal dimension to our perception of databases. When the
database is designed, we are interested in plans for the database, while when it
is used, we are concerned with the actual data present in the database. Note
that the data in a database changes frequently, while the plans remain the same
over long periods of time (although not necessarily forever).

The current contents of a database we term an *instance of the database*.
The terms *extension of the database* and *database state* also appear in the
literature, although we shall avoid them here.

Plans consist of an enumeration of the types of entities that the database
deals with, the relationships among these types of entities, and the ways in
which the entities and relationships at one level of abstraction are expressed at
the next lower (more concrete) level. The term *scheme* is used to refer to plans,
so we talk of a *conceptual scheme* as the plan for the conceptual database, and
we call the physical database plan a *physical scheme*. The plan for a view is
often referred to simply as a *subscheme*. The term *intension* is sometimes used
for "scheme," although we shall not use it here.

Example 1.2: Let us again illustrate the concepts of scheme and instance with
an analogy from programming languages. Figure 1.3 shows a two-dimensional
table of how a file might be seen. In the upper row we see schemes on the
physical and conceptual levels; we have omitted the view level because the
analogy is hard to make. The lower level shows example instances that match
the scheme above. $\square$

Data Independence

The chain of abstractions of Fig. 1.2, from view to conceptual to physical

	Physical	Conceptual	View
Scheme	Zap = directory block plus pointers to blocks holding file	Zap: **file of integer**	?
Instance		Zap: 7,4,9,0,...	?

Fig. 1.3. Schemes and instances at different levels.

database, provides two levels of "data independence." Most obviously, in a well-designed database system the physical scheme can be changed by the database administrator without altering the conceptual scheme or requiring a redefinition of subschemes. This independence is referred to as *physical data independence*. It should be realized that modifications to the physical database organization can affect the efficiency of application programs, but it will never be required that we rewrite those programs just because the implementation of the conceptual scheme by the physical scheme has changed. The advantage to physical data independence is that it allows "tuning" of the physical database for efficiency while permitting application programs to run as if no change had occurred.

The relationship between views and the conceptual database also provides a type of independence called *logical data independence*. As the database is used, it may become necessary to modify the conceptual scheme, for example, by adding information about different types of entities or extra information about existing entities. Thus, an airline may one day discover it has to provide to the Environmental Protection Agency data about the pollution and noise levels of its flights, while the relevant information about its aircraft is not now in the database and must be added.

Many modifications to the conceptual scheme can be made without affecting existing subschemes, and other modifications to the conceptual scheme can be made if we redefine the mapping from the subscheme to the conceptual scheme. Again, no change to the application programs is necessary. The only kind of change in the conceptual scheme that could not be reflected in a redefinition of a subscheme in terms of the conceptual scheme is the deletion of information that corresponds to information present in the subscheme. Such changes would naturally require rewriting or discarding some application programs.

Database Languages

In ordinary programming languages the declarations and executable statements
are all part of one language. In the database world, however, it is normal to
separate the two functions of declaration and computation into two different
languages. The motivation is that, while in an ordinary program, the program
variables exist only while the program is running, in a database system, the
data exists "forever," and it may be declared once and for all. Thus, a separate
definition facility is a distinct convenience.

As we have mentioned, the conceptual scheme is specified in a language,
provided as part of a DBMS, called the data definition language. This language
is not a procedural language, but rather a notation for describing the types of
entities, and relationships among types of entities, in terms of a particular data
model. The data definition language is used when the database is designed,
and it is used when that design is modified. It is not used for obtaining or
modifying the data itself. The data definition language almost invariably has
statements that describe, in somewhat abstract terms, what the physical layout
of the database should be. Detailed design of the physical database is done by
DBMS routines that "compile" statements in the data definition language.

The description of subschemes and their correspondence to the conceptual scheme requires a *subscheme data definition language,* which is often
quite similar to the data definition language itself, although in some cases the
subscheme language could use a data model different from that of the data
definition language. There could, in fact, be several different subscheme languages, each using a different data model.

Manipulation of the database requires a specialized language, called a data
manipulation language or query language, in which to express commands such
as:

1. Retrieve from the database the number of seats available on flight 999 on
   July 20.
2. Set to 27 the number of seats available on flight 123 on August 31.
3. Find some flight from ORD (O'Hare airport in Chicago) to JFK (Kennedy
   airport in New York) on August 24.
4. Retrieve all flights from ORD to JFK on August 24.

Not all data manipulation languages are capable of obtaining unspecified
quantities of data in one step, as typified by command (4). In many such
languages, one issues a command like (3), to obtain the first such flight and then
a command like "get next flight from ORD to JFK on August 24" repeatedly
until the response "no more" is received.

It is usually necessary for an application program to do more than manipulate the database; it must perform a variety of ordinary computational tasks.
For example, in the previous section we mentioned an application program

program in ordinary programming language	program in extended programming language
$A := B + C$	$A := B + C$
CALL GET($\cdots$)	##GET($\cdots$)
CALL STORE($\cdots$)	##STORE($\cdots$)

Fig. 1.4. Two styles of host language.

called BOOK that made reservations for the airline. This program must print on and read from a terminal, make decisions (is seat_count = 0?), and do arithmetic (seat_count := seat_count−1). For these reasons, an application program is normally written in a conventional programming language, such as PL/I or COBOL, called the *host language*. The commands of the data manipulation language are invoked by the program in one of two ways, depending on the characteristics of the DBMS.

1. The commands of the data manipulation language are invoked by host-language calls to procedures provided by the DBMS. In this arrangement, the called procedures serve as the query processor in Fig. 1.1 and also invoke the lower levels of the DBMS (database and file managers).
2. The commands are statements in a language that is an extension of the host language. Possibly there is a preprocessor that handles the data manipulation statements, or a compiler may handle both host and data manipulation language statements. The commands of the data manipulation language will thereby be converted into calls to procedures provided by the DBMS, so the distinction between approaches (1) and (2) is not a great one.

The two forms of program are illustrated in Fig. 1.4. In the second column, the double #'s are meant to suggest a way to mark those statements that are to be preprocessed.

The view of the data seen by the application program is illustrated in Fig. 1.5. The solid lines represent transfer and manipulation of data, and dashed lines represent causation. Thus data transfers beteen the program's work area and the data base are caused by data manipulation commands, which are in turn invoked by the application program. Data transfer and calculation within the workspace is caused by the statements of the application program as in any ordinary programming situation.

1.3 A MODEL OF THE REAL WORLD

The preceding synopsis of a DBMS raises a number of important questions, which we shall consider in following chapters. Among these questions are:

1. What are appropriate data structures with which to implement a typical

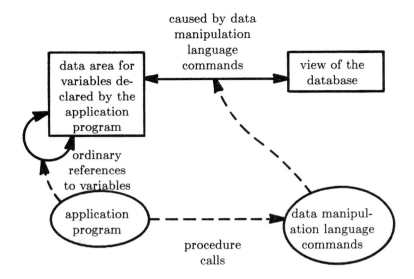

Fig. 1.5. The data seen by an application program.

physical database?

2. What are the properties of typical data, and how should it be represented by physical structures?

In order to attack these two questions, we should have a firm grasp of the kinds of information a database system would likely be required to store. Let us introduce an informal model called the *entity-relationship model* of data. This model is not a data model that has been used in data definition languages, although it is closely related to some of these models. Rather, the entity-relationship model will serve to justify the kinds of data structures and data models we introduce later, since the ability of these structures and models to represent entity-relationship structures will be apparent. It will also be intuitively clear that the entity-relationship model does an adequate, albeit imperfect, job of modeling real-world situations, such as business enterprises or the records kept by schools, hospitals, governments, and so on, where database systems are likely to be used. However, if we view the structures defined in the entity-relationship model as conceptual schemes, we shall not be grossly deceived.

Entities

The term "entity" defies an all-inclusive definition. Suffice it to say an *entity* is a thing that exists and is distinguishable; that is, we can tell one entity from another. For example, each chair is an entity. So is each person and each automobile. We could regard each ant as an entity if we had a way to distinguish one from another; otherwise we would not regard an ant as an entity. Higher-level concepts can be entities too. For example, in a biological database, terms like Arachnid, Rodent, Baboon, and Plant would be entities. If we stretch a point, concepts like love and hate are entities.

A group of all similar entities forms an *entity set*. Examples of entity sets are

1. all persons
2. all living persons
3. all automobiles
4. all emotions

Notice from examples (1) and (2), persons and living persons, that the term "similar entities" is not precisely defined, and one can establish an infinite number of different properties by which to define an entity set. One of the key steps in selecting a model for the real world, as it pertains to a particular database, is choosing the entity sets.

Attributes and Keys

Entities have properties, called *attributes,* which associate a value from a *domain* of values for that attribute with each entity in an entity set. Usually, the domain for an attribute will be a set of integers, real numbers, or character strings, but we do not rule out other types of values. For example, the entities in the entity set of persons may be said to have attributes such as name (a character string), height (a real number), and so on.

The selection of relevant attributes for entity sets is another critical step in the design of a real-world model. An attribute or set of attributes whose values uniquely identify each entity in an entity set is called a *key* for that entity set. In principle, each entity set has a key, since we hypothesized that each entity is distinguishable from all others. But if we do not choose, for an entity set, a collection of attributes that includes a key, then we shall not be able to distinguish one entity in the set from another. Often an arbitrary serial number is supplied as an attribute to serve as a key. For example, an entity set that included only U.S. nationals could use the single attribute "Social Security number" as a key.

There will be occasional cases in which the entities of an entity set are not distinguished by their attributes, but rather by their relationship to entities of another type. A most important kind of "built-in" relationship (user-defined relationships will be described subsequently) is **isa**. We say A **isa** B, read "A is a B," if entity set B is a generalization of entity set A, or equivalently, A is a special kind of B.

Example 1.3: Suppose we had a database consisting of automobiles with entity set BRANDS having attributes MAKE and MODEL. An entity in set BRANDS would be "Datsun, 280Z." We might have an entity set AUTOS with attribute SERIAL _ NO. We might also suppose SERIAL _ NO is a key for AUTO, but it is conceivable that two makes of cars use the same serial numbers. To make the entities in set AUTOS unique, we need a relationship between AUTOS and BRANDS representing the fact that an auto is of a particular brand. Then we could consider each instance of entity set AUTOS to be defined uniquely by its SERIAL _ NO and the attribute MAKE of the related entity of set BRANDS. □

Example 1.4: An example of an **isa** relationship concerns the airline database mentioned before. We may have an entity set EMPLOYEES, with attributes including EMP _ NO, a unique employee number for each employee. Another entity set PILOTS might be used. Obviously PILOTS **isa** EMPLOYEES. The entity set PILOTS might have no attributes, but only a relationship with another entity set PLANES, indicating which pilots were capable of flying 747's, DC-10's, and so on. However, because each pilot is an employee, the **isa** relationship from PILOTS to EMPLOYEES provides a unique identifier for each pilot, the EMP _ NO. □

Relationships

A *relationship* among entity sets is simply an ordered list of entity sets. A particular entity set may appear more than once on the list. If there is a relationship REL among entity sets $E_1, E_2, \ldots, E_k$, then it is presumed that a set of k-tuples named REL exists. We call such a set a *relationship set*. Each k-tuple $(e_1, e_2, \ldots, e_k)$ in set REL implies that entities $e_1, e_2, \ldots, e_k$, where e_1 is in set E_1, e_2 is in set E_2, and so on, stand in relationship REL to each other as a group. The most common case, by far, is where $k = 2$, but lists of three or more entity sets are sometimes related.

Example 1.5: Suppose we have an entity set PERSONS and we have a relationship MOTHER _ OF, whose list of entity sets is PERSONS, PERSONS. We presume that the relationship set MOTHER _ OF includes all pairs (p_1, p_2) such that person p_2 is the mother of person p_1.

An alternative way of representing this information is to postulate the existence of entity set MOTHERS and relationship MOTHERS **isa** PERSONS. This arrangement would be more appropriate if the database stored values for attributes of mothers that it did not store for persons in general. Then the relationship MOTHER _ OF would be a list of entity sets PERSONS, MOTHERS, and to get information about a person's mother as a person, we would compose (in the sense of ordinary set-theoretic relations) the relationships MOTHER _ OF and **isa**. □

Functionality

To implement a database efficiently, it is often necessary to classify relationships according to how many entities from one entity set can be associated with how many entities of another entity set. The simplest and rarest form of relationship on two sets is *one-to-one*, meaning that for each entity in either set there is at most one associated member of the other set. An example of such a situation might occur in the database of a business, where two entity sets EMPLOYEES and DEPARTMENTS exist. The relationship HEAD_OF between these two entity sets, indicating the department head of each department, might be assumed to be a one-to-one relationship. Note that the one-to-oneness of this relationship is an assumption about the real world that the database designer could choose to make or not to make. It is just as possible, in fact more plausible, to assume that the same person could head two departments, or even that a department could have two heads. However, if one head for one department is the rule in this organization, then it may be possible to take advantage of the fact that HEAD_OF is one-to-one, when designing the physical database. Also observe that a one-to-one relationship does not imply that for every entity of one set there actually exists a related entity of the other set. For example, certainly most employees are not head of any department, and there may be departments that at a given time have no head.

More common is the *many-one* relationship, where one entity in set E_2 is associated with zero or more entities in set E_1, but each entity in E_1 is associated with at most one entity in E_2. This relationship is said to be many-one *from E_1 to E_2*. That is, the relationship is a (partial) function from E_1 to E_2. For example, if each course is taught by one teacher, there is a many-one relationship TAUGHT_BY from entity set COURSES to entity set TEACHERS.

As a generalization of the many-one concept, if there is a relationship among entity sets $E_1, E_2, \ldots, E_k$, and given entities for all sets but E_i, there is at most one related entity of set E_i, then we say the relationship is many-one from $E_1, \ldots, E_{i-1}, E_{i+1}, \ldots, E_k$ to E_i.

Also common is the *many-many* relationship, where there are no restrictions on the sets of pairs of entities that may appear in a relationship set. This form of relationship is supported only with difficulty in two of the principal data models, network and hierarchical. An example of a many-many relationship is EXPORTS between entity sets COUNTRIES and PRODUCTS, since a country usually exports more than one product, and few products are exported by only one country.

Example 1.6: Let us undertake the design of a (somewhat) complete database for an airline using the entity-relationship model. Below we list the entity sets and their attributes. The domain of each attribute is declared as in a typical programming language; CHAR(n) means character string of length n, and INT(n) means integer of up to n digits. Comments are set off by /* · · · */.

1. entity set PASSENGERS with attributes:

    NAME: CHAR(30)
    ADDRESS: CHAR(30)
    PHONE: INT(10)

    NAME and ADDRESS together form a key for this entity set.

2. entity set FLIGHTS with attributes

    NUMBER: INT(3)
    SOURCE: CHAR(3) /* the source is an airport; all
        commercial aiports have three-letter codes,
        e.g. LAX, SFO, ORD, JFK */
    DEST: CHAR(3) /* the destination airport */
    DEP_TIME: INT(4) /* the departure time is given as in
        military form, e.g. 2330 for 11:30 PM */
    ARR_TIME: INT(4) /* the arrival time */

    For simplicity, we have assumed that flights never make intermediate stops, though in practice, airlines often use the same flight number for a sequence of legs of a flight. The attribute NUMBER is a key here. So is the set of attributes SOURCE, DEST, and DEP_TIME. In practice, one key, probably NUMBER because it is a singleton set, would be chosen and referred to as "the key."

3. entity set DEPARTURES with attribute

    DATE: INT(3) /* we assume dates are numbered from the
        beginning of the year, and information about flights
        is kept no more than a year in advance.
        For example, date 33 is Feb. 2 */

    Each entity of this set is a particular flight on a particular date. The attribute DATE by itself does not define an entity of this set. We shall later introduce the relationship INSTANCE_OF between DEPARTURES and FLIGHTS to define entities of set DEPARTURES completely.

4. entity set PLANES with attributes

    MANUFACTURER: CHAR(10)
    MODEL_NO: CHAR(10)

    The two attributes together form a key.

5. entity set AIRCRAFT with attribute

    SERIAL_NO: INT(5)

    We presume serial numbers are assigned by the airline and serve as a key for each aircraft owned by the airline. Note that the entity set PLANES consists of generic designations such as Boeing 747, rather than individual aircraft as are in the set AIRCRAFT.

6. entity set PERSONNEL with attributes

    EMP _ NO: INT(6) /∗ the employee number ∗/
    NAME: CHAR(30)
    ADDRESS: CHAR(30)
    SALARY: INT(6)

    EMP _ NO is a key for PERSONNEL. The fact that PERSONNEL and PASSENGERS both have attributes NAME and ADDRESS is of no significance.

7. entity set PILOTS with no attributes. We have the relationship PILOTS **isa** PERSONNEL to identify individual pilots. The reason for singling out PILOTS as a separate entity set is so that PILOTS can be related to PLANES by the relationship CAN _ FLY, while it might waste space in the database to retain this information about nonflying personnel.

The relationships, in addition to the **isa** relationship between PILOTS and PERSONNEL, are listed below.

1. relationship BOOKED _ ON between PASSENGERS and DEPARTURES, indicating reservations. This is a many-many relationship.

2. relationship INSTANCE _ OF between DEPARTURES and FLIGHTS. This relationship is many-one from DEPARTURES to FLIGHTS, since each departure has a unique flight number, although the same flight number is used from day to day.

3. relationship ASSIGNED _ TO between PERSONNEL and DEPARTURES, indicating the flight crew for each departure. This relationship is many-many.

4. relationship CAN _ FLY between PILOTS and PLANES. Here is another many-many relationship.

5. relationship TYPE between AIRCRAFT and PLANES, indicating the generic type of each aircraft. The relationship is many-one from AIRCRAFT to PLANES, since each aircraft is of one generic type, but the airline may own many DC-10's, for example.

Entity-Relationship Diagrams

It is useful to summarize the information in a design using *entity-relationship diagrams*, where

1. Rectangles represent entity sets.

2. Circles represent attributes. They are linked to their entity sets by (undirected) edges. As a special case, we sometimes identify an entity set having only one attribute with the attribute itself, calling the entity set by the

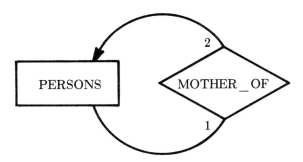

Fig. 1.6. Entity-relationship diagram of motherhood.

name of the attribute. In that case, the entity set appears as a circle attached to whatever relationships the entity set is involved in.

3. Diamonds represent relationships. They are linked to their constituent entity sets by undirected edges. Order of entity sets in the list for the relationship can be indicated by numbering edges, although the order is irrelevant unless the same entity set appears more than once on a list. However, in the case of a many-one relationship from A to B we draw an arc (directed edge) to B. More generally, if the relationship involves three or more entity sets and is many-one to some entity set A, we draw an arc to A and undirected edges to the other sets. More complicated mappings that are many-one to two or more entity sets will not be represented by an edge convention. In case of a one-one relationship, an edge with arrows at both ends is shown. As an exception, if A **isa** B, we draw an arc only to B.

Example 1.7: The diagram for the entity set PERSONS with relationship MOTHER_OF (from Example 1.5) is shown in Fig. 1.6. Figure 1.7 shows the diagram for the database scheme of Example 1.6. □

1.4 DATA MODELS

Let us now turn our attention briefly to the three most important "data models," the models that have been used in the great bulk of commercial database systems. These models, called, relational, network, and hierarchical, are each similar in many respects to the entity-relationship model, yet they have certain features that make them better tuned to the physical structures that are used to implement databases. That is, we can construct, from the description of a database in terms of one of these models, a reasonable physical organization, one in which common queries can be answered rapidly.

In general, a data model consists of two elements.

1. A mathematical notation for expressing data and relationships.
2. Operations on the data that serve to express queries and other manipula-

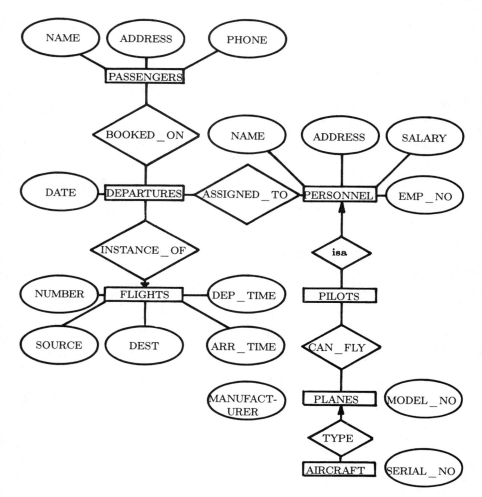

Fig. 1.7. Entity-relationship diagram of the airline database.

tions of the data.

The Relational Data Model

The mathematical concept underlying the relational model is the set-theoretic
relation, which is a subset of the Cartesian product of a list of domains. A
domain is simply a set of values. For example, the set of integers is a domain.
So are the set of character strings, the set of character strings of length 20, the
real numbers, the set $\{0, 1\}$, and so on. The *Cartesian product* of domains
$D_1, D_2, \ldots, D_k$, written $D_1 \times D_2 \times \cdots \times D_k$, is the set of all k-tuples
$(v_1, v_2, \ldots, v_k)$ such that v_1 is in D_1, v_2 is in D_2, and so on. For example,

CITY	STATE	POP
San Diego	Texas	4490
Miami	Oklahoma	13880
Pittsburg	Iowa	509

Fig. 1.8. A relation.

if we have $k = 2$, $D_1 = \{0, 1\}$, and $D_2 = \{a, b, c\}$, then $D_1 \times D_2$ is $\{(0, a), (0, b), (0, c), (1, a), (1, b), (1, c)\}$.

A *relation* is any subset of the Cartesian product of one or more domains. As far as databases are concerned, it is pointless to discuss infinite relations, so we shall assume that a relation is finite unless we state otherwise. For example, $\{(0, a), (0, c), (1, b)\}$ is a relation, a subset of $D_1 \times D_2$ defined above. The empty set is another example of a relation.

The members of a relation are called *tuples*. Each relation that is a subset of $D_1 \times D_2 \times \cdots \times D_k$ is said to have *arity* k; another term for arity is *degree*. A tuple $(v_1, v_2, \ldots, v_k)$ has k *components*; the ith component is v_i. Often we use the shorthand $v_1 v_2 \cdots v_k$ to denote the tuple $(v_1, v_2, \ldots, v_k)$.

It helps to view a relation as a table, where each row is a tuple and each column corresponds to one component. The columns are often given names, called *attributes*. The set of attribute names for a relation is called the *relation scheme*. If we name a relation REL, and its relation scheme has attributes $A_1, A_2, \ldots, A_k$, we often write the relation scheme as $REL(A_1, A_2, \ldots, A_k)$.

Example 1.8: In Fig. 1.8 we see a relation whose attributes are CITY, STATE, and POP. The arity of the relation is three. For example,

(Miami, Oklahoma, 13880)

is a tuple. The relation scheme for this relation is { CITY, STATE, POP }; if the relation were named CITYINFO, we might write the relation scheme as CITYINFO(CITY, STATE, POP). □

An Alternative Formulation of Relations

If we attach attribute names to columns of a relation, then the order of the columns becomes unimportant. In mathematical terms we view tuples as mappings from attributes' names to values in the domains of the attributes. This change in viewpoint makes certain relations equal that were not equal under the more traditional definition of a relation.

Example 1.9: Figure 1.9 shows two versions of the same relation in the set-of-mappings point of view. For example, as a mapping f, the tuple

(Buffalo, W. Va., 831)

CITY	STATE	POP		STATE	POP	CITY
Buffalo	W. Va.	831		Utah	1608	Providence
Providence	Utah	1608		W. Va.	831	Buffalo
Las Vegas	N. M.	13865		N.M.	13865	Las Vegas

Fig. 1.9. Two presentations of the same relation.

is defined by f(CITY) = Buffalo, f(STATE) = W. Va., and f(POP) = 831. Note that the order in which the tuples are listed makes no difference in either viewpoint. However, in the traditional view of a tuple as a list of values, the tuples (Buffalo, W. Va., 831) and (W. Va., 831, Buffalo) would not be the same, and the two relations of Fig. 1.9 would not be considered the same. $\square$

As existing relational database systems allow the printing of columns of a relation in any order, we shall take the set-of-mappings definition of relations as the standard one. However, there are situations, such as when we discuss relational algebra in Chapter 5, where we shall want to use the set-of-lists definition for relations. Fortunately, there is an obvious method of converting between the two viewpoints. Given a relation in the set-of-lists sense, we can give arbitrary attribute names to its columns, whereupon it can be viewed as a set of mappings. Conversely, given a relation in the set-of-mappings sense, we can fix an order for the attributes and convert it to a set of lists.

Representing Data in the Relational Model

The collection of relation schemes used to represent information is called a (*relational*) *database scheme*, and the current values of the corresponding relations is called the (*relational*) *database*. We are, of course, free to create relations with any set of attributes as a relation scheme, and we can place any interpretation we wish on tuples. However, we can see the typical pattern of usage if we recall our discussion of the entity-relationship model from Section 1.3. The data of an entity-relationship diagram is represented by two sorts of relations.

1. An entity set can be represented by a relation whose relation scheme consists of all the attributes of the entity set. Each tuple of the relation represents one entity in the entity set. If this entity set is one whose entities are identified by a relationship with some other entity set, then the relation scheme also has the attributes in the key for the second entity set, but not its non-key attributes. For example, the PILOTS entity from Example 1.6 is represented by a relation whose scheme has attribute EMP_NO from PERSONNEL and attributes for whatever information is recorded about pilots but not about personnel in general.

2. A relationship among entity sets $E_1, E_2, \ldots, E_k$ is represented by a relation

whose relation scheme consists of the attributes in the keys for each of $E_1, E_2, \ldots, E_k$. We assume, by renaming attributes if necessary, that no two entity sets in the list have attributes with the same name, even if they are the same entity set. A tuple t in this relation denotes a list of entities $e_1, e_2, \ldots, e_k$, where e_i is a member of set E_i, for each i. That is, e_i is the unique entity in E_i whose attribute values for the key attributes of E_i are found in the components of tuple t for these attributes. The presence of tuple t in the relation indicates that the entities $e_1, e_2, \ldots, e_k$ are related by the relationship in question.

Example 1.10: Let us explore a database that records baseball players, the teams they played for, their batting averages and positions played. Before showing how data of this nature can be represented as relations, let us consider the entity-relationship diagram that represents the "real world" as it pertains to this example. The entities are

1. PLAYERS, with attributes

    NAME
    HOME /* place of birth */
    BDATE /* date of birth */

    attribute NAME is a key.

2. POSITIONS, with attributes

    POSNAME /* e.g., pitcher */
    POSNUMBER /* 1 for pitcher, 2 for catcher $\cdots$ */

    Either attribute can serve as a key, but we shall take POSNAME as the key.

3. TEAMS, with attributes

    FRANCHISE /* explained below */
    CITY
    YEAR

    The FRANCHISE attribute is a unique identifier we give to a baseball franchise. As a franchise is property, it has existence as an entity even when it moves to another city or changes its name (e.g., the Cincinnati "Reds" have been called the "Redlegs" for two different periods of their history). In all example cases, we use the current name of the franchise as the value of FRANCHISE. A *team* (as opposed to a franchise) is the collection of players, coaches, etc., working for a franchise in a given year. The key for the entity set TEAMS is FRANCHISE and YEAR.

4. BA, the set of batting averages. This entity set has one attribute, whose values are three digit decimal numbers between 0 and 1. We shall identify this attribute, which clearly forms a key, with the entity set BA itself.

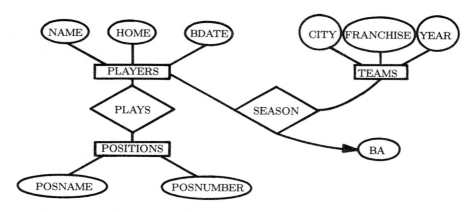

Fig. 1.10. The entity-relationship diagram for the baseball database.

Following our convention from Section 1.3, we represent the BA entity set by a circle, as if it were an attribute attached to relationships that involve entity set BA.

We shall also discuss the following relationships.

1. The relationship SEASON, between PLAYERS, TEAMS, and BA. Player p, team t and batting average b are related by SEASON if p played on team t, and his batting average was b. Notice that SEASON is a ternary relationship. It is many-one from PLAYERS and TEAMS to BA, in the sense that given a player and a team, that player has a unique batting average. Recall that a "team" exists for one particular year, so the typical player is on many teams and has many batting averages, but just one batting average per year.

2. The relationship PLAYS between PLAYERS and POSITIONS. This is a many-many relationship indicating what positions were played by a player, over the course of his career.

The entity-relationship diagram is shown in Fig. 1.10. We draw an arrow from SEASON to BA to indicate that SEASON is many-one from PLAYERS-TEAMS to BA.

The reader should observe that the notion of "season" is somewhat contrived. It's purpose is to represent the fact that the batting average is a function of both the player and the team.† Since the entity-relationship model does not permit attributes that are possessed jointly by two or more entity sets, we are forced to make the batting average an entity set by itself and connect it via a relationship to the two entity sets on which it depends.

Now let us select relation schemes to represent the entity sets and relationships. First, we have a relation scheme for each entity except BA. While there

---

† Remember that a "team" is a one-year entity; it is really the year of the team, along with the player, that detemines the batting average.

is no prohibition against a one-component relation (called a *unary* relation), such a relation would tell us nothing. It is merely a set consisting of all the possible batting averages. The three relations for the other entity sets are:

> PLAYERS(NAME, HOME, BDATE)
> TEAMS(FRANCHISE, CITY, YEAR)
> POSITIONS(POSNAME, POSNUMBER)

The relationship PLAYS is represented by a relation whose attributes form the keys for entity sets PLAYERS and POSITIONS. Each of these sets has a one-attribute key, NAME and POSNAME, respectively. Thus we introduce a relation

> PLAYS(NAME, POSNAME)

For relationship SEASON we need the keys of PLAYERS, TEAMS and BA. These are NAME, (FRANCHISE, YEAR), and BA, respectively, so we also have the relation

> SEASON(NAME, FRANCHISE, YEAR, BA)

In Fig. 1.11 we see some sample tuples that would appear in these five relations if they contained all current data.† Notice that tuples need not appear in any particular order, and we certainly do not show all of them. For example, the SEASON relation has tuples for Ruth for all years between 1914 and 1935. □

Operations on Relational Databases

We have seen the mathematical model that underlies the relational data model, but what of the operations that are necessary to make a complete data model? There are a great variety of operations that have been defined, and we shall cover in Chapters 5 and 6 both the abstract operations and their implementation in real query languages. Here, let us content ourselves with a sample only.

One way we might like to query the database is to ask for all those tuples in a certain relation that meet a certain criterion. This operation is called a *selection*. For example, we might ask, referring to the relations in Fig. 1.11, to "Print all tuples in the SEASON relation where BA is at least .300." The result would be a list in which each player would appear as many times as he batted at least .300, with the franchise, year, and average in each case.

To connect the data of two or more relations we shall define in Chapter 5 an operation called *join*, which is a generalized composition. For example, if we wish to find all the cities in which Musial played, we could find all his tuples in the SEASON relation (by a selection operation), take the FRANCHISE and YEAR components from each of these and then find the tuples in the TEAMS relation whose FRANCHISE and YEAR components matched. The

---

† Source: Turkin and Thompson *The Official Encyclopedia of Baseball,* Barnes and Co.

NAME	HOME	BDATE
Ruth, George	Baltimore, Md.	2/6/1895
Cobb, Tyrus	Narrows, Ga.	2/18/1866
Robinson, Jack	Cairo, Ga.	1/31/1919
...	...	...

PLAYERS

FRANCHISE	CITY	YEAR
Red Sox	Boston	1917
Dodgers	Brooklyn	1949
Tigers	Detroit	1911
...	...	...

TEAMS

POSNAME	POSNUMBER
Pitcher	1
Catcher	2
First base	3
...	...

NAME	POSNAME
Musial, Stanley	First base
Cobb, Tyrus	Center field
Cobb, Tyrus	First base
...	...

POSITIONS   PLAYS

NAME	FRANCHISE	YEAR	BA
Musial, Stanley	Cardinals	1948	.376
Ruth, George	Red Sox	1917	.325
Ruth, George	Yankees	1923	.393
Cobb, Tyrus	Tigers	1911	.420
Robinson, Jack	Dodgers	1949	.342
...	...	...	...

SEASON

Fig. 1.11. Part of the five relations for the baseball database.

CITY components in these TEAMS tuples are the ones we want.

The Network Data Model

Roughly, the network data model is the entity-relationship model with all relationships restricted to be binary, many-one relationships. This restriction allows us to use a simple directed graph model for data. It also makes implementation of relationships simpler, as we shall see when we discuss a concrete implementation of the network model in Chapter 3.

There is no consistent terminology for the network model, so we shall adopt our own, trying to be consistent with terms we have used, or shall use, for files and for the other data models. In place of entity sets, we shall talk about *logical record types,* in the network model. A logical record type is essentially a relation, that is, a named set of tuples. However, as in the entity-relationship model, we admit the possibility that two identical records of the same logical record type exist; these records are distinguished only by their relationship to records of another logical type. In the network model, we use the term *logical record* in place of "tuple," and *logical record format*† in place of "relation scheme." We call the component names in a logical record format *fields*.

Let us at the outset justify our decision to change terminology between the relational and the network model by reminding the reader that in the network model, logical record types are used principally to represent what we have called entity sets, while in the relational model, we use relations to represent both entities and relationships. While we cannot rule out bizarre uses of any data model, we feel it would do violence to the intuitive purposes of relations and logical record types if we tried to merge the two concepts.

Instead of "binary many-one relationships" we talk about *links* in the network model. We draw a directed graph, called a *network,* which is really a simplified entity-relationship diagram, to represent record types and their links. Nodes correspond to record types. If there is a link between two record types T_1 and T_2, and the link is many-one from T_1 to T_2, then we draw an arc from the node for T_1 to that for T_2,‡ and we say the link is from T_1 to T_2. Nodes and arcs are labeled by the names of their record types and links.

Representing Entity-Relationship Diagrams in the Network Model

As we have stated, entity sets are represented directly by logical record types. The attributes of an entity set become fields of the logical record format. In the case that an entity is determined uniquely only through a relationship with another entity, we shall add another field that is a serial number for the entity set, uniquely identifying each entity. This serial number might be a field only on the logical level; in the implementation we could use the physical location of the record representing the entity as its "serial number."

Among relationships, only those that are binary and many-one (or one-one as a special case) are representable directly by links. However, we can use the following trick to represent arbitrary relationships. Say we have a relationship

---

† We drop the word "logical" from "logical record," or "logical record type/format" whenever no confusion results.

‡ Some works on the subject draw the arc in the opposite direction. However, we chose this direction to be consistent with the notion of functional dependency discussed in Chapter 7. Our point of view is that arrows mean "determines uniquely." Thus, as each record of type T_1 is linked to at most one record of type T_2, we draw the arrow into T_2.

R among entity sets $E_1, E_2, \ldots, E_k$. We create a new logical record type T representing k-tuples $(e_1, e_2, \ldots, e_k)$ of entities that stand in the relationship R. The format for this record type might consist of a single field on the logical level that is a serial number identifying logical records of that type, although there are many situations where it is convenient to add other information-carrying fields in the format for the new record type T. We then create links $L_1, L_2, \ldots, L_k$. Link L_i is from record type T to the record type T_i for entity set E_i. The intention is that the record of type T for $(e_1, e_2, \ldots, e_k)$ is linked to the record of type T_i for e_i, so each link is many-one.

Example 1.11: Let us represent in the network model the information about baseball players and teams in the entity-relationship diagram of Fig. 1.10. First we shall have logical record types PLAYERS, TEAMS and POSITIONS. The fields of their logical record formats are the same as the attributes of the relations of the same name, from Example 1.10. There is no logical record type for entity set BA, for reasons we shall discuss in connection with the relationship SEASON.

Consider now the many-many relationship PLAYS, between PLAYERS and POSITIONS. To represent PLAYS we need a new record type, which we call PP. The record format for PP consists of a serial number PPID. There are two links, PP_PLAYERS from PP to PLAYERS, and PP_POSITIONS, from PP to POSITIONS.

We also need to represent the ternary relationship SEASON among entity sets PLAYERS, TEAMS, and BA. We create a new logical record type PTB with a serial number field named PTBID. We create links PTB_PLAYERS, from PTB to PLAYERS, and PTB_TEAMS, from PTB to TEAMS. We could also create a link from PTB to BA, but we do not need to do so, because the SEASON relationship uniquely determines a batting average, given a player and team. Thus we could include the BA attribute in the PTB record format, allowing us to avoid the existence of a BA record type and a link from PTB to BA. Notice that we could, in principle, include the attributes of PLAYERS and TEAMS in the PTB format, as well, but to do so would waste a considerable amount of space; the attribute values for each team would be repeated once for each player on the team, and the attributes of a player would be repeated once for each team he was on.

The logical record types we have defined are listed below. As for relation schemes, we use the notation $R(A_1, A_2, \ldots, A_k)$ for record type R with format $A_1, A_2, \ldots, A_k$.

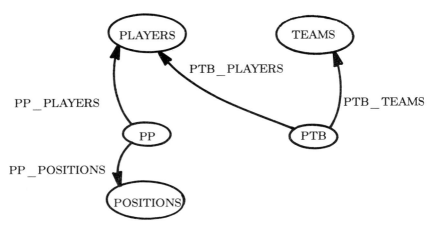

Fig. 1.12. Network for baseball database.

PLAYERS(NAME, HOME, BDATE)
TEAMS(FRANCHISE, CITY, YEAR)
POSITIONS(POSNAME, POSNUMBER)
PP(PPID)
PTB(PTBID, BA)

The links are:

    PP _ PLAYERS from PP to PLAYERS
    PP _ POSITIONS from PP to POSITIONS
    PTB _ PLAYERS from PTB to PLAYERS
    PTB _ TEAMS from PTB to TEAMS

The network is shown in Fig. 1.12.

In Fig. 1.13 we show some sample logical records of each type and the occurrences of links among these records. There may, of course, be other link occurrences involving some of the records shown. For example, the PP record with number 1 tells us that Cobb played first base, and the PTB record with number 1 says that Ruth played for the Red Sox in 1917 and batted .325. □

Operations on Networks

There are two kinds of operations we perform on network databases. First, there are selections on logical record types, which are similar to the selections on relations discussed earlier. Thus, referring to Fig. 1.13, we could print all the franchises that ever played in Boston by selecting out of the TEAMS logical record type those records with field CITY=Boston.

The other type of operation is the following of links in one direction or the other. For example, to find the highest Ty Cobb ever batted, we could follow the PTB _ PLAYERS link in reverse, from the Cobb PLAYERS record to all

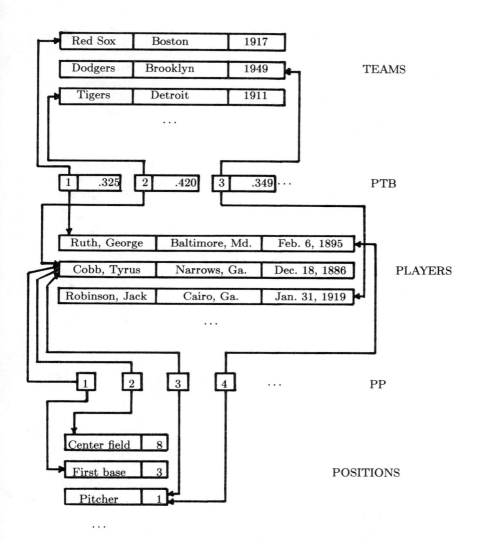

Fig. 1.13. Some logical records in the baseball database.

the associated PTB records, and examine the BA field of each of those records in turn. As another example, to find the franchise Cobb played for in 1911, we could follow the PTB_PLAYERS link in reverse, as before, and for each PTB record found, follow the PTB_TEAMS link in the forward direction to find the associated TEAMS record. The TEAMS records associated with each of these PTB records are examined until one with YEAR=1911 is found, at which time we print the FRANCHISE field of that record.

We give the process of following links, or more generally, relationships the name *navigation*. The reader should notice that in the relational model the operation of joining relations can be construed as navigation. However, we can navigate through relations that represent many-many relationships using the join, which suggests that query languages for the relational model could be made more powerful than those for the network model, where we are constrained to navigate over many-one mappings only.

While network query languages with dictions as powerful as the join could be developed, there is some validity to the intuition that relational languages have natural dictions that are more powerful than the natural dictions for network languages, as we shall see when we cover network languages in Chapter 3 and relational languages in Chapter 6. The other side of the coin is that efficient implementation of relational operations like join are difficult to achieve, while the simpler navigation of the network model can be done efficiently if we use one of several data structures discussed in Chapters 2 and 3.

The Hierarchical Data Model

A *hierarchy* is simply a network that is a *forest* (collection of trees) in which all links point in the direction from child to parent. We shall continue to use the network terminology "logical record type," and so on, when we speak of hierarchies.

Just as any entity-relationship diagram can be represented in the relational and network models, such a diagram can always be represented in the hierarchical model. However, there is a subtlety embodied in our use of the vague term "represented." In the previous two models, the constructions used to convert entity-relationship diagrams had the property that relationships could be followed easily by operations of the model, the join in the relational case and link-following in the network case. The same is true in the hierarchical model only if we introduce "virtual records," a topic we shall defer until Chapter 4. Let us content ourselves here with an example of how the baseball database might be represented in this model.

Example 1.12: Figure 1.14 shows a possible representation of the baseball database. There are three trees in the forest. Each node represents a logical record type and is displayed by a list of its fields. The children of a node represent sets of records that are associated with each record of the parent type, since the many-to-one relationship is from child to parent. For example, the tree with root PLAYERS tells us that for every player there will be a set of positions he played, a set of homes (obviously only one), and a set of birthdates (again, only one). A second tree consists only of (POSNAME, POSNUMBER) pairs; it is a tree in a trivial sense only. It is used to list the positions and their corresponding numbers. The third tree represents the franchises, with each

(POSNAME, POSNUMBER)

FRANCHISE
|
(CITY, YEAR)
|
(PLAYER, BA)

Fig. 1.14. A hierarchical scheme for the baseball database.

franchise given a number of children equal to the number of years the franchise was in existence. Each child consists of a (CITY, YEAR) pair to tell what city the franchise played in that year. Each (CITY, YEAR) pair, which represents what we have called a "team," has children for each player on the team; the child for a player indicates his name and batting average.

Let us emphasize that the many-one relationship from child logical record type to parent type is from records to records, not values to values. For example, there is a many-one relationship from POSITIONS to PLAYERS records in Fig. 1.14, meaning that each POSITIONS record is the child of only one PLAYERS record, not that each position was played by only one player. Another way to see this distinction is to imagine that the POSITIONS records have a logical field that is a serial number, as we placed in dummy records in the network model. The serial numbers represent the location of the record and are invisible on the physical level, yet they serve to distinguish different occurrences of POSITIONS records with the same data.

Figure 1.15 suggests part of a database instance of which the tree with root FRANCHISE in Fig. 1.14 is the scheme. Note that a dummy root node is introduced to reflect the fact that the root FRANCHISE really represents many different franchises stored in the database. □

Operations on Hierarchies

The basic operation on a hierarchical database is a tree walk; that is, given

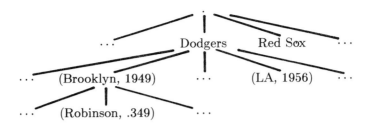

Fig. 1.15. Instance of a hierarchical database.

a node of the database instance, we scan all its descendants of a given logical record type. Thus, in the database of Fig. 1.15, we might answer the query "print those Dodgers who batted at least .300 in 1949" as follows. Beginning at the root (shown as a dot in Fig. 1.15) we find the child FRANCHISE record for the Dodgers. Then we scan the children of the Dodgers record for a (CITY, YEAR) record with YEAR=1949. Finally, we scan the children of that record, examining the BA field of each and printing the NAME field if BA≥.300.

It is important to notice that although the links in a network are bidirectional, allowing us to travel either from the many to the one or from the one to the many, in the hierarchical model, the basic operation is unidirectional, proceeding from parent to child only. That convention causes certain relationships to be hard to extract from the database, even though they may be implicit in the data. The virtual record type convention, which we discuss in Chapter 4, allows us to make direct connections that go up the tree or even from tree to tree in the forest, and thus facilitates the retrieval of facts about relationships.

EXERCISES

1.1: Many ordinary programming languages can be viewed as based on a particular data model. For example SNOBOL can be said to use a character string model of data. Can you think of any other programming languages that use a particular data model? What data models do they use? Are any of them well suited to database implementation?

1.2: Suppose that in the conceptual scheme of some enterprise, the attributes DATE, which is an integer from 1 to 366, and YEAR, an integer, appear. Suppose also that we wish to design a view in which the attributes MONTH and DAY appear. How can we define these attributes in terms of the DATE and YEAR attributes in the conceptual scheme?

1.3: Suppose we informally define the data in the database of a department store as follows.

    i)   Each employee is represented. The data about an employee are his employee number, name, address, and the department he works for.

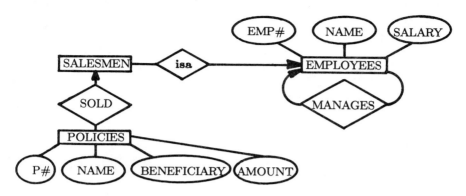

Fig. 1.16. An insurance company database.

ii) Each department is represented. The data about departments are its name, employees, manager, and items sold.

iii) Each item sold is represented. The data about items are its name, manufacturer, price, model number (assigned by the manufacturer), and an internal item number (assigned by the store).

iv) Each manufacturer is represented. The data about a manufacturer are its name, address, items supplied to the store, and their prices.

Give an entity-relationship diagram for this database. Note that some information may be represented by attributes; other information may be represented by relationships.

1.4: For the entity-relationship diagram of Exercise 1.3 indicate

a) a key for each entity set, and

b) which relationships are one-one and which are many-one.

Indicate any assumptions you make that might or might not hold depending on factors not stated in Exercise 1.3.

* 1.5: Modify the conceptual scheme for the airline database (Example 1.6) to allow flights consisting of more than one leg. That is, instead of a source and destination, a flight has an associated list of cities.

1.6: Give an entity-relationship diagram for a database showing fatherhood, motherhood and spouse relationships among men and women.

1.7: Use the entity-relationship model to describe the data connected with an organization with which you are familiar, such as a school or business.

1.8: In Fig. 1.16 we see the entity-relationship diagram of an insurance company. The keys for EMPLOYEES and POLICIES are EMP# and P#, respectively; SALESMEN are identified by their **isa** relationship to EMPLOYEES. Represent this diagram in the (a) relational (b) network (c) hierarchical models.

1.9: Figure 1.17 shows a genealogy database, with key attributes NAME and LIC#. The intuition behind the diagram is that a marriage consists of

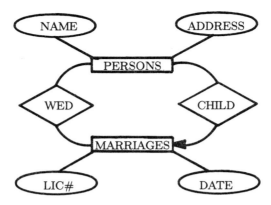

Fig. 1.17. A genealogy database.

two people, and each person is the child of a marriage, i.e., the marriage of his mother and father. Represent this diagram in the (a) relational (b) network, and (c) hierarchical models.

1.10: The recipe for *moo shoo roe* includes bamboo shoots, sliced pork, wood ears, golden needles, and assorted vegetables. *Hot and sour soup* is made from wood ears, bean curd, and golden needles, while *family style bean curd* is made from bean curd, sliced pork, and assorted vegetables.

a)   Suppose we wish to store this information in a relation RECIPE(DISH, INGREDIENT). Show the current value of the relation as a table (use suitable abbreviations for the dishes and ingredients).

b)   Suppose we wish to represent the above information as a network with record types DISH, INGREDIENT and DUMMY, where a DUMMY record represents a pair consisting of one ingredient for one dish. Suppose also that there are links USES from DUMMY to DISH and PART_OF from DUMMY to INGREDIENT. Draw the INGREDI-ENT, DISH, and DUMMY record occurrences and represent the links USES and PART_OF for this database instance.

∗ 1.11: We mentioned in Section 1.4 that two tables represent the same relation if one can be converted to the other by permuting rows and/or columns, provided the attribute heading a column moves along with the column. If a relation has a scheme with m attributes and the relation has n tuples, how many tables represent this relation?

BIBLIOGRAPHIC NOTES

The three levels of abstraction, physical-conceptual-view, appear in the "DBTG Report" (CODASYL [1971]); they are also a feature of the "ANSI/SPARC report" (ANSI [1975]), where they are called internal, conceptual, and external, respectively. Tsichritzis and Klug [1978] is an informal introduction to a revised version of that report. The three levels are present in a large number of existing database systems; we shall describe some of these systems in Chapters 3, 4, and 6. The entity-relationship model is from Chen [1976]. See also the collection of papers Chen [1980] on the subject.

A variety of other models have been proposed. Bachman [1969] was one of the earliest. The reader may wish to consult the books by Nijssen [1976], Douque and Nijssen [1976], or Tsichritzis and Lochovsky [1982], or consult the papers by Nijssen [1977] or Kerschberg, Klug, and Tsichritzis [1977] for more information.

Some more recent developments of data models include the structural model of El Masri and Wiederhold [1979] and Wiederhold and El Masri [1980], and the semantic data model of Hammer and McLeod [1981].

The subject of data manipulation languages and their role in a database system is discussed in Stonebraker and Rowe [1977].

The reader should consult the bibliographic notes for Chapters 3, 4, and 5 for references about the network, hierarchical, and relational models, respectively. Several works have been devoted to comparisons of the three models, of which we note the compendium Rustin [1974] and the issue of *Computer Surveys* edited by Sibley [1976].

The reader may also wish to consult the bibliography Kambayashi [1981].

2

PHYSICAL DATA ORGANIZATION

Before discussing design and implementation of databases further, we should first develop an understanding of what is easy and what is hard to do on the physical level. The basic problem in physical database representation is to store a *file* consisting of *records,* each record having an identical format. A *record format* consists of a list of field names, with each field possessing a fixed number of bytes and having a fixed data type. A *record* consists of values for each field. The typical operations we desire to perform on a file are:

1. insert a record.
2. delete a record.
3. modify a record.
4. find a record with a particular value in a particular field or a combination of values in a combination of fields.

The complexity of organizing a file for storage depends on the particular combination of these operations that we intend to perform on the file. If operation (4), called *lookup,* is permitted, as it usually is, we also need to consider whether desired records are specified by value, by location, or a combination of both, and whether only one or several different fields may be involved in different lookups. We shall discuss the principal file organization methods in Sections 2.2–2.5. Then in Section 2.6 we consider storage of files whose records may contain more than one value for a field; we call such records *variable length records.* Finally, Sections 2.7–2.9 discuss file organizations for handling some more general kinds of lookup.

2.1 A MODEL FOR EXTERNAL STORAGE ORGANIZATION

When we refer to "external" or "secondary" storage, we usually mean disk storage, although what we say applies to drums and, to a lesser extent, to magnetic tape or the newer kinds of circulating storage devices such as magnetic bubble memories. A file system using disk storage usually divides the disk into equal sized *physical blocks.* A typical size for a physical block is in the range 2^9 to 2^{12} bytes, but we shall not assume any particular size, except in examples. Each physical block (or just *block)* has an *address,* which is an absolute address on a disk or another storage device.

A file is stored among one or more blocks, with one or more records stored in each block. We assume there is a file system that translates between file names and the absolute addresses of the blocks occupied by the file. A block may have within it bytes that are not used for any record. Some of these are unused, while others are devoted to a *header*, which is a collection of bytes, usually at the beginning of the block, used for special purposes. For example, the header may contain information connecting the block to other blocks used to store the same file or information about how the individual bytes of the block represent the file in question.

Records have an address, which may be viewed either as the absolute address of the first byte of the record, or as the address of the block in which the record is found, together with an *offset,* the number of bytes in the block preceding the beginning of the record.

Pointers

We shall often speak of pointers to records or blocks. A pointer to a block can be its absolute address. Sometimes, secondary storage is organized as a virtual memory, and blocks or records can be pointed to by giving their offset from the beginning of an imaginary area of virtual memory,† with the file system used to translate between offsets in the area and absolute addresses. Another possible way to point to a record is to point to its block. If we choose this representation for pointers, we must be able to find the desired record within the block, once we have found the block. To do so, we must know enough about the record to identify it, a situation which comes up sufficiently frequently that we should be aware of the possibility. The advantage of pointing to blocks is that records can be moved within blocks without causing pointers to *dangle* (i.e., point to the wrong place).

Estimating the Speed of Database Operations

The basic external storage operation is the transfer of a block from secondary to main memory or vice versa; we call either operation a *block access*. It is important to note that in most present day systems, a data transfer involving secondary storage usually takes as long, or longer than searching the block for desired data once it is in main memory. Also, it is necessary in all but some hypothetical or experimental systems, to have the data in main memory before it can be used in any way. Thus when we talk about the speed of various algorithms for accessing data we shall count the number of blocks that must be read into or written from main memory, and this number will represent our

---

† Such an area can be viewed as a large random access memory, where bytes are numbered 0, 1, . . . , up to some maximum number.

estimate of the speed of the algorithm.

Interpreting Raw Data

In the simplest organization, we assume that each file has a fixed record format, although we shall later study more complex files. In each stored record of the file the fields appear in the same order, and for each field there is an associated number of bytes, which does not vary from record to record. There is also an associated data type for each field, such as character string, real, or integer, which allows us to interpret the bits of the field. As a consequence of these assumptions, if records are packed from the beginning of blocks, immediately following the header, we can decode uniquely the records of the block.

The only problem is distinguishing records from empty space, since we do not assume a block is packed with as many records as it can hold. One solution is to place a count of the number of records in the header. It is then sufficient that whatever records are in the block be packed as far forward as possible. We shall discuss some alternative schemes for distinguishing used from unused space later.

Keys

If we recall the entity-relationship model discussed in Section 1.3, we observe that files will be used to store information of two types.

1. There are files representing entity sets. Here each record represents one entity and the fields correspond to the attributes of the entity.
2. There are files representing relationships. If the relationship is many-many, we might represent the relationship by a file of records with two fields (or k fields if we had a relationship among k entity sets). Each field is of pointer type. Assuming a relationship on two entity sets, each record consists of a pair of pointers (p1, p2), where p1 points to the record for an entity of the first entity set, and p2 points to a related entity of the second entity set. If the relationship is one-to-one or many-to-one, other representations are possible and will be discussed later.

An important difference between these two types of files is that the first has a nontrivial *key,* one or more fields that together uniquely identify the record, while the second type of file is not guaranteed to have a key other than the set of all the fields. There are many cases where all interrogations of a file are of the form: given the value of the field or fields in the key, find the record.† Such queries are generally easier to handle than more general queries, and it is with these sorts of files that we shall begin our examination of file implementation.

---

† Much of what we say in this chapter is not predicated on the key uniquely defining a record. We could just as well ask for all records matching a "key" value and retrieve them all with little additional effort.

Pinned and Unpinned Records

Another issue of importance in determining a file implementation strategy is whether or not records of a file are "pinned down" to a fixed location. Records become pinned because there may exist pointers to them somewhere in the database. For example, we mentioned a possible implementation of mappings in which associated entities were represented by pairs of pointers to their records. We also mentioned in Section 1.3 the possibility of an entity being uniquely identified only by a link to some other entity, in which case the former entity's record needs a pointer to the record of the latter. In such cases, we can never move the records for these entities, or the pointers will "dangle," that is, they will no longer point to the data they pointed to at the time they were created.

In the most general case, we cannot use a file organization in which records move around (say in response to insertions of other records), as we may have no idea of where in the entire database a pointer or several pointers to a record may be. The deletion of records is also dangerous, since any pointers to them must be found or allowed to dangle. If the deleted record were replaced, the dangling pointer would then point to the new record, a clear error. Fortunately we may be able to determine that there are no pointers to records of a particular file by studying the overall database organization. In that case we have available some more flexible organizations than if we must assume that records are pinned down to their original location.

The Heap File Organization

The most obvious approach to storing a file of records is simply to list them in as many blocks as they require, although one does not generally allow records to overlap block boundaries. This organization is sometimes called a *heap* when it is necessary to dignify it with a name. The blocks used for a heap may be linked by pointers, or a table of their addresses may be stored elsewhere, perhaps on one or more additional blocks. To insert a record, we place the record in the last block if there is space, or get a new block if there is no more space. Deletions can be performed by setting a *deletion bit* in the deleted record. Reusing the space of deleted records by storing newly inserted records in their space is dangerous if pointers to records exist, as we mentioned in the previous paragraph. However, if we are sure the file is unpinned, one of a number of "garbage collection" strategies (see Aho et al. [1982], e.g.) can be used to keep track of the reusable space.

Given a key value, record lookup requires a scan of the entire heap-organized file, or at least half the file on the average, until the desired record is found. It is this operation whose cost is prohibitive if the file in question is spread over more than a few blocks. Much of the rest of this chapter is devoted to the consideration of alternative file organizations that allow arbitrary lookups without scanning more than a small fraction of the file. In designing a better file organization we must try to avoid using too much extra space, and we must refrain from making insertion and deletion too complicated. In the next four sections we describe some of the ideas that have been used.

2.2 HASHED FILES

The basic idea behind a *hashed access* file organization is that we divide the records of a file among *buckets,* which each consist of one or more blocks of storage. For each file stored in this manner there is a *hash function h* that takes as argument a value for the key of the file and produces an integer from 0 up to some maximum value. If v is a key value, $h(v)$ indicates the number of the bucket in which the record with key value v is to be found, if it is present at all.

It is desirable that h "hashes" v, that is, $h(v)$ takes on all its possible values with roughly equal probability as v ranges over likely collections of values for the key. A great deal has been said about suitable hash functions, and we do not intend to go into the subject deeply here (see Knuth [1973], e.g.). The following strategy is useful in many situations.

1.   Treat the key value as a sequence of bits, formed by concatenating together the value for each field of the key. This bit sequence is of fixed length, since each field is of fixed length.
2.   Divide the bit sequence into groups of a fixed number of bits, say 16 bits, padding the last group with 0's if necessary.
3.   Add the groups of bits as integers.
4.   Divide the sum by the number of buckets, and use the remainder as the bucket number.

In Fig. 2.1 we see a hashed file organization with B buckets. There is a bucket directory consisting of B pointers, one for each bucket. Each pointer is the address of the first block for that bucket.

A bucket consisting of only one block, such as bucket number 1 in Fig. 2.1, has in that block a header with a *null pointer,* a value that cannot be the address of a block. A bucket consisting of more than one block has in the header of the first block a pointer to the second block, in the header of the second block a pointer to the third, and so on. The header of the last block has a null pointer. For example, bucket $B-1$ in Fig. 2.1 consists of blocks b_4, b_5, and b_6.

If B is small, the bucket directory could reside in main memory; otherwise it will be stored on as many blocks as necessary, and the block of the bucket directory containing the pointer to the first block of bucket i will be called into main memory when a hash value i is computed.

The blocks each have room for a fixed number of records; If a record requires r bytes, then we assume each record begins at a multiple of r bytes

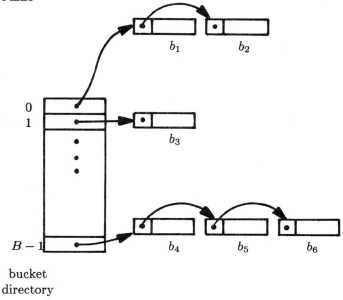

b_1 b_2

0
1
                                          b_3

$B-1$ b_4 b_5 b_6

bucket
directory

Fig. 2.1. Hashed file organization.

from the first byte following the header. The space used to hold a single record will be called a *subblock*. In certain circumstances the first r bytes could be empty while a subsequent subblock of r bytes holds a record. We assume there is some way of distinguishing full and empty subblocks of r bytes. In some circumstances, a possible but dangerous method is to place in an empty subblock a sequence of bits that could not be a real record. This is feasible if we know a bit sequence that now and forever after could not be the value of a record.

A safer method, and the one we shall assume from here on, is to place in the header one bit for each subblock, with 0 indicating that the subblock is empty and 1 indicating that it holds a record. It is sometimes useful to place in the record itself a *deletion bit,* which indicates whether the record has been deleted. It then becomes possible to avoid reusing subblocks that may have dangling pointers to them. Note the difference between an empty subblock, one that never contained a record, and a subblock containing a deleted record, which may be pointed to from elsewhere. The former is distinguished by having its full/empty bit in the header set to 0, while the latter has a full/empty bit of 1 and a deletion bit of 1.

Lookup

Suppose we are given value v, which, if there is one field in the key, is the value of that field, or, if the key consists of more than one field, is the list of values for the fields of the key, in a fixed order. We compute $h(v)$, which gives us a bucket number, say i. We consult the bucket directory to find the first block for bucket i. Next, search each nonempty subblock in the block to see if it holds a record with key value v. If so we have found the record. If the record is not found, and the header of the block has a pointer to further blocks in bucket i, search each of these blocks in turn until either the record with key value v is found, or the last block on the chain of blocks for bucket i has been searched.

Modification

Suppose we must modify one or more fields of the record with key value v. If some field to be modified is part of the key, treat this modification as a deletion followed by an insertion (insertion will be described subsequently), since the modified record probably belongs in a different bucket.† If the key value is not to be modified, search for the record with key value v as described under "lookup." If found, modify the fields of the record as desired. If the record is not found we have an error, as it makes no sense to modify a nonexistent record.

Insertion

Apply the previously described lookup procedure. If a record with the given key value v is found, there is an error, as it does not make sense to insert a record if it or a record with the same key value is present. (Perhaps the programmer intended to modify rather than insert.) Having determined that there is no existing record with key value v, we find the first empty subblock in the blocks for bucket $h(v)$. The location of this subblock can be remembered as we search the bucket in the lookup procedure.‡ Place the record to be inserted in this subblock. If no empty subblocks exist in all the blocks of the bucket $h(v)$, call upon the file system to provide a new block. Place in the header of the last block for the bucket a pointer to this new block, and in the header of the new block put the null pointer. Place the inserted record in the first subblock of the new block.

Deletion

To delete the record with key value v, use the lookup procedure to find the record. We may simply make the subblock for this record empty by setting to 0 its full/empty bit in the header. So doing makes the subblock available for reuse. However, if there may be pointers to records, we don't want to allow the

† If records are pinned, it is not possible to make such a modification.

‡ A subblock can only become empty in the middle of a bucket if deletions actually result in disappearance of a record, rather than the setting of a deletion bit. The former strategy is safe only if no pointers to records in the file exist.

subblock to be refilled, as a dangling pointer may then erroneously point to the new record. In this case, we leave the full/empty bit for the deleted record at 1, so its subblock cannot be refilled, and we set a deletion bit in the record itself to 1, indicating the record has been deleted. Then if we ever follow a pointer to the deleted record, we know the pointer is dangling, and the pointer itself may be deleted or set to null.

If records are not pinned down, we have the option of designing the deletion routine so that when a record other than the last in the bucket is deleted, we find the last record and move it to the subblock of the deleted record. By so doing we shall free the last block of the bucket if it contained only one record. This block may be returned to the file system for use later.

Example 2.1: Our file consists of information about dinosaurs, with the following fields comprising a record.

NAME: CHAR(20)
PERIOD: CHAR(10)
HABITAT: CHAR(5)
DIET: CHAR(5)
LENGTH: INT(4) /* in feet */
WEIGHT: INT(4) /* in tons */

The field NAME by itself forms a key for this file. On the assumption that two bytes hold an integer, a record takes 44 bytes. Let us assume blocks are 100 bytes long (a number too low to be realistic), so each block consists of two subblocks for records preceded by a header with a pointer (say 4 bytes) and two full/empty bits for the two subblocks. The two bits may as well occupy a full byte, which leaves 7 bytes of wasted space in each block.

Let us choose the simple hashing function $h(v)$ equal to the length of string v modulo 5, that is, the remainder when the length is divided by 5.†
Consequently there are five buckets. In Fig. 2.2 we see the file with ten dinosaur genera.‡ Notice that bucket 4 is empty, and there is a null pointer for that bucket in the directory.

Suppose we wish to insert the record

(Elasmosaurus, Cretaceous, sea, carn., 40, 5)

We hash "Elasmosaurus" and get the value 2, since the name has 12 characters. We follow the pointer in the entry numbered 2 in the bucket directory to find the first (and only, it turns out) block in bucket 2. We consult byte 5 of the

_____

† This is a particularly bad function for names of dinosaurs, since these names tend to cluster around 11–13 characters in length, and therefore the buckets will tend not to be approximately equally full.

‡ Actually some of these creatures are members of extinct orders of reptiles not usually classified as "dinosaurs."

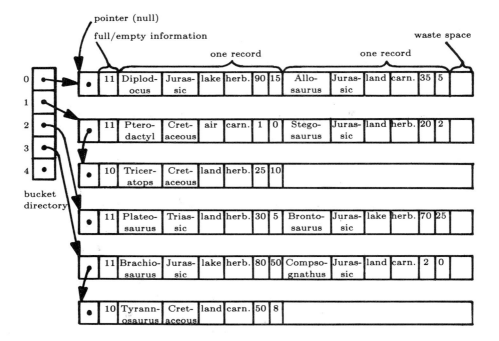

Fig. 2.2. A hashed file.

block to discover that both subblocks hold records. The key value for the first record is found in bytes 6–25, which hold "Plateosaurus," not what we want. The key value for the second record is found in bytes 50–69, and these hold "Brontosaurus," not "Elasmosaurus." We consult bytes 1–4 of the block to find the next block in the bucket. As there is a null pointer in these bytes, we have scanned the entire bucket. We find that "Elasmosaurus" is not present and can be inserted. We also note that no empty subblocks were found, so we must get a new block and insert the record for Elasmosaurus there. The pointer in the fourth block in Fig. 2.2 is made to point to the new block, bytes 1–4 of the new block are given the null pointers and the fifth byte is made to hold the bits 10.

Now suppose it is recalled that the true scientific name of Brontosaurus (thunder lizard) is really Apatosaurus (unbelievable lizard). We must modify the Brontosaurus record, and since a key is involved, we delete the record for Brontosaurus, first recording the nonkey field values in the workspace of the application program making the change, and then we insert a record for Apatosaurus with the same information. To execute these steps, we hash "Brontosaurus" and obtain value 2. Following the pointer for bucket 2, we find a block whose second subblock has key value "Brontosaurus." We copy this record and delete it by setting byte 5 of the block to 10. It is assumed that

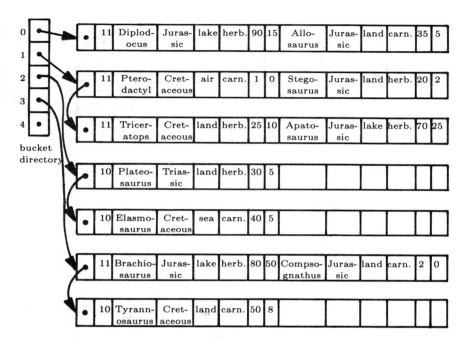

Fig. 2.3. Revised file of dinosaurs.

records are pinned down, so the record for Elasmosaurus cannot replace that for Brontosaurus.† We then assemble the record

(Apatosaurus, Jurassic, lake, herb., 70, 25)

and insert it. As the hash value for "Apatosaurus" is 1, we place the record in the second subblock of the second block for bucket 1. The file at this time is shown in Fig. 2.3. □

Time Analysis of Hashing

Each of the operations lookup, modify, insert, and delete require one access to secondary storage to get the relevant block of the bucket directory (assuming that directory is not kept in main memory) and no more accesses to secondary storage to examine the bucket than there are blocks in the bucket. If the searched-for record is present we shall look at half the blocks on the average. For any operation other than a lookup, we must write the modified block back

---

† It also is useful to note that since the Brontosaurus record is pinned, when we changed the key to Apatosaurus we really did a deletion and an insertion, not a simple update. The difference is that pointers to Brontosaurus still point there, not to Apatosaurus, and if we now moved Elasmosaurus to where the Brontosaurus record was, the pointers would point to Elasmosaurus.

into secondary storage.

The best we could hope for is that each bucket consists of one block, on the average, in which case operations take two (for lookup) or three (for the other operations) accesses independent of the size of the file. In order that buckets consist of a small number of blocks, the number of buckets must be approximately the number of records in the file divided by the number of records that can fit in one block. If the file is constantly growing, as many do, it will be necessary on occasion to reorganize the file by changing the hash function and increasing the size of the bucket directory. This reorganization need not be as chaotic as it seems, if we make two restrictions.

1. We assume the hash function is computed by taking a key value v, computing from it a very large integer (much larger than the maximum number of buckets that could ever be needed), dividing this number by the number of buckets, and taking the remainder.

2. We assume that when we reorganize, the number of buckets is multiplied by a fixed integer c (usually $c = 2$ is selected).

If we decide to double the number of buckets from n to $2n$, by assumption (1) the records in bucket i will all go into bucket i or $i + n$, and no records in other buckets will go into i or $i + n$. Thus we can split one bucket at a time. The same idea applies if we multiply the number of buckets by some integer $c > 2$. Then each old bucket can be divided into c new buckets, independent of the other buckets.

2.3 INDEXED FILES

We now consider a second representation for files that are to be accessed via a key. This method is often called *isam*, standing for *indexed sequential access method*. In this representation, we begin by sorting the records of a file by their key values. We should first observe that no matter what the domain of values for a field, we can in principle compare values from the domain, and therefore we can sort these values. The justification is that to be stored in a file, the values must be representable as bit strings, which can be ordered if we treat them as integers and use numerical order. The usual domains of values, such as character strings, integers and reals have conventional orders placed on them. For integers and reals we have numerical order. For character strings we have *lexicographic*, or *dictionary* order defined by $X_1 X_2 \cdots X_k < Y_1 Y_2 \cdots Y_m$, where the X's and Y's represent characters, if and only if either

1. $k < m$ and $X_1 \cdots X_k = Y_1 \cdots Y_k$, or
2. For some $i \le min(k, m)$, we have $X_1 = Y_1, X_2 = Y_2, \ldots, X_{i-1} = Y_{i-1}$, and the binary code for X_i is numerically less than the binary code for Y_i.

Whatever code for characters is used by a machine, we have a right to expect that the order of the codes for letters of the same case is alphabetical order and the order of the codes for digits is the numerical order of the digits. Thus, for example, 'AN' < 'AND' by rule (1), and 'BANANA' < 'BANDANA' by rule (2) with $i = 4$.

If we have a key of more than one field, we can sort key values by first arbitrarily picking an order for the key fields. Records are sorted by the first field, which will result in clusters of records with the same value in the first field. Each cluster is sorted by the value of the second field, which will result in clusters of records with the same value in the first two fields. These clusters are sorted on the third field, and so on. Note that this ordering is a generalization of lexicographic ordering for character strings where, instead of ordering lists of characters we order lists of values from arbitrary domains.

Example 2.2: Suppose we have a key with two fields, both with integer values, and we are given the list of key values (2,3), (1,2), (2,2), (3,1), (1,3). We sort these on the value of the first field to get (1,2), (1,3), (2,3), (2,2), (3,1). The first cluster, with 1 in the first field, is already sorted by the second field. The second cluster, consisting of (2,3) and (2,2), needs to be interchanged to sort on the second field. The third cluster, consisting of one record, naturally is sorted already. The sorted order is (1,2), (1,3), (2,2), (2,3), (3,1). □

If we are willing to maintain a file of records sorted by key values, we can take advantage of the known order to find a record quickly given its key value. We are probably familiar with at least two examples of searching for key values in a sorted list: using the dictionary and using the phone book. In both cases each page has in the upper left corner the first word or name on the page.† By scanning these first words, we can determine the one page on which our word (if a dictionary) or name (if a phone book) could be found.‡ This strategy is far better than looking at every entry on every page. Except for one page, which we must scan completely, we need only look at one entry per page.

Turning now to the representation of a sorted file, (which we call the *main* file), we could create a second file called a (*sparse*) *index*, consisting of pairs (key value, block address). In the index file the pair (v, b) appears if the first record in the block with address b has key value v. The first field is a key for the index file, and the index file is kept sorted by its key value. In a sense, an index file is like any other file with a key. Moreover, we may take advantage of the fact that in an index file, records are never pinned down by pointers from elsewhere.

However, there is an important difference between index files and the general files we have been discussing. In addition to (possibly) wishing to do

---

† The upper right contains the last word/name, but this information is redundant, since the first word/name of the next page provides equivalent information. It is inconvenient for a human to flip pages, but the analogous task for the computer presents no difficulty.

‡ In practice we use our intuitive feeling about the distribution of words/names to take an educated guess as to where our goal lies, and we do not search stolidly starting at page 1. We shall have more to say about adapting this idea to computer search later.

insertions, deletions, and modifications on index files, we wish to obtain the answer to questions of the form: given a key value v_1 for the file being indexed, find that record (v_2, b) in the index such that $v_2 \leq v_1$† and either (v_2, b) is the last record in the index, or the next record (v_3, b') has $v_1 < v_3$. (Say that v_2 *covers* v_1 in this situation.) This is how we find the block b of the main file that contains a record with key value v_1, since the index file is guaranteed to be sorted.

Queries of the above type rule out certain organizations for index files. For example, it would not be convenient to use the hashed file organization of Section 2.2 for index files, since there is no way to find the value v_2 that covers v_1 in a hashed file without searching the entire file.

Searching an Index

Let us assume the index file is stored over a known collection of blocks, and we must find that record (v_2, b) such that v_2 covers a given key value v_1. One strategy is to use *linear search*. Scan the index from the beginning, looking at each record until the one that covers v_1 is found. This method is undesirable for all but the smallest indices, as the entire index may be called into main memory, and on the average, half the index blocks will be accessed in a successful lookup. Yet even linear search of an index is superior to linear search of the main file; if the main file has c records per block, then the index has only $1/c^{th}$ as many records as the main file. In addition, index records may be shorter than records of the main file, allowing more to be packed on one block.

A better strategy is to use *binary search*. Given key value v_1, and an index on blocks $B_1, B_2, \ldots, B_n$, look at the middle block, $B_{\lceil n/2 \rceil}$‡ and compare v_1 with the key value v_2 in the first record on that block.§ If $v_1 < v_2$, repeat the process as if the index were on blocks $B_1 \cdots B_{\lceil n/2 \rceil - 1}$. If $v_1 \geq v_2$, repeat the process as if the index were on $B_{\lceil n/2 \rceil} \cdots B_n$. Eventually, only one block will remain to be considered. At this time, use linear search on the remaining block to find the key value in the index that covers v_1.

As we divide the number of blocks by two at each step, in $\lceil \log_2(n + 1) \rceil$ steps at the most we narrow our search to one block. Thus the binary search of an index file requires that about $\log_2 n$ blocks be brought into main memory. Once we have searched the index, we know exactly which block of the main file must be examined and perhaps must be rewritten to perform an operation on that file. The total number of block accesses, $3 + \log_2 n$, is not prohibitive, as

---

† $\leq$ is whatever order on key values is being used, e.g., lexicographic order if key values are character strings.

‡ $\lceil x \rceil$ is the ceiling of x, the least integer equal to or greater than x.

§ Note that we need a table of block addresses, which could be resident in main memory or called into main memory when needed, so we can translate from integer i to the location of block B_i.

an example will show.

Example 2.3: Suppose we have a main file of a million records, and ten records fit on a block. The index for this file thus has 100,000 records; since the index records are short, perhaps 100 will fit on a block. Hence 1,000 blocks are needed for the index, that is $n = 1000$ in the above calculation. Linear search would require about 500 block accesses on the average for a successful lookup. However, if we use a binary search, accessing and rewriting a record of the main file requires $3 + \log_2 1000$, or about 13 block accesses. This figure compares with 3 for the hashed organization. However, there are some advantages to the sorted organization. For example, with the hashed organization it is very difficult to process or list records in the order of their keys, while it is simple to do so with an indexed organization. Section 2.9 discusses "range queries," another situation where hashing is useless and a sorted organization is called for. $\square$

A method of searching an index that can be superior to binary search is known as *interpolation* or *address calculation* search. This method is predicated on our knowing the statistics of the expected distribution of key values, and on that distribution being fairly reliable. For example, if we are asked to look up John Smith in the phone book, we do not open it to the middle, but to about 75% of the way through, "knowing" that this is roughly where we find the S's. If we find ourselves among the T's, we go back perhaps 5% of the way, not halfway to the beginning as we would for the second step of a binary search.

In general, suppose we have an algorithm that given a key value v_1, tells us what fraction of the way between two other key values, v_2 and v_3, we can expect v_1 to lie. Call this fraction $f(v_1, v_2, v_3)$. If an index or part of an index lies on blocks $B_1, \ldots, B_n$, let v_2 be the first key value in B_1 and v_3 the last key value in B_n.† Look at block B_i, where $i = \lceil nf(v_1, v_2, v_3) \rceil$ to see how its first key value compares with v_1. Then, as in binary search, repeat the process on either $B_1, \ldots, B_{i-1}$ or $B_i, \ldots, B_n$, whichever could contain the value that covers v_1, until only one block remains.

It can be shown that if we know the expected distribution of keys, then we can expect to examine about $1 + \log_2 \log_2 n$ blocks of the index file. When we add to this the two accesses to read and write a block of the main file, we get $3 + \log_2 \log_2 n$. For example, under the assumptions of Example 2.3, this number is a little over 6, compared with 13 for binary search.

Operating on a Sorted File with Unpinned Records

Let us consider how to do the operations of lookup, insertion, deletion, and modification on a sorted file with records that are not pinned down, by pointers,

---

† If $B_1, \ldots, B_n$ is the entire index, then we can estimate v_2 and v_3 without looking at B_1 and B_n, since we assume the distribution of keys is known.

to a fixed location. These four operations will require insertions, deletions and modifications to the index file, so it is important to bear in mind that the index file itself is sorted and has unpinned records. Thus in describing operations on the main file, we call for the same operations to be done to the index file, assuming that the reader sees how to implement these operations on the index. Note that since the index file has no index, and lookup strategies for the index file have been described already, we are not using circular reasoning.

The original sorted file is kept on a sequence of blocks $B_1, B_2, \ldots, B_k$, with the records of each block in sorted order, and the records of B_i preceding those of B_{i+1} in the ordering, for $i = 1, 2, \ldots, k - 1$. In the header of each block is information indicating which of the subblocks hold records and which are empty, as for the blocks used in the hashed organization. We now describe each of the four operations, assuming no errors such as trying to modify a nonexistent record occur. Such errors are detected in the same manner as for the hashed organization.

Lookup

Suppose we want to find the record in the main file with key value v_1. Examine the index file to find the block whose first record has a key value v_2 that covers v_1. Search this block for a record with the key v_1. The search of the block may as well be linear, since reading the block normally takes more time than searching it, but we can use a binary search if we wish. We must make sure to consult the bits in the header so we don't accidentally find an empty subblock and decide it holds a record with key value v_1.

Modification

To modify a record with key value v_1, use the lookup procedure to find the record. If the modification changes the key, treat the operation as an insertion and deletion. If not, make the modification and rewrite the record.

Insertion

To insert a record with key value v_1, use the lookup procedure to find the block B_i on which a record with key value v_1 would be found. In the special case that v_1 precedes the key value of the first record of B_1 (and hence v_1 precedes every key value in the file) let $i = 1$. Place the new record in its correct place in block B_i, keeping the records sorted and moving records with key values greater than v_1 to the right, to make room for the new record. If block B_i had at least one empty subblock, all records will fit. If v_1 precedes the key value v_2 of the first record of B_i (this can only happen if $i = 1$) then we must modify the index file entry for B_i, for which we use the modification procedure just described. Note that even though the record in the index file with key value

v_2 has its key value changed to v_1, we do not have to delete and insert, since the position of this record in the index file will not change. Finally, we must change the full/empty information in the header of B_i to reflect the additional record. On the assumption that B_i had at least one empty subblock, we are now done.

Now suppose B_i was originally full, so the last record has no place to go. There are a variety of strategies we could follow here. In the next section we shall discuss a strategy in which B_i is split into two half-empty blocks, and this strategy could be used here. An alternative is to examine B_{i+1}. We can find B_{i+1}, if it exists, through the index file, since a pointer to B_{i+1} is in the record of the index file that follows the record just accessed to find B_i. If B_{i+1} has an empty subblock, move the excess record from B_i to the first subblock of B_{i+1}, shifting other records right until the first empty subblock is filled. Change the full/empty information in the header of B_{i+1} appropriately, and modify the index record for B_{i+1} to reflect the new key value in its first record.

If B_{i+1} does not exist, because $i = k$, or B_{i+1} exists but is full, we must get a new block, which will follow B_i in the order. Place the excess record from B_i in the new block, and insert a record for the new block in the index file, using the same strategy as we have described for inserting a record into the main file.

Deletion

As for insertion, a variety of strategies exist, and in the next section we shall discuss one in which blocks are not allowed to get less than half full. Here, let us mention only the simplest strategy, which is appropriate if relatively few deletions are made. To delete the record with key value v_1, use lookup to find it. Move any records to its right one subblock left to close the gap,† and adjust the full/empty bits in the header. If the block is now completely empty, return it to the file system, and delete the record for that block in the index, using the same deletion strategy. If the block is not empty after deleting the record with key value v_1, we are done unless the deleted record was the first in the block. In that case we must modify the index record for that block.

Example 2.4: Suppose we again have our file of dinosaurs, with blocks of 100 bytes. Recall from Example 2.1 that a dinosaur record takes 44 bytes, so we can pack two to a block. An index record consists of the dinosaur name (20 bytes) plus a pointer to a block, which we assume takes 4 bytes. Thus we can pack four to a block. The initial database is shown in Fig. 2.4. The information about the dinosaurs is omitted.

† This step is not essential. If we do choose to close up gaps, we can use a count of the full subblocks in the header in place of a full/empty bit for each subblock. The reader should again be reminded that if records are pinned we do not even have the option of moving records into subblocks whose records have been deleted.

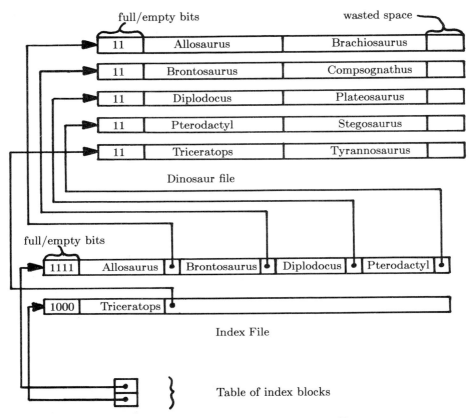

Fig. 2.4. Sorted, indexed dinosaur file.

Suppose now that we add Elasmosaurus to the file. Examination of the index file, say by linear search, discloses that "Elasmosaurus" is covered by "Diplodocus." We follow the pointer in the Diplodocus record of the index file to the third block of the dinosaur file. Scanning that block, we ascertain that "Elasmosaurus" comes between "Diplodocus" and "Plateosaurus." We therefore move the Elasmosaurus record into the subblock that held the Plateosaurus record, and the latter record becomes excess. We locate the fourth block of the dinosaur file through the index file and find that the fourth block is also full. We therefore create a new block, placed between the third and fourth blocks in the order, initially holding only the Plateosaurus record.

We then insert a record for this block in the index file. That record replaces the Pterodactyl record in the first block of the index file, and the latter record becomes excess. By consulting the table of index blocks, we find the next index block, discover it has room, and insert the Pterodactyl index record ahead of

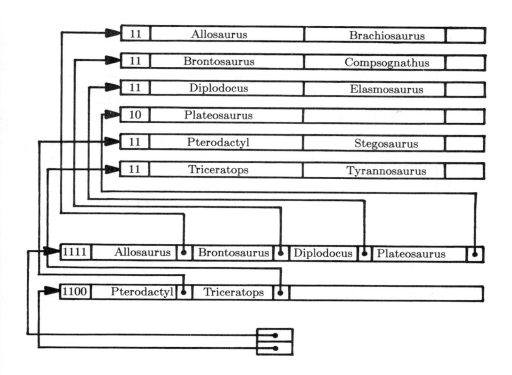

Fig. 2.5. Dinosaur file with added Elasmosaurus record.

the Triceratops record. The database at this time is shown in Fig. 2.5.

Now recall that the true name of Brontosaurus is Apatosaurus. We therefore find the Brontosaurus record through the index and delete it from the second dinosaur file block, moving the Compsognathus record left and setting the full/empty bits to 10. We modify the record in the index file for block 2 of the dinosaur file by changing its key value from "Brontosaurus" to "Compsognathus." Notice that although the key field is changed, the order of this record is not changed, so we do not have to delete and insert in the index file.

Now we add the Apatosaurus record. We find "Apatosaurus" is covered by "Allosaurus" in the index file, so we are sent to block 1 of the index file. There we insert the Apatosaurus record in the second subblock, and the Brachiosaurus record becomes excess. Fortunately, there is room in the next block, and we insert it ahead of Compsognathus, which is moved back to where it began. We modify the index record for the second dinosaur block, changing its key value

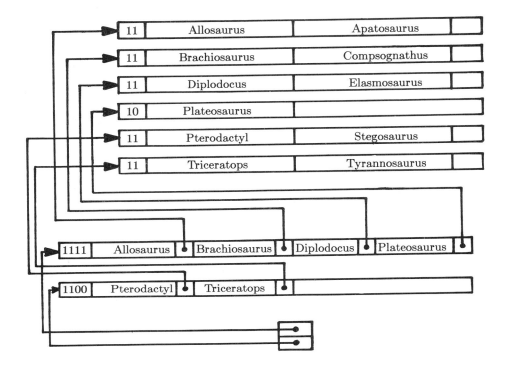

Fig. 2.6. Dinosaur file after changing "Brontosaurus" to "Apatosaurus".

to "Brachiosaurus." The final organization is shown in Fig. 2.6. □

Chaining the Blocks

We should observe that when inserting it is sometimes necessary to find the next block of the main file. Instead of going through the index file we could put a pointer in the header of each block to the next block in the file. Similarly, we could put a pointer to the next block in each index file block. This would obviate the need for a table of index blocks if linear search of the index file were used. We would then need only the address of the first block of the index file.

An Organization for Sorted Files with Pinned Records

If records are pinned down to the place in which they are first stored, we cannot in general keep records sorted within a block. We can even have trouble making sure that the records of each block precede the records of the next block. One solution is to start the file with essentially the same organization as if records were unpinned, as in Fig. 2.4. However, we view each block of the main file as the first block of a bucket. As records are inserted, additional blocks will be added to the bucket, and new blocks are chained by a series of pointers extending from the original block for that bucket. We also create an empty block to begin a bucket that will hold any records that precede the first record of the first block in the initial file. The index never changes in this organization, and the first records of each block of the initial file determine the distribution of records into buckets forever, or at least until the file has gotten so large that it is worthwhile reorganizing it into a larger number of buckets. Let us now describe the way in which operations are performed on a file with this organization.

Initialization

Sort the file and distribute its records among blocks. We might consider filling each block to less than its capacity to make room for expected growth and avoid long chains of blocks in one bucket. Get one additional block to head the bucket for those records inserted later that precede all records of the initial file. Create the index with a record for each block, including the empty block at the front. The index record for the latter block has no key, just a pointer.

Lookup

Find the index record whose key value v_2 covers the desired key value v_1. If v_1 is less than than the first key value of the index file (note that the second index record has the first key value) then the desired index record is the first record. Follow the pointer in the selected index record to the first block of the desired bucket. Scan this block and any blocks of the bucket chained to it to find the record with key v_1.

Modification

The strategy to use here is analogous to that described for the previous organization.

Insertion

Use the lookup procedure to find the desired bucket. Scan the blocks of the bucket to find the first empty place. If no empty subblock exists, get a new block and place a pointer to it in the header of the last block of the bucket. Insert the new record in the new block.

Deletion

Use the lookup procedure to find the desired record. We might consider setting

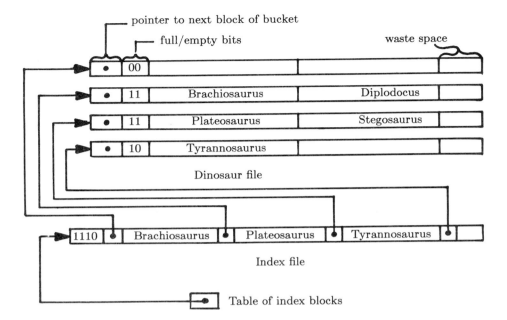

Fig. 2.7. Initial file organization.

the full/empty bit for its subblock to 0. However, as discussed in Section 2.2, if there may exist pointers to the record being deleted, another deletion strategy must be used. The full/empty bit is kept at 1, and to indicate removal of the record, a deletion bit in the record itself is set to 1.

Example 2.5: Suppose we start with a database consisting of the five dinosaurs Brachiosaurus, Diplodocus, Plateosaurus, Stegosaurus and Tyrannosaurus, and we fill blocks as completely as possible in the original database. As in previous examples, blocks are 100 bytes long and so can hold two dinosaur records. The initial database is shown in Fig. 2.7. There are four buckets, which will contain

1. any name preceding "Brachiosaurus."
2. any name from "Brachiosaurus" up to but not including "Plateosaurus."
3. any name from "Plateosaurus" up to but not including "Tyrannosaurus."
4. "Tyrannosaurus" and any following names.

Now we add the following dinosaurs. After each name we indicate where the corresponding record goes.

i) Allosaurus. This record goes in the first subblock of the initially empty block for the first bucket.

ii) Brontosaurus. This record is put into the second bucket. As the only block for that bucket is full, we get a new block and place the Brontosaurus record in the first subblock of that block.

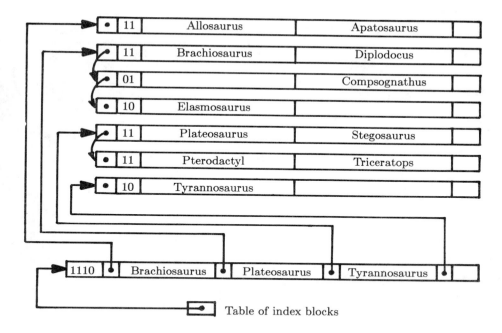

Fig. 2.8. Final file organization.

iii) Compsognathus. Another record for bucket 2, it is placed in the second subblock of the second block.

iv) Elasmosaurus. Again the record is destined for bucket 2. We get a third block for that bucket and place Elasmosaurus in its first subblock.

v) Pterodactyl. This record blongs in bucket 3, and goes in a new block.

vi) Triceratops. Another record for bucket 3, we place it in the second subblock of the second block of that bucket.

Now we discover that the name of Brontosaurus is changed to Apatosaurus. We delete the record for Brontosaurus from bucket 2; no other records for that bucket are moved. The Apatosaurus record is placed in bucket 1 and it occupies the second subblock of the first block for that bucket. The resulting structure is shown in Fig. 2.8. □

Additional Links

As for the sorted organization with unpinned records, we may find it useful to link the index blocks in order. We can also link the buckets in order. One way to do so is to leave space for another pointer in each header, and link the first blocks of successive buckets. A way that may save space is to replace the null pointer at the end of the chain for each bucket by a pointer to the first block

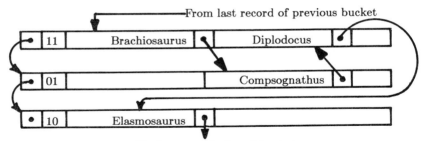

Fig. 2.9. A bucket with pointers to indicate sorted order.

of the next bucket. A single bit in the header tells whether the pointer is to the next bucket or to the next block of the same bucket.

As records are not placed in a bucket in sorted order after the initialization, we may have difficulty if we wish to examine records in sorted order. To help we can add a pointer in each record to the next record in sorted order. These pointers are somewhat different from the pointers we have been using, since they not only indicate a block, but they also indicate an offset within the block; the offset is the number of the byte that begins the stored record, relative to the beginning of the block. The algorithms needed to maintain such pointers should be familiar from an elementary study of list processing.

Example 2.6: The second bucket of Fig. 2.8 with pointers indicating the sorted order is shown in Fig. 2.9. □

2.4 B-TREES

An index being nothing more than a file with unpinned records, there is no reason why we cannot have an index of an index, an index of that, and so on, until an index fits on one block. In fact, such an arrangement can be considerably more efficient than a file with a single level of indexing. A common scheme for extremely large files is to induce a hierarchy of indices that follows the hierarchical nature of the secondary storage devices on which the file resides.

For example, if the file covers several disk units, we could arrange that all records on the first disk unit have key values that precede those on unit 2, which have key values that precede those on unit 3, and so on. The first level index gives the first key value on each unit. Within a unit, the cylinders are ordered, and the second level of index gives the first key value on each cylinder. Then, perhaps, within a cylinder we may order the tracks and use a third level of index to give the first key value of each track. Tracks may be partitioned into blocks and a fourth level of index used. If this organization is used, it is helpful, when the file is initialized, to leave free blocks on each track, free tracks

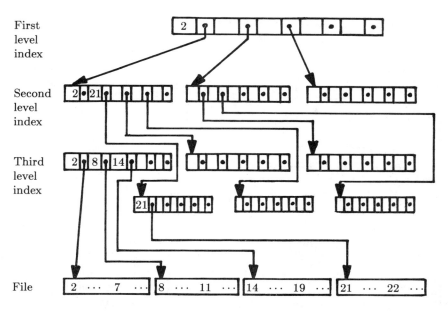

Fig. 2.10. An index hierarchy.

on each cylinder, and so on. Then if, say, a cylinder fills up, we may find a free cylinder on the same disk to hold the overflow, just as we used extra blocks to hold the overflow from the first block of a bucket in Section 2.2. In this way, the database can exist for a long time without reorganization of storage.

With an adequate file system, we can use a more general scheme in which blocks are treated uniformly, independent of where they are in secondary storage. We can view the hierarchy of indices as a tree, as suggested by Fig. 2.10. We assume in that figure that each block used as an index has space for five records, although, as discussed in Section 2.3, some blocks will hold fewer than the maximum number of records. Since records of an index are not pinned, we shall assume that the full subblocks of any block are to the left of any empty subblocks in that block. In Fig. 2.10 we take key values to be integers, and we have filled in sample key values in the original file, as well as filling in as many key values in the index files as can be determined from what is shown of the main file.

The methods for performing lookups, modifications, insertions, and deletions on a multilevel index are straightforward generalizations of the techniques discussed previously. The only problem is what happens when the first level index exceeds the capacity of a block. It should be apparent that the multilevel index idea is not dependent on how may levels of index there are, so we are free to add another level of index, to index what was formerly the first level, should the first level grow beyond the capacity of a block. We are thus led to the idea of a *B-tree* (balanced tree), which is a tree structure similar to that illustrated in Fig. 2.10, but with an unspecified number of levels. We do insist, however, that the tree be *balanced*. That is, as in Fig. 2.10, every path from the root (the first level index block) to a leaf is of the same length.

We shall assume that the records of the main file are unpinned. The variant of B-trees that we shall describe shows the blocks of the main file as part of the B-tree. This style does not use space as efficiently as possible, and we introduce the subject of B-trees this way only because of its conceptual simplicity. A superior approach, which saves space in most situations, and is also suitable for storing pinned records, is described in Section 2.5. There we keep the main file packed tightly on blocks with records in no particular order. Then the leaves of the B-tree contain not the main file records, but pointers to those records.

For insertion and deletion on a B-tree, we could use the same strategy as was described in the previous section, applying the insertion and deletion operations to the nodes (blocks) of the tree at all levels. This strategy would result in nodes having between one and the maximum possible number of records. Rather, B-trees are usually defined to use a particular insertion/deletion strategy that ensures no node, except possibly the root, is less than half full. For convenience, we assume that the number of index records a block can hold is an odd integer $2d - 1 \geq 3$, and the number of records of the main file a block can hold is also an odd integer $2e - 1 \geq 3$.

Before proceeding, let us point out one more difference between B-trees and the index hierarchy depicted in Fig. 2.10. In index blocks of a B-tree the key value in the first record is omitted, to save space. During lookups, all key values less than the value in the second record of a block are deemed to be covered by the first key value.

Lookup

Let us search for a record with key value v. We find a path from the root of the B-tree to some leaf, where the desired record will be found if it exists. We begin our path at the root. Suppose at some time during the search we have reached node (block) B. If B is a leaf (we can tell when we reach a leaf if we keep the current number of levels of the tree available) then simply examine block B for a record with key value v.

If B is not a leaf, it is an index block. Determine which key value in block B covers v. Recall that the first record in B holds no key value, and the missing value is deemed to cover any value less than the key value in the second record. In the record of B that covers v is a pointer to another block. That block follows B in the path being constructed, and we repeat the above steps with the block just found in place of B.

Modification

As with the other organizations discussed, a modification involving a key field is really a deletion and insertion, while a modification that leaves the key value fixed is a lookup followed by the rewriting of the record involved.

Insertion

To insert a record with key value v, apply the lookup procedure to find the block B in which this record belongs. If there are fewer than $2e - 1$ records in B, simply insert the new record in sorted order in the block. One can show that the new record can never be the first in block B, unless B is the leftmost leaf. It follows that in no circumstances is it necessary to modify a key value in an ancestor of B, since the first record in each index block omits the key value anyway.

If there are already $2e - 1$ records in block B, create a new block B_1 and divide the records from B and the inserted record into two groups of e records each. The first e records go in block B and the remaining e go in block B_1.

Now let P be the parent block of B. Recall that the lookup procedure finds the path from the root to B, so P is already known. Apply the insert procedure recursively, with constant d in place of e, to insert a record for B_1 to the right of the record for B in index block P. Notice that if many ancestors of block B have the maximum $2d - 1$ records, the effects of inserting a record into B can ripple up the tree for several levels. However, it is only ancestors of B that are affected. If the effects ripple up to the root, we split the root, and create a new root with two children. This is the only situation in which an index block may have fewer than d records.

Deletion

If we wish to delete the record with key value v, we use the lookup procedure to find the path from the root to a block B containing this record. If after deletion, block B still has e or more records, we are usually done. However, if the deleted record was the first in block B, then we must go to the parent of B to change the key value in the record for B, to agree with the new first key value of B. If B is the first child of its parent, the parent has no key value for B, so we must go to the parent's parent, the parent of that, and so on, until we find an ancestor A_1 of B such that A_1 is not the first child of its parent A_2. Then the new lowest key value of B goes in the record of A_2 that points to A_1. In this manner, every record (v_1, p_1) in every index block has key value v_1 equal to the lowest of all those key values of the original file found among the leaves that are descendants of the block pointed to by p_1. That is, the B-tree, even after deletion, continues to behave as a multilevel index.†

If, after deletion, block B has $e-1$ records, we look at the block B_1 having the same parent as B and residing either immediately to the left or right of B. If B_1 has more than e records, we distribute the records of B and B_1 as evenly as possible, keeping the order sorted, of course. We then modify the key values for B and/or B_1 in the parent of B, and if necessary, ripple the change to as many ancestors of B as have their key values affected. If B_1 has only e records, then combine B with B_1, which will then have exactly $2e-1$ records, and in the parent of B, modify the record for B_1 (which may require modification of some ancestors of B) and delete the record for B. The deletion of this record requires a recursive use of the deletion procedure, with constant d in place of e.

If the deletion ripples all the way up to the children of the root, we may find that we combine the only two children of the root. In this case, the node formed from the combined children becomes the root, and the old root is deleted. This is the one situation in which the number of levels decreases.

Example 2.7: Nontrivial examples of B-trees are hard to show on the page. Let us therefore take the minimum possible values of d and e, namely two. That is, each block, whether interior or a leaf, holds three records. Also to save space, we shall use small integers as key values and shall omit any other fields, including full/empty bits in the header. In Fig. 2.11 we see an initial B-tree.

Suppose we wish to insert a record with key value 32. We find a path to the block in which this record belongs by starting at the root, B_1. We find that 32 is covered by 25, the key value in the second record of B_1. We therefore progress to B_3, the block pointed to by the second record of B_1. At B_3 we find that 32 is less than 64, the value in the second record of B_3, so we follow the first pointer in B_3, to arrive at B_7. Clearly 32 belongs between 25 and 36 in B_7, but now B_7 has four records. We therefore get a new block, B_{12}, and place 25 and 32 in B_7, while 36 and 49 go in B_{12}.

We now must insert a record with key value 36 and a pointer to B_{12} into B_3. This causes B_3 to have four records, so we get a new block B_{13}. The records with pointers to B_7 and B_{12} go in B_3, while the records with pointers to B_8 and B_9 go in B_{13}. Next, we insert a record with key value 64 and a pointer to B_{13} into B_1. Now B_1 has four records, so we get a new block B_{14}, and place the records with pointers to B_2 and B_3 in B_1, while the records with pointers to B_{13} and B_4 go in B_{14}. As B_1 was the root, we create a new block B_{15}, which becomes the root and has pointers to B_1 and B_{14}. The resulting B-tree is shown in Fig. 2.12.

---

† This property is not essential, and we could dispense with the modification of keys in index blocks. Then v_1 would be a lower bound on the keys of descendants of the block pointed to by p_1. The descendants to the left of that block will still have keys less than v_1, as they must for the B-tree to be useful for finding records.

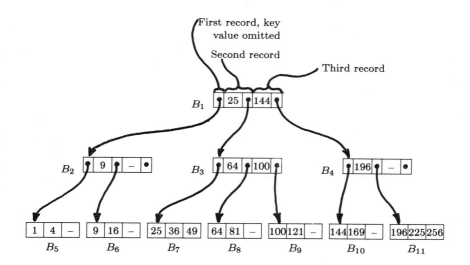

Fig. 2.11. Initial B-tree.

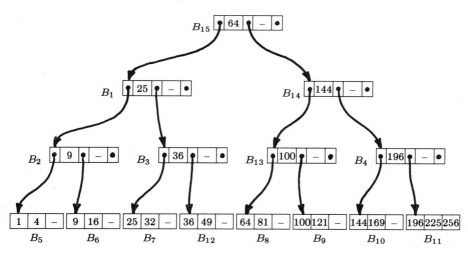

Fig. 2.12. B-tree after insertion of 32.

Next, let us delete the record with key value 64. The lookup procedure tells us the path to the block that holds this record is B_{15}, B_{14}, B_{13}, B_8. We delete the record from B_8 and find that it was the first record of that block. We therefore must propagate upwards the fact that the new lowest key value

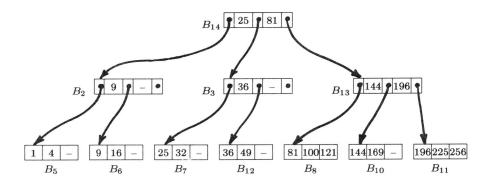

Fig. 2.13. B-tree after deleting 64.

in B_8 is 81. As B_8 is the leftmost child of B_{13}, we do not change B_{13}, nor do we change B_{14}, since B_{13} is its leftmost child. However, B_{14} is not the leftmost child of B_{15}, so there is a key value in B_{15} that must be changed, and we change 64 to 81 there. Notice that a deletion never causes more than one key value to be changed.

We have another problem when we delete 64. Block B_8 now has only one record. We go to its parent, B_{13}, and find that B_8 has no sibling to its left. We therefore examine B_8's right sibling, B_9. As B_9 has only two records, we can combine B_9 with B_8. Now we discover that B_{13} has only one child, and we must combine B_{13} with a sibling, B_4. Block B_{13} will now have pointers to B_{10} and B_{11}. The key value 196 to go with the pointer to B_{11} is found in B_4, while the key value 144 to go with B_{10} is found in B_{14}. In general, when we merge blocks in a deletion, the necessary key values are found either in the merged blocks or in their common parent.

On combining B_{13} and B_4, we find B_{14} has only one child, and so combine B_{14} with B_1. At this time, B_{15} has only one child, and since it is the root, we delete it, leaving the B-tree of Fig. 2.13. $\square$

Time Analysis of B-tree Operations

Suppose we have a file with n records organized into a B-tree with parameters d and e. The tree will have no more than n/e leaves, no more than n/de parents of leaves, n/d^2e parents of parents of leaves and so on. If there are i nodes on paths from the root to leaves, then $n \geq d^{i-1}e$, or else there would be fewer than one node at the level of the root, which is impossible. It follows that

$$i \leq 1 + \log_d(n/e)$$

To perform a lookup, i read operations on blocks suffices. For an insertion, deletion or modification, usually only one block, the leaf holding the record involved, needs to be written, although in pathological cases, about i additional reads and i additional writes may be necessary. Exact analysis of the probability of finding blocks with too many records in an insert or too few records in a delete is very difficult. However, it is not hard to show that even for $d = e = 2$, the expected number of extra reads and writes (in excess of the i reads to find the leaf and one write to store the leaf) is a proper fraction. We shall thus neglect this fraction and estimate the number of read/writes at $2 + \log_d(n/e)$. Even this figure is conservative, since in the expected case many blocks will have more than the minimum number of records, and therefore the height of the tree may well be less than $1 + \log_d(n/e)$.

Example 2.8: If $n = 1{,}000{,}000$, $e = 5$, and $d = 50$, the expected number of read/writes of blocks in an operation is $2 + \log_{50}(200000) \leq 6$. This figure is greater than for hashed access (about 3 read/writes), but is superior to methods using a single level of indexing, except perhaps in those situations where an interpolation search can be performed. The B-tree shares with the methods of Section 2.3 the advantage over hashed access of permitting the file to be listed or searched conveniently in sorted order. $\square$

2.5 FILES WITH A DENSE INDEX

Suppose we do not wish to keep our file sorted. By allowing records to appear in a random order, we can avoid having many partially filled blocks in the main file. Moreover, insertions are very easily made. We have only to keep track of the last block in the file and insert a new record there. When the last block is filled up, we simply get a new block from the file system. If deletions are frequent, "holes" will appear in the file. We could simply ignore the fact that certain subblocks are made empty by deletions, or we could keep a separate file with records consisting of one field, that being a pointer to a block with one or more empty subblocks. We could even make the pointers point to an empty subblock within the block, although doing so will not save block accesses.

The problem with using an unsorted file is that we must have a way of finding a record, given its key value. To do so efficiently, we need another file, called a *dense index,* that consists of records (v, p) for each key value v in the main file, where p is a pointer to the main file record having key value v.

To lookup, modify, or delete a record of the main file we perform a lookup on the dense index file, which tells us the block of the main file we must search for the desired record. We must then read this block of the main file. If the record is to be modified, we change the record and rewrite its block onto secondary storage. We thus make two more block accesses than are necessary to perform a lookup in the dense index file. (Recall that an "access" is either a read or write of a block.)

If we are to delete the record, we again rewrite its block and also delete the record with that key value from the dense index file. This operation takes two more accesses than a lookup and deletion from the dense index. To perform an insertion, we insert the record at the end of the main file and then insert a pointer to that record in the dense index file. Again this operation takes two more accesses than does the same operation on the dense index file.

It would thus seem that a file with a dense index always requires two more accesses than if we used, for the main file, whatever organization (e.g., hashed, indexed, or B-tree) we use on the dense index file. However, there are two factors that work in the opposite direction, to justify the use of dense indices in some situations.

1. The records of the main file may be pinned, but the records of the dense index file need not be pinned, so we may use a simpler or more efficient organization on the dense index file than we could on the main file.

2. If records of the main file are large, the total number of blocks used in the dense index may be much less than would be used for a sparse index or B-tree on the main file. By the same token, the number of buckets, or the average number of blocks per bucket, need not be so great if hashed access is used on the dense index as if hashed access were used on the main file.

Example 2.9: Let us consider the same file discussed in Example 2.8, where we used a B-tree with $d = 50$ and $e = 5$ on a file of a million records. Since dense index records are the same size as the records in the interior nodes of a B-tree, if we use a B-tree organization for the dense index, we may take $d = e = 50$. Thus the typical number of accesses to search the dense index is $2+\log_{50}(20000)$, which is less than 5. To this we must add 2 accesses of the main file, so the dense index plus B-tree organization takes slightly less than two more block accesses (the actual figure is $2 - \log_{50}(10)$) than the simple B-tree organization.

There are, however, compensating factors for the dense index. We can pack the blocks of the main file fully, if a dense index is used, while in the B-tree organization, the leaf blocks, which contain the main file, are between half full and completely full, so we can save about 25% in storage space for the main file. The space used for the leaves of the B-tree in the dense index is only 10% of the space of the main file, so we still have a net savings of approximately 15% of the space. Moreover, if the main file has pinned records, we could not use the B-tree organization described in Section 2.4 at all. □

Methods for Unpinning Records

Another use for a dense index is as a place to receive pointers to records. That is, a pointer to record r of the main file goes instead to the record in the dense index that points to r. The disadvantage is that to follow a pointer to r we must follow an extra pointer from the dense index to the main file. The compensation is that now records of the main file are not pinned (although the records of the index file are). When we wish to move a record of the main file, we have only to change the one pointer in the dense index that points to the moved record. We may thus be able to use a more compact storage organization for the main file, and the storage savings could more than cover the cost of the dense index. For example, if the main file is unpinned, we can reuse the subblocks of deleted records.

Another similar idea avoids a dense index for the entire main file and instead places pointers in each block header to the records of that block. All pointers to a record r now go to the pointer to r in the header of r's block. We are free to move records around in their block if we change the pointer in the block header, although unlike the situation where we have a dense index for the entire file, we cannot move records between blocks with impunity. That is to say, records are unpinned within a block, but are pinned to their block. A generalization of this idea is to point to the bucket of a record (assuming, say, a hashed organization). However, since buckets can grow without bound, care must be given to provide storage within the bucket for pointers to all its records; these pointers could take several blocks.

The cost of this freedom is the extra space for pointers in the block headers; the time for following those pointers is negligible, since no extra block access is involved. One situation in which the arrangement is worthwhile is when records have varying length, and therefore, adjustments within blocks are frequently required (although sometimes a growing record will have to be moved to another block because it just won't fit anymore). For example, System R (Astrahan et al. [1976]) uses this scheme for that purpose, among others.

Another technique for making files unpinned is to use the key values of records in place of pointers. That is, instead of storing the address of a record r, we store the value of the key for r, and to find r we do a standard lookup given the key value.

The IMS database system (IBM [1978b]), for example, makes heavy use of this technique. In this way, both the dense index file and the main file can be unpinned. The disadvantage is that to follow a "pointer" to the main file, we must search for the key value of that record in the dense index, or whatever structure is used for accessing the main file, which will probably take several block accesses. In comparison, we would need only one block access if we could go directly to the record of the main file, or two accesses if we went directly to the record in the dense index and then to the record in the main file.

Summary

In Fig. 2.14 we list the four types of organizations for files allowing lookup, modification, insertion, and deletion of records given the key value. In the timing analyses, we take n to be the number of records in the main file and, for uniformity with B-trees, we assume the records of the main file can be packed

Organization	Time per Operation	Advantages and Disadvantages	Problems with Pinned Records
Hashed	≥ 3	Fastest of all methods. If file grows, access slows, as buckets get large. Cannot access records easily in order of sorted key values.	Must search buckets for empty space during insertion or allow more blocks per bucket than optimal
sparse index	$\approx 2 + \log n$ for binary search $\approx 2 + \log \log n$ if address calculation is feasible and is used.	Fast access if address calculation can be used. Records can be accessed in sorted order.	Same as above.
B-tree	$\approx 2 + \log_d(n/e)$	Fast access. Records can be accessed in sorted order. Blocks tend not to be solidly packed.	Use B-tree as dense index.
dense index	$\leq 2 +$ time for operation on dense index file.	Often slower by one or two block accesses than if same access method used for index file were used for the main file. May save space.	None.

Fig. 2.14. Summary of access methods.

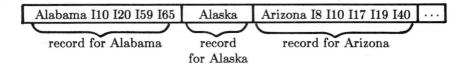

Fig. 2.15. File of states and highways.

$2e - 1$ to a block and records of any index files can be packed $2d - 1$ to a block.

2.6 FILES WITH VARIABLE LENGTH RECORDS

There are many situations in which it is useful to store files whose records have more general structure than those considered in the previous section. In particular, it is convenient to allow fields to be replaced by repeating groups of fields, each field in the group representing the same kind of object. For example, one way to store a many-many mapping from entity set E_1 to entity set E_2 is to create a file with one variable length record for each entity of type E_1. Such records consist of fields representing an entity, say e, of type E_1, and a repeating group of values, each of which is an entity of type E_2 related to e.

Example 2.10: Suppose we have a file of the states and the interstate highways within their boundaries. The states will form entity set E_1 and the highways form set E_2. A variable length record for this file consists of a field whose value is the state name, say a character string of length 15, and a repeating group of highway designators, each of which is a character string of length 3. The file might begin as shown in Fig. 2.15. Notice that the Alaska record has zero elements in its repeating group of highways. □

We should emphasize that a file such as Fig. 2.15 is a *logical file,* that is, a file at a higher level of abstraction than the files of fixed length records considered in previous sections. Indeed, the principal point of the present section is how one goes about implementing a logical file of variable length records with a file or files of fixed length records.

While in Fig. 2.15 we show actual values for entities, they could just as well be replaced by pointers to records for the states and highways, and attributes of those entities could be kept in another file. In fact, it would be wasteful to keep information about highways in the repeating groups, as this information would have to be repeated once for each state that the highway entered. Moreover, there would be the danger that two copies of the information about a highway could differ. However there is nothing inefficient or dangerous about keeping attributes of the states in their records, as each state appears only once in the file. In fact, if the relationship between entity sets E_1 and E_2 is many-one from E_2 to E_1 (note that the states-highways relationship is not many-one), we could just as well keep the attributes of an entity of type E_2 in the unique record for the entity of type E_1 to which it belongs.

We are thus led to the possibility that elements of repeating groups consist of more than one field. In fact, the fields of a repeating group could themselves be repeating groups, and in this manner we could represent in one file a many-one relationship from entity set E_2 to entity set E_1, another many-one relationship from an entity set E_3 to E_2, and so on. The general definition of a *variable length record format* we shall use is:

1. A variable length record format is a list of "elements."

2. An *element* is either a single field name or a variable length record format, which represents a repeating group of zero or more variable length records with that format.

We can represent variable length record formats in a regular-expression-like notation as follows. An element that is a field name is represented by that name. An element that is a repeating group with format α we represent by $(\alpha)^*$. A variable length record format consisting of elements with representations $\alpha_1, \alpha_2, \ldots, \alpha_k$ is represented by $\alpha_1 \alpha_2 \cdots \alpha_k$. The reader who is familar with regular expressions will notice that the set of possible sequences of field names in a record with the given format is exactly the language denoted by the regular expression constructed in this manner, but it is not essential to one's understanding of variable length record formats that one know about regular expressions. It suffices to remember that * applied to a formula means "repeat zero or more times."

We call a sequence of values that match the fields of a variable length record format an *occurrence* of that record format. Thus the term "occurrence" applies not only to full records, but we may talk about occurrences of a repeating group that is an element of some larger variable length record format. Recall that the possible formats for a repeating group and for a variable length record are one and the same.

Example 2.11:

a) The record format for the file of Example 2.10 is STATE(HIGHWAY)*. That is, the record format consists of two elements. The first is a field, named STATE, and the second is a repeating group of "variable length records." The latter records are not really varying in length and each consists of one field, called HIGHWAY. A typical occurrence of the repeating group HIGHWAY is I95, and an occurrence of the entire record format is:

New Jersey   I78   I80   I95

b) If we wished to include the attribute POPULATION in these records we could use the record format

STATE POPULATION (HIGHWAY)*

An example of an occurrence of this format is:

New Jersey   7,168,164   I78   I80   I95

c) For a more complicated example, we might include with each highway in
each state the number of miles of roadway and the set of terminal or entry
points for that highway within the state. The format for records with this
information is

STATE POPULATION (HIGHWAY LENGTH (TERMINAL)*)*

A typical record with this format is

New Jersey   7,168,164   I78   55   Phillipsburg   Newark   I80   73
Hainesburg   Ft. Lee   I95   68   W. Trenton   Ft. Lee

☐

Storing Variable Length Records

A record with repeating groups cannot be placed indiscriminately in a block
or blocks of storage, because we shall have no way of knowing what type of
field appears where. One possibility is to store each field in sequence, packing
as many to a block as will fit; it is not usual to allow fields to extend across
two blocks, however. A moment's reflection will indicate that if we simply pack
fields into blocks, we shall have great trouble decoding a block into fields, since
to determine where a field begins, we have to know how long the previous field
is. We cannot know how long a field is unless we know its type. Thus there
must be an indication of the field name or data type along with each field.

This information could be kept in a block header or with the fields themselves. The former approach requires us to leave space in the header for the
maximum possible number of fields in a block, and most of this space may be
unused in the average block. The latter approach requires that we examine the
entire block from the beginning to isolate any given field in that block.

Another approach is to represent each variable length record by one or
more fixed length records, and there are three basic strategies for doing so.

1) The Reserved Space Method

Assume there is a limit c to the number of occurrences of a repeating group.
Replace the repeating group by c groups of fields. Thus, in Example 2.11(c) we
could assume that no highway enters, leaves and then reenters a state. If so,
then the repeating group (TERMINAL)* could be replaced by TERMINAL1
TERMINAL2, and the revised record format

STATE POPULATION
        (HIGHWAY LENGTH TERMINAL1 TERMINAL 2)*

would suffice.

If the repeating group occurs no more than c times but could occur fewer than c times, we must have a way of indicating empty fields. One way is by using a "null value," one that could not be a legitimate value in that field. An alternative, which must be used if there is no suitable null value, is to add a field giving the actual number of occurrences of the repeating group; we assume that the empty fields follow the nonempty fields in the group. Thus we might decide that no state has more than ten highways and replace the repeating group for highways by a field COUNT and ten copies of the group. That is, the new record format is:

> STATE POPULATION COUNT
> HIGHWAY1 LENGTH1 TERMINAL1.1 TERMINAL2.1 ···
> HIGHWAY10 LENGTH10 TERMINAL1.10 TERMINAL2.10

We now have a fixed length record format and can store a file of such records as discussed in Sections 2.2–2.5.

2) The Pointer Method

We could replace a repeating group by a pointer to the first block of a chain of blocks used to store the occurrences of the repeating group. For example, we could replace the variable length record format of Example 2.11(c) by the three fixed length record formats

> STATE POPULATION HPTR
> HIGHWAY LENGTH TPTR
> TERMINAL

Figure 2.16 shows how our variable length record might be stored on blocks.

3) The Combined Method

There are various combinations of strategies (1) and (2) that can be used. Obviously, we could use pointers for one repeating group and a fixed repetition for another group. In general, we would prefer fixed repetition if there were a reliable maximum number of occurrences, and the average number of occurrences was close to this maximum. If the average and maximum number of occurrences differed greatly, we would waste too much space. Pointer based methods tend to use less space, but they require more block accesses to find a field than do fixed repetition methods. Thus, for the record format of Example 2.11(c), we might prefer to use fixed repetition for the TERMINAL repeating group and pointers for the HIGHWAY repeating group.

Another mode of combination of strategies (1) and (2) is to replace a repeating group by room for a small number of occurrences and a pointer to a chain of blocks where additional occurrences may be found. This strategy is useful if the number of occurrences tends to cluster around the average number.

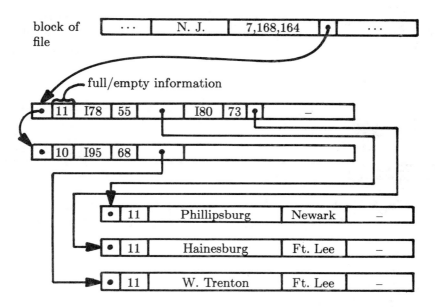

Fig. 2.16. Representing a variable length record with pointers.

Then if we choose to make room for slightly more than the average number of occurrences in the fixed length record, we shall have few pointers to chase and we shall not waste too much space.

Example 2.12: Let us reconsider Example 2.11(a), where the record format was STATE(HIGHWAY)*. Suppose we decide to allow room for three highways in the record for a state. The format of a fixed length record would then be

STATE COUNT HIGHWAY1 HIGHWAY2 HIGHWAY3 POINTER

Field COUNT indicates how many of the three highway fields are filled. We assume it is possible to fill these fields from the left, so the count is sufficient to tell us which fields are full. If values in the three highway fields were pinned, we could, instead of a count, use a bit vector indicating which fields were empty. The field POINTER will indicate the first block of a chain of blocks holding highways in excess of three for a state. The null pointer indicates that there are no extra highways. In Fig. 2.17 we see the records for three states; assuming two state records and four highway records fit in a block. □

Operations on Variable Length Records

Suppose we have a logical file of variable length records that we have implemented by a main file with a fixed length record format, perhaps with additional pointers and blocks not part of the main file, as discussed in connection with

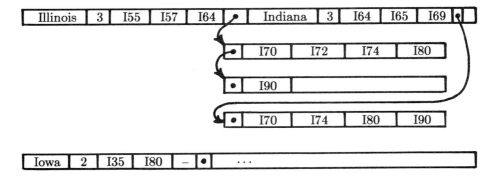

Fig. 2.17. State-highway records using reserved space and pointers.

implementation methods (2) and (3) above. We shall assume that some subset of the fields in the fixed length record format (excluding fields that are pointers to blocks holding occurrences of repeating groups) serves as a key for the variable length records of the logical file. This assumption makes sense if we recall our original motivation for considering variable length records, the representation of a many-many or many-one relationship from an entity set E_2 to another entity set E_1. Then the records will contain the attributes of a unique entity of type E_1, with the repeating group used for the associated entities of type E_2. In this case, the attributes of the key for entity set E_1 serve as a key for both the logical file and the file used in its implementation. Files with variable length records could be used for purposes other than the representation of relationships, and in those cases the main file of the implementation might not possess a key other than the entire set of fields. However, such situations occur rarely.

Assuming now that some set of fields of the implementing file of fixed length records forms a key, we can organize the implementing file for lookup, insertion, deletion, and modification using any of the organizations of previous sections. The only additional details concern the creation of blocks or chains of blocks for repeating groups during an insertion (if a pointer based implementation is used) and the return of such blocks to the file system if a deletion occurs. The algorithms involved are straightforward and we shall not elaborate on them.

We must also consider a new class of operations on variable length records, operations that have no counterpart for fixed length records. We should consider insertion and deletion of occurrences within a repeating group. These operations correspond to modifications of a relationship, if that is what the logical file represents. Whether the repeating groups are represented by the reserved space method, the pointer method, or a combination, we can view each repeating group as a small file by itself. As for the main file, we assume that there is a key for the repeating group; this key is formed from the fields of the repeating group, but does not include any pointer fields.

We could use any of the methods of previous sections to maintain a small file for a repeating group, but these files are usually sufficiently short that no special organization is used, and given a key value for the repeating group, we simply search linearly through the occurrences of the group. In that case, given a key value, lookup within the group is straightforward; we can delete an occurrence once this occurrence is found, and we can insert, either at the beginning, at the end, or in sorted order, once we have searched the occurrences and determined that no occurrence with the given key value exists.

If occurrences within a repeating group are pinned by pointers to those occurrences, then we must exercise care in how we do insertions and deletions. The ideas are covered in Section 2.2 (hashed files), where we discussed these operations on a bucket of pinned records.

2.7 DATA STRUCTURES FOR LOOKUP ON NONKEY FIELDS

Until now, we have considered only those operations on files where, given a key value, we searched for a record with that key value, and perhaps did something to that record. However, a versatile database system allows queries in which we obtain information from records that are identified by values in a field or fields that do not form a key. For example, referring to our dinosaur file introduced in Example 2.1, the data manipulation language might well allow us to express commands such as:

1. Find all dinosaurs from the Jurassic period.
2. Find the habitats with carnivorous dinosaurs.
3. Find all dinosaurs that lived on land and were at least 50 feet long.

In this section we shall consider how to organize a file so that given values for some particular sets of fields, other than the key, we can obtain efficiently those records with the correct values. The method most generally useful is the creation of "secondary indices," which relate values of a field or fields to the records with those values. We consider secondary indices in the present section; the next section considers the more general "partial match retrieval" problem of finding matching records given values for an arbitrary subset of the fields.

Secondary Indices

Let us consider a file whose records have a certain field F whose possible values are taken from the set of values D, the *domain* for F. Field F may be part of a set of fields that form a key, or it may be outside the key. It is possible that the value of field F uniquely determines a record, although we do not assume so. A *secondary index* for field F is a relationship between domain D and the set of records of the file in question.† A file with a secondary index on a field

---

† In contrast, the index discussed in Section 2.3, relating key values to records, is called a *primary index*.

F is said to be an *inverted file* (on field F). In terms of Section 2.6, we can represent a secondary index as a logical file with format

VALUE (RECORD)*

An instance of VALUE is a value from D. An instance of RECORD could be either
1.   a pointer to a record with the associated value in field F, or
2.   a key value for a record with the desired value in field F.

If option (1) is used, the pointer could point to the subblock containing the record, or it could point to the block containing the record, in which case a search of the block would be necessary to find the desired record or records. In either case, the records of the file are consequently pinned, at least to within the block. The pointer could also point to the bucket (for those organizations of fixed length records using buckets) containing the desired record or records. In this case search of a whole bucket for the record is necessary, but records are not pinned (except to within the bucket) unless there are pointers to the file other than those used by the secondary index.

As was mentioned in Section 2.5, with option (2) records of the main file are not pinned by pointers from the secondary index. However, compared with method (1), method (2) will require several additional block accesses to perform a lookup of a record given its key value, while method (1) goes directly to that record, or at least to its block or bucket.

Example 2.13: In Fig. 2.18 we see a file of dinosaurs again. Presumably there is some sort of primary index on the key field, NAME, but we do not show this index, nor do we indicate how the records are distributed among blocks. We do show a secondary index on the field PERIOD, using method (2). This secondary index has only three variable length records, implemented using the pointer method. The secondary index has no index on its own key field VALUE; as there are only three geological periods during which dinosaurs flourished, there is no need for one.

We also show a secondary index on the WEIGHT field. This index uses approach (1) with pointers to the records of the main file. This secondary index has records sorted by their key, the VALUE field, and lookup is by a sparse primary index as discussed in Section 2.3.

Suppose we wish to find the lengths of all dinosaurs from the Jurassic period. We examine the initial block for this index and find a record for "Jurassic." We follow that pointer to a chain of blocks holding the names of these dinosaurs. We then look up in the main file each of the records with these names as key values, using whatever lookup algorithm is appropriate for the unspecified primary index organization of the main file.

Next consider the query: find the names of all dinosaurs with weights between 5 and 10 tons. We begin at the primary index for the secondary index

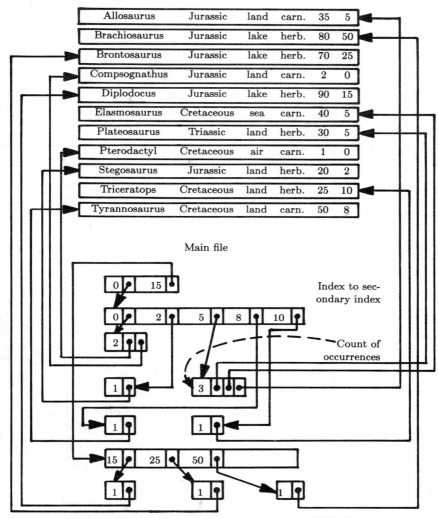

Fig. 2.18a. Secondary index for WEIGHT.

on WEIGHT. The only two records there have WEIGHT values 0 and 15. Since 0 covers both 5 and 10, we need only follow the pointer for 0. In general, if we are looking for the range between m and n we shall have to follow the pointers in the records whose key values cover m and n, and the pointers in any records between those two. In this example, we follow only one pointer, and this leads to a block with WEIGHT values 0, 2, 5, 8, and 10. The last three of these are in the desired range, so we follow their pointers. The pointer for 5 sends us to a

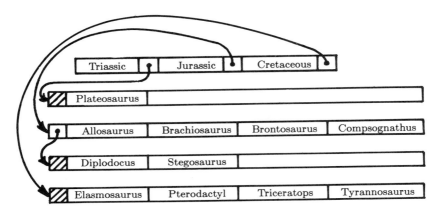

Fig. 2.18b. Secondary index for PERIOD.

block with three pointers to records of the main file, and when we follow these
we obtain the names "Allosaurus," "Elasmosaurus," and "Plateosaurus." The
pointers for 8 and 10 each lead to a block with one pointer, and following these
pointers we obtain the names "Tyrannosaurus" and "Triceratops." □

2.8 PARTIAL MATCH RETRIEVAL

In this section and the next, we shall study two common types of queries that
are more complex than the kinds considered in the previous sections. In the
first type of query, the values from one or more fields are specified, yet these
fields do not include all of the key fields. Suppose we are told to find the
records with value v_1 in field F_1, v_2 in field $F_2, \ldots, v_k$ in field F_k. If S_i is the
set of records with value v_i in field F_i, for $i = 1, 2, \ldots, k$, what we want is
$S_1 \cap S_2 \cap \cdots \cap S_k$. We shall describe two methods to solve this problem.
The first uses multiple secondary indices, and the second involves a specialized
form of hashing function. Since the problem involves finding partially specified
records, it has become known as the *partial match retrieval* problem.

Use of Multiple Secondary Indices

To solve the above problem, we do not actually have to retrieve all the records
in S_1, then those in S_2, and so on. Rather, if we have secondary indices for some
or all of the fields F_i, we can obtain only the pointers to the records in those
sets S_i for which a secondary index for F_i exists. These sets of pointers can, if
they are not too large, be intersected in main memory. Then we follow each
pointer in the intersection and check that the record pointed to has the desired
value in the remaining fields, those for which no secondary index exists. Note
that if pointers are to blocks or buckets, rather than to individual records, we

have to consider each record in the block or bucket, and we cannot be sure that even one record there has all the specified values in all the fields with secondary indices. It might be, for example, that a block has one record with value v_1 in field F_1 and a different record with value v_2 in field F_2. In that case a pointer to the block would be in $S_1 \cap S_2$ even though no record of the block had v_1 in F_1 and v_2 in F_2. Such a situation is called a *false drop*.

To minimize the size of the list of pointers with which we must deal, we should first get the set S_i for that field F_i, having a secondary index, for which we expect S_i to be smallest. As a heuristic, we might choose that field F_i with the largest set of different values present in the database, if such statistics are known or can be guessed at. For example, if we are asked for carnivorous dinosaurs of the Jurassic period, we might first look up the secondary index for PERIOD, then DIET, assuming such indices existed, as there are three periods but only two diets.

Extending this principle, the second set S_j in the intersection should be that with the second smallest expected size, and so on. Thus the intersection will shrink as rapidly as possible, on the average.

Partitioned Hash Functions

We shall now mention an interesting method of organization that uses no indices whatsoever, either primary or secondary, yet the organization usually provides significant help in narrowing down the search for records when any set of values for any set of fields is given. Naturally, the more fields there are for which values are specified, the faster the search will be.

The number of blocks to be accessed, when the method to be described is used, is large compared with the number of blocks accessed when the file organization has secondary indices for all fields, so we would not recommend this method of partial match retrieval for extremely large files. However, because no space is used for indices, this method may be a suitable alternative for files requiring a thousand blocks or so. Also, as no secondary indices are present, no time is spent modifying these indices during insertions or deletions to the main file. Finally, the structure is promising for files on which we perform range queries, as discussed in the next section.

The essential idea is that we take all the fields to be the key, even if some subset of the fields could serve as a key, and we hash records using the full set of fields as the key. Now if we used an ordinary hash function, we could obtain the bucket to which a record belongs only if we knew the record exactly. However, if we design the hash function carefully, we can limit the number of buckets in which matching records could be found whenever we know the value of one or more fields. The "trick" is to divide the bits of the bucket number into several pieces and let each field determine one of the pieces. Then, whenever we know one or more fields, we know something about the numbers of the buckets in which the desired record or records could lie.

First, we assume the number of buckets is a power of two, say 2^B, and that a logical bucket address is a sequence of B bits. Translation of logical bucket addresses to physical block addresses can be done by a simple calculation if we can choose the physical addresses ourselves; if the file system assigns block addresses, a table translating logical to physical addresses must be used. Next, we partition the B bits of bucket addresses into groups, one group for each field (a field may be assigned zero bits for its group).

If the fields are $F_1, F_2, \ldots, F_k$, and field F_i is assigned b_i bits, we determine the bucket of a record $(v_1, v_2, \ldots, v_k)$, where v_i is the value in field F_i, by computing $h_i(v_i)$ for $i = 1, 2, \ldots, k$. Here, h_i is a hash function for values in field i, and the value produced by h_i is an integer between 0 and $2^{b_i} - 1$. Thus $h_i(v_i)$ is a sequence of b_i bits. We take the logical address of the bucket for record $(v_1, v_2, \ldots, v_k)$ to be the sequence of B bits $h_1(v_1)h_2(v_2)\cdots h_k(v_k)$.

Example 2.14: Suppose we have records with three fields

> EMP_NO: INT(5)
> SS_NO: INT(9) /* Social Security number */
> DEPT: CHAR(10)

and we wish to store records in $2^9 = 512$ buckets. Suppose also that the nine bits of a bucket address are divided, four for EMP_NO, three for SS_NO, and two for DEPT. The hash function we use for EMP_NO is to divide the employee number by 16 and take the remainder. For SS_NO we divide by 8 and take the remainder. For DEPT we divide the number of nonblank characters in the department name by 4 and take the remainder.†

If we are given the record (58651, 130326734, Sales) we divide 58651 by 16 to get the remainder, eleven, or 1011 as a four-bit binary number. The social security number modulo 8 is 6, or 110 in binary, and the length of "Sales" modulo 4 is 1, or 01 as a two-bit binary number. Thus the bucket in which this record will be found is 101111001, the concatenation of hash values 1011, 110, and 01. □

Whenever we are given the value for field F_i, we can compute b_i bits of the bucket address, independently of whether the values in the other fields are known or unknown. Thus, if we know the value in field F_i, we cut down the number of buckets we must search by a factor of 2^{b_i}. For example, if we are looking for the department of the employee with number 58651 in Example 2.14, we must search 32 buckets, corresponding to the 32 possible values of the five bits belonging to fields SS_NO and DEPT. If we know both the EMP_NO and SS_NO of an employee, we need look at only four buckets.

---

† As with dinosaur names, this hash function is probably inadequate for department names but will make the example easier.

Optimizing the Distribution of Bits Among Fields

Suppose we know the statistics of queries; that is, we know the probability that any given set of fields will have their values specified in a query. Suppose also that when we specify a value for field F_i, any of the possible values for F_i are equally likely. The following theorem provides an important result on bucket addressing in this case.

Theorem 2.1: If all values for a field are equally likely when a value for that field is specified, then the minimum expected number of buckets to be examined to satisfy a query is obtained when, for some $n_1, n_2, \ldots, n_k$ whose product equals the number of buckets, the bucket address for record $(v_1, v_2, \ldots, v_k)$ is expressed as

$$h_k(v_k) + n_k(h_{k-1}(v_{k-1}) + n_{k-1}(h_{k-2}(v_{k-2}) + \cdots + n_2 h_1(v_1)\cdots))$$

where hash function $h_i(v_i)$ ranges from 0 to n_i. $\square$

The above formula is really a generalization of our approach of using a sequence of bits, calculated separately from the various fields, as a bucket address. That is, in our formulation, $n_i = 2^{b_i}$. Thus our approach is not guaranteed to be optimal, but it is never too far from optimal, and the simplicity of using a sequence of independently derived bits as a bucket address, rather than a formula such as $h_3(v_3) + 3h_2(v_2) + 12h_1(v_1)$, is worthwhile.

The proof of Theorem 2.1 is beyond the scope of this book. It should be intuitively clear that by having each bit of the bucket address only depend on the value of one field, as opposed to the values of two or more fields, we are most likely to know the value of a bit, and therefore are most likely to be able to eliminate a given bucket from the search dictated by a random query. The generalization of this plausibility argument to the bucket address formula of Theorem 2.1, which can be viewed as a variable radix notation for integers† is straightfoward. A proof of Theorem 2.1 is found in Bolour [1979].

While Theorem 2.1 supports our approach of building bucket addresses by concatenating bit strings obtained independently from the several fields, it gives us no hint as to what the values of the n_i's should be, or in our restriction, where $n_i = 2^{b_i}$, what the integer b_i should be. Obviously, the b_i's depend on the frequencies with which various sets of fields have their values specified in a query.

For example, if all queries specified a value for field F_1 and no other field, then we would be best off setting $b_1 = B$ and $b_2 = b_3 = \cdots = b_k = 0$. This situation corresponds to the case where F_1 is a key and in this case, our organization is the same as the hashing scheme of Section 2.2. In this example, each query requires that only one bucket be examined.

---

† The rightmost digit is the one's place, the next digit the "n_k's place" the third digit the "$n_{k-1}n_k$'s place" and so on.

As another example, if half the queries only specify F_1 while the other half specify F_2 and F_3, we would expect to be best off if we set $b_1 = B/2$ and $b_2 = b_3 = B/4$, with $b_i = 0$ for $i > 3$. Then we would examine $2^{B/2}$ buckets per query, not only on the average, but in all cases. $\Box$

In only a few cases has the formula for the b_i's been obtained in closed form. We mention these cases here.

If a Value is Specified for Only One Field

One such case is when a value is specified for only one field. The following theorem determines the value of b_i that minimizes the expected number of bucket searches in this case.

Theorem 2.2: If all queries specify one field, and p_i is the probability that F_i is the field specified, then assuming no b_i is less than 0 or greater than B, the expected number of buckets to be searched is minimized if we set

$$b_i = \frac{B - \sum_{j=1}^{k} \log_2 p_j}{k} + \log_2 p_i$$

where k is the number of fields and 2^B is the number of buckets. Note that only the last term, $\log_2 p_i$, depends on i.

Proof: If F_i is specified, we look at 2^{B-b_i} buckets. Thus the expected number of buckets searched is $\sum_{i=1}^{k} p_i 2^{B-b_i}$. As $\sum_{i=1}^{k} b_i = B$, using the method of Lagrangian multipliers, we know the above expression will be minimized when for all i,

$$\frac{\partial}{\partial b_i}\left[\sum_{j=1}^{k} p_j 2^{B-b_j} + \lambda(B - \sum_{j=1}^{k} b_j)\right] = 0$$

or equivalently:

$$(-\log_e 2)p_i 2^{B-b_i} - \lambda = 0$$

for all i. Thus there is some constant c such that for all i,

$$p_i 2^{-b_i} = c$$

or

$$\log_2 p_i = b_i + \log_2 c \tag{2.1}$$

Since the b_i's sum to B we see that summing (2.1) gives:

$$\sum_{j=1}^{k} \log_2 p_j = B + k \log_2 c$$

so

$$\log_2 c = \frac{\sum_{j=1}^{k} \log_2 p_j - B}{k}$$

and substituting for $\log_2 c$ in (2.1):

$$b_i = \log_2 p_i - \log_2 c = \frac{B - \sum_{j=1}^{k} \log_2 p_j}{k} + \log_2 p_i$$

as was to be proved. $\square$

There are several problems with the formula of Theorem 2.2. First, what if $b_i < 0$ or $b_i > B$? In the former case, we set b_i to 0, eliminate field F_i from consideration and reapply Theorem 2.2. Note that more than one reapplication of the theorem may be necessary, as some b_j that was positive may become negative on the second application. In the case $b_i > B$, we set $b_i = B$, set all other b_i's to 0, and we are done.

Another problem is that the formula for b_i in Theorem 2.2 may yield a nonintegral number of bits. The rule to be followed to find the optimal apportionment of bits is the following. Let $b_i = c_i + d_i$, where c_i is an integer and $0 \le d_i < 1$. Then the d_i's will always sum to an integer if B is an integer. Let $\sum_{i=1}^{k} d_i = D$. Then pick the D b_i's with the largest values of d_i, and raise them to $c_i + 1$. Lower the remaining b_j's to c_j.

Example 2.15: Let us consider the file of Example 2.14. Suppose 75% of the queries specify an employee's EMP_NO, 24% specify the SS_NO, and 1% specify the DEPT. That is, $p_1 = .75$, $p_2 = .24$, and $p_3 = .01$. Suppose $B = 9$. As $k = 3$, and $\sum_{j=1}^{3} \log_2 p_j = (-0.41) + (-2.05) + (-6.64) = -9.10$, the formula of Theorem 2.2 tells us

$$b_i = \frac{9 - (-9.10)}{3} + \log_2 p_i = 6.03 + \log_2 p_i$$

Thus $b_1 = 5.62$, $b_2 = 3.98$, and $b_3 = -0.61$.

As b_3 is negative, we set b_3, the number of bits allocated to field DEPT, to 0 and resolve the problem as though there were only two fields with probabilities $p_1 = \frac{.75}{1-.01} = .758$, and $p_2 = \frac{.24}{1-.01} = .242$. Now, $k = 2$, so $\sum_{j=1}^{2} \log_2 p_j = (-0.40) + (-2.04) = -2.44$, and

$$b_i = \frac{9 - (-2.44)}{2} + \log_2 p_i = 5.72 + \log_2 p_i$$

whereupon we obtain $b_1 = 5.32$ and $b_2 = 3.68$. As the proper fractions in 5.32 and 3.68 total 1, we select the larger fraction, .68, and raise it to 1; the other fraction, .32 is lowered to 0. Thus the optimal apportionment of bits is $b_1 = 5$, $b_2 = 4$, and $b_3 = 0$. that is, five bits from the EMP_NO field, four from the SS_NO field and none from the DEPT field. With this distribution, the expected number of buckets to be searched is

$$.75(2^4) + .24(2^5) + .01(2^9) = 24.8 \text{ buckets}$$

□

If Values for Fields are Specified Independently

The second known case where the values of the b_i's can be found explicitly is if there is a probability p_i that a value will be specified for field i, and this probability is independent of which, if any, of the other fields have values specified. For example, if there are three fields, then the probability that a query specifies values for the first two fields but not the third is $p_1 p_2 (1 - p_3)$. Notice that unlike the case of Theorem 2.2, the p_i's need not sum to one.

Theorem 2.3: If the probability is p_i that a value for field F_i is specified, independent of which other fields have values specified, then assuming no b_i is less than zero or greater than B, the expected number of buckets to be searched is minimized when we set

$$b_i = \frac{B - \sum_{j=1}^{k} \log_2(\frac{p_j}{1-p_j})}{k} + \log_2(\frac{p_i}{1 - p_i})$$

Notice that the above formula is the formula of Theorem 2.2 with p_m replaced by $\frac{p_m}{1-p_m}$.

Proof: The expected number of buckets searched is

$$\sum_{S \subseteq \{1,2,...,k\}} \prod_{i \text{ in } S} p_i \prod_{i \text{ not in } S} (1 - p_i)2^{b_i}$$

The key observations are first that the above formula is equivalent to

$$2^B \prod_{i=1}^{k} (1 - p_i) \sum_{S \subseteq \{1,2,...,k\}} \prod_{i \text{ in } S} (\frac{p_i}{1 - p_i})2^{-b_i}$$

and then that for any values of the a_i's the following formula holds:

$$\sum_{S \subseteq \{1,2,...,k\}} \prod_{i \text{ in } S} a_i = \prod_{i=1}^{k} (1 + a_i)$$

Letting $a_i = (\frac{p_i}{1-p_i})2^{-b_i}$ we see that the original formula is equivalent to

$$2^B \prod_{i=1}^{k} (1 - p_i)(1 + \frac{p_i}{1 - p_i}2^{-b_i}) \tag{2.2}$$

The balance of the proof follows the lines of Theorem 2.2; we use Lagrangian multipliers and take partial derivatives with respect to each b_i. We leave this part as an exercise for the reader. □

We deal with b_i's that are negative or exceed B as in Theorem 2.2. We also adjust fractions in the optimal b_i's as discussed following that theorem.

Example 2.16: Suppose we have a billing file with the following fields

> (F_1) NAME: CHAR(20) /* the purchaser */
> (F_2) ITEM: CHAR(20) /* the item purchased */
> (F_3) QUANTITY: INT(9)
> (F_4) DATE: INT(6)

Let us assume that the probabilities that the various fields are specified in a query are $p_1=.8$, $p_2=.5$, $p_3=.01$, and $p_4=.2$, and that these probabilities are independent of the other fields specified. For example, the probability of a query like: "find the names and/or quantities of all bills for shirts on July 20, 1982" is $(1-.8)(.5)(1-.01)(.2) = .0198$. That is, about 2% of the queries specify the ITEM and DATE but not the other two fields. Let $B = 9$. Then

$$\sum_{j=1}^{4} \log_2(\tfrac{p_j}{1-p_j})$$

$$= \log_2(\tfrac{.8}{1-.8}) + \log_2(\tfrac{.5}{1-.5}) + \log_2(\tfrac{.01}{1-.01}) + \log_2(\tfrac{.2}{1-.2})$$

$$= 2 + 0 + (-6.63) + (-2) = -6.63$$

Thus Theorem 2.3 tells us

$$b_i = \frac{9-(-6.63)}{4} + \log_2(\frac{p_i}{1-p_i}) = 3.91 + \log_2(\frac{p_i}{1-p_i})$$

That is, $b_1=5.91$, $b_2=3.91$, $b_3=-2.73$, and $b_4=1.91$.

As b_3 is negative, we eliminate the QUANTITY field from consideration and set $b_3 = 0$. Note that unlike Theorem 2.2, no adjustment of probabilities is necessary when we eliminate a field. On reapplying Theorem 2.3 we obtain

$$b_i = 3 + \log_2(\frac{p_i}{1-p_i})$$

for $i = 1, \ldots, 4$. Thus $b_1=5$, $b_2=3$, $b_3=0$, and $b_4=1$. and no adjustment of fractions is necessary.

If we apply formula (2.2) to get the average number of buckets, we obtain

$$2^9 \prod_{i=1}^{4}(1-p_i)(1 + \tfrac{p_i}{1-p_i}2^{-b_i})$$

$$= 2^9(.2)(1 + \tfrac{4}{2^5})(.5)(1 + \tfrac{1}{2^3})(.99)(1 + \tfrac{.0101}{2^0})(.8)(1 + \tfrac{.25}{2^1})$$

$$= 58.3 \text{ buckets}$$

☐

2.9 DATA STRUCTURES FOR RANGE QUERIES

Another common kind of query is one where we are given a range for several fields of the key and we want to retrieve all those records whose values in all the specified fields fall within the desired ranges. For example, we might request all records for which $10 \leq F_1 < 50$, $F_2 < 5$, and $F_3 = 14$. Note that the last of these conditions is a trivial range, $14 \leq F_3 \leq 14$, and points up the fact that a partial match query is a special case of a range query.

Many specialized tree structures have been proposed for handling range queries. In this section, we shall only consider one possibility. However, first, let us examine the structure from the previous section and see how it might help us with range queries.

Use of Partitioned Hash Functions

Suppose that we are trying to answer the example range query above, and our data is stored in a partitioned hash table. Our first thought might be to generate a list of all the records that could fall within the ranges, and search for them each in turn. The notion of "all records within a range" doesn't even make sense in some circumstances. For example, a simple range like $10 \leq F_1 < 50$ defines an infinite number of possibilities if the value of F_1 is a real number. Even if all fields have integer values, a range like $F_2 < 5$ implies an infinite number of values for F_2, since we must presume F_2 could be negative.

Finally, even supposing that $0 \leq F_2 < 5$ were implied by the range for F_2, and also supposing that all fields have integer values, we would still have 200 combinations of values for the specified fields to consider. That would not be so bad if we expect that for each combination of values there is at least one record to retrieve. However, typically, there are astronomically more possible records, that is, possible combinations of values in the key fields, than there are actual records, and most of the 200 searches will be futile. For example, one field might be the name of a subject, another field the address, a third the age, and so on. We would hardly expect that at every address there is a person with each possible name and of every possible age.

In many cases, we can use partitioned hashing functions and avoid all these problems. In particular, we shall be able to arrange that the fraction of buckets searched is close to the fraction of the records that satisfy the range query, so the cost of answering the query is roughly proportional to the time needed just to retrieve the answer. Suppose, for example, that the values of field F_1 are known to be distributed fairly evenly in the range 0 to 100, and that the partitioned hash function devotes three bits to F_1. As there are 101 different values of F_1, and we would like to divide them into eight ranges, corresponding to the eight sequences of three bits, we should choose ranges of twelve or thirteen values each. For example, we might let bits 000 correspond to the range 0–12, 001 correspond to the range 13–24, 010 correspond to range 25–37, 011 correspond to 38–50, and so on.

If that were the case, all the records with F_1 in the range 10 to 49 would be in buckets whose bucket addresses have 000, 001, 010, or 011 for the three bits devoted to F_1. This fact reduces the number of buckets to be searched by a factor of 0.5, which is not bad, considering that the range desired in the field F_1 covers fraction 0.39 of the possible values in that field.

It might seem that there is nothing more to the matter. Each of the hash functions has only to map the value for the corresponding field to one of several ranges, using comparisons with fixed values to do so. Not every range appearing in a query will consist exactly of some subset of the ranges that correspond to the bit sequences produced by the hash function for that field, but there cannot be too much overlap. That is, suppose the ranges corresponding to the hash function values are $a_0 \leq F < a_1$, $a_1 \leq F < a_2, \ldots, a_{k-1} \leq F < a_k$. The requested range $b \leq F < c$ requires us to look at the ranges i through j, where i is the largest integer such that $a_{i-1} \leq b$, and j is the smallest integer such that $a_j \geq c$.

Observe that all the records out of the range for field F, except for those that fall in the ith or j^{th} range but are not between b and c, are in buckets whose addresses do not match, in the bits for field F, any of the selected hash values. Suppose $j - i$ is larger than, say, 2 or 3. Then the "edge effect" due to the fact that the first and last selected ranges do not consist wholly of records with an F-value in the desired range is not too significant; that is, the fraction of buckets we must search has been cut down by a factor roughly proportional to the fraction of the total range for field F that lies between b and c.

Since the same argument applies to the range for each field in turn, we can now see why this method allows us to focus on a fraction of the buckets equal to

$$\prod_{i=1}^{k} \frac{r_i}{t_i}$$

where r_i is the size of the range specified for field i, and t_i is the total range for the ith field; if no range is specified by the query for the ith field, then we take r_i to be t_i. That is, fields not mentioned by the query do not help to restrict the search.

To get a more accurate value, we should round each fraction r_i/t_i up, to the nearest multiple of 2^{-b}, where b is the number of bits devoted to the ith field. Thus, for example, the tiny range defined by the term $F_3 = 14$, if, say, two bits are devoted to F_3, only restricts the number of buckets to be searched by factor 0.25, still a significant restriction, but not as powerful as the estimate $1/t_3$, if t_3 were, say, 1000.

However, the above analysis is predicated on values being distributed evenly among the ranges that define the hash values for a field. In many cases, we can develop ways to distribute approximately evenly the values for a given field, yet there are pitfalls. For example, if two bits are devoted to field AGE, we might suppose that four ranges like 0–15, 16–34, 35–54, and 55 and up would be appropriate. Yet what if we turned out to be dealing with a database for the Boy Scouts, or a database of social security recipients? In most cases, a little thought would prevent such problems, and it is reasonable to expect that in a well designed database the records would distribute evenly enough among ranges. There is, however, the danger of drift in the values for a field. For example, there might be a lowering of the minimum age for receiving social security, in which case, the lowest AGE range would suddenly be flooded with records. In that situation, a restructuring of the database, while hardly the most important social consequence of the change, would nevertheless be required.

A B-tree Based Organization

As mentioned, there are a variety of data structures, mostly variants of tree structures, that have been proposed to deal efficiently with range queries. The interested reader is encouraged to consult the bibliographic notes in this regard. We shall here discuss only the use of B-tree indices as an appropriate tree structure for handling range queries on data to which our secondary storage model of data applies. Recall that B-trees are preferable to hashing for indices whenever the retrieval of records in order of key value is important, and range queries are a good example of such a situation. The isam index is another suitable structure for finding ranges of values, but it is probably inferior to the B-tree.

Let us pick one field, say A, and maintain the records in a B-tree, as if A were the entire key. The only difference between what we do here and Section 2.4 is that A isn't really a key, and there may be many records with a particular A-value. As a consequence, we need to place at a node both the lowest and highest A-value found among each of its descendants. As a particular A-value may be found among the descendants of more than one child of a node, we must consult the range for each child before deciding which of the children of a node to follow, and which not to follow, during a search for a particular range of values for field A.

Because the records are grouped by A-value, there is a considerable advantage in picking field A to be one that frequently has a small range specified in queries. The reason is that whenever a small range for A is specified, we can limit the number of blocks of the main file that must be retrieved, while if no range restriction is specified for A, we are likely to find ourselves reading a few records from every block of the main file, with a resulting large cost in blocks retrieved.

For all the other fields of the key, we create secondary indices, also structured as B-trees. As for the primary index, it is useful to record the range of values for that field found among the descendants of each node.

Given a query, we consult the indices for all the fields that have a range restriction, obtaining sets of pointers to the records satisfying one of the range restrictions. These sets of pointers can be intersected in main memory, preferably starting with the smallest set, as discussed at the beginning of Section 2.8. The records that appear in all the sets are retrieved. The number of blocks retrieved to perform the intersection depends on the number of fields for which ranges are specified. The total number is

$$B \sum_i \frac{r_i}{t_i}$$

where the sum ranges over all fields for which a range is specified, and r_i and t_i are the range size and total range, as before. B is the number of blocks required to hold a secondary index stored as a B-tree.

Example 2.17: Figure 2.19 shows a file of ten records, with each record represented by a pair (a, b) of values for the fields A and B of the key. The primary index is on A, and there is a secondary index on B. We have assumed parameter $d = 2$ for each B-tree, i.e., each node has two or three children, so we can exhibit a nontrivial example. Ranges for A are shown at the interior nodes of the upper tree, and ranges for B in the lower. Note that the records themselves are stored in order of A-value, and that two children of the node with range 1–3 have ranges that include 2. $\square$

Comparison of Methods

There is no convenient way to make a direct comparison between the two approaches to range queries we have covered, but we can make a few observations. First, the existence of a field to play the role of A in the B-tree method, that is, a field that frequently appears in queries with a small range, favors the B-tree method. However, if we tune the partitioned hash function to devote many bits to A, we can obtain much of the same advantage with that method. Second, let us observe that queries with range restrictions on many fields actually increase the number of index blocks that must be retrieved, while the partitioned hash method performs better if additional fields are restricted. Third, the size of blocks influences our choice of method, since a bucket must be at least one block in size, on the average. If the main file fits on a small number of blocks, edge effects may make it difficult for the hashing approach to eliminate many buckets, while the B-tree method could do most of its work in main memory, after consulting a small number of index blocks.

It should be emphasized that neither of the methods attain the ideal of a number of retrieved blocks close to the minimum number that will hold the records satisfying the query. In cases where the ranges are large, the hashing approach comes closer to this goal than the B-tree method.

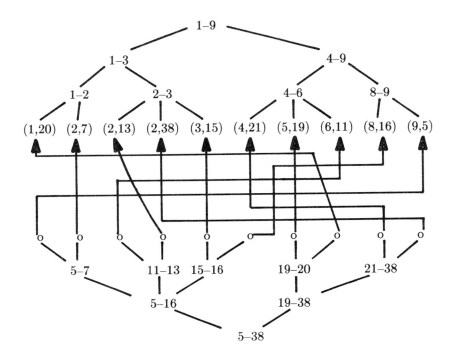

Fig. 2.19. B-tree structure for range queries.

EXERCISES

2.1: Suppose we have a file of one million records. Each record takes 200 bytes, of which 50 are for fields of the key. A block has room for 1000 bytes, exclusive of space for the header. A pointer to a block or subblock takes 5 bytes.

a)   If we use a hashed file organization with 1000 buckets, how many blocks are needed for the bucket directory?

b)   How many blocks are needed for the buckets, assuming all buckets have the average number of records?

c)   On the assumption of (b), what is the average number of block accesses to lookup a record that is actually present in the file?

d)   If we assume pinned records and use a sparse index that has just been created for the file (all file blocks are full, with no overflow), how many blocks are used for the index?

e)   If we use binary search for the index, how many block accesses are needed to lookup a record?

f)   If we use a B-tree and assume all blocks are as full as possible, how many index blocks are used (among all nonleaf levels)?

2.2: Suppose keys are integers, and we have a file consisting of records with keys 1, 4, 9, ..., $15^2 = 225$. Assume that three records will fit in one block.

- a) If we use the hashed organization of Section 2.2, with the hash function "divide by 7 and take the remainder," what is the distribution of records into buckets?

** b) Explain why the perfect squares hash so nonuniformly in part (a).

- c) Suppose we begin a sparse index organization as in Section 2.3 by packing the perfect squares into blocks as tightly as possible. Assuming the records are unpinned, show the file organization after inserting the even perfect squares.
- d) Repeat part (c) assuming pinned records.
- e) Show a B-tree organization of the file if the fifteen records are inserted in order of their keys. Assume the parameters of the B-tree are $d = e = 2$.
- f) Suppose we use a B-tree with d=2 as a dense index on the file. Show the organization if the records are inserted even squares first, in numerical order, then odd squares in numerical order.

2.3: Suppose we keep a file of information about states. Each state has a variable-length record with a field for the state name and a repeating group for the counties of the state. Each county group has fields for the name and population, a repeating group for township names, and a repeating group for city names. Give the record format for variable-length state records.

2.4: Suppose we have variable-length records of format $A(B)^*$. An A field takes 20 bytes and a B field 30 bytes. A pointer requires 4 bytes and a count field one byte. Each A has associated with it from 2 to 8 B's with probabilities .05, .1, .2, .3, .2, .1, and .05, respectively. If blocks are 100 bytes long, compare the average number of blocks per record used if we adopt

- a) the reserved space method,
- b) the pointer method with as many records as possible packed into one block, and,
- c) the mixed method with room for p B fields along with each A field. What is the optimal value of p?

* 2.5: Suppose we have a file with three fields F, G, and H. There are 10 possible values for F, 100 possible values for G, and 20 possible values for H. All 20,000 possible (F, G, H) records are equally likely to appear in the file. We assume that all queries specify values for exactly two fields; with probability .8, F and G are specified, with probability .15, F and H are specified, and with probability .05, G and H are specified. Finally, suppose we are allowed to select two fields on which to create secondary indices. Which two fields should we choose to minimize the expected number of retrieved

records in response to a query? Assume that in the case where secondary indices for both specified fields exist, we may intersect sets of pointers in memory before we retrieve any records.

2.6: When we create secondary indices, there is a tradeoff between insertion and deletion time on one hand, and lookup time on the other, because each index speeds up the lookup time while requiring us to do more work each time we insert or delete a record. Suppose as an oversimplified example that if we use s secondary indices the expected time to find a record is 3^{-s} seconds, while the insertion/deletion time is $.1(s + 1)$ seconds. If on the average there are 100 lookups for every insertion or deletion, what value of s gives the minimum expected time per operation?

2.7: Complete the proof of Theorem 2.3.

2.8: Suppose we use a partitioned hashing scheme for partial match retrieval as discussed in Section 2.8, and the bucket addresses have 12 bits. If there are four fields, and each query specifies exactly one of them, with probabilities $1/2$, $1/4$, $1/8$, and $1/8$, what is the optimal distribution of bits in the bucket addresses to the fields?

2.9: Suppose all is as in Exercise 2.8, but queries specify any number of fields independently, and the probability that values are specified for the four fields are $8/9$, $1/2$, $1/9$, and $1/17$. What is the optimal distribution of bits in the bucket address?

2.10: Suppose keys have three fields, A, B, and C, and we attempt to handle range queries by using a partitioned hash function with 2, 3, and 4 bits devoted to A, B, and C, respectively. Let the number of values in the total allowable range for these fields be 100, 200, and 500, respectively, and suppose that a particular query specifies ranges of size 10, 20, and 30, for A, B, and C, respectively. Taking into account the edge effects due to the fact that entire buckets must be searched if they may contain even one record in the desired set, estimate the total number of buckets that must be retrieved.

2.11: Suppose we are again handling range queries, and our file consists of a million records. All queries specify a range for A equal to $1/10^{th}$ of the total range for that field, and also specify a range for either field B or field C, but not both, equal to half the total range for the field specified.

** a) Suppose we wish to use a partitioned hash function with 16 bit addresses. How many bits should be devote to each of the fields A, B, and C?

* b) Compare the performance in average number of blocks retrieved of a partitioned hash table with 6, 5, and 5 bits devoted to A, B, and C, respectively, against a B-tree organization. You may assume each bucket fits on two blocks, and in the B-trees, each block contains 100 (key, pointer) pairs.

BIBLIOGRAPHIC NOTES

A variety of books discuss data structures. Among those that emphasize structures for organization of large-scale secondary storage devices are Knuth [1973], Horowitz and Sahni [1976], Wiederhold [1977], Martin [1977], Gotlieb and Gotlieb [1978], and Aho, Hopcroft, and Ullman [1982]. Hashing techniques are surveyed in Morris [1968], Knuth [1973], and Maurer and Lewis [1975]. The selection of physical database schemes from among alternatives is discussed by Gotlieb and Tompa [1973].

Fast ordered list searching is discussed by Yao and Yao [1976]. The $\log \log n$ complexity of interpolation search is shown there; see also Perl, Itai, and Avni [1978]. The B-tree is from Bayer and McCreight [1972], where it was presented as a dense index, as described in Section 2.5. The articles by Held and Stonebraker [1978] and Snyder [1978] contain an interesting discussion of the merits of their use in database systems. Yao [1978] analyzes the expected occupancy of 2-3 trees (B-trees with $d = e = 2$) and shows that on the average, interior nodes have between 21% and 30% waste space. Gudes and Tsur [1980] provide some experimental evidence regarding the average performance of B-trees.

The choice of secondary indices is discussed by many articles, including Lum and Ling [1970] and Schkolnick [1975]. The point of view generally taken is that the contents of the database can be known before the indices are selected. Comer [1978] shows optimal selection to be $\mathcal{N}P$-complete. (See Aho, Hopcroft, and Ullman [1974] or Garey and Johnson [1979] for an explanation of how $\mathcal{N}P$-completeness implies a problem cannot be solved efficiently.)

The use of partitioned hashing functions for partial match retrieval was considered in its generality by Rivest [1976], and the design of such hashing functions was also investigated by Burkhard [1976]. Theorem 2.1 on the shape of optimal hashing functions is from Bolour [1979]; Theorem 2.2, the case where queries specify one field, is from Rothnie and Lozano [1974], while Theorem 2.3 is from Bolour [1979] and Aho and Ullman [1979a]. A related idea, called "superimposed codes," also has applications to database systems, as described in Roberts [1978], for example.

The use of partitioned hashing functions for range queries is covered in Bolour [1981]. Tree structures for range queries are discussed by Finkel and Bentley [1974], Bentley [1975], Bentley and Stanat [1975], Lueker [1978], Willard [1978a, b], and Culik, Ottmann, and Wood [1981]. Bentley and Friedman [1979] surveys the subject. There is a well-developed theory of the limitations as to how fast range queries can be answered. See Burkhard, Fredman, and Kleitman [1981] and Fredman [1982].

3

THE NETWORK MODEL
and
THE DBTG PROPOSAL

The dominant influence in the development of the network data model and database systems using that model has been a series of proposals put forth by the Data Base Task Group (DBTG) of the Conference on Data Systems Languages (CODASYL), the group responsible for the standardization of the programming language COBOL. In addition to proposing a formal notation for networks (the *Data Definition Language* or *DDL*), the DBTG has proposed a *Subschema Data Definition Language* (*Subschema DDL*) for defining views of a conceptual scheme that was itself defined using the data definition language. Also proposed is a *Data Manipulation Language* (*DML*) suitable for writing applications programs that manipulate the conceptual scheme or a view.

We shall begin with a treatment of the data definition language and the concept of "DBTG sets," which are related to the links, or many-one mappings, mentioned in Section 1.4. We shall then study the implementation of network databases in general and the way the DBTG data definition language allows us to specify our choice of physical organization from among options. Finally, we shall cover the data manipulation language in some detail.

3.1 THE DBTG DATA DEFINITION LANGUAGE

The underlying model of data is the network model, as discussed in Section 1.4. What we have called logical record types are referred to as *record types* in the DBTG proposal. The fields in a logical record format are called *data items,* and what we called logical records are known simply as *records*. We shall use the terms "record" and "record type," since we are inclined to drop the term "logical" anyway, when no confusion results. However, let us continue to use "field," rather than "data item," since the latter term is used rarely outside the DBTG proposal itself. The database can, naturally, contain many occurrences of records of the same type. There is no requirement that occurrences of the same type be distinct, and indeed, record types with no fields are possible; they would be used to connect records of other types, and in the implementation, the seemingly empty record occurrences would have one or more pointers.

DBTG Sets

By an unfortunate turn of fate, the concept of a link, that is, a many-one mapping from one record type to another, is known in the DBTG world as a *set*. To avoid the obvious confusions that would occur should the term "set" be allowed this meaning, many substitute names have been proposed; the term *DBTG set* is a common choice, and we shall adopt it here.

When we have a many-one mapping m from records of type R_2 to records of type R_1, we can associate with each record r of type R_1 the set S_r, consisting of those records s of type R_2 such that $m(s)$ - r. Since m is many-one, the sets S_{r_1} and S_{r_2} are disjoint if $r_1 \neq r_2$. If SET is the name of the DBTG set representing the link m, then each set S_r, together with r itself, is said to be a *set occurrence* of SET. Record r is the *owner* of the set occurrence, and each s such that $m(s) = r$ is a *member* of the set occurrence. Record type R_1 is called the *owner type* of SET, and R_2 is the *member type* of SET. We shall observe the DBTG restriction that the owner and member types of a DBTG set are distinct.

The requirement that owner and member types be distinct produces some awkwardness, but it is considered necessary because many DBTG operations assume that we can distinguish the owner from members in a set occurrence. We can get around the requirement by introducing dummy record types. For example, we might have a record type PEOPLE, which we would like to be both the owner and member types of DBTG set MOTHER_OF, where the owner record in a set occurrence is intended to be the mother of all its member records. The solution is to create a record type DUMMY, with the following DBTG sets.

1. IS, with owner DUMMY and member PEOPLE. The intention is that each DUMMY record owns an IS set occurrence with exactly one PEOPLE record. Thus, each DUMMY record is effectively identified with the person represented by the PEOPLE record owned by that DUMMY record.

2. MOTHER_OF, with owner PEOPLE and member DUMMY. The intention is that a PEOPLE record r owns the DUMMY records that own (in the IS set occurrence) the PEOPLE records of which r is the mother.

We now consider an extended example of how a network database can be defined using the data definition language.

Example 3.1: Let us now introduce a sample database that we shall use throughout the book as we discuss various query languages. The Happy Valley Food Coop (HVFC) keeps a database in which its members' balances, their orders,

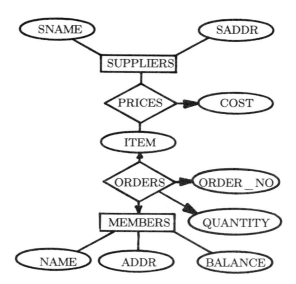

Fig. 3.1. Entity-relationship diagram for the HVFC database.

and possible suppliers and prices are recorded. Figure 3.1 shows an entity-relationship diagram of the database.

The PRICES relationship indicates the price charged by each supplier for each item; note that the entity set COST is simply a set of real numbers, and that we have identified the one attribute of COST with the entity set itself. Also note that the cost of an item can differ for different suppliers, so we could not make COST an attribute of ITEM or SUPPLIER. The ORDERS relationship gives for each order number, the club member placing the order, the item ordered, and the quantity ordered. The entity sets ITEM, QUANTITY, and ORDER_NO are additional examples of entity sets with single attributes.

Figure 3.2 shows some sample data, which we shall in the future take to be the "current" instance of the database. Figure 3.2(a) gives data about members, (b) summarizes the ORDERS relationship, and (c) gives the information about suppliers, their addresses and the prices they charge for the items they are willing to supply. This data is expressed as three tables, i.e., relations, for compactness; we shall later illustrate the representation of some of this data as a network.

In Fig. 3.3 we see a possible network to represent the database of Fig. 3.1. Essentially, the entity-relationship diagram of Fig. 3.1 is two many-many relationships, one between items and suppliers, indicating who supplies what, and the second between members (which we call "persons" here to avoid confusion with "member of a DBTG set") and items, indicating who ordered what. As was mentioned in Section 1.4, we must break a many-many relationship

NAME	ADDRESS	BALANCE
Brooks, B.	7 Apple Rd.	+10.50
Field, W.	43 Cherry La.	0
Robin, R.	12 Heather St.	−123, 45
Hart, W.	65 Lark Rd.	−43.00

(a) MEMBERS

ORDER_NO	NAME	ITEM	QUANTITY
1	Brooks, B.	Granola	5
2	Brooks, B.	Unbleached Flour	10
3	Robin, R.	Granola	3
4	Hart, W.	Whey	5
5	Robin, R.	Sunflower Seeds	2
6	Robin, R.	Lettuce	8

(b) ORDERS

SNAME	SADDRESS	ITEM	PRICE
Sunshine Produce	16 River St.	Granola	1.29
Sunshine Produce	16 River St.	Lettuce	.89
Sunshine Produce	16 River St.	Sunflower Seeds	1.09
Purity Foodstuffs	180 Industrial Rd.	Whey	.70
Purity Foodstuffs	180 Industrial Rd.	Curds	.80
Purity Foodstuffs	180 Industrial Rd.	Granola	1.25
Purity Foodstuffs	180 Industrial Rd.	Unbleached Flour	.65
Tasti Supply Co.	17 River St.	Lettuce	.79
Tasti Supply Co.	17 River St.	Whey	.79
Tasti Supply Co.	17 River St.	Sunflower Seeds	1.19

(c) SUPPLIERS

Fig. 3.2. Current relations in HVFC database.

Notes: All addresses are in the town of Happy Valley. QUANTITY is in pounds.
PRICE is per pound. Lettuce is union-picked only.

into two many-one links, and we have done so in Fig. 3.3. The logical record type PRICES not only serves as a dummy to relate SUPPLIERS and ITEMS; it can record the cost of an item from a supplier, since in Fig. 3.1, PRICES is many-one from ITEMS and SUPPLIERS to COST. Also, since an order number determines an item, quantity, and member, it is possible to place order numbers and quantities in the ORDERS logical record type that was created in Fig. 3.3

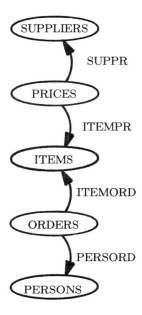

Fig. 3.3. Network diagram for HVFC database.

to serve as a dummy between ITEMS and PERSONS.

In Fig. 3.4 we see the declaration of the record types and DBTG sets needed to describe the network of Fig. 3.3. These declarations are in a "Pidgin" language based on the DBTG proposal. The actual DBTG data manipulation language requires that certain other items of information, the nature of which we have not yet touched upon, be included in the declaration of DBTG sets and record types.

The fields for each record type, with the data type of each field, are listed in the declaration of the record type. The integer 1 preceding each field name is a level number, as in the declaration of PL/I record structures. Level numbers up to 99 are permitted, allowing fields to have structure. The typical use of such structure is to declare, within a field such as ADDRESS, subfields like STREET, CITY, and ZIP at level 2.

Figure 3.4 also contains the declaration of four DBTG sets, corresponding to the four links in Fig. 3.3. Each link is many-one from the member type for the DBTG set to the owner of that DBTG set. For example, one set occurrence of the ITEMORD set consists of an owner, which is an ITEMS record, and zero or more members, which are ORDERS records representing all the orders for that item.

Let us consider how the database instance of Fig. 3.2 would be represented by records and set occurrences. For example, the PERSORD DBTG set would

```
RECORD SUPPLIERS
    1 SNAME CHAR(20),
    1 SADDR CHAR(30);
RECORD ITEMS
    1 INAME CHAR(15);
RECORD PRICES
    1 PRICE REAL,
    1 INAME VIRTUAL
        SOURCE IS ITEMS.INAME OF OWNER OF ITEMPR
    1 SNAME VIRTUAL
        SOURCE IS SUPPLIERS.SNAME OF OWNER OF SUPPR;
RECORD PERSONS
    1 NAME CHAR(20),
    1 ADDR CHAR(30),
    1 BALANCE REAL;
RECORD ORDERS
    1 ORDER _ NO INTEGER,
    1 QUANTITY REAL;
DBTG SET SUPPR
    OWNER IS SUPPLIERS
    MEMBER IS PRICES;
DBTG SET ITEMPR
    OWNER IS ITEMS
    MEMBER IS PRICES;
DBTG SET ITEMORD
    OWNER IS ITEMS
    MEMBER IS ORDERS;
DBTG SET PERSORD
    OWNER IS PERSONS
    MEMBER IS ORDERS;
```

Fig. 3.4. A DDL description of records and DBTG sets.

have four set occurrences, each owned by a PERSONS record; the owners are Brooks, Field, Robin, and Hart. Each of these records has a name, address, and balance, as:

Brooks, B.   7 Apple Rd.   +10.50

These four set occurrences have ORDERS records as members. The member records for the set occurrence owned by Brooks are records $(1, 5)$ and $(2, 10)$. The first of these records means order number 1, with quantity 5 pounds, and other ORDERS records are interpreted similarly. The set occurrence owned by Robin has member records $(3,3)$, $(5,2)$, and $(6,8)$; the set occurrence owned by Hart has one member record, $(4,5)$, while the set occurrence for Field has no member records.

The ITEMORD DBTG set has six set occurrences, each owned by an ITEMS record. For example, the granola record owns a set occurrence with ORDERS member records $(1,5)$ and $(3,3)$. The other set occurrences are owned by unbleached flour, whey, sunflower seeds, lettuce, and curds. The last of these owns no member records, because no one has ordered curds.

To determine the items ordered by Brooks, we must navigate through PERSORD and ITEMORD set occurrences, taking advantage of the fact that each ORDERS record is owned by both a PERSONS and an ITEMS record. Starting at the record for Brooks, we find its set occurrence in the PERSORD DBTG set. This set occurrence has member records $(1,5)$ and $(2,10)$ of type ORDERS. To find the items these orders represent, we find the owners of their set occurrences in the ITEMORD DBTG set. ORDERS record $(1,5)$ is owned by the granola ITEMS record and $(2,10)$ by the unbleached flour ITEMS record, so these are the items ordered by Brooks.

The SUPPR DBTG set has three occurrences, owned by the three SUP-PLIERS records for the three suppliers, Sunshine Produce, Purity Foodstuffs, and Tasti Supply Co. For example, the SUPPR set occurrence for Sunshine Produce owns three member records of PRICES type:

1.29	Granola	Sunshine Produce
.89	Lettuce	Sunshine Produce
1.09	Sunflower seeds	Sunshine Produce

Recall that only the prices actually appear in the records, item and supplier names being virtual fields.

Lastly, the DBTG set ITEMPR has six occurrences, each owned by one of the six items. For example, the ITEMPR set occurrence for lettuce owns the member records of PRICES type:

| .89 | Lettuce | Sunshine Produce |
| .79 | Lettuce | Tasti Supply Co. |

□

Virtual Fields and Redundancy Avoidance

One important nuance in Fig. 3.4 is the declaration of "virtual" item names and supplier names in the PRICES logical record type. These fields are declared VIRTUAL, meaning that although they are not actually present in PRICES records, even as pointers, we may write programs as if they were. The clause

SOURCE IS ITEMS.INAME OF OWNER OF ITEMPR

in the INAME declaration of PRICES says that to find the value of INAME for a PRICES record, we first find the owner of that record's set occurrence for the ITEMPR DBTG set.† This owner must be an ITEMS record (see the declaration of the ITEMPR set), and we can extract its INAME field, which becomes the value of the virtual INAME field in the PRICES record. The virtual field SNAME is evaluated analogously, by going to the owner of the PRICES record in the SUPPR DBTG set occurrence to which it belongs.

The virtual field concept is the DBTG response to a fundamental problem of database design, the desire to avoid redundancy. That is, while there is no reason in principle why each PRICES record could not have the item and supplier appearing, we would waste considerable space if we did so. There is another reason, besides space waste, why we do not like to repeat information in a database; there is always the potential that two copies of the same information will be changed so that they no longer agree. Thus, if we had a PRICES record with item "Granola" literally appearing in the record, and the record was also owned by the granola ITEMS record, we might change the INAME field in the PRICES record without also changing the owner of the record, or vice-versa. By making only one copy of the information, and causing all other places where the information might logically appear to refer to that one place (the INAME field in the owning ITEMS record, in our example), we ensure that the information will at least be consistent, although we cannot, of course, ensure that it is correct.

Incidentally, we shall, as we cover the hierarchical and relational models, see how each has developed a response to the redundancy problem. As a brief example, notice in Fig. 3.2(c), that the SADDRESS column appears to have some redundancy, since each address appears as many times as the supplier has items to sell. We shall see in Chapter 7 that this table, regarded as a relation, is faulty, and we should instead replace it by two relations, one with scheme { SNAME, SADDRESS }, and the other with scheme { SNAME, ITEM, PRICE }.

View Definition

The DBTG proposal calls for a subschema data definition language, in which one can define views. In a view one is permitted to use a different name for any record type, field, or DBTG set. We can omit from the view fields that are present in a record type, we can eliminate record types altogether, and we can eliminate DBTG sets from the view.

As the view facility of the DBTG proposal contains no concepts not present in the data definition language for the conceptual scheme, we shall in the following sections write programs that act on the conceptual scheme directly,

---

† We use the notation $A.B$ to mean field B of record type A. Incidentally, the DBTG proposal uses B IN A for the more common $A.B$.

as if it were a complete view of itself. Thus, views play no role in what follows.

3.2 IMPLEMENTATION OF NETWORKS

We can represent the logical records of a given record type by a file in the obvious manner, with one field of each record for each field of the logical record. As we shall see, even if a logical record format consists only of virtual fields, its records need not disappear entirely, and the presence of those records surely will influence the organization of the database, no matter what representation we choose for the network.

There are several ways we can represent links so that we can travel efficiently from owner to members or vice-versa. Suppose we have a link from record type T_1 to record type T_2. Since the link is many-one from T_1 to T_2, we could represent it by variable length records of the format $T_2(T_1)^*$. That is, after each record of type T_2, list all the associated records of type T_1. The variable length records can then be represented in one of the ways discussed in Section 2.6. If there is another link from record type T_3 to T_2, we can list the occurrences of T_3 records with the corresponding T_2 records, using a variable length record format like $T_2(T_1)^*(T_3)^*$. Again, the methodology of Section 2.6 can be used to implement such variable length records.

However, suppose there is another link from T_1 to some record type T_4. We cannot list T_1 records after T_2 records and also list them after T_4 records, or at least, it would hardly be efficient or convenient to do so. If we duplicated T_1 records and placed them after both T_2 and T_4 records owning them, we would introduce the redundancy and potential for inconsistency we discussed earlier and wish to avoid.

We therefore need another way of representing links, one that does not force records of one type to be adjacent to records of another type. In this organization, called a *multilist,* each record has one pointer for each link in which it is involved, although we do have the option of eliminating the pointer for one link and representing that link by variable length records as discussed above.

Suppose we have a link L from T_1 to T_2. For each record R of type T_2 we create a circular chain beginning at R, then to all the records $R_1, R_2, \ldots, R_k$ of type T_1 linked to R by L, and finally back to R. The pointers for link L in records of types T_1 and T_2 are used for this purpose. We show an example chain in Fig. 3.5. Note how we can follow the chain from R to visit each of $R_1, R_2, \ldots, R_k$ and, if records of type T_2 are identifiable in some way (e.g., each record begins with a few bits indicating its record type, or the record address determines the type) we can go from any of $R_1, R_2, \ldots, R_k$ to R.

It is important to remember that in a multilist organization, each record has as many pointers as its record type has links. As the pointers are fields in the records, and therefore appear in fixed positions, we can follow the chain for

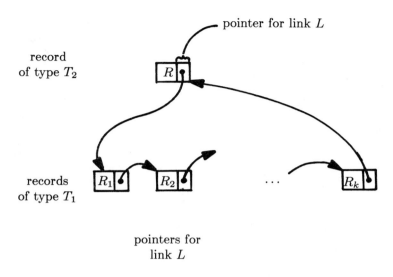

Fig. 3.5. A circular chain.

a particular link without fear of accidentally following some other link. Also remember that since links are many-one, each circular chain has exactly one record of one type and zero or more records of the second type. Notice that if we tried to represent many-many relationships by multilists, we would face severe problems, since each record could be on many chains for the same relationship. We would not know in advance how many pointers were needed in a record for each link, and we would have trouble determining which link was for which chain. This problem is not conveniently solved, which in a sense justifies why the network model restricts us to many-one links.

Example 3.2: Let us illustrate multilists with part of the database of Fig. 3.2. We shall consider only the ITEMS, ORDERS, and PERSONS record types and implement the ITEMORD and PERSORD links by a multilist. each PERSONS record has a pointer for PERSORD; each ORDERS record has two pointers, one dedicated to PERSORD and the other to ITEMORD. We shall show the ITEMS records with a pointer for ITEMORD only, leaving open the question whether the ITEMPR link is implemented by a multilist structure or another way. The multilist structure is shown in Fig. 3.6. □

Implementation Options in the DBTG Proposal

As mentioned, logical record types are implemented by files of records, one record of the file for each logical record. This file is organized in one of several ways, called *location modes*. One important location mode is called *CALC*, and

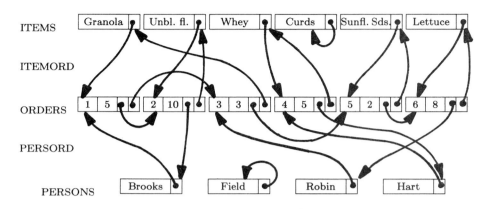

Fig. 3.6. A multilist structure for part of the HVFC database.

is indicated by the clause

LOCATION MODE IS CALC $<$procedure$>$ USING $<$field list$>$

in the declaration of the record type. For example, in Fig. 3.4 we could include with the declaration for SUPPLIERS the information

LOCATION MODE IS CALC PROC1 USING SNAME, SADDR

Presumably, PROC1 is the name of a procedure that takes values for the SNAME and SADDR fields, producing a "hash value." In general, the CALC location mode suggests, but does not require, that the file for a record type declared this way be stored in buckets, one for each value produced by the "hashing" $<$procedure$>$ applied to the values of the fields in the $<$field list$>$, as described in Section 2.2. As a perfectly reasonable alternative, the $<$procedure$>$ could examine a sparse index to find the bucket in which a record belongs, as described in Section 2.3, or it could examine a dense index organized as a B-tree, as suggested in Section 2.5. There are no fundamental limits on what the $<$procedure$>$ can do, but the user is entitled to rely on the assumption that, given values for the $<$field list$>$, locating some record (there may be several) with those values in the $<$field list$>$ can be done efficiently; it is the responsibility of the system to provide built-in procedures that make this search efficient.

A second location mode is DIRECT, declared by

LOCATION MODE IS DIRECT

This mode declares that records of the type are found only by their addresses in the file system; addresses are called *database keys* in the DBTG proposal. In principle, the file of records of this type can be kept in any order; a record will be accessed by providing a database key, that is, the location of the record. In a sense, the "serial number" fields discussed in Section 1.4 are a symbolism for database keys.

A third location mode, VIA, is declared for a record type T_1 by

LOCATION MODE IS VIA $<$set name$>$ SET

This declaration implies that type T_1 is the member type of the designated $<$set name$>$, S, and each record of type T_1 will be grouped with the owner of the S occurrence of which it is a member. That is, if the owner type for S is T_2, the file of T_2 records can be viewed as a file of variable length records, with format $T_2(T_1)^*$. This file can be implemented by fixed length records as suggested in Section 2.6. The presumption, when the VIA location mode is chosen, is that all members of a set occurrence can be read together, with roughly as few block accesses as possible.

The VIA location mode leads to some very complex structures. For example, it is possible that record type T_2 is given declaration

LOCATION MODE IS VIA R SET

where T_2 is the member type for DBTG set R, whose owner type is T_3. Then records of types T_1, T_2, and T_3 are organized as if in variable length records with format $T_3(T_2(T_1)^*)^*$.

Each location mode makes certain operations efficient but not others. The direct mode allows us to use minimum area for a file, but makes search for records, given values for certain fields, almost impossible. The CALC mode is very good for lookup of records given their CALC-key, but navigation through links involving a member type stored in this way may be inefficient. That is, to get all members of a given set occurrence requires that we make almost as many block accesses as there are members in the occurrence, since there is no reason to believe that two members will live on the same block.

One the other hand, the VIA mode makes that sort of navigation efficient, but lookup of a record is difficult if we don't know its owner. We can, however, create a secondary index† on the key values for some record type stored VIA a set and thus have the advantage of fast lookup inherent in the CALC mode. The price we pay is having to maintain the index when we do insertion and deletion.

As always, we can only decide what organization to use for a physical database if we have a clear idea of what sorts of operations we shall do, i.e., shall we be doing more lookup or more navigation. Thus, we might prefer to store ORDERS records by CALC-key if the most frequent type of query about orders asks for the quantity on a particular order, since this sort of query requires no navigation. However, if we frequently ask for all the orders placed by a particular person, then we would prefer to store ORDERS via the PERSORD

---

† Secondary indices are called *search keys* in the DBTG proposal, and we can declare any number of these for a logical record type.

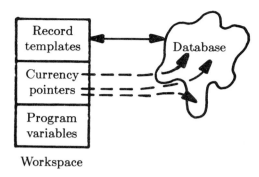

Fig. 3.7. The program environment.

set. If we most frequently ask for the orders for a particular item, then storing ORDERS via the ITEMORD set is indicated.

Set Modes

There are also options regarding how DBTG sets are to be stored. The DBTG proposal allows us to declare *set modes* for DBTG sets. While the proposal is somewhat vague about what all the options should be, it includes the multilist structure, called *chain mode*, and an arrangement called *pointer array mode*, in which each owner record has an array of pointers to its members. Presumably, any DBMS implementing the proposal would also allow users to declare other set modes, such as some of those discussed in Section 2.6 to implement variable length records. Another sensible option is to include a pointer from each member record directly to its owner, in addition to any other structure used.

3.3 THE PROGRAM ENVIRONMENT

Programs are written in a host language (COBOL in the DBTG proposal) augmented by the commands of the data manipulation language, such as FIND (locate a described record), GET (read a record from the database), and STORE (a record into the database). This arrangement is essentially the one illustrated in the second column of Fig. 1.4, although it is not intended that statements of the extended language would be marked for a preprocessor as we showed in Fig. 1.4. The environment in which a program operates is depicted in Fig. 3.7. There is a workspace, called the *user working area,* in which is found space for three kinds of data.

1. Variables defined by the program.
2. *Currency pointers,* which are the database keys of certain records in the database; we shall describe currency pointers in more detail next.
3. *Templates* for the various record types. The template for a record type

T consists of space for each field F of the record type, and that space is referred to as $T.F$ (or just F if the field name is unique) in programs. A record is stored into the database only after assembling the record in the template for its type, and the STORE command copies the contents of the template into the database. Similarly, the GET command reads a record from the database into the appropriate template. We also use the template as a way of "passing parameters" to certain commands that at first glance do not appear to have parameters, especially to the FIND command.

Currency Pointers

As a program runs, it is necessary for it to locate various records by a FIND command, and to operate upon them by other commands. To keep track of recently accessed records, a collection of currency pointers is maintained automatically by the database system, and the values of these pointers, which are actually the database keys of the records, are made available to the program. The currency pointers with which we deal are:

1. The *current of run-unit*. The term "run-unit" means "program" in the DBTG proposal. The most recently accessed record, of any type whatsoever, has its database key in a currency pointer called the "current of run-unit."

2. The *current of record type*. For each record type T, the most recently accessed record of this type is pointed to by the "current of T."

3. The *current of set type*. For each DBTG set S, consisting of owner record type T_1 and member record type T_2, the most recently accessed record of type T_1 or T_2 is called the "current of S." Note that sometimes the current of S will be an owner, and sometimes it will be a member. Also understand that the current of S is a record, rather than a set occurrence. Sometimes it is convenient to talk of the set occurrence containing the record "current of S" as if this set occurrence itself were the "current S occurrence," but there is no such thing as a pointer to a set occurrence.

Example 3.3: Let us return to the database of Example 3.1. Suppose we wish to find the items ordered by Brooks. In Example 3.1 we showed how we might use the PERSORD and ITEMORD DBTG sets to navigate from Brooks to the items, granola and unbleached flour, that he ordered. It is convenient to view a set occurrence as a ring of records consisting of the owner and any members, as described in Section 3.2 when we discussed the multilist data structure. Thus the set occurrence of the PERSORD DBTG set for Brooks might consist of an owner record for Brooks and two member records (1,5) and (2,10), in that order around a ring. While we have not yet discussed how the FIND statement works, suffice it to say that one thing we can do, starting at an owner record, is to find each member record around the ring in turn. Another thing we can do is find

Current of

Step	PERSONS	ORDERS	ITEMS	PERSORD	ITEMORD	run-unit
1. find Brooks record	Brooks	–	–	Brooks	–	Brooks
2. find (1,5) ORDERS record	Brooks	(1,5)	–	(1,5)	(1,5)	(1,5)
3. find owner of (1,5) in ITEMORD	Brooks	(1,5)	Granola	(1,5)	Granola	Granola
4. find (2,10) ORDERS record	Brooks	(2,10)	Granola	(2,10)	(2,10)	(2,10)
5. find owner of (2,10) in ITEMORD	Brooks	(2,10)	Unbleached flour	(2,10)	Unbleached flour	Unbleached flour

Fig. 3.8. A program and its effect on currency pointers.

the owner of a set occurrence if we are given a member of that set occurrence. In Fig. 3.8 we see a sequence of steps that a program might execute, and we indicate the current of the PERSONS, ORDERS, and ITEMS record types, the current of the PERSORD and ITEMORD DBTG sets, and the current of run-unit after each step. □

3.4 NAVIGATION WITHIN THE DATABASE

Reading a record from the database to the workspace is a two stage process. First, using a sequence of FIND statements, we locate the desired record; that is, the desired record becomes the current of run-unit. At this point, nothing has been copied into the template for the record type. To copy the record into the template in the workspace, we simply execute the command GET. This command always copies the current of run-unit into the template for whatever record type is the current of run-unit. If we wish to copy only a subset of the fields of the current of run-unit, we can list the desired fields after GET, as in

GET <record type>; <list of fields>

Example 3.4: If the current of run-unit is a PRICES record (we are continuing with the HVFC example), we can read the INAME and PRICE fields by saying

GET PRICES; INAME, PRICE

The SNAME field in the template for PRICES is not affected. Notice that even though INAME is a virtual field of PRICES, we can program as though it actually existed, relying on the system to get the correct value from the ITEMS.INAME field of the owner of the PRICES record in its ITEMPR set occurrence. □

For debugging purposes, we can append the record type to the command GET, even if we want all fields of the record. For example

GET PRICES

will copy the current of run-unit into the PRICES template, if the current of run-unit is a PRICES record. Otherwise, the system will warn the user of an error when the GET PRICES statement is executed. Let us emphasize that one cannot use GET to read a record other than the current of run-unit, even if we follow GET by the type of that record.

The FIND Statement

The FIND command in the DBTG proposal is really a collection of different commands, distinguished by the keywords following FIND, with the common purpose of locating a particular record by some designated strategy. The variety of FIND statements is extensive, and we shall here consider only a useful subset of the possibilities. In brief, the FIND statement can be used in the following ways.†

1. Find a record given its database key.
2. Find a record given a value for its CALC-key. Recall that record types are given a location mode, and frequently that location mode is CALC, where there is a "hash function" applied to the values in certain fields (those fields that form the CALC-key) of any record of that type. Given values for these fields, we can find some record (it need not be unique) with those values in the designated fields.
3. We can scan the file of records of a given type, and in their turn find all the records with a given value in the CALC-key field or fields.
4. We can scan all the members of a set occurrence in turn.
5. We can scan a set occurrence for those member records having specified values in certain of the fields.
6. We can find the owner of a given record in a given DBTG set.
7. We can find the current of any record or DBTG set. At first, this statement seems paradoxical, since if a record is "current of something" it is, in principle, "found." However, we observed that GET operates only on the current of run-unit, not on a current of set or record. Most of the other commands, which we have not yet introduced, also require the current of run-unit as the sole possible operand. Thus the purpose of this FIND statement is to make a "current of something" record be the current of run-unit, for further processing.

---

† These seven types of FIND statement are not the "seven formats" spoken of in the literature. Rather, we have grouped the formats mentioned in the DBTG proposal into what we regard as logical units.

Finding a Record Directly

The first two sorts of FIND access records by a "key," either the database key or the CALC-key. To access by database key in our "Pidgin" language† we write:

> FIND <record type> RECORD BY DATABASE KEY <variable>

where the <variable> is a variable in the workspace that has previously been given a database key as value. For example, to read the current of ITEMS into its template in the workspace, we could write:

> XYZ := CURRENT OF ITEMS
> FIND ITEMS RECORD BY DATABASE KEY XYZ
> GET ITEMS

Here XYZ is the name of a variable in the workspace.

To find a record given values for its CALC-key fields, we "pass" those values to FIND by placing the values in the corresponding fields of the template, then issue the command

> FIND <record type> RECORD BY CALC-KEY

For example, suppose PERSONS records are given location mode CALC with a CALC-key consisting only of the field NAME. Then we could find the balance for Brooks by:

> PERSONS.NAME := "Brooks, B."
> FIND PERSONS RECORD BY CALC-KEY
> GET PERSONS; BALANCE

Note that PERSONS.NAME and PERSONS.BALANCE could have been written NAME and BALANCE, as no ambiguity would arise. We should also observe that although NAME is a CALC-key, there is no guarantee that two persons with the same name do not exist, and the above sequence of steps will only find one record with NAME = "Brooks, B.," not all of them.

Scanning a Record Type

To find all the records of a given type with a given value for the CALC-key, we can find the first such record as above, and then find additional records with the same CALC-key by executing, in a loop,

> FIND DUPLICATE <record type> RECORD BY CALC-KEY

---

† There are several differences between the notation used here and that used in the DBTG proposal. First, the proposal calls for many optional "noise words" in its syntax. We have arbitrarily chosen to include or exclude them, with an eye toward maximizing clarity. Second, we have inserted the words RECORD, SET, and other explanatory words, in certain places where they help to remind the reader of what the variables represent.

```
print "SUPPLIER" , "PRICE"  /* print header */
PRICES.INAME := "Granola"
FIND PRICES RECORD BY CALC-KEY
while ¬FAIL do
     GET PRICES; SNAME, PRICE
     print PRICES.SNAME, PRICE
     FIND DUPLICATE PRICES RECORD BY CALC-KEY
end
```

Fig. 3.9. Print suppliers and prices for granola.

Assuming the current of run-unit is of the type <record type>, and its values in the CALC-key fields equal the corresponding values in the template for <record type>, then the next <record type> record with those values is found.

When performing any sort of scan, we must be prepared to find no record matching the specifications. In the DBTG proposal, there is a global *error-status* word, that indicates when a FIND operation fails to find a record, among other abnormal conditions. We shall here assume for convenience that a variable FAIL becomes true if and only if a FIND fails to find a record.

Example 3.5: Suppose we wish to print all the suppliers of granola and the prices they charge. Suppose for convenience that the CALC-key for PRICES is INAME. Then the desired table could be printed by the routine shown in Fig. 3.9. □

Scanning a Set Occurrence

To begin, suppose we have a current set occurrence for some DBTG set S. Recall that the set occurrence can be viewed as a ring consisting of the owner and each of the members. If we get to the owner, we can scan around the ring and come back to the owner, causing FAIL to become true when we do. The FIND statement

        FIND OWNER OF CURRENT <set name> SET

finds the owner of the current of <set name>, making it the current of run-unit and, most importantly, the current of <set name>.

        The statement

        FIND NEXT <record type> RECORD IN
              CURRENT <set name> SET

goes one position around the ring from the current of <set name>, setting FAIL to true† if the next record is not of the <record type>. Normally, the

---

† Technically, the error-status word treats reaching the last member of a set occurrence as a different "abnormality" from failing to find a record, but we trust no confusion will occur if we use FAIL to indicate all abnormalities.

```
NAME := "Brooks, B."
FIND PERSONS RECORD BY CALC-KEY
/* CALC-key for PERSONS is NAME */
FIND FIRST ORDERS RECORD IN CURRENT PERSORD SET
while ¬FAIL do
        FIND OWNER OF CURRENT ITEMORD SET
        GET ITEMS /* read item that owns current order record */
        print ITEMS.INAME
        FIND NEXT ORDERS RECORD IN CURRENT PERSORD SET
end
```

Fig. 3.10. Print the items ordered by Brooks.

<record type> is the member type of the <set name>, so we fail when we get back to the owner.

An alternative way to scan around the ring is to issue the command

FIND FIRST <record type> RECORD IN
CURRENT <set name> SET

to get the first member record of the current <set name> DBTG set. If there are no members of this set, FAIL becomes true. Otherwise, we can continue around the ring with a loop containing a FIND NEXT··· command, as above.

Example 3.6: Let us print the items ordered by Brooks. The program of Fig. 3.10 does the job. We begin by finding the PERSONS record for Brooks. This record owns the PERSORD set occurrence we wish to scan. We find the first member record of this set occurrence, and in the loop, we check whether we have gone around the ring already. If not, we use FIND OWNER to get the ITEMS record owning the order and read it, to get the name of the item. We print the item, find the next member of the PERSORD set occurrence owned by Brooks, and go around the loop once more. □

Singular Sets

There are times when we would like to scan all the records of a certain type, for example, to find all PERSONS with negative balances. We cannot directly access all the PERSONS records by CALC-key or database key, unless we know the name of every person belonging to the HVFC, or if we know all the database keys for these records, which are two unlikely situations. Scanning set occurrences for PERSONS records won't work either, unless we have some way of locating every set occurrence of some DBTG set.

We may define, for a given record type, what is known as a *singular* DBTG set. A singular set has two special properties.

1.   The owner type is a special record type called SYSTEM. Having SYSTEM as the owner distinguishes singular DBTG sets.

```
print "PERSON", "BALANCE"
FIND FIRST PERSONS RECORD IN CURRENT ALLPERS SET
/* the lone set occurrence of ALLPERS is always current */
while ¬FAIL do
      GET PERSONS
      if BALANCE < 0 then
            print NAME, BALANCE
      FIND NEXT PERSONS RECORD IN CURRENT ALLPERS SET
end
```

Fig. 3.11. Print HVFC members with negative balances.

2.   There is exactly one set occurrence, whose members are all the records of
the member type. The records are made members automatically, with no
specific direction required from the user.

Example 3.7: If we wish the capability of searching all the PERSONS records
conveniently, we could add to the DBTG set declarations in Fig. 3.4 the definition
of the following singular set.

> DBTG SET ALLPERS
>   OWNER IS SYSTEM
>   MEMBER IS PERSONS;

To print all the persons with negative balances we could execute the program
of Fig. 3.11. □

Scanning a Set Occurrence for Fields of Specified Value

The next type of FIND statement also scans the members of a set occurrence,
but it allows us to look at only those records with specified values in certain
fields. The values for these fields are stored in the template for the member
record type before using the FIND. To get the first member record having the
desired values, in the current set occurrence of the <set name> DBTG set, we
can write

> FIND <record type> RECORD IN CURRENT
> <set name> SET USING <field list>

Here, <record type> is the member type for the DBTG set whose name is <set
name>, and the <field list> is a list of fields of the <record type> whose
values, stored in the template for <record type>, must match the values of
these fields in the record found. To get subsequent records in the same set
occurrence with the same values we say

> FIND DUPLICATE <record type> RECORD IN CURRENT
> <set name> SET USING <field list>

SUPPLIERS.SNAME := "Tasti Supply Co."
FIND SUPPLIERS RECORD USING CALC-KEY
/* establishes a current SUPPR occurrence */
PRICES.INAME := "Whey"
FIND PRICES RECORD IN CURRENT SUPPR SET USING INAME
GET PRICES; PRICE
print PRICE

Fig. 3.12. Find the price charged by Tasti for whey.

BALANCE := 0
FIND PERSONS RECORD IN CURRENT ALLPERS
    SET USING BALANCE
while ¬FAIL **do**
    GET PERSONS; NAME
    print NAME
    FIND DUPLICATE PERSONS RECORD IN
        CURRENT ALLPERS SET USING BALANCE
end

Fig. 3.13. Find persons with zero balance.

Example 3.8: To find the price charged by Tasti Supply Co. for whey, we could use the program of Fig. 3.12. As an example of a situation where we might wish to scan for several matching records, consider Fig. 3.13, where we scan the singular set ALLPERS, introduced in Example 3.7, for all persons with zero balance. □

Establishing a Current of Run-Unit

The last sort of FIND we shall cover is a FIND statement whose purpose is to make a current of record or set become the current of run-unit. The syntax is:

    FIND CURRENT OF <set name> SET

or

    FIND CURRENT OF <record type> RECORD

Example 3.9: Suppose we wish to find if Brooks ordered granola, and if so, how much. We scan the PERSORD set occurrence owned by Brooks. For each order, we consult its owner in the ITEMORD DBTG set to see if the item is granola. We could read the ORDERS record before consulting its owner, but then we would waste time reading orders for items other than granola. One solution is to reestablish an ORDERS record as the current of run-unit when

```
NAME := "Brooks, B."
FIND PERSONS RECORD USING CALC-KEY
LOOP: repeat forever
        FIND NEXT ORDERS RECORD IN CURRENT PERSORD SET
        if FAIL then break LOOP
        FIND OWNER OF CURRENT ITEMORD SET
        GET ITEMS; INAME
        if ITEMS.INAME = "Granola" then do
                FIND CURRENT OF ORDERS RECORD
                GET ORDERS; QUANTITY
                print QUANTITY
                break LOOP
        end
end LOOP
```

Fig. 3.14. Find how much granola Brooks ordered.

we discover it is an order for granola.† Remember that having made an ITEMS record be the current of run-unit, we cannot immediately apply GET to any other record. The program is given in Fig. 3.14. □

3.5 INSERTION, DELETION, AND MODIFICATION

In addition to FIND and GET, the DBTG proposal includes commands to insert or delete the current of run unit from set occurrences and from the list of records of a type, and a command to modify the current of run unit. The user is given, by the DDL, a variety of *existence constraints* that he may choose to have the system enforce. For example, if there is a DBTG set S with owner type T_1 and member type T_2, we may wish that whenever we create a T_2 type record, it has some S set occurrence to which it belongs. To do so, when the DBTG set S is declared, we also declare

INSERTION IS AUTOMATIC

and give a *set selection* clause, to be illustrated shortly, that tells how to select the set occurrence into which the T_2 record should be placed. Among other uses of such constraints, we can check that we do not do meaningless operations such as inserting an order from a nonexistent person.

Another form of constraint we may place on DBTG set members is to declare a *retention class* for them. If we declare retention to be MANDATORY, then once a record is a member of some set occurrence, it cannot be removed from that occurrence and placed in another; we must copy the record into the working area, delete it from the database, and then store it again, putting it in

† While we do not discuss the matter here, it is possible to suppress the updating of the currency pointers, which provides another solution to this problem.

the desired set occurrence. If, however, retention is declared OPTIONAL, then by INSERT and REMOVE commands to be discussed, we can shift it from one set occurrence to another. The purpose of mandatory retention is not to make things difficult, but to offer the user a check on possible program bugs.

A third form of constraint concerns deletion. When we delete the owner of a nonempty set occurrence, should we simply delete all members of the set, all those that are in the MANDATORY retention class only, or should we, as a form of program error detection, refuse to do the deletion at all? These options are available with a DELETE command to be discussed subsequently.

The STORE Command

To store a new record of type T into the database, we create the record r in the template for record type T and then issue the command

STORE T

This command adds r to the collection of records of type T and makes r be the current of run-unit, the current of T, and the current of any DBTG set of which T is the owner or member type.

As mentioned above, if T is the member type of any DBTG sets in which it is declared to have automatic insertion, then r becomes a member of one set occurrence for each of these sets; exactly which occurrences depends on the set selection clauses that are part of the DDL database description. The opposite of AUTOMATIC is MANUAL. If DBTG set S is declared this way, then member records are not inserted into any set occurrence of S when the records are stored, and we must "manually" insert records into set occurrences of S by an INSERT command, to be discussed later in this chapter.

Set Selection

Granted that we have declared insertion of records of type T into set occurrences of S to be AUTOMATIC, we need a mechanism for deciding which set occurrence of S gets the new record. The STORE command itself cannot specify the correct set occurrence. Rather, when we declare DBTG set S, we include a SET SELECTION clause that tells how to select the set occurrence of S into which a newly stored member record is to be placed. There are many different ways in which the set occurrence could be chosen. We shall describe only the two simplest kinds of set selection clauses. Remember that each of the following statements belongs in the declaration for a set S; it is not part of the executable portion of a program. Also note that we use a "Pidgin" syntax to make the meaning of the clauses more apparent.

1.   SET SELECTION IS THRU CURRENT OF <set name> SET. Here, before storing a record, the program itself establishes a current set occurrence for the <set name> set (presumably S is the set name). When the record

```
read N, I, Q /* the name, item, and quantity */
NEXTORD := NEXTORD + 1 /* get a new order number */
PERSONS.NAME := N /* prepare PERSORD set selection */
ITEMS.INAME := I
FIND ITEMS RECORD USING CALC-KEY
/* the above prepares ITEMORD set selection */
ORDERS.ORDER_NO := NEXTORD
ORDERS.QUANTITY := Q
/* the above creates new ORDERS record in template */
STORE ORDERS /* automatically places the record in the
    PERSORD set occurrence owned by N and in the current ITEMORD
    set, which is that owned by I */
```

Fig. 3.15. Read and store new order.

is stored, it becomes a member of the current *S* occurrence.

2. SET SELECTION IS THRU OWNER USING <field list>. The <field list> is the CALC-key for the owner type of *S*, which must therefore have location mode CALC, if this particular type of set selection is to be used. The current values of these fields in the template for the owner type must determine a unique record of the owner type for *S*, and the stored record goes into the set occurrence of *S* owned by that record.

Example 3.10: Suppose we wish to store ORDERS records and insert them automatically into PERSORD and ITEMORD set occurrences when we do. If NAME is the CALC-key for PERSONS, we can use a person's name to select the set occurrence for PERSORD, by including in the declaration for PERSORD the clause

> SET SELECTION IS THRU OWNER USING NAME

We might choose to select the ITEMORD occurrence through the owner identifier INAME, but for variety, let us select the ITEMORD occurrence by placing

> SET SELECTION IS THRU CURRENT OF ITEMORD SET

in the declaration of ITEMORD. The clause

> INSERTION IS AUTOMATIC

must be placed in the declarations of both PERSORD and ITEMORD. The program in Fig. 3.15 reads an order, stores it in the ORDERS file, and inserts it into the desired set occurrences of PERSORD and ITEMORD, automatically.
☐

Manual Insertion and Deletion

If we do not wish to use set selection to place records in set occurrences, we can do so by an explicit command. A record type can be declared an AUTOMATIC

```
read N, I, Q
NEXTORD := NEXTORD + 1
PERSONS.NAME := N
FIND PERSONS RECORD USING CALC-KEY
/* establishes the correct current of PERSORD */
ITEMS.INAME := I
FIND ITEMS RECORD USING CALC-KEY
/* establishes the correct current of ITEMORD */
ORDERS.ORDER_NO := NEXTORD
ORDERS.QUANTITY := Q
STORE ORDERS /* new order is now the current of run unit,
    but not a member of any set occurrences */
INSERT ORDERS INTO PERSORD, ITEMORD
```

Fig. 3.16. Manual instertion of a new ORDERS record.

member of some DBTG sets, in which case set selection is used, and the same record type can be declared

INSERTION IS MANUAL

for some other DBTG set of which it is a member, in which case a record, when stored, is not made a member of any set occurrence for this DBTG set.

To insert a record r (which already exists in the database) of the member type T for DBTG set S, into a designated set occurrence of S, we first make this set occurrence be the current of S, by whatever means we find suitable. Then we make r be the current of run-unit and issue the command

INSERT T INTO S

Note that r must be the current of run-unit, not just the current of T. It is permissible to follow INTO by a list of DBTG sets, and if so, insertion of r into the current of each set will occur.

Example 3.11: In Example 3.10 we read an ORDERS record and inserted it automatically into PERSONS and ITEMS set occurrences. If we instead declare ORDERS to be a MANUAL member of the PERSORD and ITEMORD DBTG sets, we can do the insertion manually by the procedure of Fig. 3.16. □

To remove the current of run-unit, which is a record of type T, from its set occurrence for DBTG set S, we issue the command

REMOVE T FROM S

As with insertion, S could be replaced by a list of DBTG sets. Remember, the record removed must be the current of run-unit, not just the current of T. Also, we are not permitted to execute the REMOVE statement if mandatory retention has been specified for S.

PRICES.INAME := "Lettuce"
PRICES.SNAME := "Sunshine Produce"
FIND PRICES RECORD USING CALC-KEY
/* above assumes CALC-key for PRICES is { INAME, SNAME } */
PRICES.PRICE := .75
MODIFY PRICES; PRICE

Fig. 3.17. Set price of lettuce sold by Sunshine Produce to .75.

Record Modification

The command

MODIFY <record type>

has the effect of copying the template for <record type> into the current of run-unit. If the current of run-unit is not of the designated record type, it is an error. We can also modify a selected subset of the fields in the current of run-unit by writing

MODIFY <record type>; <field list>

If T is the record type for the current of run-unit, the values of the fields in the list are copied from the template for T into the fields of the current of run-unit. Other fields in the current of run-unit are unchanged. Thus to change the price charged by Sunshine Produce for lettuce to .75 we could execute the program of Fig. 3.17.

Deletion of Records from the Database

The command

DELETE <record type>

deletes the current of run-unit, which must be of the specified <record type>, from the file of records of that type. Naturally, if the current of run-unit is a member of any set occurrences, it is removed from those occurrences. If the current of run-unit is the owner of any set occurrences, those occurrences must presently have no members, or it is an error, and the deletion cannot take place.

Another form of DELETE statement is

DELETE <record type> ALL

This instruction is applicable even if the current of run-unit is the owner of some nonempty set occurrences. The DELETE ALL statement not only erases the current of run-unit, as the simple DELETE does, but recursively, DELETE ALL is applied to any members of set occurrences owned by the deleted record. Thus it is conceivable that DELETE ALL could destroy the entire database.

Example 3.12: To cancel an order given its order number we could write

> **read** ORDERS.ORDER_NO
> FIND ORDERS RECORD USING CALC-KEY
> DELETE ORDERS

Since ORDERS records are not owners in any DBTG set, the given order is simply deleted from the file of ORDERS records and from whatever PERSORD and ITEMORD records it belongs to.

As another example, if Robin quits the HVFC, we can execute

> NAME := "Robin, R."
> FIND PERSONS RECORD USING CALC-KEY
> DELETE PERSONS ALL

This erasure has the effect of deleting the record for Robin from the PERSONS file and deleting the entire PERSORD set occurrence of which Robin is the owner. Recursively, each order in the deleted set occurrence is itself deleted from the ORDERS file and from the ITEMORD set occurrence of which it is a member. Since ORDERS records do not own any set occurrences, the recursion stops here, and no further alterations to the database are made. □

EXERCISES

3.1: Define, using the DBTG data manipulation language, the network of Fig. 1.12.

3.2: In Exercise 1.10 we discussed information about the ingredients of certain dishes.
  a) Define a network to represent the data, using the DBTG DDL.
  b) Show the links in your network for the particular data given in Exercise 1.10.
  c) Show your links represented by a multilist structure.

3.3: Suppose we have the following record types:

> COMPANY(CNAME, CADDR)
> STOCK(SH_NO, QUANTITY)
> PERSON(PNAME, PADDR)

Let there also be the following DBTG sets.
  1. EMP, with member PERSON and owner COMPANY, indicating the employees of a company.
  2. OWNS, with member STOCK and owner PERSON, indicating which person owns which stock certificates.
  3. ST_CO, with member STOCK and owner COMPANY, indicating the company to which a stock certificate pertains.

You may assume the location mode for each record is CALC, with keys CNAME, SH_NO, and PNAME, respectively. Write programs in the "Pidgin" data manipulation language of this chapter, to do the following.

a) Read a share number and print the name and address of the person owning the share.

b) List all persons owning stock in IBM. You may list a person owning two certificates twice.

c) List all persons owning stock in the company they work for. (Assume a singular set of persons exists.)

d) Determine the total quantity of stock in IBM owned by its employees.

3.4: Suppose we wish to enter new shares into the database of Exercise 3.2, and we want a new share to be entered into the correct OWNS and ST _ CO set occurrences when the stock record is stored.

a) Suggest set selection clauses that will enable the automatic insertion to be performed.

b) Write a program to read the necessary data and store the new stock record correctly.

c) Suppose we wish to use manual insertion instead of automatic. Write a program to store STOCK records and insert them in the proper OWNS and ST _ CO occurrences manually.

BIBLIOGRAPHIC NOTES

The DBTG proposal is contained in the document CODASYL [1971]. Periodic updates are available in the *COBOL Journal of Development* (CODASYL [1978]). Olle [1978] is a tutorial on the network model.

TOTAL (see Cincom [1978]) is a major commercial system based on the network model. IDMS (Cullinane [1978]) and ADABAS (Software AG [1978]) are other important realizations of some of these ideas. Each of these systems is described in Tsichritzis and Lochovsky [1977], and TOTAL is also described in Cardenas [1979]. Wiederhold [1977] enumerates many commercial systems based on DBTG ideas.

4

THE HIERARCHICAL MODEL

In this chapter we shall introduce the basic ideas behind the hierarchical data model. We shall show how to design a hierarchy from a network, and we shall introduce the concept of virtual record types that makes this translation possible. Like the multilist structure for networks, there are certain data structures that are especially important for the implementation of hierarchies, and we shall introduce them in the second section. Then we shall discuss data definition and manipulation languages that are based loosely on IBM's IMS database system.

4.1 FROM NETWORKS TO HIERARCHIES

Recall from Section 1.4 that a hierarchy is a network whose links form a forest, with each link a many-one relationship from child to parent. Our first impression might be that only a few networks are hierarchies, and therefore the hierarchical model does not have the power to represent information that the relational and network models have. Our second thought might be that with sufficient duplication of records, every network can be put in a hierarchical form. Such may be true, but recall that an important design consideration is the necessity to avoid redundancy, as we discussed in Section 3.1. Therefore, our final approach to the issue of construction of hierarchies will be to introduce "virtual" record types, which are pointers to other record types; these will enable us to have apparent duplication of records, without the attendant redundancy.

To begin our discussion, let us focus on the HVFC database restricted to the items, orders, and members. Each item has a set of orders for it, and each member has placed a set of orders, so we might design a forest like that of Fig. 4.1(a), where there are two trees, one with root MEMBERS and the other with root ITEMS; each has one child, ORDERS. Note that the trees of Fig. 4.1(a) are quite simple, in that each root has only one child, but in general, the root can have many children, the children can have many children, and so on. Figure 4.1(b) shows the data of Fig. 3.2(b) represented in this hierarchy. Notice that ORDERS records appear twice. There is redundancy because the order

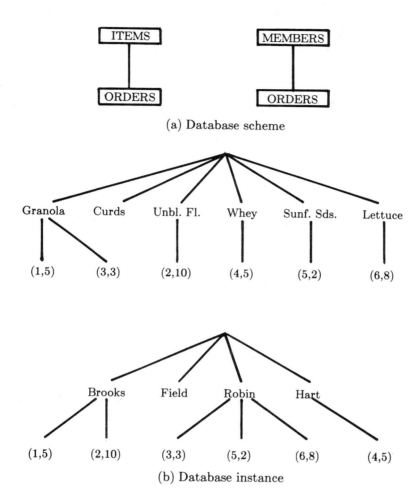

(a) Database scheme

(b) Database instance

Fig. 4.1. A redundant form of hierarchy.

numbers and quantities are each repeated, and there is the associated risk of inconsistency, because we might change the quantity ordered in one occurence of an order, yet not make the same change in the other occurrence of the same order.

Virtual Records

In the hierarchical model, the preferred solution to the redundancy problem is to allow the use of *virtual* logical record types; a virtual type T record should be interpreted as a pointer to a physical record of type T. Figure 4.2 shows what happens to Fig. 4.1 if we replace the ORDERS child of MEMBERS by

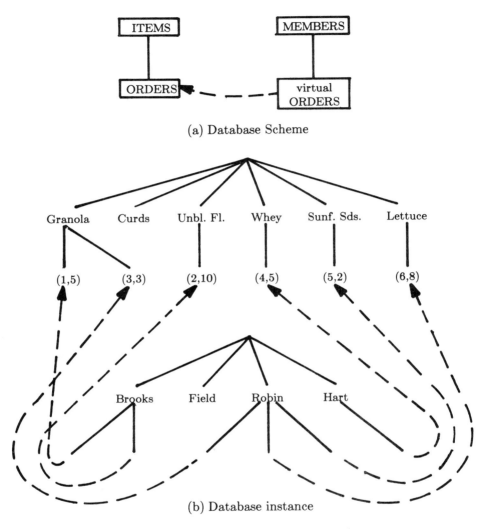

(a) Database Scheme

(b) Database instance

Fig. 4.2. Hierarchy with virtual record type.

a virtual ORDERS field. We could, of course, have decided to leave orders as children of members, and made the children of items be virtual instead.

Let us also recall from Section 1.4 that links in a hierarchy are unidirectional, proceeding from parent to child and not vice-versa, unless we explicitly create a pointer from child to parent. Thus, while the relation of Fig. 3.2(b) tells us directly who placed each order and for what the order was placed, the hierarchy does not give us that information simply, if all we can do is proceed from parent to child and follow the pointers that are implied by virtual children. For example, to tell what items Brooks has ordered, we must find the Brooks MEMBERS record, follow the pointers in each of its virtual ORDERS children, and for each real ORDERS record found, examine all the ITEMS records to see which had that ORDERS record as a child—a very time-consuming process. Or to find all the members that ordered granola, we would have to find all the ORDERS records that were children of the ITEMS record for granola, then scan each of the MEMBERS records and their virtual ORDERS children to see which of these pointed to one of the selected ORDERS records.

A pointer in each ORDERS record to its parent ITEMS record will help us find the items ordered by a member, but pointers in virtual ORDERS records to their MEMBERS parent will not help find the members ordering a given item. A more general, and usually preferable, way to represent many-many relationships in the hierarchical model, say between logical record types A and B, is to make virtual B a child of A and virtual A a child of B.

Example 4.1: In Fig. 4.3(a) we see the database scheme, and in Fig. 4.3(b) is shown the database instance if the relationship between A and B consists of the $A - B$ pairs (a_1, b_1), (a_1, b_2), (a_2, b_1), and (a_3, b_1). $\square$

In our running HVFC example, there is essentially a many-many relationship between items and members, although it is complicated somewhat by having orders acting as a connection between the two. Figure 4.4(a) shows one way we might represent the many-many relationship so we can go directly from an item to the members ordering it or vice-versa. Note that there is a potential for inconsistency in this scheme, because the pairs of pointers linking members and items are required to represent exactly the pairs of members and items found in the orders.

Figure 4.4(b) is a better way to design the scheme. There, to go from an item to its orderers, we find the ORDERS records that are children of the item, and for each such order we find its virtual MEMBERS children (there will in practice be only one child of each ORDERS record). To go from a member to the items he ordered, we find the virtual ORDERS children of the member, follow the pointers therein, and from each order follow its pointer to its parent.

The advantage of the second scheme is that we can find the member placing an order even if we are "at" the record for the order, rather than at its parent ITEMS record. The disadvantage is that to find the members ordering an item we must follow an extra pointer in Fig. 4.4(b). However, we should remember that there is still the potential for inconsistency since we expect that an order has a virtual MEMBERS pointer to exactly that member record that has a virtual ORDERS pointer to that order. That form of potential inconsistency is inherent in the style of representing many-many relationships, and we consider it less odious than the problems found in Fig. 4.4(a), which involved not only members and items, but orders as well.

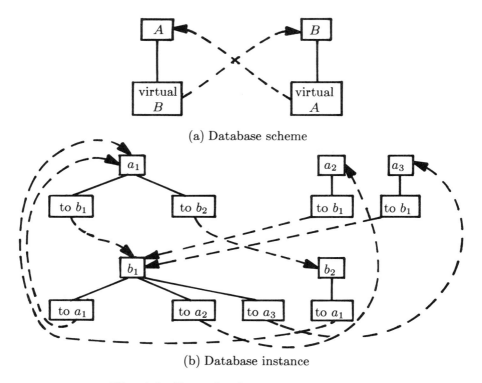

(a) Database scheme

(b) Database instance

Fig. 4.3. Example of a many-many mapping.

An Algorithm to Construct Hierarchies

We can now show that it is possible to construct for each entity-relationship diagram a hierarchy that represents its information and allows relationships to be followed efficiently. What we actually do is start from a network representation and mechanically convert it to a hierarchy. So that links can be followed in both directions, we shall assume that each child record has a pointer to its parent record. The result is really only of theoretical interest. Even though the hierarchies constructed satisfy our intent that the information in the network should be obtained easily from the hierarchy, the designs produced tend to be rather unintuitive and to rely on virtual record types rather than on the natural hierarchical structure of the information.

Figure 4.5 shows the algorithm that "selects" each logical record type of a given network and places it into a forest. The idea behind the algorithm is to select nodes n and "build" a tree with root n by attaching as many nodes as have arcs entering n in the network. Then we attach to the children of n the nodes of the network entering them, and so on. We only attach a node to

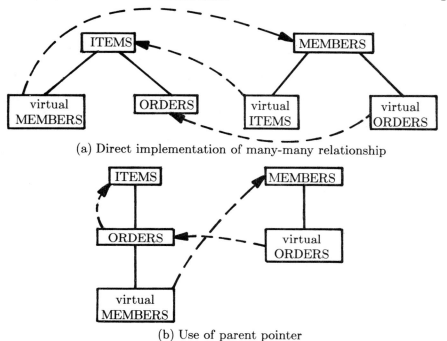

(a) Direct implementation of many-many relationship

(b) Use of parent pointer

Fig. 4.4. Implementations of a many-many relationship
between ORDERS and MEMBERS

one tree, however, so if a node is already attached to another tree we make a
"virtual" version of the node and attach that instead.

Example 4.2: Let us consider the baseball network of Fig. 1.12. We might
begin with PLAYERS as node n, since that node has two incoming arcs but no
outgoing arcs, while no other node has more than one entering arc. We build
the tree with root PLAYERS by considering each entering arc in turn. These
arcs come from PP and PTB, so we make them each children of PLAYERS
in the hierarchy. We then proceed to build the trees dangling from PP and
PTB, but since neither has any incoming arcs, those trees are empty, and we
are through with the recursive use of the procedure BUILD(PLAYERS).

We might then select TEAMS as node n; we find it has one incoming arc,
from PTB, but the latter is already selected so we make virtual PTB a child
of TEAMS and do not attempt to build from virtual PTB. Similarly, we would
next select POSITIONS as n and give it a virtual PP child but not attempt
to build further from the virtual PP node. The resulting hierarchy is shown
in Fig. 4.6. The reader should compare it with the ad-hoc design of Fig. 1.14
and notice how the latter captures the structure of the data better than Fig.
4.6 does.

while not all nodes in the network have been selected **do**
    pick an unselected node n with no arcs leaving
    /∗ prefer a node with many entering arcs ∗/
    BUILD(n)
end

procedure BUILD(n)
    make n selected
    for each node m with a link from m to n **do**
        if m is not selected **then do**
            make m a child of n
            BUILD(m)
        end
        else /∗ m was previously selected ∗/
            make virtual m be a child of n
    end
end

Fig. 4.5. Algorithm to convert networks to hierarchies.

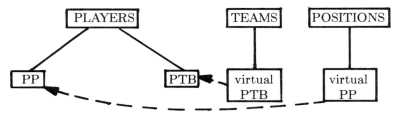

Fig. 4.6. Hierarchy constructed by algorithm of Fig. 4.5.

A Data Definition Language for the Hierarchical Model

Let us take the ideas just developed regarding the need for virtual logical record types and other sorts of pointers and set down a formal DDL for the hierarchical model. The notation we use is patterned loosely after that used in the previous chapter for the network DDL and also draws from the IMS notation somewhat.

In our DDL we are allowed to declare three kinds of objects: trees, logical record types, and fields. We declare a tree by

    TREE <name> <list of logical record types>

Each logical record type is declared by

    RECORD <name> <information>

The <information> is of the following types.
1.   Fields. Each field is declared as in the network DDL, e.g.,

```
TREE ITEMSTREE
    RECORD ITEMS ROOT
        1 INAME CHAR(15)
    RECORD ORDERS PARENT=ITEMS POINTER=PARENT
        1 ORDER _ NO INTEGER
        1 QUANTITY REAL
    RECORD VIRT _ MEMBERS PARENT=ORDERS
        VIRTUAL MEMBERS IN MEMBERSTREE

TREE MEMBERSTREE
    RECORD MEMBERS ROOT
        1 NAME CHAR(20)
        1 ADDR CHAR(30)
        1 BALANCE REAL
    RECORD VIRT _ ORDERS PARENT=MEMBERS
        VIRTUAL ORDERS IN ITEMSTREE
```

Fig. 4.7. Declaration of Fig. 4.4(b) in our hierarchical DDL.

1 QUANTITY INTEGER;

2. Information telling the position of the logical record type in its tree. Either the word ROOT will appear, or the parent will be declared by a clause

    PARENT=<parent name>

3. An (optional) indication that the record type is virtual, in which case no fields are declared for it and the clause

    VIRTUAL <record name> IN <tree name>

    appears, designating the node of which the present record type is a virtual version.

4. Pointer information. We shall go into various kinds of pointers that might be declared in Section 4.2. For the moment let us just introduce the declaration that says a logical record type has a pointer in each record occurrence to the parent of that record:

    POINTER=PARENT

    The general form of pointer declarations is

    POINTER=<list of pointer types>

Example 4.3: The formal declaration of the hierarchy of Fig. 4.4(b) is shown in Fig. 4.7. □

4.2 IMPLEMENTATION OF HIERARCHICAL DATABASES

In one sense, we already know how to implement a hierarchy, since we covered implementation of networks in Section 3.2, and hierarchies are special cases of

procedure PREORDER(n)
list n
for each child c of n from the left **do**
    PREORDER(c)
end

Fig. 4.8. Procedure for listing a tree in preorder.

networks. However, the way hierarchical databases tend to be designed makes a particular approach to implementation very common and appropriate. For each tree in the hierarchical database scheme we construct a variable length record format by the following rules.

1. The format for a leaf is $(\alpha)^*$, where α is the list of fields in the logical record format for that leaf.

2. If a node has k children with variable length record formats $\alpha_1, \ldots, \alpha_k$, and the list of fields in the logical record format for this node is β, then the variable length record format for the node is $(\beta\alpha_1, \ldots, \alpha_k)^*$.

Example 4.4: Consider the tree with root ITEMS in Fig. 4.4(a). The leaf ORDERS has two fields, ORDER_NO and QUANTITY, so its variable length record format is

   (ORDER_NO QUANTITY)*

The other leaf is a virtual logical record type, so we shall give it a single field, say P_MEMBER to represent a pointer to a MEMBER record. The root logical record type has only one field, INAME, so the entire variable length record format is

   (INAME (P_MEMBER)* (ORDER_NO QUANTITY)*)*

□

We could implement these variable length records in any of the ways discussed in Section 2.6. However, a specialized approach seems to be quite valuable as a way to provide the needed efficient accesses to parts of the database without wasting too much space. We list all the records in an entire tree of the physical database in preorder. Figure 4.8 defines the preorder traversal or listing of a tree for those unfamiliar with the concept. We obtain the preorder listing of a tree by applying the recursive PREORDER procedure to its root.

Example 4.5: The preorder listing of the upper tree in Fig. 4.1(b) is

Granola, $(1, 5)$, $(3, 3)$, Curds, Unbleached flour, $(2, 10)$, Whey, $(4, 5)$, Sunflower seeds, $(5, 2)$, Lettuce, $(6, 8)$

Strictly speaking, the dummy root node of that tree precedes all of the above in the listing. □

Another way to view this organization is that each logical record type that is not a root is stored "via" the DBTG set of which its parent is the owner and it is the member type. The result of such an organization is that given a node, we can find its descendants in the tree in very few block accesses on the average, since they collectively follow the node in the preorder sequence. It is this property of the preorder listing, together with the assumption that the most frequent type of query will ask for the descendants of a node, that justifies the preorder sequence as an important way in which to store hierarchical data.

Methods for Storing the Preorder Sequence

In addition to the already discussed methods for storing hierarchical data as if it was a collection of variable length records, there are methods for storing the data in its preorder sequence efficiently. The key issues in selecting such an organization are that the descendants of a node must be kept "near" the node, that is, spread over as few blocks as possible, and that we should be capable of doing insertions and deletions of nodes efficiently.

In such organizations, it helps to think of storage as by *database record*, which is an occurrence of the root record type and all of its descendants. For example, in the upper tree of Fig. 4.1(b), the records Granola, $(1, 5)$, and $(3, 3)$ form one database record. We divide the database records into buckets; the bucket to which a database record belongs is determined by the values in fields of the root record that form the key for that type. In effect, we are going to store each root record type by CALC-key and all its descendants VIA some DBTG set, the one that relates that record type to its parent in the tree. The two most obvious methods for dividing database records into buckets is to use a sparse index, as in Section 2.3 or a hashing scheme as in Section 2.2.

We can view each bucket as arranged in a two-dimensional way. The rows correspond to single database records, and each database record will be, in general, spread over some list of blocks. Each record of the database record contains a few bits that indicate its type, so we can scan a block and determine where the records begin and end, knowing the length of each record type. We shall assume that no block holds data from more than one database record and that, as usual, records are not spread over more than one block. The former constraint is for implementation convenience; if we select the block size to be somewhat smaller than the typical database record, there will be little waste space because of it. The latter constraint is to save block accesses when reading a single record, and if blocks are much bigger than typical records, again little waste occurs.

Example 4.6: Figure 4.9(a) shows a simple hierarchy and Fig. 4.9(b) shows three database records that might form a tiny instance of the database. We have made some unstated assumptions about the relative sizes of A, B, and C

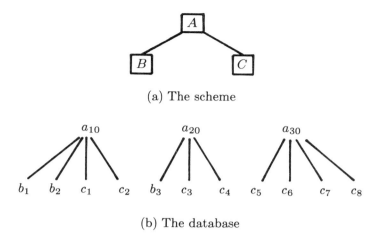

(a) The scheme

(b) The database

Fig. 4.9. Example database and its scheme.

Bucket
headers

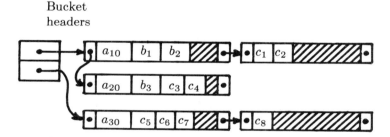

Fig. 4.10. Two-dimensional organization of database records.

records, and we have, for convenience assumed that the key value for an A-type record a_i is i. We have assumed that the database records whose roots have key values 10 and 20 belong in one bucket and the one with key value 30 belongs in a second bucket. Perhaps the bucket scheme is a sparse index in which we initially place two database records per bucket, or it could as well be a hash table in which 10 and 20 happen to hash to the same value.

Figure 4.10 shows the three database records stored among blocks. Each block has a pointer in the front to the first block of the next database record in the same bucket. This pointer is unused if the block is not the first block for its database record. We also show a pointer at the end of each block, linking the block to the next block for the same database record if there is one. In practice this pointer would probably be part of the header and appear near the front of the block. $\square$

Insertions and Deletions from Database Records

The way in which we implement insertions and deletions depends on whether records are pinned or not. Recall that a virtual T type record is a pointer to a record of type T. If virtual T records exist, then T records are pinned unless we represent pointers very carefully, in a way we shall discuss. In general, if one or more record types in a tree are pinned, we may as well consider all record types pinned, because it is generally useless to move some of the records around if we cannot order the records of a database records exactly as we like. Thus, we shall consider the question of whether records are pinned to be one of how pointers are represented, rather than an issue of what virtual record types exist.

We might ask ourselves, given the organization suggested by Fig. 4.10, what sort of pointers would allow us to insert, delete, and move around records within a single database record, without causing pointers to dangle? First of all, the record of the root type in any database record will never be moved; presumably we cannot allow a database record to exist without a record of the root type. Thus, ordinary pointers to the root type are feasible. We must, of course, set a deletion bit if the root record is deleted, rather than trying to reuse its space, or dangling pointers may result.

For records other than the root type, we may move them around in the blocks holding a database record, to keep them in the preorder sequence, only if pointers direct us to the database record itself. We must then look in the entire database record to find the intended record, which means that a pointer must consist of

1. The address of the first block of the database record, and
2. The value of the key field or fields for the record in question.

Note that this type of "pointer" will not support the movement of records among different database records. Deletion by setting a deletion bit instead of reusing space is not mandatory, since we shall not find the designated key value if we go searching for the record. However, for the sake of catching errors, and also to avoid a situation where we delete a record with key value v and later insert a record with the same key value that then becomes the target of pointers to the deleted record, we suggest the use of a deletion bit.

Example 4.7: Suppose that in the database of Fig. 4.10 we insert b_4 as a second B-child of a_{30}. Using our relative size assumptions it will be necessary to move c_7 to the block now occupied by c_8, while shifting c_5, c_6, and c_8 to the right. If we then delete c_6, we simply set a deletion bit in that record; no motion of records is made.

Now, imagine that we are using a sparse index, and we insert a database record with root a_{12} and children b_5 and c_9, then insert a database record with root a_{15} and children b_6, b_7, and b_8. Each of these database records goes in the first bucket, and we can place them in sorted order within the bucket. The

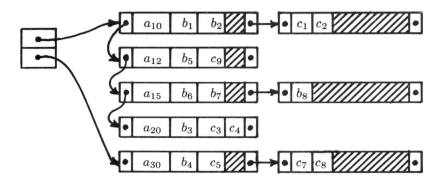

Fig. 4.11. Database records after some insertions and deletions.

resulting arrangement of blocks and records is shown in Fig. 4.11. □

The pointers we have described above do not give very fast access, as we must frequently scan most of the blocks of a database record to follow a pointer. There is a good case, therefore, for using true pointers and pinning the records. If we make this choice, we can still delete by setting a deletion bit, but we cannot slide records to make room for an inserted record. We must instead place an inserted record at the end of the last block for the database record, or create a new block for the database record if there is no room. In order to maintain the preorder information, we shall use a network of pointers, as described next.

Pointer Networks

There are two reasons why we might want to represent the preorder sequence by a collection of pointers.

1. As just mentioned above, we might, because records are pinned, be forced to keep the records of a database record in other than the preorder sequence as they appear within the blocks, and thus, we must represent the preorder sequence some other way.

2. The pointers might help us skip some blocks of the database record. For example, if all the children of the root were linked by a chain of pointers, we could visit each child in turn, even though many blocks holding the descendants of each child of the root appear between blocks that hold two consecutive children.

There are two common methods of representing the preorder sequence by pointers. The first is the obvious one: each record points to the next record in the preorder listing. This arrangement is called *preorder threads*. The second arrangement is for each record to have a pointer to its leftmost child and a pointer to its *right sibling*, where the right sibling of a node n is that child of the parent of n that is immediately to the right of n. For example, in the

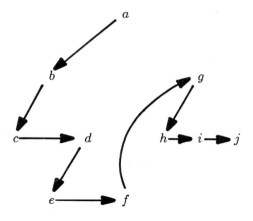

(a) Preorder threads

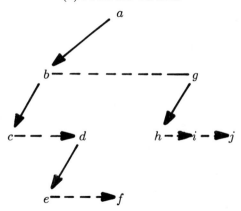

(b) Leftmost child/right sibling pointers

Fig. 4.12. Pointer arrangements.

upper tree of Fig. 4.1(b), $(3,3)$ is the right sibling of $(1,5)$, and $(3,3)$ has no right sibling.

Example 4.8: Figure 4.12(a) shows a tree with preorder threads, and Fig. 4.12(b) shows the same tree with leftmost child (solid) and right sibling (dashed) pointers. □

Each of these networks of pointers can be specified in a pointer clause associated with the tree as a whole, similarly to the way we specified parent pointers for one particular logical record type in Fig. 4.7. Each method has its advantages. We might prefer preorder threads because there is only one pointer per record, while leftmost child/right sibling pointers require space for two pointers per record, even though many of these pointers are null (e.g., no leaf node has a leftmost child). On the other hand, leftmost child/right sibling pointers enable us to travel from left to right through the children of a node quickly, even though many desdcendants intervene in the preorder sequence. Observe, for example, how we can go from b to g directly in Fig. 4.12(b), while we must travel through c, d, e, and f in Fig. 4.12(a).

4.3 A HIERARCHICAL DATA MANIPULATION LANGUAGE

We shall introduce the reader to a hierarchical query language that is loosely based on IMS's data manipulation language called DL/I, and we shall refer to our language as "Pidgin DL/I." This language is a collection of commands that are embedded in a host language. In IMS, these commands are actually procedure calls, and we can regard them as such here.

The Program Environment

The database consists of a collection of trees, as covered in Sections 1.4 and 4.1. As in the DBTG model, we may assume there is a workspace in which a template for each logical record type is kept. These templates can be filled by particular records of the correct type chosen from the database by the GET command. Also in analogy with the DBTG proposal, it is convenient to assume that there is a "current record" of each tree. This record could be of any type in the scheme for that tree. We shall also have some use for the notion of a "current parent," the parent of the current record. In the more complex forms of DL/I queries, there is some use for a "current of record type" for each record type, but we shall not discuss such queries here.

We shall also assume that there is a variable FAIL that is accessible both to the host language program and to the commands of the query language; FAIL will be used to indicate whether or not certain database searches have found a record meeting the desired conditions.

The GET Command

The basic retrieval command of Pidgin DL/I, called GET LEFTMOST, specifies a path from a root record occurrence to a (*target*) record of a particular type, not necessarily a leaf record type. This command causes to be retrieved, and placed in the template for the target record type, the leftmost record occurrence of that type to satisfy whatever conditions are placed on it and on its ancestors by the GET LEFTMOST command.

The syntax we shall use in our "Pidgin DL/I" for GET LEFTMOST is

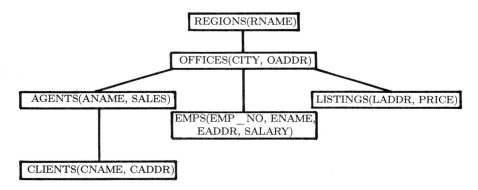

Fig. 4.13. Scheme for the real estate database.

GET LEFTMOST <target record name>
WHERE <condition list>

The <condition list> consists of a sequence of conditions of the form

<record name> . <field name> θ <value>

possibly connected by "and" and "or." Each <record name> is an ancestor
(not necessarily proper) of the target record type. The <field name> is a field
of the <record name>, and θ is one of the arithmetic comparison operators,
=, <, and so on. The <value> can be a constant or a variable of the host
language program; the latter option helps us pass "parameters" to the calls
represented by the Pidgin DL/I commands. We can omit the <record name>
if it is uniquely determined by the <field name>.

Example 4.9: The examples with which we have been dealing do not provide
interesting enough hierarchies, so we shall introduce a new example, about a
real estate company, for the purposes of this section. The database scheme is
shown in Fig. 4.13, and a formal definition of the scheme in our hierarchical
DDL is given in Fig. 4.14. The company is divided into regions, each with
several offices, so in the database, each REGIONS record has one child for each
office in the region. Offices have agents, and employees in general. Offices also
have "listings," properties that they offer for sale. Thus, each OFFICES record
has children of three types: AGENTS, EMPS, and LISTINGS.† Finally, agents
have clients, so AGENTS records are given CLIENTS records as children. It
is assumed that each client has only one agent, that is, there is a many-one

---

† An agent is also an employee, so an agent may have two records, one of AGENTS type and
one of EMPS type, the latter holding information relevant to all employees and the former
holding information relevant to agents only. However, the correspondence between AGENTS
and EMPS records is through the equality of their ANAME and ENAME fields and does not
concern us here.

```
TREE REALESTATE
    RECORD REGIONS ROOT
        1 RNAME CHAR(20)
    RECORD OFFICES PARENT=REGIONS
        1 CITY CHAR(20)
        1 OADDR CHAR(30)
    RECORD AGENTS PARENT=OFFICES
        1 ANAME CHAR(20)
        1 SALES INTEGER
    RECORD EMPS PARENT=OFFICES
        1 EMP_NO INTEGER
        1 ENAME CHAR(20)
        1 EADDR CHAR(30)
        1 SALARY INTEGER
    RECORD LISTINGS PARENT=OFFICES
        1 LADDR CHAR(30)
        1 PRICE INTEGER
    RECORD CLIENTS PARENT=AGENTS
        1 CNAME CHAR(20)
        1 CADDR CHAR(30)
```

Fig. 4.14. DDL definition of real estate database.

relationship from clients to agents.

The Pidgin DL/I command

```
GET LEFTMOST AGENTS
    WHERE SALES>1000000
```

finds the first (leftmost in the tree) agent whose sales total exceeds one million dollars. It is implemented by scanning the database in preorder,† effectively examining each AGENTS record from the left, until finding one whose sales total exceeds one million dollars. When found, this record is placed in the AGENTS template in the workspace.

Suppose now we wished to find an agent in the Princeton office with over a million in sales. We could write:

```
GET LEFTMOST AGENTS
    WHERE CITY="Princeton" AND SALES>1000000
```

If the agency had offices in both Princeton, N.J. and Princeton, Tex., we could specify

```
GET LEFTMOST AGENTS
    WHERE RNAME="Northeast" AND CITY="Princeton"
    AND SALES>1000000
```

assuming that New Jersey is in the Northeast region and Texas is not.

---

† Recall we assume all REGIONS records are children of a dummy root.

```
read REG, OFF
GET LEFTMOST AGENTS
    WHERE RNAME=REG AND CITY=OFF
    AND SALES>1000000
```

Fig. 4.15. Use of variables in record search arguments.

```
GET LEFTMOST AGENTS
    WHERE SALES>1000000
while ¬ FAIL do
    print AGENTS.ANAME /* "print" refers to the template
    for the appropriate record type in the workspace */
    GET NEXT AGENTS
        WHERE SALES>1000000
end
```

Fig. 4.16. Print all agents with sales over a million.

We could even write a program that reads a region and city and **produces** an agent with over a million in sales in that city's office. The program in Fig. 4.15 performs this operation. □

Another version of the GET command allows us to scan the entire database for all records satisfying certain conditions. We use the word NEXT in place of LEFTMOST to cause a scan rightward from the last record accessed (i.e., from the "current of view") until we next meet a record of the same type satisfying the conditions in the GET NEXT statement. These conditions could differ from the conditions that established the "current of view," but in practice they are usually the same.

Example 4.10: Suppose we wish to find all agents with sales over a million. We could write the program of Fig. 4.16 to accomplish this task. Note that in Fig. 4.16 we use the variable FAIL to indicate the success or failure of a Pidgin DL/I statement. Recall that FAIL is a global variable that is accessible to both the host language program and the procedures that implement the Pidgin DL/I statements. The value of FAIL becomes true whenever no record satisfying the desired conditions can be found. In our example, if no agents have sales over a million, GET LEFTMOST will cause FAIL to become true. Otherwise, FAIL becomes true on the execution of GET NEXT immediately after the rightmost agent with sales over a million was found. □

A third form of GET, written GET NEXT WITHIN PARENT, permits us to visit all the children of a particular record occurrence in the actual database. It utilizes the informal concept of "current parent," which is the record occurrence most recently accessed by any variety of GET other than

```
GET LEFTMOST AGENTS
    WHERE CITY="Princeton" AND ANAME="Slick,Sam"
    /* above establishes the current parent */
GET NEXT WITHIN PARENT CLIENTS
    /* above gets Slick's first client */
while ¬ FAIL do
    print CLIENTS.CNAME
    GET NEXT WITHIN PARENT CLIENTS
end
```

Fig. 4.17. Print all the clients of Slick.

GET NEXT WITHIN PARENT. The record type accessed by a GET NEXT WITHIN PARENT command need not be a child record type for the type of the current parent; it could be any descendant record type. The important difference between GET NEXT and GET NEXT WITHIN PARENT is that the latter fails when it has scanned all the descendants of the current parent; the former searches rightward for any record occurrence such that it and its ancestors satisfy the associated conditions.

Example 4.11: In Fig. 4.17 we show a program that prints all the clients of agent Sam Slick, who works in the Princeton office (we assume this information uniquely identifies the agent). If instead, we wanted to print the clients of all the agents in the Princeton office (assuming there is only one office with CITY = "Princeton") we could simply change the GET LEFTMOST statement in Fig. 4.17 to

```
GET LEFTMOST OFFICES
    WHERE CITY="Princeton"
```

Note that in this case, "within parent" effectively means "within grandparent," and all clients of all agents in the Princeton office would be printed. □

Insertions

An INSERT command, for which we use the same "Pidgin" syntax as for the varieties of GET, allows us to insert a record of type S, first created in the workspace, as a child of a designated record occurrence of the parent type for S. If the "current of view" is either of the parent type for S, or any descendant of the parent type, simply writing

```
INSERT S
```

will make the record of type S sitting in the workspace a child of that occurrence of the parent type that is the current of view or an ancestor of the current of view. The order of children is a matter we have not discussed. Some declaration

CLIENTS.CNAME := "Nebbish, Joe"
CLIENTS.ADDR := "74 Family Way"
/* the above assignments take place in the CLIENTS template
   of the workspace */
INSERT CLIENTS
    WHERE CITY= "Princeton" AND ANAME= "Slick,Sam"

Fig. 4.18. Nebbish becomes a client of Slick.

mechanism is needed in the DDL to indicate which of several options should
be taken. Reasonable options include making each record the rightmost (or
perhaps leftmost) child of its parent at the time it is inserted, or keeping children
in sorted order according to a key field or fields.

Example 4.12: Suppose Joe Nebbish agrees to become Sam Slick's client. We
could enter a record for Nebbish as a child of the record for Slick, by executing
the program of Fig. 4.18. If Slick's record was already the current of view, or
even if some client of Slick were the current of view, we could insert the Nebbish
record by putting the correct field values for the record in the workspace, as in
Fig. 4.18, and then issuing the command

    INSERT CLIENTS

□

Deletion and Modification

In order to delete or modify a record we must first "hold" it by issuing some
variety of GET command that will make the desired record the current of view,
but adding the word HOLD after GET in the command. The requirement for
holding a record before deleting or modifying it is motivated by the possibility
that there is concurrent processing of the database by two or more application
programs. Upon executing GET HOLD, any other program is prevented from
accessing the record. See Chapter 11 for a description of the need for "holding"
a record before modifying it. "Hold" here corresponds to "lock" or "write-lock"
in Chapter 11.

To delete a record after finding and holding it, simply issue the Pidgin
DL/I command

    DELETE

The effect of this statement is to delete the record that is the current of view
and also to delete any of its children in the underlying database.

To modify a record after finding and holding it, we first change the copy of
the record found in the workspace. When we issue the Pidgin DL/I command

    REPLACE

```
GET HOLD LEFTMOST AGENTS
    WHERE CITY= "Princeton" AND ANAME= "Slick,Sam"
AGENTS.SALES := AGENTS.SALES+100000
/* the above takes place in the AGENTS template
   of the workspace */
REPLACE
```

Fig. 4.19. Add 100,000 to the sales of Slick.

the version of the current record in the workspace replaces the corresponding record in the database.

Example 4.13: Suppose agent Slick sells a lonely tropical island for one hundred thousand dollars. We can add this amount to his sales total with the program shown in Fig. 4.19.

Unfortunately, shortly thereafter, the tropical island swims away. It is therefore decided that Slick must be fired, which is done with the commands

```
GET HOLD LEFTMOST AGENTS
    WHERE CITY= "Princeton" AND ANAME= "Slick,Sam"
DELETE
```

Note that the DELETE command deletes not only Slick's record but also the records of all clients of Slick. Perhaps we should have transferred them to another agent first. □

EXERCISES

4.1: Apply the algorithm of Section 4.1 to construct hierarchies from the network of Fig. 3.3.

4.2: Describe your answer to Exercise 4.1 using the hierarchical DDL of Section 4.1.

4.3: Suppose blocks hold 1000 bytes of data, in addition to a few pointers, and there are records of three types, A, B, and C, of length 300, 200, and 400 bytes, respectively. Let C be a child of B, and B a child of A in the hierarchy. Suppose that the key for record a_i of type A is taken to be i, and that database records are to be distributed into three buckets, based on the key value of their root records. The three buckets take keys (i) below 10 (ii) 10–20, and (iii) above 20, respectively. Show the structure of blocks if the database records of Fig. 4.20 are inserted, in the order shown, assuming the "two-dimensional" organization of Fig. 4.10.

4.4: Show (a) preorder threads, and (b) leftmost child/right sibling pointers on the database records of Exercise 4.3.

4.5: Show the effect of deleting c_7 and inserting c_{13} as the rightmost child of b_2 (a) assuming records are unpinned and can slide within a bucket, and

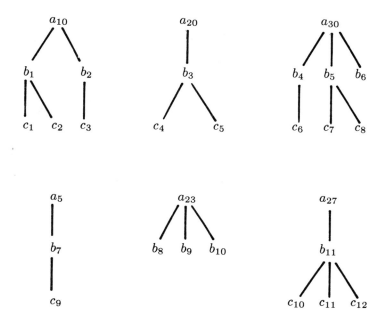

Fig. 4.20. Database records.

(b) assuming records are pinned and preorder threads are maintained.

* 4.6: Give algorithms to update (a) preorder threads (b) leftmost child/right sibling pointers when a record is inserted or deleted.

4.7: In Fig. 4.21 is a hierarchical database scheme representing the navies of the world. Assume for convenience that each record type has a field NAME that serves as a key. Write queries in Pidgin DL/I to do the following.

a) Print all squadrons that have at least one submarine.

b) Print all countries that have a squadron with at least two cruisers.

* c) Print all countries that have a fleet with at least two cruisers.

* d) Read a naval base and print the country to which it belongs.

e) Read a country, fleet, squadron, and the name of a submarine and enter the submarine into the proper squadron.

4.8: What additional structure added to the database scheme would make it possible to execute the query of Exercise 4.7(d) easily?

* 4.9: If the queries in Section 4.3 are typical of the way the real estate database will be used, what pointer options would be advisable in the physical database. Make reasonable assumptions about how many children the nodes of each type could be expected to have.

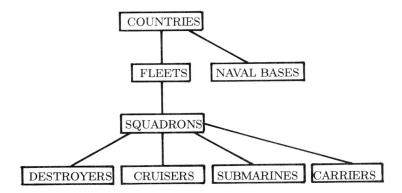

Fig. 4.21. Naval database.

BIBLIOGRAPHIC NOTES

The reader may wish to read about the IMS system (IBM [1978b]) or an equally important hierarchical system, System 2000 (MRI [1978]). An extensive treatment of IMS can be found in Date [1981], while both these systems are covered in Tsichritzis and Lochovsky [1977] and Cardenas [1979].

5

THE RELATIONAL MODEL

This chapter begins an extended coverage of the relational data model. We shall follow the pattern of previous chapters, first discussing storage organization ideas, and then covering query languages. However, here we cover only abstract query languages, called relational algebra and calculus. The real query languages based on these abstractions are covered in Chapter 6.

5.1 STORAGE STRATEGIES FOR RELATIONS

The obvious way to represent a relation is as a file whose record format consists of one field for each attribute of the relation scheme. Many data definition languages for the relational model allow the user to specify, from among options, the organization of this file. The options available are usually a subset of those described in Sections 2.2–2.5, such as hashed and indexed-sequential. Another alternative, which may be best for relations with a small number of tuples (say, a few hundred), is the "heap," that is, no particular order to the records of the file, and no way to find records except by examining the whole file. In addition to these organization options, the user should be given the ability to create secondary indices on arbitrary sets of attributes.

As many file organizations are dependent on the existence of a key for records, a relational DDL should also provide a mechanism for specifying a set of one or more attributes as the key for the relation. The notion of "key" for a relation is essentially identical to that of "key" in the context of files or entity sets; a relation is guaranteed not to have two tuples that agree on all the attributes of the key.

Example 5.1: In the HVFC database of Fig. 3.2, NAME forms a key for the MEMBERS relation, since we do not expect to find two tuples with the same name but different addresses or balances.†

---

† There is a fundamental assumption about the HVFC database that names are sufficient to identify members, that is, the co-op would find some way (e.g., a nickname) of dealing with two members who went by the same name. In practice, it is almost essential for an organization to identify people uniquely, either by a unique number such as a social security number, or by a specially assigned number, such as an employee number or account number.

The appropriate key for the SUPPLIERS relation is SNAME and ITEM together. That is, the supplier name determines the address, but not the price, since a supplier may charge different amounts for different items. However, given both the supplier and the item, we expect there to be only one associated price. □

Clearly the attributes that form a key for the relation can also serve as a key for the file. It is interesting to note that if we design our relations from an entity-relationship diagram, then the relations for the entity sets adopt a key from the entity set. Also, relations constructed to represent many-one relationships from an entity set E_1 to E_2 can adopt the key of E_1. Relations for many-many relationships must use the keys for all related entity sets as the key for the relation. The general subject of finding and using keys in relations has been well developed, and we shall explore some of this theory in Chapter 7.

The purpose of using specialized storage strategies such as hashing or secondary indexing is to make certain kinds of queries answerable in an efficient way. For example, if we organize the MEMBERS relation by hashing or indexing on the key NAME, then we can respond rapidly to queries like "print the balance of Brooks." If we had a secondary index on NAME in the ORDERS relation, we could answer quickly a question like "print the items ordered by Brooks," since the secondary index would get us to only those blocks containing tuples of the ORDERS relation that had Brooks in the NAME field.

Storage of Relations in INGRES

Before proceeding to more complex storage organizations for relations, let us consider one existing system and how it handles storage. INGRES (Stonebraker, Wong, Kreps and Held [1976]) is a pioneer among relational database systems. It was designed at Berkeley and runs under the UNIX operating system. In this system, relations are stored as UNIX files, spread over a sequence of 512-byte blocks. Tuples are represented by records, and records are packed into blocks as tightly as possible, but with no record split over two blocks.

There are three options for organization of relations. When a relation R is created, it has a "heap" organization; that is, the tuples are in any order, with no access structure. Tuples of such a relation can be found only by scanning the file.

We can arrange for hashed access to the file for relation R, as discussed in Section 2.2, by saying†

† INGRES does not make a strong distinction between the data definition language and the data manipulation language, so commands to change the structure of a relation's storage, which properly belong to the DDL, can be interspersed with queries in the language QUEL, which we shall take up in Section 6.4.

modify R to hash on $A_1, \ldots, A_k$

where $A_1, \ldots, A_k$ is the list of attributes of R that serve as a key. The INGRES implementation of the file for R becomes that of Section 2.2; records may be pinned because of secondary indices, which we shall discuss later. As an alternative to a hashed access structure, a primary index can be created for the file R, by writing

modify R to isam on $A_1, \ldots, A_k$

Again, $A_1, \ldots, A_k$ is the assumed key for R_j. Recall that the acronym isam stands for indexed sequential access method; the structure created is that of Section 2.3.

We can create a secondary index for R by the statement

index on R is $S(A_1, \ldots, A_k)$

The relation S becomes a secondary index on attributes $A_1, \ldots, A_k$ for R, using a structure similar to that described in Section 2.7. The relation S has $k + 1$ components, the first k being $A_1, \ldots, A_k$, and the last being a pointer to a record of R; the last component has no attribute name, so the user cannot access its values or change them (a good design decision, if you think about it). The file for secondary index S is automatically made isam on $A_1, \ldots, A_k$, although this organization can be changed by a modify command, just as for any other relation, if the user so desires.

Implementation Ideas from the Network Model

It is not necessary that relations be stored straightforwardly as files. Existing systems can, and have, borrowed ideas that were developed to implement data in the network and hierarchical model. For example, the DBTG proposal suggests that certain record types be stored VIA set. The purpose of doing so is to reduce the number of block accesses when we scan the members of a set.

We can adopt the same idea to relations if we store the tuples of one relation interspersed with those of another in a certain way. As an example, suppose we have the relations MEMBERS and ORDERS from our HVFC database of Fig. 3.2. We might choose to store all ORDERS tuples for a particular member immediately after the MEMBERS tuple for that member. The effect is as if the MEMBERS tuple "owned" a set occurrence consisting of itself and all the ORDERS tuples for the member whose name appears in that MEMBERS tuple. As in the network model, this arrangement makes a query of the form "print all the orders from a particular member" answerable with comparatively few block accesses.

Example 5.2: Figure 5.1 shows the MEMBERS and ORDERS tuples from Fig. 3.2 stored with ORDERS tuples with a particular value in the NAME attribute

Brooks,B. 7 Apple Rd. +10.50
  1 Brooks,B. Granola 5
  2 Brooks,B. Unbleached Flour 10
Field,W. 43 Cherry La. 0
Robin,R. 12 Heather St. −123.45
  3 Robin,R. Granola 3
  5 Robin,R. Sunflower Seeds 2
  6 Robin,R. Lettuce 8
Hart,W. 65 Lark Rd. −43.00
  4 Hart,W. Whey 5

Fig. 5.1. HVFC data stored "VIA set".

following the MEMBERS tuple with the same value for the NAME attribute. Notice how if these records were distributed, in the order shown, over blocks, that queries like "print the items ordered by Brooks" could be answered in very few block accesses, provided we could find the MEMBERS record for Brooks efficiently, say because there is an index on NAME for the MEMBERS relation. In fact, the organization of Fig. 5.1 is preferable even to a secondary index on NAME for the ORDERS relation, since the latter requires a number of block accesses close to the number of orders placed by Brooks, and we may assume most of these orders are on different blocks. In comparison, the arrangement of Fig. 5.1 groups many of the desired orders onto one block, so we expect the total number of blocks we must retrieve to be significantly less than the number of orders records we want. □

It should be understood that the above example is typical of what can be done whenever there are two relations, R and S, and a set of attributes X such that

1. X is present in the relation schemes for both R and S,†
2. X is a key for R, and
3. whenever a tuple t is in S, there is a tuple of R that has the same values as t in all the attributes in set X.

Then there is a many-one relationship from the tuples of S to the tuples of R, where each tuple of S is mapped to the unique tuple of R that has the same value in the attributes of set X. We can store tuples of S immediately after the tuple of R with the same value in attributes X. In our informal example, R was MEMBERS, S was ORDERS, and X is the set consisting of NAME alone.

In fact, just as the VIA set structure in the network model allows us to set up any variable length record structure, we can arrange to store any variable length record format, in which the fields are relation names, in an obvious

---

† Strictly speaking, the names of the attributes need not even be the same in R and S, as long as we understand that corresponding attributes from R and S refer to the same thing.

NAME	ADDRESS	BAL	PTR		PTR	O#	NAME	ITEM	QTY
Brooks,B	7 Apple Rd.	+10.50				1	Brooks,B.	Granola	5
Field,W.	43 Cherry La.	0				2	Brooks,B.	Unbl. Fl.	10
Robin,R.	12 Heather St.	−123.45				3	Robin,R.	Granola	3
Hart,W.	65 Lark Rd.	−43.00				4	Hart,W.	Whey	5
						5	Robin,R.	Sunfl. Sds.	2
						6	Robin,R.	Lettuce	8

Fig. 5.2. Ring structure for HVFC relations.

generalization of the above idea. For example, we could store after each tuple t of relation R all the tuples of S that agreed with t on certain attributes and then all the tuples of another relation T that agreed with t on certain (possibly different) attributes. We could also nest the storage of relations, where after each tuple of a relation R follow the associated tuples of a relation S, each followed by the tuples of a relation T that were associated with that tuple from S.

Another way to store relations that is borrowed from network ideas and that makes navigation between relations easier is to use multilists on the tuples to represent "set occurrences." If two relations R and S and a set of attributes X satisfy (1)–(3) above, we can add a pointer field to the record types for both relations, and use that field to link in a ring the tuple from R with a given X-value and all the tuples from S with the same X-value. Like the arrangement where tuples of S are stored with those of R, this arrangement makes it possible to find the tuples in S with a given X-value without scanning all of S. However, with the ring arrangement, we do not have any reason to believe that we shall find many of these tuples on one block; we shall in general have to make one block access per tuple. The reason we might prefer the ring structure is that a relation like S can be stored VIA only one other relation, while it can have a ring structure connecting it to any number of relations.

Example 5.3: In Fig. 5.2 we see the MEMBERS and ORDERS relations with a multilist structure for the attribute NAME. □

Storage Organization in System R

System R (Astrahan et al. [1976]) is a relational database system developed at IBM, San Jose. In this DBMS we are allowed to store one relation "VIA" another, as we have described above. We are also allowed to create multilist structures connecting the tuples of two relations. Finally, we can create an index to any relation on any set of attributes. This index is a dense index, as described in Section 2.5, with a B-tree structure. There is no distinction between a "primary" and "secondary" index; that is, it doesn't matter to the system whether the set of attributes for an index forms a key for the relation.

The interior nodes of the B-tree are blocks filled, as much as the B-tree scheme allows, with pairs consisting of a pointer to another block and a value for the attributes of the index. Leaf nodes of the B-tree consist of values for these attributes and associated lists of *tuple identifiers*; there is one tuple identifier for each tuple having the given values for the attributes of the index. Actually, tuple identifiers point not to the tuple, but to a place near the end of the block, where a pointer to the tuple itself can be found. This double indirection does not cost us extra block accesses, and it has the advantage that tuples may be moved around within blocks, as was discussed in Section 2.5.†

The reader should note that this arrangement is a little more than the B-tree scheme we discussed in Sections 2.4 and 2.5. In the terms of Chapter 2, there is a file of variable length records of the form value(pointer)* that serves as a secondary index into the main file. This (logical) file is implemented by packing fields as well as possible using the strategy of splitting overfull blocks into two, and merging blocks less than half full, according to the B-tree style of handling insertions and deletions. The blocks implementing this file are the "leaves of the B-tree" mentioned above. The interior nodes of the B-tree are used in the manner of Section 2.5 to serve as a dense index to the first values in each of the leaf blocks.

Storage Ideas from the Hierarchical Model

There is at least one idea we can borrow from the hierarchical model and use to save space in the storage of relations. Consider Fig. 5.1, which we can view as the preorder sequence for a hierarchical database where records of type ORDERS are children of MEMBERS records. However, if we had designed a hierarchical database in the first place, we would not have put the NAME field into the ORDERS records. Rather, the member placing each order would be found in the parent of each ORDERS record in the database.

Suppose R and S are two relations stored together as MEMBERS and ORDERS are in Fig. 5.1. If the relational system allows, we could declare an attribute A of relation S to be "virtual," in the sense that it is found by looking for the previous tuple from relation R in the merged list of tuples, and getting the value of some other attribute (not necessarily called A) in that tuple.

For example, we could dispense with the NAME field in the records for the ORDERS relation in Fig. 5.1. Then, every time we wanted a value for NAME in a particular tuple, we would back up the sequence of blocks holding

† In System R, tuples can have varying length, so it is not always possible to leave tuples where they are without wasting space.

MEMBERS and ORDERS until we came to a MEMBERS tuple. The desired value would be found in the NAME field of that tuple. The advantage of this scheme is that we avoid using space for the NAME attribute in the ORDERS tuples. We need space to identify which tuples are from ORDERS and which from MEMBERS in the combined file, but that space was necessary anyway if we are to be capable of disambiguating the combined file. The disadvantage is that extra time is needed to retrieve the value for certain attributes, but the number of extra block accesses required for such searches may not be large if there are not too many orders placed per member.

5.2 RELATIONAL ALGEBRA

In this and the next section we discuss the three principal approaches to the design of languages for expressing queries about relations. The notation for expressing queries is usually the most significant part of a data manipulation language. The nonquery aspects of a relational data manipulation language, or "query language," are often straightforward, being concerned with the insertion, deletion and modification of tuples. On the other hand, queries, which in the most general case are arbitrary functions applied to relations, often use a rich, high-level language for their expression.

Query languages for the relational model break down into two broad classes:
1. Algebraic languages, where queries are expressed by applying specialized operators to relations, and
2. Predicate calculus languages, where queries describe a desired set of tuples by specifying a predicate the tuples must satisfy.

We further divide the calculus-based languages into two classes, depending on whether the primitive objects are tuples or are elements of the domain of some attribute, making a total of three distinct kinds of query languages.

We introduce relational algebra in this section and the two forms of relational calculus, called tuple relational calculus and domain relational calculus, in the next section. These abstract query languages are not implemented exactly as described here in any existing DBMS, but they serve as a benchmark for evaluating existing systems. That is, each of the three abstract query languages is equivalent in expressive power to the others, and they were proposed by Codd [1972b] to represent the minimum capability of any reasonable query language using the relational model. Real query languages usually provide the capabilities of the abstract languages and additional capabilities as well.

In the next chapter we shall discuss one typical query language of each of the three types: ISBL, an algebraic language, QUEL, a tuple calculus language, and Query-by-Example, a domain calculus language. We shall also discuss SQUARE and its cousin, SEQUEL, which are languages intermediate between algebra and calculus.

Operators and Operands in Relational Algebra

Recall that a relation is a set of k-tuples for some fixed k, the arity of the relation. We sometimes find it convenient to give the components of the tuples names, which are the attributes of its relation, of course, while sometimes it is convenient to let the components be anonymous and to refer to them by number. When defining relational algebra, we assume columns need not be named, and order in tuples is significant. This point of view differs from that of Section 1.4, but is compatible with it, when we use the obvious conversions. When dealing with relations as a database, it is assumed that all relations are finite, and we shall adopt this assumption without explicit mention in the future. The constraint of finiteness introduces some difficulties into the definition of relational algebra and calculus. For example, we cannot allow the algebraic operation of complementation, since $-R$ generally denotes an infinite relation, the set of all tuples not in R. There is no way to list the relation $-R$, even if the query language permitted such an expression.

The operands of relational algebra are either constant relations or variables denoting relations of a fixed arity. The arity associated with a variable will be mentioned only when it is important. There are five basic operations that serve to define relational algebra. After introducing them we shall mention a few more operations that do not add to the set of functions expressible in the language, but serve as useful shorthand.

1. *Union.* The union of relations R or S, denoted $R \cup S$, is the set of tuples that are in R or S or both. We only apply the union operator to relations of the same arity, so all tuples in the result have the same number of components.

2. *Set difference.* The difference of relations R and S, denoted $R - S$, is the set of tuples in R but not in S. We again require that R and S have the same arity.

3. *Cartesian product.* Let R and S be relations of arity k_1 and k_2, respectively. Then $R \times S$, the Cartesian product of R and S, is the set of $(k_1 + k_2)$-tuples whose first k_1 components form a tuple in R and whose last k_2 components form a tuple in S.

4. *Projection.* The idea behind this operation is that we take a relation R, remove some of the components and/or rearrange some of the remaining components. If R is a relation of arity k, we let $\pi_{i_1,i_2,\ldots,i_m}(R)$, where the i_j's are distinct integers in the range 1 to k, denote the projection of R onto components $i_1, i_2, \ldots, i_m$, that is, the set of m-tuples $a_1 a_2 \cdots a_m$ such that there is some k-tuple $b_1 b_2 \cdots b_k$ in R for which $a_j = b_{i_j}$ for $j = 1, 2, \ldots, m$. For example, $\pi_{3,1}(R)$ is computed by taking each tuple t in R and forming a 2-tuple from the third and first components of t, in that order. If R has attributes labeling its columns, then we may substitute attribute names

A	B	C
a	b	c
d	a	f
c	b	d

D	E	F
b	g	a
d	a	f

(a) Relation R (b) Relation S

Fig. 5.3. Two relations.

for component numbers, and we may use the same attribute names in the projected relation. For example, if relation R is $R(A, B, C, D)$, then $\pi_{C,A}(R)$ is the same as $\pi_{3,1}(R)$, and the resulting relation has attribute C naming its first column and attribute A naming its second column.

5.   *Selection.* Let F be a formula involving

   i)   operands that are constants or component numbers,

   ii) the arithmetic comparison operators $<, =, >, \leq, \neq$, and $\geq$, and

   iii) the logical operators $\wedge$ (and), $\vee$ (or), and $\neg$ (not).

Then $\sigma_F(R)$ is the set of tuples t in R such that when, for all i, we substitute the ith component of t for any occurrences of the number i in formula F, the formula F becomes true. For example, $\sigma_{2>3}(R)$ denotes the set of tuples in R whose second component exceeds its third component, while $\sigma_{1=\text{'Smith'}\vee 1=\text{'Jones'}}(R)$ is the set of tuples in R whose first component has the value 'Smith' or 'Jones'. As with projection, if a relation has named columns, then the formula in a selection can refer to columns by name instead of number. Notice also that even numerical constants must be quoted in formulas, to distinguish them from column numbers or names.

Example 5.4: Let R and S be the two relations of Fig. 5.3. In Fig. 5.4(a) and (b), respectively, we see the relations $R \cup S$ and $R - S$. Note that we can take unions and differences even though the columns of the two relations have different names, as long as the relations have the same number of components. However, the resulting relation has no obvious names for its columns. Figure 5.4(c) shows $R \times S$. Since R and S have disjoint sets of attributes, we can carry the column names over to $R \times S$. If R and S had a column name in common, say G, we could distinguish the two columns by calling them $R.G$ and $S.G$. Figure 5.4(d) shows $\pi_{A,C}(R)$, and Fig. 5.4(e) shows $\sigma_{B=b}(R)$. $\square$

Some Additional Algebraic Operations

There are a number of useful operations that can be expressed in terms of the five previously mentioned operations, but which have been given names in the literature and sometimes used as primitive operations.

1.   *Intersection.* $R \cap S$ is shorthand for $R - (R - S)$.

2.   *Quotient.* Let R and S be relations of arity r and s, respectively, where

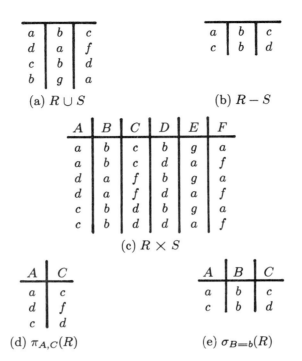

a	b	c
d	a	f
c	b	d
b	g	a

(a) $R \cup S$

a	b	c
c	b	d

(b) $R - S$

A	B	C	D	E	F
a	b	c	b	g	a
a	b	c	d	a	f
d	a	f	b	g	a
d	a	f	d	a	f
c	b	d	b	g	a
c	b	d	d	a	f

(c) $R \times S$

A	C
a	c
d	f
c	d

(d) $\pi_{A,C}(R)$

A	B	C
a	b	c
c	b	d

(e) $\sigma_{B=b}(R)$

Fig. 5.4. Results of some relational algebra operations.

$r > s$, and $S \neq \emptyset$. Then $R \div S$ is the set of $(r - s)$-tuples t such that for all s-tuples u in S, the tuple tu is in R. To express $R \div S$ using the five basic relational algebra operations, let T stand for $\pi_{1,2,...,r-s}(R)$. Then $(T \times S) - R$ is the set of r-tuples that are not in R, but are formed by taking the first $r - s$ components of a tuple in R and following it by a tuple in S. Then let

$$V = \pi_{1,2,...,r-s}((T \times S) - R)$$

V is the set of $(r - s)$-tuples t that are the first $r - s$ components of a tuple in R such that for some s-tuple u in S, tu is not in R. Hence $T - V$ is $R \div S$. We can write $R \div S$ as a single expression in relational algebra by replacing T and V by the expressions they stand for. That is,

$$R \div S = \pi_{1,2,...,r-s}(R) - \pi_{1,2,...,r-s}((\pi_{1,2,...,r-s}(R) \times S) - R)$$

Example 5.5: Let R and S be the relations shown in Fig. 5.5(a) and (b). Then $R \div S$ is the relation shown in Fig. 5.5(c). Tuple ab is in $R \div S$ because $abcd$ and $abef$ are in R, and tuple ed is in $R \div S$ for a similar reason. Tuple bc, which is the only other pair appearing in the first two columns of R, is not in

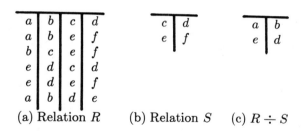

(a) Relation R (b) Relation S (c) $R \div S$

Fig. 5.5. Example of a quotient calculation.

A	B	C
1	2	3
4	5	6
7	8	9

(a) Relation R

D	E
3	1
6	2

(b) Relation S

A	B	C	D	E
1	2	3	3	1
1	2	3	6	2
4	5	6	6	2

(c) $R \underset{B<D}{\bowtie} S$

Fig. 5.6. Example of a $<$-join.

$R \div S$ because $bccd$ is not in R. □

3. *Join.* The θ-join of R and S on columns i and j written $R \underset{i\theta j}{\bowtie} S$, where θ is an arithmetic comparison operator ($=$, $<$, and so on), is shorthand for $\sigma_{i\theta(r+j)}(R \times S)$, if R is of arity r. That is, the θ-join of R and S is those tuples in the Cartesian product of R and S such that the ith component of R stands in relation θ to the jth component of S. If θ is $=$, the operation is often called an *equijoin*.

Example 5.6: Let R and S be the relations given in Fig. 5.6(a) and (b). Then $R \underset{B<D}{\bowtie} S$ is given in Fig. 5.6(c). As with all algebraic operations, when columns have names we are free to use them. Thus $\underset{B<D}{\bowtie}$ is the same as $\underset{2<1}{\bowtie}$ in this case. □

4. *Natural Join.* The natural join, written $R \bowtie S$, is applicable only when both R and S have columns that are named by attributes. To compute $R \bowtie S$ we

i) Compute $R \times S$.

ii) For each attribute A that names both a column in R and a column in S select from $R \times S$ those tuples whose values agree in the columns for $R.A$ and $S.A$. Recall that $R.A$ is the name of the column of $R \times S$ corresponding to the column A of R, and $S.A$ is defined analogously.

iii) For each attribute A above, project out the column $S.A$.

Formally then, if $A_1, A_2, \ldots, A_k$ are all the attribute names used for both

A	B	C
a	b	c
d	b	c
b	b	f
c	a	d

B	C	D
b	c	d
b	c	e
a	d	b

A	B	C	D
a	b	c	d
a	b	c	e
d	b	c	d
d	b	c	e
c	a	d	b

(a) Relation R (b) Relation S (c) $R \bowtie S$

Fig. 5.7. Example of a natural join.

R and S, $R \bowtie S$ is $\pi_{i_1,i_2,\ldots,i_m} \sigma_{R.A_1=S.A_1 \wedge \cdots \wedge R.A_k=S.A_k}(R \times S)$, where $i_1,i_2,\ldots,i_m$ is the list of all components of $R \times S$, in order, except the components $S.A_1,\ldots,S.A_k$.

Example 5.7: Let R and S be the relations given in Fig. 5.7(a) and (b). Then $R \bowtie S$ stands for $\pi_{A,R.B,R.C,D} \sigma_{R.B=S.B \wedge R.C=S.C}(R \times S)$. To construct $R \bowtie S$, we consider each tuple in R to see which tuples of S agree with it in both columns B and C. For example, abc in R agrees with bcd and bce in S, so we get $abcd$ and $abce$ in $R \bowtie S$. Similarly, dbc gives us $dbcd$ and $dbce$ for $R \bowtie S$. Tuple bbf agrees with no tuple of S in columns B and C, so we obtain no tuple in $R \bowtie S$ that begins with bbf. Lastly, cad matches adb, so we get tuple $cadb$. $\square$

The significance of the natural join will become clear when we discuss the theory of decomposition of relations in Chapter 7.

5.3 RELATIONAL CALCULUS

We shall begin our study of relational calculus by first defining the tuple relational calculus. To make things easy, we shall initially present a calculus that permits infinite relations to be defined. Then we shall discuss the modifications needed to assure that each formula in relational calculus denotes a finite relation. Incidentally, the term "relational calculus" does not imply any connection with the branch of mathematics usually called "calculus," or more precisely, "differential and integral calculus." Rather, relational calculus comes from the first order predicate calculus, from the field of logic.

Expressions in tuple relational calculus are of the form $\{ t \mid \psi(t) \}$, where t is a *tuple variable,* that is, a variable denoting a tuple of some fixed length,† and ψ is a formula built from atoms and a collection of operators to be defined shortly.

The *atoms* of formulas ψ are of three types.

1. $R(s)$, where R is a relation name and s is a tuple variable. This atom stands for the assertion that s is a tuple in relation R.

---
† We use $t^{(i)}$ to denote the fact that t is of arity i.

2. $s[i]$ θ $u[j]$, where s and u are tuple variables and θ is an arithmetic comp-
    arison operator ($<$, $=$, and so on). This atom stands for the assertion that
    the ith component of s stands in relation θ to the jth component of u. For
    example, $s[1] < u[2]$ means that the first component of s is less than the
    second component of u.

3. $s[i]$ θ a and a θ $s[i]$, where θ and $s[i]$ are as in (2) above, and a is a constant.
    The first of these atoms asserts that the ith component of s stands in
    relation θ to the constant a, and the second has an analogous meaning.
    For example, $s[1] = 3$ means that the value of the first component of s is
    3.

When defining the operators of relational calculus, it is useful at the same
time to define the notions of "free" and "bound" tuple variables. These notions
are exactly the same as in predicate calculus. (A familiarity with predicate
calculus is not a prerequisite for what follows.) Informally, an occurrence of a
variable in a formula is "bound" if that variable has been introduced by a "for
all" or "there exists" quantifier, and we say the variable is "free" if not.

The notion of a "free variable" is analogous to that of a global variable
in a programming language, that is, a variable defined outside the current
procedure. A "bound variable" is like a local variable, one that is defined in
the procedure at hand and cannot be referenced from the outside. In effect, the
quantifiers of relational calculus play the role of declarations in a programming
language.

Formulas, and *free* and *bound* occurrences of tuple variables in these formulas, are defined recursively, as follows.

1. Every atom is a formula. All occurrences of tuple variables mentioned in
    the atom are free in this formula.

2. If ψ_1 and ψ_2 are formulas, then $\psi_1 \wedge \psi_2$, $\psi_1 \vee \psi_2$, and $\neg\psi_1$ are formulas
    asserting "ψ_1 and ψ_2 are both true," "ψ_1 or ψ_2, or both, are true," and
    "ψ_1 is not true," respectively. Occurrences of tuple variables are free or
    bound in $\psi_1 \wedge \psi_2$, $\psi_1 \vee \psi_2$, and $\neg\psi_1$ as they are free or bound in ψ_1 or
    ψ_2, depending on where they occur. Note that an occurrence of a variable
    s could be bound in ψ_1, while another occurrence of s is free in ψ_2, or
    conversely.

3. If ψ is a formula, then $(\exists s)(\psi)$ is a formula. The symbol $\exists$ is a *quantifier,*
    read "there exists." The only other quantifier used is $\forall$, "for all," described
    in (4) below. Occurrences of s that are free in ψ are bound to $(\exists s)$
    in $(\exists s)(\psi)$.† Other occurrences of tuple variables in ψ, including possible
    occurrences of s that were bound in ψ, are free or bound in $(\exists s)(\psi)$ as they
    were in ψ. The formula $(\exists s)(\psi)$ asserts that there exists a value of s such
    that when we substitute this value for all free occurrences of s in ψ, the

---

† If we think of free variable s of ψ as "global" to ψ, then $(\exists s)$ constitutes the "declaration"
of s.

formula ψ becomes true. For example, $(\exists s)(R(s))$ says that relation R is not empty, that is, there exists a tuple s in R.

4. If ψ is a formula, then $(\forall s)(\psi)$ is a formula. Free occurrences of s in ψ are bound to $(\forall s)$ in $(\forall s)(\psi)$, and other occurrences of variables in ψ are treated as in (3) above. The formula $(\forall s)(\psi)$ asserts that whatever value of the appropriate arity we substitute for free occurrences of s in ψ, the formula ψ becomes true.

5. Parentheses may be placed around formulas as needed. We assume the order of precedence is: arithmetic comparison operators highest, then the quantifiers $\exists$ and $\forall$, then $\neg$, $\wedge$, and $\vee$, in that order.

6. Nothing else is a formula.

    A *tuple relational calculus expression* is an expression of the form

$$\{ t \mid \psi(t) \}$$

where t is the only free tuple variable in ψ.

Example 5.8: The union of R and S is expressed by the calculus expression

$$\{ t \mid R(t) \vee S(t) \}$$

In words, the above is "the set of tuples t such that t is in R or t is in S." Note that union only makes sense if R and S have the same arity, and similarly, the formula $R(t) \vee S(t)$ only makes sense if R and S have the same arity, since tuple variable t is assumed to have some fixed length.

The difference $R - S$ is expressed by $\{ t \mid R(t) \wedge \neg S(t) \}$. If R and S are relations of arity r and s, respectively, then $R \times S$ can be expressed in calculus by:

$$\{ t^{(r+s)} \mid (\exists u^{(r)})(\exists v^{(s)})(R(u) \wedge S(v)$$
$$\wedge \, t[1] = u[1] \wedge \cdots \wedge t[r] = u[r]$$
$$\wedge \, t[r+1] = v[1] \wedge \cdots \wedge t[r+s] = v[s]) \}$$

Recall that $t^{(i)}$ indicates that t has arity i. In words, $R \times S$ is the set of tuples t (which we understand to be of length $r + s$) such that there exist u and v, with u in R, v in S; the first r components of t form u, and the next s components of t form v.

The projection $\pi_{i_1, i_2, \ldots, i_k}(R)$ is expressed by

$$\{ t^{(k)} \mid (\exists u)(R(u) \wedge t[1] = u[i_1] \wedge \cdots \wedge t[k] = u[i_k]) \}$$

The selection $\sigma_F(R)$ is expressed by $\{ t \mid R(t) \wedge F' \}$, where F' is the formula F with each operand i, denoting the ith component, replaced by $t[i]$.

As a last example, if R is a relation of arity two, then

$$\{ t^{(2)} \mid (\exists u)(R(t) \wedge R(u) \wedge (t[1] \neq u[1] \vee t[2] \neq u[2])) \}$$

is a calculus expression that denotes R if R has two or more members and denotes the empty relation if R is empty or has only one member. $\Box$

Restricting Relational Calculus to Yield only Finite Relations

The tuple relational calculus as we have defined it allows us to define some infinite relations such as $\{\, t \mid \neg R(t) \,\}$, which denotes all possible tuples that are not in R, but are of the length we associate with t (that length must also be the arity of R for the expression to make sense). As we could not expect to print "all possible tuples" (over what domain?), we must rule out such meaningless expressions. What is usually done is to restrict consideration to certain expressions $\{\, t \mid \psi(t) \,\}$, called "safe."

To define safety, let us first define $DOM(\psi)$ to be the set of symbols that either appear explicitly in expression ψ or are components of some tuple in some relation R mentioned in ψ. This choice of $DOM(\psi)$ is not necessarily the smallest set of symbols we could use, but it will suffice. Informally, an expression ψ is "safe" if each component of any t that satisfies ψ must be a member of $DOM(\psi)$. A more formal definition follows.

Notice that $DOM(\psi)$ is not determined by looking at ψ, but is a function of the actual relations to be substituted for the relation variables in ψ. However, as all relations are assumed finite, $DOM(\psi)$ is always finite. For example, if $\psi(t)$ is $t[1] = a \vee R(t)$, where R is a binary relation, then $DOM(\psi)$ is the unary relation† given by the relational algebra formula $\{\, a \,\} \cup \pi_1(R) \cup \pi_2(R)$.

We say a tuple calculus expression $\{\, t \mid \psi(t) \,\}$ is *safe* if

1. Whenever t satisfies ψ, each component of t is a member of $DOM(\psi)$.
2. For each subformula of ψ of the form $(\exists u)(\omega(u))$,‡ if ω is satisfied by u for any values of the other free variables in ω, then each component of u is a member of $DOM(\omega)$.
3. For each subformula of ψ of the form $(\forall u)(\omega(u))$, if any component of u is not in $DOM(\omega)$, then u satisfies ω for all values of the other free variables in ω.

The purpose of points (2) and (3) is to assure that we can determine the truth of a quantified formula $(\exists u)(\omega(u))$ or $(\forall u)(\omega(u))$ by considering only those u's composed of symbols in $DOM(\omega)$. For example, any formula

$$(\exists u)(R(u) \wedge \cdots)$$

satisfies (2), and any formula $(\forall u)(\neg R(u) \vee \cdots)$ satisfies (3). Note that in the definition of safety, we do not assume that any free variables of ω, besides u, necessarily have values in $DOM(\omega)$. Rules (2) and (3) must hold independently of the value of those variables.

---

† For all practical purposes, a unary relation is a set of symbols, and we shall so treat it here.

‡ We allow the possibility that ω has bound variables within it, and possibly other free variables besides u. As a general convention, we show only free variables as arguments of formulas, but we shall not necessarily list all the free variables.

While rule (3) may appear unintuitive, we should observe that the formula $(\forall u)(\omega(u))$ is logically equivalent to $\neg(\exists u)(\neg\omega(u))$. The latter formula is unsafe if and only if there is a u_0 for which $\neg\omega(u_0)$ is true, and u_0 is not in the domain of the formula $\neg\omega$. As the domains of ω and $\neg\omega$ are the same, rule (3) says that formula $(\forall u)(\omega(u))$ is safe exactly when formula $\neg(\exists u)(\neg\omega(u))$ is safe.

We shall see that the safe expressions of tuple relational calculus are equivalent to relational algebra. It is an interesting and nontrivial exercise to determine those tuple calculus expressions that are safe. Fortunately, in showing the equivalence of relational algebra and calculus, we never need to know exactly which calculus expressions are safe. However, we can give some examples of constructions in the tuple calculus that are guaranteed to be safe.

Example 5.9: In what follows, let $\psi(t)$ be a formula such that no subformula of the form $(\exists u)(\omega(u))$ or $(\forall u)(\omega(u))$ violates safety. Then any expression of the form $\{\, t \mid R(t) \wedge \psi(t) \,\}$ is safe, since any tuple t satisfying $R(t) \wedge \psi(t)$ is in R, whereupon each of its components is in $\text{DOM}(R(t) \wedge \psi(t))$. For example, the formula for set difference, $\{\, t \mid R(t) \wedge \neg S(t) \,\}$, is of this form, with $\psi(t) = \neg S(t)$. The formula for selection in Example 5.8 is also of this form, with $\psi(t) = F'$.

As a generalization of the above, we observe that any formula

$$\{\, t \mid (R_1(t) \vee R_2(t) \vee \cdots \vee R_k(t)) \wedge \psi(t) \,\}$$

is also safe; $t[i]$ must be a symbol appearing in the ith component of some tuple of some relation R_j. For example, the formula for union in Example 5.8 is of this form, but ψ is missing, i.e., we may take ψ to be an always true formula like $t[1] = t[1]$.

Another form of safe expression is

$$\{\, t^{(m)} \mid (\exists u_1)(\exists u_2)\cdots(\exists u_k)(R_1(u_1) \wedge R_2(u_2) \wedge \cdots \wedge R_k(u_k)$$
$$\wedge\ t[1] = u_{i_1}[j_1] \wedge t[2] = u_{i_2}[j_2] \wedge \cdots \wedge t[m] = u_{i_m}[j_m]$$
$$\wedge\ \psi(t, u_1, u_2, \ldots, u_k)) \,\}$$

Component $t[l]$ is restricted to be a symbol appearing in the j_l^{th} component of a tuple of R_{i_l}. The formulas for Cartesian product and projection in Example 5.8 are of the above form. $\square$

Reduction of Relational Algebra to Tuple Relational Calculus

We shall prove that the set of functions of relations expressible in relational algebra is exactly the same as the set of functions expressible by safe formulas in the tuple relational calculus. One direction of this equivalence will be proved now, and the other direction will be shown after we introduce the domain relational calculus, which is a third equivalent notation.

Theorem 5.1: If E is a relational algebra expression, then there is a safe expression in tuple relational calculus equivalent to E.

Proof: We proceed by induction on the number of occurrences of operators in E.

Basis: Zero operators. Then E is either a constant relation $\{\, t_1, t_2, \ldots, t_n \,\}$ or a relation variable R. In the latter case, E is equivalent to $\{\, t \mid R(t) \,\}$, which is a safe expression, as pointed out in Example 5.9. In the former case, E is equivalent to $\{\, t \mid t = t_1 \vee t = t_2 \vee \cdots \vee t = t_n \,\}$, where $t = t_i$ is shorthand for $t[1] = t_i[1] \wedge \cdots \wedge t[k] = t_i[k]$; k is the assumed arity of t. It is easy to see that $t[i]$ is one of the finite set of symbols appearing explicitly as the ith component of some constant tuple t_j; it is therefore in DOM for this expression.

Induction: Assume that E has at least one operator, and that the theorem is true for expressions with fewer occurrences of operators than E has.

Case 1: $E = E_1 \cup E_2$. Then E_1 and E_2 each have fewer operator occurrences than E, and by the inductive hypothesis we can find safe relational calculus expressions $\{\, t \mid \psi_1(t) \,\}$ and $\{\, t \mid \psi_2(t) \,\}$ equivalent to E_1 and E_2, respectively. Then E is equivalent to $\{\, t \mid \psi_1(t) \vee \psi_2(t) \,\}$. If t satisfies $\psi_1(t) \vee \psi_2(t)$, then each component of t is in $\mathrm{DOM}(\psi_1)$ or each component is in $\mathrm{DOM}(\psi_2)$. As $\mathrm{DOM}(\psi_1(t) \vee \psi_2(t)) = \mathrm{DOM}(\psi_1) \cup \mathrm{DOM}(\psi_2)$, E is equivalent to a safe expression. That is, the complete formula $\psi(t) = \psi_1(t) \vee \psi_2(t)$ is true only when t is in $\mathrm{DOM}(\psi)$, and any subformula $(\exists u)(\omega(u))$ or $(\forall u)(\omega(u))$ in ψ must be within ψ_1 or ψ_2, so the inductive hypothesis assures that these subformulas do not violate safety.

Case 2: $E = E_1 - E_2$. Then E_1 and E_2 have safe expressions, as in Case 1. Clearly E is equivalent to $\{\, t \mid \psi_1(t) \wedge \neg\psi_2(t) \,\}$. As $\mathrm{DOM}(\psi_1(t) \wedge \neg\psi_2(t)) = \mathrm{DOM}(\psi_1) \cup \mathrm{DOM}(\psi_2)$, the above expression is safe.

Case 3: $E = E_1 \times E_2$. Let E_1 and E_2 be equivalent to safe expressions as in Case 1, and let E_1 and E_2 denote relations of arity k and m, respectively. Then E is equivalent to

$$
\begin{aligned}
\{\, t^{(k+m)} \mid &(\exists u)(\exists v)(\psi_1(u) \wedge \psi_2(v) \\
&\wedge\; t[1] = u[1] \wedge \cdots \wedge t[k] = u[k] \\
&\wedge\; t[k+1] = v[1] \wedge \cdots \wedge t[k+m] = v[m]) \,\}
\end{aligned}
$$

It is easy to check that the above expression is safe, since $t[i]$ is restricted to values that $u[i]$ may take, if $i \le k$, and to values that $v[i-k]$ may take if $k < i \le k+m$.

Case 4: $E = \pi_{i_1, i_2, \ldots, i_k}(E_1)$. Let E_1 be equivalent to safe expression $\{\, t \mid \psi_1(t) \,\}$. Then E is equivalent to

$$
\{\, t^{(k)} \mid (\exists u)(\psi_1(u) \wedge t[1] = u[i_1] \wedge \cdots \wedge t[k] = u[i_k]) \,\}
$$

Safety of the above expression is easy to show, as in Case 3.

Case 5: $E = \sigma_F(E_1)$. Let E_1 be equivalent to the safe expression $\{\, t \mid \psi_1(t) \,\}$. Then E is equivalent to $\{\, t \mid \psi_1(t) \wedge F' \,\}$, where F' is F with each operand that denotes component i replaced by $t[i]$. This expression is safe, because each component of t is restricted to those symbols to which $\psi_1(t)$ restricts the component. □

Example 5.10: If R and S are binary relations, their composition in the ordinary set-theoretic sense is expressed by the relational algebra expression $\pi_{1,4}(\sigma_{2=3}(R \times S))$. Using the algorithm of Theorem 5.1, we construct for $R \times S$ the relational calculus expression

$$\{\, t \mid (\exists u)(\exists v)(R(u) \wedge S(v)$$
$$\wedge\, t[1] = u[1] \wedge t[2] = u[2] \wedge t[3] = v[1] \wedge t[4] = v[2])\,\}$$

For $\sigma_{2=3}(R \times S)$ we add to the above formula the term $\wedge\, t[2] = t[3]$. Then, for $\pi_{1,4}(\sigma_{2=3}(R \times S))$ we get the expression

$$\{\, w \mid (\exists t)(\exists u)(\exists v)(R(u) \wedge S(v)$$
$$\wedge\, t[1] = u[1] \wedge t[2] = u[2] \wedge t[3] = v[1] \wedge t[4] = v[2]$$
$$\wedge\, t[2] = t[3] \wedge w[1] = t[1] \wedge w[2] = t[4])\,\}$$

Note that the above expression is not as succinct as possible; we can eliminate t if we replace each of its components by the appropriate component of u or v. If we do so, we get

$$\{\, w \mid (\exists u)(\exists v)(R(u) \wedge S(v)$$
$$\wedge\, u[2] = v[1] \wedge w[1] = u[1] \wedge w[2] = v[2])\,\}$$

The above expression should be recognizable as the usual set-theoretic definition of composition, translated into the language of tuple relational calculus. □

Domain Relational Calculus

The domain relational calculus is built from the same operators as the tuple relational calculus. The essential differences are that

1.   There are no tuple variables in the domain calculus, but there are *domain variables* to represent components of tuples, instead.
2.   An atom is either of the form
     i) $R(x_1 x_2 \cdots x_k)$, where R is a k-ary relation and every x_i is a constant or domain variable, or
     ii) $x \,\theta\, y$, where x and y are constants or domain variables and θ is an arithmetic relational operator.
     $R(x_1 x_2 \cdots x_k)$ asserts that the values of those x_i's that are variables must be chosen so that $x_1 x_2 \cdots x_k$ is a tuple in R. The meaning of atom $x \,\theta\, y$ is that x and y must have values that make $x \,\theta\, y$ true.
3.   Formulas in the domain relational calculus use the connectives $\wedge$, $\vee$, and $\neg$, as in the tuple calculus. We also use $(\exists x)$ and $(\forall x)$ to form expressions of the domain calculus, but x is a domain variable instead of a tuple variable.
     The notions of free and bound domain variables and the scope of a bound variable are defined in the domain calculus exactly as in the tuple calculus, and

we shall not repeat these definitions here. A domain calculus expression is of the form $\{ x_1 x_2 \cdots x_k \mid \psi(x_1, x_2, \ldots, x_k) \}$, where ψ is a formula whose only free domain variables are the distinct variables $x_1, x_2, \ldots, x_k$.

In analogy with tuple calculus, we define a domain calculus expression $\{ x_1 x_2 \cdots x_k \mid \psi(x_1, x_2, \ldots, x_k) \}$ to be *safe* if

1. $\psi(x_1, x_2, \ldots, x_k)$ true implies x_i is in $\text{DOM}(\psi)$,
2. if $(\exists u)(\omega(u))$ is a subformula of ψ, then $\omega(u)$ true for any values of the free variables of ω (besides u) implies that u is in $\text{DOM}(\omega)$, and
3. if $(\forall u)(\omega(u))$ is a subformula of ψ, then $\omega(u)$ false for any values of the free variables of ω (besides u) implies u is in $\text{DOM}(\omega)$.

Example 5.11: Let us reconsider the last part of Example 5.8, where we were given a binary relation R and asked to write an expression that was equal to R if R had two or more members and was the empty set otherwise. In domain relational calculus, one such expression is

$$\{ wx \mid (\exists y)(\exists z)(R(wx) \wedge R(yz) \wedge (w \neq y \vee x \neq z)) \}$$

Let $\psi(w, x, y, z)$ stand for the formula

$$R(wx) \wedge R(yz) \wedge (w \neq y \vee x \neq z)$$

and let R be the relation $\{ 12, 13 \}$. If we let $w = 1$ and $x = 2$, then the formula $(\exists y)(\exists z)(\psi(1, 2, y, z))$ is true, since we may pick $y = 1$ and $z = 3$ to make ψ true. Similarly, if we let $w = 1$ and $x = 3$, this formula is true, as we may pick $y = 1$ and $z = 2$. Thus tuples 12 and 13 are both in the set denoted by our domain calculus expression. However, if we pick any other values for w and x, then $(\exists y)(\exists z)(\psi(w, x, y, z))$ must be false, since the clause $R(wx)$ of ψ will be false. Thus the domain calculus expression denotes a set equal to R when $R = \{ 12, 13 \}$.

If we let R be a singleton set, like $\{ 12 \}$, then no values of w and x satisfy $(\exists y)(\exists z)(\psi(w, x, y, z))$, since the first clause of ψ, $R(wx)$, is only satisfied if $w = 1$ and $x = 2$, the second clause $R(yz)$ is only satisfied if $y = 1$ and $z = 2$, and then the third clause, $(w \neq y \vee x \neq z)$ is not satisfied. $\square$

Reducing Tuple Calculus to Domain Calculus

The construction of a domain calculus expression equivalent to a given tuple calculus expression $\{ t \mid \psi(t) \}$ is straightforward. If t has arity k, introduce k new domain variables $t_1, t_2, \ldots, t_k$ and replace the expression by

$$\{ t_1 t_2 \cdots t_k \mid \psi'(t_1, t_2, \ldots, t_k) \}$$

where ψ' is ψ with any atom $R(t)$ replaced by $R(t_1 t_2 \cdots t_k)$, and each free occurrence of $t[i]$ replaced by t_i. Note that there could be bound occurrences of t within ψ, if there were a quantifier $(\exists t)$ or $(\forall t)$; uses of this t refer to a "different" tuple variable and are not replaced.†

Next, for each quantifier $(\exists u)$ or $(\forall u)$, if u has arity m, introduce m new domain variables $u_1, u_2, \ldots, u_m$, and, within the scope of this quantification of u, replace $u[i]$ by u_i and $R(u)$ by $R(u_1 u_2 \cdots u_m)$. Replace $(\exists u)$ by $(\exists u_1)\cdots(\exists u_m)$ and replace $(\forall u)$ by $(\forall u_1)\cdots(\forall u_m)$. The result is an expression in the domain calculus that is equivalent to the original tuple calculus expression.

It should also be clear that the values that may be assumed by t_i are exactly those that could be assumed by $t[i]$ in the original expression. Thus if $\{\, t \mid \psi(t)\,\}$ is safe, so is the resulting domain calculus expression. We therefore state the following theorem without further proof.

Theorem 5.2: For every safe tuple relational calculus expression there is an equivalent safe domain relational calculus expression. $\square$

Example 5.12: The algorithm described above was used to produce the domain calculus expression of Example 5.11 from the last tuple calculus expression of Example 5.8.

For another example, let us take the simpler expression for composition given in Example 5.10, that is:

$$\{\, w \mid (\exists u)(\exists v)(R(u) \wedge S(v) \wedge u[2] = v[1] \wedge w[1] = u[1] \wedge w[2] = v[2])\,\}$$

We replace w by $w_1 w_2$, u by $u_1 u_2$ and v by $v_1 v_2$ to get

$$\{\, w_1 w_2 \mid (\exists u_1)(\exists u_2)(\exists v_1)(\exists v_2)(R(u_1 u_2) \wedge S(v_1 v_2)$$
$$\wedge\, u_2 = v_1 \wedge w_1 = u_1 \wedge w_2 = v_2)\,\}$$

$\square$

Reduction of Domain Calculus to Relational Algebra

Our plan is to take any safe domain calculus formula $\psi(x_1, x_2, \ldots, x_k)$, with free variables $x_1, x_2, \ldots, x_k$, and construct, by induction on the number of operators in ψ, an algebraic expression whose value is $\{\, x_1 x_2 \cdots x_k \mid \psi(x_1, x_2, \ldots, x_k)\,\}$. To do so, we prove by induction on the size (number of operators) of a subformula ω of ψ with free variables $y_1, y_2, \ldots, y_m$, that there is a relational algebra expression for

$$\mathrm{DOM}(\psi)^m \cap \{\, y_1 y_2 \cdots y_m \mid \omega(y_1, y_2, \ldots, y_m)\,\}$$

where D^m denotes $D \times D \times \cdots \times D$, ($m$ times).

Note that for convenience, we restrict our consideration to $\mathrm{DOM}(\psi)$ for all subformulas ω of ψ, even though we could have restricted ourselves to the various $\mathrm{DOM}(\omega)$'s, each of which must be a subset of $\mathrm{DOM}(\psi)$.

The following lemmas will be useful in the proof.

---

† This situation is analogous to a local and global variable having the same identifier, in an ordinary programming language possessing block structure.

Lemma 5.1: If ψ is any formula in domain calculus (or tuple calculus, for that matter) then there is an expression in relational algebra denoting the unary relation (set) DOM(ψ).

Proof: If R is a relation of arity k, let

$$E(R) = \pi_1(R) \cup \pi_2(R) \cup \cdots \cup \pi_k(R)$$

Then the desired expression is the union of $E(R)$, for each relation variable R appearing in ψ, and the constant relation $\{a_1, a_2, \ldots, a_n\}$, where the a_i's are all the constant symbols appearing in ψ. $\square$

Lemma 5.2: If ψ is any formula in domain calculus (or tuple calculus, for that matter) then there is an equivalent formula ψ' of domain calculus (respectively tuple calculus) with no occurrences of $\wedge$ or $\forall$. If ψ is safe, so is ψ'.

Proof: Replace each subformula $\psi_1 \wedge \psi_2$ of ψ by $\neg(\neg\psi_1 \vee \neg\psi_2)$. This equivalence-preserving transformation is called *DeMorgan's law,* and says that ψ_1 and ψ_2 are both true if and only if it is not true that ψ_1 or ψ_2 is false. Next, replace each subformula $(\forall u)(\psi_1(u))$ by $\neg(\exists u)(\neg\psi_1(u))$. This transformation also preserves equivalence, saying in essence that ψ_1 is true for all u if and only if there does not exist a u for which ψ_1 is false.

Let the resulting formula be ψ'. Surely ψ' is equivalent to ψ. If ψ is safe, then for each subformula $(\forall u)(\psi_1(u))$, we know that $\psi_1(u)$ is true whenever u has a value outside the set DOM(ψ_1). Hence $\neg\psi_1(u)$ is false whenever u is outside DOM(ψ_1), which equals DOM($\neg\psi_1$). Thus the introduced quantified subformula $(\exists u)(\neg\psi_1(u))$ of ψ' satisfies the safety condition. $\square$

Theorem 5.3: For every safe expression of the domain relational calculus, there is an equivalent expression in relational algebra.

Proof: Let $\{x_1 \cdots x_k \mid \psi(x_1, \ldots, x_k)\}$ be a safe formula of domain calculus. By Lemma 5.2 we may assume that ψ has only the operators $\vee$, $\neg$, and $\exists$. By Lemma 5.1, we may take E to be a relational algebra expression for the set DOM(ψ), and as usual, we let E^k stand for $E \times E \times \cdots \times E$ (k times). We prove by induction on the number of operators in a subformula ω of ψ that if ω has free domain variables $y_1, y_2, \ldots, y_m$, then

$$\text{DOM}(\psi)^m \cap \{y_1 \cdots y_m \mid \omega(y_1, \ldots, y_m)\}$$

has an equivalent expression in relational algebra. Then, as a special case, when ω is ψ itself, we have an algebraic expression for

$$\text{DOM}(\psi)^k \cap \{x_1 \cdots x_k \mid \psi(x_1, \ldots, x_k)\}$$

Since ψ is safe, intersection with DOM(ψ)^k does not change the relation denoted, so we shall have proved the theorem. We therefore turn to the inductive proof. *Basis*: Zero operators in ω. Then ω is an atom, which we may take without loss of generality to be in one of the forms $x_1 \theta x_2$, $x_1 \theta x_1$, $x_1 \theta a$, or $R(x_{i_1} x_{i_2} \cdots x_{i_l})$, where θ is an arithmetic comparison operator, and a is a constant. If the atom is $x_1 \, \theta \, x_2$, then the desired algebraic expression is $\sigma_{1\theta2}(E \times E)$. Atoms $x_1 \, \theta \, x_1$ and $x_1 \, \theta \, a$ are handled similarly.

Finally, if the atom is $R(x_{i_1} x_{i_2} \cdots x_{i_l})$ we construct the expression

$$\pi_{j_1, j_2, \ldots, j_k}(\sigma_F(R))$$

where F is a formula that has term $u = v$ whenever x_{i_u} and x_{i_v} are the same variable, and $u < v$; all terms are connected by the $\wedge$ operator.† The list $j_1, j_2, \ldots, j_k$ is any list such that $x_{i_{j_1}} = x_1, \ldots, x_{i_{j_k}} = x_k$. For example, if ω is $R(x_2 x_1 x_2 x_3)$, then our expression is $\pi_{2,1,4}(\sigma_{1=3}(R))$.

Induction: Assume ω has at least one operator and that the inductive hypothesis is true for all subformulas of ψ having fewer operators than ω.

Case 1: $\omega(y_1, \ldots, y_m) = \omega_1(u_1, \ldots, u_n) \vee \omega_2(v_1, \ldots, v_p)$, where each u_i is a distinct y_j and each v_i is a distinct y_j (although some of the u's and v's may be the same y_j). Let E_1 be an algebraic expression for

$$\mathrm{DOM}(\psi)^n \cap \{\, u_1 \cdots u_n \mid \omega_1(u_1, \ldots, u_n) \,\}$$

and E_2 an algebraic expression for

$$\mathrm{DOM}(\psi)^p \cap \{\, v_1 \cdots v_p \mid \omega_2(v_1, \ldots, v_p) \,\}$$

Define E_1', by:

$$E_1' = \pi_{i_1, \ldots, i_m}(E_1 \times E^{m-n})$$

where i_l is that q such that $u_q = y_l$ if such a u_q exists, and i_l is a unique integer between $n + 1$ and m otherwise. Similarly define

$$E_2' = \pi_{j_1, \ldots, j_m}(E_2 \times E^{m-p})$$

where j_l is that q such that $v_q = y_l$ if such a v_q exists, and j_l is a unique integer between $p + 1$ and m otherwise. Then the desired expression is $E_1' \cup E_2'$.

For example, if $\omega(y_1, y_2, y_3, y_4)$ is

$$\omega_1(y_1, y_3, y_4) \vee \omega_2(y_2, y_4)$$

then

$$E_1' = \pi_{1,4,2,3}(E_1 \times E)$$

and

$$E_2' = \pi_{3,1,4,2}(E_2 \times E \times E)$$

The correctness of the formula $E_1' \cup E_2'$ follows from the fact that E_1' denotes $\mathrm{DOM}(\psi)^m \cap \{\, y_1 \cdots y_m \mid \omega_1(u_1, \ldots, u_n) \,\}$ and E_2' denotes

---

† Note that if there are three or more occurrences of one variable, some of these terms will be redundant and can be eliminated.

$$\text{DOM}(\psi)^m \cap \{\, y_1 \cdots y_m \mid \omega_2(v_1, \ldots, v_p)\,\}$$

(Recall that each of the u's and v's is one of the y's.) It follows that $E_1' \cup E_2'$ denotes $\text{DOM}(\psi)^m \cap \{\, y_1 \cdots y_m \mid \omega(y_1, \ldots, y_m)\,\}$.

Case 2: $\omega(y_1, \ldots, y_m) = \neg\omega_1(y_1, \ldots, y_m)$. Let E_1 be an algebraic expression for $\text{DOM}(\psi)^m \cap \{\, y_1 \cdots y_m \mid \omega_1(y_1, \ldots, y_m)\,\}$. Then $E^m - E_1$ is an expression for $\text{DOM}(\psi)^m - \{\, y_1 \cdots y_m \mid \omega_1(y_1, \ldots, y_m)\,\}$, which is equivalent to

$$\text{DOM}(\psi)^m \cap \{\, y_1 \cdots y_m \mid \neg\omega_1(y_1, \ldots, y_m)\,\}$$

Note that $\{\, y_1 \cdots y_m \mid \neg\omega_1(y_1, \ldots, y_m)\,\}$ is likely to be an infinite set, but we get all we need of it by intersecting with the finite set $\text{DOM}(\psi)^m$.

Case 3: $\omega(y_1, \ldots, y_m) = (\exists y_{m+1})(\omega_1(y_1, \ldots, y_{m+1}))$. Let E_1 be an algebraic expression for $\text{DOM}(\psi)^{m+1} \cap \{\, y_1 \cdots y_{m+1} \mid \omega_1(y_1, \ldots, y_{m+1})\,\}$. Since ψ is safe, and therefore ω is safe, $\omega_1(y_1, \ldots, y_{m+1})$ is never true unless y_{m+1} is in the set $\text{DOM}(\omega)$, which is a subset of $\text{DOM}(\psi)$. Therefore $\pi_{1,2,\ldots,m}(E_1)$ denotes the relation $\text{DOM}(\psi)^m \cap \{\, y_1 \cdots y_m \mid (\exists y_{m+1})(\omega_1(y_1, \ldots, y_{m+1}))\,\}$, which completes the induction and proves the theorem. $\square$

Example 5.13: Let R and S be binary relations. The domain calculus expression

$$\{\, wx \mid R(wx) \wedge (\forall y)(\neg S(wy) \wedge \neg S(xy))\,\}$$

denotes the set of tuples in R neither of whose components are the first component of any tuple in S. This expression is safe, since

1. The formula is not satisfied for w and x unless wx is a tuple of R, and

2. Whenever y is not a symbol appearing in a tuple of S, $\neg S(wy) \wedge \neg S(xy)$ is surely true.

Let E stand for $\pi_1(R) \cup \pi_2(R) \cup \pi_1(S) \cup \pi_2(S)$. We begin by eliminating $\wedge$ and $\forall$ using the construction of Lemma 5.2. After "cancelling" pairs of $\neg$'s, we obtain the expression

$$\{\, wx \mid \neg(\neg R(wx) \vee (\exists y)(S(wy) \vee S(xy)))\,\}$$

Now we apply the construction of Theorem 5.3, beginning at the atoms and progressing to larger subformulas. The trivial algebraic expression R serves for $E^2 \cap \{\, wx \mid R(wx)\,\}$, so R is the expression constructed in the basis of the proof for the atom $R(wx)$. Similarly, the expression S denotes $E^2 \cap \{\, wy \mid S(wy)\,\}$ as well as $E^2 \cap \{\, xy \mid S(xy)\,\}$,† so we construct algebraic expression S for atoms $S(wy)$ and $S(xy)$. Next, let us apply Case 1 of Theorem 5.3 to get an expression for $E^3 \cap \{\, wxy \mid S(wy) \vee S(xy)\,\}$ corresponding to the single-operator formula $S(wy) \vee S(xy)$. The expression constructed in Case 1 of the proof of Theorem 5.3 is

---

† The "formulas" R and S are substantially simpler than the formulas given in the basis of Theorem 5.3. We can use the relations themselves here, because no atom has a domain variable appearing in two components.

$$E_1 = \pi_{1,3,2}(S \times E) \cup \pi_{3,1,2}(S \times E)$$

Then, apply the construction of Case 3 to get an expression for

$$E^2 \cap \{\, wx \mid (\exists y)(S(wy) \vee S(xy)) \,\}$$

That expression is $E_2 = \pi_{1,2}(E_1)$. If we compose cascaded projections in the obvious way we obtain $E_2 = \pi_{1,3}(S \times E) \cup \pi_{3,1}(S \times E)$. This expression denotes the set of pairs one of whose components is a first component of a tuple of S and whose other component appears in some tuple of R or S.

The expression for $E^2 \cap \{\, wx \mid \neg R(wx) \,\}$ is $E^2 - R$ by Case 2. By Case 1, the formula for $E^2 \cap \{\, wx \mid \neg R(wx) \vee (\exists y)(S(wy) \vee S(xy)) \,\}$ is $(E^2 - R) \cup E_2$. Notice that no projection is necessary, since the projections for both $E^2 - R$ and E_2 are $\pi_{1,2}$, which leaves all tuples intact. Finally, the entire domain calculus expression has algebraic expression $E^2 - ((E^2 - R) \cup E_2)$, by the Case 2 construction. Since R and E_2 both denote subsets of E^2, this expression is equivalent to $R - E_2$, that is $R - (\pi_{1,3}(S \times E) \cup \pi_{3,1}(S \times E))$. $\square$

5.4 COMPARISON OF THE MODELS

To evaluate the three models discussed in this chapter we must first state the criteria by which they should be judged. We see two primary concerns.

1. *Ease of use.* Especially in small databases, on the order of thousands or tens of thousands of records, the principal cost may be the time spent by the programmer writing applications programs and by the user posing queries. We want a model that makes accurate programming and the phrasing of queries easy.

2. *Efficiency of implementation.* When databases are large, the cost of storage space and computer time dominate the total cost of implementing a database. We need a data model in which it is easy for the DBMS to translate a specification of the conceptual scheme and the conceptual-to-physical mapping into an implementation that is space efficient and in which queries can be answered efficiently.

By the criterion of easy use, there is no doubt that the relational model is superior. It provides only one concept, the relation, that the programmer or user must understand. Moreover, the relational algebra and calculus clearly provide a notation that is quite succinct and powerful, and we shall see in the next chapter that this power carries over naturally to real relational query languages. These languages make systems based on the relational model available to persons whose programming skill is not great. Compare, for example, the effort needed to specify the join of relations with the work required to write a program in the DBTG data manipulation language or the Pidgin DL/I of Section 4.3.

Further, the network model requires our understanding of both record types and links, and their interrelationships. The implementation of many-many relationships and relationships on three or more entity sets is not straightforward, although with practice one gets used to the technique, discussed in Section 1.4, of introducing dummy record types. Similarly, the hierarchical model requires understanding the use of pointers (virtual record types) and has the same problems as the network model regarding the representation of relationships that are more complex than many-one relationships between two entity sets.

When we consider the potential for efficient implementation, the network and hierarchical models score high marks. We saw in Section 3.2 how implementations of variable length records can facilitate the task of following links. We also mentioned that data structures such as the multilist and the pointer-based implementation of variable length records do not generalize readily to many-many mappings. Since relations can, and often do, represent many-many mappings, we see that efficient implementation can be more difficult for relations than for networks or hierarchies.

Fortunately, there is no fundamental reason why all these implementation ideas for networks and hierarchies cannot be carried over to the implementation of relations, and indeed, as we discussed in Section 5.1, many of them have been.

Language Level

The level of the data manipulation language can affect profoundly the ease with which a DBMS can be used, just as it is often easier to program in FORTRAN than in assembly language, and often easier to program in APL than in FORTRAN. It has been the case that relational DBMS's have stressed languages of very high-level, while DBMS's based on the other models have tended to have languages of lower-level. That is to say, the examples of network and hierarchical languages we covered in Chapters 3 and 4, and the examples of relational languages we covered in this chapter and will cover in the next, are typical of languages for their respective models.

One might wonder if there is an inherent reason why these examples are typical. It is hard to argue that there is, although we should point out that the principal general-purpose languages of very high level, such as APL, SNOBOL, LISP, or SETL, are each based on a single data type (the array, string, list structure, and set, respectively), just as the relational model provides but a single "data type", the relation. In contrast, lower level languages have a variety of data types at the programmer's disposal, in much the way the relational and hierarchical models place a variety of constructs in the hands of the user.

Conclusions

Early commercial database systems were almost uniformly based on the network or hierarchical model, because the emphasis of such systems has been on the maintenance of large databases, and these models lend themselves most easily to the necessary efficient implementation. However, there are in 1982 several successful commercializations of the relational model, and we feel that the relational systems will become progressively more accepted for two reasons. First, it is becoming clear that the same concepts used to design large databases apply as well to small and medium scale databases, and there are many more small (i.e., thousands of records rather than millions) databases than large ones. With small databases, the ease of use inherent in the relational model assumes increased importance.

Second, many of the apparent inefficiencies of the relational model can be eliminated. We have mentioned already how the physical implementation ideas of the other two models have been carried over to the relational model. The other potential source of inefficiency in the relational model is in the response to queries. The powerful operators can be used carelessly, resulting in queries that, if literally obeyed, would involve the calculation of huge amounts of useless data. A typical example occurs when given relations $R(A, B)$ and $S(B, C)$, we want to relate a particular A-value, say a, to those C-values that connect to it by being associated with a common B-value; that is, we want to find the C-values associated with a in the composition of R and S. A natural way to express this query is $\pi_C(\sigma_{A=a}(R \bowtie S))$. However, that expression, if literally followed, causes us to take the join of R and S first, including the many tuples that do not have A-value a.

In comparison, if we wrote an equivalent query in a navigation-oriented language, we would surely first find the B-values related to a through the relationship represented by R, then find the C-values related to these B-values through S, which will normally require much less computation. Even this difficulty is not a serious impediment to using the relational model. Chapter 8 discusses some of the techniques that have been developed for optimizing relational queries, that is, processing them in ways that are more efficient than the obvious ways. Largely, such optimizers produce implementations of relational queries that are just as efficient as programs developed in one of the navigation-oriented languages such as those mentioned in Sections 3.4 and 4.3.

EXERCISES

5.1: Let R and S be the relations shown in Fig. 5.8. Compute (a) $R \cup S$ (b) $R - S$ (c) $R \bowtie S$ (the natural join) (d) $\pi_A(R)$ (e) $\sigma_{A=C}(R \times S)$. Ignore attribute names in the result of union and difference.

5.2: Assuming R and S are of arity 3 and 2, respectively, convert the expression $\pi_{1,5}(\sigma_{2=4 \vee 3=4}(R \times S))$ to
   a)   tuple relational calculus
   b)   domain relational calculus.

5.3: Convert the tuple calculus formula

A	B
a	b
c	b
d	e

B	C
b	c
e	a
b	d

Fig. 5.8. Example relations.

$$\{\, t^{(2)} \mid R(t) \land (\exists u^{(2)})(S(u) \land \lnot u[1] = t[2]) \,\}$$

to

a) an English statement
b) domain relational calculus
c) relational algebra.

5.4: Convert the domain calculus formula

$$\{\, ab \mid R(ab) \land R(ba) \,\}$$

to

a) an English statement
b) tuple relational calculus
c) relational algebra.

5.5: Are the expressions of Exercises 5.3 and 5.4 safe?

5.6: Suppose we have a database consisting of the following three relations

FREQUENTS(DRINKER, BAR)
SERVES(BAR, BEER)
LIKES(DRINKER, BEER)

The first indicates the bars each drinker visits, the second tells what beers each bar serves, and the last indicates which beers each drinker likes to drink. Express in (i) relational algebra (ii) tuple calculus (iii) domain calculus

a) Print the bars that serve a beer that drinker Charles Chugamug likes.
b) Print the drinkers that frequent at least one bar that serves a beer they like.
* c) Print the drinkers that frequent only bars that serve some beer that they like. (Assume each drinker likes at least one beer and frequents at least one bar.)
* d) Print the drinkers that frequent no bar that serves a beer that they like.

** 5.7: The *transitive closure* of a binary relation R, denoted R^+, is the set of pairs (a, b) such that for some sequence $c_1, c_2, \ldots, c_n$:

i) $c_1 = a$
ii) $c_n = b$

iii) for $i = 1, 2, \ldots, n - 1$, we have (c_i, c_{i+1}) in R.
Prove that there is no expression of relational algebra equivalent to the transitive closure operation on finite relations.

* 5.8: Show that the five relational algebra operators (union, difference, selection, projection, and Cartesian product) are *independent*, meaning that none can be expressed as a formula involving only the other four operators. *Hint:* For each operator you need to discover a property that is not possessed by any expression in the other four operators. For example, to show independence of union, suppose there were an expression $E(R, S)$ that used only difference, selection, projection, and product, but was equal to $R \cup S$ for any R and S. Let R_0 consist of the single tuple (a, b) and S_0 of the single tuple (c, d), where a, b, c, and d do not appear as constants in E. Show by induction on the number of operators used in any subexpression F of E that the relation that is the value of $F(R_0, S_0)$ cannot have a component in which one tuple has a and another tuple has c. Since $R_0 \cup S_0$ has such a component, it follows that $E(R_0, S_0) \neq R_0 \cup S_0$.

BIBLIOGRAPHIC NOTES

Relational algebra was introduced in Codd [1970], and its equivalence to tuple relational calculus was shown in Codd [1972b]. The latter paper is also the source of the principle that a query language should at least be complete for relational calculus. Childs [1968] was a primitive forerunner of the idea of relations as databases.

The notion that predicate calculus could be used for stating queries has been attributed to Kuhns [1967]. Jacobs [1979, 1980, 1982] generalizes the algebra-calculus correspondence to other data models, such as network and hierarchical and suggests the possible influence of predicate calculus on other aspects of database systems. Also, Klug [1981] generalizes the correspondence between algebra and calculus to include aggregate operators (sum, max, and so on). See Gallaire and Minker [1978] for a variety of applications of predicate calculus to relational databases.

A number of relational systems are now available commercially or have been distributed widely. These include System R (Astrahan et al. [1976], Chamberlin et al. [1981b], Blasgen et al. [1981]), INGRES (Stonebraker, Wong, Kreps, and Held [1976], Stonebraker [1980], Zook et al. [1977]), DaTaSyS (DTSS [1980]), ORACLE (RSI [1980]), NOMAD (McCracken [1980]), and RELGRAF (Simpson [1981]). Surveys of relational systems are given by Pirotte [1978] and Kim [1979]. The former divides languages into the three classes: algrebraic, tuple calculus, and domain calculus, as we attempt to do here.

Exercise 5.7, on the transitive closure, is from Aho and Ullman [1979]. That paper and Chandra and Harel [1980, 1982] explore the possiblility of relational query languages that perform only manipulation of data (as opposed to arithmetic on data), yet are richer than relational calculus. In contrast, Bancilhon [1978] and Paredaens [1978] attempt to argue that relational calculus can express all operations that do not involve arithmetic. However, they allow functions like R^+ to be computed by a different expression for each R, so there is no contradiction of Exercise 5.7. Zloof [1975] explains how the transitive closure can be computed in Query-by-Example (a query language discussed in the next chapter), demonstrating that Query-by-Example is more powerful that relational calculus. A result on operator independence similar to Exercise 5.8 was shown by Beck [1978].

There have been a number of attempts to improve the relational model, usually by providing more "semantics," that is, by specializing the meaning of certain relations. Works such as Schmid and Swenson [1976], Furtado [1978], El Masri and Wiederhold [1979], Codd [1979], and Sciore [1979], have attempted to distinguish the roles played by different attributes or relations. Without going into detail, we noted in Section 1.4 how some attributes in relation schemes might represent entities, while others represent relationships among entities. These distinctions have been further refined in the papers cited. Kent [1979] points out some of the problems with representing data in the relational model.

Of additional interest are the concepts called "aggregation and generalization" in Smith and Smith [1977]. Essentially, this paper extends the relational model by allowing the domain of an attribute to be a set of relation names. This extension facilitates generalization (e.g., the entity set "students" generalizes the entity sets "grad students," "female students," and so on) by permitting us to associate with each member of an entity set a relation that gives information germaine to that entity (e.g., "advisor" is an attribute appropriate only for grad students).

Another area in which problems remain is the extension of the relational model to handle "null values," that is, entries in tuples that represent unknown, irrelevant, or inconsistent values. Attempts to deal with nulls have been made by Codd [1975], Lacroix and Pirotte [1976], Zaniolo [1977], Lipsky [1981], Vassilou [1979, 1980], and Maier [1980]. However, problems arise when we try to define algebraic operations. For example, when taking an equijoin, should two nulls be regarded as equal? No answer is wholly satisfactory.

6

RELATIONAL QUERY LANGUAGES

Let us now look at how the abstract query languages of Chapter 5 are made available in real systems. Section 6.2 discusses ISBL, an almost pure embodiment of relational algebra. The next section covers SQUARE and SEQUEL, which are two languages that have features from both relational algebra and calculus, as well as some set-theoretic operations. Section 6.4 is devoted to QUEL, a tuple calculus language, and Section 6.5 covers Query-by-Example, a domain calculus language.

6.1 GENERAL COMMENTS REGARDING QUERY LANGUAGES

We have seen three abstract notations that can serve as the part of a data manupulation language that extracts information from relations. These notations are relational algebra, tuple relational calculus, and domain relational calculus. As we saw in Theorems 5.1, 5.2, and 5.3, the three notations are equivalent in their expressive power.

Historically, Codd [1972b] first proposed tuple relational calculus (in a formulation somewhat different from that given in Section 5.3) as a benchmark for evaluating data manipulation languages based on the relational model. That is, a language without at least the expressive power of the safe formulas of relational calculus, or equivalently of relational algebra, was deemed inadequate. It is the case that almost all modern query languages embed within them one of the three notations discussed in the previous section; some are best viewed as embedding a combination of these notations. A language that can (at least) simulate tuple calculus, or equivalently, relational algebra or domain calculus, is said to be *complete*. We shall in the remainder of this chapter consider some important relational query languages and show their completeness.

Additional Features of Data Manipulation Languages

In truth, data manipulation languages generally have capabilities beyond those of relational calculus. Of course, all data manipulation languages include insertion, deletion, and modification commands, which are not part of relational algebra or calculus. Some additional features frequently available are:

1. *Arithmetic capability.* Often, atoms in calculus expressions or selections in algebraic expressions can involve arithmetic computation as well as comparisons, such as $A < B + 3$. Note that $+$ and other arithmetic operators appear in neither relational algebra nor calculus.

2. *Assignment and Print Commands.* Languages generally allow the printing of the relation constructed by an algebraic or calculus expression or the assignment of a computed relation to be the value of a relation name.

3. *Aggregate Functions.* Operations such as average, sum, min, or max can often be applied to columns of a relation to obtain a single quantity.

For these reasons, the languages we shall discuss are really "more than complete"; that is, they can do things with no counterpart in relational algebra or calculus. Many, but not all, become equivalent to relational calculus when we throw away arithmetic and aggregate operators. It is an interesting exercise to prove this by showing how to convert to relational calculus or algebra all expressions in the language that do not involve arithmetic or aggregation. However, the reader should be warned that we do not give the entire set of features of those languages we discuss, so the design document for the language must be consulted before attempting such a proof. Also, some languages, like Query-by-Example (Section 6.5), are more than complete even after eliminating arithmetic and aggregation. In particular, Query-by-Example allows computation of the transitive closure of a relation, although we do not discuss this feature here.

Comparison of Algebraic and Calculus Languages

It is often said that relational calculus-based languages are higher-level than the algebraic languages because the algebra specifies the order of operations while the calculus leaves it to a compiler or interpreter to determine the most efficient order of evaluation. For example, in Section 5.4 we discussed a situation where we had relations $R(A, B)$ and $S(B, C)$, and we formulated the algebraic query

$$\pi_C(\sigma_{A=a}(R \bowtie S)) \tag{6.1}$$

where $\bowtie$ stands for the natural join, and a is a constant. This query says: "print the C-values associated with A-value a in the joined relation with columns A, B, and C." An equivalent domain calculus expression is

$$\{\, c \mid (\exists b)(R(ab) \wedge S(bc)) \,\} \tag{6.2}$$

If we compare (6.1) and (6.2) we see that the calculus expression does in fact tell only what we want, not how to get it; that is, (6.2) only specifies the properties of the desired values c. In comparison, (6.1) specifies a particular order of operations. It is not immediately obvious that (6.1) is equivalent to:

$$\pi_C(\pi_B(\sigma_{A=a}(R)) \bowtie S) \tag{6.3}$$

To evaluate (6.3) we need only look up R for the tuples with A-value a and find the associated B-values. This step computes $\pi_B(\sigma_{A=a}(R))$. Then we look up the tuples of S with those B-values and print the associated C-values. The lookup is reflected by the natural join, since the left operand of that join is a relation over attribute B, and its right operand is over B and C.

In comparison, (6.1) requires that we evaluate the natural join of R and S, which could involve sorting both relations on their B-values and running through the sorted relations. The resulting relation could be very large compared to R and S. Typically, the evaluation of (6.1) would take much more time than (6.3), even though the answers are the same.

In principle, we can always evaluate (6.2) like (6.3) rather than (6.1), which appears to be an advantage of calculus over algebra, especially as (6.1) is simpler, and therefore more likely to be written than is (6.3). However, an optimization pass in an algebra-based query language compiler can convert (6.1) into (6.3) immediately, and relational calculus expressions require optimization as well if we are to receive the full benefit of their nonprocedurality.†

We shall consider such optimization in Chapter 8. Thus we feel that it is specious to regard calculus as higher-level than algebra, if for no other reason than that the first step in the optimization of an algebraic expression could be to convert it by Theorem 5.1 to an equivalent calculus expression. We must admit, however, that calculus-based languages are today more prevalent than algebraic languages. We prefer to attribute the dominance of calculus languages to the desirability of their nonprocedurality from the programmer's point of view, rather than from the point of view of efficiency or ease of compilation.

Select-Project-Join Expressions

While we expect a query language to be complete, there is a subset of the expressions of relational algebra that appear with great frequency, and it is important to consider how easily a language handles these expressions. The class of expressions we have in mind is formed from the operators select, project, and natural join. Intuitively, many queries can be viewed as taking an entity (described by the selection clause), connecting it to an entity of another type, perhaps through many relationships (the natural join expresses the connection), and then printing some attributes of the latter entity (the projection determines the attributes printed). We call such expressions *select-project-join* expressions. The reader is encouraged to look at how the query languages to be described each handle select-project-join queries in a succinct way.

---

† A *nonprocedural* language is one that expresses what we want without necessarily saying how to obtain it.

Relational algebra	ISBL
$R \cup S$	$R + S$
$R - S$	$R - S$
$R \cap S$	$R.S$
$\sigma_F(R)$	$R : F$
$\pi_{A_1,\ldots,A_n}(R)$	$R \% A_1, \ldots, A_n$
$R \bowtie S$	$R * S$

Fig. 6.1. Correspondence between ISBL and relational algebra.

6.2 ISBL: A "PURE" RELATIONAL ALGEBRA LANGUAGE

ISBL (Information System Base Language) is a query language developed at the IBM United Kingdom Scientific Center in Peterlee, England, for use in the experimental PRTV (Peterlee Relational Test Vehicle) system. It closely approximates the relational algebra given in Section 5.2, so the completeness of ISBL is easy to show. The correspondence of syntax is shown in Fig. 6.1. In both ISBL and relational algebra, R and S can be any relational expressions, and F is a Boolean formula. Components of a relation are given names (the attributes of the relation), and we refer to components by these names in F.

To print the value of an expression, precede it by LIST. To assign the value of an expression E to a relation named R, we write $R = E$. An interesting feature of assignment is that we can delay the binding of relations to names in an expression until the name on the left of the assignment is used. To delay evaluation of a name, preceed it by N!. The N! calls for evaluation "by name."

Example 6.1: Suppose we want to use the composition of binary relations $R(A, B)$ and $S(C, D)$ from time to time. If we write

> RCS = (R * S) : B=C % A, D

the composition of the current relations R and S would be computed and assigned to relation name RCS. Note that as R and S have attributes with different names, the *, or natural join, operator is here a Cartesian product.

However, suppose we wanted RCS to stand not for the composition of the current values of $R(A, B)$ and $S(C, D)$ but for the formula for composing R and S. Then we could write

> RCS = (N!R * N!S) : B=C % A, D

The above ISBL statement causes no evaluation of relations. Rather, it defines RCS to stand for the formula $(R * S) : B=C \% A, D$. If we ever use RCS in a statement that requires its evaluation, such as

> LIST RCS

or

$$T = RCS + U$$

the values of R and S are at that time substituted into the formula for RCS to get a value for RCS. □

The delayed evaluation operator N! serves two important purposes. First, large relational expressions are hard to write down correctly the first time. Delayed evaluation allows the programmer to construct an expression in easy stages, by giving temporary names to important subexpressions. More importantly, delayed evaluation serves as a rudimentary facility for defining views. By defining relation names by expressions with delayed evaluation, the programmer can use these names as if the defined relations really existed. Thus, a set of defined relations forms a view of the database.

Renaming of Attributes

The purely set theoretic operators, union, intersection, and difference, have definitions that are modified from their standard definitions in relational algebra, to take account of the fact that components have attribute names in ISBL. The union and intersection operators are only applicable when the two relations involved have the same set of attribute names. The difference operator, $R - S$, is the ordinary set-theoretic difference when R and S have the same set of attribute names. However, if some of the attributes of R and S differ, then $R - S$ denotes the set of tuples t in R such that t agrees with no tuple in S on those attributes that R and S have in common. Thus, for example, in ISBL the expression $R - S$, where R is $R(A, B)$ and S is $S(A, C)$, denotes the relational algebra expression

$$R - (\pi_A(S) \times \pi_B(R))$$

To allow these operators to be used at will, a special form of projection permits the renaming of attributes. In a list of attributes following the projection (%) operator, an item $A \rightarrow B$ means that the component for attribute A is included in the projection but is renamed B. For example, to take the union of $R(A, B)$ with $S(A, C)$ we could write

(R % A, B→C) + S

The resulting relation has attributes A and C.

We can also use renaming to take the Cartesian product of relations whose sets of attributes are not disjoint. Observe that the natural join $R(A, B) * S(C, D)$ is really a Cartesian product, but $R(A, B) * S(B, C)$ is a natural join in which the B-components of R and S are equated. If we want to take the Cartesian product of $R(A, B)$ with $S(B, C)$ we can write

(R % A, B→D) * S

As the left operand of the * has attributes A and D, while S has attibutes B and C, the result is a Cartesian product.

With attribute renaming, we have a way to simulate any of the five basic relational algebra operations in ISBL. Thus it is immediately obvious that ISBL is complete.

Some Sample Queries

Example 6.2: Recall that the Happy Valley Food Coop (HVFC) keeps a database in which its members' balances, their orders, and possible suppliers and prices are recorded. We saw in Fig. 3.2 what we shall, for the duration of this chapter, regard as the "current value" of the three relations that hold the information of the HVFC database. These relations are

MEMBERS(NAME, ADDRESS, BALANCE)
ORDERS(ORDER_NO, NAME, ITEM, QUANTITY)
SUPPLIERS(SNAME, SADDRESS, ITEM, PRICE)

We shall now consider some typical queries on the HVFC database and their expression in ISBL. For comparison, we shall use these same queries, which we refer to as "queries 1, 2, and 3," as examples in subsequent sections.

The simplest queries often involve a selection and projection on a single relation. That is, we specify some condition that tuples must have, and we print some or all of the components of these tuples. The specific example query we shall use is

(1) *Print the names of members with negative balances.*

In ISBL we can write

LIST MEMBERS : BALANCE < 0 % NAME

The clause BALANCE < 0 selects the third and fourth tuples, because their values in column 3 (BALANCE) is negative. The projection operator leaves only the first column, NAME, so LIST causes the table

Robin, R.
Hart, W.

to be printed.

A more complicated type of query involves taking the natural join, or perhaps a more general join or Cartesian product of several relations, then selecting tuples from this relation and printing some of the components. Our example query is:

(2) *Print the supplier names, items, and prices of all suppliers*
  that supply at least one item ordered by Brooks.

We could write the expression for this query directly, but it is conceptually

SNAME	ITEM	PRICE
Sunshine Produce	Granola	1.29
Purity Foodstuffs	Granola	1.25
Purity Foodstuffs	Unbleached Flour	.65

Fig. 6.2. Result of the second query.

simpler first to define the natural join of ORDERS and SUPPLIERS by

OS = N!ORDERS * N!SUPPLIERS

Note that the evaluation of OS is deferred. If OS were evaluated, it would have a tuple with name n, item i, and supplier s for every set of values n, i, s for which n ordered i and s supplies i. Thus, each member is associated with all the suppliers of any of the items he ordered.

Now with the natural join

OS(ORDER_NO, NAME ITEM, QUANTITY,
SNAME, SADDRESS, PRICE)

available, we select NAME = "Brooks,B." and project onto the desired attributes SNAME, ITEM, and PRICE. The formula is

LIST OS : NAME = "Brooks,B" % SNAME ITEM PRICE

The result of this expression is the table of Fig. 6.2.

A still more complicated sort of query involves what amounts to a "for all" quantifier. The particular query we shall consider is:

(3) *Print the suppliers that supply every item ordered by Brooks.*

Such queries are easier in calculus languages than algebraic languages. The reader will note that in the proof of Theorem 5 ˙, we eliminated ∀ quantifiers before converting to algebra, by converting them to ∃ quantifiers with negations. The same strategy works here. We first construct the set of suppliers that do not supply some item ordered by Brooks. Define

S = N!SUPPLIERS % SNAME /* the set of suppliers */
I = N!SUPPLIERS % ITEM /* the set of supplied items */
B = N!ORDERS; NAME="Brooks,B." % ITEM
/* above are the items ordered by Brooks */
NS = (N!S * N!I) − (N!SUPPLIERS % SNAME, ITEM)
/* the pairs of suppliers and items not supplied by that supplier */
NSB = N!NS . (N!S * N!B) /* the set of supplier-item pairs such that
the supplier doesn't supply the item, and Brooks ordered the item */

Then the desired expression is S − (NSB % SNAME). It evaluates to the list consisting of one entry: Purity Foodstuffs. □

ISBL Extensions

The ISBL language is fairly limited, when compared with query languages to be discussed in the next sections. For example, it has no aggregate operators (e.g., average, min), and there are no facilities for insertion, deletion, or modification of tuples. However, there exists in the surrounding PRTV system the facility to write arbitrary PL/I programs and integrate them into the processing of relations.

The simplest use of PL/I programs in ISBL is as tuple-at-a-time processors, which serve as generalized selection operators. For example, we could write a PL/I program LOWADDR(S) that examines the character string S and determines whether S, as a street address, has a number lower than 50, returning "true" if so. We can then apply LOWADDR to an attribute in an ISBL expression, with the result that the component for that attribute in each tuple is passed to LOWADDR, and the tuple is "selected" if LOWADDR returns "true." The syntax of ISBL calls for the join operator to be used for these generalized selections. Thus

LIST (MEMBERS * LOWADDR(ADDRESS)) % NAME

prints the names of members whose street number does not exceed 49.

PL/I programs that operate on whole relations, rather than tuples, can also be defined. To facilitate such processing, the PRTV system allows relations to be passed to PL/I programs, either as *relational read files,* or *relational write files.* These are ordinary files in the PL/I sense, opened for reading or writing, respectively. A PL/I program can read or write the next record, which is a tuple of the underlying relation, into or from a PL/I record structure. The reader should be able to envision how to write PL/I programs to compute aggregate operators like sums or averages, to delete or modify tuples in arbitrarily specified ways, or to read tuples from an input file (not necessarily a relational read file; it could be a terminal, e.g.) and append them to a relation.

6.3 SQUARE AND SEQUEL

The language SQUARE was one step in the development of a query language for the System R DBMS designed at IBM in San Jose. It has evolved into a language called SEQUEL (also called SQL), which is similar in concept to SQUARE, but has a syntax that is reminiscent of tuple relational calculus. We shall discuss the evolution of SQUARE into SEQUEL after presenting the important ideas in SQUARE.

SQUARE itself has a number of features not present in pure relational algebra, such as the ability to name tuples in relations or to compare sets by conditions such as $\subseteq$. In SQUARE, the union and difference operators are expressed as in relational algebra; intersection is treated likewise. The Cartesian product of R and S is expressed by

$$r \in R, s \in S$$

Projection of relation R onto attributes $A_1, A_2, \ldots, A_n$ is expressed:

$$_{A_1, A_2, \ldots, A_n} R$$

Selection is not done exactly as in relational algebra. Rather, the style is that of tuple calculus. The expression of $\sigma_F(R)$ in SQUARE is

$$r \in R : F'$$

where F' is F with r_A replacing the attribute A or the component number of attribute A in F.

We can immediately confirm that SQUARE is complete, since in SQUARE there is the capability to assign a computed relation to another relation name, using the assignment operator $\leftarrow$. An assignment

$$R_{A_1, A_2, \ldots, A_n} \leftarrow \text{<expression>}$$

where the <expression> denotes an n-component relation, causes the expression to be evaluated and the result to be assigned to relation name R, whose attributes are then named $A_1, A_2, \ldots, A_n$. Thus, if no more convenient feature is present in the language, we can evaluate any relational expression by applying one operator at a time and assigning the result a temporary name. Note that unlike ISBL, assignment in SQUARE always implies immediate evaluation; deferred evaluation is not possible.

Mappings

One of the central features of SQUARE is the *mapping*, which is a special kind of selection followed by a projection. The general form of a mapping is

$$_{A_1, A_2, \ldots, A_n} R_{B_1, B_2, \ldots, B_m} (\theta_1 b_1, \theta_2 b_2, \ldots, \theta_m b_m)$$

where R is a relation name, the A's and B's are lists of attributes of R, θ_i is an arithmetic comparison operator ($=, \neq, <, \leq, >,$ or $\geq$) and is followed by a constant, b_i. The operator $=$ is understood if θ_i is missing. This mapping stands for

$$\pi_{A_1, A_2, \ldots, A_n} (\sigma_{B_1 \theta_1 b_1 \wedge \cdots \wedge B_m \theta_m b_m} (R))$$

Mappings can be composed using the operator $\circ$. Composition will be seen to effect an equijoin of relations, so to a large extent the mapping embodies the select-project-join core of relational algebra.

Example 6.3: The first query of Example 6.2 can be expressed in SQUARE as

$$_{\text{NAME}} \text{MEMBERS}_{\text{BALANCE}} (< 0)$$

and the second query can be expressed

$$\text{SNAME,ITEM,PRICE}\text{SUPPLIERS}_{\text{ITEM}} \circ {}_{\text{ITEM}}\text{ORDERS}_{\text{NAME}}(\text{``Brooks,B."})$$

The mapping on the right is applied first, and it produces the set of items ordered by Brooks. Notice that the equality operator before "Brooks,B." is assumed, since no other operator is present. Then the second mapping looks up the tuples in SUPPLIERS with one of those items in the third component and produces the first, third and fourth components of those tuples. $\square$

Free Variables

SQUARE permits tuple variables, called *free variables*, just as the tuple relational calculus does. We have met free variables already, in the formulas for Cartesian product and selection. In SQUARE, free variables may be subscripted by a list of attribute names to indicate which components of the tuple represented by the variable are to be taken. The following expressions in SQUARE can be likened to tuple relational calculus expressions.

$$(t_1)_{\alpha_1} \in R_1, \ldots, (t_k)_{\alpha_k} \in R_k \colon \psi \tag{6.4}$$

Here, t_i is a free variable denoting a tuple in R_i; α_i is the list of attributes of R_i that we want printed. If α_i is missing, then the list of all attributes of R_i is assumed. Formula ψ takes operands that are constants or variables among the t_i's, perhaps subscripted by arbitrary lists of attributes.

The meaning of (6.4) is

$$\{\, u \mid (\exists t_1)\cdots(\exists t_k)(R_1(t_1) \wedge \cdots \wedge R_k(t_k) \wedge \omega \wedge \psi)\,\}$$

where ω asserts that $u[j] = t_i[m]$, if i and m are chosen such that the sum of the lengths of $\alpha_1, \alpha_2, \ldots, \alpha_{i-1}$ plus m totals j, and the length of α_i is no more than m. That is, form the list of components represented by $(t_1)_{\alpha_1}$, then those represented by $(t_2)_{\alpha_2}$, and so on. The jth component of u is equal to the jth component on this list. The form of ω, plus the clauses $R_i(t_i)$ for each i, guarantee safety of the expression, since ψ is not allowed to have quantifiers.

The operators that can appear in ψ include mappings, as defined previously, the algebraic operations $\cup$, $\cap$, and $-$, the Boolean operators, arithmetic operators and comparisons, and set comparisons ($=$, $\neq$, $\subseteq$, and so on).

Example 6.4: The first query of Example 6.2 can be written with free variables as

$$t_{\text{NAME}} \in \text{MEMBERS} \colon t_{\text{BALANCE}} < 0$$

The second query is not expressed in a very convenient way using free variables, but the third query, asking for suppliers that supply every item ordered by Brooks can be expressed succinctly as:

$s_{\text{SNAME}} \in \text{SUPPLIERS}: ({}_{\text{ITEM}}\text{ORDERS}_{\text{NAME}}(\text{"Brooks,B."})$
$\subseteq {}_{\text{ITEM}}\text{SUPPLIERS}_{\text{SNAME}}(s_{\text{SNAME}}))$

That is, ${}_{\text{ITEM}}\text{ORDERS}_{\text{NAME}}(\text{"Brooks,B."})$ is a mapping that produces the set of items ordered by Brooks. ${}_{\text{ITEM}}\text{SUPPLIERS}_{\text{SNAME}}(s_{\text{SNAME}})$ gives the set of items supplied by the supplier whose name is in the SNAME component of the tuple s. Therefore, the formula to the right of the colon is true exactly when the supplier mentioned in the tuple s supplies all items ordered by Brooks. As s ranges over all tuples in the SUPPLIERS relation, the expression causes all suppliers that supply all items ordered by Brooks to be printed.

As a last example, note that the expression for $R \times S$ given earlier:

$r \in R, s \in S$

is a special case of a free variable expression where the formula ψ is missing, and therefore considered always true. Thus the concatenation of every tuple in R with every tuple in S is printed. $\square$

Insertions, Deletions, and Modifications

The way to insert a tuple into relation R is to write $\downarrow R_{A_1,\ldots,A_n}(a_1,\ldots,a_n)$, where $A_1,\ldots,A_n$ is a list of some or all of the attributes of relation scheme R, and a_i is the value of attribute A_i in the new tuple. If R has attributes not listed among $A_1,\ldots,A_n$, the new tuple has the *null value* in the components for the unlisted attributes.

Example 6.5: The tuple ("Sunshine, L.M.", "29 Blue Sky Dr.", 0) can be added to the MEMBERS relation of Fig. 3.2 by the SQUARE statement

$\downarrow \text{MEMBERS}_{\text{NAME,ADDRESS,BALANCE}}(\text{"Sunshine,L.M."},$
"29 Blue Sky Dr.", 0)

$\square$

It is also permitted to write

$\downarrow R_{A_1,\ldots,A_n}(<\text{expression}>)$

where the $<\text{expression}>$'s value is an n-ary relation S. This statement has the same effect as the sequence of statements

$\downarrow R_{A_1,\ldots,A_n}(a_1,\ldots,a_n)$

where $(a_1,\ldots,a_n)$ ranges over all tuples in S.

The deletion statement has the same syntax as insertion, but $\uparrow$ is used in place of $\downarrow$.

$\uparrow R_{A_1,\ldots,A_n}(a_1,\ldots,a_n)$

deletes from R all tuples whose value in the component for attribute A_i is a_i, for each i between 1 and n. The command

$$\uparrow R_{A_1,\ldots,A_n}(<\text{expression}>)$$

where $<\text{expression}>$ evaluates to an n-ary relation S, deletes from R all tuples that match some tuple of S in the components for $A_1,\ldots,A_n$.

Example 6.6: If Tasti Supply Co. stops selling lettuce, we could update the database of Fig. 3.2 by

$$\uparrow \text{SUPPLIERS}_{\text{SNAME,ITEM}}(\text{``Tasti Supply Co.''}, \text{``lettuce''})$$

This will delete the tuple

$$(\text{``Tasti Supply Co.''}, \text{``17 River St.''}, \text{``lettuce''}, .79)$$

from SUPPLIERS.

If we wish to cancel the orders of all members with negative balances, we can use the expression $_{\text{NAME}}\text{MEMBERS}_{\text{BALANCE}}(<0)$ to denote the set of all members with negative balances. A set is a unary relation, so we may use it as the argument of a deletion and write

$$\uparrow \text{ORDERS}_{\text{NAME}}(_{\text{NAME}}\text{MEMBERS}_{\text{BALANCE}}(<0))$$

☐

The syntax for a modification is

$$\to R_{A_1,\ldots,A_n;B_1,\ldots,B_m}(a_1,\ldots,a_n,b_1,\ldots,b_m)$$

The A's and B's are (not necessarily disjoint) lists of attributes of relation R; the B's, but not the A's, may be preceded by arithmetic operators, $+$, $-$, $\times$, or $/$. The a's and b's are constants. The statement causes R to be searched for tuples whose value in the A_i component is a_i, for all i between 1 and n. For each such tuple, it replaces the value in the component B_i by b_i, for $1 \leq i \leq m$. However, if B_i is preceded by arithmetic operator α, the old value c in component B_i is replaced by $c\alpha b_i$. For example, $+B_i$ causes c to be replaced by $c + b_i$.

Example 6.7: To set Hart's balance to 0, write

$$\to \text{MEMBERS}_{\text{NAME;BALANCE}}(\text{``Hart,W.''}, 0)$$

If Robin pays 200 dollars, we can increase her balance by that amount if we write

$$\to \text{MEMBERS}_{\text{NAME;+BALANCE}}(\text{``Robin,R.''}, 200)$$

If Purity Foodstuffs cuts the price of whey in half we can write

$$\to \text{SUPPLIERS}_{\text{SNAME,ITEM;/PRICE}}(\text{``Purity Foodstuffs''}, \text{``Whey''}, 2)$$

☐

Aggregate Functions

Functions such as COUNT, AVG, SUM, MIN, or MAX can be applied to the collection of values in a set (unary relation). For example, if we wished to determine the net balance of all members of the HVFC, we could write

$$\text{SUM}(_{\text{BALANCE}}\text{MEMBERS}')$$

As another example, if we wished to find the supplier or suppliers with the lowest price for granola we could write

$$_{\text{SNAME}} \in \text{SUPPLIERS}: s_{\text{ITEM}} = \text{``Granola''}$$
$$\land s_{\text{PRICE}} = \text{MIN}(_{\text{PRICE}}\text{SUPPLIERS}_{\text{ITEM}}(\text{``Granola''}))$$

The reader may note the prime on MEMBERS in the first of these formulas. Its presence is to remind SQUARE not to merge two identical elements when it computes a set. That is, if we wrote

$$\text{SUM}(_{\text{BALANCE}}\text{MEMBERS})$$

two members balances that happened to be the same would be counted only once in the sum. The prime indicates that the result of the mapping

$$_{\text{BALANCE}}\text{MEMBERS}'$$

is to be a multiset, with repetitions allowed, rather than the usual set, with repetitions combined.

The Query Language SEQUEL

One of the problems with SQUARE is its reliance on subscripts in its syntax. While we can develop a syntax for the language that places everything on a line (and we must do this for use with a computer) such syntax is not appealing. One way in which SEQUEL differs from SQUARE is that SEQUEL solves the two-dimensional syntax problem by using keywords to indicate the role of relation and attribute names.

The SQUARE mapping

$$_{A_1,\ldots,A_n}R_{B_1,\ldots,B_m}(\theta_1 b_1, \ldots, \theta_m b_m)$$

is expressed in SEQUEL by

> SELECT $A_1, \ldots, A_n$
> FROM R
> WHERE $B_1\theta_1 b_1$ AND $\cdots$ AND $B_m\theta_m b_m$

Recall that if θ_i is missing in the SQUARE mapping, it is assumed to be $=$. Thus the first query of Example 6.2 can be written

```
SELECT NAME
FROM MEMBERS
WHERE BALANCE < 0
```

Once we have adopted this style of representation for mappings, we see that the restrictions on what follows the WHERE can be relaxed somewhat. In SEQUEL the expression following WHERE can be any expression involving the attributes of the relation followng FROM, arithmetic comparisons and operations, Boolean connectives (written AND, OR, NOT), set operations (UNION, INTERSECT, MINUS), set membership (X IN S, or equivalently S CONTAINS X, where S is a set) and the negation of set membership (X NOT IN S or S DOES NOT CONTAIN X). The same operators can serve for set inclusion if X is a set rather than an element or tuple. The expression following WHERE can also contain operands that are relations formed from another SELECT-FROM-WHERE clause.

Example 6.8: To print the names and addresses of suppliers that supply either curds or whey, we write

```
SELECT UNIQUE SNAME, SADDRESS
FROM SUPPLIERS
WHERE ITEM = 'curds' OR ITEM = 'whey'
```

The word UNIQUE is needed after SELECT here because unlike SQUARE, when SEQUEL applies a mapping it does not eliminate duplicates unless told to do so by the keyword UNIQUE. Without UNIQUE, this query would print Purity Foodstuffs twice, since it supplies both curds and whey.

The composition of mappings is achieved by nesting SELECT-FROM-WHERE clauses. Thus the second query of Example 6.2 in SEQUEL is

```
SELECT UNIQUE SNAME, ITEM, PRICE
FROM SUPPLIERS
WHERE ITEM IN
    SELECT ITEM
    FROM ORDERS
    WHERE NAME = 'Brooks,B.'
```

☐

There are two features of SEQUEL that are like free variable expressions in SQUARE. First, we can give a name T to a typical tuple of relation R by writing

SELECT $\cdots$ FROM $R\ T$ WHERE $\cdots$

Then, inside the WHERE clause we may refer to the value of component A of tuple T by $T.A$.

Example 6.9: To print the names of all members who have ordered ten or more

```
SELECT SNAME
FROM SUPPLIERS T
WHERE
        (SELECT ITEM
        FROM SUPPLIERS
        WHERE SNAME = T.SNAME)
     CONTAINS
        (SELECT ITEM
        FROM ORDERS
        WHERE NAME = 'Brooks,B.')
```

Fig. 6.3. A SEQUEL query.

pounds of food, we could write

```
SELECT NAME
FROM MEMBERS T
WHERE 10 <=
     SELECT SUM(QUANTITY)
     FROM ORDERS
     WHERE NAME = T.NAME
```

Here SUM is an aggregate function as in SQUARE. In the clause

WHERE NAME = T.NAME

the attribute NAME refers to the NAME component of ORDERS, while the term T.NAME refers to the NAME component of the tuple T from MEMBERS. The result printed is

Brooks,B.
Robin,R.

The third query of Example 6.2 can be written as in Fig. 6.3. It is analogous to the SQUARE query from Example 6.4. □

Another feature of SEQUEL that can be used like free variables in SQUARE is the ability to list more than one relation in the FROM-clause. The values of attributes of any of the relations following FROM can be referred to either in the SELECT- or WHERE-clauses. If there is potential ambiguity, because A is an attribute of more than one relation, we can use $R.A$ to indicate that attribute A from relation R is meant.

If we have clause FROM $R_1, \ldots, R_n$ in a query, we consider all lists $t_1, \ldots, t_n$ of tuples, where t_i is taken from R_i. If the list satisfies the conditions following WHERE, we include in the output the list of components specified in the SELECT-clause.

Example 6.10: We can produce the join of relations by listing them in the

FROM-clause and putting the necessary relationships among the attributes in the WHERE-clause. Thus, the second query in Example 6.2 could be written

        SELECT SNAME, SUPPLIERS.ITEM, PRICE
        FROM SUPPLIERS, ORDERS
        WHERE NAME = 'Brooks,B.' AND
            SUPPLIERS.ITEM = ORDERS.ITEM

Note that as ITEM appears in both relations SUPPLIERS and ORDERS, it must be qualified by the relation from which it comes. The other attributes mentioned in the query appear in only one of the two relations, and they need not be qualified.

As another example, we can take the Cartesian product of relations R and S by

        SELECT *
        FROM R, S

The symbol * stands for all components of all the relations folllowing FROM.
□

The insertion, deletion and modification operations of SEQUEL are syntactically-sugared versions of the corresponding operations of SQUARE, just as the SELECT-FROM-WHERE construction is a syntactically sugared version of the SQUARE mapping. We shall not go into these operations here.

Completeness of SEQUEL

We saw in Example 6.10 how to compute a Cartesian product. The operations union and set difference are obtained by the UNION and MINUS operations. For example, the union of R and S is

        (SELECT *
        FROM R)
        UNION
        (SELECT *
        FROM S)

The SELECT-FROM-WHERE construct obviously includes both the selection and projection operators of relational algebra. In SEQUEL, assignment is indicated by preceding a query by

        ASSIGN TO R:

if we wish to assign the result to relation R. Thus we have the means to evaluate any relational algebra expression in SEQUEL by applying one operator at a time and thereby computing each subexpression. hence SEQUEL is complete.

SEQUEL and System R

As we have mentioned, SEQUEL is the principal query language used by the System R DBMS. SEQUEL can be used as a "stand alone" query language, in which the user simply expresses SEQUEL queries and database updates and has these operations executed directly by System R. It is also possible to embed SEQUEL queries in PL/I programs. The SEQUEL statements are prefixed with a ∗, and a preprocessor translates them into calls from the surrounding PL/I program, which is then compiled. These calls are to special procedures provided by System R. For example, the procedure named SEQUEL takes a string argument that is the query itself, and a call to this procedure causes the string to be executed.

When used with PL/I as a host language, SEQUEL queries can use variables of the surrounding program. For example, we could write a program to read an item I and then print all suppliers of I, by embedding the SEQUEL query

    ∗ SELECT SNAME
    ∗ FROM SUPPLIERS
    ∗ WHERE ITEM $= I$

in the program. It is also possible, using a mechanism we shall not discuss in detail, to retrieve the result of a query, one tuple at a time, into designated variables of the surrounding program.

6.4 QUEL: A TUPLE RELATIONAL CALCULUS LANGUAGE

QUEL is the query language of INGRES, a relational DBMS developed at the University of California, Berkeley, to run under the UNIX operating system. The language can be used either in a stand-alone manner, by typing commands to the QUEL processor, or embedded in the C programming language. In the latter case, QUEL statements are preceded by ## and handled by a preprocessor. It is therefore possible for QUEL statements to make reference to variables of the surrounding C program.

QUEL has a powerful statement form that covers a wide variety of tuple calculus statements. The calculus statement

$$\{ u^{(r)} \mid (\exists t_1) \cdots (\exists t_k)(R_1(t_1) \wedge \cdots \wedge R_k(t_k) \tag{6.5}$$
$$\wedge\, u[1] = t_{i_1}[j_1] \wedge \cdots \wedge u[r] = t_{i_r}[j_r]$$
$$\wedge\, \psi) \}$$

states that t_i is in R_i, that u is composed of r particular components of the t_i's, and also asserts some additional condition ψ. If ψ is any tuple calculus formula with no quantifiers, (6.5) can be written in QUEL as:

range of t_1 is R_1

.

.

.

range of t_k is R_k
retrieve $(t_{i_1}.A_1, \ldots, t_{i_r}.A_r)$
    where ψ'

In the above, A_m is the j_m^{th} attribute of relation R_{i_m}, for $m = 1, 2, \ldots, k$, and ψ' is the translation of condition ψ into a QUEL expression. To perform the translation we must:

1.   replace ψ's references to a component $u[m]$ by a reference to $t_{i_m}[j_m]$. Note that $u[m]$ and $t_{i_m}[j_m]$ are equated by formula (6.5).
2.   replace any reference to $t_m[n]$ by $t_m.B$, where B is the nth attribute of relation R_m, for any n and m.
3.   replace $\leq$ by $<=$, $\geq$ by $>=$, and $\neq$ by $!=$.
4.   replace $\wedge$, $\vee$, $\neg$ by and, or, not, respectively.

The intuitive meaning of statement

range of t is R

is that any subsequent operations, until t is redeclared by another range statement, are to be carried out once for each tuple in R, with t equal to each of these tuples in turn.

The retrieve statement prints a table whose columns are headed $A_1, \ldots, A_r$. If we wish a different name, say TITLE, for column m, use TITLE $= t_{i_m}.A_m$ in place of $t_{i_m}.A_m$.

Example 6.11: The first query of Example 6.2 is written

range of t is MEMBERS
retrieve (t.NAME)
    where t.BALANCE < 0

The second query of that example can be written

range of t is ORDERS
range of s is SUPPLIERS
retrieve (s.SNAME, s.ITEM, s.PRICE)
    where t.NAME $=$ "Brooks,B." and t.ITEM $=$ s.ITEM.

□

The reader should observe that since ψ in (6.5) has no quantifiers, it is easy to show that expression (6.5) is always safe. The form of (6.5) is not quite general enough to be complete; in particular, we cannot express the union or difference of relations. Fortunately, QUEL provides a delete statement to compute set differences among other functions. One can write

range of t is R
delete t
    where $\psi(t)$

Here, $\psi(t)$ is a QUEL expression like those that can follow "where" in the retrieve statement. The effect of this statement is to delete from R all tuples t that satisfy ψ.

Similarly, QUEL has an append statement to perform unions, among other tasks. We can write

range of t_1 is R_1
    .
    .
    .
range of t_k is R_k
append to $S(A_1 = \omega_1, \ldots, A_n = \omega_n)$
    where $\psi(t_1, \ldots, t_k)$

Here ψ is a QUEL expression as above, and the ω_i's are expressions involving components of the t_i's and/or constants, connected by arithmetic operators. For each assignment of values to the t_j's such that $\psi(t_1, \ldots, t_k)$ is true, we add to relation S the tuple whose component for attribute A_p is the value of ω_p, for $p = 1, 2, \ldots, n$. For example, if we wish to add an order for 10 pounds of curds for each member of HVFC with a nonnegative balance we could write

range of t is MEMBERS
append to ORDERS(ORDER _ NO=nextorder++,† NAME=t.NAME,
    ITEM="Curds", QUANTITY=10)
    where t.BALANCE $>= 0$

Note that the where clause is not required in the append statement, and it is possible, indeed usual, for the append statement to be used with no tuple variables, for the purpose of appending a single tuple to a relation.

We are still not ready to simulate any relational algebra expression in QUEL; we need the capability to assign values to new relations. If S is the name of a new relation we can write

---

† In order for this operation to make sense, we must suppose that this QUEL program is embedded in the programming language c. The c expression nextorder++ stands for the current value of variable nextorder, which we presume keeps the curently next available order number, with the side effect of adding one to the value of nextorder, after taking its value.

range of t_1 is R_1

.

.

.

range of t_k is R_k
retrieve into $S(A_1 = \omega_1, \ldots, A_n = \omega_n)$
    where $\psi(t_1, \ldots, t_k)$

this statement will find all lists of tuples $t_1, \ldots, t_k$ such that t_i is in R_i, and $\psi(t_1, \ldots, t_k)$ is true, and create a tuple for new relation S whose i^{th} component is ω_i. Here, ω_i is a formula as in the append statement. Note that the use of formulas, the ω_i's, to compute the components of tuples is permitted in all retrieve statements, not just those that have an "into" term.

The attribute names $A_1, \ldots, A_n$ become the names of the components of S. We may omit "$A_i =$" if ω_i is of the form t_j.NAME, whereupon NAME becomes the name of the ith attribute of S.

Example 6.12: QUEL, like SEQUEL, does not automatically remove duplicates when it computes a relation. Suppose we wanted to print the names and addresses of all suppliers. We could write

    range of t is SUPPLIERS
    retrieve (t.SNAME, t.SADDRESS)

but then each supplier would be printed once for each item it supplied. QUEL provides a sort command to eliminate duplicates while it sorts a relation, initially on the first component, then on the second component for tuples with the same first component, and so on. To print each supplier only once, and incidentally print them in alphabetical order, we could write

    range of t is SUPPLIERS
    retrieve into JUNK(NAME=t.SNAME, ADDR=t.SADDRESS)
    sort JUNK
    print JUNK

The columns of JUNK would be headed NAME and ADDR. □

Completeness of QUEL

Since we now know how to create temporary relations, all we have to do to evaluate any relational algebra expression is to show how to apply the five basic operators. Suppose in what follows that $R(A_1, \ldots, A_n)$ and $S(B_1, \ldots, B_m)$ are relations, and T is a new relation name. To compute $T = R \cup S$ (assuming $m = n$) we could write

range of r is R
append to $T(C_1 = r.A_1, \ldots, C_n = r.A_n)$
range of s is S
append to $T(C_1 = s.B_1, \ldots, C_n = s.B_n)$

To compute $T = R - S$, write

range of r is R
append to $T(C_1 = r.A_1, \ldots, C_n = r.A_n)$
range of s is S
range of t is T
delete t
    where $s.B_1 = t.C_1$ and $\cdots$ and $s.B_n = t.C_n$

For $T = R \times S$ write

range of r is R
range of s is S
append to $T(C_1 = r.A_1, \ldots, C_n = r.A_n,$
    $C_{n+1} = s.B_1, \ldots, C_{n+m} = s.B_m)$

To compute the selection $\sigma_F(R)$, write

range of r is R
append to $T(C_1 = r.A_1, \ldots, C_n = r.A_n)$
    where F'

Here F' is the formula F translated into QUEL notation (component i of R becomes $r.A_i$, $\wedge$ becomes "and," and so on). Finally, to express the projection $\pi_{i_1, \ldots, i_k}(R)$ we can write

range of r is R
append to $T(C_1 = r.A_{i_1}, \ldots, C_k = r.A_{i_k})$

Example 6.13: The third query of Example 6.2 can be evaluated in QUEL by following the relational algebra formula developed in that example. Let us first write a program to compute the set of supplier-item pairs.

range of s is SUPPLIERS
range of i is SUPPLIERS
retrieve into DUMMY(S=s.SNAME, I=i.ITEM)

Now we follow this by statements to delete from DUMMY those supplier-item pairs (S, I) such that S supplies I. The result is those (S, I) pairs such that S does not supply I.

> range of s is SUPPLIERS
> range of t is DUMMY
> delete t
> > where t.S=s.SNAME and t.I=s.ITEM

Next create a relation of (S, I) pairs such that S is any supplier and I is not supplied by S but I is ordered by Brooks by writing

> range of r is ORDERS
> range of t is DUMMY
> retrieve into JUNK(S=t.S, I=t.I)
> > where r.NAME= "Brooks,B." and r.ITEM=t.I

Then, we list only those SUPPLIERS that do not appear as a first component of a tuple in JUNK. To get the set of suppliers, write

> range of s is SUPPLIERS
> retrieve into SUPS(S=s.SNAME)

Finally, to print the desired set, say

> range of u is SUPS
> range of j is JUNK
> delete u
> > where u.S=j.S
> sort SUPS
> print SUPS

While the above may look like a lot of code, it can be simplified if we realize that range statements declare a variable to range over a particular relation "forever," or until another range statement for that variable is given. Thus we could condense range statements and write the QUEL program of Fig. 6.4.

Aggregate Operators

QUEL uses the aggregate functions sum, avg, count, min, and max, as do SQUARE or SEQUEL. The argument of such a function can be any expression involving components of a single relation, constants and arithmetic operators. The components must all be referred to as $t.A$ for some one tuple variable t and various attributes A. For example, if we want the net balance of all members of HVFC, we could write

> range of t is MEMBERS
> retrieve(sum(t.BALANCE))

We can also partition the tuples of a relation according to the value of one or more expressions computed from each tuple and take aggregates separately for each set of tuples having values in common for each of the expressions.†

```
range of s is SUPPLIERS
range of i is SUPPLIERS
retrieve into DUMMY(S=s.SNAME, I=i.ITEM)
range of t is DUMMY
delete t
    where t.S=s.SNAME and t.I=s.ITEM
range of r is ORDERS
retrieve into JUNK(S=t.S, I=t.I)
    where r.NAME="Brooks,B." and r.ITEM=t.I
retrieve into SUPS(S=s.SNAME)
range of u is SUPS
range of j is JUNK
delete u
    where u.S=j.S
sort SUPS
print SUPS
```

Fig. 6.4. QUEL program for query three.

This partitioning is achieved by writing

$$\text{ag\_op}(E \text{ by } F_1, F_2, \ldots, F_k) \tag{6.6}$$

where E and the F's are expressions whose operands are chosen from among constants and terms $t.A$ for one tuple variable t only. The operands in an expression may be connected by arithmetic operators. If t ranges over R, the value of (6.6) for a given value of t is computed by finding all those tuples of R that give the same value as t for $F_1, \ldots, F_k$. Then, apply the aggregate operator ag_op to the value of E for each of those tuples.

Example 6.14: To print the items supplied with their average prices, we could write

```
range of s is SUPPLIERS
retrieve into DUMMY(ITEM=s.ITEM,
    AP = avg(s.PRICE by s.ITEM))
sort DUMMY
print DUMMY
```

We sort DUMMY to remove duplicates, as DUMMY will have, for each item, as many tuples as the SUPPLIERS relation has for that item. The result of running the above program on relation SUPPLIERS of Fig. 3.2 is shown in Fig. 6.5. □

---

† SEQUEL and Query-by-Example (to be discussed in the next section) also have such a feature, although we discuss the concept only in the context of QUEL.

ITEM	AP
Curds	.80
Granola	1.27
Lettuce	.84
Sunflower Seeds	1.14
Unbleached Flour	.65
Whey	.74

Fig. 6.5. Average prices of items.

6.5 QUERY-BY-EXAMPLE: A DOMAIN CALCULUS LANGUAGE

Query-by-Example (*QBE*) is a language developed at IBM, Yorktown Hts. It contains a number of features not present in relational algebra or calculus, or in any of the implemented query languages we have discussed. Not the least of its special features is that QBE is designed to be used sitting at a terminal, using a special screen editor to compose queries. A button on the terminal allows the user to call for one or more *table skeletons,* as shown in Fig. 6.6, to be displayed on the screen. The user then names the relations and attributes represented by the skeleton, using the screen editor.

Queries are posed by using domain variables and constants, as in domain relational calculus, to form tuples that we assert are in one of the relations whose skeletons appear on the screen. Certain of the variables, indicated by prefixing their name with P., are printed. (All operators in QBE end in dot, and the dot is not itself an operator.) When a tuple or combination of tuples matching the conditions specified by the query are found, the components for those attributes preceded by P. are printed.

Before going into detail regarding the expression and meaning of queries in QBE, let us take an example of what a typical query looks like. Suppose we want to answer the second query of Example 6.2, and we have the ORDERS and SUPPLIERS relations available in the database. We call for two table skeletons to be displayed. In the box reserved for the relation name, in one skeleton, we type ORDERS P. In response to the P., the attributes of ORDERS will appear along the first row of that skeleton, as shown in Fig. 6.7. Similarly, we type SUPPLIERS P. in the upper left corner of the other skeleton to get the attributes of the SUPPLIERS relation.

The essence of query two in Example 6.2 is that we want to find a tuple in the ORDERS relation whose NAME component is "Brooks,B." and whose ITEM component is some item, for example "banana." Then we look for a tuple in the SUPPLIERS relation with the same item in the ITEM component, and we print the SNAME, SADDR, and ITEM components of each such tuple found.

for relation name		for attributes (additional columns available if used)	
for commands on tuples			

for tuples mentioned
in queries

Fig. 6.6. A QBE table skeleton.

ORDERS	ORDER _ NO	NAME	ITEM	QUANTITY
		Brooks,B.	_ banana	

SUPPLIERS	SNAME	SADDR	ITEM	PRICE
	P.	P.	P._ banana	

Fig. 6.7. An example of a query in QBE: for each item
ordered by Brooks, print the suppliers
their addresses and the item

In Fig. 6.7 we see this query expressed in QBE. We write the important features of the tuple we want to find in the ORDERS relation in the second line of the skeleton for that relation. The example item "banana" is preceded by an underscore to indicate that it is only an example. The entry in the NAME component, "Brooks,B.," is written with no quote marks or underscore, to indicate that it is a literal.† In the SUPPLIERS skeleton we see the important feature of the tuple we wish to find in that relation, namely that the item be the same as the item in the tuple found in the ORDERS relation. The fact

---

† Note that this convention, preceding names of domain variables by an underscore and leaving literals unadorned, is diametrically opposed to the usual style of query languages and programming languages, where character string literals are adorned with quotes, and variables are unadorned. Also observe that Query-by-Example takes its name from the suggestion that variable names be chosen to be examples of the object desired. However, as with variables of other languages, the name "banana" has no semantic meaning, and it could be replaced in all its occurrences by junk, a, or xyz.

that the two ITEM components must be the same is expressed by the fact that the domain variable, _banana, is the same in both tuples. We also see, from the tuple written into the SUPPLIERS skeleton, that components SNAME, SADDR, and ITEM are to be printed. The operator P. in these columns indicates the components printed.

A large family of QBE queries correspond to domain calculus expressions of the form

$$\{\, a_1 a_2 \cdots a_n \mid (\exists b_1)(\exists b_2) \cdots (\exists b_m)(R_1(c_{11}, \ldots, c_{1k_1}) \wedge \\ \cdots \wedge R_p(c_{p1}, \ldots, c_{pk_p})) \,\}$$

where each c_{ij} is an a_l, a b_l, or a constant, and each a_l and b_l appears at least once among the c's. To express any such query, we display the table skeletons for all the relations mentioned among $R_1, \ldots, R_p$, and create a variable name for each of the a's and b's. Duplicate skeletons, if two of the R_i's are the same relation, may be used. In general, it is a good mnemonic to use variable names that are examples of objects actually found in the appropriate domains, but any character string preceded by an underscore will do. Now, for each term $R_i(c_{i1}, \ldots, c_{ik_i})$ write a tuple in the skeleton for R_i. If c_{ij} is a constant, place that constant in the jth component. If c_{ij} is one of the a's or b's, place the variable corresponding to that symbol there instead. However, if one of the a's or b's appears only once among all the terms, then we can leave the corresponding component blank if we wish.

It will often be the case that all the a's appear as components of one term $R_i(c_{i1}, \ldots, c_{ik_i})$. If so, in the tuple for this term we prefix each of the a's by the operator P., and we are done. However, if no such term exists, we can create another table skeleton, whose components we can optionally name, and enter into the table skeleton the tuple

P._A1 P._A2 $\cdots$ P._An

where _Ai is the variable name for a_i.

Example 6.15: Suppose we wish to print the name and quantity ordered, for all granola orders. We can express this query in domain calculus as

$$\{\, a_1 a_2 \mid \text{ORDERS}(a_1, \text{``Granola''}, a_2) \,\}$$

and in QBE as

ORDERS	ORDER_NO	NAME	ITEM	QUANTITY
		P._Oakes	Granola	P.

Here variable _Oakes replaces a_1. We could have omitted _Oakes altogether, since it appears only once. We have taken our option not to create a variable for a_2, since it also appears only once.

MEMBERS	NAME	ADDRESS	BALANCE
	_ Oakes		_ 999

ORDERS	ORDER _ NO	NAME	ITEM	QUANTITY
		_ Oakes	_ hotdog	_ mucho

	P. _ Oakes	P. _ hotdog	P. _ mucho	P. _ 999

Fig. 6.8. Print names, items, quantities ordered, and balances.

Let us consider another problem: print the name, item, quantity and balance of the person named, for each order. In domain calculus this query is:

$$\{ a_1 a_2 a_3 a_4 \mid (\exists b_1)(\exists b_2)(\text{MEMBERS}(a_1 b_1 a_4) \land \text{ORDERS}(b_2 a_1 a_2 a_3)) \}$$

As no term has all the a's, we call for a new table skeleton, as well as the skeletons of MEMBERS and ORDERS. The query is shown in Fig. 6.8.

It would also have been permissible to write the unnamed relation of Fig. 4.16 as

P.	_ Oakes	_ hotdog	_ mucho	_ 999

since a command such as P. in the first column (the column corresponding to the relation name) applies to all components of the tuple. □

Implementation of QBE Queries

The general rule for implementing a query in QBE† is that the system creates a tuple variable for each row entered into the table skeletons of existing relations. For the second query of Example 6.15 we would create a tuple variable t for the row (_ Oakes, , _ 999) of MEMBERS and a tuple variable s for the row (, _ Oakes, _ hotdog, _ mucho) of ORDERS. Note that no variable is created for the row of the unnamed relation in Fig. 4.16, since that relation does not exist in the database. If there are k such tuple variables we create k nested loops; each loop causes one of the variables to range over all tuples in its relation. For

---

† That is not to say that QBE must be implemented this way. Rather, the procedure to be described serves as a definition of queries in QBE.

ORDERS	ORDER _ NO	NAME	ITEM	QUANTITY
P.			Granola	$>= 5$

(a)

ORDERS	ORDER _ NO	NAME	ITEM	QUANTITY
		Robin,R	Granola	_ x
P.			Granola	$>$ _ x

(b)

Fig. 6.9. Two queries.

each assignment of values to the tuple variables (each "value" is a tuple in the corresponding relation), we check whether the domain variables of the query can be given consistent values. In the above example, we only have to check that the NAME components of s and t agree, so that we can give a consistent value to domain variable _ Oakes.

Each time we are successful in obtaining values for the domain variables, we take whatever action the query calls for. For example, if one or more rows of the query has some print commands, we print the values of the domain variables to which P. is prefixed. In Fig. 6.8, only the tuple in the unnamed relation has P. operators, so we obtain the values for the variables mentioned in that tuple and print them. If more than one row has print commands, whether or not the rows are in the same relation, we print the values for those rows in separate tables. Other actions that might be taken when we find a successful match include the insertion or deletion of a tuple into or from a relation; we shall discuss these actions later.

Entries Representing Sets

An entry in a skeleton can be made to match more than one, but less than all, the elements of some domain. A primary example is an entry θc, where θ is an arithmetic comparison and c a constant. For example, $>=3$ matches any value three or greater. We can also write θv, where v is a domain variable. For example, $<$ _ amount matches any value less than the value of _ amount. Presumably, the value of _ amount is determined by some other entry of the query, and that value changes as we allow tuple variables to range over all tuples in the implementation procedure just described.

Example 6.16: To print all orders for at least 5 pounds of granola, we may write the query of Fig. 6.9(a). The query in Fig. 6.9(b) prints all orders for more granola than Robin ordered.

The query of Fig. 6.9(b) is implemented by creating tuple variables t and s for the rows of the skeleton.† As we allow t and s to range over the various tuples in ORDERS, we check for matches. Tuple t must have NAME component "Robin,R." and ITEM component "Granola." If so, it defines a value for _x. This value happens to be 3 whenever a match occurs (ref. Fig. 3.2). We then look at the tuple s. If it has ITEM "Granola," and its QUANTITY exceeds the value of _x, we print s. $\Box$

Another way to designate a set is to use an entry that is part constant and part variable. Juxtaposition represents concatenation, so if the domain for this entry is character strings, we can try to match any constant character strings in the entry to substrings of the string that forms the corresponding component of some tuple. If we find such a match, we can assign pieces of the remainder of the string to the variables in the entry.

Example 6.17: Suppose we wish to print the names of all suppliers on River St. We could write:

SUPPLIERS	SNAME	SADDR	ITEM	PRICE
	P.	_ 999 River St.		

Whenever the address ended in "River St.," the variable _999 would take on the street number, and we would have a match. Thus, given the relation of Fig. 3.2(c), we would print

Sunshine Produce
Tasti Supply Co.

Note that QBE, unlike QUEL or SEQUEL, automatically eliminates duplicates. $\Box$

Negation of Rows

We may place the symbol $\neg$ in the first column (the column with the relation name R) of any row. Intuitively, the query then requires that any tuple matching the row not be a tuple of R. We shall try to be more precise later, but first let us consider an example.

Example 6.18: Suppose we wished to print the order or orders with the largest quantity. We could use the aggregate function MAX, to be described later, but we can also do it with a negation. Rephrase the query as: "print an order if there is no order with a larger quantity." This is expressed in QBE in Fig. 6.10. $\Box$

The implementation of queries with a negation requires that we modify the algorithm described earlier. If in Fig. 6.10 we created tuples t and s for

---

† The term *row* is used here to refer to any row except the header, which is the line containing the relation and attribute names.

ORDERS	ORDER_NO	NAME	ITEM	QUANTITY
P.				_x
¬				> _x

Fig. 6.10. Print orders such that no order has a larger quantity.

the two rows (t for the first row), and we ranged over all possible values of t and s, we would not want to print t just because we found a tuple s whose QUANTITY component was not greater than the QUANTITY of t. This would cause each tuple in ORDERS, whose QUANTITY was not the minimum, to be printed eventually. Rather, we must arrange our loops on the variables so that the variables corresponding to negated rows are the innermost loops. Then for each set of values for the tuples corresponding to unnegated rows, we check that all values of the tuple variables for negated rows fail to produce a consistent assignment of values for the domain variables in the query.

Aggregate Operators

QBE has the usual five aggregate operators, denoted SUM., AVG., MAX., MIN., and CNT. (count). There are two other operators, ALL. and UN. (unique) that often are used in conjunction with aggregate operators. ALL. applied to a domain variable produces the multiset of values that the variable takes on as we run through all the tuples in the relevant relation. Recall that a *multiset* is a set with repetitions allowed, so the ALL. operator effectively leaves duplicates in, while most other QBE operations eliminate duplicates. Thus, to compute the average balance of HVFC members we write

MEMBERS	NAME	ADDRESS	BALANCE
			P.AVG.ALL._999

The operator UN. converts a multiset into a set, by eliminating duplicates. For example, suppose we wanted to know how many suppliers there were in the HVFC database. If we (incorrectly) wrote

SUPPLIERS	SNAME	SADDR	ITEM	PRICE
	P.CNT.ALL._x			

and applied it to the relation of Fig. 3.2(c) we would get the answer 9, since variable _x takes on a multiset of nine values, one for each tuple in the relation. The correct way to pose the query is

SUPPLIERS	SNAME	SADDR	ITEM	PRICE
	P.CNT.UN.ALL._x			

In this way, before counting the set of suppliers produced by the expression ALL._x, the operator UN. removes duplicates.

Insertion and Deletion

If a row in a query has the operator I. or D. in the first column, then when implementing the query we do not create a tuple variable for this row. Rather, when a match for all the tuple variables is found, we insert (I.) or delete (D.) into or from the relation in whose skeleton one of these commands is found. Variables in the row or rows to be inserted, deleted, or updated take their values from the appropriate components of the tuple variables.

Example 6.19: If Sunshine Produce starts selling whey at 59 cents per pound, we write:

SUPPLIERS	SNAME	SADDR	ITEM	PRICE
I.	Sunshine Produce	16 River St.	Whey	.59

Notice that this query is implemented by a special case of the QBE implementation rule. Since there are no tuple variables on which to loop, we simply execute the insert operation once. The row to be inserted has no variables, so the components of the tuple to be inserted are well defined.

If we forget the address of Sunshine Produce, we can obtain it from the database at the same time we perform the insert, as follows.

SUPPLIERS	SNAME	SADDR	ITEM	PRICE
I.	Sunshine Produce	_address	Whey	.59
	Sunshine Produce	_address		

A tuple variable for the second row ranges over all tuples in SUPPLIERS. The value "16 River St." is given to variable _address whenever the tuple variable for the second row takes on a value with "Sunshine Produce" in the first component. □

Updates

The update operation can only be understood if we are aware that the QBE system allows one to define *key* and *nonkey* attributes of relations, by a mechanism to be discussed shortly. The set of key attributes must uniquely determine a tuple; that is, two tuples in a relation cannot agree on all key attributes. If we use the update (U.) operator in the first column of a row, then entries in key fields must match the tuple updated, and any tuple of the relation that does match the row of the skeleton in the key attributes will have its nonkey attributes updated to match the values in the row with U.

Example 6.20: In the SUPPLIERS relation, SNAME and ITEM are key attributes and the others are nonkey. If Sunshine Produce changes the price of Granola to $1.33 per pound, we write

SUPPLIERS	SNAME	SADDR	ITEM	PRICE
U.	Sunshine Produce		Granola	1.33

If all items supplied by Sunshine Produce are increased in price by $.10 per pound write

SUPPLIERS	SNAME	SADDR	ITEM	PRICE
U.	Sunshine Produce		_hotdog	_x+.10
	Sunshine Produce		_hotdog	_x

Note the use of an arithmetic expression in the row to be updated. The use of arithmetic is permitted where it makes sense, such as in rows to be updated or inserted, and in "condition boxes," a concept to be described next. □

Condition Boxes

There are times when we wish to include a condition on a query, insertion, deletion, or update that is not expressed by terms such as <3 in the rows of the query. We can then call for a *condition box* to be displayed and enter into the box any relationships we wish satisfied. Entries of a condition box are essentially conditions as in a language like PL/I, but without the use of the "not" operator, $\neg$. Either AND or ampersand can be used for logical "and," while OR or a vertical bar is used for "or." When the query is implemented, a match is deemed to occur only when the current values of the tuple variables allow a consistent assignment of values to the domain variables in the query, and these values also satisfy the conditions.

Example 6.21: Suppose we wish to print all those suppliers of granola that charge more than Tasti Supply Co. charges for sunflower seeds and no more than twice what Purity Foodstuffs charges for curds. The query, expressed with the aid of a condition box, is shown in Fig. 6.11. □

The Table Directory

The QBE system maintains a list, called the *table directory*, of all the relation names in the database, their attributes and certain information about the attributes. One can query, insert, or delete from this list using the same

SUPPLIERS	SNAME	SADDR	ITEM	PRICE
	P.		Granola	_p1
	Tasti Supply		Sunfl. Seeds	_p2
	Purity Foodstuffs		Curds	_p3

CONDITIONS
_p1 > _p2
_p1 ≤ _p3 * 2

Fig. 6.11. Example of a condition box.

notation as for general queries. For example, typing P. _ relname, or just P.,
in the upper left hand box of a table skeleton will cause the system to print the
current list of relation names. Typing P. _relname P. in that box will print the
relation names and their attribute names. The second P. refers to the attribute
names. To insert a new relation REL into the table directory, type I.REL I. in
the upper left box and then type the attributes of REL along the top of the
skeleton. Again, the second I. refers to the attributes, while the first I. refers
to the relation name.

The attributes may be declared to have certain properties. These properties
are:

1. KEY, telling whether or not the attribute is part of the key (recall that
    updates require the system to distinguish between key and nonkey fields).
    The values of this property are Y (key) and N (nonkey).

2. TYPE, the data type of the attribute, such as CHAR (variable length
    character string), CHAR(n) (character string of length n), FLOAT (real
    number), or FIXED (integer).

3. DOMAIN, a name for the domain of values for this attribute. If a domain
    variable in a query appears in two different columns, those columns must
    come from the same domain. The system rejects queries that violate this
    rule, a useful check on the meaningfulness of queries.

4. INVERSION, indicating whether an index on the attribute is (Y) or is not
    (N) to be created and maintained.

Example 6.22: To create the SUPPLIERS relation we might fill a table skeleton
with some of its properties, as shown in Fig. 6.12. The domain AMOUNTS
might also be used for the domain of BALANCE in MEMBERS, for example.
□

I.SUPPLIERS I.	SNAME	SADDR	ITEM	PRICE
KEY I.	Y	N	Y	N
TYPE I.	CHAR	CHAR	CHAR	FLOAT
DOMAIN I.	NAMES	ADDRS	ITEMS	AMOUNTS
INVERSION I.	N	N	N	N

Fig. 6.12. Creation of SUPPLIERS relation.

R				
	_a1	_a2	$\cdots$	_an

S				
	_b1	_b2	$\cdots$	_bn

T				
I.	_a1	_a2	$\cdots$	_an
I.	_b1	_b2	$\cdots$	_bn

Fig. 6.13. QBE command for taking unions.

Completeness of QBE

As with the other languages we have studied, it appears simplest to prove completeness by showing how to apply each of the five relational algebra operations and store the result in a new relation. For instance, to compute $T = R \cup S$ we can execute the QBE command shown in Fig. 6.13, assuming T is initially empty. The operation of set difference is achieved with an insertion command, then a deletion command; Cartesian product and projection are performed with an insertion. We leave these commands as exercises.

The knottiest problem comes when we try to compute the selection $T = \sigma_F(R)$ for an arbitrary condition F.

Conditions in condition boxes do not use the logical "not" operator. However, we can remove $\neg$'s from the selection condition F as follows. To perform the conversion, the first step is to use DeMorgan's laws:

$$\neg(F_1 \wedge F_2) = \neg F_1 \vee \neg F_2$$
$$\neg(F_1 \vee F_2) = \neg F_1 \wedge \neg F_2$$

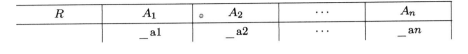

R	A_1	∘	A_2	$\cdots$	A_n
	_a1		_a2	$\cdots$	_an

CONDITIONS
F'

T				
I.	_a1	_a2	$\cdots$	_an

Fig. 6.14. Selection in QBE.

to move all negations inside $\wedge$ and $\vee$ until $\neg$ applies only to atoms. Second, any atom can be negated by changing its comparison. For example $\neg(A \neq B)$ is the same as $A = B$, and $\neg(A < B)$ is the same as $A \geq B$. Now we have only $\wedge$ and $\vee$ operators applied to atoms, and the result is a legal QBE formula.

Example 6.23: The formula $\neg(A < B \vee (C = D \wedge E \neq F))$ is first converted by moving $\neg$ inside $\vee$ and $\wedge$, as:

$$\neg(A < B) \wedge \neg(C = D \wedge E \neq F)$$
$$\neg(A < B) \wedge (\neg(C = D) \vee \neg(E \neq F))$$

The negations are applied to the atoms to yield

$$A \geq B \wedge (C \neq D \vee E = F)$$

or in the QBE notation

$$A \geq B \text{ AND } (C \neg = D \text{ OR } E = F)$$

□

Now, to compute $\sigma_F(R)$ in QBE, we have only to execute the query of Fig. 6.14, where F' is F with "not" operators eliminated as above.

Views

QBE contains a delayed evaluation feature similar to ISBL. When we wish to create a view V, we insert V into the table directly as a relation, prefixing the name V by the keyword VIEW. We then formulate in QBE the method whereby V is to be calculated. V is not actually computed at the time. Rather, it is computed whenever V is used in a subsequent query, and its value is computed then, from the current relations mentioned in the formula for V.

Example 6.24: Suppose we wish to create a view BILLS, that gives the items

I.VIEW BILLS I.	NAME	ITEM	CHARGE
I.	_ Oakes	_ hotdog	_ q*MIN.ALL. _ p

ORDERS	ORDER _ NO	NAME	ITEM	QUANTITY
		_ Oakes	_ hotdog	_ q

SUPPLIERS	SNAME	SADDR	ITEM	PRICE
			_ hotdog	_ p

Fig. 6.15. Definition of View BILLS.

ordered with the person ordering them, along with a charge for the item. The charge is computed by taking the lowest price for the item among all the suppliers of that item and multiplying the lowest price per pound by the number of pounds ordered. This view can be defined as in Fig. 6.15. We could then use it as a relation in a query such as

BILLS	NAME	ITEM	CHARGE
P.	Brooks,B.	_ hotdog	_ 999

The value of relation BILLS is computed from ORDERS and SUPPLIERS when the above query is executed. □

EXERCISES

6.1: Write the queries of Exercise 5.6 about the beer drinkers' database in (*i*) ISBL (*ii*) SQUARE (*iii*) SEQUEL (*iv*) QUEL, and (*v*) Query-by-example.

6.2: Using (*i*) SQUARE (*ii*) QUEL (*iii*) Query-by-Example write programs to perform the following operations on the beer drinkers' database.
   a) Delete from SERVES all tuples for Potgold Beer.
   b) Insert the fact that drinker Chugamug likes Potgold.
   c) Insert the fact that Chugamug likes all beers served at the Bent Elbow Bar and Grill.

6.3: Suppose that the database of Exercise 5.6 has relation SELLS(BAR, BEER, AMOUNT). Write in QUEL, queries to print the (a) sum and (b) average per bar (excluding bars that do not sell the beer) of each beer sold.

6.4: Suppose that in the database of Exercise 5.6 we want a view

   WHERE(DRINKER, BEER, BAR)

containing those tuples (d, b, r) such that drinker d likes beer b, bar r serves b, and d frequents r. Write in (a) ISBL and (b) Query-by-Example view definitions for the view WHERE.

* 6.5 Show that every select-project-join query can be written (a) in SEQUEL, using a single SELECT-FROM-WHERE statement, and (b) in QUEL, using a single retrieve-statement. *Hint*: The key to the proof is showing how every select-project-join expression can be converted to one in which we first take a Cartesian product, then do a selection, then a projection. Chapter 8 provides clues, but the reader should be able to attempt this problem now.

BIBLIOGRAPHIC NOTES

ISBL and the PRTV system are discussed in Todd [1976]. SQUARE is described in Boyce et al. [1975], while SEQUEL is described in Chamberlin et al. [1976, 1981a], and an earlier version of the language is covered in Astrahan and Chamberlin [1975]. For information about QUEL see Stonebraker, Wong, Kreps, and Held [1976], Wong and Youssefi [1976], and Zook et al. [1977]. A description of the commercially available Query-by-Example is in IBM [1978a], while the experimental version is described in Zloof [1977].

Greenblatt and Waxman [1978] compare the ease of learning QBE, SEQUEL, and relational algebra; apparently the advantage is with QBE.

Aho, Kernighan, and Weinberger [1979] describe a relational database "tool" for use with the UNIX system. The system, called AWK, combines selection and projection on a single relation with powerful regular expression based pattern matching primitives.

Several authors, such as Schmidt [1977] and Van de Reit et al. [1981], have developed extensions to ordinary programming languages that enable us to do tuple-at-a-time operations as well as the more powerful relational algebra operators.

There has also been a considerable amount of effort directed towards the use of natural language as a relational query language. Typical is the work by Dell'Orco, Spadavecchio, and King [1977], SODA (Moore [1979]), and the Rendezvous system of Codd et al. [1978] and Codd [1978]. While the problem of translating natural languages, such as English, into queries a machine can understand is always difficult, the relational model does provide a useful framework for such translation. In particular, it is possible to identify certain nouns and verbs with relations, attributes, and domain values. The fact that a relation scheme has a fixed set of attributes, known in advance, often provides valuable clues to understanding.

7

DESIGN THEORY
for
RELATIONAL DATABASES

When designing a database using the relational model, we are often faced with a choice among alternative sets of relation schemes.† Some choices are more convenient than others for various reasons. We shall study some of the desirable properties of relation schemes and consider several algorithms for obtaining a database scheme (set of relation schemes) with good properties.

Central to the design of database schemes is the idea of a *data dependency,* that is, a constraint on the possible relations that can be the current value for a relation scheme. For example, if one attribute uniquely determines another, as NAME apparently determines ADDRESS in relation MEMBERS of Example 3.1, we say there is a "functional dependency" of ADDRESS on NAME. We shall consider functional dependencies and a more complex type of dependency called "multivalued," where some attributes determine a set of values for some other attributes, but the set is not restricted to size one, as it is in the case of a functional dependency.

After studying these dependencies, we shall return to the question of picking a good set of relation schemes to represent given information. The reader should bear in mind that much mathematical preliminaries are needed to deal successfully with the difficult topic of automatic database design, so our digression to study dependencies is a lengthy one.

We then close the chapter with a discussion of more complex forms of dependencies that, while not bearing directly on the database design problem as described here, serve to unify the theory and to introduce certain subjects that become important in the next two chapters.

7.1 WHAT CONSTITUTES A BAD DATABASE DESIGN?

Before telling how to design a good database scheme, let us see why some

---

† Recall a relation scheme is the set of attributes associated with a relation name.

schemes might prove inadequate. In particular let us focus on the relation scheme

SUPPLIERS(SNAME, SADDRESS, ITEM, PRICE)

of Example 3.1. We can see several problems with this scheme.

1. *Redundancy.* The address of the supplier is repeated once for each item supplied.

2. *Potential inconsistency (update anomalies).* As a consequence of the redundancy, we could update the address for a supplier in one tuple, while leaving it fixed in another. Thus we would not have a unique address for each supplier as we feel intuitively we should.

3. *Insertion anomalies.* We cannot record an address for a supplier if that supplier does not currently supply at least one item. We might put null values in the ITEM and PRICE components of a tuple for that supplier, but then, when we enter an item for that supplier, will we remember to delete the tuple with the nulls? Worse, ITEM and SNAME form a key for the relation,† and it might be awkward or impossible to look up tuples with null values in the key.

4. *Deletion anomalies.* The inverse to problem (3) is that should we delete all the items supplied by one supplier, we unintentionally lose track of its address.

The reader should appreciate that the problems of redundancy and potential inconsistency are ones we have seen before and dealt with in other models. In the network model, virtual fields were introduced for the purpose of eliminating redundancy and inconsistency. In the hierarchical model, we used virtual record types for the same purpose.

In this example, all the above problems go away if we replace SUPPLIERS by two relation schemes

SA(SNAME, SADDRESS)
SIP(SNAME, ITEM, PRICE)

The first, SA, gives the address for each supplier exactly once; hence there is no redundancy. Moreover, we can enter an address for a supplier even if it currently supplies no items. The second relation scheme, SIP, gives the suppliers, the items they supply, and the price each supplier charges for each item.

Yet some questions remain. For example, there is a disadvantage to the above decomposition; to find the addresses of suppliers of whey, we must now

---

† Informally, a key for a relation scheme is a set of attributes such that we never expect to find two different tuples in the relation that agree on all the attributes in the key. Thus the notion of "key" for relations is quite similar to the same notion for entity sets. However, once we cover functional dependencies formally in the next section, we shall see that there are some subtle differences as well. For the time being, the analogy with entity sets is adequate.

take a join, which is expensive, while with the single relation SUPPLIERS we could simply do a selection and projection. How do we determine that the above replacement is beneficial? Are there other problems of the same four kinds present in the two new relation schemes? How do we find a good replacement for a bad relation scheme?

Dependencies and Redundancy

The balance of the chapter is devoted to answering these questions. Before proceeding though, let us emphasize the relationship between dependencies and redundancy. Recall that in generality, a dependency is simply a statement that only a subset of all possible relations are "legal," i.e., only certain relations reflect a possible state of the real world. If not all relations are possible, it stands to reason that there will be some sort of redundancy in each legal relation. That is to say, given the fact that a relation R is legal, i.e., satisfies certain dependencies, and given certain information about the value of R, we should be able to deduce other things about R.

In the case that the dependencies are functional, the form of the redundancy is obvious. When we see the first tuple in the SUPPLIERS relation of Fig. 3.2(c), we know that 16 River St. is the address of Sunshine Produce. If we know that SNAME functionally determines SADDRESS in this relation, and we see the SNAME value Sunshine Produce in the second tuple of Fig. 3.2(c), we do not have to look at the SADDRESS component of the second tuple; we know it is 16 River St. Thus, all but one of the SADDRESS components in the first three tuples (those with SNAME="Sunshine Produce") are redundant.

In the case of more general kinds of dependencies, the form redundancy takes may not be so clear. However, in all cases, it appears that the cause and cure of the redundancy go hand-in-hand. That is, the dependency, such as that of SADDRESS on SNAME, not only causes the redundancy, but it permits the decomposition of the SUPPLIERS relation into the SA and SIP relations in such a way that the original SUPPLIERS relation can be recovered from the SA and SIP relations. We shall discuss these concepts more fully in Section 7.3.

7.2 FUNCTIONAL DEPENDENCIES

This section and the next represent a digression into the necessary theory of functional dependencies. We shall return to the business at hand, the design of database schemes, in Section 7.4.

In Section 1.4 we asserted that relations could be used to model the "real world" in several ways; for example, each tuple of a relation could represent an entity and its attributes or it could represent a relationship between entities. In many cases, the known facts about the real world imply that not every finite set of tuples could be the current value of some relation, even if the tuples were of the right arity and had components chosen from the right domains. We can distinguish two kinds of restrictions on relations.

1. *Restrictions that depend on the semantics of domain elements.* These restrictions depend on understanding what components of tuples mean. For example, no one is 60 feet tall, and no one with an employment history going back 37 years has age 27. It is useful to have a DBMS check for such implausible values, which probably arose due to an error when entering or computing data. Chapter 10 covers the expression and use of this sort of "integrity constraint." Unfortunately, they tell us little or nothing about the design of database schemes.

2. *Restrictions on relations that depend only on the equality or inequality of values.* There are other constraints that do not depend on what value a tuple has in any given component, but only on whether two tuples agree in certain components. We shall discuss the most important of these constraints, called functional dependencies, in this section, but there are other types of value-oblivious constraints that will be touched on in later sections. It is value-oblivious constraints that turn out to have the greatest impact on the design of database schemes.

Let $R(A_1, A_2, \ldots, A_n)$ be a relation scheme, and let X and Y be subsets of $\{ A_1, A_2, \ldots, A_n \}$. We say $X \rightarrow Y$, read "X functionally determines Y" or "Y functionally depends on X" if whatever relation r is the current value for R, it is not possible that r has two tuples that agree in the components for all attributes in the set X yet disagree in one or more components for attributes in the set Y.

Functional dependencies arise naturally in many ways. For example, if R represents an entity set whose attributes are $A_1, \ldots, A_n$, and X is a set of attributes that forms a key for the entity set, then we may assert $X \rightarrow Y$ for any subset Y of the attributes. This follows because the tuples of each possible relation r represent entities, and entities are identified by the value of attributes in the key. Therefore, two tuples that agreed on the attributes in X would have to represent the same entity and thus be the same tuple. Similarly, if R represents a many-one mapping from entity set E_1 to entity set E_2, and among the A_i's are attributes that form a key X for E_1 and a key Y for E_2, then $X \rightarrow Y$ would hold, and in fact, X functionally determines any set of attributes of R. However, $Y \rightarrow X$ would not hold unless the mapping were one-to-one.

It should be emphasized that functional dependencies are statements about all possible relations that could be the value of relation scheme R. We cannot look at a particular relation r for scheme R and deduce what functional dependencies hold for R. For example, if r is the empty set, then all dependencies appear to hold, but they might not hold in general, as the value of the relation denoted by R changes. We might, however, be able to look at a particular relation for R and discover some dependencies that did not hold.

The only way to determine the functional dependencies that hold for relation scheme R is to consider carefully what the attributes mean. In this sense, dependencies are actually assertions about the real world; they cannot be proved, but we might expect them to be enforced by a DBMS if told to do so by the database designer. Many existing systems will enforce those functional dependencies that follow from the fact that a key determines the other attributes of a relation, and some will even enforce arbitrary functional dependencies.

There could even be a more efficient implementation of the relation possible because the functional dependency is asserted to hold. However, there is a price to pay, in that the storage of certain information becomes impossible. For example, if we declare that NAME functionally determines ADDRESS, then under no circumstances can we store two addresses for one person in our database.

Example 7.1: Let us consider the functional dependencies that we expect to hold in the HVFC database of Example 3.1. We might suppose that each member has a unique address and a unique balance, and the co-op will never have two members with the same name. (Perhaps it would use a nickname if the need arose.) If we make these assumptions, then we can assert

NAME → ADDRESS BALANCE

Note that it is customary to use concatenation of attribute names to denote sets of attributes, so $A_1 A_2 \cdots A_n$ is shorthand for $\{ A_1, A_2, \ldots, A_n \}$. We also use concatention of sets of attributes in place of union, so XY stands for $X \cup Y$, if X and Y are sets of attributes.

In the ORDERS relation, ORDER_NO determines everything, since we expect that no two orders will have the same number. That is,

ORDER_NO → NAME ITEM QUANTITY

In relation SUPPLIERS, we observe the following dependencies.

SNAME → SADDRESS
SNAME ITEM → PRICE

One might wonder whether a dependency like SADDRESS → SNAME or ADDRESS → NAME is valid. By looking at Fig. 3.2 we might suspect they were valid. However, in principle, there is nothing stopping HVFC from enrolling two members with the same address, or stopping two suppliers from having the same address. Thus we do not assert these dependencies. There are other trivial dependencies that do hold, such as

NAME → NAME or
NAME ITEM → ITEM

The first of these says that any two tuples that agree in the NAME component agree in the NAME component, a fact we could hardly argue with. The second says that if two tuples agree in both the NAME and ITEM components, then they agree in the ITEM component, which is another transparent observation. There are also some nontrivial dependencies that follow from those we have already asserted, such as

SNAME ITEM → SADDRESS PRICE

This dependency says that two tuples that agree in SNAME and ITEM agree in both SADDRESS and PRICE. We know they agree in SADDRESS because the SNAME component alone determines the address, while we also stated above that the name of the supplier and the item together determine a price. $\square$

Logical Implications of Dependencies

Suppose R is a relation scheme and A, B, and C are some of its attributes. Suppose also that the functional dependencies $A \to B$ and $B \to C$ are known to hold in R. We claim that $A \to C$ must also hold in R. In proof, suppose r is a relation that satisfies $A \to B$ and $B \to C$, but there are two tuples t and u in r such that t and u agree in the component for A but disagree in C. Then we must ask whether t and u agree on attribute B. If not, then r would violate $A \to B$. If they do agree on B, then since they disagree on C, r would violate $B \to C$. Hence r must satisfy $A \to C$.

In general, let F be a set of functional dependencies for relation scheme R, and let $X \to Y$ be a functional dependency. We say F *logically implies* $X \to Y$, written $F \models X \to Y$, if every relation r for R that satisfies the dependencies in F also satisfies $X \to Y$. We saw above that if F contains $A \to B$ and $B \to C$, then $A \to C$ is logically implied by F. That is, $\{A \to B, B \to C\} \models A \to C$. Let F^+, the *closure* of F, be the set of functional dependencies that are logically implied by F, i.e., $F^+ = \{X \to Y \mid F \models X \to Y\}$.

Example 7.2: Let $R = ABC$ and $F = \{A \to B, B \to C\}$. Then F^+ consists of all those dependencies $X \to Y$ such that either
1. X contains A, e.g., $ABC \to AB$, $AB \to BC$, or $A \to C$,
2. X contains B but not A, and Y does not contain A, e.g., $BC \to B$, $B \to C$, or $B \to \emptyset$, and
3. $X \to Y$ is one of the two dependencies $C \to C$ or $C \to \emptyset$.

We shall discuss how to prove the above contention shortly. $\square$

Keys

When talking about entity sets we assumed that there was a key, a set of attributes that uniquely determined an entity. There is an analogous concept for relations with functional dependencies. If R is a relation scheme with attributes $A_1 A_2 \cdots A_n$ and functional dependencies F, and X is a subset of $A_1 A_2 \cdots A_n$, we say X is a *key* of R if:

1. $X \to A_1 A_2 \cdots A_n$ is in F^+, that is, the dependency of all attributes on the set of attributes X is given or follows logically from what is given, and
2. for no proper subset $Y \subseteq X$ is $Y \to A_1 A_2 \cdots A_n$ in F^+.

We should observe that minimality, condition (2) above, was not present when we talked of keys for entity sets in Chapter 1 or keys for files in Chapter 2. The reason is that without a formalism like functional dependencies, we could not verify that a given set of attributes was minimal. The reader should be aware that in this chapter the term "key" does imply minimality. Thus, the given key for an entity set will only be a key for the relation representing that entity set if the given key was minimal. Otherwise, one or more subsets of the key for the entity set will serve as a key for the relation.

As there may be more than one key for a relation, we sometimes designate one as the "primary key." The primary key might serve as the file key when the relation is implemented, for example. However, any key could be the primary key if we desired. The term *candidate key* is sometimes used in the literature to denote any minimal set of attributes that functionally determine all attributes, with the term "key" reserved for one designated candidate key. We also use the term *superkey* for any superset of a key. Remember that therefore a key is a special case of a superkey.

Example 7.3: For relation R and set of dependencies F of Example 7.2 there is only one key, A, since $A \to ABC$ is in F^+, but no X not containing A functionally determines ABC.

A more interesting example is the relation scheme R(CITY, ST, ZIP), where ST stands for street address and ZIP for zip code. We expect tuple (c, s, z) in a relation for R only if city c has a building with street address s, and z is the zip code for that address in that city. It is assumed that the nontrivial functional dependencies are:

$$\text{CITY ST} \to \text{ZIP}$$
$$\text{ZIP} \to \text{CITY}$$

That is, the address (city and street) determines the zip code, and the zip code determines the city, although not the street address. One can easily check that { CITY, ST } and { ST, ZIP } are both keys. $\square$

Axioms for Functional Dependencies

To determine keys, and to understand logical implications among functional dependencies in general, we need to compute F^+ from F, or at least, to tell, given F and functional dependency $X \to Y$, whether $X \to Y$ is in F^+. To do so requires that we have inference rules telling how one or more dependencies imply other dependencies. In fact, we can do more; we can provide a *complete* set of inference rules, meaning that given set of dependencies F, the rules allow us to deduce all the dependencies in F^+. Moreover, the rules are *sound*, meaning that using them, we cannot deduce from F any dependency that is not in F^+.

The set of rules is often called *Armstrong's axioms,* from Armstrong [1974], although the particular rules we shall present differ from Armstrong's. In what follows we assume we are given a relation scheme with set of attributes U, the *universal set* of attributes, and a set of functional dependencies F involving only attributes in U. The inference rules are:

A1: *(reflexivity).* If $Y \subseteq X \subseteq U$, then $X \to Y$ is logically implied by F. Note that this rule gives the *trivial dependencies,* those that have a right side contained in the left side, and the use of this rule depends only on U, not on F.

A2: *(augmentation).* If $X \to Y$ holds, and $Z \subseteq U$, then $XZ \to YZ$. Recall that X, Y, and Z are sets of attributes, and XZ is conventional shorthand for $X \cup Z$. It is also important to remember that the given dependency $X \to Y$ might be in F, or it might have been derived from dependencies in F using the axioms we are in the process of describing.

A3: *(transitivity)* If $X \to Y$ and $Y \to Z$ hold, then $X \to Z$ holds.

Example 7.4: Let us reconsider the situation of Example 7.3, where we claimed that ST, ZIP was a key; that is:

> ST ZIP → CITY ST ZIP

In proof we can state the following.
1. ZIP → CITY (given)
2. ST ZIP → CITY ST (augmentation of (1) by ST)
3. CITY ST → ZIP (given)
4. CITY ST → CITY ST ZIP (augmentation of (3) by CITY ST)
5. ST ZIP → CITY ST ZIP (transitivity with (2) and (4))
□

It is relatively easy to prove that Armstrong's axioms are sound; that is, they lead only to true conclusions. It is rather more difficult to prove completeness, that they can be used to make every valid inference about dependencies. We shall tackle the soundness issue first.

Lemma 7.1: Armstrong's axioms are sound. That is, if $X \to Y$ is deduced from F using the axioms, then $X \to Y$ is true in any relation in which the dependencies of F are true.

Proof: A1, the reflexivity axiom, is clearly sound. We cannot have a relation r with two tuples that agree on X yet disagree on some subset of X. To prove A2, augmentation, suppose we have a relation r that satisfies $X \to Y$, yet there are two tuples t and u that agree on the attributes of XZ but disagree on YZ. Since they cannot disagree on any attribute of Z, t and u must disagree on some attribute in Y. But then t and u agree on X but disagree on Y, violating our assumption that $X \to Y$ holds for r. The soundness of A3, the transitivity axiom, is a simple extension of the argument given previously that $A{\to}B$ and $B{\to}C$ imply $A{\to}C$. We leave this part of the proof as an exercise. $\square$

There are several other inference rules that follow from Armstrong's axioms. We state three of them in the next lemma. Since we have proved the soundness of A1, A2, and A3, we are entitled to use them in the proof that follows.

Lemma 7.2:
a) *The union rule.* $\{X{\to}Y, X{\to}Z\} \models X{\to}YZ$.
b) *The pseudotransitivity rule.* $\{X{\to}Y, WY{\to}Z\} \models XW{\to}Z$.
c) *The decomposition rule.* If $X{\to}Y$ holds, and $Z \subseteq Y$, then $X{\to}Z$ holds.

Proof:
a) We are given $X{\to}Y$, so we may augment by X to infer $X{\to}XY$. We are also given $X{\to}Z$, so we may augment by Y to get $XY{\to}YZ$. By transitivity, $X{\to}XY$ and $XY{\to}YZ$ imply $X{\to}YZ$.
b) Given $X{\to}Y$, we may augment by W to get $WX{\to}WY$. Since we are given $WY{\to}Z$, transitivity tells us $WX{\to}Z$.
c) The decomposition rule follows easily from A1 and A3. $\square$

An important consequence of the union and decomposition rules is that if $A_1, \ldots, A_n$ are attributes, then $X{\to}A_1, \ldots, A_n$ holds if and only if $X{\to}A_i$ holds for each i. Thus, singleton right sides on functional dependencies are sufficient. We shall discuss this matter in more detail when we take up the subject of "covers" for sets of functional dependencies.

Before tackling the completeness issue, it is important to define the closure of a set of attributes with respect to a set of functional dependencies. Let F be a set of functional dependencies on set of attributes U, and let X be a subset of U. Then X^+, the *closure* of X (with respect to F) is the set of attributes A such that $X{\to}A$ can be deduced from F by Armstrong's axioms. The central fact about the closure of a set of attributes is that it enables us to tell at a glance whether a dependency $X{\to}Y$ follows from F by Armstrong's axioms. The next lemma tells how.

Lemma 7.3: $X{\to}Y$ follows from Armstrong's axioms if and only if $Y \subseteq X^+$.

Proof: Let $Y = A_1 \cdots A_n$ for attributes $A_1, \ldots, A_n$, and suppose $Y \subseteq X^+$. By definition of X^+, $X{\to}A_i$ is implied by Armstrong's axioms for all i. By the union rule, Lemma 7.2(a), $X{\to}Y$ follows. Conversely, suppose $X{\to}Y$ follows from the axioms. For each i, $X{\to}A_i$ holds by the decomposition rule, so $Y \subseteq X^+$. $\square$

We are now ready to prove that Armstrong's axioms are complete. We do so by showing that if F is the given set of dependencies, and $X{\to}Y$ cannot be proved by Armstrong's axioms, then there must be a relation in which the dependencies of F all hold but $X{\to}Y$ does not; that is, F does not logically imply $X{\to}Y$.

Theorem 7.1: Armstrong's axioms are sound and complete.

Attributes of X^+				Other attributes			
1	1	$\cdots$	1	1	1	$\cdots$	1
1	1	$\cdots$	1	0	0	$\cdots$	0

Fig. 7.1. A relation r showing F does not logically imply $X{\to}Y$.

Proof: Soundness is Lemma 7.1, so we have to prove completeness. Let F be a set of dependencies over attribute set U, and suppose $X{\to}Y$ cannot be inferred from the axioms. Consider the relation r with two tuples shown in Fig. 7.1. First we show that all dependencies in F are satisfied by r. Suppose $V{\to}W$ is in F but is not satisfied by r. Then $V \subseteq X^+$, or else the two tuples of r disagree on some attribute of V, and therefore could not violate $V{\to}W$. Also, W cannot be a subset of X^+, or $V{\to}W$ would be satisfied by the relation r. Let A be an attribute of W not in X^+. Since $V \subseteq X^+$, $X{\to}V$ follows from the axioms by Lemma 7.3. Dependency $V{\to}W$ is in F, so by transitivity we have $X{\to}W$. By reflexivity, $W{\to}A$, so by transitivity again, $X{\to}A$ follows from the axioms. But then, by definition of the closure, A is in X^+, which we assumed not to be the case. We conclude by contradiction that each $V{\to}W$ in F is satisfied by r.

Now we must show that $X{\to}Y$ is not satisfied by r. Suppose it is satisfied. As $X \subseteq X^+$ is obvious, it follows that $Y \subseteq X^+$, else the two tuples of r agree on X but disagree on Y. But then Lemma 7.3 tells us that $X{\to}Y$ can be inferred from the axioms, a contradiction. Therefore, $X{\to}Y$ is not satisfied by r, even though each dependency in F is. We conclude that whenever $X{\to}Y$ does not follow from F by Armstrong's axioms, F does not logically imply $X{\to}Y$. That is, the axioms are complete. $\square$

Theorem 7.1 has some interesting consequences. We defined X^+ to be the set of attributes A such that $X{\to}A$ followed from the given dependencies F using the axioms. We now see that an equivalent definition of X^+ is the set of A such that $F \models X{\to}A$. Another consequence is that although we defined F^+ to be the set of dependencies that were logically implied by F, we could as well have defined F^+ to be the set of dependencies that follow from F by Armstrong's axioms.

Computing Closures

It turns out that computing F^+ for a set of dependencies F is a time-consuming task in general, simply because the set of dependencies in F^+ can be large even if F itself is small. Consider the set $F = \{ A{\to}B_1, A{\to}B_2, \ldots, A{\to}B_n \}$. Then F^+ includes all the dependencies $A{\to}Y$, where Y is a subset of $\{ B_1, B_2, \ldots, B_n \}$. As there are 2^n such sets Y, we could not expect to list F^+ conveniently, even for reasonably sized n.

At the other extreme, computing X^+, for a set of attributes X, is not hard; it takes time proportional to the length of all the dependencies in F, written out. By Lemma 7.3, telling whether $X \rightarrow Y$ is in F^+ is no harder than computing X^+. A simple way to compute X^+ is the following.

Algorithm 7.1: Computation of the Closure of a Set of Attributes with Respect to a Set of Functional Dependencies.

Input: A finite set of attributes U, a set of functional dependencies F on U, and a set $X \subseteq U$.

Output: X^+, the closure of X with respect to F.

Method: We compute a sequence of sets of attributes $X^{(0)}$, $X^{(1)}, \ldots$ by the rules:

1. $X^{(0)}$ is X.
2. $X^{(i+1)}$ is $X^{(i)}$ plus the set of attributes A such that there is some dependency $Y \rightarrow Z$, in F, A is in Z, and $Y \subseteq X^{(i)}$. Since $X = X^{(0)} \subseteq \cdots \subseteq X^{(i)} \subseteq \cdots \subseteq U$, and U is finite, we must eventually reach i such that $X^{(i)} = X^{(i+1)}$. It then follows that $X^{(i)} = X^{(i+1)} = X^{(i+2)} = \cdots$. There is no need to compute beyond $X^{(i)}$ once we discover $X^{(i)} = X^{(i+1)}$. We can (and shall) prove that X^+ is $X^{(i)}$ for this value of i. $\square$

Example 7.5: Let F consist of the following eight dependencies:

$$
\begin{array}{ll}
AB \rightarrow C & D \rightarrow EG \\
C \rightarrow A & BE \rightarrow C \\
BC \rightarrow D & CG \rightarrow BD \\
ACD \rightarrow B & CE \rightarrow AG
\end{array}
$$

and let $X = BD$. To apply Algorithm 7.1, we let $X^{(0)} = BD$. To compute $X^{(1)}$ we look for dependencies that have a left side $B, D,$ or BD. There is only one, $D \rightarrow EG$, so we adjoin E and G to $X^{(0)}$ and make $X^{(1)} = BDEG$. For $X^{(2)}$, we look for left sides contained in $X^{(1)}$ and find $D \rightarrow EG$ and $BE \rightarrow C$. Thus $X^{(2)} = BCDEG$. Then, for $X^{(3)}$ we look for left sides contained in $BCDEG$ and find, in addition to the two previously found, $C \rightarrow A$, $BC \rightarrow D$, $CG \rightarrow BD$, and $CE \rightarrow AG$. Thus $X^{(3)} = ABCDEG$, the set of all attributes. It therefore comes as no surprise that $X^{(3)} = X^{(4)} = \cdots$. Thus $(BD)^+ = ABCDEG$. $\square$

Algorithm 7.1 can be implemented to run in time proportional to the sum of the lengths of the dependencies if we keep, for each dependency $Y \rightarrow Z$, a count of the number of attributes in Y that are not yet in $X^{(i)}$. We must also create a list, for each attribute A, of the dependencies on whose left side A appears. When A is adjoined to some $X^{(i)}$, we decrement by one the count for each dependency on A's list. When the count for $Y \rightarrow Z$ becomes 0, we know $Y \subseteq X^{(i)}$. Lastly, we must maintain $X^{(i)}$ as a Boolean array, indexed by attribute numbers, so when we discover $Y \subseteq X^{(i)}$, where $Y \rightarrow Z$ is a dependency, we can tell in time proportional to the size of Z those attributes in Z that need to be adjoined to $X^{(i)}$. When computing $X^{(i+1)}$ from $X^{(i)}$ we have only to set to true the cells of the array corresponding to attributes added to $X^{(i)}$; there is no need to copy $X^{(i)}$. The details of this modification to Algorithm 7.1 are found in Bernstein [1976], although Algorithm 7.1 itself is probably efficient enough for most purposes.

Now we must address ourselves to the problem of proving that Algorithm 7.1 is correct. It is easy to prove that every attribute placed in some $X^{(j)}$ belongs in X^+, but harder to show that every attribute in X^+ is placed in some $X^{(j)}$.

Theorem 7.2: Algorithm 7.1 correctly computes X^+.

Proof: First we show by induction on j that if A is placed in $X^{(j)}$, then A is in X^+.

Basis: $j = 0$. Then A is in X, so by reflexivity, $X \rightarrow A$.

Induction: Let $j > 0$ and assume that $X^{(j-1)}$ consists only of attributes in X^+. Suppose A is placed in $X^{(j)}$ because A is in Z, $Y \rightarrow Z$ is in F, and $Y \subseteq X^{(j-1)}$. Since $Y \subseteq X^{(j-1)}$, we know $Y \subseteq X^+$ by the inductive hypothesis. Thus $X \rightarrow Y$ by Lemma 7.3. By transitivity, $X \rightarrow Y$ and $Y \rightarrow Z$ imply $X \rightarrow Z$. By reflexivity, $Z \rightarrow A$, so $X \rightarrow A$ by transitivity. Thus A is in X^+.

Now we show the converse, that if A is in X^+, then A is in some $X^{(j)}$. It does not matter whether or not Algorithm 7.1 ends before computing $X^{(j)}$, because if it stops when $X^{(i)} = X^{(i+1)}$, for some $i < j$, we know that $X^{(i)} = X^{(j)}$. Therefore the value returned for X^+, which is $X^{(i)}$, includes A. What we actually show is that if there is a proof by Armstrong's axioms that $F \models X \rightarrow Y$, then every attribute of Y is placed in some $X^{(j)}$. The proof is by induction on the number of lines in the proof, where a *line* is a dependency that is either in F, follows from reflexivity or follows from a previous line or lines by augmentation or transitivity; the last line is $X \rightarrow Y$.

Before proceeding to the induction, let us remark on an inference we make repeatedly.

Observation (∗) If X_1 and X_2 are two sets of attributes, and $X_1 \subseteq X_2$, then for all j, $X_1^{(j)} \subseteq X_2^{(j)}$

Informally, when we start Algorithm 7.1 with more attributes, we don't wind up with fewer. A formal proof of (∗) by induction on j is easy and left as an exercise. Now we prove by induction on p, the number of lines in a proof of $X \rightarrow Y$ from F, that Y is a subset of some $X^{(j)}$.

Basis: One line. Then $X \rightarrow Y$ either follows by reflexivity, in which case $Y \subseteq X^{(0)}$, or $X \rightarrow Y$ is in F, in which case each attribute of Y is certainly in $X^{(1)}$.

Induction: Suppose the claim is true for proofs of fewer than p lines, and $X \rightarrow Y$ has a p line proof. If $X \rightarrow Y$ is in F, or follows by reflexivity, then we may argue as in the basis. If $X \rightarrow Y$ follows by transitivity from two previous lines of the proof, say $X \rightarrow Z$ and $Z \rightarrow Y$, then both these dependencies have proofs of fewer than p lines. By the inductive hypothesis there is some $X^{(j)}$ that includes all the attributes of Z, so $Z \subseteq X^{(j)}$. Now consider running Algorithm 7.1 with Z in place of X. By the inductive hypothesis there is some k such that $Z^{(k)}$ contains all the attributes of Y. By observation (*), with $X^{(j)}$ in place of X_2 and Z for X_1, we know that $X^{(j+k)}$ contains all the attributes in Y.

The last case to consider is where $X \rightarrow Y$ follows by augmenting some previous line $V \rightarrow W$ by set of attributes Z. Then $VZ = X$ and $WZ = Y$. We know $V \rightarrow W$ has a proof of fewer than p lines, so by the inductive hypothesis, if we run Algorithm 7.1 starting with V, there is some j such that $W \subseteq V^{(j)}$. By (*), if we run Algorithm 7.1 starting with $X = VZ$, then $W \subseteq X^{(j)}$. Since $Z \subseteq X$, surely $Z \subseteq X^{(j)}$, so WZ, which is Y, is a subset of $X^{(j)}$. This completes the induction.

By Lemma 7.3, if A is in X^+, then $X \rightarrow A$ has a proof from F using the axioms. Therefore, by the above induction, A is in some $X^{(j)}$, and hence A is in the set returned by Algorithm 7.1 as the value of X^+. Hence the algorithm returns neither too much nor too little; it returns exactly X^+. $\square$

Covers of Sets of Dependencies.

Let F and G be sets of dependencies. We say F and G are *equivalent* if $F^+ = G^+$. If F and G are equivalent we sometimes say F *covers* G (and G covers F). It is easy to test whether F and G are equivalent. For each dependency $Y \rightarrow Z$ in F, test whether $Y \rightarrow Z$ is in G^+ using Algorithm 7.1 to compute Y^+ and then checking whether $Z \subseteq Y^+$. If some dependency $Y \rightarrow Z$ in F is not in G^+, then surely $F^+ \neq G^+$. If every dependency in F is in G^+, then every dependency $V \rightarrow W$ in F^+ is in G^+, because a proof that $V \rightarrow W$ is in G^+ can be formed by taking a proof that each $Y \rightarrow Z$ in F is in G^+, and following it by a proof from F that $V \rightarrow W$ is in F^+. To test whether each dependency in G is also in F^+, we proceed in an analogous manner. Then F and G are equivalent if and only if every dependency in F is in G^+, and every dependency in G is in F^+.

A useful fact about equivalence is stated in the next lemma.

Lemma 7.4: Every set of functional dependencies F is covered by a set of dependencies G in which no right side has more than one attribute.

Proof: Let G be the set of dependencies $X \rightarrow A$ such that for some $X \rightarrow Y$ in F, A is in Y. Then $X \rightarrow A$ follows from $X \rightarrow Y$ by the decomposition rule. Thus $G \subseteq F^+$. But $F \subseteq G^+$, since if $Y = A_1 \cdots A_n$, then $X \rightarrow Y$ follows from $X \rightarrow A_1, \ldots, X \rightarrow A_n$ using the union rule. $\square$

It turns out to be useful, when we develop a design theory for database schemes, to consider a stronger restriction on covers than that the right sides have but one attribute. We say a set of dependencies F is *minimal* if:

1. Every right side of a dependency in F is a single attribute.
2. For no $X \rightarrow A$ in F is the set $F - \{X \rightarrow A\}$ equivalent to F.

3.   For no $X{\rightarrow}A$ in F and proper subset Z of X is $F - \{\,X{\rightarrow}A\,\} \cup \{\,Z{\rightarrow}A\,\}$ equivalent to F.

Intuitively, (2) guarantees that no dependency in F is redundant, and (3) guarantees that no attribute on any left side is redundant. As each right side has only one attribute by (1), surely no attribute on the right is redundant.

Theorem 7.3: Every set of dependencies F is equivalent to a set F' that is minimal.

Proof: By Lemma 7.4, assume no right side in F has more than one attribute. To satisfy condition (2), consider each dependency $X{\rightarrow}Y$ in F, in some order, and if $F - \{\,X{\rightarrow}Y\,\}$ is equivalent to F, then delete $X{\rightarrow}Y$ from F. Note that considering dependencies in different orders may result in the elimination of different sets of dependencies. For example, given the set F:

$$A{\rightarrow}B \qquad A{\rightarrow}C$$
$$B{\rightarrow}A \qquad C{\rightarrow}A$$
$$B{\rightarrow}C$$

we can eliminate both $B{\rightarrow}A$ and $A{\rightarrow}C$, or we can eliminate $B{\rightarrow}C$, but we cannot eliminate all three.

Having satisfied (2), we proceed to satisfy (3) by considering each dependency remaining in F, and each attribute in its left side, in some order. If we can eliminate an attribute from a left side and still have an equivalent set of attributes, we do so, until no more attributes can be eliminated from any left side. Again, the order in which attributes are eliminated may affect the result. For example, given

$$AB{\rightarrow}C$$
$$A{\rightarrow}B$$
$$B{\rightarrow}A$$

we can eliminate either A or B from $AB{\rightarrow}C$, but we cannot eliminate them both. $\square$

Example 7.6: Let us consider the dependency set F of Example 7.5. If we use the algorithm of Lemma 7.4 to split right sides we are left with:

$$AB{\rightarrow}C \qquad BE{\rightarrow}C$$
$$C{\rightarrow}A \qquad CG{\rightarrow}B$$
$$BC{\rightarrow}D \qquad CG{\rightarrow}D$$
$$ACD{\rightarrow}B \qquad CE{\rightarrow}A$$
$$D{\rightarrow}E \qquad CE{\rightarrow}G$$
$$D{\rightarrow}G$$

Clearly $CE{\rightarrow}A$ is redundant, since it is implied by $C{\rightarrow}A$. $CG{\rightarrow}B$ is redundant, since $CG{\rightarrow}D$, $C{\rightarrow}A$, and $ACD{\rightarrow}B$ imply $CG{\rightarrow}B$, as can be checked by computing $(CG)^+$. Then no more dependencies are redundant. However,

$$
\begin{array}{cc}
AB \rightarrow C & AB \rightarrow C \\
C \rightarrow A & C \rightarrow A \\
BC \rightarrow D & BC \rightarrow D \\
CD \rightarrow B & D \rightarrow E \\
D \rightarrow E & D \rightarrow G \\
D \rightarrow G & BE \rightarrow C \\
BE \rightarrow C & CG \rightarrow B \\
CG \rightarrow D & CE \rightarrow G \\
CE \rightarrow G &
\end{array}
$$

(a)   (b)

Fig. 7.2. Two minimal covers.

$ACD \rightarrow B$ can be replaced by $CD \rightarrow B$, since $C \rightarrow A$ is given. Thus one minimal cover for F is shown in Fig. 7.2(a). Another minimal cover, constructed from F by eliminating $CE \rightarrow A$, $CG \rightarrow D$, and $ACD \rightarrow B$, is shown in Fig. 7.2(b). Note that the two minimal covers have different numbers of dependencies. □

7.3 DECOMPOSITION OF RELATION SCHEMES

The *decomposition* of a relation scheme $R = \{ A_1, A_2, \ldots, A_n \}$ is its replacement by a collection $\rho = \{ R_1, R_2, \ldots, R_k \}$ of subsets of R such that

$$R = R_1 \cup R_2 \cup \cdots \cup R_k$$

There is no requirement that the R_i's be disjoint. One of the motivations for performing a decomposition is that it may eliminate some of the problems mentioned in Section 7.1. In general, it is the responsibility of the person designing a database (the "database administrator") to decompose an initial set of relation schemes when warranted.

Example 7.7: Let us reconsider the SUPPLIERS relation scheme introduced in Example 3.1, but as a shorthand, let the attributes be S (SNAME), A (SADDRESS), I (ITEM), and P (PRICE). The functional dependencies we shall assume are $S \rightarrow A$ and $SI \rightarrow P$. We mentioned in Section 7.1 that replacement of the relation scheme $SAIP$ by the two schemes SA and SIP makes certain problems go away. For example, in $SAIP$ we cannot store the address of a supplier unless the supplier provides at least one item. In SA, there does not have to be an item supplied to record an address for the supplier. □

One might question whether all is as rosey as it looks, when we replace $SAIP$ by SA and SIP in Example 7.7. For example, suppose we have a relation r as the current value of $SAIP$. If the database uses SA and SIP instead of $SAIP$, we would naturally expect the current relation for these two relation schemes to be the projection of r onto SA and SIP, that is $r_{SA} = \pi_{SA}(r)$

and $r_{SIP} = \pi_{SIP}(r)$. How do we know that r_{SA} and r_{SIP} contain the same information as r? One way to tell is to check that r can be computed knowing only r_{SA} and r_{SIP}. We claim that the only way to recover r is by taking the natural join of r_{SA} and r_{SIP}.† The reason is that, as we shall prove in the next lemma, if we let $s = r_{SA} \bowtie r_{SIP}$, then $\pi_{SA}(s) = r_{SA}$, and $\pi_{SIP}(s) = r_{SIP}$. If $s \neq r$, then given r_{SA} and r_{SIP} there is no way to tell whether r or s was the original relation for scheme $SAIP$. That is, if the natural join doesn't recover the original relation, then there is no way whatsoever to recover it uniquely.

Lossless Joins

If R is a relation scheme decomposed into schemes $R_1, R_2, \ldots, R_k$, and D is a set of dependencies, we say the decomposition is a *lossless join decomposition* (with respect to D) if for every relation r for R satisfying D:

$$r = \pi_{R_1}(r) \bowtie \pi_{R_2}(r) \bowtie \cdots \bowtie \pi_{R_k}(r)$$

that is, r is the natural join of its projections onto the R_i's. From our remarks above, it is apparent that the lossless join property is a desirable condition for a decomposition to satisfy, so we shall study the subject of lossless joins in some detail.

Some basic facts about project-join mappings follow in Lemma 7.5. First we introduce some notation. If $\rho = (R_1, R_2, \ldots, R_k)$, then m_ρ is the mapping defined by $m_\rho(r) = \bowtie_{i=1}^{k} \pi_{R_i}(r)$. That is, $m_\rho(r)$ is the join of the projections of r onto the relation schemes in ρ. Thus the lossless join condition with respect to a set of dependencies D can be expressed as: for all r satisfying D, $r = m_\rho(r)$. As another useful notational convention, if t is a tuple, we define $t[X]$, where X is a set of attributes, to be the components of t for the attributes of X.‡ For example, we could express $\pi_X(r)$ as $\{ t[X] \mid t \text{ is in } r \}$.

Lemma 7.5: Let R be a relation scheme, $\rho = (R_1, \ldots, R_k)$ a decomposition of R, r a relation for R, and $r_i = \pi_{R_i}(r)$. Then

a) $r \subseteq m_\rho(r)$.

b)   If $s = m_\rho(r)$, then $\pi_{R_i}(s) = r_i$.

c) $m_\rho(m_\rho(r)) = m_\rho(r)$.

Proof:

a)   Let t be in r. Then for each i, $t_i = t[R_i]$ is in r_i. By definition of the natural join, t is in $m_\rho(r)$, since t agrees with t_i on the attributes of R_i for all i.

b)   As $r \subseteq s$ by (a), it follows that $\pi_{R_i}(r) \subseteq \pi_{R_i}(s)$. That is, $r_i \subseteq \pi_{R_i}(s)$. To

---

† Recall Section 5.2 for a definition of the natural join.

‡ Recall that t is a mapping from attributes to values, so $t[X]$ is that mapping restricted to domain X. In practice, we always pick some ordering for the attributes and show tuples, or restricted tuples such as $t[X]$, as lists of values.

show $\pi_{R_i}(s) \subseteq r_i$, suppose for some particular i that t_i is in $\pi_{R_i}(s)$. Then there is some tuple t in s such that $t[R_i] = t_i$. As t is in s, there is some u_j in r_j for each j such that $t[R_j] = u_j$. Thus, in particular, $t[R_i]$ is in r_i. But $t[R_i] = t_i$, so t_i is in r_i, and therefore $\pi_{R_i}(s) \subseteq r_i$. We conclude that $r_i = \pi_{R_i}(s)$.

c) If $s = m_\rho(r)$, then by (b), $\pi_{R_i}(s) = r_i$. Thus $m_\rho(s) = \bowtie_{i=1}^{k} r_i = m_\rho(r)$.
$\square$

Let us observe that if for each i, r_i is some relation for R_i, and

$$s = \bowtie_{i=1}^{k} r_i$$

then $\pi_{R_i}(s)$ is not necessarily equal to r_i. The reason is that r_i may contain "dangling" tuples that do not match with anything when we take the join. For example, if $R_1 = AB$, $R_2 = BC$, $r_1 = \{a_1 b_1\}$, and $r_2 = \{b_1 c_1, b_2 c_2\}$, then $s = \{a_1 b_1 c_1\}$ and $\pi_{BC}(s) = \{b_1 c_1\} \neq r_2$. However, in general, $\pi_{R_i}(s) \subseteq r_i$, and if the r_i's are each the projection of some one relation r, then $\pi_{R_i}(s) = r_i$.

The ability to store "dangling" tuples is an advantage of decomposition. As we mentioned previously, this advantage must be balanced against the need to compute more joins when we answer queries, if relation schemes are decomposed, than if they are not. When all things are considered, it is generally believed that decomposition is desirable when necessary to cure the problems, such as redundancy, described in Section 7.1, but not otherwise.

Testing Lossless Joins

It turns out to be fairly easy to tell whether a decomposition has a lossless join with respect to a set of functional dependencies.

Algorithm 7.2: Testing for a Lossless Join.
Input: A relation scheme $R = A_1 \cdots A_n$, a set of functional dependencies F, and a decomposition $\rho = (R_1, \ldots, R_k)$.
Output: A decision whether ρ is a decomposition with a lossless join.
Method: We construct a table with n columns and k rows; column j corresponds to attribute A_j, and row i corresponds to relation scheme R_i. In row i and column j put the symbol a_j if A_j is in R_i. If not, put the symbol b_{ij} there.

Repeatedly "consider" each of the dependencies $X \rightarrow Y$ in F, until no more changes can be made to the table. Each time we "consider" $X \rightarrow Y$, we look for rows that agree in all the columns for the attributes of X. If we find two such rows, equate the symbols of those rows for the attributes of Y. When we equate two symbols, if one of them is a_j, make the other be a_j. If they are b_{ij} and $b_{\ell j}$, make them both b_{ij} or $b_{\ell j}$, arbitrarily.

If after modifying the rows of the table as above, we discover that some row has become $a_1 \cdots a_k$, then the join is lossless. If not, the join is lossy (not lossless). $\square$

Example 7.8: Let us consider the decomposition of $SAIP$ into SA and SIP as in Example 7.7. The dependencies are $S{\to}A$ and $SI{\to}P$, and the initial table is

S	A	I	P
a_1	a_2	b_{13}	b_{14}
a_1	b_{22}	a_3	a_4

Since $S{\to}A$, and the two rows agree on S, we may equate their symbols for A, making b_{22} become a_2. The resulting table is

S	A	I	P
a_1	a_2	b_{13}	b_{14}
a_1	a_2	a_3	a_4

Since one row has all a's, the join is lossless.

For a more complicated example, let $R = ABCDE$, $R_1 = AD$, $R_2 = AB$, $R_3 = BE$, $R_4 = CDE$, and $R_5 = AE$. Let the functional dependencies be:

$$A{\to}C \qquad DE{\to}C$$
$$B{\to}C \qquad CE{\to}A$$
$$C{\to}D$$

The initial table is shown in Fig. 7.3(a). We can apply $A{\to}C$ to equate b_{13}, b_{23}, and b_{53}. Then we use $B{\to}C$ to equate these symbols with b_{33}; the result is shown in Fig. 7.3(b), where b_{13} has been chosen as the representative symbol. Now use $C{\to}D$ to equate a_4, b_{24}, b_{34}, and b_{54}; the resulting symbol is a_4. Then $DE{\to}C$ enables us to equate b_{13} with a_3, and $CE{\to}A$ lets us equate b_{31}, b_{41}, and a_1. The result is shown in Fig. 7.3(c). Since the middle row is all a's, the decomposition has a lossless join. $\square$

It is interesting to note that one might assume Algorithm 7.2 could be simplified by only equating symbols if one was an a_i. The above example shows this is not the case; if we do not begin by equating b_{13}, b_{23}, b_{33}, and b_{53}, we can never get a row of all a's.

Theorem 7.4: Algorithm 7.2 correctly determines if a decomposition has a lossless join.

Proof: Suppose the final table produced by Algorithm 7.2 does not have a row of all a's. We may view this table as a relation r for scheme R; the rows are tuples, and the a_j's and b_{ij}'s are distinct symbols chosen from the domain of A_j. Relation r satisfies the dependencies F, since Algorithm 7.2 modifies the table whenever a violation of the dependencies is found. We claim that $r \neq m_\rho(r)$. Clearly r does not contain the tuple $a_1 a_2 \cdots a_n$. But for each R_i, there is a tuple t_i in r, namely the tuple that is row i, such that $t_i[R_i]$ consists of all a's. Thus the join of the $\pi_{R_i}(r)$'s contains the tuple with all a's, since that tuple agrees with t_i for all i. We conclude that if the final table from Algorithm 7.2 does

A	B	C	D	E
a_1	b_{12}	b_{13}	a_4	b_{15}
a_1	a_2	b_{23}	b_{24}	b_{25}
b_{31}	a_2	b_{33}	b_{34}	a_5
b_{41}	b_{42}	a_3	a_4	a_5
a_1	b_{52}	b_{53}	b_{54}	a_5

(a)

A	B	C	D	E
a_1	b_{12}	b_{13}	a_4	b_{15}
a_1	a_2	b_{13}	b_{24}	b_{25}
b_{31}	a_2	b_{13}	b_{34}	a_5
b_{41}	b_{42}	a_3	a_4	a_5
a_1	b_{52}	b_{13}	b_{54}	a_5

(b)

A	B	C	D	E
a_1	b_{12}	a_3	a_4	b_{15}
a_1	a_2	a_3	a_4	b_{25}
a_1	a_2	a_3	a_4	a_5
a_1	b_{42}	a_3	a_4	a_5
a_1	b_{52}	a_3	a_4	a_5

(c)

Fig. 7.3. Applying Algorithm 7.2.

not have a row with all a's, then the decomposition ρ does not have a lossless join; we have found a relation r for R such that $m_\rho(r) \neq r$.

Conversely, suppose the final table has a row with all a's. We can in general view the table as shorthand for the domain relational calculus expression

$$\{\, a_1 a_2 \cdots a_n \mid (\exists b_{11}) \cdots (\exists b_{kn})(R(w_1) \wedge \cdots \wedge R(w_k)) \,\} \qquad (7.1)$$

where w_i is the ith row of the initial table. Formula (7.1) defines the function m_ρ, since $m_\rho(r)$ contains an arbitrary tuple $a_1 \cdots a_n$ if and only if for each i, r contains a tuple with a's in the attributes of R_i and arbitrary values in the other attributes.

Since we assume that any relation r for scheme R, to which (7.1) could be applied, satisfies the dependencies F, we can infer that (7.1) is equivalent to a set of similar formulas with some of the a's and/or b's identified. The modifications made to the table by Algorithm 7.2 are such that the table is

	$R_1 \cap R_2$	$R_1 - R_2$	$R_2 - R_1$
row for R_1	$aa\cdots a$	$aa\cdots a$	$bb\cdots b$
row for R_2	$aa\cdots a$	$bb\cdots b$	$aa\cdots a$

Fig. 7.4. A general two row table.

always shorthand for some formula whose value on relation r is $m_\rho(r)$ whenever r satisfies F, as can be proved by an easy induction on the number of symbols identified. Since the final table contains a row with all a's, the domain calculus expression for the final table is of the form.

$$\{\, a_1\cdots a_n \mid R(a_1\cdots a_n) \wedge \cdots \,\} \tag{7.2}$$

Clearly the value of (7.2) applied to relation r for R, is a subset of r. However, if r satisfies F, then the value of (7.2) is $m_\rho(r)$, and by Lemma 7.5(a), $r \subseteq m_\rho(r)$. Thus whenever r satisfies F, (7.2) computes r, so $r = m_\rho(r)$. That is to say, the decomposition ρ has a lossless join with respect to F. $\square$

Algorithm 7.2 can be applied to decompositions into any number of relation schemes. However, for decompositions into two schemes we can give a simpler test, the subject of the next theorem.

Theorem 7.5: If $\rho = (R_1, R_2)$ is a decomposition of R, and F is a set of functional dependencies, then ρ has a lossless join with respect to F if and only if $(R_1 \cap R_2)\to(R_1 - R_2)$ or $(R_1 \cap R_2)\to(R_2 - R_1)$. Note that these dependencies need not be in the given set F; it is sufficient that they be in F^+.

Proof: The initial table used in an application of Algorithm 7.2 is shown in Fig. 7.4, although we have omitted the subscripts on a and b, which are easily determined and immaterial anyway. It is easy to show by induction on the number of symbols identified by Algorithm 7.2 that if the b in the column for attribute A is changed to an a, then A is in $(R_1 \cap R_2)^+$. It is also easy to show by induction on the number of steps needed to prove $(R_1 \cap R_2)\to Y$ by Armstrong's axioms, that any b's in the columns for attributes in Y are changed to a's. Thus the row for R_1 becomes all a's if and only if $R_2 - R_1 \subseteq (R_1 \cap R_2)^+$, that is $(R_1 \cap R_2)\to(R_2 - R_1)$, and similarly, the row for R_2 becomes all a's if and only if $(R_1 \cap R_2)\to(R_1 - R_2)$. $\square$

Example 7.9: Suppose $R = ABC$ and $F = \{A\to B\}$. Then the decomposition of R into AB and AC has a lossless join, since $AB \cap AC = A$, $AB - AC = B$,† and $A\to B$ holds. However if we decompose R into $R_1 = AB$ and $R_2 = BC$, we discover that $R_1 \cap R_2 = B$, and B functionally determines neither $R_1 - R_2 = A$ nor $R_2 - R_1 = C$. Thus the decomposition AB and BC does not have a lossless join with respect to $F = \{A\to B\}$, as can be seen by considering the

---
† To make sense of equations like these do not forget that $A_1 A_2 \cdots A_n$ stands for the set of attributes $\{A_1, A_2, \ldots, A_n\}$.

relation $r = \{\, a_1 b_1 c_1,\ a_2 b_1 c_2 \,\}$ for R. Then $\pi_{AB}(r) = \{\, a_1 b_1,\ a_2 b_1 \,\}$, $\pi_{BC}(r) = \{\, b_1 c_1,\ b_1 c_2 \,\}$, and $\pi_{AB}(r) \bowtie \pi_{BC}(r) = \{\, a_1 b_1 c_1,\ a_1 b_1 c_2,\ a_2 b_1 c_1,\ a_2 b_1 c_2 \,\}$. $\square$

Decompositions that Preserve Dependencies

We have seen that it is desirable for a decomposition to have the lossless join property, because it guarantees that any relation can be recovered from its projections. Another important property of a decomposition of relation scheme R into $\rho = (R_1, \ldots, R_k)$ is that the set of dependencies F for R be implied by the projection of F onto the R_i's. Formally, the *projection* of F onto a set of attributes Z, denoted $\pi_Z(F)$, is the set of dependencies $X \to Y$ in F^+ such that $XY \subseteq Z$. (Note that $X \to Y$ need not be in F; it need only be in F^+.) We say decomposition ρ *preserves* a set of dependencies F if the union of all the dependencies in $\pi_{R_i}(F)$, for $i = 1, 2, \ldots, k$ logically implies all the dependencies in F.

The reason it is desirable that ρ preserve F is that the dependencies in F can be viewed as integrity constraints for the relation R. If the projected dependencies do not imply F, then should we represent R by $\rho = (R_1, \ldots, R_k)$, we could find that the current value of the R_i's represented a relation R that did not satisfy F, even if ρ had the lossless join property with respect to F. Alternatively, every update to one of the R_i's would require a join to check that the constraints were not violated.

Example 7.10: Let us reconsider the problem of Example 7.3, where we had attributes CITY, ST, and ZIP, which we here abbreviate C, S, and Z. We observed the dependencies $CS \to Z$ and $Z \to C$. The decomposition of the relation scheme CSZ into SZ and CZ has a lossless join, since

$$(SZ \cap CZ) \to (CZ - SZ)$$

However, the projection of $F = \{\, CS \to Z,\ Z \to C \,\}$ onto SZ gives only the trivial dependencies that follow from reflexivity, while the projection onto CZ gives $Z \to C$ and the trivial dependencies. It can be checked that $Z \to C$ and trivial dependencies do not imply $CS \to Z$, so the decomposition does not preserve dependencies.

For example, the join of the two relations in Fig. 7.5(a) and (b) is the relation of Fig. 7.5(c). Figure 7.5(a) satisfies the trivial dependencies, as any relation must. Figure 7.5(b) satisfies the trivial dependencies and the dependency $Z \to C$. However, their join in Fig. 7.5(c) violates $CS \to Z$. $\square$

We should note that a decomposition may have a lossless join with respect to set of dependencies F, yet not preserve F. Example 7.10 gave one such instance. Also, the decomposition could preserve F yet not have a lossless join. For example, let $F = \{\, A \to B,\ C \to D \,\}$, $R = ABCD$, and $\rho = (AB, CD)$.

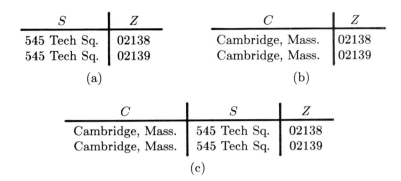

Fig. 7.5. A join violating a functional dependency.

Testing Preservation of Dependencies

In principle, it is easy to test whether a decomposition $\rho = (R_1, \ldots, R_k)$ preserves a set of dependencies F. Just compute F^+ and project it onto all the R_i's. Take the union of the resulting sets of dependencies, and test whether this set covers F.

However, in practice, just computing F^+ is a formidable task, since the number of dependencies it contains will be exponential in the size of F. Therefore, it is fortunate that there is a way to test preservation without actually computing F^+; this method takes time that is polynomial in the size of F.

Algorithm 7.3: Testing Preservation of Dependencies.

Input: A decompostion $\rho = (R_1, \ldots, R_k)$ and a set of functional dependencies F.

Output: A decision whether ρ preserves F.

Method: Define G to be $\cup_{i=1}^k \pi_{R_i}(F)$. Note that we do not compute G; we merely wish to see whether it covers F. To test whether G covers F, we must consider each $X \to Y$ in F and determine whether X^+, computed with respect to G, contains Y. The trick we use to compute X^+ without having G available is to consider repeatedly what the effect is of closing X with respect to the projections of F onto the various R_i's.

That is, define an *R-operation* on set of attributes Z with respect to a set of dependencies F to be the replacement of Z by $Z \cup ((Z \cap R)^+ \cap R)$, the closure being taken with respect to F. This operation adjoins to Z those attributes A such that $(Z \cap R) \to A$ is in $\pi_R(F)$. Then we compute X^+ with respect to G by starting with X, and repeatedly running through the list of R_i's, performing the R_i-operation for each i in turn. If at some pass, none of the R_i-operations make any change in the current set of attributes, then we are done; the resulting set is X^+. More formally, the algorithm is:

$$Z = X$$
while changes to Z occur **do**
  for $i = 1$ **to** k **do**
    $Z = Z \cup ((Z \cap R_i)^+ \cap R_i)$

If Y is a subset of the Z that results from executing the above steps, then $X \rightarrow Y$ is in G. If each $X \rightarrow Y$ in F is thus found to be in G, answer "yes," otherwise answer "no." $\square$

Example 7.11: Consider set of attributes $ABCD$ with decomposition

$$\{\, AB, BC, CD \,\}$$

and set of dependencies $F = \{\, A \rightarrow B,\ B \rightarrow C,\ C \rightarrow D,\ D \rightarrow A \,\}$. That is, in F^+, each attribute functionally determines all the others. We might first imagine that when we project F onto AB, BC, and CD, we fail to get the dependency $D \rightarrow A$, but that intuition is wrong. When we project F, we really project F^+ onto the relation schemes, so projecting onto AB we get not only $A \rightarrow B$, but also $B \rightarrow A$. Similarly, we get $C \rightarrow B$ in $\pi_{BC}(F)$ and $D \rightarrow C$ in $\pi_{CD}(F)$, and these three dependencies logically imply $D \rightarrow A$. Thus, we should expect that Algorithm 7.3 will tell us that $D \rightarrow A$ follows logically from

$$G = \pi_{AB}(F) \cup \pi_{BC}(F) \cup \pi_{CD}(F)$$

We start with $Z = \{\, D \,\}$. Applying the AB-operation does not help, since $\{\, D \,\} \cup ((\{\, D \,\} \cap \{\, A, B \,\})^+ \cap \{\, A, B \,\})$ is just $\{\, D \,\}$. Similarly, the BC-operation does not change Z. However, when we apply the CD-operation we get

$$
\begin{aligned}
Z &= \{\, D \,\} \cup ((\{\, D \,\} \cap \{\, C, D \,\})^+ \cap \{\, C, D \,\}) \\
  &= \{\, D \,\} \cup (\{\, D \,\}^+ \cap \{\, C, D \,\}) \\
  &= \{\, D \,\} \cup (\{\, A, B, C, D \,\} \cap \{\, C, D \,\}) \\
  &= \{\, C, D \,\}
\end{aligned}
$$

Similarly, on the next pass, the BC-operation applied to the current $Z = \{\, C, D \,\}$ produces $Z = \{\, B, C, D \,\}$, and on the third pass, the AB-operation sets Z to $\{\, A, B, C, D \,\}$, whereupon no more changes to Z are possible.

Thus, with respect to G, $\{\, D \,\}^+ = \{\, A, B, C, D \,\}$, which contains A, so we conclude that $G \models D \rightarrow A$. Since it is easy to check that the other members of F are in G^+ (in fact they are in G), we conclude that this decomposition preserves the set of dependencies F. $\square$

Theorem 7.6: Algorithm 7.3 correctly determines if $X \rightarrow Y$ is in G^+.

Proof: Each time we add an attribute to Z, we are using a dependency in G, so when the algorithm says "yes," it must be correct. Conversely, suppose $X \rightarrow Y$ is in G^+. Then there is a sequence of steps whereby, using Algorithm 7.1 to take the closure of X with respect to G, we eventually include all the attributes of Y. Each of these steps involves the application of a dependency in G, and therefore it is a dependency in $\pi_{R_i}(F)$ for some i. Let one such dependency be $U \to V$. An easy induction on the number of dependencies applied in Algorithm 7.1 shows that eventually U becomes a subset of Z, and then on the next pass the R_i-operation will surely cause all attributes of V to be added to Z if they are not already there. $\square$

7.4 NORMAL FORMS FOR RELATION SCHEMES

A number of different properties, or "normal forms" for relation schemes with dependencies have been defined. The most significant of these are called "third normal form"† and "Boyce-Codd normal form." These normal forms guarantee that most of the problems of redundancy and anomalies discussed in Section 7.1 do not occur.

Boyce-Codd Normal Form

The strongest of these normal forms is called Boyce-Codd. A relation scheme R with dependencies F is said to be in *Boyce-Codd normal form* if whenever $X \to A$ holds in R, and A is not in X, then X is a superkey for R; that is, X is or contains a key. Put another way, the only nontrivial dependencies are those in which a key functionally determines one or more other attributes.

Example 7.12: The relation scheme CSZ of Example 7.10, with dependencies $CS \to Z$ and $Z \to C$, is not in Boyce-Codd normal form (although we shall see it is in third normal form). The reason is that $Z \to C$ holds (in fact it is a given dependency), but Z is not a key of CSZ, nor does it contain a key.

The MEMBERS and ORDERS relations of Example 3.1 are in Boyce-Codd normal form, since their keys, NAME and ORDER_NO respectively, are the left sides of the only dependencies that were given for their respective relations. We shall see that the SUPPLIERS relation is neither in Boyce-Codd normal form nor third normal form. $\square$

Third Normal Form

It turns out that in some circumstances, Boyce-Codd normal form is too strong a condition, in the sense that it is not possible to bring a relation scheme into that form by decomposition without losing the ability to preserve dependencies. Thus third normal form has seen use as a condition that has almost the benefits of Boyce-Codd normal form, as far as elimination of anomalies is concerned, yet that we can achieve for an arbitrary database scheme without giving up either dependency preservation or the lossless join property.

Before defining third normal form, we need a preliminary definition. Call

---

† Yes Virginia, there is a first normal form and a second normal form. There's even a fourth normal form. All in good time $\cdots$

an attribute A in relation scheme R a *prime* attribute if A is a member of any key for R (recall there may be many keys). If A is not a member of any key, then A is *nonprime*.

Example 7.13: In the relation scheme CSZ of Example 7.10, all attributes are prime, since given the dependencies $CS \rightarrow Z$ and $Z \rightarrow C$, both CS and SZ are keys.

In the relation scheme $ABCD$ with dependencies $AB \rightarrow C$, $B \rightarrow D$, and $BC \rightarrow A$ we can check that AB and BC are the only keys, so A, B, and C are prime; D is nonprime. $\square$

A relation scheme R is in *third normal form* if whenever $X \rightarrow A$ holds in R and A is not in X, then either X is a superkey for R, or A is prime. Notice that the definitions of Boyce-Codd and third normal forms are identical except for the clause "or A is prime" that makes third normal form a weaker condition than Boyce-Codd normal form.

If $X \rightarrow A$ violates third normal form, then one of two cases can occur. Either
1. X is a proper subset of a key, or
2. X is a proper subset of no key.
In the first case, we say that $X \rightarrow A$ is a *partial dependency*, and in the second case we call it a *transitive dependency*. The term "transitive" comes from the fact that if Y is a key, then $Y \rightarrow X \rightarrow A$ is a nontrivial chain of dependencies. It is nontrivial because we know that X is not a subset of Y, by (2), A is given not to be in X, and A cannot be in Y because A is nonprime. If R has no partial dependencies, although it may have transitive dependencies, we say R is in *second normal form*.†

Example 7.14: The relation scheme $SAIP$ from Example 7.7, with dependencies $SI \rightarrow P$ and $S \rightarrow A$ violates third normal form, and in fact violates second normal form. A is a nonprime attribute, since the only key is SI. Then $S \rightarrow A$ violates the third normal form condition, since S is not a superkey. Note that in this case, the violating dependency, $S \rightarrow A$, not only holds, it is even a given dependency. In general, however, it is sufficient that the violating dependency follow from the given set of dependencies, even if it is not itself a given dependency.

As another example, the relation scheme CSZ from Example 7.12 is in third normal form. Since all of its attributes are prime, the conditions for third normal form hold vacuously.

For an example of a relation scheme in second normal form but not third, consider the attributes S (Store) I (Item) D (Department number), and M

---

† O.K., we might as well mention "first normal form." That form simply requires that the domain of each attribute consists of indivisible values, not sets or tuples of values from a more elementary domain or domains. We have not considered set-valued domains and so feel free to ignore first normal form. In effect, "relation" is for us synonymous with "first normal form relation" in some works appearing in the literature.

(Manager). The functional dependencies we assume are $SI \rightarrow D$ (each item in each store is sold by at most one department) and $SD \rightarrow M$ (each department in each store has one manager). The only key is SI. Then $SD \rightarrow M$ violates third normal form, since SD is not a superset of a key. Note the application of transitivity implied by the chain $SI \rightarrow SD \rightarrow M$. However, there are no partial dependencies, since no proper subset of the key SI functionally determines D or M. $\square$

Motivation Behind Normal Forms

We may suppose that the functional dependencies $X \rightarrow Y$ not only represent an integrity constraint on relations, but also represent a relationship that the database is intended to store. That is, we regard it important to know, given an assignment of values to the attributes in X, what value for each of the Y attributes is associated with this assignment of X-values. If we have a partial dependency $Y \rightarrow A$, where X is a key and Y a proper subset of X, then in every tuple used to associate an X-value with values for other attributes besides A and those in X, the same association between Y and A must appear. This situation is best seen in the running example of the $SAIP$ scheme, where $S \rightarrow A$ is a partial dependency, and the supplier's address must be repeated once for each item supplied by the supplier. The third normal form condition eliminates this possibility and the resultant redundancy and update anomalies.

If we have a transitive dependency $X \rightarrow Y \rightarrow A$, then we cannot associate a Y-value with an X-value unless there is an A-value associated with the Y value. This situation leads to insertion and deletion anomalies, where we cannot insert an X-to-Y association without a Y-to-A association, and if we delete the A-value associated with a given Y-value, we may lose track of an X-to-Y association. For example, in the relation scheme $SIDM$ with dependencies $SI \rightarrow D$ and $SD \rightarrow M$, mentioned in Example 7.14, we cannot record the department selling hats in Bloomingdales if that department has no manager.

As we saw from Example 7.14, a relation scheme can be in third normal form but not Boyce-Codd normal form. However, every Boyce-Codd normal form relation scheme is in third normal form. The benefits of Boyce-Codd normal form are the same as for third normal form—freedom from insertion and deletion anomalies and redundancies. Note how Boyce-Codd normal form eliminates some anomalies not prevented by third normal form. For instance, in the CSZ example, we cannot record the city to which a zip code belongs unless we know a street address with that zip code.

It is worth mentioning that relations intended to represent an entity set or a many-one mapping between entity sets will be in Boyce-Codd normal form unless there are unexpected relationships among attributes. It is interesting to conjecture that all functional dependencies that satisfy third normal form but violate Boyce-Codd normal form are in a sense irrelevant. That is, they tell us something about the structure of the real world that is of no use to the database designer. For example, $Z \rightarrow C$ in the above example tells us how cities are broken into zip codes, but the information is not really useful, since the apparent application of the CSZ database is not to relate zip codes to cities, but to store zip codes for addresses.

Lossless Join Decomposition into Boyce-Codd Normal Form

We have now been introduced to the properties we desire for relation schemes: Boyce-Codd normal form or, failing that, third normal form. In the last section we saw the two most important properties of database schemes as a whole, the lossless join and dependency preservation properties. Now we must attempt to put these ideas together, that is, construct database schemes with the properties we desire for database schemes, and with each individual relation scheme having the properties we desire for relation schemes.

It turns out that any relation scheme has a lossless join decomposition into Boyce-Codd Normal Form, and it has a decomposition into third normal form that has a lossless join and is also dependency-preserving. However, there may be no decomposition of a relation scheme into Boyce-Codd normal form that is dependency-preserving. The CSZ relation scheme is the canonical example. It is not in Boyce-Codd normal form because the dependency $Z \rightarrow C$ holds, yet if we decompose CSZ in any way such that CSZ is not one of the schemes in the decomposition, then the dependency $CS \rightarrow Z$ is not implied by the projected dependencies. Before giving the decomposition algorithms, we shall state some properties of natural joins that we shall need.

Lemma 7.6:

a)   Suppose R is a relation scheme with functional dependencies F. Let $\rho = (R_1, \ldots, R_k)$ be a decomposition of R with a lossless join with respect to F. For a particular i, let $F_i = \pi_{R_i}(F)$, and let $\sigma = (S_1, \ldots, S_m)$ be a decomposition of R_i whose join is lossless with respect to F_i. Then the decomposition of R into $(R_1, \ldots, R_{i-1}, S_1, \ldots, S_m, R_{i+1}, \ldots, R_k)$ has a lossless join with respect to F.

b)   Suppose R, F and ρ are as in (a), and let $\tau = (R_1, \ldots, R_k, R_{k+1}, \ldots, R_n)$ be a decomposition of R into a set of relation schemes that includes those of ρ. Then τ also has a lossless join with respect to F.

Proof: Each of these statements follows by algebraic manipulation from the definition of a lossless join decomposition. We shall leave formal proofs as exercises and only give the intuition here. The reason (a) holds is that if we take relation r for R and project it to relations r_j for each R_j, and then project r_i to relations s_p for each S_p, the lossless join property tells us we can join the s_p's to recover r_i. Then we can join the r_j's to recover r. Since the natural join is an associative operation (another exercise for the reader) the order in which we perform the join doesn't matter, so we recover r no matter in what order we take the join of the r_j's, for $i \neq j$, and the s_p's.

For part (b), we again appeal to the associativity of the natural join. Observe that if we project relation r for R onto the R_i's, $i = 1, 2, \ldots, n$, then when we take the join of the projections onto $R_1, \ldots, R_k$ we recover r. Since $R_1, \ldots, R_k$ include all the attributes of R, further joins can only produce a subset of what we already have, which is r. But by Lemma 7.5(a), $r \subseteq m_\tau(r)$, so we cannot wind up with less than r. That is, $m_\tau(r) = r$, and τ is a lossless join decomposition. $\square$

Algorithm 7.4: Lossless Join Decomposition into Boyce-Codd Normal Form.
Input: Relation scheme R and functional dependencies F.
Output: A decomposition of R with a lossless join, such that every relation scheme in the decomposition is in Boyce-Codd normal form with respect to the projection of F onto that scheme.
Method: We iteratively construct a decomposition ρ for R. At all times, ρ will have a lossless join with respect to F. Initially, ρ consists of R alone. If S is a relation scheme in ρ, and S is not in Boyce-Codd normal form, let $X \rightarrow A$ be a dependency that holds in S, where X is not a superkey for S, and A is not in X. Replace S in ρ by S_1 and S_2, where S_1 consists of A and the attributes of X, and S_2 consists of all the attributes of S except for A. S_2 is surely a proper subset of S. S_1 is also a proper subset, or else $X = S - A$, so X is a superkey for S.

By Theorem 7.5, the decomposition of S into S_1 and S_2 has a lossless join with respect to the set of dependencies projected onto S, since $S_1 \cap S_2 = X$, $S_1 - S_2 = A$, and therefore $(S_1 \cap S_2) \rightarrow (S_1 - S_2)$. By Lemma 7.6(a), ρ with S replaced by S_1 and S_2 has a lossless join, if ρ does. As S_1 and S_2 each have fewer attributes then S, and any relation scheme with two or fewer attributes must be in Boyce-Codd normal form, we eventually reach a point where each relation scheme in ρ is in Boyce-Codd normal form. At that time, ρ still has a lossless join, since the initial ρ consisting of R alone does, and each modification of ρ preserves the lossless join property. $\square$

Example 7.15: Let us consider the relation scheme $CTHRSG$, where $C =$ course, $T =$ teacher, $H =$ hour, $R =$ room, $S =$ student, and $G =$ grade. The functional dependencies F we assume are

$$C \rightarrow T \quad \text{each course has one teacher}$$
$$HR \rightarrow C \quad \text{only one course can meet in a room at one time}$$
$$HT \rightarrow R \quad \text{a teacher can be in only one room at one time}$$
$$CS \rightarrow G \quad \text{each student has one grade in each course}$$
$$HS \rightarrow R \quad \text{a student can be in only one room at one time}$$

The only key for $CTHRSG$ is HS.

To decompose this relation scheme into Boyce-Codd normal form, we might first consider the dependency $CS \rightarrow G$, which violates the condition, since CS does not contain a key. Thus, by Algorithm 7.4, we first decompose $CTHRSG$ into CSG and $CTHRS$. For further decompositions we must compute F^+ and project it onto CSG and $CTHRS$.

Note that this process is in general time consuming, as the size of F^+ can be exponential in the size of F. Even in this relatively simple example, F^+, naturally, has all the trivial dependencies that follow by reflexivity and, in addition to those in F, some other nontrivial dependencies like $CH \rightarrow R$, $HS \rightarrow C$, and $HR \rightarrow T$. Once we have F^+, we select those involving only C, S, and G. This is $\pi_{CSG}(F)$. This set has a minimal cover consisting of $CS \rightarrow G$ alone; all other dependencies in the set follow from this dependency by Armstrong's axioms. We also project F^+ onto $CTHRS$. $\pi_{CTHRS}(F)$ has a minimal cover

$$C \rightarrow T \qquad TH \rightarrow R$$
$$HR \rightarrow C \qquad HS \rightarrow R$$

and the only key for $CTHRS$ is HS.

It is easy to check that CSG is in Boyce-Codd normal form with respect to its projected dependencies. $CTHRS$ must be decomposed further, and we might choose the dependency $C \rightarrow T$ to break it into CT and $CHRS$. Minimal covers for the projected dependencies are $C \rightarrow T$ for CT and $CH \rightarrow R$, $HS \rightarrow R$, and $HR \rightarrow C$ for $CHRS$; HS is the only key of the latter scheme. Observe that $CH \rightarrow R$ is needed in a cover of $CHRS$, although in $CTHRS$ it followed from $C \rightarrow T$ and $TH \rightarrow R$.

CT is in Boyce-Codd normal form, and one more decomposition of $CHRS$, say using $CH \rightarrow R$, puts the entire database scheme into the desired form. In Fig. 7.6 we see the tree of decompositions, with the keys and minimal covers for the sets of projected dependencies also shown.

The final decomposition of $CTHRSG$ is CSG, CT, CHR, and CHS. This is not a bad database design, since its four relation schemes tabulate, respectively,

1. grades for students in courses,
2. the teacher of each course,
3. the hours at which each course meets and the room for each hour, and
4. the schedule of courses and hours for each student.

In fairness it should be noted that not every decomposition produces a database scheme that matches so well our intuition about what information should be tabulated in the database. For example, if at the last decomposition step we had used dependency $HR \rightarrow C$ instead of $CH \rightarrow R$, we would have scheme HRS instead of CHS, and HRS represents the room in which a student can be found at a given hour, rather than the class he is attending. Surely the latter is more fundamental information than the former.

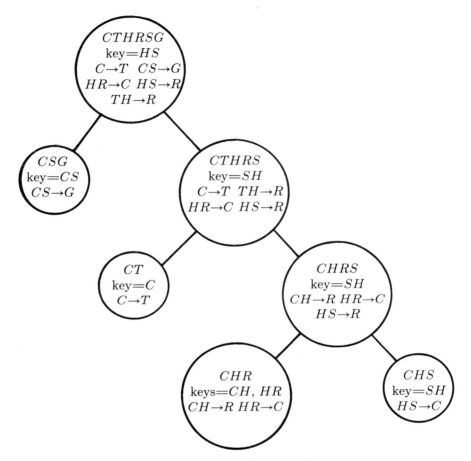

Fig. 7.6. Tree of decomposition.

Another problem with the decomposition of Fig. 7.6 is that the dependency $TH \rightarrow R$ is not preserved by the decomposition. That is, the projection of F onto CSG, CT, CHR, and CHS, which can be represented by the cover

$$
\begin{aligned}
CS &\rightarrow G & HR &\rightarrow C \\
C &\rightarrow T & HS &\rightarrow C \\
CH &\rightarrow R
\end{aligned}
$$

found by taking the minimal covers in each of the leaves of Fig. 7.6, does not imply $TH \rightarrow R$. For example, the relation for $CTHRSG$ shown below

C	T	H	R	S	G
c_1	t	h	r_1	s_1	g_1
c_2	t	h	r_2	s_2	g_2

does not satisfy $TH{\to}R$, yet its projections onto CSG, CT, CHR, and CHS satisfy all the projected dependencies. $\square$

We mentioned that the process of projecting dependencies, where we construct F^+ from F and then select out those with a particular set of attributes, can be exponential in the number of dependencies in F. One might wonder whether Algorithm 7.4 can be made to run in less than exponential time by using another approach to decomposition. Unfortunately, Beeri and Bernstein [1979] proved that it is $\mathcal{NP}$-complete† just to determine whether a relation scheme is in Boyce-Codd normal form. Thus it is extremely unlikely that one will find a substantially better algorithm.

Dependency Preserving Decompositions into Third Normal Form

We saw from Examples 7.12 and 7.14 that it is not always possible to decompose a relation scheme into Boyce-Codd normal form and still preserve the dependencies. However, we can always find a dependency-preserving decomposition into third normal form, as the next algorithm and theorem show.

Algorithm 7.5: Dependency-Preserving Decomposition into Third Normal Form.

Input: Relation scheme R and set of functional dependencies F, which we assume without loss of generality to be a minimal cover.

Output: A dependency-preserving decomposition of R such that each relation scheme is in third normal form with respect to the projection of F onto that scheme.

Method: If there are any attributes of R not involved in any dependency of F, either on the left or right, then that attribute can, in principle, form a relation scheme by itself, and we shall eliminate it from R.‡ If one of the dependencies in F involves all the attributes of R, then output R itself. Otherwise, the decomposition ρ to be output consists of scheme XA for each dependency $X{\to}A$ in F. However, if $X{\to}A_1$, $X{\to}A_2,\ldots,X{\to}A_n$ are in F, we may use scheme $XA_1{\cdots}A_n$ instead of XA_i for $1 \le i \le n$, and in fact, this substitution is usually preferable. $\square$

Example 7.16: Reconsider the relation scheme $CTHRSG$ of Example 7.15, whose dependencies have minimal cover

---

† $\mathcal{NP}$-completeness of a problem almost certainly implies that it is inherently exponential. See Aho, Hopcroft, and Ullman [1974] or Garey and Johnson [1979] for a description of the theory.

‡ Sometimes it is desirable to have two or more attributes, say A and B, appear together in a relation scheme, even though there is no functional dependency involving them. There may simply be a many-many relationship between A and B. An idea of Bernstein [1976] is to introduce a dummy attribute θ and functional dependency $AB{\to}\theta$, to force this association. After completing the design, attribute θ is eliminated.

$$C \rightarrow T \qquad CS \rightarrow G$$
$$HR \rightarrow C \qquad HS \rightarrow R$$
$$HT \rightarrow R$$

Algorithm 7.5 yields the set of relation schemes CT, CHR, HRT, CGS, and HRS. $\square$

Theorem 7.7: Algorithm 7.5 yields a dependency-preserving decomposition into third normal form.

Proof: Since the projected dependencies include a cover for F, the decomposition clearly preserves dependencies. We must show that the relation scheme YB, for each functional dependency $Y \rightarrow B$ in the minimal cover, is in third normal form. Suppose $X \rightarrow A$ violates third normal form for YB, that is, A is not in X, X is not a superkey for YB, and A is nonprime. Of course, we also know that $XA \subseteq YB$, and $X \rightarrow A$ follows logically from F. We shall consider two cases, depending on whether or not $A = B$.

Case 1: $A = B$. Then since A is not in X, we know $X \subseteq Y$, and since X is not a superkey for YB, X must be a proper subset of Y. But then $X \rightarrow B$, which is $X \rightarrow A$, could replace $Y \rightarrow B$ in the supposed minimal cover, contradicting the assumption that $Y \rightarrow B$ was part of the given minimal cover.

Case 2: $A \neq B$. Since Y is a superkey for YB, there must be some $Z \subseteq Y$ that is a key for YB. But A is in Y, since we are assuming $A \neq B$, and A cannot be in Z, because A is nonprime. Thus Z is a proper subset of Y, yet $Z \rightarrow B$ can replace $Y \rightarrow B$ in the supposedly minimal cover, again providing a contradiction. $\square$

Decompositions into Third Normal Form with a Lossless Join and Preservation of Dependencies

We have seen that we can decompose any relation scheme R into a set of schemes $\rho = (R_1, \ldots, R_k)$ such that ρ has a lossless join and each R_i is in Boyce-Codd normal form (and therefore in third normal form). We can also decompose R into $\sigma = (S_1, \ldots, S_m)$ such that σ preserves the set of dependencies F, and each S_j is in third normal form. Can we find a decomposition into third normal form that has both the lossless join and dependency-preservation properties? We can, if we simply adjoin to σ a relation scheme X that is a key for R, as the next theorem shows.

Theorem 7.8: Let σ be the third normal form decomposition of R constructed by Algorithm 7.5, and let X be a key for R. Then $\tau = \sigma \cup \{X\}$ is a decomposition of R with all relation schemes in third normal form; the decomposition preserves dependencies and has the lossless join property.

Proof: It is easy to show that any transitive or partial dependency in X implies that a proper subset of X functionally determines X, and therefore R, so X

would not be a key in that case. Thus X, as well as the members of σ, are in third normal form. Clearly τ preserves dependencies, since σ does.

To show that τ has a lossless join, apply the tabular test of Algorithm 7.2. We can show that the row for X becomes all a's, as follows. Consider the order $A_1, A_2, \ldots, A_k$ in which the attributes of $R - X$ are added to X^+ in Algorithm 7.1. Surely all attributes are added eventually, since X is a key. We show by induction on i that the column corresponding to A_i in the row for X is set to a_i in the test of Algorithm 7.2.

The basis, $i = 0$, is trivial. Assume the result for $i - 1$. Then A_i is added to X^+ because of some given functional dependency $Y \rightarrow A_i$, where

$$Y \subseteq X \cup \{A_1, \ldots, A_{i-1}\}$$

Then YA_i is in σ, and the rows for YA_i and X agree on Y (they are all a's) after the columns of the X-row for $A_1, \ldots, A_{i-1}$ are made a's. Thus these rows are made to agree on A_i during the execution of Algorithm 7.2. Since the YA_i-row has a_i there, so must the X-row. $\square$

Obviously, in some cases τ is not the smallest set of relation schemes with the properties of Theorem 7.8. We can throw out relation schemes in τ one at a time as long as the desired properties are preserved. Many different database schemes may result, depending on the order in which we throw out schemes, since eliminating one may preclude the elimination of others.

Example 7.17: We could take the union of the database scheme produced for $CTHRSG$ in Example 7.16 with the key SH, to get a decomposition that has a lossless join and preserves dependencies. It happens that SH is a subset of HRS, which is one of the relation schemes already selected. Thus, SH may be eliminated, and the database scheme of Example 7.16, that is CT, CHR, HRT, CGS, and HRS, suffices. Although some proper subsets of this set of five relation schemes are lossless join decompositions, we can check that the projected dependencies for any four of them do not imply the complete set of dependencies F, last mentioned in Example 7.16. $\square$

7.5 MULTIVALUED DEPENDENCIES

In previous sections we have assumed that the only possible kind of data dependency is functional. In fact there are many plausible kinds of dependencies, and at least one other, the multivalued dependency, appears in the "real world." Suppose we are given a relation scheme R, and X and Y are subsets of R. Intuitively, we say that $X \rightarrow\!\!\!\rightarrow Y$, read "$X$ *multidetermines* Y," or "there is a *multivalued dependency* of Y on X," if given values for the attributes of X there is a set of zero or more associated values for the attributes of Y, and this set of Y-values is not connected in any way to values of the attributes in $R - X - Y$.

C	T	H	R	S	G
CS101	Deadwood, J.	M9	222	Klunk, A.	B+
CS101	Deadwood, J.	W9	333	Klunk, A.	B+
CS101	Deadwood, J.	F9	222	Klunk, A.	B+
CS101	Deadwood, J.	M9	222	Zonker, B.	C
CS101	Deadwood, J.	W9	333	Zonker, B.	C
CS101	Deadwood, J.	F9	222	Zonker, B.	C

Fig. 7.7. A sample relation for scheme $CTHRSG$.

Formally, we say $X \twoheadrightarrow Y$ holds in R if whenever r is a relation for R, and t and s are two tuples in r, with $t[X] = s[X]$ (that is, t and s agree on the attributes of X), then r also contains tuples u and v, where
1. $u[X] = v[X] = t[X] = s[X]$,
2. $u[Y] = t[Y]$ and $u[R - X - Y] = s[R - X - Y]$, and
3. $v[Y] = s[Y]$ and $v[R - X - Y] = t[R - X - Y]$.†

That is, we can exchange the Y values of t and s to obtain two new tuples that must also be in r. Note we did not assume that X and Y are disjoint in the above definition.

Example 7.18: Let us reconsider the relation scheme $CTHRSG$ of the previous section. In Fig. 7.7 we see a possible relation for this relation scheme. In this simple case there is only one course with two students, but we see several salient facts that we would expect to hold in any relation for this relation scheme. A course can meet for several hours, in different rooms each time. Each student has a tuple for each class taken and each session of that class. His grade for the class is repeated for each tuple.

Thus we expect that in general the multivalued dependency $C \twoheadrightarrow HR$ holds, that is, there is a set of hour-room pairs associated with each course and disassociated from the other attributes. For example, if in the formal definition of a multivalued dependency we let

    $t = $ CS101   Deadwood, J.   M9   222   Klunk, A.   B+
    $s = $ CS101   Deadwood, J.   W9   333   Zonker, B.   C

then we would expect to be able to exchange (M9, 222) from t with (W9, 333) in s to get the two tuples

    $u = $ CS101   Deadwood, J.   M9   222   Zonker, B.   C
    $v = $ CS101   Deadwood, J.   W9   333   Klunk, A.   B+

A glance at Fig. 7.7 affirms that u and v are indeed in r.

It should be emphasized that $C \twoheadrightarrow HR$ holds not because it held in the

---

† Note we could have eliminated clause (3). The existence of tuple v follows from the existence of u when we apply the definition with t and s interchanged.

one relation of Fig. 7.7. It holds because for any course c, if it meets at hour h_1 in room r_1, with teacher t_1 and student s_1 who is getting grade g_1, and it also meets at hour h_2 in room r_2 with teacher t_2 and student s_2 who is getting grade g_2, then we expect from our understanding of the attributes' meanings that the course c also meets at hour h_1 in room r_1 with teacher t_2 and student s_2 with grade g_2.

Note also that $C \rightarrow\!\!\!\rightarrow H$ does not hold, nor does $C \rightarrow\!\!\!\rightarrow R$. In proof, consider relation r of Fig. 7.7 with tuples t and s as above. If $C \rightarrow\!\!\!\rightarrow H$ held, we would expect to find tuple

CS101	Deadwood, J.	M9	333	Zonker, B.	C

in r, which we do not. There are a number of other multivalued dependencies that hold, however, such as $C \rightarrow\!\!\!\rightarrow SG$ and $HR \rightarrow\!\!\!\rightarrow SG$. There are also trivial multivalued dependencies like $HR \rightarrow\!\!\!\rightarrow R$. We shall in fact prove that every functional dependency $X \rightarrow Y$ that holds implies that the multivalued dependency $X \rightarrow\!\!\!\rightarrow Y$ holds as well. $\square$

Axioms for Functional and Multivalued Dependencies

We shall now present a sound and complete set of axioms for making inferences about a set of functional and multivalued dependencies over a set of attributes U. The first three are Armstrong's axioms for functional dependencies only; we repeat them here.

A1: *(reflexivity for functional dependencies)* If $Y \subseteq X \subseteq U$, then $X \rightarrow Y$.

A2: *(augmentation for functional dependencies)* If $X \rightarrow Y$ holds, and $Z \subseteq U$, then $XZ \rightarrow YZ$.

A3: *(transitivity for functional dependencies)* $\{ X \rightarrow Y, Y \rightarrow Z \} \models X \rightarrow Z$.

The next three axioms apply to multivalued dependencies.

A4: *(complementation for multivalued dependencies)*

$$\{ X \rightarrow\!\!\!\rightarrow Y \} \models X \rightarrow\!\!\!\rightarrow (U - X - Y)$$

A5: *(augmentation for multivalued dependencies)* If $X \rightarrow\!\!\!\rightarrow Y$ holds, and $V \subseteq W$, then $WX \rightarrow\!\!\!\rightarrow VY$.

A6: *(transitivity for multivalued dependencies)*

$$\{ X \rightarrow\!\!\!\rightarrow Y, Y \rightarrow\!\!\!\rightarrow Z \} \models X \rightarrow\!\!\!\rightarrow (Z - Y)$$

It is worthwhile comparing A4–A6 with A1–A3. Axiom A4, the complementation rule, has no counterpart for functional dependencies. Axiom A1, reflexivity, appears to have no counterpart for multivalued dependencies, but the fact that $X \rightarrow\!\!\!\rightarrow Y$ whenever $Y \subseteq X$ follows from A1 and the rule (Axiom A7, to be given) that if $X \rightarrow Y$ then $X \rightarrow\!\!\!\rightarrow Y$. A6 is more restrictive than its counterpart transitivity axiom, A3. The more general statement, that $X \rightarrow\!\!\!\rightarrow Y$ and $Y \rightarrow\!\!\!\rightarrow Z$ imply $X \rightarrow\!\!\!\rightarrow Z$ is false. For instance, we saw in Example 7.18 that

$C \twoheadrightarrow HR$ holds, and surely $HR \twoheadrightarrow H$ is true, yet $C \twoheadrightarrow H$ is false. To compensate partially for the fact that A6 is weaker than A3, we use a stronger version of A5 than the analogous augmentation axiom for functional dependencies, A2. We could have replaced A2 by: $X \rightarrow Y$ and $V \subseteq W$ imply $WX \rightarrow VY$, but for functional dependencies, this rule is easily proved from A1, A2, and A3.

Our last two axioms relate functional and multivalued dependencies.

A7: $\{X \rightarrow Y\} \models X \twoheadrightarrow Y$.

A8: If $X \twoheadrightarrow Y$ holds, $Z \subseteq Y$, and for some W disjoint from Y, we have $W \rightarrow Z$, then $X \rightarrow Z$ also holds.

We shall not give a proof that axioms A1–A8 are sound and complete. Rather, we shall prove that some of the axioms are sound, that is, they follow from the definitions of functional and multivalued dependencies, leaving the soundness of the rest of the axioms, as well as a proof that any valid inference can be made using the axioms (completeness of the axioms), for an exercise.

Let us begin by proving A6, the transitivity axiom for multivalued dependencies. Suppose in some relation r over set of attributes U, $X \twoheadrightarrow Y$ and $Y \twoheadrightarrow Z$ hold, but $X \twoheadrightarrow (Z - Y)$ does not hold. Then there are tuples t and s in r, where $t[X] = s[X]$, but the tuple u, where $u[X] = t[X]$, $u[Z - Y] = t[Z - Y]$, and $u[U - X - (Z - Y)] = s[U - X - (Z - Y)]$, is not in r. Since $X \twoheadrightarrow Y$ holds, it follows that the tuple v, where $v[X] = t[X]$, $v[Y] = s[Y]$, and $v[U - X - Y] = t[U - X - Y]$, is in r. Now v and s agree on Y, so since $Y \twoheadrightarrow Z$, it follows that r has a tuple w, where $w[Y] = s[Y]$, $w[Z] = v[Z]$, and $w[U - Y - Z] = s[U - Y - Z]$.

We claim that $w[X] = t[X]$, since on attributes in $Z \cap X$, w agrees with v, which agrees with t. On attributes of $X - Z$, w agrees with s, and s agrees with t on X. We also claim that $w[Z - Y] = t[Z - Y]$, since w agrees with v on $Z - Y$, and v agrees with t on $Z - Y$. Finally, we claim that $w[V] = s[V]$, where $V = U - X - (Z - Y)$. In proof, surely w agrees with s on $V - Z$, and by manipulating sets we can show $V \cap Z = (Y \cap Z) - X$. But w agrees with v on Z, and v agrees with s on Y, so w agrees with s on $V \cap Z$ as well as on $V - Z$. Therefore w agrees with s on V. If we look at the definition of u, we now see that $w = u$. But we claimed that w is in r, so u is in r, contrary to our assumption. Thus $X \twoheadrightarrow Z - Y$ holds after all, and we have proved A6.

Now let us prove A8. Suppose we have a relation r in which $X \twoheadrightarrow Y$ and $W \rightarrow Z$ hold, where $Z \subseteq Y$, and $W \cap Y$ is empty, but $X \rightarrow Z$ does not hold. Then there are tuples s and t in r such that $s[X] = t[X]$, but $s[Z] \neq t[Z]$. By $X \twoheadrightarrow Y$ applied to s and t, there is a tuple u in r, such that $u[X] = t[X] = s[X]$, $u[Y] = t[Y]$, and $u[U - X - Y] = s[U - X - Y]$. Since $W \cap Y$ is empty, u and s agree on W. As $Z \subseteq Y$, u and t agree on Z. Since s and t disagree on Z, it follows that u and s disagree on Z. But this contradicts $W \rightarrow Z$, since u and s agree on W but disagree on Z. We conclude that $X \rightarrow Z$ did not fail to hold, and we have verified rule A8.

The remainder of the proof of the following theorem is left as an exercise.

Theorem 7.9: (Beeri, Fagin, and Howard [1977]). Axioms A1–A8 are sound and complete for functional and multivalued dependencies. That is, if D is a set of functional and multivalued dependencies over a set of attributes U, and D^+ is the set of functional and multivalued dependencies that follow logically from D, in the sense that every relation over U that satisfies D also satisfies the dependencies in D^+, then D^+ is exactly the set of dependencies that follow from D by A1–A8. $\square$

Additional Inference Rules for Multivalued Dependencies

There are a number of other rules that are useful for making inferences about functional and multivalued dependencies. Of course, the union, decomposition, and pseudotransitivity rules for functional dependencies mentioned in Lemma 7.1 still apply. Some other rules are:

1. (union rule for multivalued dependencies) $\{\, X \twoheadrightarrow Y,\, X \twoheadrightarrow Z \,\} \models X \twoheadrightarrow YZ$.
2. (pseudotransitivity rule for multivalued dependencies)

$$\{\, X \twoheadrightarrow Y,\, WY \twoheadrightarrow Z \,\} \models WX \twoheadrightarrow (Z - WY)$$

3. (mixed pseudotransitivity rule) $\{\, X \twoheadrightarrow Y,\, XY \rightarrow Z \,\} \models X \rightarrow (Z - Y)$.
4. (decomposition rule for multivalued dependencies) If $X \twoheadrightarrow Y$ and $X \twoheadrightarrow Z$ hold, then $X \twoheadrightarrow (Y \cap X)$, $X \twoheadrightarrow (Y - Z)$, and $X \twoheadrightarrow (Z - Y)$ hold.

We leave the proof that these rules are valid as an exercise; techniques similar to those used for A6 and A8 above will suffice, or we can prove them from axioms A1–A8.

We should note that the decomposition rule for multivalued dependencies is weaker than the corresponding rule for functional dependencies. The latter rule allows us to deduce immediately from $X \rightarrow Y$ that $X \rightarrow A$ for each attribute A in Y. The rule for multivalued dependencies only allows us to conclude $X \twoheadrightarrow A$ from $X \twoheadrightarrow Y$ if we can find some Z such that $X \twoheadrightarrow Z$, and either $Z \cap Y = A$ or $Y - Z = A$.

However, the decomposition rule for multivalued dependencies, along with the union rule, allows us to make the following statement about the sets Y such that $X \twoheadrightarrow Y$ for a given X.

Theorem 7.10: If U is the set of all attributes, then we can partition $U - X$ into sets of attributes $Y_1, Y_2, \ldots, Y_k$, such that if $Z \subseteq U - X$, then $X \twoheadrightarrow Z$ if and only if Z is the union of some of the Y_i's.

Proof: Start the partition of $U - X$ with all of $U - X$ in one block. Suppose at some point we have partition $W_1, \ldots, W_n$, and $X \twoheadrightarrow W_i$ for $i = 1, 2, \ldots, n$. If $X \twoheadrightarrow Z$, and Z is not the union of some W_i's, replace each W_i such that $W_i \cap Z$ and $W_i - Z$ are both nonempty by $W_i \cap Z$ and $W_i - Z$. By the decomposition rule, $X \twoheadrightarrow (W_i \cap Z)$ and $X \twoheadrightarrow (W_i - Z)$. As we cannot partition a finite set of attributes indefinitely, we shall eventually find that every Z such that $X \twoheadrightarrow Z$ is the union of some blocks of the partition. By the union rule, X multidetermines the union of any set of blocks. $\square$

We call the above sets $Y_1, \ldots, Y_k$ constructed for X from a set of functional and multivalued dependencies D the *dependency basis* for X (with respect to D).

Example 7.19: In Example 7.18 we observed that $C \twoheadrightarrow HR$. Thus, by the complementation rule, $C \twoheadrightarrow TSG$. We also know that $C \to T$. Thus, by axiom A7, $C \twoheadrightarrow T$. By the decomposition rule, $C \twoheadrightarrow SG$. One can check that no single attribute except T or C itself is multidetermined by C. Thus the dependency basis for C is $\{T, HR, SG\}$. $\square$

Closures of Functional and Multivalued Dependencies

Given a set of functional and multivalued dependencies D, we would like to find the set D^+ of all functional and multivalued dependencies logically implied by D. We can compute D^+ by starting with D and applying axioms A1–A8 until no more new dependencies can be derived. However, this process can take time that is exponential in the size of D. Often we only want to know whether a particular dependency $X \to Y$ or $X \twoheadrightarrow Y$ follows from D, if for example, we should wish to eliminate redundant dependencies.

To test whether a multivalued dependency $X \twoheadrightarrow Y$ holds, it suffices to determine the dependency basis of X and see whether $Y - X$ is the union of some sets thereof. For example, referring to Example 7.19, we know that $C \twoheadrightarrow CTSG$, since TSG is the union of T and SG. Also, $C \twoheadrightarrow HRSG$, but $C \twoheadrightarrow TH$ is false, since TH intersects block HR of the dependency basis, yet TH does not include all of HR. In computing the dependency basis of X with respect to D, a theorem of Beeri [1980] tells us it suffices to compute the basis with respect to the set of multivalued dependencies M, where M consists of

1. all multivalued dependencies in D, and
2. for each functional dependency $X \to Y$ in D, the set of multivalued dependencies $X \twoheadrightarrow A_1, \ldots, X \twoheadrightarrow A_n$, where $Y = A_1 \cdots A_n$, and each A_i is a single attribute.

Another theorem of Beeri [1980] gives us a way to extract the nontrivial functional dependencies from the dependency basis computed according to the set of multivalued dependencies M. It can be shown that if X does not include A, then $X \to A$ holds if and only if

1. A is a singleton set of the dependency basis for X according to the set of dependencies M, and
2. there is some set of attributes Y, excluding A, such that $Y \to Z$ is in D, and A is in Z.

Furthermore, Beeri [1980] gives the following polynomial time algorithm for computing the dependency basis of X with respect to M. Note that while Theorem 7.10 convinces us that the dependency basis exists, it does not tell us how to find the multivalued dependencies needed to apply the decomposition rule.

Algorithm 7.6: Computing the Dependency Basis.
Input: A set of multivalued dependencies M over set of attributes U, and a set $X \subseteq U$.
Output: The dependency basis for X with respect to M.
Method:
1. Let T be the set of sets $Z \subseteq U$ such that for some $W \twoheadrightarrow Y$ in M, we have $W \subseteq X$, and Z is either $Y - X$ or $U - X - Y$.
2. Until T consists of a disjoint collection of sets, find a pair of sets Z_1 and Z_2 in T that are not disjoint and replace them by the sets $Z_1 - Z_2$, $Z_2 - Z_1$, and $Z_1 \cap Z_2$, throwing away the empty set, in case one of Z_1 and Z_2 is contained in the other. Let S be the final collection of sets.
3. Until no more changes can be made to S, look for dependencies $V \twoheadrightarrow W$ in M and a set Y in S such that Y intersects W but not V. Replace Y by $Y \cap W$ and $Y - W$ in S.
4. The final collection of sets S is the dependency basis for X. $\square$

Since steps (2) and (3) only cause sets to be split, and they terminate when no more splitting can be done, it is straightforward that Algorithm 7.6 takes time that is polynomial in the size of M and U. In fact, careful implementation allows the algorithm to run in time proportional to the number of dependencies in M times the cube of the number of attributes in U. A proof of this fact and a proof of correctness for Algorithm 7.6 can be found in Beeri [1980].

Lossless Joins

Algorithm 7.2 helps us determine when a decomposition of a relation scheme R into $(R_1, \ldots, R_k)$ has a lossless join, on the assumption that the only dependencies to be satisfied by the relations for R are functional. The algorithm can be generalized to handle multivalued dependencies, as we shall see in the next section. In the case of a decomposition of R into two schemes, there is a simple test for a lossless join.

Theorem 7.11: Let R be a relation scheme and $\rho = (R_1, R_2)$ a decomposition of R. Let D be a set of functional and multivalued dependencies on the attributes of R. Then ρ has a lossless join if and only if $(R_1 \cap R_2) \twoheadrightarrow (R_1 - R_2)$ [or equivalently, by the complementation rule, $(R_1 \cap R_2) \twoheadrightarrow (R_2 - R_1)$].

Proof: ρ has a lossless join if and only if for any relation r satisfying D, and any two tuples t and s in r, the tuple u such that $u[R_1] = t[R_1]$ and $u[R_2] = s[R_2]$ is in r if it exists. But u exists if and only if $t[R_1 \cap R_2] = s[R_1 \cap R_2]$. Thus, the condition that u is always in r is exactly the condition that

$$(R_1 \cap R_2) \twoheadrightarrow (R_1 - R_2)$$

or equivalently, $(R_1 \cap R_2) \twoheadrightarrow (R_2 - R_1)$. $\square$

Note that by axiom A7, Theorem 7.5 implies Theorem 7.11 when the only dependencies are functional, but Theorem 7.5 says nothing at all if there are multivalued dependencies that must be satisfied.

Fourth Normal Form

There is a generalization of Boyce-Codd normal form, called fourth normal form, that applies to relation schemes with multivalued dependencies. Let R be a relation scheme and D the set of dependencies applicable to R. We say R is in *fourth normal form* if whenever there is a multivalued dependency $X \twoheadrightarrow Y$, where Y is not empty or a subset of X, and XY does not include all the attributes of R, then X is a superkey of R. Note that the definitions of "key" and "superkey" have not changed because multivalued dependencies are present; "key" still means a set of attributes that functionally determines R.

Observe that if D includes only functional dependencies, then whenever R is in fourth normal form it is in Boyce-Codd normal form. For then $X \twoheadrightarrow Y$ must mean that $X \rightarrow Y$. Suppose R is not in Boyce-Codd normal form, because there is some functional dependency $X \rightarrow A$, where X is not a superkey. If $XA = R$, then surely X includes a key. Therefore XA does not include all attributes, and a violation of fourth normal form, with $X \rightarrow A$ as a special case of $X \twoheadrightarrow Y$, is immediate.

We can find a decomposition of R into $\rho = (R_1, \ldots, R_k)$, such that ρ has a lossless join with respect to D, and each R_i is in fourth normal form, as follows. We start with ρ consisting only of R, as in Algorithm 7.4 (decomposition into Boyce-Codd normal form). If there is a relation scheme in ρ not in fourth normal form with respect to D projected onto some set of attributes S,† then there must be in S a dependency $X \twoheadrightarrow Y$, where X is not a superkey of S, Y is not empty or a subset of X, and $XY \neq S$. We may assume X and Y are disjoint, since $X \twoheadrightarrow (Y - X)$ follows from $X \twoheadrightarrow Y$ using A1, A7, and the decomposition rule. Then replace S by $S_1 = XY$ and $S_2 = S - Y$, which must be two relation schemes with fewer attributes than S. By Theorem 7.11, since $(S_1 \cap S_2) \twoheadrightarrow (S_1 - S_2)$, the join of S_1 and S_2 is lossless with respect to D projected onto S.

We leave it as an exercise that the repeated decomposition as above produces a set of relation schemes that has a lossless join with respect to D. The only important detail remaining is to determine how one computes, given R, D, and $S \subseteq R$, the set of functional and multivalued dependencies that hold in S, that is, $\pi_S(D)$, the projection of D onto S. It is a theorem of Aho, Beeri, and Ullman

---

† We shall discuss later how to find the projection of a set of functional and multivalued dependencies.

[1978] that $\pi_S(D)$ can be computed as follows.

1. Compute D^+.
2. For each $X \to Y$ in D^+, if $X \subseteq S$, then $X \to (Y \cap S)$ holds in S.†
3. For each $X \twoheadrightarrow Y$ in D^+, if $X \subseteq S$, then $X \twoheadrightarrow (Y \cap S)$ holds in S.
4. No other functional or multivalued dependencies for S may be deduced from the fact that D holds for R.

Example 7.20: Let us reinvestigate the $CTHRSG$ relation scheme first introduced in Example 7.15. We have several times noted the minimal cover

$$
\begin{array}{ll}
C \to T & CS \to G \\
HR \to C & HS \to R \\
HT \to R &
\end{array}
$$

for the pertinent functional dependencies. It turns out that one multivalued dependency, $C \twoheadrightarrow HR$, together with the above functional dependencies, allows us to derive all the multivalued dependencies that we would intuitively feel are valid. We saw, for example, that $C \twoheadrightarrow HR$ and $C \to T$ imply $C \twoheadrightarrow SG$. We also know that $HR \to CT$, so $HR \twoheadrightarrow CT$. By the complementation rule, $HR \twoheadrightarrow SG$. That is to say, given an hour and room, there is an associated set of student-grade pairs, namely the students enrolled in the course meeting in that room and that hour, paired with the grades they got in that course. The reader is invited to explore further the set of multivalued dependencies following from the given five functional dependencies and one multivalued dependency.

To place relation scheme $CTHRSG$ in fourth normal form, we might start with $C \twoheadrightarrow HR$, which violates the fourth normal form conditions since C is not a superkey (recall that SH is the only key for $CTHRSG$). We decompose $CTHRSG$ into CHR and $CTSG$. The relation scheme CHR has key HR. The multivalued dependency $C \twoheadrightarrow HR$ does not violate fourth normal form for CHR, since the left and right sides together include all the attributes of CHR. No other functional or multivalued dependency projected onto CHR violates fourth normal form, so we need not decompose CHR any further.

Such is not the case for $CTSG$. The only key is CS, yet we see the multivalued dependency $C \twoheadrightarrow T$, which follows from $C \to T$. We therefore split $CTSG$ into CT and CSG. These are both in fourth normal form with respect to their projected dependencies, so we have obtained the decomposition CHR, CT, and CSG, which has a lossless join and all relation schemes in fourth normal form.

It is interesting to note that when in Example 7.15 we decomposed relation scheme $CTHRSG$ into Boyce-Codd normal form using only functional dependencies, we obtained these three relation schemes and the scheme CHS as well. When we ignore the multivalued dependency $C \twoheadrightarrow HR$, the decomposition into

† Note that since $X \to Y \cap S$ is also in D^+, this rule is equivalent to the rule for projecting functional dependencies given earlier.

three schemes $\rho = (CHR, CT, CSG)$ does not necessarily have a lossless join, but if we are allowed to use $C \twoheadrightarrow HR$, it is easy to prove by Theorem 7.11 that their join is lossless. As an exercise, the reader should find a relation r for $CTHRSG$ such that $m_\rho(r) \neq r$, yet r satisfies all the given functional dependencies (but not $C \twoheadrightarrow HR$, of course). $\square$

Embedded Multivalued Dependencies

One further complication that enters when we try to decompose a relation scheme R into fourth normal form is that there may be certain multivalued dependencies that we expect to hold when we project any plausible relation r for R onto a subset $X \subseteq R$, yet we do not expect these dependencies to hold in r itself. Such a dependency is said to be *embedded* in R, and we must be alert, when writing down all the constraints that we believe hold in relations r for R, not to ignore an embedded multivalued dependency. Incidentally, embedded functional dependencies never occur; it is easy to show that if $Y \rightarrow Z$ holds when relation r over R is projected onto X, then $Y \rightarrow Z$ holds in r as well. The same is not true for multivalued dependencies, as the following example shows.

Example 7.21: Suppose we have the attributes C (course), S (student), P (prerequisite), and Y (year in which the student took the prerequisite). The only nontrivial functional or multivalued dependency is $SP \rightarrow Y$, so we may decompose $CSPY$ into CSP and SPY; the resulting schemes are apparently in fourth normal form.

The multivalued dependency $C \twoheadrightarrow S$ does not hold. For example, we might have in relation r for $CSPY$ the tuples

CS402	Jones	CS311	1978
CS402	Smith	CS401	1979

yet not find the tuple

CS402	Jones	CS401	1979

Presumably Jones took CS401, since it is a prerequisite for CS402, but perhaps he did not take it in 1979. Similarly, $C \twoheadrightarrow P$ does not hold in $CSPY$.

However, if we project any legal r for $CSPY$ onto CSP, we would expect $C \twoheadrightarrow S$ and, by the complementation rule, $C \twoheadrightarrow P$ to hold, provided every student enrolled in a course is required to have taken each prerequisite for the course at some time. Thus $C \twoheadrightarrow S$ and $C \twoheadrightarrow P$ are embedded multivalued dependencies for CSP. As a consequence, CSP is really not in fourth normal form, and it should be decomposed into CS and CP. This replacement avoids repeating the student name once for each prerequisite of a course in which he is enrolled.

It is interesting to observe that the decomposition $\rho = (CS, CP, SPY)$ has a lossless join if we acknowledge that $C \twoheadrightarrow S$ is an embedded dependency for CSP. For then, given any relation r for $CSPY$ that satisfies $SP{\to}Y$ and the dependency $C{\to\!\!\!\to}S$ in CSP, we can prove that $m_\rho(r) = r$. Yet we could not prove this assuming only the functional dependency $SP{\to}Y$; the reader can as an exercise find a relation r satisfying $SP{\to}Y$ (but not the embedded dependency) such that $m_\rho(r) \neq r$. $\square$

We shall consider embedded multivalued dependencies further in the next section. Here let us introduce the standard notation for such dependencies. A relation r over relation scheme R satisfies the embedded multivaued dependency $X{\to\!\!\!\to}Y \mid Z$ if the multivalued dependency $X{\to\!\!\!\to}Y$ is satisfied by the relation $\pi_{X\cup Y\cup Z}(r)$, which is the projection of r onto the set of attributes mentioned in the embedded dependency. Note that there is no requirement that X, Y, and Z be disjoint, and by the union, decomposition, and complementation rules, $X{\to\!\!\!\to}Y$ holds in $\pi_{X\cup Y\cup Z}(r)$ if and only if $X{\to\!\!\!\to}Z$ does, so $X{\to\!\!\!\to}Y \mid Z$ means the same as $X{\to\!\!\!\to}Z \mid Y$. As an example, the embedded multivalued dependency from Example 7.21 is written $C{\to\!\!\!\to}S \mid P$ or $C{\to\!\!\!\to}P \mid S$.

7.6 OTHER KINDS OF DEPENDENCIES

We have seen functional and multivalued dependencies and the embedded version of multivalued dependencies.† That just about covers the sorts of dependencies we encounter in practice, with the exception of the *join dependency*, written $\bowtie(R_1, R_2, \ldots, R_n)$, which is satisfied by a relation r over the union of the sets of attributes $R_1 \cup \cdots \cup R_n$ if and only if the join of the projections of r onto the R_i's equals r. That is, $m_\rho(r) = r$, where ρ is the decomposition $(R_1, \ldots, R_n)$. We shall discuss join dependencies later in this section, after we make a brief excursion into the subject of generalized dependencies, and a crucial application of join dependencies occurs in Chapter 9.

Generalized Dependencies

We shall introduce a broad class of dependencies not because we believe the real world requires them for accurate description; functional, multivalued, and join dependencies are most likely all we need. Rather, there are some key ideas, such as the "chase" algorithm, that are better described in the general context to which the ideas apply than in the special case of functional or multivalued dependencies. Further, the general algorithm will be applied to optimization of queries in the next chapter and to "universal relation" database systems in Chapter 9.

We view both functional and multivalued dependencies as saying of relations that "if you see a certain pattern, then you must also see this." In the case of functional dependencies, "this" refers to the equality of certain of the

---

† Recall from our discussion of embedded multivalued dependencies in the previous section there is no distinct notion of an "embedded functional dependency."

a	b_1	c_1	d_1
a	b_2	c_2	d_2

$$b_1 = b_2$$

(a) The functional dependency $A{\rightarrow}B$.

a	b_1	c_1	d_1
a	b_2	c_2	d_2
a	b_1	c_2	d_2

(b) The multivalued dependency $A{\rightarrow}{\rightarrow}B$.

Fig. 7.8. Dependencies in tabular notation.

symbols seen, while for multivalued dependencies, "this" is another tuple that must also be in the relation. For example, let $U = ABCD$ be the universal set of attributes. Then the functional dependency $A{\rightarrow}B$ says that whenever we see, in some relation r, two tuples $ab_1c_1d_1$ and $ab_2c_2d_2$, then $b_1 = b_2$ in those tuples. The multivalued dependency $A{\rightarrow}{\rightarrow}B$ says of the same two tuples that we must also see the tuple $ab_1c_2d_2$† in r, which is a weaker assertion than saying $b_1 = b_2$. A convenient tabular form of such dependencies is shown in Fig. 7.8.

We do not wish to generalize the sorts of conclusions we can draw. Rather, the two classes of generalized dependencies, represented by Fig. 7.8(a), where the conclusion is the equality of two symbols, and by Fig. 7.8(b), where the conclusion is the existence of another tuple, seem quite general enough. We call these two types *equality-generating* and *tuple-generating*, respectively. The generalization we need is in the sorts of patterns we shall look for among the tuples of the given relation. We wish to allow more than two tuples, and we wish to allow various combinations of symbols appearing in their components.

Define a generalized dependency over a relation scheme $A_1 \cdots A_n$ to be an expression of the form $(t_1, \ldots, t_k)/t$, where the t_i's are n-tuples of symbols, and t is either another n-tuple (in which case we have a tuple-generating dependency) or an expression $x = y$, where x and y are symbols appearing among the t_i's (then we have an equality-generating dependency). We call the t_i's the *hypotheses* and t the *conclusion*. Intuitively, the dependency means that every relation in which we find the hypotheses, the conclusion holds. To find the hypothesis tuples, we may have to rename some or all of the symbols used in the hypotheses to make them match the symbols used in the relation. Any renaming of

---

† Recall that in the formal definition of multivalued dependencies in Section 7.5, we asserted the existence of two tuples, u and v, but that definition was redundant. Since in the original definition, either given tuple could play the role of t or s, asserting the existence of u asserts the existence of v.

symbols that is done applies to the conclusion as well as the hypotheses. We shall give a more formal definition after some examples.

Frequently we shall display these dependencies as in Fig. 7.8, with the hypotheses listed in rows above a line and the conclusion below. It is sometimes useful as well to show the attributes to which the columns correspond, above a line at the top. In all cases, we assume that the order of the attributes in the relation scheme is fixed and understood.

We shall make the assumption that no symbol of the t_i's or t appears in more than one column.† We shall not require that a symbol appearing in the conclusion of a tuple-generating dependency also appear in the hypotheses. A symbol of the conclusion appearing nowhere else is called *unique*. A generalized dependency is called *embedded* if it has one or more unique symbols and *full* if it has no unique symbols. This use of the term "embedded" generalizes our use of the term in connection with multivalued dependencies. That is, if a multivalued dependency is embedded, it must have unique symbols in all the components not in the set of attributes onto which the projection is made.

Example 7.22: We could write the embedded multivalued dependency $C \twoheadrightarrow S \mid P$ of Example 7.21 as

C	S	P	Y
c	s_1	p_1	y_1
c	s_2	p_2	y_2
c	s_1	p_2	y_3

Notice that y_3 is a unique symbol.

As a general rule, we can write any embedded multivalued dependency $X \twoheadrightarrow Y \mid Z$ over a set of attributes U by writing two hypothesis rows that agree in the columns for the attributes in X and disagree in all other attributes. The conclusion agrees with both hypotheses on X, agrees with the first hypothesis on Y, agrees with the second on the attributes in Z, and has a unique symbol everywhere else. The justification is that the embedded multivalued dependency $X \twoheadrightarrow Y \mid Z$ says that if we have two tuples t and s in relation r that project onto $X \cup Y \cup Z$ to give tuples t' and s', and $t'[X] = s'[X]$, then there is some tuple u in r that projects to u' and satisfies $u'[X] = t'[X] = s'[X]$, $u'[Y] = t'[Y]$, and $u'[Z] = s'[Z]$. Notice that nothing at all is said about the value of u for attributes in $U - X - Y - Z$. Clearly, we can express all the above in our generalized dependency notation, where t and s are the first and second hypotheses, and u is the conclusion. Since we can only conclude that the tuple u has some values in the attributes $U - X - Y - Z$, but we cannot relate those values to the values in t or s, we must use unique symbols in our conclusion.

† This constraint is made primarily because it is satisfied by the kinds of dependencies we find in nature. Relaxing the constraint gives us what are called *typeless* dependencies, and the bibliographic notes have some interesting facts to tell about these.

A	B	C	D	E
a			d	
a	b			
	b			e
		c	d	e
a				e
a	b	c	d	e

Fig. 7.9. A join dependency in tabular notation.

For another example, the second part of Example 7.8 showed that given a certain collection of functional dependencies, the decomposition

$$(AD, AB, BE, CDE, AE)$$

is a lossless join decomposition. What was really shown there was that any relation that satisfies the functional dependencies $A{\to}C$, $B{\to}C$, $C{\to}D$, $DE{\to}C$, and $CE{\to}A$ must also satisfy the join dependency $\bowtie (AD, AB, BE, CDE, AE)$. We can display this join dependency as in Fig. 7.9. In that figure, and several subsequent ones, we shall use blanks to denote symbols that appear only once. The reader should appreciate the similarity between the tabular representation of generalized dependencies and the Query-by-Example notation, and the convention that a blank stands for a symbol that appears nowhere else is borrowed from there.

In general, the join dependency $\bowtie (R_1, \ldots, R_n)$, expressed in the tabular notation, has one hypothesis row for each R_i, and this row has the same symbol as the conclusion row in the columns for the attributes in R_i and elsewhere has a symbol that appears nowhere else. The justification is that the join dependency says about a relation r that whenever we have a tuple, such as the conclusion row, that agrees with some tuple t_i in r in the attributes R_i for all $1 \leq i \leq n$, then that tuple is itself in r. $\square$

One reason for introducing the generalized dependency notation is that it leads to a conceptually simple way to infer dependencies. The test works for full dependencies of all sorts, although it may take exponential time, and therefore is not preferable to the method outlined before Algorithm 7.6 (computation of the dependency basis) when only functional and multivalued dependencies are concerned. When there are embedded dependencies, the method may succeed in making the inference, but it may also give an inconclusive result. There is in fact, no known algorithm for testing whether a dependency follows logically from others, even when the dependencies are restricted to an apparently simple class, such as embedded multivalued dependencies. (Of course, if we restrict the class still further, to full multivalued dependencies, then there is such an algorithm, as we saw in the last section.)

Symbol Mappings

Before giving the inference test, we need to introduce an important concept, the *symbol mapping*, which is a function h from one set of symbols S to another set T; that is, for each symbol a in S, $h(a)$ is a symbol in T. We allow $h(a)$ and $h(b)$ to be the same member of T, even if $a \neq b$. If $s = a_1 a_2 \cdots a_n$ is a tuple whose symbols are in S, we may apply the symbol mapping h to s and obtain the tuple $h(s) = h(a_1)h(a_2)\cdots h(a_n)$. If $s_1, \ldots, s_k$ is a set of tuples whose symbols are in S, and $t_1, \ldots, t_m$ are tuples whose symbols are in T, we say there is a symbol mapping from the first set of tuples to the second if there is some h such that for all i, $1 \leq i \leq k$, $h(s_i)$ is t_j for some j. It is possible that two or more s_i's are mapped to the same t_j, and some t_j's may be the target of no s_i.

Example 7.23: Let $A = \{abc, ade, fbe\}$ and $B = \{xyz, wyz\}$. There are several symbol mappings from A to B. One has $h(a) = h(f) = x$, $h(b) = h(d) = y$, and $h(c) = h(e) = z$. This one maps all three tuples in A to xyz. Another symbol mapping has $g(a) = x$, $g(b) = g(d) = y$, $g(c) = g(e) = z$, and $g(f) = w$. Symbol mapping g sends abc and ade to xyz, but sends fbe to wyz. □

Our most important use for symbol mappings is as maps between sets of rows as in Example 7.23. The reader should observe a duality that holds in that situation. We defined symbol mappings as functions on symbols, and when applied to sets of rows, we added the requirement that the mapping applied to each row of the first set is a row of the second set. Dually, we could have defined mappings from rows to rows, and added the requirement that no symbol be mapped by two different rows to different symbols. Thus, in Example 7.23, we could not map abc to xyz and also map ade to wyz, because a would be mapped to both x and w.

Formal Definition of Generalized Dependency

With the notion of a symbol mapping, we can formally define the meaning of generalized dependencies. We say a relation r *satisfies* the tuple-generating dependency $(t_1, \ldots, t_n)/t$ if whenever h is a symbol mapping from all the hypotheses $\{t_1, \ldots, t_n\}$ to r, we can extend h to any unique symbols in t in such a way that $h(t)$ is in r. We also say that r *satisfies* the equality-generating dependency $(t_1, \ldots, t_n)/a = b$ if whenever h is a symbol mapping from the hypotheses to r, it must be that $h(a) = h(b)$.

Example 7.24: Let d be the generalized dependency in Fig. 7.10(a), and let r be the relation of Fig. 7.10(b). Notice that d is not the same as the multivalued dependency $A \twoheadrightarrow B$, since the symbol a_2, which is a unique symbol in Fig. 7.10(a), would have to be a_1 instead. In fact, Fig. 7.10(a) is an example of a two-hypothesis tuple-generating dependency that is neither a full nor embedded multivalued dependency; such dependencies were called *subset dependencies* by

a_1	b_1	c_1
a_1	b_2	c_2
a_2	b_1	c_2

0	1	2
0	3	4
0	3	2
5	1	4

(a) The dependency d (b) The relation r

Fig. 7.10. A generalized dependency and a relation satisfying it.

Sagiv and Walecka [1982].

To see that r satisfies d, let us consider a symbol mapping h and the tuples of r to which each of the hypotheses of d could be mapped. Since the two hypotheses agree in the A-column, and $h(a_1)$ can have only one value, we know that either both hypotheses are mapped to the last tuple of r (if $h(a_1) = 5$), or both are mapped among the first three tuples (if $h(a_1) = 0$). In the first case, h maps b_1 and b_2 to 1 and c_1 and c_2 to 4. Then we can extend h to the unique symbol by defining $h(a_2) = 5$. In that case, $h(a_2b_1c_2) = 514$, which is a member of r, so we obtain no violation of d with mappings that have $h(a_1) = 5$.

Now consider what happens if $h(a_1) = 0$, so the only possible mappings send the two hypotheses into the first three tuples of r. Any such mapping h has $h(b_1)$ equal to either 1 or 3, and it has $h(c_2)$ equal to either 2 or 4. In any of the four combinations, there is a tuple in r that has that combination of values in its B and C components. Thus, we can extend h to the unique symbol a_2 by setting $h(a_2) = 5$ if $h(b_1) = 1$ and $h(c_2) = 4$, and setting $h(a_2) = 0$ otherwise.

We have now considered all symbol mappings that map each of the hypotheses of d into a tuple in r, and have found that in each case, we can extend the mapping to the unique symbol a_2 in such a way that the conclusion of d is present in r. Therefore, r satisfies d. $\square$

Applying Dependencies to Relations

To test whether a dependency d follows logically from a set of dependencies D, we shall attempt to prove the conclusion of d from the hypotheses of d. We shall begin with the hypotheses of d and use the dependencies in D to transform them, by drawing conclusions about the equality of their symbols or about other tuples that must be in any relation satisfying D. The process of making these inferences is called "applying" the dependency to the relation that is formed from the hypotheses of d. We shall thus study first the matter of applying dependencies.

Suppose we have an equality-generating dependency

$$d = (s_1, \ldots, s_k)/a = b$$

and a relation $r = \{t_1, \ldots, t_m\}$. We can *apply* d to r if we find a symbol mapping h from $\{s_1, \ldots, s_k\}$ to $\{t_1, \ldots, t_m\}$. The effect of applying d to r

using symbol mapping h is to equate the symbols $h(a)$ and $h(b)$ wherever they appear among the t_i's; either may replace the other.

If we have a tuple-generating dependency instead, say $e = (s_1, \ldots, s_k)/s$, we apply e to r using h by adjoining to r the tuple $h(s)$. However, if e is an embedded dependency, then s will have one or more unique symbols, so h will not be defined for all symbols of s. In that case, if c is a unique symbol in s, create a new symbol, one that appears nowhere else in r, and extend h by defining $h(c)$ to be that symbol. Of course, we create distinct symbols for each of the unique symbols of s.

In certain cases, however, the new symbols can all be replaced by existing symbols of r so that $h(s)$ becomes a member of r. In that case, e with symbol mapping h has no effect upon r.

Example 7.25: Let us consider the equality-generating dependency

$$(abc, ade, fbe)/a = f$$

applied to the relation $r = \{\, xyz, wyz \,\}$. If we use the symbol mapping g of Example 7.23, we find that $g(a) = x$ and $g(f) = w$. We apply the dependency using this symbol mapping, by equating x and w; say we replace them both by x. Then the effect on r of applying the dependency in this way is to change r into $\{\, xyz \,\}$.

Suppose instead we had the tuple-generating dependency $(abc, ade, fbe)/abq$. Then using the same symbol mapping, we would adjoin to r a tuple whose first two components were $g(a) = x$ and $g(b) = y$ and whose third component was a new symbol, not appearing in r, say u; that is, r becomes $\{\, xyz, wyz, xyu \,\}$. However, we could replace u by the existing symbol z, and the result would be xyz, a tuple already in r. Thus we have the option (which we should take, because it simplifies matters) of not changing r at all. $\square$

The Chase Algorithm for Inference of Dependencies

Now we can exhibit a process that helps us resolve the question whether $D \models d$, where D is a set of generalized dependencies, and d is another generalized dependency. The procedure is an algorithm when D has full dependencies only, but if D has some embedded dependencies, it tells the truth if it answers at all, but it may run on forever inconclusively. We call the process the *chase*, because we "chase down" all the consequences of the dependencies D.

As we mentioned in connection with the application of dependencies, the intuitive idea behind the chase process is that we start with the hypotheses of the dependency d we wish to test, and we see what inferences we can make by applying the given dependencies D. If we can obtain the conclusion of d, then we have a proof that d follows from D. The reason the test works both ways is that, in a generalization of Algorithm 7.4, if we fail to draw the desired conclusion, the relation that results when we finish the process is a counterexample; it satisfies D but not d.†

First suppose that d is a tuple-generating dependency $(t_1, \ldots, t_m)/t$. We begin with the relation $r = \{ t_1, \ldots, t_m \}$. We then apply all the dependencies in D, in any order, repeatedly, until either

1. we cannot apply the dependencies in any way that changes r, or
2. we discover in r a tuple that agrees with t on all components except, perhaps, those places where t has a unique symbol.

However, when applying an equality-generating dependency, if one of the symbols being equated appears in t, change the other symbol to that one.‡ In case (2) above, we conclude that $D \models d$ is true. If (1) holds, but not (2), then we say that $D \models d$ is false. In fact, the resulting r will be a counterexample. It is a relation that satisfies all dependencies in D (or else one of them could be applied). However, r does not satisfy d, because there is a symbol mapping from the hypotheses of d to the original m tuples of r that implies the tuple t, or a tuple that agrees with it in nonunique symbols, should be present in r, which, since (2) is false, is not the case. This symbol mapping is the one that maps $t_1 \ldots, t_m$ to what each of these hypothesis rows has become after equality-generating dependencies in D were applied to these rows in r.

To see why the implication holds whenever case (2) applies, let us recall the proof of Theorem 7.4, which is really a special case of our present claim. That is, Algorithm 7.2, the lossless join test, can now be seen as a use of the chase process to test whether $F \models j$, where j is the join dependency made from the decomposition to which the algorithm applies, that is $\bowtie (R_1, \ldots, R_k)$. As in Theorem 7.4, we can see the relation r used in the chase as saying that certain tuples are in a hypothetical relation that satisfies D. Initially, these tuples are the hypotheses of the dependency being tested. Each time we apply a dependency, we are making an inference about other tuples that must be in the hypothetical relation that satisfies D (if we use a tuple-generating dependency), or about two symbols that must be equal (if we use an equality-generating dependency). Thus, each application is a valid inference from D, and if we infer the presence of t, that too is valid, i.e., we have shown that any relation containing $t_1, \ldots, t_m$ also contains t (or a tuple that agrees with t on nonunique symbols).

However, the dependency d says more than that; it says that if a relation contains any symbol mapping h of the t_i's, then h can be extended to the unique symbols of t, and $h(t)$ will also be in the relation. We need only to observe that

---

† However, there is the problem that if some dependencies are embedded, the process may not stop. In principle, it generates an infinite relation, and that infinite relation forms a counterexample. Unfortunately, with embedded dependencies we cannot tell, as we work, whether the process will go on forever or not, so the "test" is sometimes inconclusive.

‡ Notice how the assumption that no symbol appears in two columns is essential here, or we might try to equate two symbols of t.

this too can be shown by following the sequence of applications of dependencies in D. That is, start with $\{\,h(t_1),\ldots,h(t_m)\,\}$ and apply the same sequence of dependencies from D by composing the symbol mapping used to apply each dependency, with the symbol mapping h, to get another symbol mapping. The result will be the image, under h, of the sequence of changes made to the original relation $r = \{\,t_1,\ldots,t_m\,\}$.

We must also explain how to test, using the chase process, whether an equality-generating dependency $(t_1,\ldots,t_m)/a = b$ follows from a set of dependencies D. Follow the same process, but end and say yes if we ever equate the symbols a and b; say no as for tuple-generating dependencies, if we can make no more changes to r, yet we have not equated a and b. The validity of the inferences follows in essentially the same way as for tuple-generating dependencies.

We can sum up what we have claimed in the following theorem.

Theorem 7.12: The chase process applied to a set of full generalized dependencies D and a (possibly embedded) generalized dependency d determines correctly whether $D \models d$.

Proof: We have argued informally above why the procedure, if it makes an answer at all, answers correctly. We shall not go into further detail; the bibliographic notes provide directions into the literature where full proofs may be found.

We must, however, show that if D has only full dependencies, then the process is an algorithm, that is, it always halts. The observation is a simple one. When we apply a full dependency, we need introduce no new symbols. Thus, the relation r never has a tuple that is not made up of the original symbols of the hypotheses of d. But there are only a finite number of such symbols, and therefore r is always a subset of some finite set. We have only to rule out the possibility that r exhibits an oscillatory behavior; that is, it assumes after successive applications of dependencies, a sequence of values $r_1, r_2, \ldots, r_n = r_1$.

Tuple-generating dependencies always make the size of r increase, so it is not possible that the cycle involves no equality-generating dependencies. But an equality of symbols permanently reduces the number of symbols, since only the application of an embedded dependency could increase the number of different symbols in r. Thus no cycle could involve an equality-generating dependency and full tuple-generating dependencies only, proving that no cycle exists. We conclude that either we reach a condition where no change to r is possible, or we discover that the conclusion of d is in r. $\square$

Example 7.26: We can now see Example 7.8 as being an application of the chase algorithm to make the inferences $\{\,S{\to}A,\ SI{\to}P\,\} \models \bowtie(SA, SIP)$ and

$$
\begin{array}{cccc}
a_1 & b_1 & c_1 & d_1 \\
a_1 & b_2 & c_2 & d_2 \\
\hline
a_1 & b_1 & c_2 & d_3
\end{array}
$$

(a) $A \twoheadrightarrow B \mid C$

$$
\begin{array}{cccc}
a_2 & b_3 & c_3 & d_4 \\
a_3 & b_3 & c_4 & d_5 \\
\hline
\end{array}
$$

$$d_4 = d_5$$

(b) $B \rightarrow D$

$$
\begin{array}{cccc}
a_4 & b_4 & c_5 & d_6 \\
a_4 & b_5 & c_6 & d_7 \\
\hline
a_4 & b_6 & c_5 & d_7
\end{array}
$$

(c) $A \twoheadrightarrow C \mid D$

Fig. 7.11. Example dependencies.

$$\{\, A \rightarrow C,\ B \rightarrow C,\ C \rightarrow D,\ DE \rightarrow C,\ CE \rightarrow A \,\} \models$$
$$\bowtie (AD, AB, BE, CDE, AE)$$

As another example, we can show that over the set of attributes $ABCD$

$$\{\, A \twoheadrightarrow B \mid C,\ B \rightarrow D \,\} \models A \twoheadrightarrow C \mid D$$

We can write the three dependencies in tabular notation as in Fig. 7.11.

We begin with the hypotheses of Fig. 7.11(c), as shown in Fig. 7.12(a). We can apply the dependency of Fig. 7.11(a) by using the symbol mapping $h(a_1) = a_4$, $h(b_1) = b_5$, $h(c_1) = c_6$, $h(d_1) = d_7$, $h(b_2) = b_4$, $h(c_2) = c_5$, and $h(d_2) = d_6$. This mapping sends the two hypothesis rows of Fig. 7.11(a) to the two rows of Fig. 7.12(a), in the opposite order. If we extend h to map d_3 to a new symbol, say d_8, then we can infer that the tuple $a_4 b_5 c_5 d_8$ is in r, as in Fig. 7.12(b). Then, we can apply the dependency of Fig. 7.11(b), using a symbol mapping that the reader can deduce, to map the two hypotheses of Fig. 7.11(b) to the second and third rows of Fig. 7.12(b) and prove that $d_7 = d_8$. The substitution of d_7 for d_8 is reflected in Fig. 7.12(c). This tuple agrees with the conclusion of Fig. 7.11(c), except in the B-column, where the latter has a unique symbol, b_6. We conclude that the inference is valid. $\square$

EXERCISES

7.1: Suppose we have a database for an investment firm, consisting of the following attributes: B (broker), O (office of a broker), I (investor), S (stock), Q (quantity of stock owned by an investor), and D (dividend

a_4	b_4	c_5	d_6
a_4	b_5	c_6	d_7

(a) Initial relation.

a_4	b_4	c_5	d_6
a_4	b_5	c_6	d_7
a_4	b_5	c_5	d_8

(b) After applying Fig. 7.11(a).

a_4	b_4	c_5	d_6
a_4	b_5	c_6	d_7
a_4	b_5	c_5	d_7

(c) After applying Fig. 7.11(b).

Fig. 7.12. Sequence of relations constructed by the chase.

paid by a stock), with the following functional dependencies: $S \rightarrow D$, $I \rightarrow B$, $IS \rightarrow Q$, and $B \rightarrow O$.

a)   Find a key for the relation scheme $R = BOSQID$.

b)   How many keys does relation scheme R have? Prove your answer.

c)   Find a lossless join decomposition of R into Boyce-Codd normal form.

d)   Find a decomposition of R into third normal form, having a lossless join and preserving dependencies.

7.2: Suppose we choose to represent the relation scheme R of Exercise 7.1 by the two schemes $ISQD$ and IBO. What redundancies and anomalies do you forsee?

7.3: Suppose we instead represent R by SD, IB, ISQ, and BO. Does this decomposition have a lossless join?

7.4: Suppose we represent R of Exercise 7.1 by ISQ, IB, SD, and ISO. Find minimal covers for the dependencies (from Exercise 7.1) projected onto each of these relation schemes. Find a minimal cover for the union of the projected dependencies. Does this decomposition preserve dependencies?

7.5: In the database of Exercise 7.1, replace the functional dependency $S \rightarrow D$ by the multivalued dependency $S \rightarrow\!\!\!\rightarrow D$. That is, D now represents the dividend "history" of the stock.

a)   Find the dependency basis of I.

b)   Find the dependency basis of BS

c)   Find a fourth normal form decomposition of R.

* 7.6: Complete the proof of Theorem 7.5 by providing a formal proof that in the row for R_1, an a is entered if and only if $R_1 \cap R_2 \rightarrow A$.

7.7: Complete the proof of Lemma 7.5 by showing that if $r \subseteq s$ then $\pi_{R_i}(r) \subseteq \pi_{R_i}(s)$.

7.8: In Example 7.10 we contended that $Z \rightarrow C$ does not imply $CS \rightarrow Z$. Prove this contention.

7.9: At the end of Section 7.3 it was claimed that $\rho = (AB, CD)$ was a dependency-preserving, but not lossless join decomposition of $ABCD$, given the dependencies $A \rightarrow B$ and $C \rightarrow D$. Verify this claim.

** 7.10: Complete the proof of Theorem 7.9 by showing that axioms A1–A8 are sound and complete.

* 7.11: Verify the union, pseudotransitivity, and decomposition rules for multivalued dependencies.

* 7.12: Give a formal proof of Lemma 7.6(a), that the iteration of lossless join decompositions itself has a lossless join. Also prove Lemma 7.6(b), that the addition of schemes (with no new attributes) to a lossless join decomposition preserves the lossless join property.

* 7.13: Verify the contention in Example 7.21, that there is a relation r satisfying $SP \rightarrow Y$, such that $\pi_{CS}(r) \bowtie \pi_{CP}(r) \bowtie \pi_{SPY}(r) \neq r$. Check that your relation does not satisfy $C \rightarrow\!\!\!\rightarrow S$ in CSP.

** 7.14: Show that it is $\mathcal{NP}$-complete to determine
   a)   Whether a relation scheme has a key of size k or less.
   b)   If a relation scheme is in Boyce-Codd normal form.

7.15: Use the chase algorithm to tell whether the following inferences are valid over the set of attributes $ABCD$.
   a) $\{ A \rightarrow\!\!\!\rightarrow B, A \rightarrow C \} \models A \rightarrow\!\!\!\rightarrow D$
   b) $\{ A \rightarrow\!\!\!\rightarrow B \mid C, B \rightarrow\!\!\!\rightarrow C \mid D \} \models A \rightarrow\!\!\!\rightarrow C \mid D$
   c) $\{ A \rightarrow\!\!\!\rightarrow B \mid C, A \rightarrow D \} \models A \rightarrow\!\!\!\rightarrow C \mid D$
   ** d) $\{ A \rightarrow\!\!\!\rightarrow B \mid C, A \rightarrow\!\!\!\rightarrow C \mid D \} \models A \rightarrow\!\!\!\rightarrow B \mid D$

* 7.16: Show that no collection of tuple-generating dependencies can imply an equality-generating dependency.

7.17: Give an algorithm to determine, given a collection of functional, (full) multivalued, and (full) join dependencies, whether a given decomposition has a lossless join.

7.18: Show that the multivalued dependency $X \rightarrow\!\!\!\rightarrow Y$ over the set of attributes U is equivalent to the join dependency $\bowtie (XY, XZ)$, where $Z = U - X - Y$. *Hint*: Write both as generalized dependencies.

BIBLIOGRAPHIC NOTES

Functional dependencies were first studied by Codd [1970]. Axioms for functional dependencies were first given by Armstrong [1974]; the axioms used here are from Beeri, Fagin, and Howard [1977]. Algorithm 7.1, the computation of the closure of a set of attributes, is from Bernstein [1976]. Algorithm 7.2, the lossless join test, is from Aho, Beeri, and Ullman [1978]. The special case of the join of two relations, Theorem 7.5, was shown in the "if" direction by Heath

[1971] and Delobel and Casey [1972] and in the opposite direction by Rissanen [1977].

Algorithm 7.3, the test for preservation of dependencies, is by Beeri and Honeyman [1982]. The paper by Ginsburg and Zaiddan [1982] points out that when projected, functional dependencies imply certain other dependencies, which happen to be equality-generating, generalized dependencies, but are not themselves functional. As a result, when we discuss projected dependencies, we must be very careful to establish the class of dependencies about which we speak.

Third normal form is defined in Codd [1970] and Boyce-Codd normal form in Codd [1972a]. The dependency-preserving decomposition into third normal form, Algorithm 7.5, is from Bernstein [1976], although he there uses a "synthetic" approach, designing a scheme without starting with a universal relation. Theorem 7.3, the minimal cover theorem used in Algorithm 7.5, is also from Bernstein [1976], and a stronger theorem of that type appears in Maier [1980b].

Theorem 7.8, giving a third normal form decomposition with lossless join and dependency preservation is from Biskup, Dayal, and Bernstein [1979]. A related result appears in Osborn [1977]. The equivalence problem for decompositions of a given relation was solved by Beeri, Mendelzon, Sagiv, and Ullman [1981]. Ling, Tompa, and Kameda [1981] generalize the notion of third normal form to account for redundancies across several different relation schemes. Relatons satisfying Boyce-Codd normal form are characterized by Ginsburg and Hull [1981]. Schkolnick and Sorenson [1981] consider the positive and negative consequences of failing to normalize relation schemes.

The problem of adequacy of a decomposition has been considered from several points of view. Arora and Carlson [1978] regard the lossless join and dependency-preservation conditions as a notion of adequacy, while Rissanen [1977] defines a decomposition to have *independent components* if there is a one-to-one correspondence between relations for the universal scheme that satisfy the dependencies, and projections of relations that satisfy the projected dependencies. Maier, Mendelzon, Sadri, and Ullman [1980] show that these notions are equivalent for functional dependencies, but not for multivalued dependencies.

Multivalued dependencies were invented independently by Fagin [1977], Delobel [1978], and Zaniolo [1976] (see also Zaniolo and Menkanoff [1981]), although the earliest manifestation of the concept is in Delobel's thesis in 1973. The axioms for multivalued dependencies are from Beeri, Fagin, and Howard [1977]. The independence of subsets of these axioms was considered by Mendelzon [1979], while Biskup [1980] shows that if one does not assume a universal relation, then without the complementation axiom, they form a sound and complete set. Lein [1979] develops axioms for multivalued dependencies on the assumption that null values are permitted. Sagiv et al. show the equivalence of multivalued dependency theory to a fragment of propositional calculus, thus providing a convenient notation in which to reason about such dependencies.

The dependency basis and Algorithm 7.6 are from Beeri [1980]. Hagihara et al. [1979] give a more efficient test whether a given multivalued dependency is implied by others, and Galil [1979] gives an even faster way to compute the dependency basis. Embedded multivalued dependencies were considered by Fagin [1977], Delobel [1978] and Tanaka, Kambayashi, and Yajima [1978].

Join dependencies were first formalized by Rissanen [1979]. The condition on relations corresponding to a join dependency on their schemes was considered by Nicolas [1978] and Mendelzon and Maier [1979]. Fagin [1979] provides a "fifth" normal form, based on the absence of nontrivial join dependencies within a relation scheme, and Fagin [1981a] goes beyond this, showing that it is possible to decompose relation schemes so that the only dependencies remaining are functional dependencies of a nonkey attribute on a key and constraints that reflect the limited sizes of domains for attributes.

Lossless join testing by the "chase" process, given multivalued and functional dependencies was considered in Aho, Beeri, and Ullman [1978], while Maier, Mendelzon, and Sagiv [1979] generalize the chase to handle the case where join dependencies are included. While there appears to be great power in the "chase" technique, Goodman and Shmueli [1981a] give a more general situation in which the "chase" is not adequate to make inferences. Liu and Demers [1978] provide a more efficient lossless join test when functional dependencies are involved, while Vardi [1980] and Maier, Sagiv, and Yannakakis [1980] cover polynomial time cases of the more general lossless join testing problem.

The notion of generalized dependencies was discovered independently several times. It appears in Beeri and Vardi [1980], Paredaens and Janssens [1980], Paredaens [1981], and Sadri and Ullman [1980a, 1980b]. A somewhat more general class, called implicational dependencies in Fagin [1980] and algebraic dependencies in Yannakakis and Papadimitriou [1980], has also been investigated.

The undecidability of implication for generalized equality-generating dependencies was shown independently by Gurevich and Lewis [1982] and Vardi [1982]. Key results leading to the undecidability proof were contained in earlier papers by Beeri and Vardi [1981a] and Chandra, Lewis, and Makowsky [1981].

Several sound and complete axiom systems for generalized dependencies are found in Beeri and Vardi [1981b] and Sadri and Ullman [1980a, 1980b]. Yannakakis and Papadimitriou [1980] gives an axiom system for algebraic dependencies. Fagin et al. [1981] give some other interesting properties of generalized dependencies. No axiom system is known for embedded multivalued dependencies, and Sagiv and Walecka [1982] provides reason to believe there can be none. The axioms for join dependencies were studied by Beeri and Vardi [1979], and Sciore [1982] provides a sound and complete axiomatization for a slightly more general class of dependencies.

Another form of dependency, called "inclusion dependencies," where symbols appearing in one component of a relation are required to appear elsewhere as well, were studied by Casanova, Fagin, and Papadimitriou [1982]. These dependencies model existence constraints, such as we discussed in Section 3.5 concerning automatic insertion in the network model.

A number of problems concerning the subject matter of this chapter have been shown $\mathcal{NP}$-complete. For example, testing whether a relation scheme is in Boyce-Codd normal form is $\mathcal{NP}$-complete (Beeri and Bernstein [1979]), as are finding a minimal sized key for a relation scheme (Lucchesi and Osborn [1978]) and inferring a join dependency from multivalued dependencies (Fischer and Tsou [1981]).

Surveys of relational database theory, with additional references, are found in Beeri, Bernstein, and Goodman [1978], and Ullman [1981].

8

QUERY OPTIMIZATION

High level query languages such as those discussed in Chapter 6 allow us to write queries that take a great deal of time to execute, and whose execution time can be reduced greatly if the query language processor rephrases the query before executing it. Such improvements are commonly called "optimizations," although the rephrased query need not be optimal over all possible ways of implementing the query, and the terms "amelioration" or "improvement" would be more appropriate. In this chapter we shall consider several different kinds of optimization strategies that have been used.

First we look at algebraic manipulations that improve the running time of queries. Then, we shall look at a much lower level of optimization, as we consider how System R optimizes selections on a single relation. Here the issues are not algebraic, but are concerned with how to use indices and other facts about the organization of the file holding the relation to minimize the number of block accesses required to answer the query. Next, we consider the QUEL optimizer for retrieve-where queries. This optimizer represents one methodology for performing the right algebraic manipulations on queries. Last, we consider tableau minimization, a method for producing the minimum number of joins required to perform a select-project-join query. In addition to being interesting in its own right, this technique will be used in the next chapter for a purpose somewhat unrelated to optimization.

8.1 BASIC OPTIMIZATION STRATEGIES

One might begin a study of optimization by asking what operations take a long time to execute. More specifically, we should ask what operations are likely to take a long time to execute and can frequently be avoided by rephrasing the query. In a relational query language, the greatest offender is a Cartesian product, but a join is another heavy consumer of time and is much more frequently used than a Cartesian product.

To see how much time a Cartesian product can take, consider the expression

$AB \times CD$.† To produce the value for this product, we have no choice but to run through the file for one of the relations, say AB, in an outer loop, and for each record r (representing a tuple), to run through the entire file CD in an inner loop and concatenate r with each record of the latter file. If we are clever, we shall load main memory with as many blocks of the AB file as we can, while still leaving room for one block of the CD file. While keeping the selection of AB blocks in main memory fixed, we run through the CD file completely. Then we can concatenate each AB record in main memory with each of the records in the block from the CD file, before we bring in the next block from the CD file. This strategy reduces the number of times we must load each CD block by a factor equal to the number of AB records that can fit in main memory.

Let us assume that each relation is stored in one file by itself, so blocks containing the tuples of a relation contain nothing but tuples of that relation. Suppose

1. relations AB and CD have n_{AB} and n_{CD} records, respectively,

2. b_{AB} and b_{CD} records of AB and CD, respectively, fit on a block, and

3. main memory can hold m blocks.

Then the total number of block accesses required to read file AB is n_{AB}/b_{AB}. We must read file CD $n_{AB}/(m-1)b_{AB}$ times, and each time requires n_{CD}/b_{CD} block accesses, so the total number of block accesses is

$$\frac{n_{AB}}{b_{AB}}(1 + \frac{n_{CD}}{(m-1)b_{CD}})$$

If $n_{AB} = n_{CD} = 10,000$, $b_{AB} = b_{CD} = 5$, and $m = 100$, the number of accesses is 42,400. At 20 block accesses per second, the evaluation of this Cartesian product takes 35 minutes. In general, since m will probably be large, we see from the above formula that the time taken is less sensitive to the ratio n_{CD}/b_{CD} than to the ratio n_{AB}/b_{AB}. Thus, we would speed the process by picking in the role of AB the relation with the smaller ratio, that is, the one that fits on fewer blocks.

Implementation of Joins

If the query asks that a Cartesian product be printed, there is little we can do except make the best of a few options such as which relation to run though in the inner loop and which in the outer, as discussed above. However, often the query will be something like the following (QUEL) program.

---

† In this chapter an subsequently, we find it convenient to name a relation by the set of attributes in its scheme, so AB refers to a relation with attributes A and B, and so on.

range of x is AB
range of y is CD
retrieve($x.A$)
    where $x.B = y.C$ and $y.D = 99$

In algebraic terms, this query is asking for the value of

$$\pi_A(\sigma_{B=C \wedge D=99}(AB \times CD))$$

If we migrate the selection $D = 99$ inside the Cartesian product to get

$$\pi_A(\sigma_{B=C}(AB \times \sigma_{D=99}(CD)))$$

we save considerably, as the following analysis shows. Most importantly, the Cartesian product and selection for $B = C$ convert to an equijoin; this is a very typical situation, as joins are very much more common than Cartesian products. If we group the selection and product, our expression becomes

$$\pi_A(AB \underset{B=C}{\bowtie} \sigma_{D=99}(CD))$$

The above formula is a common configuration. In essence, it asks for the A's that are associated with a particular D-value, 99, with the connection defined by an equijoin between two other attributes; the equijoin serves to connect the relations that hold A- and D-values. Let us therefore consider how best to implement this query. One way would be to take the join first, then select for $D = 99$, and project the result onto A. However, since we are only interested in a small fraction of the tuples in the join, namely those with $D = 99$, it would be better to do the selection first, then take the join with the selected subset of the CD relation.

Should the file for CD be indexed on D, a few block accesses would likely suffice to find those records with $D = 99$. Even if there is no index, we need only scan the CD file once to find the records with $D = 99$, which takes n_{CD}/b_{CD} block accesses, or 2,000 accesses using the numbers from the above example concerning the Cartesian product. From this set of tuples we really only need the projection onto C, since the D components are all 99 and are not involved in the operations to be performed subsequently, the equijoin and projection onto A.

The set of C-values becomes a set of B-values for us to look up in the AB file, thereby performing the equijoin. If this set of B-values is small, and there is an index on B for the AB file, then only a few block accesses are necessary to get the tuples in $AB \underset{B=C}{\bowtie} \sigma_{D=99}(CD)$ and their projection onto A. Even if there is no such index, a pass through the entire AB file, requiring another 2,000 block accesses, is sufficient to gather the tuples with the correct B-values and collect the A-values in those tuples.

We see that the rewritten query, using an equijoin, takes no more than one tenth (4000 vs. 42,400) the block accesses, and if the right indices are available, the ratio could be several orders of magnitude smaller.

The above example made the plausible assumption that when we select for a particular value, the resulting set of tuples is small enough to fit in main memory. There are times when we must take an equijoin in which neither side is so small, and we must consider how to handle such a case. Suppose we need the value of $AB \underset{B=C}{\bowtie} CD$, and neither AB nor CD fits in main memory. If we compare all AB tuples with all CD tuples, we must perform the same sequence of operations as we did for the Cartesian product $AB \times CD$ above, and we shall take just as much time, an amount that grows as the product of the lengths of the two files.

However, there are methods of taking this equijoin that require time closer to the sum, rather than the product, of the relation sizes. We can sort both files, the AB file on the value of B and the CD file on the value of C. If we then run through each file once, we can find all pairs of tuples with equality in the B and C components, thereby computing the equijoin. The number of block accesses for comparison of the files is $n_{AB}/b_{AB} + n_{CD}/b_{CD}$, while the number of block accesses needed to sort a file that extends over m blocks (m is n_{AB}/b_{AB} or n_{CD}/b_{CD}) is proportional to $m \log m$, which dominates the time to compare the files.

Another way to take the equijoin is to use an index on B or C. For example, if AB has an index on B, we can run once through the CD file, and for each C-value c found, look up the records of the AB file having B-value c, using the index on B.

Let us make the simplifying assumption that each record of the CD file has a different C-value, that is, C is a key for CD. Also, we shall assume that all, or almost all, B-values in the AB file appear as C-values in the CD file. Finally, let us assume that the AB records are not bunched by B-value, so given a particular B-value, the number of different blocks to be accessed when finding the AB records with that value approximately equals the total number of records with that B-value.

The number of block accesses for this approach is roughly n_{CD}/b_{CD} for scanning the CD file and n_{AB} for looking up the matching tuples in the AB file. Whether this approach is superior to the method of sorting depends on whether $n_{CD}/b_{CD} + n_{AB}$ exceeds $(n_{AB}/b_{AB}) \log(n_{AB}/b_{AB}) + (n_{CD}/b_{CD}) \log(n_{CD}/b_{CD})$. Using our sample values of the n's and b's, these numbers are 12,000 and 44,000, respectively, so indexing would be preferred in this case.†

Several variations on the above comparison exist. For example, the records of the AB file with a fixed B-value may be bunched on very few blocks, if B

---

† Note that the formulas are not exact; for example, sorting m elements doesn't take exactly $m \log_2 m$ steps. Thus, the actual numbers should be viewed as approximations, perhaps to within a factor of two, of the true values.

were the key for the file, say. In that case, we would need many fewer than n_{AB} block accesses to retrieve the desired records; the number would be closer to n_{AB}/b_{AB} if most of the blocks consisted of records with identical B-values. In this case, our example numbers would give a cost of 4,000 for indexing. On the other hand, there could be many CD records with a given C-value, which would cause AB records to be looked up more than once, on the average, when computing the join, and giving a cost for indexing significantly greater than n_{AB} (if no bunching by B-value is present) or n_{AB}/b_{AB} (with bunching).

A second consideration is that there may not be an index on B, nor might there be an index on C for the CD file. In that case, we would have to create one. If there is enough room in main memory to hold a block for every different B-value or C-value, then it would take only n_{AB}/b_{AB} block accesses to create an index on B or n_{CD}/b_{CD} to create one on C, as we could assemble the lists of pointers to tuples having each B- or C-value in one pass through the file. However, if all these blocks did not fit in main memory, almost every record of the file would require a read and write of a block from secondary memory, to make an index entry. Thus n_{AB} or n_{CD} block accesses, respectively, would be a closer approximation to the true cost of making an index on B or C. Then the indexing method would require n_{AB} to create the index on B, n_{CD}/b_{CD} to run through the CD file, and n_{AB} to look up tuples of AB having each particular B-value. This cost is 22,000, using our sample numbers.

A third consideration is that the files may already be sorted on B and C, respectively. Then the cost of the sorting method goes down to $n_{AB}/b_{AB} + n_{CD}/b_{CD}$, or 4,000, using our sample numbers.

General Strategies for Optimization

We have had a rambling introduction to the subject of optimization, which should offer a flavor for the kinds of issues that come up when designing an optimizer for a relation query language or other high-level query language. Optimization ideas can be divided into two groups. One group consists of algebraic manipulations—transformations that are applied with no concern, or little concern, for how the relations are stored. The second group consists of strategies to take advantage of the storage of the relations, features such as keys and indices. We shall treat optimizations in both areas much more systematically in later sections. Let us here list the major themes from the two areas. First is a list of important algebraic ideas.

1. *Perform selections as early as possible.* This transformation on queries, more than any other, is responsible for saving orders of magnitude in execution time, since it tends to make the intermediate results of multistep evaluations small.

2. *Combine certain selections with a prior Cartesian product to make a join.* As we have seen, a join, especially an equijoin, can be considerably cheaper

than a Cartesian product of the same relations. When the result of Cartesian product $R \times S$ is the argument of a selection, and that selection involves comparisons between attributes of R and S, the product is really a join. Note that a comparison involving no attribute of R or no attribute of S can be moved ahead of the product and be applied to S or R, respectively, which is even better than converting the product to a join.

3. *Combine sequences of unary operations, such as selections and projections.* Any sequence of unary operations, such as selection or projection, whose result depends on the tuples of the argument relation individually, can be combined by applying them in a group as we scan each tuple. Similarly, we can combine these unary operations with a prior binary operation, if we apply the unary operations to each tuple in the result of the binary operation as we construct it.

4. *Look for common subexpressions in an expression.* If the result of a common subexpression (an expression appearing more than once) is not a large relation, and it can be read from secondary memory in much less time than it takes to compute it, then it is advantageous to precompute the common subexpression once. Subexpressions involving a join that cannot be modified by moving a selection inside it generally fall in this category. It is interesting to observe that common subexpressions will appear frequently when the query is expressed in terms of views, since to execute the query we must substitute a fixed expression for the view. If several queries are part of one compiled program, then we also have the opportunity of looking for common subexpressions among all the queries at once.

The following are two recurrent themes concerning the physical implementation of relations and optimization of queries.

5. *Preprocess files appropriately.* We mentioned two important preprocessing ideas above, sorting files and creating indices. Each allows common values in the two files to be associated efficiently. While it may not be economical to maintain an index permanently or keep the file sorted (because the cost of insertions goes up), it may make sense to create an index or to sort temporarily in response to a query.

6. *Evaluate options before computing.* Whenever we have a choice in the order of operations, or we are allowed to treat one argument of a binary operation differently from the other, we should compute the cost of doing it either way. Above, we gave examples of how a Cartesian product could be performed more efficiently if we compared n_{AB}/b_{AB} with n_{CD}/b_{CD} to decide which file to run thorugh in the outer loop, and of how comparison of sorting and indexing strategies could speed up the computation of an equijoin. The justification for spending time considering options is that there are great differences among the costs of various ways of implementing the query, and the time spent considering all options is normally much less

than the time spent executing the query in an inferior way.

8.2 ALGEBRAIC MANIPULATION

Most of the above strategies involve transforming algebraic expressions. A good place to begin a study of optimization is therefore by cataloging some of the algebraic laws that apply to the relational algebra operators. We envision a query processor that begins by building a parse tree for an algebraic expression. The query language itself might be a pure relational algebra language, like ISBL. It might be a language like SQUARE or SEQUEL, with certain algebraic features, in which case the parse of a query could yield a tree in which some nodes represent relational algebra operators, and others represent operators special to the language. Yet again, the query language might be a relational calculus language whose calculus-like expressions are translated into algebraic expressions. For example, the QUEL optimizer, to be discussed in the next section, begins by assuming a Cartesian product of relations

$$R_1 \times R_2 \times \cdots \times R_k$$

if the applicable range statements are of the form

$$\text{range of } t_i \text{ is } R_i$$

for $i = 1, 2, \ldots, k$. Then the where-clause of the QUEL query is replaced by a selection, and the components mentioned in the retrieve-clause are obtained by a projection.

Equivalence of Expressions

Before we can "optimize" expressions we must understand clearly when two expressions are equivalent. First, let us recall that there are two definitions of relations in use (see Section 1.4), and they have somewhat different mathematical properties. The first viewpoint is that a relation is a set of k-tuples for a fixed k, and two relations are equal if and only if they are the same sets of tuples. The second viewpoint is that a relation is a set of mappings from a set of attribute names to values. Two relations are deemed equal if they are the same set of mappings. A relation in the first sense can be converted to a relation in the second sense by providing attribute names for the columns. We can convert from the second definition of relation to the first by picking a fixed order for the attributes.

We shall here use only the second definition, that a relation is a set of mappings from attributes to values. The justification is that existing query languages all allow, or even require, names for columns in a relation. More importantly, in any application of which we are aware, the order in which the columns of a table are printed is not significant, as long as each column is labeled by the proper attribute name. Where possible, we adopt names for attributes of a relation that is the result of an algebraic expression, from the names of attributes for the expression's arguments. We also require that names be provided for the result of a union or set difference.

An expression in relational algebra whose operands are relation variables $R_1, R_2, \ldots, R_k$ defines a mapping from k-tuples of relations $(r_1, r_2, \ldots, r_k)$, each r_i being a relation of the arity appropriate to R_i. The mapping is to a single relation, that which results when we substitute each r_i for R_i and evaluate the expression. Two expressions E_1 and E_2 are *equivalent*, written $E_1 \equiv E_2$, if they represent the same mappings; that is, when we substitute the same relations for identical names in the two expressions, we get the same result.† With this definition of equivalence, we can list some useful algebraic transformations.

Laws Involving Joins and Cartesian Products

1. *Commutative laws for joins and products.* If E_1 and E_2 are relational expressions, and F is a condition on attributes of E_1 and E_2,‡ then

$$E_1 \underset{F}{\bowtie} E_2 \equiv E_2 \underset{F}{\bowtie} E_1$$

$$E_1 \bowtie E_2 \equiv E_2 \bowtie E_1$$

$$E_1 \times E_2 \equiv E_2 \times E_1$$

Let us prove the first of these, the commutative law for joins. Let E_1 have attributes $A_1, \ldots, A_n$ and E_2 have attributes $B_1, \ldots, B_m$. We shall assume the A's and B's are distinct, since in the join, their columns must be renamed to be distinct anyway. Let r_1 and r_2 be arbitrary relations for E_1 and E_2 respectively. Then the value of $E_1 \underset{F}{\bowtie} E_2$ is the set of mappings ν from $A_1, \ldots, A_n, B_1, \ldots, B_m$ to values, such that there are mappings μ_1 and μ_2 in r_1 and r_2, respectively, for which

a) $\nu[A_i] = \mu_1[A_i]$, for $i = 1, 2, \ldots, n$,

b) $\nu[B_i] = \mu_2[B_i]$, for $i = 1, 2, \ldots, m$, and

c) the condition F becomes true when we substitute $\nu[C]$ for each attribute name C in F.

If we express the value of $E_2 \underset{F}{\bowtie} E_1$ in this style, we see it is exactly the same, with the order of clauses (a) and (b) interchanged, proving the equivalence. Note that if we viewed relations as tuples rather than mappings, the join, natural join, and Cartesian product operations would not

---

† In Section 8.6, we shall discuss "weak equivalence," which, as the name implies, is a less stringent requirement to be satisfied by expressions that are deemed "equivalent." That notion also has its motivation, but the definition of "equivalence" given here is the normal one used by query optimizers.

‡ We refer to an attribute by its name. If two or more attributes of the same name A exist, we denote them $R.A$, $S.A$, and so on, to distinguish one from another in a condition such as F.

be commutative, since the order of components in the resulting relations would be of significance.

2. *Associative laws for joins and products.* If E_1, E_2, and E_3 are relational expressions, and F_1 and F_2 are conditions, then

$$(E_1 \underset{F_1}{\bowtie} E_2) \underset{F_2}{\bowtie} E_3 \equiv E_1 \underset{F_1}{\bowtie} (E_2 \underset{F_2}{\bowtie} E_3)$$

$$(E_1 \bowtie E_2) \bowtie E_3 \equiv E_1 \bowtie (E_2 \bowtie E_3)$$

$$(E_1 \times E_2) \times E_3 \equiv E_1 \times (E_2 \times E_3)$$

We leave the verification of these laws as easy exercises.

Laws Involving Selections and Projections

The cascade of several projections can be combined into one. We express this fact by:

3. *Cascade of projections.*

$$\pi_{A_1,\ldots,A_n}(\pi_{B_1,\ldots,B_m}(E)) \equiv \pi_{A_1,\ldots,A_n}(E)$$

Note that the attribute names $A_1,\ldots,A_n$ must be among the B_i's for the cascade to be legal.

Similarly, the cascade of selections can be combined into one selection that checks for all conditions at once, as expressed by:

4. *Cascade of selections.*

$$\sigma_{F_1}(\sigma_{F_2}(E)) \equiv \sigma_{F_1 \wedge F_2}(E)$$

Since $F_1 \wedge F_2 = F_2 \wedge F_1$, it follows immediately that selections can be commuted, i.e.,

$$\sigma_{F_1}(\sigma_{F_2}(E)) \equiv \sigma_{F_2}(\sigma_{F_1}(E))$$

5. *Commuting selections and projections.* If condition F involves only attributes $A_1,\ldots,A_n$, then

$$\pi_{A_1,\ldots,A_n}(\sigma_F(E)) \equiv \sigma_F(\pi_{A_1,\ldots,A_n}(E))$$

More generally, if condition F also involves attributes $B_1,\ldots,B_m$ that are not among $A_1,\ldots,A_n$, then

$$\pi_{A_1,\ldots,A_n}(\sigma_F(E)) \equiv \pi_{A_1,\ldots,A_n}(\sigma_F(\pi_{A_1,\ldots,A_n,B_1,\ldots,B_m}(E)))$$

6. *Commuting selection with Cartesian product.* If all the attributes mentioned in F are attributes of E_1, then

$$\sigma_F(E_1 \times E_2) \equiv \sigma_F(E_1) \times E_2$$

As a useful corollary, if F is of the form $F_1 \wedge F_2$, where F_1 involves only attributes of E_1, and F_2 involves only attributes of E_2, we can use rules (1), (4) and (6) to obtain

$$\sigma_F(E_1 \times E_2) \equiv \sigma_{F_1}(E_1) \times \sigma_{F_2}(E_2)$$

Moreover, if F_1 involves only attributes of E_1, but F_2 involves attributes of both E_1 and E_2, we can still assert

$$\sigma_F(E_1 \times E_2) \equiv \sigma_{F_2}(\sigma_{F_1}(E_1) \times E_2)$$

thereby pushing part of the selection ahead of the product.

7. *Commuting selection with a union.* If we have an expression $E = E_1 \cup E_2$, we may assume the attributes of E_1 and E_2 have the same names as those of E, or at least, that there is a given correspondence that associates each attribute of E with a unique attribute of E_1 and a unique attribute of E_2. Thus we may write

$$\sigma_F(E_1 \cup E_2) \equiv \sigma_F(E_1) \cup \sigma_F(E_2)$$

If the attribute names for E_1 and/or E_2 actually differ from those of E, then the formulas F on the right must be modified to use the appropriate names.

8. *Commuting selection with a set difference.*

$$\sigma_F(E_1 - E_2) \equiv \sigma_F(E_1) - \sigma_F(E_2)$$

As in (7), if the attribute names of E_1 and E_2 differ, we must replace the attributes in F on the right by the corresponding names for E_1. Note also that the selection $\sigma_F(E_2)$ on the right is not necessary; we could replace it by E_2 if we wished. However, it is usually at least as efficient to perform the selection as it is to obtain the value of the expression E_2, and in many cases, $\sigma_F(E_2)$ is much easier to compute than E_2, because the former is a smaller set than the latter.

We shall not state the laws for pushing a selection ahead of a join, since a join can always be expressed as a Cartesian product followed by a selection, and, in the case of the natural join, a projection. The rules for passing a selection ahead of a join thus follow from rules (4), (5), and (6).

The rules for moving a projection ahead of a Cartesian product or union are similar to rules (6) and (7). However, note that there is no general way to move a projection ahead of a set difference.

9. *Commuting a projection with a Cartesian product.* Let E_1 and E_2 be two relational expressions. Let $A_1, \ldots, A_n$ be a list of attributes, of which $B_1, \ldots, B_m$ are attributes of E_1, and the remaining attributes, $C_1, \ldots, C_k$, are from E_2. Then

$$\pi_{A_1,\ldots,A_n}(E_1 \times E_2) \equiv \pi_{B_1,\ldots,B_m}(E_1) \times \pi_{C_1,\ldots,C_k}(E_2)$$

10. *Commuting a projection with a union.*

$$\pi_{A_1,\ldots,A_n}(E_1 \cup E_2) \equiv \pi_{A_1,\ldots,A_n}(E_1) \cup \pi_{A_1,\ldots,A_n}(E_2)$$

As in rule (7), if the names of attributes for E_1 and/or E_2 differ from those in $E_1 \cup E_2$, we must replace $A_1, \ldots, A_n$ on the right by the appropriate names.

An Algorithm for Optimizing Relational Expressions

We can apply the above laws to "optimize" relational expressions. The resulting "optimized" expressions obey the principles set down in Section 8.1, although they are in no sense guaranteed to be optimal over all equivalent expressions. We shall attempt to move selections and projections as far down the parse tree of the expression as we can, although we want a cascade of these operations to be organized into one selection followed by one projection. We also group selections and projections with the preceding binary operation, such as union, Cartesian product, or set difference, where possible.

Some special cases occur when a binary operation has operands that are selections and/or projections applied to leaves of the tree. We must consider carefully how the binary operation is to be done, and in some cases we wish to incorporate the selection or projection with the binary operation. For example, if the binary operation is union, we can incorporate selections and projections below it in the tree with no loss of efficiency, as we must copy the operands anyway to form the union. However, if the binary operation is Cartesian product, with no following selection to make it an equijoin, we would prefer to do selection and projection first, leaving the result in a temporary file, as the size of the operand files greatly influences the time it takes to execute a full Cartesian product.

The output of our algorithm is a *program,* consisting of the following kinds of steps.

1. the application of a single selection or projection,
2. the application of a selection and projection, or
3. the application of a Cartesian product, union, or set difference to two operands, perhaps preceded by selections and/or projections applied to one or both operands, and possibly followed by these operations.

We assume steps (1) and (2) are implemented by a pass through the operand relation, creating a temporary relation. Steps of type (3) are implemented by applying selection and/or projection to each tuple of operand relations, if appropriate, each time the operand tuple is accessed, and applying the following selection and/or projection, if appropriate, to each tuple generated as part of the resulting relation. The result goes into a temporary relation.

Algorithm 8.1: Optimization of Relational Expressions.

Input: A tree representing an expression of relational algebra.

Output: A program for evaluating that expression.

Method:

1. Use rule (4) to separate each selection $\sigma_{F_1 \wedge \cdots \wedge F_n}(E)$ into the cascade

$$\sigma_{F_1}(\cdots(\sigma_{F_n}(E))\cdots)$$

2. For each selection, use rules (4)–(8) to move the selection as far down the tree as possible.

3. For each projection, use rules (3), (9), (10), and the generalized rule (5) to move the projection as far down the tree as possible. Note that rule (3) causes some projections to disappear, while the generalized rule (5) splits a projection into two projections, one of which can be migrated down the tree if possible. Also, eliminate a projection if it projects an expression onto all its attributes.

4. Use rules (3)–(5) to combine cascades of selections and projections into a single selection, a single projection, or a selection followed by a projection. Note that this alteration may violate the heuristic "do projection as early as possible," but a moment's reflection will serve to convince one that it is more efficient to do all selections, then all projections, in one pass over a relation than it is to alternate selections and projections in several passes.

5. Partition the interior nodes of the resulting tree into *groups*, as follows. Every interior node representing a binary operator $\times$, $\cup$, or $-$ is in a group along with any of its immediate ancestors that are labeled by a unary operator (σ or π). Also include in the group any chain of descendants labeled by unary operators and terminating at a leaf, except in the case that the binary operator is a Cartesian product and not followed by a selection that combines with the product to form an equijoin.

6. Produce a program consisting of a step to evaluate each group in any order such that no group is evaluated prior to its descendant groups. $\square$

Example 8.1: Let us consider a library database consisting of the following relations.

> BOOKS(TITLE, AUTHOR, PNAME, LC_NO)
> PUBLISHERS(PNAME, PADDR, PCITY)
> BORROWERS(NAME, ADDR, CITY, CARD_NO)
> LOANS(CARD_NO, LC_NO, DATE)

The attributes used above that are not self explanatory are:

PNAME	=	publisher's name
LC_NO	=	Library of Congress number
PADDR	=	the street address of a publisher
PCITY	=	the city in which a publisher is located
CARD_NO	=	library card number
DATE	=	the date on which a book was borrowed

To keep track of books, we might suppose that there is a view XLOANS that contains additional information about books borrowed. XLOANS is the natural join of BOOKS, BORROWERS, and LOANS, which might, for example, be

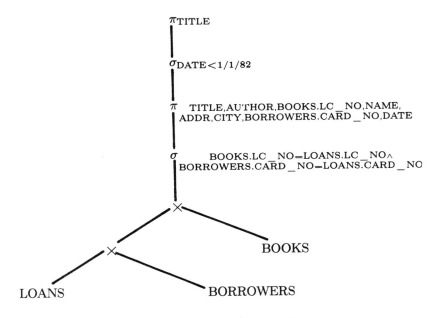

Fig. 8.1. Parse tree of expression.

defined as

$$\pi_S(\sigma_F(\text{LOANS}\times\text{BORROWERS}\times\text{BOOKS}))$$

where

$F =$BORROWERS.CARD $\_$ NO=LOANS.CARD $\_$ NO
    AND BOOKS.LC $\_$ NO=LOANS.LC $\_$ NO

while

$S =$TITLE, AUTHOR, PNAME, LC $\_$ NO, NAME,
    ADDR, CITY, CARD $\_$ NO, DATE

We might wish to list the books that been borrowed before some date in the distant past, say 1/1/82 by:

$$\pi_{\text{TITLE}}\sigma_{\text{DATE}<1/1/82}(\text{XLOANS})$$

After substituting for XLOANS, the expression above has the parse tree shown in Fig. 8.1.

The first step of the optimization is to split the selection F into two, with conditions BOOKS.LC $\_$ NO = LOANS.LC $\_$ NO and

BORROWERS.CARD $\_$ NO = LOANS.CARD $\_$ NO

respectively. Then we move each of the three selections as far down the tree as possible. The selection $\sigma_{\text{DATE}<1/1/82}$ moves below the projection and the two selections by rules (4) and (5). This selection then applies to the product (LOANS $\times$ BORROWERS) $\times$ BOOKS. Since DATE is the only attribute mentioned by the selection, and DATE is an attribute only of LOANS, we can replace

$$\sigma_{\text{DATE}<1/1/82}((\text{LOANS} \times \text{BORROWERS}) \times \text{BOOKS})$$

by

$$(\sigma_{\text{DATE}<1/1/82}(\text{LOANS} \times \text{BORROWERS})) \times \text{BOOKS}$$

then by

$$((\sigma_{\text{DATE}<1/1/82}(\text{LOANS})) \times \text{BORROWERS}) \times \text{BOOKS}$$

We have now moved this selection as far down as possible. The selection with condition BOOKS.LC_NO = LOANS.LC_NO cannot be moved below either Cartesian product, since it involves an attribute of BOOKS and an attribute not belonging to BOOKS.† However, the selection on

BORROWERS.CARD_NO = LOANS.CARD_NO

can be moved down to apply to the product

$$\sigma_{\text{DATE}<1/1/82}(\text{LOANS}) \times \text{BORROWERS}$$

Note that LOANS.CARD_NO is the name of an attribute of

$$\sigma_{\text{DATE}<1/1/82}(\text{LOANS})$$

since it is an attribute of LOANS, and the result of a selection takes its attributes to be the same as those of the expression to which the selection is applied.

Next, we can combine the two projections into one, π_{TITLE}, by rule (3). The resulting tree is shown in Fig. 8.2. Then by the extended rule (5) we can replace π_{TITLE} and $\sigma_{\text{BOOKS.LC\_NO}=\text{LOANS.LC\_NO}}$ by the cascade

π_{TITLE}
$\sigma_{\text{BOOKS.LC\_NO}=\text{LOANS.LC\_NO}}$
$\pi_{\text{TITLE,BOOKS.LC\_NO,LOANS.LC\_NO}}$

We apply rule (9) to replace the last of these projections by

$\pi_{\text{TITLE,BOOKS.LC\_NO}}$

applied to BOOKS, and $\pi_{\text{LOANS.LC\_NO}}$ applied to the left operand of the higher Cartesian product in Fig. 8.2.

---

† We could use the commutative and associative laws of products and then move this selection down one level, but then we could not move the selection on BORROWERS.CARD_NO = LOANS.CARD_NO down.

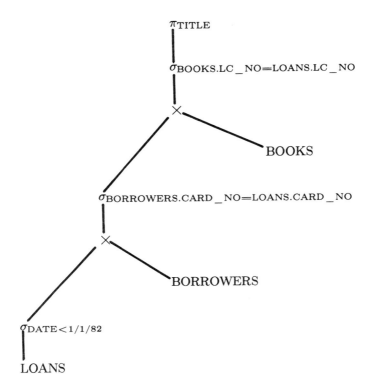

Fig. 8.2. Tree with selections lowered and projections combined.

The latter projection interacts with the selection below it by the extended rule (5) to produce the cascade

πLOANS.LC _ NO
σBORROWERS.CARD _ NO=LOANS.CARD _ NO
πLOANS.LC _ NO,BORROWERS.CARD _ NO,LOANS.CARD _ NO

The last of these projections passes through the Cartesian product by rule (9) and passes partially through the selection $\sigma_{\text{DATE}<1/1/82}$ by the extended rule (5). We then discover that in the expression

πLOANS.LC _ NO,LOANS.CARD _ NO,DATE

the projection is superfluous, since all attributes of LOANS are mentioned. We therefore eliminate this projection. The final tree is shown in Fig. 8.3. In that figure we have indicated groups of operators by dashed lines. Each of the Cartesian products is effectively an equijoin, when combined with the selection above. In particular, the selection on LOANS and the projection of

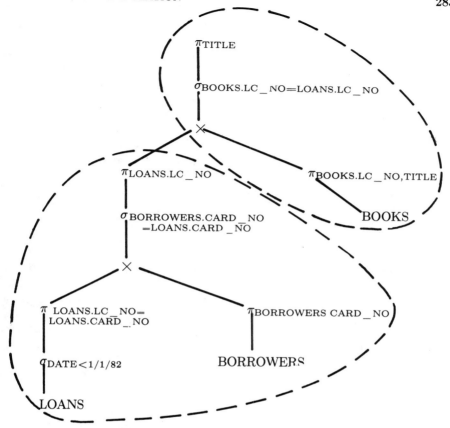

Fig. 8.3. Final tree with grouping of operators.

BORROWERS below the first product can be successfully combined with that product. Obviously a program executing Fig. 8.3 will perform the lower group of operations before the upper. □

8.3 OPTIMIZATION OF SELECTIONS IN SYSTEM R

We shall focus in this section on a problem that is instructive for several reasons. First, it shows a great deal about the opportunities for optimization in even a simple kind of query. Second, it lets us sample the issues at the implementation level, and third, it is representative of the way System R does all its optimization, which is quite different from the methodology followed by most other systems (although the results are largely the same).

The problem we consider is one in which we are given a query of the form

SELECT $A_1, \ldots, A_n$
FROM R (8.1)
WHERE P_1 AND P_2 AND $\cdots$

Here the P_i's are predicates involving the attributes of relation R. These predicates may be composed of subpredicates connected by AND, OR, NOT, IN, and so on, as for all SEQUEL conditions. However, we assume that none of them are of the form Q_1 AND Q_2. That is, it is important in this algorithm, and actually in most code optimization algorithms, that the predicates be broken as finely as possible into predicates connected by logical "and".

One may wonder where the implementation issues arise in queries as simple as these. First, System R takes advantage of indices whenever it can. For example, if one of the P_i's is of the form $A = c$, and there is an index on attribute A, System R will tend to favor an approach that begins by obtaining the set of tuples that have c in their A component, using the index. Then these tuples can be examined for satisfaction of the other predicates and the answer to the query obtained.

The second source of difficulty is that System R allows a great deal of flexibility in how relations are stored. For example, we noticed in Fig. 5.1 how System R might store the ORDERS relation of the HVFC database with the MEMBERS relation, so each order would follow the member who placed the order. The result is that while ORDERS tuples are relatively compact, the MEMBERS tuples tend to be spread widely. The practical consequence of this situation is that if we have to get certain MEMBERS tuples, even using an index, we shall have to take about one block access per member retrieved, since it is unlikely that we shall find two members' tuples in one block.

On the other hand, certain retrievals of ORDERS tuples can proceed much more efficiently. For example, if there is an index for ORDERS on attribute NAME, we would expect to retrieve all the orders for a given member in a number of block accesses that was just a little more than the minimum number in which those ORDERS tuples would fit. The reason is that the ORDERS tuples for a given member are packed in blocks almost as tightly as possible; only an occasional MEMBERS tuple intervenes, and the first and last blocks holding orders for a given member may also hold orders for the preceding and following members. Thus, the work per tuple retrieved is much less in this case than in the first example, where MEMBERS tuples are retrieved.

Problem Parameters

Define a *clustering index* to be an index on an attribute or attributes such that tuples with the same value for those attributes will tend to fill blocks almost entirely. The canonical example is the way ORDERS tuples are spread over blocks in Fig. 5.1, and the consequence is that an index on NAME for the

ORDERS relation would be a clustering index. Another example is that if a file were sorted on an attribute A, then an index on A would be a clustering index. Note that in general it is impossible for a relation to have more than one clustering index, because it is not usually possible for a file to have its records grouped by the values of two different fields at once.

Let us also say that a predicate of the form $A = c$, where A is an attribute and c is a constant, *matches* an index on A. No other predicate matches any index; the comparison must be equality. Evidently, if a predicate matches an index, we can use that index to look up all the tuples that satisfy the predicate, and no index not matched by a predicate can be so used.

Let us agree that T will denote the number of tuples in the relation R mentioned in the from-clause of the query with which we introduced the chapter. Also, let B be the number of blocks that would theoretically be needed to store R, if R were stored contiguously, i.e., with its tuples packed into blocks as tightly as possible. Then B is T divided by the number of tuples of R that will fit on one block. Note that B is well-defined even if R happens to be spread widely over blocks. Finally, if there is an index on an attribute A, the *image size* of that index is the number of different values for A appearing in the relation.

We shall see how knowing T, B, and the various image sizes helps us select the proper way to implement the query. Maintaining the value of T only requires that we keep a running count of the number of tuples in R, updating the count when we insert or delete. Calculating B from T, the length of a block, and the length of a record is easy, if records in the file for R have a fixed block length. Unfortunately, in System R, the records that represent tuples may have variable length, since variable length strings are allowed as domains of attributes. In that case, an estimation based on a sample of records must be used. It is not hard to get an estimate of the image size of an index in System R. Recall that all indices are implemented by B-trees in which the leaf blocks consist of key values followed by pointers to all the records that have that key value. It is easy to record the number of leaf blocks, and a sample tells us how many keys per leaf block there are on the average. The image size is the number of leaf blocks times the average number of keys per leaf block.

While these parameters may be difficult to estimate accurately without examining the entire relation, let us emphasize that approximations are usually good enough. Thus the methodology should carry over to other storage organizations besides the one used by System R, as we would expect some way of estimating the parameters to be available.

An Algorithm for Optimizing Simple Queries

Let us now give the details of the System R approach to optimization of queries of the form (8.1), found at the beginning of the section. Like all of System R optimization, the approach is enumerative. That is, all the options on a preselected "menu" are enumerated, and the query processor estimates the cost of using each option and takes the best choice. In more complicated situations, such as queries that involve several joins, there can be thousands of possible options, although in the simple case we cover, the number of options is usually not that great. The designers of the optimizer evidently felt that time spent optimizing the query will be paid back in reduced time to execute the query, and most likely that is the case, especially if the relations are large.

It is not feasible to enumerate all the possible ways to implement a query, so System R, like any optimizing system, has to pick the space of strategies it will search for the best choice. The strategies considered by System R include those of the form in which we pick one of the predicates P_i, find all the tuples satisfying that predicate, and then examine those tuples to see which of them satisfy the other predicates, if any. We also consider strategies in which we begin by examining all the tuples of R and see which of them satisfy all the predicates.

Algorithm 8.2: System R Optimization Algorithm for Simple Selection Queries.
Input: A SEQUEL query of the form (8.1), together with information about what indices on relation R exist, the estimated values of parameters T and B for this relation, and the estimated image sizes for those indices.
Output: A way of computing the response to this query.
Method: We consider the following list of methods for obtaining either R itself, or R with selection by one of the predicates applied. For those methods that involve a choice of which index or predicate to use, consider all possible choices. The methods are listed in approximate order of desirability, but in each case we must use the parameters T and B, possibly with estimates of image sizes as well, to judge the cost. The method with the lowest estimated cost is the output of the algorithm.

1. Get those tuples of R that satisfy a predicate of the form $A = c$ that matches a clustering index. Then apply the remaining predicates to the tuples obtained.† If I is the image size for this index, we must read about $(1/I)^{th}$ of the tuples on the average. Since we have a clustering index, the number of block accesses required to read these tuples will be about equal to the number of blocks they would fit on if packed tightly. Thus the estimated number of block accesses for this method is B/I.

2. Use a clustering index on an attribute A, where $A \theta c$ is one of the predi-
    cates, and θ is $<$, $\leq$, $>$, or $\geq$, to obtain the subset of R that satisfies

---

† We might also consider the possibility that there is more than one predicate matching an index, for example "WHERE $A = 1$ AND $B = 17$." In this case, we could do better than any of the strategies System R considers if we intersect in main memory the collections of pointers obtained, and then use block accesses only to obtain those tuples that satisfy all the predicates. System R does not consider this strategy because it would have to inhibit concurrent access to the relation during the time it was intersecting the pointers.

this predicate. Then apply the remaining predicates to the result. Here we require about $B/2$ block accesses, since on the average we shall have to read about half the tuples, and because we have a clustering index, these will be packed onto about $B/2$ blocks. Note that the case where θ is $\neq$ is not included here, since we can expect very limited selection to take place, and essentially all the tuples will have to be retrieved. This case is covered under (5), below.

3. If there is a nonclustering index that matches a predicate $A = c$, use that index to find all the tuples with A-value c and apply the other predicates to those tuples. If I is the image size for this index, then we shall have to retrieve about T/I tuples. They will likely be on different blocks, since the index is nonclustering, so T/I is the estimated cost for this method.

4. If R is stored in a file by itself, we can simply read all the tuples of R and apply the predicates to the tuples. The cost here is B, since that is the number of blocks over which R will be spread.

5. If R is not stored by itself, but it has a clustering index on any attributes, whether or not those attributes are involved in a predicate, use the index to obtain all the tuples of R and apply the predicates to them. The cost of this method is also B, since any clustering index guarantees that we can obtain the tuples in not many more block accesses than it takes to store them.

6. If there is a nonclustering index on attribute A, and $A \; \theta \; c$ is a predicate, where θ is $<$, $\leq$, $>$, or $\geq$, use that index to get the tuples of R satisfying $A \; \theta \; c$ and apply the other predicates to the result. The cost is $T/2$, since we may expect to retrieve about half of R, and these tuples will be spread over blocks independently.

7. Use a nonclustering index of any sort to find the tuples of R and apply all the predicates to them. The cost of this method is T.

8. If none of the above methods are available, simply scan all blocks that might contain tuples of R to retrieve them. The cost of this method is T or perhaps even more. $\square$

Example 8.2: Let us consider the response of Algorithm 8.2 to the query

> SELECT ORDER_NO
> FROM ORDERS
> WHERE QUANTITY $\geq$ 5 AND ITEM="Granola"

where ORDERS is the usual HVFC database relation. Suppose that there is a clustering index for ORDERS on NAME and nonclustering indices on ITEM and QUANTITY. Suppose also that there are 1000 orders ($T = 1000$), and that ten orders fit in one block, so $B = 100$, i.e., the ORDERS relation fits on 100 blocks. Let the image size for the ITEM index be 50, i.e., we assume that there are about 50 different items on order at any time. The image sizes for the other indices are irrelevant in what follows, so we do not make an assumption about them. There are no options under choice (1) of Algorithm 8.2, because the only predicate that matches an index is ITEM="Granola," and ITEM does not have a clustering index. Similarly, there are no options under choice (2).

For choice (3), a nonclustering index that matches a predicate, we have the ITEM index and the predicate ITEM="Granola." The estimated cost of making this choice is $T/I = 1000/50 = 20$.

Choice (4), reading the ORDERS relation from its blocks, on the assumption that the relation is stored by itself, would have cost $B = 100$, if in fact ORDERS was stored by itself. If ORDERS is stored with the MEMBERS relation as suggested earlier, then choice (4) is not applicable. However, choice (5), the use of the clustering index on NAME, has the same effect, and its estimated cost is $B = 100$.

Choice (6) is the use of a nonclustering index on an attribute involved in a predicate whose comparison is neither $=$ nor $\neq$. Our opportunity here is to use the index on QUANTITY and the predicate QUANTITY ≥ 5. The cost of this choice is $T/2 = 500$. Choices (7) and (8) each have cost at least $T = 1000$.

Thus, the least cost is achieved from the option under choice (3), where we use the ITEM index to obtain the approximately 20 tuples with ITEM="Granola" and examine each to see if the quantity is at least 5. Since each of the 20 tuples is likely to be on a different block, because the ITEM index is nonclustering, we estimate the retrieval cost at 20 block accesses. $\square$

8.4 THE QUEL DECOMPOSITION ALGORITHM

We shall now consider in some detail the optimization algorithm used in the QUEL processor. This algorithm, while it is tailored to a calculus-based language, has application to algebraic languages as well. In addition to using the idea that selections should be performed as early as possible, the QUEL algorithm has at least one important idea not encountered so far, the judicious decomposition of Cartesian products and joins.

Consider the QUEL query

>   range of t_1 is R_1
>
>   .
>   .
>   .
>
>   range of t_k is R_k
>   retrieve (α)
>   where F

where α is a list of attributes belonging to the relations $R_1, \ldots, R_k$, and F is a condition on attributes of the R_i's. The formal meaning of this query is given by the expression

$$\pi_\alpha(\sigma_F(R_1 \times R_2 \times \cdots \times R_k)) \tag{8.2}$$

Note that some of the R_i's may be the same relation. Since the attributes in α and F are associated with t_i's, we can determine which copy of a relation is referred to by terms in α and F, should two or more of the R_i's be the same.

If we use the algebraic manipulation techniques of Section 8.2, we can move the selection and projection as far inside the Cartesian products as possible. However, we can also take advantage of the associativity and commutativity of the product to pick a good ordering for these products. There is a nonobvious technique used in the QUEL optimizer that helps select a good order for the products. To motivate this method, suppose we wish to take the natural join of relations AB, BC, and CD, where A, B, C, and D are attribute names. By the commutative and associative laws, we can join in any order we wish. The worst thing we could do is to start by taking $AB \bowtie CD$, since this join is really a Cartesian product. Better is to take the join $AB \bowtie BC$, and then join the result with CD. Starting with $BC \bowtie CD$ is an equally good way, on the average, because of the symmetry of the situation.

To analyze the relative merits of approaches to this problem, let us assume for simplicity that each of the three relations has n tuples, and that when we take a natural join of relations with one common attribute, the resulting relation has $p \geq 1$ times the maximum of the number of tuples in either operand. We also assume that the domain of each attribute is sufficiently small that we can create conveniently an index on any attribute, and the time to create the index is a constant c times the number of tuples in the relation. We also assume that the time to compute a join, once the necessary indices have been created, is d times the size of the result.

Then the time to compute $AB \bowtie BC$ is cn to create an index for one of the two relations on attribute B, and dpn to compute the join. Then to compute $(AB \bowtie BC) \bowtie CD$ takes cn to compute an index on C for CD, the smaller relation, then dp^2n to compute the join. The total time is thus

$$2cn + d(p^2 + p)n \tag{8.3}$$

There is another way we might compute the join. First create an index for AB on B and for CD on C. This step takes time $2cn$. Then run through the tuples (b_1, c_1) of BC. Use the indices to find all the tuples in AB with B-value b_1 and all the tuples in CD with C-value c_1. Accumulate the Cartesian products of these sets to produce the value of the join $AB \bowtie BC \bowtie CD$. This step takes time proportional to the number of tuples produced, which is $0(p^2n)$, so the entire join is computed in time

$$2cn + ep^2n \tag{8.4}$$

for some constant e.

If we consider the details of this process and the details of computing a join like $AB \bowtie BC$, we realize that d and e are about the same. As long as $d = e$, the value of (8.3) exceeds that of (8.4). Furthermore, our second approach uses no extra space, except for indices, while taking two joins requires space for a temporary relation.

Thus we see the desirability of implementing a natural join of three relations, two of which have sets of attributes that do not overlap, by *decomposing* the relation that overlaps the other two, that is, by running through the tuples of the latter relation. If we now reconsider the basic QUEL query, formula (8.2) at the beginning of the section, we see that we have a Cartesian product, not a join. However, suppose condition F is the logical "and" of one or more terms, and each term involves the equality of two attributes. Then the Cartesian product might be equivalent to a collection of equijoins. We can apply the decomposition approach to equijoins just as we did to natural joins, simply by taking account of the fact that the attributes providing the link between two relations have different names in the two relations. Of course the selection condition F need not be the logical "and" of terms; it could involve "or" and "not." Moreover, F might involve comparisons other than $=$ among attributes. These situations complicate the decomposition algorithm to be described, but the method works very well on a large fraction of the queries, those for which selection conditions are the logical "and" of equalities among attributes and constant values.

The Connection Graph

Suppose we have the Cartesian product of relations $R_1, \ldots, R_k$, to which a selection $\sigma_{F_1 \wedge \cdots \wedge F_n}$ is to be applied. Each F_i may be an arbitrarily complex condition, but we assume it is not the logical "and" of two or more conditions. We construct a graph G† with a node for each R_i, $i = 1, 2, \ldots, k$, and a node for each occurrence of a constant in any of the F_j's. Two occurrences of the same relation name or the same constant are given two distinct nodes. For each F_j, find the set of relations R_i such that F_j involves one or more attributes of R_i, and find the set of constants appearing in F_j. These sets of relations and constants determine a set of nodes of G. Create an "edge," which in general is a hyperedge, connecting this set of nodes, and label the hyperedge F_j. In the common case where F_j is of the form $R_1.A = a$ or $R_i.A = R_m.B$, the "edge" will be a true edge connecting two nodes, although in more complex cases the "edge" will connect many nodes. A useful observation is that since each occurrence of a constant has a unique node in G, the nodes for constants

---

† Technically, G is a *hypergraph* since its "edges" are in general *hyperedges,* that is, sets of one, two, or more nodes, rather than being pairs of nodes as in an ordinary graph. In the most important and frequent case, the edges will turn out to be pairs of nodes.

range of t is BOOKS
range of s is PUBLISHERS
range of u is BORROWERS
range of v is LOANS
retrieve(u.NAME)
    where t.LC_NO $= v$.LC_NO
        and u.CARD_NO $= v$.CARD_NO
        and t.PNAME $= s$.PNAME
        and u.CITY $= s$.PCITY

Fig. 8.4. A QUEL program.

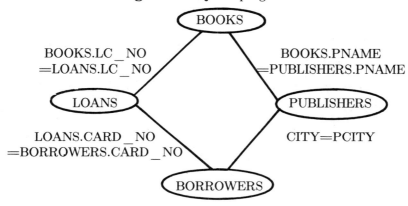

Fig. 8.5. The Connection graph for the program of Fig. 8.4.

have only one edge incident upon them.†

Example 8.3: Let us reconsider the relations of Example 8.1 and suppose we have
the QUEL program of Fig. 8.4. That is, print all persons who have borrowed
a book published in the same city that they live in. In algebra, this query is
expressed by the Cartesian product

BOOKS×PUBLISHERS×BORROWERS×LOANS

to which we apply the selection indicated in the where-clause and then project
onto BORROWERS.NAME. The connection graph for this query is shown in
Fig. 8.5. Note that all edges in Fig. 8.5 are hyperedges that happen to be
ordinary edges, that is, sets of two nodes. □

Decomposing the Connection Graph

The execution of a query can be viewed as a series of operations on the connec-

---

† An edge is *incident upon* a node if that node is a member of the edge.

tion graph, where each operation has the effect of constructing a new relation, used as an intermediate step in the evaluation of the query, as well as changing the graph itself. At the end of this process, the graph disappears, and the relation denoted by the query has been constructed. During the construction, some nodes will symbolize new relations, and others will symbolize new "constants," which may be single tuples or sets of tuples (relations) that we assume are small sets and which we treat as if they were single tuples.

In what follows, we use doubly circled nodes to symbolize constants in this generalized sense. Constant nodes will always have only one incident edge. If an edge runs between two nodes and has a label of the form $A = B$, we call it a *simple edge*. The important role played here by simple edges mirrors the role of predicates that match an index in the previous section. Note also how the division of the condition into predicates connected by logical "and" is a common theme between this section and the previous one. The constructions we use to decompose the connection graph are the following.

1. *Instantiation.* A simple edge connecting a relation to a constant is in effect a selection. We execute the selection as follows. Suppose we have a simple edge between nodes n and m, where n represents a relation r and m represents a constant that is a single value v. We eliminate node m in such a way that the relation denoted by the entire graph does not change. If the constant is a single value v, the label of a simple edge will be $A = v$, for some A that is an attribute for relation r. We eliminate the edge (n, m), eliminate the node m, and make node n represent the relation $\sigma_{A=v}(r)$. This relation is deemed to be "small," so node n now represents a constant that is a small relation.

2. *Dissection.* Suppose we have a node n representing a relation r, and let n be a member of k different edges. To evaluate the relation denoted by the entire graph, we may run through the tuples t in r and for each t create a graph that denotes the relation of the original graph, with r replaced by $\{t\}$. To do so, let e be an "edge" (which may contain more than two nodes) of which n is a member, and let F be the formula associated with e. Replace each occurrence in F of an attribute A of r, by the constant $t[A]$, and for each component of t mentioned in F, create a node representing the constant value of that component. Remove n from e, but insert into e all the nodes just created. Do the same for each edge containing n and then eliminate node n. After evaluating the resulting graph to yield a relation s, take the Cartesian product $s \times \{t\}$. Take the union of these Cartesian products over all tuples t in r. The result is the relation denoted by the original graph.

We can now give the complete decomposition algorithm for a connection graph. The algorithm is recursive, calling itself on modified graphs and returning a relation that is the value denoted by the graph on which it is called.

To get the value of a given query, we construct its connection graph, call the decomposition algorithm on the graph, and then project the resulting relation, which is a selection applied to a product, onto the components mentioned in the retrieve clause. As an exercise, the reader can modify the algorithm to perform projections as soon as possible.

Algorithm 8.3: Query Evaluation by Decomposition.
Input: A connection graph G.
Output: The relation $\text{REL}(G)$ denoted by G.
Method: We choose to apply either instantiation or dissection according to the following preferences.

1. While an instantiation is possible, do it.
2. If no instantiation is possible, select a node n for dissection. In selecting n, consider only nodes contained in one or more edges. Give first priority to nodes all of whose incident edges are simple. If there are one or more such nodes, select one representing a "small" constant relation (these are created during instantiations or dissections by a small relation); if there are none, select a node whose elimination will disconnect the graph,† and if there are none of these, select any node with only simple incident edges. If there are no nodes with only simple incident edges, select any node, giving priority to nodes representing "small" relations and then to nodes whose deletion breaks the graph into two or more connected components.
3. Having selected a node n for dissection, for each tuple t in the relation denoted by n, proceed to replace that node by nodes denoting constant values, as described in the definition of dissection, to obtain a graph G_t. Apply Algorithm 8.3 recursively to G_t, to produce a relation $\text{REL}(G_t)$. Return $\underset{t}{\cup}(\text{REL}(G_t) \times \{\,t\,\})$. Note that the method provided by Algorithm 8.3 to evaluate G_t works for arbitrary t, so the algorithm must be run on only one "generic" G_t. Also, usually t will range over a small set, so the union may not be very large.
4. We reach here only if after using instantiation wherever possible, there are no edges remaining. In this case return the Cartesian product of the relation represented by each of the remaining nodes. □

Example 8.4: Let us apply Algorithm 8.3 to the connection graph of Fig. 8.5. No instantiation is possible, so we turn to a dissection. All edges are simple, but there are no "small" relations, and no node disconnects the graph. Therefore we are free to dissect at any node, and let us choose BOOKS. Letting t be an arbitrary tuple in BOOKS we replace Fig. 8.5 by the graph of Fig. 8.6; there is, in principle, one such graph for each t, although their decompositions are

---

† It is not trivial to find such nodes, but algorithms exist for finding them; see Aho et al. [1974]. Note that the preference for disconnecting a graph corresponds to our preference to run through the tuples of BC in the join $AB \bowtie BC \bowtie CD$, as discussed in the beginning of the section.

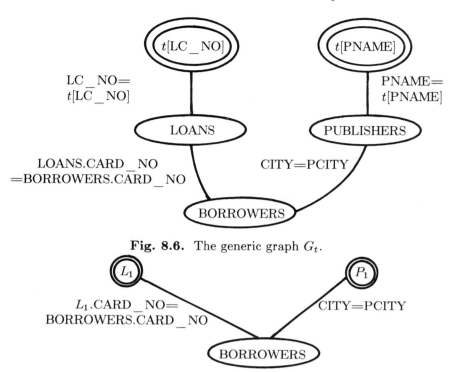

Fig. 8.6. The generic graph G_t.

Fig. 8.7. The generic graph G_t after instantiation.

essentially the same, and we need only work on one to discover how to evaluate the relation denoted by any one of them.

We now apply Algorithm 8.3 to the graph G_t represented in Fig. 8.8. There are two applications of instantiation to be made, to the constant nodes $t[\text{LC\_NO}]$ and $t[\text{PNAME}]$. As a result of these operations, the nodes of Fig. 8.6 representing LOANS and PUBLISHERS now represent the "small" relations

$$L_1 = \sigma_{\text{LC\_NO}=t[\text{LC\_NO}]}(\text{LOANS})$$
$$P_1 = \sigma_{\text{PNAME}=t[\text{PNAME}]}(\text{PUBLISHERS})$$

The resulting graph is shown in Fig. 8.7.

We now prefer to pick either of the "small" relations L_1 or P_1 on which to do dissection; say we pick L_1. Let u be a typical tuple of L_1. We create for each u the graph G_{tu} as shown in Fig. 8.8(a). Instantiation then enables us to replace BORROWERS by the relation

$$B_1 = \sigma_{\text{CARD\_NO}=u[\text{CARD\_NO}]}(\text{BORROWERS})$$

as shown in Fig. 8.8(b). A last dissection, say on B_1, produces a graph G_{tuv}, as in Fig. 8.8(c), for each v in B_1. Then an application of instantiation leaves

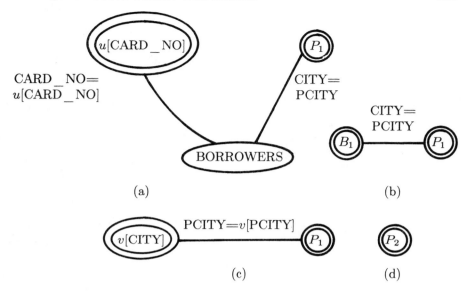

Fig. 8.8. Further steps in the decomposition process.

us with the graph of Fig. 8.8(d), where

$$P_2 = \sigma_{\text{PCITY}=v[\text{PCITY}]}(P_1)$$

By step (4) of Algorithm 8.3, $\text{REL}(G_{tuv}) = P_2$. To obtain $\text{REL}(G_{tu})$ we take $\underset{v \text{ in } B_1}{\cup} (\text{REL}(G_{tuv}) \times \{v\})$. Note that B_1 is a "small" relation, and also that the actual value of B_1 depends on t and u. Then we obtain

$$\text{REL}(G_t) = \underset{u \text{ in } L_1}{\cup} (\text{REL}(G_{tu}) \times \{u\})$$

where L_1 is the relation from Fig. 8.7. Note that L_1 depends on t, and

$$\text{REL}(G) = \underset{t \text{ in BOOKS}}{\cup} (\text{REL}(G_t) \times \{t\}).$$

□

Example 8.5: Suppose we have the QUEL program

      range of t is BOOKS
      range of u is LOANS
      range of v is BORROWERS
      retrieve(v.NAME, t.TITLE)
          where v.CARD_NO = u.CARD_NO
            and u.LC_NO = t.LC_NO

That is, print the persons borrowing books and the titles of the books they borrowed. The connection graph G is shown in Fig. 8.9. The first step must be a dissection, and we prefer LOANS, since it alone disconnects the graph, and

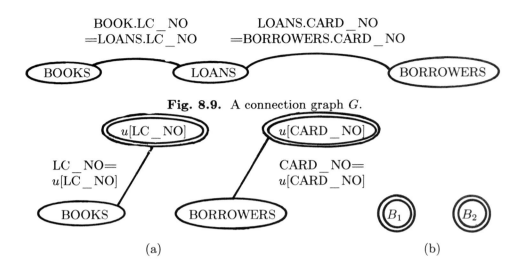

Fig. 8.9. A connection graph G.

(a)   (b)

Fig. 8.10. Decomposition steps.

there are no "small" relations. For each u in LOANS we obtain the graph G_u shown in Fig. 8.10(a). Two instantiations yield the graph of Fig. 8.10(b), where

$$B_1 = \sigma_{\text{LC\_NO}=u[\text{LC\_NO}]}(\text{BOOKS})$$
$$B_2 = \sigma_{\text{CARD\_NO}=u[\text{CARD\_NO}]}(\text{BORROWERS})$$

Now we obtain $\text{REL}(G_u) = B_1 \times B_2$, and

$$\text{REL}(G) = \underset{u \text{ in LOANS}}{\cup} (\text{REL}(G_u) \times \{ u \})$$

answering the query. □

8.5 EXACT OPTIMIZATION FOR A SUBSET OF RELATIONAL QUERIES

We have seen in the three previous sections a number of good ideas for improving the running time of queries. We might wonder whether these algorithms always produce the best implementation of those queries to which they apply. The answer is that they do not, for the simple reason that they, like any algorithm we might think of, can only consider implementations from among those that they are preprogrammed to try.

In this section, we shall consider a class of queries, and a class of options for their implementation, such that we can prove a limited result to the effect that the optimum query equivalent to a given one can be found. The class of queries we consider is select-project-join queries, and the options we consider for their implementation are all algebraic formulas involving select, project, and natural join equivalent to a given expression. The result is limited because what we produce is not the most efficient implementation over all, but simply the expression with the fewest joins. Since join is the most expensive operation among the three, there is considerable merit in minimizing joins. However, this minimization must then be followed by an algorithm such as the QUEL optimization algorithm of Section 8.4, which we hope will find the best sequence in which to apply the various selections and joins.

The question of minimizing joins may seem unimportant for the simple reason that although much can be saved by eliminating joins, very few queries are phrased in such a way that more joins than necessary are taken in the first place. We are interested in the join minimization algorithm for several reasons. First, it has intrinsic interest, for what it tells us about the equivalence of relational algebra expressions. Second, it is of practical importance in case that we have a view built by joining several relations. If queries are phrased in terms of the view, we shall begin each query by taking the join implied by the view, whether we need all the terms of the join or not. The algorithm we propose can eliminate unnecessary join terms here. As an extreme, but important example of this phenomenon, we shall discuss in the next chapter the support of a "universal relation," which we often can see as the natural join of all the relations in the database. A natural way to implement queries about the universal relation is to take the join of all relations and eliminate the unnecessary terms.

Conjunctive Queries and Tableaux

A *conjunctive query* is one of the form

$$\{\, a_1 \cdots a_n \mid (\exists b_1) \cdots (\exists b_m)(P_1 \wedge \cdots \wedge P_k)\,\} \tag{8.5}$$

where the P_i's are either of the form

1. $R(c_1 c_2 \cdots c_r)$, meaning that the tuple $c_1 c_2 \cdots c_r$ is asserted to be in the relation R; the c_j's are either among the a's or b's, or are constants, or

2. $c \,\theta\, d$, where c and d are among the a's, b's, and constants, and θ is one of $<$, $>$, $\leq$, or $\geq$. Note we exclude $=$ and $\neq$ from this list. Equality can be taken care of by identifying symbols, and $\neq$ can only have the effect of deriving contradictions, i.e., forcing the set of tuples defined to be vacuous, as in sets of terms like $a \leq b \wedge a \geq b \wedge a \neq b$.

One useful way to display conjunctive queries is by a *tableau*. To begin the description of tableaux, we first assume that we have agreed upon a set of attributes for all the relations under discussion. Attributes that mean the same thing in different relations must be given the same name, while attributes with different meanings are given different names.

Example 8.6: In the library database of Example 8.1, we might consider PADDR in the PUBLISHERS relation and ADDR in the BORROWERS relation to be the same thing; that is, if a publisher's address is literally equal to a borrower's address, then the addresses really are the same.† Similarly, let us agree that PCITY and CITY are really the same thing. However, we shall assume that PNAME from PUBLISHERS and NAME from BORROWERS are really different and not identify these two attributes. Thus the set of attributes that we use is: T (title), Au (author), P (publisher's name), L (library of congress number), Ad (address), Ci (city), B (borrower's name), Cn (card number), and D (date). □

A tableau is a two-dimensional array, possibly with some additional constraints listed below it. The first row of a tableau lists the attributes. We may optionally omit the attributes if the correspondence between columns and attributes is understood. The next row, called the *summary*, consists of blanks and *distinguished variables* (or *distinguished symbols*), which are the a's in the generic conjunctive query (8.5). The existentially quantified b's in (8.5) are called *nondistinguished variables* (or *nondistinguished symbols*).

Note that in the tableau, components of the relation resulting from the conjunctive query are each assigned to the column of a particular attribute. In comparison, the distinguished variables in (8.5) are simply listed in a particular order, without any association with an attribute. This distinction is not an important one; it is a typical manifestation of the fact, first mentioned in Section 1.4, that we can view relations from either the "mathematical" or "database" viewpoint.

The remaining rows, called simply *rows*, represent the terms of the conjunctive query of the form $R(c_1 \cdots c_k)$, that is, terms asserting that a particular tuple is in a particular relation. We place c_i in that column corresponding to the ith attribute of R, and we place blanks in columns that do not correspond to attributes in the relation scheme of R. Optionally, we *tag* the row with the relation name R to remind us where the row came from. Finally, we write below the matrix all those predicates of the conjunctive query of the form $c \; \theta \; d$, which we term *constraints*.

The tableau should be interpreted, like the conjunctive query (8.5), as a mapping from values of the relation variables to a relation. The result relation is over the attributes with distinguished symbols in the summary. It is the set of all tuples $v_1 v_2 \cdots v_n$, where v_i is a value for the distinguished variable a_i, for $1 \leq i \leq n$, such that we can find values for the existentially quantified b's (nondistinguished symbols) in (8.5), making each row become a tuple in relation R, where R is the tag of the row. Also, each of the constraints must be satisfied for the given values of the distinguished and nondistinguished variables. More formally, the relation produced by the tableau, given an assignment of relations

---

† In contrast, the publisher's address could be "Charles Street" and the borrower's name could be "Charles Street," yet the two would not be the same in any useful sense.

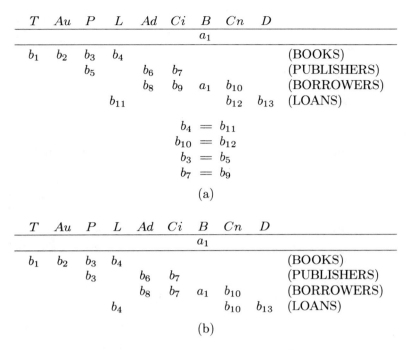

Fig. 8.11. Tableau representations of a query.

to the relation variables, is the set of tuples $h(s)$, where s is the summary with blanks removed, and h is a symbol mapping from the distinguished and nondistinguished symbols of the tableau, such that

1. for each row t, $h(t)$ is in the relation R, where R is the tag of row t, and
2. for each constraint $c \, \theta \, d$, $h(c) \, \theta \, h(d)$ is true.

The reader should check that the above definition of the tableau's mapping is a restatement of what is meant by Formula (8.5).

Example 8.7: The query of Fig. 8.4 can be represented by the tableau shown in Fig. 8.11(a). Alternatively, it could be represented by the tableau of Fig. 8.11(b), which differs from the first only in that the equalities following the matrix in Fig. 8.11(a) have been removed, and the equated symbols replaced by one symbol in each case.

The summary of the tableau in Fig. 8.11(a) has a distinguished symbol, a_1, in the column B (borrower name), because that is the only attribute retrieved in Fig. 8.4, or put another way, only a_1 would appear on the left of the bar in the set former defining the conjunctive query in the style of Equation (8.5). The four rows below the summary correspond to the tuple variables t, s, u, and v in Fig. 8.4. The four constraints below the matrix correspond to the four conditions in the where-clause of Fig. 8.4. □

Constructing Tableaux

There is a straightforward way of constructing tableaux for a wide variety of relational algebra expressions, although not for all expressions. The operations we can handle are:

1.   Selections.
2.   Projections.
3.   Natural joins. As a special case of the natural join, we can handle intersection of two relations over the same set of attributes. We can also handle equijoins if the attributes of the relations involved are renamed so the equated attributes have the same name, and no others do. Even Cartesian product can be handled if the attributes are renamed to be disjoint; all these operations become special cases of a natural join.

Algorithm 8.4: Construction of Tableaux for Select-Project-Join Expressions.

Input: An algebraic expression involving relation variables as arguments, and selections, projections, and natural joins as operators.

Output: A tableau that, treated as a conjunctive query of domain relational calculus, is equivalent to the expression.

Method: We construct tableaux for each subexpression of the given algebraic expression, working up the tree from the leaves.

Basis: The basis is a leaf, i.e., a relation variable $R(A_1, \ldots, A_n)$. The tableau we create has a summary and a single row. Both have distinguished variables in the columns for each of the A_i's and blanks elsewhere. The row is tagged R.

Induction: Suppose we have a subexpression $\pi_{A_1,\ldots,A_n}(E)$, and we have constructed the tableau T for E. To reflect the projection, we delete from the summary of T all the distinguished symbols in columns not among the A_i's. The symbols still appear in the rows, and in any constraints of T in which they appear, but they are now nondistinguished symbols. The reader should compare the construction on tableaux used here to Case (4) of Theorem 5.1, where we constructed a relational calculus expression from an algebraic one. Remembering that the tableau is really shorthand for a domain relational calculus expression, we see that the idea, projecting out an attribute by moving a symbol representing it from the left of the bar in the set former to an existentially quantified position on the right of the bar, is the same in both places.

Suppose instead that we have subexpression $\sigma_F(E)$, where we may assume without loss of generality that condition F cannot be broken up into the logical "and" of two or more conditions, i.e., F is not of the form $G \wedge H$. If T is the tableau for E, we modify T by appending the condition F', where F' is F, with any attribute A replaced by the distinguished symbol in the column for A of the summary of T. Note that T must have a distinguished symbol there, or else the expression E produces a relation that has no attribute A, and the selection makes no sense. Also observe the similarity between this construction and Case (5) of Theorem 5.1.

As a special case, if the condition F is $A = B$, then instead, identify the distinguished symbols in the summary of T for the columns A and B.† If the condition F is $A = c$, where c is a constant, we replace the distinguished variable for A by the constant c.‡

The third case occurs when we have a subexpression $E_1 \bowtie E_2$. Let T_1 and T_2 be the tableaux constructed for E_1 and E_2, respectively. Let us assume without loss of generality that if both T_1 and T_2 have distinguished symbols in the summary column for attribute A, then those symbols are the same, but that otherwise, T_1 and T_2 have no symbols in common. Then the tableau for $E_1 \bowtie E_2$ has a summary in which a column has a distinguished symbol a if a appears as a distinguished symbol in that column of the summary of T_1 or T_2, or both. Otherwise, the summary has a blank in that column. The new tableau has as rows all the rows of T_1 and T_2, and has as constraints all the constraints of those tableaux. $\square$

Example 8.8: Consider the expression $\pi_A \sigma_{C=0}(AB \bowtie BC)$. We begin by constructing tableaux for the basis expressions AB and BC, that is, the relation operands themselves. Assuming the tableaux to have columns corresponding to A, B, and C, in that order, these two tableaux are

$$
\begin{array}{cc}
a_1 & a_2 \\
\hline
a_1 & a_2 \quad (AB)
\end{array}
$$

$$
\begin{array}{cc}
a_3 & a_4 \\
\hline
a_3 & a_4 \quad (BC)
\end{array}
$$

Working up the tree, we need a tableau for the subexpression $AB \bowtie BC$. This tableau is formed from the two tableaux above by identifying the distinguished symbols in the columns for B, since B is a common attribute of both relation schemes. Say we replace a_3 by a_2. No other changes of symbols are needed, since the two tableaux had no common symbols. The resulting tableau is

---

† By *identifying* two symbols we mean to replace one by the other or replace both by a third symbol. Each occurrence of the symbols must be replaced by this common symbol, not just the occurrences in the summary. It is irrelevant what symbol we choose as the common symbol, as long as it is not one of the other symbols of the tableau.

‡ This replacement is a liberty taken with notation, since constants do not, strictly speaking, appear in the summary. It is a shorthand for the condition $a = c$, where a is the distinguished symbol in the column for A.

$$\begin{array}{ccc} a_1 & a_2 & a_4 \\ \hline a_1 & a_2 & \quad (AB) \\ & a_2 & a_4 \quad (BC) \end{array}$$

Next, we apply $\sigma_{C=0}$ to the above tableau. The result is obtained by replacing the distinguished symbol in the C column, that is, a_4, by the constant 0, that is

$$\begin{array}{ccc} a_1 & a_2 & 0 \\ \hline a_1 & a_2 & \quad (AB) \\ & a_2 & 0 \quad (BC) \end{array}$$

Finally, we perform the projection onto A by simply removing the symbols a_2 and 0 from the summary of the above tableau. The symbol a_2 continues to appear in the rows, but since it is now nondistinguished, we shall replace it by the symbol b_1. The resulting tableau is

$$\begin{array}{cc} a_1 & \\ \hline a_1 & b_1 \quad (AB) \\ & b_1 \quad 0 \quad (BC) \end{array}$$

In words, this tableau represents the set of a_1 such that for some b_1, $a_1 b_1$ is in AB and $b_1 0$ is in BC. $\square$

Tableau Containment and Equivalence

An examination of Algorithm 8.4 tells us that the number of rows of any tableau is equal to one plus the number of joins in the expression from which it came. Conversely, given any tableau with n rows, we can build from it an algebraic expression with $n-1$ joins (which are really Cartesian products). Start by taking the product of the relations that correspond to each of the rows, apply the selections necessary to reflect the constraints in the tableau and to equate any components that are represented by the same symbol in the tableau. Finally, project onto those components that correspond to distinguished variables in the summary.

Example 8.9: For the last tableau of Example 8.8 we begin by taking the product $AB \times BC$. We then note that the second component of the row for AB and the first component of the row for BC use the same symbol, b_1, so these components must be equated in the product by the selection

$$\sigma_{2=3}(AB \times BC)$$

Note this expression is really the natural join of AB and BC. We also note that the C component of the second row is the constant 0, so we must select for this component, which is the fourth component of the product $AB \times BC$, equal to 0. The expression to reflect both selections is

$$\sigma_{2=3 \wedge 4='0'}(AB \times BC)$$

Finally, the only distinguished symbol, a_1, appears in the first component of the row for AB, and we may therefore produce for the tableau the algebraic expression $\pi_1(\sigma_{2=3 \wedge 4='0'}(AB \times BC))$. When we recognize that the selection $2=3$ and the product is really the natural join, and we identify component numbers with their appropriate attribute names, we see that the expression we have constructed is the same as the one with which we started Example 8.8. $\square$

Now, understanding the close relationship between rows and number of joins, we can attempt to minimize the number of joins in an expression equivalent to a given one by asking which, among all the tableaux that represent the same mapping, has the fewest joins. True, simply minimizing the number of joins does not guarantee that we have the most efficient way to answer the query, but minimizing the joins is surely a good heuristic, because joins take much more time, on the average, than selections or projections. In addition, given the tableau with the fewest rows, we can build a connection graph for its expression, since the expression from the tableau, constructed as in Example 8.9, is a Cartesian product followed by a selection, as are the expressions for which the QUEL algorithm of Section 8.4 was designed. Therefore, a complete algorithm for finding an efficient way to implement a given select-project-join expression is

1. Construct a tableau for the expression by Algorithm 8.4.
2. Find the equivalent tableau with the fewest rows, by a method to be discussed.
3. Convert the minimal tableau back to an expression by the method described prior to Example 8.9.
4. Implement the resulting expression by Algorithm 8.3.

We shall now deal with the question of how to minimize the rows of a tableau. An essential intermediate step is to learn how to tell whether the mapping defined by one tableau, T_1, is contained in that of another, T_2. We say that $T_1 \subseteq T_2$ if

1. the tableaux are defined over the same sets of attributes and have distinguished variables in exactly the same summary positions, and
2. for any assignment of relations to the relation variables that tag the rows of the tableaux, the relation produced by T_1 is a subset of that produced by T_2.

The rule for testing containment of tableaux is fairly simple and is stated in the next theorem.

Theorem 8.1: $T_1 \subseteq T_2$ if and only if there is a symbol mapping h from the symbols of T_2 to those of T_1, such that

1. h applied to the summary of T_2 is the summary of T_1,
2. h applied to each row of T_2 (h maps any constants to themselves) is a row

of T_1 with the same tag, and

3. Each constraint of T_2 is implied by the hypothesis that the constraints of T_1 hold for the symbols to which h maps the symbols of T_2.†

Proof: We shall only sketch the ideas of this theorem, which are similar to those in Theorem 7.11 on infering dependencies. Suppose first that such a mapping h exists, and let T_1, when applied to a certain list of relations, produce a relation containing the particular tuple t. That means there is some symbol mapping f from T_1 to the symbols used in the relations, such that f applied to the summary of T_1 is t, f applied to each row of T_1 is a tuple in the relation whose name tags that row, and the constraints associated with T_1 are satisfied when f is applied to the symbols in the constraints.

Now consider the mapping g defined by $g(x) = f(h(x))$. That is, g maps the symbols of T_2 to the symbols of the given relations by first applying h to produce a symbol of T_1, and then mapping that symbol according to the mapping f from the symbols of T_1 to the relations' symbols. Since h maps the summary of T_2 to the summary of T_1, it follows that g maps the summary of T_2 to t. Similarly, for every row r of T_2, $h(r)$ is a row of T_1, so $g(r)$ is a tuple in the relation tagging row $h(r)$. That tag must be the same as the tag of r by condition (2). Likewise, we can check that (3) holds for each constraint of T_2. Thus, every tuple t in the relation produced by T_1 when applied to the given relations is also produced by T_2; that is, $T_1 \subseteq T_2$.

Conversely, suppose that $T_1 \subseteq T_2$. We shall form particular relations such that the fact that T_2 applied to these relations produces every tuple that T_1 produces implies the existence of a mapping h as in the statement of the theorem. We essentially make the rows of T_1 into relations. That is, if R tags one or more rows of T_1, then the relation for R consists of those rows of T_1, projected onto the relation scheme of R. We should think of the symbols of T_1 as abstract constants; they satisfy no ordering relationship ($a \leq b$, e.g.), unless it follows from the constraints associated with T_1. Then the tuple that is the summary of T_1 is surely in T_1 applied to these relations; the identity mapping from the symbols of T_1 sends each row of T_1 into the tuple that was derived from the row itself.

Since $T_1 \subseteq T_2$ is assumed, T_2 applied to these relations must also produce the summary of T_1. Then there must be a symbol mapping from the symbols of T_2 to the symbols of these relations, i.e., to the symbols of T_1, that maps rows of T_2 to rows of T_1, maps the summary to the summary, and maps each constraint of T_2 into a constraint on the symbols of T_1 that follows logically from the constraints of T_1 (because no other inequalities hold about the abstract constants that the symbols of T_1 have become). □

In less formal terms, the first two conditions of Theorem 8.1 tell us that

---

† We shall discuss how to test condition (3) shortly.

h must map distinguished symbols of one tableau to the corresponding distinguished symbols of the other tableau. They also tell us that the symbol mapping h can be viewed as a mapping on the rows.

Example 8.10: Let T_1 be the tableau

a		
a	b	(R)
c	d	(R)
e	f	(R)

$$b < d, d < f$$

and let T_2 be the tableau

w		
w	x	(R)
y	z	(R)

$$x < z$$

Informally, T_2 is the set of first components of a relation R such that this first component is associated with a second component that is not the largest. Similarly, T_1 is the set of first components of R that are associated with second components that are no more than third largest. Clearly we expect T_2 applied to any relation R, to produce all that T_1 does, and probably more.

To prove that that is the case, consider the mapping h defined by $h(w) = a$, $h(x) = b$, $h(y) = c$, and $h(z) = d$. Then h maps the two rows of T_2 to the first two rows of T_1, respectively, and it maps the summary to the summary. Likewise, the constraint $x < z$ is mapped to $h(x) < h(z)$, which is $b < d$, one of the given constraints of T_1.

Alternatively, we could prove the same fact by using the symbol mapping g defined by $g(w) = a$, $g(x) = b$, $g(y) = e$, and $g(z) = f$. This mapping sends the first row of T_2 to the first row of T_1 and the second row of T_2 to the third row of T_1. The constraint $x < z$ becomes $b < f$. This constraint is not a given constraint of T_1, but it follows logically from $b < d$ and $d < f$ in an obvious manner. $\square$

Testing Logical Consequences of Inequalities

Since we see from the above example the importance of making inferences about arithmetic inequalities, let us digress for a moment and see how such inferences are made.

Algorithm 8.5: Testing Consequences of Inequalities.

Input: A collection of inequalities of the form $a < b$ or $a \leq b$, and a particular

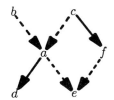

Fig. 8.12. Graph representing inequalities.

inequality $x < y$ or $x \leq y$ to be tested.

Output: A decision whether the inequality being tested holds, independent of the values assigned to the variables, as long as the given inequalities hold.

Method: Construct a graph whose nodes correspond to the variables mentioned in the inequalities. If there is an inequality $a < b$, place a directed edge from the node b to the node a, and mark that edge *solid*. For each inequality $a \leq b$, place a directed edge from b to a and mark it *dashed*. If there are any cycles that contain a solid edge, then the constraints are inconsistent; they clearly imply that some variable is strictly less than itself. There may be cycles of dashed edges; these involve variables that are implied by the constraints to have equal values.

Then $x < y$ holds if and only if there is a path in the graph from y to x with at least one solid edge. Also, $x \leq y$ holds if there is any path at all from y to x. $\square$

Example 8.11: Suppose we are given the constraints $a \leq b$, $a \leq c$, $d < a$, $e \leq a$, $f < c$, and $e \leq f$. Figure 8.12 shows the graph that results. The conclusions we can draw in addition to the given ones are $d < b$, $d < c$, $e \leq b$, and $e < c$. $\square$

Equivalence of Tableaux

From the method for testing containment of tableaux, testing equivalence follows at once. That is, the mappings defined by two tableaux T_1 and T_2 are the same, written $T_1 \equiv T_2$, if and only if both $T_1 \subseteq T_2$ and $T_2 \subseteq T_1$ hold. Thus the test for equivalence is simply to find whether symbol mappings satisfying the conditions of Theorem 8.1 exist in both directions. There need not be any relationship between the two mappings.

Example 8.12: We already know from Example 8.10 that $T_1 \subseteq T_2$. Could it be that $T_2 \subseteq T_1$, so that these two tableaux are equivalent? If there is a mapping h from T_1 to T_2, then surely $h(a) = w$, since the summary must map to the summary. Therefore, $h(b) = x$, or else there is no row that the row ab could map to. The constraint $b < d$ must map to a true constraint, which could only be $x < z$, so $h(d) = z$. But then $h(d) < h(f)$ cannot be made true by any value assigned to $h(f)$, since $h(d)$, which is z, is not less than anything in T_2. We conclude that a symbol mapping h satisfying the conditions of Theorem 8.1 does not exist, and $T_2 \subseteq T_1$ is false; therefore so is $T_1 \equiv T_2$.

For another example, consider the tableau T_3

a		b	
a	c	d	(R)
a	e	f	(R)
g	c	b	(R)
h	e	b	(R)

and the tableau T_4

a		b	
a	e	f	(R)
h	e	b	(R)

The identity symbol mapping from T_4 to T_3 shows that $T_3 \subseteq T_4$. Conversely, mapping c to e, d to f, and g to h, with other symbols unchanged, sends the first two rows of T_3 to the first row of T_4 and the last two rows of T_3 to the second row of T_4. Thus $T_4 \subseteq T_3$, and the two tableaux are equivalent. $\square$

Minimization of Tableaux

Let T_0 be a given tableau, and T_m an equivalent tableau with the minimum possible number of rows. We might expect that the rows of T_m have little or nothing to do with the rows of T_0, but in fact they are very closely related. The rows of any minimal equivalent tableau T_m must be a subset of the rows of T_0, perhaps with the symbols renamed. We prove these facts in the next theorem and corollary.

Theorem 8.2: If T_0 is any tableau, there is a minimal equivalent tableau formed from T_0 by deleting zero or more rows of T_0.

Proof: Suppose T_m is any tableau equivalent to T_0 with a minimum possible number of rows. Since $T_0 \equiv T_m$, there is a symbol mapping f from T_0 to T_m satisfying Theorem 8.1, and another symbol mapping g from T_m to T_0, also satisfying the conditions of that theorem. By Theorem 8.1, f and g can be viewed as mapping rows to rows, as well as symbols to symbols. Let R be the set of rows of T_0 that are the target of rows of T_m under the mapping g, and let T_1 be T_0 with the rows not in R deleted.

T_1 has no more rows than T_m, because g cannot map one row of T_m to more than one row. Since f maps all the rows of T_0 to rows of T_m, it surely does the same for T_1. Thus the symbol mappings f and g also show $T_1 \equiv T_m$. By transitivity of equivalence, $T_1 \equiv T_0$. Since T_1 has as few rows as T_m, it has the minimum possible number of rows, and since the rows of T_1 were constructed to be a subset of the rows of T_0, T_1 satisfies the theorem. $\square$

Corollary: All the minimum row tableaux equivalent to a given tableau are the same except possibly for the names of symbols.

Proof: We have only to observe that the symbol mapping f defines the correspondence of symbols between the tableau T_1 and an arbitrary minimal tableau T_m needed to make them identical. Then, the correspondence betweeen the symbols of any two minimal tableaux for T_0 can be deduced from their correspondence to rows of T_1.

The only detail that must be considered is whether f could send the rows of T_1 to a proper subset of the rows of T_m. But if that were the case, then f followed by g would map the rows of T_1 into a proper subset of themselves, contradicting the fact that T_1 is minimal. $\square$

Example 8.13: Let us consider the tableau T_3 of Example 8.12 in the role of T_0 of Theorem 8.2. It turns out that the tableau T_4 is a minimum row tableau equivalent to T_3. We already know they are equivalent, and it is easy to show that T_4 is equivalent to no one-row tableau, which by Theorem 8.2 would have to consist of one of the rows of T_4.

To see that T_4 is minimal suppose, for example, that the first row, aef, of T_4 could be eliminated, to make an equivalent tableau

a		b	
h	e	b	(R)

Then aef must map to heb, meaning that a maps to h. But a must map to a, because the summaries of the two tableaux must map to each other, and both are ab.

A similar argument shows that the row aef alone does not yield a tableau equivalent to T_4. We conclude that T_4 is a minimal equivalent tableau for T_3. It happens that T_4's rows are exactly equal to a subset of the rows of T_3, namely the second and fourth. However, tableaux like the following are also minimal equivalent tableaux for T_3.

a		e	
d	b	e	(R)
a	b	c	(R)

The symbol correspondence between T_4 and the above tableau is a-a, b-e, e-b, f-c, and h-d. Note that the corresponding rows appear in opposite order in the two tableaux in question. $\square$

Theorem 8.2 suggests the general procedure we must follow to minimize tableaux. Look at the possible mappings from all the rows to a subset of the rows. Consider those that define symbol mappings because they do not map any one symbol into two and they do map the summary into the summary (i.e., they are the identity on distinguished symbols) and preserve constraints. The problem of finding the mapping to the fewest rows is known to be $\mathcal{NP}$-complete, but because the number of rows in tableaux occuring in practice tends to be small, that does not appear to be a severe problem.

8.6 OPTIMIZATION UNDER WEAK EQUIVALENCE

We defined "equivalence" of tableaux, and indeed, of expressions in general by saying that two tableaux are equivalent if and only if they yield the same relation when applied to any set of relations used to substitute for the relation variables. Let us agree now to call this notion *strong equivalence*.

There is a weaker notion of equivalence, which we shall, not surprisingly, call *weak equivalence*. Let E_1 and E_2 be two expressions with operand relations $R_1, \ldots, R_k$, and let U be the union of all the attributes found among the relation schemes of the R_i's. Suppose that for any relation u over U, when we substitute $\pi_{R_i}(u)$ for R_i in the two expressions,† they produce the same result. Then we say that E_1 and E_2 are weakly equivalent, written $E_1 \equiv_w E_2$. We shall use $\equiv_s$ for strong equivalence when we want to emphasize the difference.

In terms of tableaux and the construction of Algorithm 8.4, only the basis changes. That is, to construct the tableau for an expression consisting of a single operand R, we construct a tableau for the expression $\pi_R(U)$. This tableau, as can be seen from Algorithm 8.4, has distinguished symbols in the columns for R, both in the summary and in its lone row. In the other columns the tableau has blanks in the summary and nondistinguished symbols in the rows. The tag becomes irrelevant, since all rows correspond to the universal set of attributes U. Following our convention that arose in the study of Query-by-Example and was continued in Section 7.6, we shall allow a nondistinguished variable that appears only once to be replaced by a blank.

The effect of these observations is that we can use a modified Algorithm 8.4 to develop tableaux whose equivalence, by the test of Theorem 8.1 implies the weak equivalence of the expressions represented by these tableaux. The only difference between the modified and unmodified Algorithm 8.4 turns out to be that the tags are omitted in the modified algorithm. That follows because in a row that comes from relation R, the columns for attributes not in R surely are nondistinguished symbols that appear only once, and these may be left blank. The symbols appearing in the columns for R may wind up being nondistinguished symbols that appear nowhere else, but they need not be replaced by blanks if we wish not to. Thus, a row that would have been tagged R can be assumed without loss of generality to have nonblanks exactly in the columns for R.

Example 8.14: Let $U = \{A, B, C\}$, and let us have two relations AB and BC.

---

† We identify a relation name with its relation scheme, so R_i is both a name for a relation and a set of attributes onto which we can perform a projection.

The expression AB has tableau T_1 as follows

A	B	C
a_1	a_2	
a_1	a_2	

The symbol in column C of the one row is left blank, although we could put a nondistinguished symbol there.

Now consider the expression $\pi_{AB}(AB \bowtie BC)$. This expression has a tableau T_2 constructed by the modified Algorithm 8.4; it is

A	B	C
a_1	a_2	
a_1	a_2	
	a_2	b_1

We have shown the nondistinguished symbol b_1 explicitly, since it was once a distinguished symbol, representing the C column in the row for BC. Other nondistinguished symbols also appear only once and are left blank.

We claim that $T_1 \equiv_w T_2$. In proof, the identity mapping from T_1 to T_2 sends the row of T_1 to the first row of T_2, and satisfies Theorem 8.1 in all respects. Conversely, let $h(a_1) = a_1$, $h(a_2) = a_2$, and let $h(b_1)$ be the blank appearing in the C column of the row of T_1. In principle, h is also defined on the blanks in the rows of T_2, but it is easy to see that we can always define a symbol mapping on a nondistinguished symbol that appears only once and be sure that the conditions of Theorem 8.1 are not violated. That is, if a blank appears in row r, and we would like to satisfy Theorem 8.1 by mapping r to some row s, just see what symbol s has in the column of the blank, and define the symbol mapping on that blank to be that symbol.

We can easily see that the symbol mapping h sends both rows of T_2 to the one row of T_1, and sends the summary to the summary; it therefore satisfies Theorem 8.1 and shows the weak equivalence of T_1 and T_2. It does not show the strong equivalence of the two tableaux, since we did not tag the rows, and allowed any row to map to any other. Had we used the unmodified version of Algorithm 8.4, we would have obtained the tableaux of Fig. 8.13. These are inequivalent, although $T_2' \subseteq T_1'$. The reason that $T_1' \subseteq T_2'$ is easily seen not to hold is that the row tagged BC cannot be mapped to a row of T_1', since no row has that tag. $\square$

Motivation Behind Weak Equivalence

At first, strong equivalence appears so natural that we might wonder why any other notion is needed. To see the role played by weak equivalence, let us consider why the expressions AB and $\pi_{AB}(AB \bowtie BC)$ are weakly, but not strongly, equivalent. If the AB and BC relations are each the projection of

A	B	C	
a_1	a_2		
a_1	a_2		(AB)

(a) T'_1

A	B	C	
a_1	a_2		
a_1	a_2		(AB)
	a_2	b_1	(BC)

(b) T'_2

Fig. 8.13. Tableaux constructed using unmodified Algorithm 8.4.

a single relation u over ABC, then $AB \bowtie BC$ includes u, and no tuple in $AB \bowtie BC$ can have A and B components that do not appear in some tuple of u, by definition of the join. Thus, the projection of $AB \bowtie BC$ onto AB is exactly what we get by projecting u onto AB directly.

However, suppose that the relations r_{AB} for AB and r_{BC} for BC are not the projection of any one relation u. Then there might be a tuple ab in r_{AB} but no tuple with B-component b in the r_{BC} relation, thereby causing there to be no tuple abx for any x in $AB \bowtie BC$, and therefore no tuple ab in

$$\pi_{AB}(AB \bowtie BC)$$

This phenomenon was termed "dangling tuples" in Section 7.3; the ab tuple in r_{AB} is dangling because there is no tuple in the r_{BC} relation that matches ab when we form the join.

Evidently, if both r_{AB} and $_{BC}$ are the projections of a single relation, there can be no dangling tuples, and the expressions AB and $\pi_{AB}(AB \bowtie BC)$ produce the same result on r_{AB} and r_{BC}. Thus, one way to interpret weak equivalence is "equivalence assuming no dangling tuples." In a sense, saying that $AB \equiv_w \pi_{AB}(AB \bowtie BC)$ is like saying $1/(1/x) = x$; it's a true statement except in "pathological" cases, where there are dangling tuples in the former equation, and where $x = 0$ in the latter.

The trouble is that dangling tuples are hardly "pathological." Rather, we expect them as a matter of course. For example, one of the motivations for normalization of relations, as discussed in Section 7.4, is to allow meaningful dangling tuples in relations. To justify weak equivalence we have to say something stronger. We must claim that dangling tuples should not figure into the calculation of expressions. In certain cases we cannot make such an assertion. If we want those AB tuples that have a B-value for which there is an associated C-value in the BC relation, then the expression $\pi_{AB}(AB \bowtie BC)$ is what we

E	D	S	M	
			m	
e	d			(ED)
e		s		(ES)
	d		m	(DM)

$$e = \text{``Jones''}$$

Fig. 8.14. Tableau for query on a view.

want, and AB is simply not an acceptable substitute.

However, there are certain conditions under which we can very reasonably say that we do not want dangling tuples in our expressions, and it is there that weak equivalence plays an important role. These conditions most frequently occur when views of the database are involved, especially where that view is a "universal relation," or join of all the relations, as discussed in the next chapter.

For example, suppose we have attributes E (employee), D (department), S (salary), and M (manager), grouped into relations ES, ED, and DM. Suppose that we have a view, which could be a "universal relation,"

$$ESDM = ES \bowtie ED \bowtie DM$$

If we ask a query about this view, like "find the manager of employee Jones," the query is answered by forming the view and then applying the selection and projection implied by the query. That is, we ask for

$$\pi_M(\sigma_{E=\text{``Jones''}}(ES \bowtie ED \bowtie DM))$$

The tableau for this expression constructed by Algorithm 8.4 is shown in Fig. 8.14.

If we use strong equivalence as our notion of equivalence, then the tableau of Fig. 8.14 cannot be reduced. To see this, simply observe that each row has a different tag, so no row could map to any other. However, if we take weak equivalence as our standard, then we get, by the modified Algorithm 8.4, the same tableau as Fig. 8.14, but with all tags equal to the full set of attributes, i.e., $EDSM$. Then we can use a symbol mapping that is the identity on all symbols but s; it sends s to the symbol represented by the blank in the S column of the first row of Fig. 8.14. This symbol mapping sends the second row of Fig. 8.14 to the first row, and other rows to themselves. Thus, the tableau of Fig. 8.15 is a smaller tableau weakly equivalent to Fig. 8.14.

We cannot further reduce Fig. 8.15. The second row cannot map to the first, because distinguished symbol m cannot map to the nondistinguished symbol represented by the blank in the M column of the first row, because then the summary, which is m itself, would not map to the summary. The first row cannot map to the second, because e would then map to the blank in the E

E	D	S	M
			m
e	d		
	d		m

$e = $ "Jones"

Fig. 8.15. Reduced tableau weakly equivalent to Fig. 8.14.

column of the second row. Since that blank symbol is unrelated to "Jones" by the constraints given, we could not then infer the constraint $e =$ "Jones" from the constraint $h(e) =$ "Jones", if h were the symbol mapping involved.

The tableaux of Figs. 8.14 and 8.15, while weakly equivalent, produce different answers sometimes. In particular, when Jones has no salary recorded in the ES relation, Fig. 8.14 produces the empty set as the answer, because no symbol mapping from Fig. 8.14 to relations could both map e into "Jones", as required by the constraint, and also map es into a tuple of the ES relation. However, Fig. 8.15 will print the manager or managers of those departments to which Jones is assigned, as long as the necessary associations are in the ED and DM relations, independently of the value of the ES relation.

Here we see graphically how differently weak and strong equivalence interact with dangling tuples. That is, the tuple (Jones, d) in ED and dm in DM are both dangling if there is no tuple (Jones, s) in ES for any salary s. Yet we feel intuitively that m is still Jones' manager, independent of whether we have recorded Jones' salary or not. That is, the fact that Jones and manager m are related only through dangling tuples is not really a concern. Put even more strongly, we claim that when queries over views formed by joins are being optimized, there is excellent justification for optimizing according to weak, rather than strong, equivalence. Not only does weak equivalence provide an optimized query with fewer joins to take than that provided by strong equivalence, but there is reason to feel that the result of the query found by weak equivalence is more likely to meet the intent of the querier than the other.

EXERCISES

8.1: Verify each of the identities in Section 8.2.

8.2: Show that the equation

$$\pi_S(E_1 - E_2) \equiv \pi_S(E_1) - \pi_S(E_2)$$

is not valid in general.

8.3: Let us recall the beer drinkers' database first introduced in Exercise 5.6, with relations

FREQUENTS(DRINKER,BAR)
SERVES(BAR,BEER)
LIKES(DRINKER,BEER)

Write relational algebra expressions for the following queries and optimize them according to Algorithm 8.1.

a) Find the drinkers that frequent a bar that serves a beer that they like.

b) Find the drinkers that drink at the same bar with a drinker that likes "Potgold" beer.

c) Find the drinkers that drink at the same bar with a drinker that likes a brand of beer that the bar serves and Charles Chugamug likes.

8.4: Use Algorithm 8.3 to optimize the queries of Exercise 8.3.

8.5: Write tableaux for the queries of Exercise 8.3.

* 8.6: Show that every SQUARE mapping defines a conjunctive query.

* 8.7: Show that any QUEL retrieve statement, in which a list of attributes is retrieved (no aggregate operators), and the where-clause is the logical "and" of terms equating components of tuples to one another or to constants, is a conjunctive query.

* 8.8: Show that QBE queries in which all entries are variables or constants and no condition boxes are used is a conjunctive query.

8.9: Let R_1 and R_2 be relations over some set of attributes including the set S.

a) Show that the containment $\pi_S(R_1 \cap R_2) \subseteq \pi_S(R_1) \cap \pi_S(R_2)$ holds by using the test of Theorem 8.1.

b) Also prove the containment $\pi_S(R_1) - \pi_S(R_2) \subseteq \pi_S(R_1 - R_2)$.

8.10: Suppose a relation $ABCD$ has a clustering index on A and nonclustering indices on the other attributes; the four indices have image sizes of 50, 10, 20, and 100, respectively. The number of tuples in the relation is 10,000, and the relation would fit on 500 blocks. Find all the ways to evaluate the query

$$\pi_A(\sigma_{A=0 \wedge B=1 \wedge C>2 \wedge D=3}(ABCD))$$

Which method is the least costly?

8.11: Consider the following four conjunctive queries.

I $\{ a_1 a_2 \mid (\exists b_1)(\exists b_2)(R(a_1 b_1) \wedge R(b_1 b_2) \wedge R(b_2 a_2)) \}$

II $\{ a_1 a_2 \mid (\exists b_1)(\exists b_2)(\exists b_3)(R(a_1 b_1) \wedge R(b_1 b_2) \wedge R(b_2 b_3) \wedge R(b_3 a_2)) \}$

III $\{ a_1 a_2 \mid (\exists b_1)(\exists b_2)(\exists b_3)(\exists b_4)(R(a_1 b_2) \wedge R(b_3 b_4) \wedge R(b_1 a_2) \wedge R(a_1 b_3) \wedge R(b_2 b_4) \wedge R(b_4 b_1)) \}$

IV $\{ a_1 a_2 \mid (\exists b_1)(\exists b_2)(R(a_1 b_1) \wedge R(b_1 c) \wedge R(c b_2) \wedge R(b_2 a_2)) \}$

where c is a constant. Construct tableaux for these queries and find all the equalities and containments among these expressions. Note that the constant c must be simulated by a variable x and a constraint $x = c$.

A	B	C	D	
a				

A	B	C	D	
a		c		(R)
	b	c	d	(S)
	e	c	f	(S)
	g	h	f	(S)

Fig. 8.16. Tableau to be minimized.

** 8.12: Suppose $Q = Q_1 \cup Q_2 \cup \cdots \cup Q_k$, and $P = P_1 \cup P_2 \cup \cdots \cup P_r$, where the Q_i's and P_i's are mappings defined by tableaux. Prove that $Q \subseteq P$ if and only if for each Q_i there exists a P_j such that $Q_i \subseteq P_j$.

8.13: Optimize the query of Fig. 8.16 under (a) strong (b) weak equivalence.

** 8.14: Show that it is $\mathcal{NP}$-complete to determine the minimum-row tableau equivalent to a given tableau.

BIBLIOGRAPHIC NOTES

A variety of algorithms for optimization of an expression in relational algebra have been proposed in Hall [1976], Minker [1978], Pecherer [1975], and Smith and Chang [1975], for example. The heart of these algorithms is the moving of selections as far down the tree as possible, although a variety of other useful manipulations are suggested. The strategy of optimization by doing selections first is attributed to Palermo [1974]. Gotlieb [1975] discusses alternative ways to compute joins, and S. B. Yao [1979] analyses alternatives for select-project-join queries.

The QUEL decomposition algorithm is from Wong and Youssefi [1976]. ISBL optimization is described in Hall [1976], and SEQUEL optimization, including Algorithm 8.2 and its generalizations to more complex queries, in Astrahan et al. [1976] and Griffiths et al. [1979]. A theoretical study of SEQUEL optimization is found in Kim [1981].

The optimization of conjunctive queries is based on Chandra and Merlin [1977], and the solution to Exercise 8.14, the $\mathcal{NP}$-completeness of minimization, is from there. The tableau notation is from Aho, Sagiv, and Ullman [1979a, b], where the notion of equivalence was extended to take account of functional dependencies, by "chasing" the rows of the tableau in a manner similar to that of Section 7.6.

Klug [1982] extended the tableau concept to include constraints, as in Section 8.5. Sagiv and Yannakakis [1981] extended the equivalence test to unions of tableaux (Exercise 8.12) and to some even more general classes of queries. It is also possible to test for equivalence of tableaux given that they apply only to relations that satisfy a set of dependencies. Aho, Sagiv, and Ullman [1979a, b] cover the case where functional dependencies are permitted, while Johnson and Klug [1982] handle both functional and inclusion dependencies.

9

THE UNIVERSAL RELATION AS A
USER INTERFACE

This chapter is devoted to what the author considers the most promising direction in which the developing theory of relational databases can serve to make database systems easier on the user. We shall show how the user may regard the database as a single relation, and how some of the concepts developed in previous chapters can be used to make interpretation of queries about this (imaginary) relation make sense in terms of the actual relations in the database scheme.

9.1 THE UNIVERSAL RELATION CONCEPT

Let us imagine that the data of an entire database were kept in a single relation, called a *universal relation*, whose scheme consisted of all the attributes in any of the relation schemes of the database. As discussed in Section 8.5, it is helpful, when talking of attributes independently of any particular relation scheme, to assume that attributes representing the same thing in different relation schemes are given the same name, and attributes representing different things are given different names; we shall make this assumption here.

For an example of a universal relation, Section 7.4 discussed the decomposition of a hypothetical relation over set of attributes $CTHRSG$, the six attributes standing for courses, teachers, hours, rooms, students, and grades, respectively. Figure 7.7 gave an example of a hypothetical relation over this scheme, although we agreed that we would never really wish to store the data in this way, because of the various anomalies that were present. Recall, it was to avoid anomalies such as in Fig. 7.7 that the normalization process was introduced.

However, we are not proposing that the data be stored as in Fig. 7.7, only that the user be allowed to perceive the data as if it were. The advantage is that the user is thus spared memorizing details concerning which attributes are grouped with which to form relation schemes. In order that the universal relation make sense as a conceptual tool, we must sometimes use null values

to pad out (imaginary) tuples, and thereby avoid the problems associated in
Section 7.1 with unnormalized relations. For example, we could use nulls in the
S and G components of the $CTHRSG$ universal relation to record information
about courses before students registered. We shall discuss nulls in more detail
later, but for the moment, the reader should be reminded that the fact that
the universal relation is imaginary, rather than stored physically, gives us the
flexibility necessary to handle anomalies by using nulls. If we were to store
unnormalized relations in reality, we might use too much space storing tuples
with nulls, and handling updates in the presence of possible null values could
be too time consuming.

In a sense, we propose going one step further than the relational model
generally attempts to do, by removing from the user not only concern about
the physical organization of the data, but about some of the logical organization
as well. The penalty we pay is that the DBMS must work harder to interpret
queries and updates on the database, than it would if the user had to specify
the query in terms of the conceptual database itself. The penalty is not a
great one, however, and it is analogous to the additional work of optimization
that is contributed by any relational DBMS to relieve the user of specifying his
query in terms even lower than relations, as he would using systems based on
nonrelational data models.

A Simple Query Language for Universal Relations

An experimental DBMS, called System/U,† that supports the universal relation
view of data is under development at Stanford. It's query language is similar
to QUEL, with two simplifications.

1. Since all tuple variables range over the universal relation, there is no need
    for declarations of tuple variables.

2. Since most queries in ordinary QUEL that require two or more tuple
    variables involve joins, and joins, at least natural joins, are hidden by the
    universal relation view of data, it is rare that a query to System/U requires
    more than one tuple variable. Thus we make the assumption that there is
    an "invisible" tuple variable, called *blank*, and let an attribute A standing
    alone stand for blank.A.

Example 9.1: Consider the $CTHRSG$ universal relation. If we want to know
in which rooms Prof. Deadwood teaches, we write

> retrieve (R)
> where $T=$ "Deadwood"

The reader should compare the simplicity of this query with the standard
QUEL query to do the same thing, assuming the actual database scheme is

---

† The name was originated by H. Korth as a way of embarrassing the author. The "U" stands
for "universal," and nothing else.

$\{\,CT, CHR, CSG\,\}$. The QUEL query is

> range of t is CT
> range of s is CHR
> retrieve $(s.R)$
> > where $t.T=$ "Deadwood" and $t.C = s.C$

Some queries to System/U do require one or more nonblank tuple variables. For example, if we want to know all the courses that meet in the same room as CS101, we could write

> retrieve (C)
> > where $R = t.R$ and $t.C=$ "CS101"

The terms R and C stand for blank.R and blank.C, and are thereby differentiated from $t.R$ and $t.C$.

The first of these queries will be implemented in System/U by taking the natural join of CT and CHR, selecting for $T=$ "Deadwood", and then projecting onto R. However, the user does not have to know this fact. If, for example, there were a THR relation in the database scheme, the query would instead be answered by taking the selection and projection on this relation alone.†

The second example query would be answered by taking an equijoin on $R = R$ of two copies of the CHR relation, then selecting for the first C component equal to CS101, and finally projecting onto the second C component. How System/U, or any system that supports universal relations, decides on these responses to queries is the major subject of this chapter. ☐

The Object Structure of Universal Relations

In order to discuss most of the issues raised by interpretation of queries on universal relations, we must begin by examining what it is we believe are the tuples in this imaginary universal relation about which the user poses his queries. The hypothesis we take is that if the universal relation has any meaning at all, it can be expressed by writing a domain relational calculus expression that describes its tuples. For example, the contents of the universal $CTHRSG$ relation could be described as

---

† One may wonder how the user can know what answer to expect, since the knowledge of whether there is a THR relation, or CT and CHR relations, or all three is hidden, and the answer produced from the THR relation need not be the same as that produced from the join of CT and CHR. It is a fundamental assumption of universal relation systems that the normally desired response is the simplest expression, e.g., don't take a join if a single relation scheme contains the attributes needed. However, in the case that the user is aware of the particular relation schemes used in the database, and a circuitous connection among certain attributes is wanted, one can express, in a query language like System/U's, any QUEL query, by using as many tuple variables as needed.

$\{\,cthrsg\mid t$ teaches course c, and

course c meets in room r at hour h, and

student s is getting grade g in course $c\,\}$

In this expression we see that there are three fundamental relationships dictating the structure of the universal relation. One is the relationship between c and t, that is, courses and teachers, which we termed "teaches" above. A second is among c, r, and h, which we expressed as "meets in $\cdots$ at." The third is between c, s, and g, and is expressed by "getting $\cdots$ in." In this case, the fundamental relationships can be identified with the relations CT, CHR, and CSG of the database, but that need not be the case in general, as we shall see from other examples shortly. We call such sets of attributes that are involved in these fundamental relationships *objects*.

It is important to note how our expression of the universal relation in the form above reflects our understanding of how attributes relate. For example, since we said that one fundamental relationship involved all three attributes course, hour, and room, it is implied that we cannot express this relationship by factoring it into two. In contrast, if we had said "c meets in r and c is held at hour h," then we would be presenting a different view of the world, one in which courses were assigned rooms in which they met every hour at which they were held. However, as is apparent from Fig. 7.7, we believe that courses can meet in different rooms at different hours. Let us emphasize that there is no way to determine which viewpoint is correct; we should simply be aware that there is an opportunity to reflect different assumptions about the "real world" by phrasing the set former defining the universal relation in different ways.†

The above example can be generalized by saying that the current value of the universal relation is to be expressed as

$$\{\,a_1\cdots a_n\mid P_1(X_1)\wedge\cdots\wedge P_k(X_k)\,\}\tag{9.1}$$

The P_i's are predicates about sets of attributes X_i; the X_i's are what we called *objects* above. Really, P_i will be written in terms of the a_j's that correspond to the positions of the attributes in set X_i, rather than the attributes themselves, but it is useful to identify the domain variable for an attribute with the attribute itself. For example, in the $CTHRSG$ universal relation definition above, X_1 would be CT, and P_1 is "teaches." X_2 is CHR, and P_2 is "meets in $\cdots$ at." Finally, X_3 is CSG, and P_3 is "getting $\cdots$ in."

In general, we must assume that no predicate can be broken into the conjunction of two predicates; that is, we cannot write $P_i(X_i)=Q(Y)\wedge R(Z)$, where Y and Z are both proper subsets of X. We shall also assume, for reasons

---

† In fact, it is interesting to consider whether the "real world" description by objects and functional dependencies within those objects might be a viable alternative to description by entity sets and relationships.

that will become clear when we talk about interpreting queries, that each object is a subset of a relation scheme, possibly a proper subset, and possibly not.

Example 9.2: Let us give a plausible interpretation to the HVFC database seen as a universal relation. For reasons that we are not yet ready to discuss, we shall assume that addresses of members are different from addresses of suppliers. Note how this contrasts with our assumption made in Section 7.5 about the library database, where we assumed that borrowers' and publishers' addresses were the same. The consequences of these two approaches are quite significant where a universal relation definition is concerned, as we shall see in Section 9.3.

The attributes of the HVFC database are M (member), B (balance), A (member's address), O (order number), I (item), Q (quantity), S (supplier), and D (supplier address). What are the appropriate objects? There is no way of deducing the answer, although in this case, a few observations will suffice. There is a clear relationship, in fact a functional dependency, between members and balances, and a tuple of the universal relation would make no sense if it had, say, $M=$"Robin" and a B-value that was not Robin's balance. Thus one predicate is "is the balance of" on object MB. Similarly, members and addresses are fundamentally related, so another object is MA.

In contrast, there is no obvious relationship between members and suppliers. We might suppose that members and suppliers were related by a predicate like "supplies some item ordered by," but this predicate can be expressed in terms of more fundamental relationships "places order" on object MO, "orders item" on object OI, and "supplies $\cdots$ at price" on object SIP.

Note that the SIP object cannot be broken down further, since suppliers sell different items at different prices. The other objects that we shall assume are OQ, relating orders to the quantity ordered, and SD, relating suppliers and their addresses.

The structure we assume for the HVFC database is shown in Fig. 9.1. There we use some conventions that we follow throughout the chapter. Objects of two attributes are represented by edges, with an arrow indicating the direction of a functional dependency, if any. Objects of more than two attributes are represented by circles enclosing the attributes. We thus have a hypergraph defining the database structure, where the nodes are attributes and the edges are the objects.

We should observe that each of the objects in Fig. 9.1 is a subset of one of the relation schemes MBA, $OMQI$, and $SDIP$ that we have assumed for the database. Even if the $SDIP$ relation were decomposed into Boyce-Codd normal form, so it became SD and SIP, the objects would still be subsets of the relation schemes. However, the objects are not identical to even the normalized relation schemes. For example, MB and MA are proper subsets of

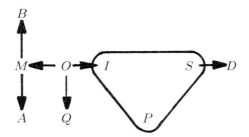

Fig. 9.1. Object structure of the HVFC database.

the MBA relation scheme.† ☐

Join Dependency Characterization of Universal Relations

There is a straightforward and important relationship between join dependencies and database structures defined by objects. To begin, observe that a relation r over the universal set of attributes is a possible value for the universal relation defined by Equation (9.1) if and only if there are relations r_i over set of attributes X_i, such that r_i is exactly the set of tuples that satisfy P_i, for $1 \le i \le k$, and $r = r_1 \bowtie \cdots \bowtie r_k$. In proof, suppose r satisfies the join dependency on the objects, that is, $\bowtie (X_1, \ldots, X_k)$. Let us define $r_i = \pi_{X_i}(r)$. If P_i is chosen to be true for exactly the tuples in r_i, then the relation defined by (9.1) is really $s = r_1 \bowtie \cdots \bowtie r_k$. We may use the fact that r satisfies the join dependency and the fact that $r_i = \pi_{X_i}(r)$ to conclude that $r = s$. That is, r is constructed from certain values of the predicates in the manner of (9.1).

Conversely, suppose r is constructed by (9.1) from some predicates

$$P_1(X_1), \ldots, P_k(X_k)$$

Then $r_i = \pi_{X_i}(r)$ must be a subset of those tuples over set of attributes X_i for which P_i is true. It follows that $r_1 \bowtie \cdots \bowtie r_k$ is a subset of r. But it cannot be a proper subset, by Lemma 7.5(a). Thus r satisfies the join dependency $\bowtie (X_1, \ldots, X_k)$. We have now proved the following result.

Theorem 9.1: A relation is constructable by Equation (9.1) from some values of the P_i's if and only if it satisfies the join dependency on the objects, that is, $\bowtie (X_1, \ldots, X_k)$. ☐

   Starting only with the assumption that the universal relation could be

---

† It appears that the most common situation in which objects are proper subsets of relation schemes is when we have a key that functionally determines several attributes. The key and any one of the attributes it determines would logically form an object, yet the key and all the functionally determined attributes together form a relation in Boyce-Codd normal form. For example, we would likely group the attribute M together with the two attributes A and B that it functionally determines, and make one Boyce-Codd normal form relation.

defined by predicates about the various attributes, we have proven, in Theorem 9.1, a surprising condition that appears to place a lot of structure on the universal relation. Of course, in the worst case, there could be but a single predicate over all the attributes, in which case Theorem 9.1 says nothing. A key assumption, which is generally true in practice, is that real-world databases do not have a trivial structure. Rather, there are many small objects, so Theorem 9.1 does in practice place significant structure on typical databases.

One significance of Theorem 9.1 is that it enables us to deduce many multivalued dependencies that hold in the universal relation. These are multivalued dependencies that follow logically from the join dependency on the objects. In fact, it appears that almost every full multivalued dependency that holds in reality either follows from this join dependency or follows from a given functional dependency trivially by axiom A7 (of Section 7.5).

As discussed in Example 9.2, we can represent the objects by a hypergraph, in which the nodes are attributes and the edges are the objects. By Theorem 9.1, we can similarly represent the join dependency on the objects by the same hypergraph. The next theorem shows how to deduce multivalued dependencies from a join dependency by inspecting its hypergraph.

Theorem 9.2: Let $X_1, \ldots, X_k$ be a set of objects, and Y any subset of

$$X_1 \cup \cdots \cup X_k$$

Then $Y \twoheadrightarrow Z$ follows logically from $j = \bowtie (X_1, \ldots, X_k)$, where Z is disjoint from Y, if and only if Z is the union of one or more of the connected components of the hypergraph of j when the nodes in Y are deleted.

Proof: We shall use the chase process of Section 7.6 to verify that the multivalued dependency $Y \twoheadrightarrow Z$ follows from j. In the chase test, we must begin with rows

Y	Z	$U - YZ$
$a_1 \cdots a_m$	$a_{m+1} \cdots a_p$	$b_{p+1} \cdots b_n$
$a_1 \cdots a_m$	$b_{m+1} \cdots b_p$	$a_{p+1} \cdots a_n$

where U is the complete set of attributes, and we must try to deduce $a_1 \cdots a_n$.

Recall that j can be represented as a generalized dependency in which there is one hypothesis row for each X_i, and we may suppose that row has distinguished symbol a_ℓ in the ℓth column if the ℓth attribute is in X_i, and a symbol appearing nowhere else otherwise. The conclusion row is $a_1 \cdots a_n$. We use this generalized dependency to produce the desired row from the hypothesis rows for $Y \twoheadrightarrow Z$ above in one step. To do so, we use the symbol mapping that is the identity on the a_i's and maps symbols appearing only once as needed. We can thus map the row for any X_i that is a subset of YZ to the first hypothesis row. If X_i is not a subset of YZ, then since Z is a connected component when Y is removed, it must be that X_i is disjoint from Z, and we can therefore map its row to the second of the hypothesis rows for $Y \twoheadrightarrow Z$.

We have thus proved that all the multivalued dependencies in which the left side is Y and the right side is the union of some of the connected components of the hypergraph of j with Y removed follow logically from j. The converse portion of Theorem 9.2, that no multivalued dependency follows logically from j unless it is one of these, or it follows logically from one of these, is true, but we leave it as an exercise for the reader. $\square$

Example 9.3: In Fig. 9.1 we saw the hypergraph for the join dependency $\bowtie (MB, MA, MO, OQ, OI, SIP, SD)$. If we delete O, the hypergraph splits into three pieces, MBA, Q, and $SIPD$. Thus multivalued dependencies like $O \twoheadrightarrow MBA$, $O \twoheadrightarrow Q$, $O \twoheadrightarrow SIPD$, and $O \twoheadrightarrow MBAQ$ hold. It happens that because of the functional dependencies indicated in Fig. 9.1, we also have $O \twoheadrightarrow M$ from $O \rightarrow M$, and we have $O \twoheadrightarrow B$ from $O \rightarrow M \rightarrow B$. Similarly, we have $O \twoheadrightarrow A$ and $O \twoheadrightarrow I$. By the decomposition rule, with $O \twoheadrightarrow I$ and $O \twoheadrightarrow SIPD$, we have $O \twoheadrightarrow SPD$. Thus, the dependency basis for O is

$$O \twoheadrightarrow M \mid B \mid A \mid Q \mid I \mid SPD$$

All but the last turn out to follow from the functional dependencies. The last, $O \twoheadrightarrow SPD$ reflects the fact that associated with any order will be a set of supplier-price-address triples that represent a supplier, its address, and the price at which the ordered item is offered.

As another example, if we let $Y = MI$, and delete both M and I from Fig. 9.1, we find that OQ becomes a connected component, so we assert the multivalued dependency $MI \twoheadrightarrow OQ$. Intuitively, this dependency says that associated with every member-item pair is a set of order-quantity pairs such that these are the orders and quantities placed by the member for the item. $\square$

Null Values and the Interpretation of Universal Relations

One important point concerning the meaning of universal relations has not yet been dealt with—the question of what happens when important information is contained in dangling tuples. It might appear that such information is lost in the universal relation. For example, in the $CTHRSG$ database, if we have not yet recorded a grade for a student, as might be the case before the end of the term, how do we keep any information about that student in the universal relation? The problem, of course, is that in the universal relation, every tuple must have a grade entry.

The solution is to allow the presence of *null values*, both in the universal relation (which, recall, is really a figment of our imagination) and in the actual relations of the database.† These null values are distinguishable from one another, and are usually written $\perp_i$ for some integer i that serves to identify

---

† Universal relation based systems are not unique in using null values, as most relational DBMS's provide them at least in certain contexts.

the null. When taking equijoins, $\perp_i$ is equal to $\perp_i$, but not to any $\perp_j$ for $j \neq i$. Also, when required to generate a null value, we never generate one that has been used before. However, two occurrences of null symbols will sometimes become identical because a functional dependency implies the equality of two nulls, or because of an explicit update.

Example 9.4: If we have not yet assigned teachers to courses or grades to students, a typical tuple in the $CTHRSG$ universal relation might look like

(CS101, $\perp_1$, M9, 222, Klunk,A., $\perp_2$)

As the universal relation doesn't really exist, what we really see is a tuple (CS101, $\perp_1$) in the CT relation, (CS101, M9, 222) in the CHR relation, and (CS101, Klunk,A., $\perp_2$) in the CSG relation. That is, the imaginary tuple in the universal relation is represented by its projections onto the database relations.

The above example is relatively simple to follow. However, a subtlety comes up if there is a null in a component of a tuple in the universal relation that appears in more than one of the database relations. For example, if we had not decided on the name of CS101, we might use $\perp_3$ for it in both the universal relation and in the CT, CHR, and CSG relations. In this case, the common null value would "glue together" the projections in the three database relations. $\square$

In order for null values to make sense, we must replace them by real values whenever we can deduce a value for a null. This replacement occurs conceptually in the universal relation, but in practice occurs in the database relations themselves. The deductions of values for nulls come from functional dependencies. For example, if we start with the tuple with two nulls mentioned in Example 9.4, and we update the database with the fact that Deadwood is assigned to teach CS101, we can see this new fact as the insertion of tuple

(CS101, Deadwood, $\perp_4$, $\perp_5$, $\perp_6$, $\perp_7$)

into the universal relation. We can then use the assumed functional dependency $C{\to}T$ to deduce that $\perp_1 =$"Deadwood".

What actually happens is that the projection of the new tuple onto CT, that is, (CS101, Deadwood), interacts with the tuple (CS101, $\perp_1$) already in CT, and we deduce $\perp_1 =$"Deadwood", whereupon the two tuples become the same and one is deleted.

This update to the universal relation can be implemented correctly because the functional dependency applied in the universal relation is also a projected dependency.† It is a difficult question to determine exactly what updates to a universal relation can be reflected correctly by an update to the actual database,

---

† Interestingly, the decomposition (CT, CHR, CSG) is not dependency preserving; e.g., $SH{\to}R$ is not implied by the projected dependencies. However, the relevant dependency, $C{\to}T$, is preserved in the projection.

and what that update should be. The algorithm we have tacitly used above, which is to insert the tuple into the universal relation by projecting it onto the actual relations, inserting it there (but only if at least one of the projected components is nonnull), and applying any functional dependencies that hold in the relation, is a reasonable alternative in many cases.

Deletions present an even more difficult problem. A possible strategy is to project the tuple to be deleted onto the database relations and delete the projection only if it has no null components. The bibliographic notes contain references to various works that have dealt with the proper formulation of updates to universal relations.

Perhaps the most sensible strategy is that adopted by "q," a universal relation system developed at Bell Laboratories. There, only the query language assumes a universal relation. Updates are done by separate commands and apply to the relations of the database themselves. The consequence of this decision is that while "naive" users can query the database, no assistance to this class of users is offered when they attempt to update the data. That is probably not too bad an approach, since we might expect that data modification should be restricted to those users that are capable of understanding the structure of the database.

9.2 A SIMPLE QUERY INTERPRETATION ALGORITHM

We shall now give a simple heuristic for interpreting queries over a universal relation. In the next section, we shall see some of the situations where this heuristic apparently goes astray, and Section 9.4 will discuss the System/U query interpretation algorithm, which fixes some of these problems.

Our query interpretation strategy is based on the assumption that a query must be answered in a relation constructed from the actual relations in the database by a lossless join. The motivation for this assumption, as discussed at the beginning of Section 7.3, is that if we view relations in the database, say AB and BC, as representing an ABC relation, but the join of AB and BC is not lossless, then some relations r and s over AB and BC, respectively, will be the projection of two or more different relations over ABC. In that case, it is not clear that our database represents a specific relation over ABC at all, so trying to answer queries about an ABC relation may lead to ambiguities that cannot be resolved.

Fortunately, we always know one way to get a lossless join that involves any set of attributes; take the join of all the objects. That join must be lossless by Theorem 9.1. However, that join often is not the simplest or most efficient lossless join to take. Thus, we shall use the weak equivalence test developed in Section 8.6 to find a minimal weakly equivalent join. We are justified in using $\equiv_w$ rather than $\equiv_s$ in minimizing joins, because we assumed the query was about a universal relation, and weak equivalence is tailored to finding equivalent

M	B	A	O	Q	I	S	P	D
			o					
m	b							
m		a						
m			o					
			o	q				
			o		"Whey"			
					"Whey"	s	p	
							p	d

Fig. 9.2. Tableau for query on HVFC universal relation.

expressions exactly under the condition that all relations are assumed to be the projection of a universal relation.

The typical effect of this minimization is that objects not required to connect the atributes involved in the query are eliminated from the join, and those found along paths in the hypergraph of the objects are retained. Because the relations of the actual database may contain dangling tuples, this minimization under weak equivalence may change the value computed, which seems to say that we should not use $\equiv_w$. However, as we argued in Section 8.6, we tend to feel this change in value is for the better, because we do not eliminate tuples from the answer if the reason they are dangling has nothing to do with the objects along those paths in the hypergraph that connect attributes in the query.†

Example 9.5: Suppose we ask of the HVFC database the query

     retrieve (O)
         where $I=$"Whey"

That is, print the numbers of all the orders for whey. Using the above approach, we interpret this as a request to take the join of the seven objects in Fig. 9.1, select for $I=$"Whey", and project onto the O attribute. This query has the tableau of Fig. 9.2.

Let us minimize this tableau. To do so, we must find a symbol mapping that sends all the rows into as few rows as possible. As discussed in Section 7.6, we can think of symbol mappings as if they were mappings on rows, subject

† The reader should observe that our decision to optimize under weak equivalence is one point that distinguishes a universal relation system from an ordinary relational database system in which we simply define a view that is the join of all the objects. In the latter arrangement, since ordinary relational database systems must optimize using strong equivalence, the terms of the join that represented objects not on paths between the attributes of the query could not be eliminated for fear of a dangling tuple changing the value of the computed expression. Thus answering queries about this universal view would often be too time consuming to be feasible.

to the constraint that no symbol is mapped into two differnet symbols, and the distinguished symbols map to themselves. In Fig. 9.2, the first four rows can be mapped to the fifth row if we use a symbol mapping that sends o to itself, and m, b, a, and q to the nondistinguished symbols represented by the blanks in columns M, B, A, and Q of row five, respectively. Of course, the blanks in rows 1–4 represent symbols that appear only once, and these are mapped to the symbols in the corresponding columns of the fifth row. Similarly, the sixth and seventh rows can be mapped to row five. This mapping of rows does not map any one symbol into two, and it preserves the distinguished symbol o, so it is a legal symbol mapping. Thus, we are left with the one-row tableau

M	B	A	O	Q	I	S	P	D
			o					
			o		"Whey"			

The row of this tableau can only be viewed as the result of taking the relation $OMQI$, and selecting for $I=$"Whey". Then, since only the atttribute O has a distinguished symbol, we must project onto O. That is, the query represented by the above tableau is

$$\pi_O(\sigma_{I=\text{"Whey"}}(OMQI))$$

This query has an obvious optimal way of obtaining the answer, which we could deduce by either Algorithm 8.2 or 8.3; it is to select on $OMQI$ for $I=$"Whey", and print the O component of the selected tuples. $\square$

Example 9.6: Let us take another example, one where there is more than one tuple variable. Consider the database consisting of ES and EM objects, where the attributes E, S, and M stand for employee, manager, and salary, respectively. A traditional query is to ask for the employees that make more than their managers, which can be expressed in the System/U query language as

retrieve(E)
    where $M = t.E$ and $S > t.S$

That is, the blank tuple variable stands for the employee, and the tuple variable t for the manager. The condition $S > t.S$ says that the salary in the tuple for the employee is larger than the salary in the tuple for the manager, and the condition $M = t.E$ says that the employee represented by t really is the manager of the employee represented by the blank tuple variable.

If we remember the discussion of the QUEL optimization algorithm from Section 8.4, we recall that optimization begins by expressing the query as a selection and projection on the Cartesian product of the relations represented by each of the tuple variables. In our case, we must begin by taking the Cartesian product of two copies of the universal relation, one corresponding to the blank, and the other to t. We shall distinguish the two copies by using subscript 1 for

E_1	S_1	M_1	E_2	S_2	M_2
e_1					
e_1	s_1				
e_1		m_1			
			e_2	s_2	
			e_2		m_2

$$m_1 = e_2, \; s_1 > s_2$$

Fig. 9.3. Find the employees that earn more than their managers.

the first and subscript 2 for the second. The reader should understand that the symbols E_1 and E_2 stand for the same attribute, E; the subscript serves only to distinguish different components of relations when both components have claim to the name E.

We obtain the first copy of the universal relation, which we denote $E_1 S_1 M_1$, by joining the two objects, which we also distinguish by subscript 1. We obtain the second copy similarly. Thus, the selection and projection of the query will be applied to the expression

$$(E_1 S_1 \bowtie E_1 M_1) \times (E_2 S_2 \bowtie E_2 M_2)$$

The first selection condition, $M = t.E$, can be performed on the above expression if we remember that an M standing alone, without a tuple variable, is associated with the blank tuple variable, i.e., subscript 1 above, and $t.E$ is associated with subscript 2. Thus the condition $M = t.E$ is expressed $M_1 = E_2$. Similarly, the second condition, $S > t.S$, is expressed $S_1 > S_2$. The projection onto E is really onto E_1, so we may write the expression for the complete query as

$$\pi_{E_1}(\sigma_{M_1=E_2 \wedge S_1 > S_2}((E_1 S_1 \bowtie E_1 M_1) \times (E_2 S_2 \bowtie E_2 M_2)))$$

The tableau for this query is shown in Fig. 9.3.

Not much can be done to reduce Fig. 9.3. We can map the last row into the third row by using a symbol mapping that sends e_2 to itself, and every other symbol in row four to the corresponding symbol in row three. Since no symbol but e_2 in row four appears anywhere else, this symbol mapping is legal.

However, we cannot map row one anywhere, because that would involve mapping s_1 to one of the symbols represented by blanks in column S_1, and since none of these symbols is involved in any inequalities, we would never be able to deduce $h(s_1) > h(s_2)$, if h were the symbol mapping. Similarly, we could not map the second row anywhere, since we could not deduce $h(m_1) = h(e_2)$. Likewise, the third row cannot map to another and still let us have $h(s_1) > h(s_2)$, since $h(s_2)$ would have to be a blank.

Thus, the minimum tableau weakly equivalent to Fig. 9.3 consists of the first three rows. These rows evidently come from objects ES, EM, and ES, respectively. On the assumption that the objects are the relations, the optimized expression can be written as

$$\pi_1(\sigma_{1=3 \wedge 4=5 \wedge 2>6}(ES \times EM \times ES))$$

The condition 1=3 enforces the fact that the two occurrences of e_1 in Fig. 9.3 represent the same individual. Condition 4=5 comes from $m_1 = e_2$, and 2>6 comes from $s_1 > s_2$. There is not much that can be done to optimize this query further, either using Algorithm 8.3 or any other approach. Probably the best way is to dissect the EM relation, thereby checking an employee and corresponding manager with each tuple of the EM relation we examine. These two individuals can have their salaries looked up in the ES relation and compared. $\square$

The Query Interpretation Algorithm

The two examples above embody most of the ideas of the general case. One detail that has not come up concerns the relationship between rows of the optimized tableau and relations. Call a symbol *essential* if it is either distinguished, appears in a constraint associated with the tableau, or appears more than once in the rows of the tableau. For example, in Fig. 9.3, all the symbols given explicit names, except for m_2, are essential, and none of the symbols represented by blanks are essential, of course.

When we must select a relation to correspond to a given row of the tableau, which, we should remember, was produced not from an expression about relations, but an expression about objects, we shall select the union of all the relations whose schemes include all the columns with essential symbols in that row. There must always be at least one such relation, because we made the assumption that each object was a subset of some relation. However, there could be more than one relation covering a given row. For instance, if in the database of Example 9.6, we simply asked to retrieve the employees, we would get the tableau

E	S	M
e		
e		

Both relations ES and EM cover the row e, so we take the union of the projections of these relations onto E. That is, we interpret the query as asking for all entries in the employee columns of the relations that have employee as an attribute. If there were no dangling tuples permitted, then either relation would do, but to play safe, we shall retrieve all employees for which either a salary or manager, or both, is listed.

We are now ready to describe our first formal approach to query interpretation in a universal relation system.

Algorithm 9.1: Simple Interpretation for Queries over a Universal Relation.

Input: A query in the System/U query language, along with the relation schemes and objects of the database.

Output: An algebraic expression that represents our interpretation of the query and is suitable for implementation using an algorithm like Algorithm 8.3.†

Method:

1. Let the tuple variables mentioned in the query be $t_1, \ldots, t_k$, the blank included among them. By convention, we always take t_1 to be the blank tuple variable. Identify the subscript i with tuple variable t_i. Begin by writing the expression $U_1 \times \cdots \times U_k$, where U_i is the copy of the universal relation associated with tuple variable i.

2. Replace each U_i in the above expression by the natural join of all the objects. We distinguish the attributes in the join for U_i by subscripting each attribute with i.

3. In the query, replace each occurrence of attribute A by A_1 (recall that t_1 is taken to be the blank tuple variable, and A_1 stands for the attribute called A in the copy of the universal relation associated with t_1). Replace each occurrence of $t_i.A$ by A_i. Complete the algebraic expression for the query by applying, to the result of (2), selection by the formula in the where-clause of the query (which is modified as above), and then projecting onto the list of attributes found in the retrieve-clause.

4. Construct the tableau for the expression from (3). Optimize it under the weak equivalence criterion.

5. Build an algebraic expression for the result of (4) by taking the product $T_1 \times \cdots \times T_m$, where each T_i is the union of the relations whose schemes include all the columns with essential symbols in the ith row, projected onto those columns. In this way, each component in the product is associated with a particular component of a particular row of the tableau, and this row is sure to hold an essential symbol. Then apply the selections needed to enforce the equality of components in the product that correspond to identical symbols in the tableau. Also apply selections to reflect the constraints associated with the tableau, again using the obvious correspondence from the essential symbols of the tableau to components in the product.

6. Apply a standard optimization algorithm that follows the $\equiv_s$ notion of equivalence, such as Algorithm 8.3, to improve the efficiency with which the expression from (5) is evaluated. $\square$

Examples 9.5 and 9.6 serve to illustrate the process described above.

---

† Note that while the algorithm involves optimization under $\equiv_w$ as part of the query interpretation process, it is not yet optimized in the broadest sense; we have merely minimized the number of joins. Algorithms like 8.3 consider issues that tableau optimization does not touch, such as order of joins and performing selections as quickly as possible.

9.3 CYCLIC AND ACYCLIC DATABASE STRUCTURES

The algorithm for interpreting queries does a reasonably good job of guessing what the user intends. For example, any query about attributes in a single object will be answered by obtaining that object from the relation or relations whose schemes contain the object. Since objects by definition embody fundamental relationships of the database, there is a high probability that a query about the attributes of an object really is asking for the relationship represented by that object.

However, Algorithm 9.1 does more than interpret queries about single objects. When confronted with a tree of objects, like Fig. 9.1, it will find the smallest subtree of objects that serves to connect all the attributes in the query, and it answers the query as if it referred to this minimal connection. The reasons this response is appropriate are that

1. Simple, short connections are asked for much more frequently than long, circuitous connections.
2. As long as the set of all objects forms a tree, adding additional objects to the join of the objects in a subtree would not make any new connections among the attributes of the query; it would only remove from the answer certain tuples that were dangling. We have argued in Section 8.6 why elimination of such dangling tuples does not appear to be the normally desired action.

However, there are databases whose object structure is not a simple tree like Fig. 9.1. For example, Fig. 9.4 shows the library database's object structure. This database, introduced in Section 8.2, has attributes T (title), Au (author), P (publisher), L (library of Congress number), Ad (address), Ci (city), B (borrower), Cn (card number), and D (date). Recall how in Section 8.5 we agreed that we would identify the attributes representing cities and addresses for publishers and for borrowers. This decision is opposite that made about addresses for members and suppliers in Section 9.1 for the HVFC database. Either decision is reasonable, but often the result of identifying attributes is that the object structure is made to have cycles, as is the case in Fig. 9.4.

Cyclic structures such as Fig. 9.4 make the connection between attributes ambiguous. For example, does the query

> retrieve P
> where $Cn=$"123"

ask for

1. the publishers of titles checked out on library card 123 (i.e., the path through objects $CnDL$, LT, and TP), or
2. the publishers with the same address as the borrower with card number 123 (i.e., the path through objects CnB, BAd, and AdP), or
3. the publishers in the same city as the borrower with card 123 (i.e., the path

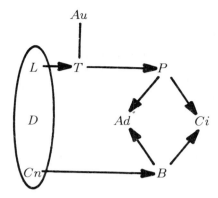

Fig. 9.4. Object structure of library database.

T	Au	P	L	Ad	Ci	B	Cn	D
		p						
t	a_u							
t		p						
t			ℓ					
		p		a_d				
		p			c_i			
				a_d		b		
					c_i	b		
						b	"123"	
			ℓ				"123"	d

Fig. 9.5. Tableau for query about library database.

through objects CnB, BCi, and CiP), or

4. something else.

We might wonder what Algorithm 9.1 will do in response to this query. The tableau for the query is shown in Fig. 9.5. Only the first row, corresponding to the object TAu can be eliminated. We claim that all the other rows are present in the minimal tableau equivalent to Fig. 9.5. For example, suppose we tried to map the last row into row 8. Then ℓ gets mapped to the symbol represented by the blank in the L column of row 8. Then, since a symbol mapping can send ℓ to only one symbol, it follows that row 3 must also map to row 8. Similarly, arguing about the variable t we may conclude that row 2 is also mapped to row 8. Then p gets mapped to the blank in the P column of row 8. But this mapping is not legal, because the summary of Fig. 9.5 would then not map to the summary of the reduced tableau.

What has happened, as always happens when we minimize tableaux under

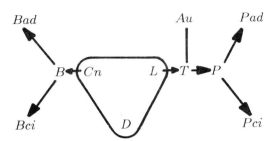

Fig. 9.6. Tree-like presentation of library database.

$\equiv_w$, is that all and only the objects that are found along one or more minimal paths (paths from which we cannot eliminate an edge and still be connected) are retained, and the other objects are eliminated. The query framed by Algorithm 9.1 will begin by taking the join of all the objects except TAu, and the effect will be that a tuple of the answer will have Cn component "123" and some publisher p only if all three conditions 1–3 above hold. That is, p must not only publish a book borrowed on card 123, but p must also have the same street address and city as the borrower with that card number, a very unlikely occurrence.

We must thus confront the fact that while Algorithm 9.1 gives intuitively plausible answers to queries involving object structures that look like trees, it doesn't seem to respond in a meaningful way to queries that involve going around cycles. There are two responses to this problem that we shall consider.

1. Duplicate attributes until all cycles are broken.
2. Restrict the range of tuple variables to certain subsets of the objects, to avoid ambiguities about which way to travel around cycles.

Attribute Duplication

We shall cover approach (2) in the next section. The first approach is quite simple in principle. For example, we might split the attributes Ad and Ci of Fig. 9.4 into two pairs of attributes, Bad and Bci for borrowers' address and city, and Pad and Pci for the publishers' address and city. We then get the tree-like hypergraph shown in Fig. 9.6.

This attribute splitting solves many of our problems. In particular, there is now a unique shortest connection among any set of attributes, and this connection will be found by Algorithm 9.1. On the negative side, the connection between a pair of attributes like Cn and P has been chosen arbitrarily; it reflects the condition that the publisher publishes a book checked out on this library card. Thus, the user must know about the particular objects assumed by the database system, which is analogous to knowing about the relations in an ordinary relational database system. In addition, the user must now remember that publishers and borrowers use different terms for their cities and street addresses, which is analogous to knowing about the attributes of the relations BORROWERS and PUBLISHERS in ordinary systems, and is another inconvenience universal relation systems were intended to avoid.

Another problem with duplication of attributes that occasionally surfaces is that while we can always remove cycles in principle, the number of new attributes we introduce can be great. Consider, for example, what happens if our objects are all pairs chosen from the set of attributes $\{A_1, \ldots, A_n\}$. We shall thus consider an alternative way to eliminate the ambiguities implied by cycles in the next section. Here we first study more formally the matter of what an acyclic hypergraph really is.

Acyclic Hypergraphs

There are many equivalent definitions of "acyclic hypergraph" in the sense used in database theory; unfortunately, the notion, while intuitively appealing, differs from that used by graph theorists. The definition of "acyclic" we shall use requires the notion of "Graham reduction," a process similar to the removal of leaves from trees until nothing is left.

Let O_1 and O_2 be two objects, i.e., sets of attributes, and let each attribute in $O_1 - O_2$ appear in no object besides O_1. Then we term O_1 an *ear*, and we term the deletion of O_1 from the hypergraph of the objects *ear removal*. As a special case, if there is only one object O_1, we may remove it by "ear removal."

The *Graham reduction*† of a hypergraph is obtained by applying ear removal until no more removals are possible. It may not be obvious that different sequences of ear removals lead to the same hypergraph. To see why, note that a potential removal will still be possible if another removal is chosen. For example, if O_1 could be removed because of O_2, but instead, we remove O_2 because of O_3, then $O_1 \cap O_2 \subseteq O_2 \cap O_3$, because any attribute in $O_2 - O_3$ cannot appear in any other object. It follows that O_1 can still be removed, now because of O_3. Thus, we are never faced with a true choice of ears to be removed; what can be removed eventually will be removed. We have thus indicated the essential idea behind an important fact.

Theorem 9.3: The Graham reduction of a hypergraph is unique, independent of the order of ear removals chosen. □

A hypergraph is *acyclic* if its Graham reduction is empty, i.e., the hypergraph with no edges. Otherwise, the hypergraph is *cyclic*.

Example 9.7: The hypergraph of Fig. 9.1 is acyclic. We might begin by removing the ear MB, in favor of the object MO, since the attribute B, which is $MB -$

---

† The term "Graham reduction" comes from Graham [1979], which is the first known work to study this process in the context of hypergraphs. However, independently and at about the same time, Yu and Oszyoglu [1979] studied the same process from a slightly different point of view, which we shall discuss in Section 12.2.

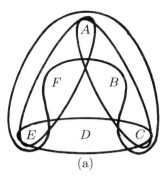
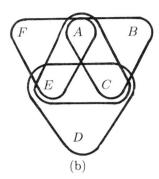

(a)   (b)

Fig. 9.7. An acyclic hypergraph.

MO, appears in no object but MB. Similarly, we can remove MA. Now we can remove MO from the remaining hypergraph, in favor of OI, say, because $MO - OI = O$, and O now appears in no object but MO. The reader can complete this example, eliminating the remaining objects in any of several orders, such as OQ, OI, SIP, SD, or SD, SIP, OI, OQ. Note that in each case, the last step is the elimination of a single object, and it does not matter which object is last; we can always remove it.

As another example, Fig. 9.4 is cyclic. While we can remove TAu in favor of TL, say, we can remove no more objects. For example, we cannot remove $LDCn$, because only D appears in no other object, and there is no object besides $LDCn$ that contains both L and Cn.

As a third example, the reader should check that Fig. 9.6 is acyclic.

A final example concerns the strange hypergraph in Fig. 9.7(a). This hypergraph appears to have a cycle, consisting of ABC, CDE, and EFA. In fact, if the hypergraph consisted of only these three edges, it would be cyclic, as the reader can easily check. However, with the edge ACE included, we find that ABC is an ear, because $ABC - ACE = B$, and B appears only in ABC. Similarly, CDE and EFA are ears, and their removal leaves only ACE, which can be removed as can any lone edge.

Fig. 9.7(b) helps explain the "paradox," since it redraws the same hypergraph in a more tree-like form, with ACE at the center. However, we should be aware of the subtlety brought out by this example; unlike ordinary graphs, it is possible for an acyclic hypergraph to have a subgraph that is cyclic. $\Box$

Connections in Acyclic Hypergraphs

With apparent anomalies like Fig. 9.7, one may wonder whether we have a useful, or even a correct definition of "acyclic," and we shall attempt to justify the definition now. Let us define the *connection* among a set of attributes S to be the set of objects that we get by the following process.

1. Construct the query that is the projection onto S of the natural join of all the objects.
2. Minimize this query under weak equivalence.
3. For each row r in the minimal tableau, find those objects that include all the attributes in whose columns r has an essential symbol. Place each such object in the connection.

Example 9.8: Suppose we want the connection for the set of attributes AC in the hypergraph of Fig. 9.7. The initial tableau

A	B	C	D	E	F
a		c			
a	b	c			
		c	d	e	
a				e	f
a		c		e	

is easily seen to reduce to either the first or last row, whereupon it becomes

A	B	C	D	E	F
a		c			
a		c			

It doesn't matter whether the row is the first, and the nondistinguished symbol b, appearing only once, was replaced by a blank, or the row is the fourth, and e was replaced by a blank. There are two objects, ABC and ACE, that contain the columns with essential symbols in the one remaining row. Thus, the connection for AC consists of these two objects.

There is good intuitive motivation for taking $\{ABC, ACE\}$ to be the connection between A and C. Essentially, we shall get the projection of both objects ABC and ACE onto AC, thereby getting whatever connection is implied by either or both of these objects. We do not get the "connection" between A and C that goes from A through EFA to E, then through CDE to C. That reflects a basic assumption: we want only the minimal connections; we never wish to take a join if we can avoid it. $\square$

The following theorem has a proof that is beyond the scope of this book. We shall state it, because it explains why we regard acyclic hypergraphs as those hypergraphs for which Algorithm 9.1 suffices to produce the appropriate connections among a set of attributes. Before proceeding, we should notice that any query that mentions only attributes in some set S, whether they are mentioned in the retrieve-clause or the where-clause, or both, will, after its tableau is optimized, only involve objects in the connection for S as defined above. Usually, exactly these objects will be involved. However, if the query is expressed in a redundant form, there may be reductions that can be done for this query but that could not be done when we compute the connection for S

In that case, only a subset of the connection will be used.

We regard the response of Algorithm 9.1 as inadequate if there are paths connecting attributes in S that go outside the connection for S, because these paths represent relationships among attributes in S that will not be taken into account when answering the query. The definition of "outside" requires a precise definition. An attribute A not in S that is found in a single edge of a path will not be regarded as part of the path, since it is not essential to the path. Only those attributes in the intersection of consecutive edges of the path are taken into account, because it is those attributes that provide the links between objects along the path. The next theorem relates acyclic hypergraphs to the ability of the connection, as we have defined it, to embody all the paths between attributes.

Theorem 9.4: Let H be an acyclic hypergraph, and S a set of nodes (attributes) of H. Let T be the set of nodes of H that are members of one or more edges (objects) in the connection for S. Let $E_1, \ldots, E_n$ be a path (sequence of edges such that $E_i \cap E_{i+1}$ is nonempty for all $1 \le i < n$) such that E_1 and E_n contain different members of S. Then every node appearing in $E_i \cap E_{i+1}$ for any i is also in T, the connection for S. Conversely, if H is cyclic, then there is always some set S and some path for which there is a node in some $E_i \cap E_{i+1}$ that is not in the connection for S. $\square$

Example 9.9: We established in Example 9.8 that the connection for AC in the hypergraph of Fig. 9.7 is $ABCE$. The path from A to C consisting of edges EFA and CDE has only E in the intersection of consecutive edges. Since E is in the connection, this path does not violate the condition of Theorem 9.4, and we may conclude that, at least as far as this evidence is concerned, Fig. 9.7 is acyclic.

However, if edge ACE were missing from Fig. 9.7, the connection between A and C would consist of only the edge ABC. Then the path EFA, CDE would demonstrate by Theorem 9.4 that the hypergraph is cyclic.

As another example, in Fig. 9.4, we see the cyclic hypergraph for the library database. The connection for BCi consists of only those two attributes, as must be the case whenever the attributes are contained in a single object. However, the path BAd, PAd, PCi contains the attributes Ad and P that are outside the connection, yet appear in the intersection of consecutive edges. $\square$

9.4 MAXIMAL OBJECTS AND QUERIES ABOUT CYCLIC DATA-BASES

We shall now consider an improved approach to interpreting queries about cyclic databases in the intuitively correct manner. What we do is back off a bit from our goal of letting the user mention any set of attributes in his query without restriction. We back off as little as possible, by allowing each tuple variable of a query, including the blank tuple variable, to range only over a set of objects that have some strong connection. There are several degrees of "strength" that we might try to enforce in these connections among sets of objects, but we shall consider only one here, the one used by System/U.

The sets of objects that are allowed as the range of tuple variables are called *maximal objects*. We build them, starting from single objects, in a way that enables us to prove at each step that we have a lossless join. Further, the losslessness of the join must follow from the given functional dependencies and the join dependency on the objects. This condition about losslessness of joins is the degree of "strength" we require to bind together sets of attributes that they may be the range of a tuple variable.

The motivation for requiring a lossless join has been discussed before; it is necessary for the objects of the database to represent a unique relation over the full set of attributes. Notice we require that not only will the set of objects in a maximal object have a lossless join, but that the subsets of objects from which the maximal object is built up will have a lossless join also. This condition is so that when we apply tableau optimization to a query about the join over a maximal object, the subset of objects that results will have a lossless join.

Algorithm 9.2: Construction of Maximal Objects.

Input: A collection of objects and functional dependencies on the attributes of those objects.

Output: The collection of maximal objects for the input structure.

Method: We begin by constructing for any object O the largest set of objects containing O such that we can adjoin each object in turn with a lossless join that follows either from

1. Theorem 7.5 and a functional dependency, or
2. Theorem 7.11 and a multivalued dependency. Further, this multivalued dependency, since none are given directly, must be one of those that follow from Theorem 9.2 and the given join dependency.

In what follows, we use $\text{ATTR}(\mathcal{M})$ to stand for the set of attributes that is the union of all the objects in $\mathcal{M}$. The following steps construct $\mathcal{M}$ from object O.

> $\mathcal{M} := \{ O \}$;
> **while** changes to $\mathcal{M}$ occur **do**
> > **for** each object P such that either $(P \cap \text{ATTR}(\mathcal{M})) \rightarrow P$
> > $(P \cap \text{ATTR}(\mathcal{M})) \rightarrow \text{ATTR}(\mathcal{M})$, or $P - \text{ATTR}(\mathcal{M})$ is disconnected
> > from $\text{ATTR}(\mathcal{M}) - P$ when $P \cap \text{ATTR}(\mathcal{M})$ is
> > deleted from the hypergraph **do**
> > > $\mathcal{M} := \mathcal{M} \cup \{ P \}$

Having constructed a set of objects by expanding each object, we may find that some sets of objects are subsets of others. Drop from consideration all that are proper subsets of others. The remaining sets of objects are the maximal objects. $\square$

Example 9.10: Let us construct the collection of maximal objects for the hypergraph of Fig. 9.4. Suppose we start with the object TP. We can add TAu because when we delete T, which is $TP \cap TAu$, Au is disconnected from P. That is, we are invoking the embedded multivalued dependency $T \twoheadrightarrow P \mid Au$ that follows from the given join dependency on the objects. We can also add TL because of the functional dependency $T \to L$, since $T = TL \cap TPAu$, and the attributes in the current set of objects is $TPAu$. Similarly, we can add PAd and PCi, but we can go no further. For example, we cannot add BAd because $BAd \cap TPLAuAdCi = Ad$, and Ad neither functionally determines B or $TPLAuCi$, nor does Ad disconnect B when deleted. Thus, starting with $\mathcal{M} = \{ TP \}$ yields $\{ TP, TL, TAu, PAd, PCi \}$, and this set turns out not to be a proper subset of what we get when we start from any object; it is therefore a maximal object.

If we start with BCn we can add BAd and BCi using functional dependencies, and $\{ BCn, BAd, BCi \}$ turns out to be another maximal object. Finally, LCD is a maximal object all by itself, so we find the maximal objects for Fig. 9.4 to be

$$\mathcal{M}_1 = \{ TP, TL, TAu, PAd, PCi \}$$
$$\mathcal{M}_2 = \{ BCn, BAd, BCi \}$$
$$\mathcal{M}_3 = \{ LCD \}$$

$\square$

An important fact about maximal objects is that they do not affect acyclic databases in any way, because there is only one maximal object, the complete set of objects. There is an easy proof by induction on the number of objects in the database. For the basis, if there is only one object, Algorithm 9.2 clearly produces only one maximal object.

Suppose the result is true for sets of up to $n - 1$ objects, and suppose we have an acyclic database with n objects. Let P be the first ear removed by the Graham reduction process. Then the inductive hypothesis applies to the remaining $n-1$ objects, and we know that starting with one of them produces a set $\mathcal{M}$ consisting of all $n-1$ objects. But since P is an ear, we know that removal of $P \cap \text{ATTR}(\mathcal{M})$ will disconnect $P - \text{ATTR}(\mathcal{M})$ from the rest of the hypergraph, since every attribute in $P - \text{ATTR}(\mathcal{M})$ appears in no other object. Thus we can adjoin P to $\mathcal{M}$ by Algorithm 9.2. We have thus proved the following theorem.

Theorem 9.5: Every acyclic hypergraph has only one maximal object. $\square$

Interpreting Queries in the Presence of Maximal Objects

Having constructed the maximal objects for a database, we shall use them to interpret queries in the following manner. Each tuple variable t in a query, including the blank, is assumed to refer to each of the maximal objects $\mathcal{M}$ that *covers* t, in the sense that every attribute A such that $t.A$ appears in the retrieve-clause or where-clause of the query is in $\text{ATTR}(\mathcal{M})$. We consider all connections among attributes that stay within one maximal object to be equally valid, so we allow t to assume as a value any tuple in the join of the objects in any of the maximal objects that covers t.

There follows an algorithm to interpret queries in this manner. It is essentially the strategy followed by System/U.

Algorithm 9.3: Interpretation of Queries Using Maximal Objects.

Input: A query in the System/U query language, along with the relation schemes, objects, and maximal objects of the database.

Output: An algebraic expression that represents our interpretation of the query. The expression is the union of terms, each of which is suitable for optimization using an algorithm such as 8.3.

Method:

1. As in Step (1) of Algorithm 9.1, let the tuple variables of the query be $t_1, \ldots, t_k$, with t_1 the blank tuple variable. Begin with the Cartesian product of k copies of the universal relation, the expression $U_1 \times \cdots \times U_k$, where subscript i is identified with tuple variable t_i, for $1 \leq i \leq k$.

2. For each i let S_i be the set of maximal objects that covers t_i. Replace each U_i by the union of the maximal objects in S_i. Then distribute the Cartesian product over the unions, so the expression becomes a union of products of maximal objects. For example, if $k = 2$, $S_1 = \{ \mathcal{M}_1, \mathcal{M}_2 \}$, and $S_2 = \{ \mathcal{M}_2, \mathcal{M}_3 \}$, then the expression $(\mathcal{M}_1 \cup \mathcal{M}_2) \times (\mathcal{M}_2 \cup \mathcal{M}_3)$ is converted to

$$(\mathcal{M}_1 \times \mathcal{M}_2) \cup (\mathcal{M}_1 \times \mathcal{M}_3) \cup (\mathcal{M}_2 \times \mathcal{M}_2) \cup (\mathcal{M}_2 \times \mathcal{M}_3)$$

3. Replace each maximal object in the expression from (2) with the natural join of all the objects in that maximal object. As in Algorithm 9.1, we shall subscript occurrences of an attribute A by the copy of the universal relation to which it corresponds. Note that each term of the union is the product of k maximal objects, with the ith maximal object corresponding to the ith copy of the universal relation.

4. As in Algorithm 9.1, rephrase the query by replacing each occurrence of $t_i.A$ by A_i, remembering that t_1 is the blank tuple variable. Apply to each term of the union from (3) the selection expressed in the where-clause and the projection onto the attributes of the retrieve-clause.

5. Construct the tableau for each term of the union from (4). Optimize it under the weak equivalence criterion.

6. Determine, using the test of Theorem 8.1, whether the mapping defined by one tableau in the list from (5) is a subset of the mapping defined by another. Eliminate any tableau that is a proper subset of another, and

eliminate all but one of a set of tableaux that are equivalent.

7. Build an expression from each of the tableaux that remain after (6), by the method of step (5) of Algorithm 9.1. The output is the union of these expressions.

□

Example 9.11: Recall from Example 9.10 that the library database has three maximal objects, $\mathcal{M}_1$, $\mathcal{M}_2$, and $\mathcal{M}_3$, where

$$\text{ATTR}(\mathcal{M}_1) = \{\, T, L, P, Au, Ad, Ci \,\}$$
$$\text{ATTR}(\mathcal{M}_2) = \{\, B, Cn, Ad, Ci \,\}$$
$$\text{ATTR}(\mathcal{M}_3) = \{\, L, C, D \,\}$$

In the query

> retrieve(P)
>   where $Cn = 123$

the blank tuple variable is the only one that appears; it is associated with the attributes P and Cn. Since no maximal object contains both these attributes, no maximal object covers the blank tuple variable, and the union of terms constructed by Algorithm 9.3 is empty. Therefore, the response to this query is the empty set. There is a good case that this response is adequate, since we never were able to assign a natural meaning to the query. Of course, the system should inform the user that the answer is empty for the reason that the query was considered by the the system to be meaningless.

As another example, the query

> retrieve(Ci)
>   where $Cn = 123$

has a blank tuple variable that is covered only by $\mathcal{M}_2$. Thus the response of Algorithm 9.3 is to replace the copy of the universal relation corresponding to the blank tuple variable by the join of the objects in $\mathcal{M}_2$, that is

$$BCn \bowtie BAd \bowtie BCi$$

After tableau-based optimization, we discover that the term BAd is not needed, so the expression we produce is a "union" of only one term

$$\pi_{Ci}(\sigma_{Cn=123}(BCn \bowtie BCi))$$

That is, we retrieve the city in which the borrower with library card number 123 lives, which seems a reasonable response. □

Example 9.12: Now let us consider an example where more than one tuple variable and more than one maximal object are involved. Figure 9.8 shows a hypothetical database of a bank, where customers are related to branches by being the owner of an account or the holder of a loan. Both accounts and loans can be shared by several customers, but each loan and each account is

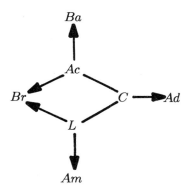

Fig. 9.8. The bank database.

at a single branch. The attributes are Br (branch), Ac (account number), Ba (balance of an account), L (loan number), Am (amount of a loan), C (customer), and Ad (customer's address).

The maximal objects are built from the CAc and CL objects. Starting from CAc, we can use the functional dependency rule to add $AcBa$, $BrAc$, and CAd. Similarly, starting from CL we can add LAm, LBr, and CAd. Starting with any other object gives us a subset of one of these. Thus, there are two maximal objects, M, with $\text{ATTR}(M) = \{ Br, Ac, Ba, C, Ad \}$, and N, with $\text{ATTR}(N) = \{ Br, L, Am, C, Ad \}$. These are shown dashed in Fig. 9.8.

The query we shall discuss is

> retrieve (C)
>   where $Br = t.Br$ and $t.C=$ "Jones"

That is, print all the customers who bank at a branch that Jones banks at.

As there are two tuple variables, blank and t, we create two copies of the universal relation, $U_1 \times U_2$. We then observe that the set of attributes associated with each tuple variable is $\{ Br, C \}$, and these attributes are members of both maximal objects. Thus, both maximal objects cover both tuple variables, and U_1 and U_2 are each to be replaced by the union of M and N. When we distribute the product over the unions, we get the expression

$$(M_1 \times M_2) \cup (M_1 \times N_2) \cup (N_1 \times M_2) \cup (N_1 \times N_2)$$

The subscripts 1 and 2 indicate the copy of the universal relation to which each of the maximal objects pertain. Now we must replace M_1 by

$$Br_1 Ac_1 \bowtie Ac_1 Ba_1 \bowtie C_1 Ac_1 \bowtie C_1 Ad_1$$

and M_2 by a similar join involving attributes subscripted with 2. Also, N_1 and N_2 are replaced by joins of the objects in the maximal object N, with all attributes subscripted 1 or 2 as appropriate.

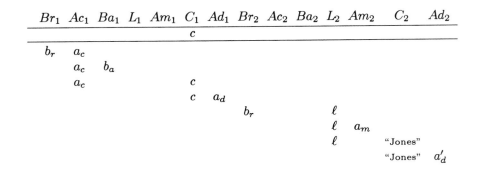

Fig. 9.9. Tableau for $\mathcal{M}_1 \times \mathcal{N}_2$.

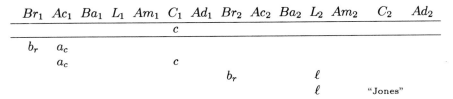

Fig. 9.10. Result of optimizing Fig. 9.9.

Now we are ready to form the tableaux for the terms. We show only one, that for $\mathcal{M}_1 \times \mathcal{N}_2$, in Fig. 9.9. Notice that we have used one symbol, b_r, for the branches of both Jones and the hypothetical customer c, rather than using different branch symbols and equating them by a constraint. Similarly, we use "Jones" in the tableau, rather than a symbol equated to "Jones" by a constraint.

It happens that there are no containment relationships among the four tableaux, so each is optimized by itself. The result of optimizing Fig. 9.9 is shown in Fig. 9.10. We can see that this expression gives us those customers c that have an account at a branch at which Jones has a loan. It is most efficiently implemented by finding the loans that Jones has, then the branches of those loans, the accounts at those branches, and the customers owning those accounts. □

The System/U Data Definition Language

In order that the system may make the response to queries indicated by Algorithm 9.3, it must be given a variety of kinds of information. Without going into notational details, let us simply list the kinds of information that the data definition language of System/U lets us provide.

1. The attributes and their data types.

2.   The relation schemes and the names of relations.

3.   The objects. Each object is defined to be a projection of one of the relations, and renaming of attributes is allowed. Thus, for example, we could have a relation PM, giving persons and their mothers. There could be an object PM, but also an object MG, or mother-grandmother, with attributes M and G of the object corresponding to P and M, respectively, in the relation. Thus, we could have a universal relation PMG supported by the single PM relation.

4.   Any functional dependencies that hold.

In addition, after calculating the maximal objects from the given functional dependencies and the objects, the maximal objects are printed and the database designer is asked if they are satisfactory. By an interactive process, the designer can delete any of the maximal objects or create new ones.

Example 9.13: In the bank database, we might suppose that the functional dependency $L \rightarrow Br$ did not hold; that is, groups of branches could get together to make one loan. If that is the case, then $\mathcal{N}$ is no longer a maximal object. It is replaced by $\mathcal{P}$ and $\mathcal{Q}$, with $\text{ATTR}(\mathcal{P}) = \{Br, L, Am\}$ and $\text{ATTR}(\mathcal{Q}) = \{L, Am, C, Ad\}$. This change has the effect that if we ask for the branches at which Jones does business, we get only those at which he has an account; there is no longer a connection between branches and customers through loans.

We might believe that there really is such a connection. If so, we are in effect saying that each person sharing loan 12345 is related to each branch making loan 12345, which is a reasonable way to view things. Formally, we are asserting the embedded multivalued dependency $L \rightarrow\!\!\!\rightarrow Br \mid C$.

We can simulate the effect of this embedded multivalued dependency by deleting the maximal objects $\mathcal{P}$ and $\mathcal{Q}$ and replacing them by the maximal object $\mathcal{N}$. Then the database will continue to respond as before, when we assumed the functional dependency $L \rightarrow Br$. $\square$

EXERCISES

9.1: Phrase the following queries in the System/U language; the queries refer to the HVFC database as in Fig. 9.1.

   a)   Print the members who ordered whey.

   b)   Print the names and addresses of all suppliers who supply an item that Robin ordered.

   c)   Print the suppliers and items such that there is another supplier supplying the same item at a lower price.

9.2: Compute the System/U response to each of the queries from Exercise 9.1.

9.3: What is the response of System/U to the following query about the library database of Fig. 9.4?

retrieve (Ci)
    where $Ad=$ "25 Maple St."

9.4: What are the objects for the beer drinker's database of Exercise 5.6? What are the maximal objects? Write the queries of Exercise 5.6(a, b) in the System/U language.

9.5: Suppose that the attributes A and D are merged in the HVFC database of Fig. 9.1; that is, the attribute A will stand for the addresses of both members and suppliers. Find the maximal objects of the resulting database, assuming the functional dependencies shown in Fig. 9.1, plus the dependency $SI \rightarrow P$.

9.6: Implement each of the queries of Exercise 9.1 on the database of Exercise 9.5.

9.7: Suppose we have a database with objects ABD, ACD, DEG, DFG, GHJ, and GIJ.
   a)   Is the hypergraph for this database cyclic or acyclic?
   b)   What is the connection for $\{ A, J \}$?

∗ 9.8: Prove the converse of Theorem 9.2, that no multivalued dependencies but those given by that theorem follow logically from the join dependency j.

∗∗ 9.9: We can modify the Graham reduction algorithm to allow a set of nodes to be *sacred*. We can only delete object O_1 in favor of O_2 if every node in O_1 is either in O_2 or is both (a) in no object but O_1 and (b) not sacred. Prove that the connection for a set of attributes X is exactly what you obtain if you perform Graham reduction with the nodes in X sacred.

∗ 9.10: Complete the proof of Theorem 9.3, that the result of Graham reduction is unique.

∗ 9.11: Express the airline database of Example 1.6 in terms of objects and functional dependencies.

BIBLIOGRAPHIC NOTES

Descriptions of the System/U query language and its interpretation appear in Korth and Ullman [1980] and Ullman [1982]. The object concept is from Sciore [1980], where is was viewed as an elementary unit for insertions and deletions. The related use of the notion made in this chapter is from Fagin, Mendelzon, and Ullman [1980]; Theorem 9.1 also appears there.

Maximal objects were first described in Maier and Ullman [1980]. An idea similar to maximal objects, but computed anew for each query and ignoring multivalued dependencies, is expressed by Sagiv [1981a, b]; this idea uses the extension joins of Honeyman [1980] to select the connections among attributes in a query over the universal relation. Maier and Warren [1981] present a more structured view of objects and maximal objects.

Historically, Carlson and Kaplan [1976] was an early study of ways to select connections among attributes automatically. The first notion of interpretation of queries over a universal relation was that of taking a lossless join that included the attributes of the query (Aho, Beeri, and Ullman [1977]). Schenk and Pinkert [1977] and Kambayashi [1978] suggested algorithms for finding minimal lossless joins. Chang [1980] and Osborn [1979] proposed taking the union of certain joins to answer queries involving attributes connected by more than one path. The latter proposed a selection criterion similar to extension joins.

Sciore [1980], Maier [1980a], Korth and Ullman [1980], and Keller [1981] deal with the problem of updates to the universal relation and some possible schemes for introducing and controlling null values.

Theorem 9.2 on computing the multivalued dependencies that follow from a join dependency is from Fagin, Mendelzon, and Ullman [1980]. A slightly weaker result was obtained previously by Lien [1982], and Maier, Sagiv, and Yannakakis [1981] earlier provided a general inference rule from which Theorem 9.2 follows easily. Sciore [1981] discusses the structure of multivalued dependencies in the "real world," indicating why we might expect them to be equivalent to a single join dependency. Theorem 9.4 is from Maier and Ullman [1982], as is Exercise 9.9.

The use of an acyclic hypergraph to describe the structure of a universal relation is from Fagin, Mendelzon, and Ullman [1980], although the same concept was studied in different contexts by Bernstein and Goodman [1981a] and Yu and Oszyoglu [1979]. Graham reduction was first introduced as a process by Graham [1979] and Yu and Oszyoglu [1979], independently. A number of useful properties of acyclic hypergraphs and equivalent definitions of the term are found in Beeri, Fagin, Maier, and Yannakakis [1981], Yannakakis [1981a], and Goodman and Shmueli [1980, 1981b].

Fagin [1981b] and Yannakakis [1981a] discuss a stronger form of acyclicity, called *acyclic Bachman diagrams*. The latter shows a theorem stronger than 9.4 about connections among attributes in this type of hypergraph. The acyclic Bachman diagram was first studied by Lein [1982].

Another approach to defining the meaning of queries over a universal relation concerns the construction of a *representative instance*, formed by taking the database relations, padding them with unique nulls in attributes not present in a particular relation scheme, taking the union of the padded relations, and applying the dependencies to the resulting universal relation. A query over set of attributes X is applied to those tuples in the representative instance that have no nulls in the X-components.

The idea originally came from Honeyman [1982], where it was used to define when a database as a whole satisfied a functional dependency. Mendelzon [1981] used the concept to define the information-carrying capacity of a database scheme, but Sagiv [1981a] and Yannakakis [1981a] were probably the first to see the representative instance as the universal relation to which queries should refer. The idea seems promising as a way of unifying different viewpoints regarding what the response of a universal relation system to queries should be, and already, Sagiv [1981b] and Yannakakis [1981a] have shown some results that relate the representative instance to unions of lossless joins in special cases.

There has been a substantial discussion in the literature about difficulties concerning the universal relation and its attendant concepts. For example, Honeyman, Ladner, and Yannakakis [1980] show it is $\mathcal{NP}$-complete to tell whether an update to a relation will cause the database to be the projection of a universal relation. We have only touched on a few of the issues here. The reader might consult such works as Kent [1979, 1981], Bernstein and Goodman [1980a], and Atenzi and Parker [1982] for a discussion of the problems, and Ullman [1982] for a rebuttal and further discussion of issues related to the feasibility of universal relation systems that we have not touched on here.

10

PROTECTING THE DATABASE
AGAINST MISUSE

In any complete DBMS we find facilities to prevent incorrect data from being stored in a database and to prevent the reading of data that should not be disclosed to the person reading. There are two sources of incorrect data: accidents, such as mistyping of input or programming errors, and malicious use of the database. We can divide the problem of protecting the database into two subproblems.

1. *Integrity preservation.* This aspect concerns nonmalicious errors and their prevention. For example, it is reasonable to expect a DBMS to provide facilities for declaring that the value of a field AGE should be less than 150. The DBMS can also help detect some programming bugs, such as a procedure that inserts a record with the same values in the key fields as a record that already exists in the database (assuming we tell the system we do not want such an insertion to be made). In this case, the program should be rewritten to check first whether a conflicting record is present.

2. *Security* (or *access control*). Here we are concerned primarily with restricting certain users so they are allowed to access and/or modify only a subset of the database. It might appear that any attempt on the part of a user to access a restricted portion of the database would be malicious, but in fact a programming error could as well cause the attempted access to restricted data.

Both integrity and security aspects of a DBMS will be considered in this chapter. We devote considerable attention to some of the subtle problems of security for *statistical databases,* such as census data, where the problem is not to restrict the user from accessing any part of the database in particular, but rather to prevent his deducing detailed data, such as the income of one particular individual, from statistical information such as the average salaries of several large classes of individuals.

10.1 INTEGRITY

There are two essentially different kinds of constraints we would like a DBMS to enforce. As discussed at the beginning of Chapter 7, one type is structural, concerning only equalities among values in the database. By far the most prevalent instances of such constraints are what we there called functional dependencies. Many, but not all, functional dependencies can be expressed if the DBMS allows the user to declare that a set of fields or attributes forms a key for a record type or relation. The need to express functional dependencies is not restricted to relational systems, nor do all relational systems have such a facility, explicitly. For example, the hierarchical system IMS allows the user to declare one field of a logical record type to be "unique," meaning that it serves as a key for that type. A unique field in the root record type serves as a key for database records, as well as for records of the root type. Also, the unique field for any record type, together with the unique fields for all its ancestor record types will serve as a key for that record type.

The second kind of integrity constraint concerns the actual values stored in the database. Typically these constraints restrict the value of a field to some range or express some arithmetic relationship among various fields. For example, a credit union might expect that the sum of the BALANCE field, taken over all members of the credit union, equals the net assets of the union. As another example, if the record for a course contained fields E%, H%, and L%, indicating the percentage of the grade devoted to exams, homework, and labs, we would expect that in each such record the sum of the values in these fields is 100.

Query Languages as Integrity Constraint Languages

A fundamental idea concerning integrity constraints is that the data manipulation language can serve as the language in which integrity constraints are expressed. The declaration of an integrity constraint has two parts. First, we must express the constraint itself; for this part the data manipulation language is generally quite suitable. That is, we express the constraint as an equality or containment relationship between the results of two queries.

Example 10.1: Referring to the HVFC database again, we could write as the containment of two queries the constraint that orders can only be entered if placed by people who are members, i.e., those listed in the MEMBERS relation. These queries can be expressed in any notation; we shall use relational algebra as an example, and write

$$\pi_{\text{NAME}}(\text{ORDERS}) \subseteq \pi_{\text{NAME}}(\text{MEMBERS}) \tag{10.1}$$

As another example, the constraint that no one be allowed to have a negative balance can be expressed by requiring that the set of names in the

MEMBERS relation be the same as the set of names after selection for a nonnegative balance, that is

$$\pi_{\text{NAME}}(\text{MEMBERS}) = \pi_{\text{NAME}}(\sigma_{\text{BALANCE} \geq 0}(\text{MEMBERS}))$$

☐

Some intelligence must be used when we plan how to check integrity constraints. For example, on inserting a new order, we should realize that only the newly inserted order could violate (10.1), so all we have to do is check its name component for membership in $\pi_{\text{NAME}}(\sigma_{\text{BALANCE} \geq 0}(\text{MEMBERS}))$.

The second part of an integrity check declaration is a description of when the constraint is to be checked. The general idea is that the integrity constraints are allowed to function as high-level "interrupts," like ON conditions in PL/I. For example, the DBTG proposal allows any number of ON clauses of the form

ON <command list> CALL <procedure>

in the declaration of DBTG sets and record types. For a DBTG set, the <command list> may include any of INSERT, REMOVE, and FIND. The <procedure> is an arbitrary routine written in the DBTG data manipulation language, which is an extension of COBOL, and thus has full computing capability as well as the ability to access any part of the database. For example, if we declare for DBTG set S:

ON INSERT CALL P1

the procedure P1 could check that certain fields of the current of run-unit, which is the member record being inserted, are not already present in the selected set occurrence, thus assuring that these fields, plus a key for the owner record type functionally determine the rest of the fields of the member type.

The <command list> for an ON clause in a record type declaration can include any of the above three commands and also the remaining four: STORE, DELETE, MODIFY, and GET. Such an ON clause is triggered whenever a command in the list is executed and the current of run-unit is of the relevant record type.

10.2 INTEGRITY CONSTRAINTS IN QUERY-BY-EXAMPLE

To demonstrate how the ideas of the previous section can be put into practice, we shall discuss integrity in the Query-by-Example system in depth. First, if we review Section 6.5, we note that when a relation is declared in QBE, we are allowed to specify whether each field is key or nonkey. The system then enforces the functional dependency of each nonkey field on the set of key fields taken together. This integrity check is triggered on each insertion or modification of a tuple in the relation, and operations that would cause a violation of the dependency are not done; a warning is printed. We shall discuss later how to set up functional dependency constraints that are not of the form key→nonkey.

The QBE system maintains a constraint table for each relation. To create a constraint on relation R, we call for a table skeleton for R. We enter one or more rows representing the constraints into the skeleton. Below the relation name we enter

I. CONSTR(<condition list>). I.

As always, the first I. refers to the entry itself and the second I. to the constraint in the portion of the row that follows. The <condition list> can consist of any or all of I.(insert), D.(delete), U.(update), and identifiers that represent user defined conditions, to be described subsequently. The terms in the <condition list> indicate when the integrity constraint is to be tested; for example, CONSTR(I.,U.). tells us to test the constraint whenever an insertion or modification occurs in the relevant relation. CONSTR. is short for CONSTR(I.,U.,D.).

What follows in the rows are entries for some or all of the attributes. An entry may be a constant, which says the tuple being inserted, deleted, or modified must have that constant value for that attribute. An entry can be of the form θc, where c is a constant and θ an arithmetic comparison, which says that the tuple must stand in relation θ to c in that attribute. It can be blank or have a variable name beginning with underscore, which means the tuple can be arbitrary in that attribute. Moreover, there can be additional rows entered in the skeleton for R or in another skeleton; these rows place additional constraints on the values that may appear in the tuple being inserted, deleted, or modified, according to the semantics of the QBE language.

Example 10.2: Let us once more consider the HVFC database of Fig. 3.2. To place the constraint on balances that no one owe more than 100 dollars, we could call for a MEMBERS skeleton and enter

MEMBERS	NAME	ADDRESS	BALANCE
I. CONSTR(I.,U.). I.			$>=-100$

To guarantee that no order be accepted for an item for which no supplier exists, we can call for ORDERS and SUPPLIERS skeletons and enter the information shown in Fig. 10.1. This constraint says that the inserted tuple, which defines a value for _ hotdog equal to the value of the ITEM attribute in the inserted tuple, must be such that some tuple in the SUPPLIERS relation has that value for its ITEM attribute. □

Defined Triggers for Integrity Checks

There is, in QBE, the capability to define a condition that, when satisfied by an inserted or modified tuple, causes an associated integrity check or checks to be made on that tuple. As we mentioned, in the phrase

ORDERS	ORDER_NO	NAME	ITEM	QUANTITY
I. CONSTR(I.). I.			_ hotdog	

SUPPLIERS	SNAME	SADDR	ITEM	PRICE
			_ hotdog	

Fig. 10.1. Constraint that orders may only be placed for supplied items.

CONSTR($<$condition list$>$).

the $<$condition list$>$ can include arbitrary character strings as well as I., D., and U. These character strings, called *defined triggers*, are the names of conditions expressed as rows in the QBE language.

Example 10.3: Suppose we wish to constrain Brooks so that he cannot owe as much as 100 dollars. We could write

MEMBERS	NAME	ADDRESS	BALANCE
BL	Brooks,B.		
I. CONSTR(BL). I.			>-100

The first row indicates that there is a defined trigger called BL that is "triggered" whenever we modify or insert a tuple for Brooks. The second row says that if the MEMBERS tuple for Brooks is inserted or modified, check that his new balance is not lower than -99.99. The tuples for other members are not affected by this constraint. □

Old-New Constraints

Sometimes one wishes to constrain updates in such a way that there is a relationship between the old and new values for certain attributes. We include in the constraint specification a line representing the old tuple as well as the constraint tuple itself. Often the QBE language allows the relationship between the old and new tuples to be expressed in the tuples themselves, but if not, a condition box can be used.

Example 10.4: To create a constraint that a supplier cannot raise the price of granola we enter:

SUPPLIERS	SNAME	SADDR	ITEM	PRICE
I. CONSTR(U.). I.	_ supl		Granola	$<= \_p$
I.	_ supl		Granola	_ p

The row with the keyword CONSTR. represents the new value, and the other row represents the old value. The presence of I. in the latter row distinguishes the old-new type of constraints from a general constraint requiring more than one row to express, as in the second part of Example 10.2. The presence of variable _ supl in both rows is necessary, or else we would only check that the new price for the supplier involved in the change is less than the price charged for granola by at least one other supplier. □

Timing of Constraint Enforcement

The QBE system allows one to enter an entire screenful of commands at once, and this collection of commands may include several insertions, deletions, or updates. It is important to note that integrity constraints are not checked as each command in the collection is executed, but only after all the commands in the collection are executed. This feature allows us certain freedoms in the order in which we specify commands, as long as the commands are entered together.

Thus, in Example 10.2 we constrained our HVFC database in such a way that we could not place an order for an item not supplied. If we enter as one "screenload" several orders for rolled oats and the fact that Tasti Supply now sells rolled oats, we would not violate the constraint. However, if the system entered the orders and checked the integrity constraints before entering the new supply information, we would have had an integrity violation.

The Constraint Table

All integrity constraints declared are available to the user. We can print the constraints pertaining to a relation R if we enter

    P. CONSTR. P.

under the relation name in a skeleton for R. Alternatively, we could print only the constraints of specified type; for example

    P. CONSTR(I.) P.

prints only the insertion constraints.

We can delete a constraint on R by entering under R in a skeleton for this relation

    D. CONSTR(<condition list>).

followed, in the columns for the attributes, by a description of the constraint. Note that a trailing D. is not needed the way a second I. or P. is needed when we insert or print a constraint.

10.3 SECURITY

The subject of database security, the protection of the database against un-authorized use, has many different aspects and approaches. First, we need to protect against both undesired modification or destruction of data and against unauthorized reading of data. Many of the problems associated with security are not unique to database systems, but must be faced by the designer of an operating system, for example. Therefore, let us touch on some of the tech-niques common to security for database systems and more general systems, and then turn to some of the specialized problems and techniques germane to existing database systems.

1. *User identification.* Generally, different users are accorded different rights to different databases or different portions of the database, such as relations or attributes. These rights may include the reading of portions of the database, and the insertion, deletion, or modification of data. The most common scheme to identify users is a password known only to the system and the individual. Presumably, the passwords are protected by the system at least as well as the data, although to be realistic, guarantees or proofs of security are nonexistent.

2. *Physical Protection.* A completely reliable protection scheme must take into account the possibility of physical attacks on the database, ranging from forced disclosure of a password to theft of the physical storage devices. We can protect against theft fairly well by encrypting the data. A high security system needs better identification than a password, such as per-sonal recognition of the user by a guard. It should not surprise the reader if we rule this topic outside the scope of the book.

3. *Maintenance and Transmittal of Rights.* The system needs to maintain a list of rights enjoyed by each user on each protected portion of the database. One of these rights may be the right to confer rights on others. For example, the DBTG proposal calls for DBTG sets, record types, and areas to be protectable; the mechanism could be a password for each protected object. The proposal does not call for a table of user rights to protected objects, and transmission of rights can be handled outside the system, by informing users of passwords, for example. Both System R and the Query-by-Example System (to be discussed further in Section 10.4) maintain a table of rights and permit the granting of rights to others.

Now let us turn to the consideration of two mechanisms of protection that are specially designed for use in database systems.

Views as Protection Mechanisms

The view, in addition to making the writing of application programs easier by allowing some redefinition of the conceptual database and promoting logical data independence, serves as a convenient protection facility in many cases. There are two distinct kinds of view facilities. The first, which we discussed in connection with ISBL and Query-by-Example (Sections 6.2 and 6.5), allows no modification to the view. We call such a view facility *read-only*. There are many situations in which the owner of a database (or of any protectable object for that matter) wishes to give the public the privilege of reading his data but wishes to reserve the privilege of modifying the database to himself or to a limited set of associates. The read-only view is ideal for this purpose.

For example, in ISBL or QBE, we may define a view equal to the current value of a given relation and allow public (read-only) access to this view. There is also the option of creating a view containing only part of the information of a relation, or parts of several relations, thus shielding certain attributes or tuples from public view.

The other type of view permits both reading and writing of the objects that are part of the view, and modifications to the view are reflected in the conceptual scheme. IMS, System R, and the DBTG proposal permit this sort of view, for example. Clearly this facility is more versatile than the read-only view, as far as the design of application programs is concerned.

A serious problem with this sort of facility is that updates to a view often have side effects on parts of the database that are not in the view. For example, in a hierarchical system, we might have a particular record type in the view, but not its descendants. If we delete an occurrence of that record type, we must delete its descendants as well, for they no longer fit anywhere in the database. This action could be a surprise to the user, or it could be illegal, as we would ordinarily not give a user authorization to delete an object that we would not even allow him to see in his view.

A similar situation occurs in the network model, where we wish to delete an owner record but do not know about its owned records because they are outside the view. Likewise, those relational systems that borrow network and hierarchical ideas for structuring the storage of their relations face exactly the same problems. It is also unclear, in relational systems, what the deletion of some components of a tuple means if there are other attributes of the relation that are outside the view and that therefore should not be deletable by a user seeing only the view. For these reasons, many updates to views must be ruled out by the system.

The Use of Query Languages to Define Rights

The second important idea concerning security as it pertains to database systems is that the data manipulation language can be used to define the privileges each user has for accessing the database, in much the same way that this language can be used to define integrity constraints. That is, we may write a selection and projection to be included automatically with every query posed by designated users about a designated relation. This selection and projection have the effect of making certain values invisible.

Example 10.5: If a user querying the HVFC database is required to project the MEMBERS relation onto NAME and ADDRESS, whether or not he specifies that projection, then that user cannot see balances. If Tasti Supply Co. is required to select for SNAME="Tasti Supply Co." in every query about the SUPPLIERS relation, then it cannot find the prices charged by other suppliers. □

Each of the four relational systems discussed in Chapter 6 follow this general approach; we shall discuss Query-by-Example's security mechanism in detail in the next section. The DBTG proposal allows the "privacy lock" for a protectable object to be an arbitrary procedure, so here too we are able to implement arbitrary checks, expressed in the DBTG data manipulation language, for granting or denying a request to access a protected object.

10.4 SECURITY IN QUERY-BY-EXAMPLE

The QBE system recognizes the four rights: insert (I.), delete (D.), update (U.), and read (P., for "print"). To confer one or more rights to a relation R upon a person or group of people, the owner of relation R enters a tuple in an R skeleton. Under the relation name R appears the entry

$\quad$ I.AUTR(<list>). <name> I.

where <list> is a list of one or more of the four rights, I., D., U., and P.; <name> is either the name of the person being given the rights or a variable, representing an arbitrary person. We may omit (<list>) if we intend to grant all four rights, and we may omit <name> if we wish to grant a set of rights to all users.

$\quad$ To complete the row with the AUTR. keyword, we enter variables or constants in some or all of the columns for the attributes. A variable indicates that the right applies to the column. A constant indicates the right applies only to tuples with that constant value in that column. A blank indicates that the column cannot be accessed. Note that this rule differs from the general QBE policy that blanks are synonymous with variables mentioned only once. The full power of the QBE language can be brought to bear to refine the set of tuples in the relation R to which the right is granted. For example, we can use condition boxes to constrain the values of variables, and we can add additional rows that also restrict values of variables.

ORDERS	ORDER _ NO	NAME	ITEM	QUANTITY
I. AUTR(P.). _Lark I.	_ n	_ i	_ q	

SUPPLIERS	SNAME	SADDR	ITEM	PRICE
	Sunshine Produce		_ i	

Fig. 10.2. Anyone may read orders for items supplied by Sunshine Produce.

Example 10.6: Let us again use the HVFC database as an example. To give user Brooks the right to read the ORDERS relation we say

ORDERS	ORDER _ NO	NAME	ITEM	QUANTITY
I. AUTR(P.). Brooks I.	_ n	_ i	_ q	

To grant Brooks all four access rights to the ORDERS relation we can write

ORDERS	ORDER _ NO	NAME	ITEM	QUANTITY
I. AUTR. Brooks I.	_ n	_ i	_ q	

To give anyone the right to read names and balances (but not addresses) from the MEMBERS relation, provided the balance is nonnegative, we say

MEMBERS	NAME	ADDRESS	BALANCE
I. AUTR(P.). _Lark I.	_ n		>0

As a final example, to allow anyone access to read orders for items supplied by Sunshine Produce, we may write the command shown in Fig. 10.2. □

Constraints on the Name of the Grantee

We have so far shown two kinds of grants: to anyone or to one specific person. We can use the QBE language to express subsets of the set of users, and we can even allow the set of accessible tuples to be different for different users. The technique is to use a variable for <name> in the AUTR. entry, and to use the same name in the tuple or tuples describing the right granted to each individual user. The system provides a facility to relate the name of the user to the representation of his name as it appears in the database.

Example 10.7: We can give everyone authorization to read only his own balance by:

MEMBERS	NAME	ADDRESS	BALANCE
I. AUTR(P.). _ Lark I.	_ Lark		_ b

☐

The Authorization Table

As for integrity constraints, all AUTR. statements are placed in a table. From this table we can print the rights granted to an individual concerning a relation, or all grants concerning a relation, in much the same manner as we print integrity constraints. Similarly, the owner of a relation can delete rights from the table concerning that relation.

10.5 SECURITY IN STATISTICAL DATABASES

A *statistical database* is a database from which aggregate information about large subsets of entities of an entity set is to be obtained, such as a database of census data, or for certain applications, a file of employees, tax returns, or hospital patients. In addition to the usual problems of forbidding unauthorized access to or modification of the database, there is, in a statistical database, the rather subtle problem of permitting queries such as "Print the average income of all persons in the state of New Jersey" while forbidding access to the income of an individual, John Jones.

It is not sufficient simply to forbid queries that ask for information pertaining to a single record. For example, Fred Smith could ask for the average income of the set { Fred Smith, John Jones }, from which, knowing his own income, Smith could deduce Jones' income. Nor can one simply insist that queries ask for aggregate information about a set of at least m individuals, for a suitably large m fixed by the security mechanism of the database. For then Smith could take a set S of $m - 1$ or more individuals, whose incomes he need not know, and obtain the average income of these individuals plus Jones. Then, Smith obtains the average income of the set consisting of himself and the individuals in set S, from which, knowing his own income, he can deduce Jones', by subtracting the two answers.

The problem with the above example was not that we allowed queries about small sets; m can be as large as we wish. Rather, the problem lies in the interrogator's ability to ask two queries that are almost the same. This possibility suggests that we put a limit not only on the size of sets about which statistics can be taken, but also that we limit the size of the intersection of two sets that are queried. We shall see that this restriction helps; we cannot prevent the disclosure of individual data, but we can make it arbitrarily difficult.

A Model of a Statistical Database

Let us assume for simplicity that a statistical database consists of a single file of records. Each record consists of several fields. A query specifies values for certain fields, and produces some aggregate information, such as a sum or average, of the values in one field, taken over all records that satisfy the conditions of the query. For example, if the records consist of name, occupation, and salary, a query might ask for the average salary of all persons named Smith or for the sum of the salaries of all lawyers.

We assume there is a protection mechanism that, in addition to performing the normal security functions discussed in Section 10.3, monitors all queries made by each user, remembering some large number of previous queries he has made. The protection mechanism can enforce a protection strategy, such as refusing to answer queries involving fewer than a predetermined minimum number of records, or refusing to answer a query that has too large an intersection with a previous query.

In general the latter rule may require that the system record a bit vector representing each set of records queried by anyone, over a long period of time, and therefore may not be practical to implement. Some limits regarding what is remembered must be imposed. For example, we could choose to remember only a limited number of queries, or we could partition the records into groups and only remember which groups had records that satisfied a given query. When deciding whether to answer a given query, we would assume the worst, that for each set of groups corresponding to a previous query, the actual query asked might have selected any subset from each of the groups. The first of these methods, remembering only a limited number of queries, may answer queries it should not answer, while the second method, blurring the records into groups, may forbid answering a query that it could safely answer.

Linear Queries

Let us consider a database of n records, and let $\mathbf{v} = (v_1, v_2, \ldots, v_n)$ be the vector of values of these records in a particular nonkey field. A *linear query* is a linear sum $\sum_{i=1}^{n} c_i v_i$, where the c_i's are arbitrary real numbers. The most important cases are sums over set S, where $c_i = 1$ if record i is in S and 0 if not, and averages, where $c_i = 1/p$ if record i is in S and 0 if not; p is the number of records in S. However, what we say about our ability to *compromise* a database (deduce the value of an individual v_i) will generally depend on the number of nonzero c_i's we allow, not on their exact values or on whether the nonzero c_i's are equal.

Suppose we have a set of q queries, where the ith query extracts from the database $r_i = \sum_{j=1}^{n} c_{ij} v_j$. The results of these queries can be expressed in matrix formulation as

$$\mathbf{r}^T = M\mathbf{v}^T \qquad\qquad (10.2)$$

where M is a q by n matrix whose entry in row i and column j is c_{ij}, and $\mathbf{v}$ and $\mathbf{r}$ are the vectors $(v_1, \ldots, v_n)$ and $(r_1, \ldots, r_q)$, respectively. Superscript T stands for the transpose, making a column vector out of a row vector such as $\mathbf{r}$ or $\mathbf{v}$. If we are to compromise the database, we need to compute some function $f(r_1, \ldots, r_q)$ that is equal to one of the v_j's, say v_1 without loss of generality. A fundamental fact is stated in the following lemma.

Lemma 10.1: If, in the notation used above, there is some function f such that $f(r_1, \ldots, r_q) = v_1$, then there is a linear such function f; that is, for some $d_1, \ldots, d_q$, $\sum_{i=1}^{q} d_i r_i = v_1$.

Proof: The proof requires some linear algebra and multivariable calculus. We omit the proof, giving hints in the exercises for those willing to tackle it. $\square$

Suppose now that f is linear. Then there is some vector $\mathbf{d} = (d_1, \ldots, d_q)$ such that $f(r_1, \ldots, r_q) = \sum_{i=1}^{q} d_i r_i = v_1$, that is, $\mathbf{d}\mathbf{r}^T = v_1$. Then substituting for $\mathbf{r}^T$ by (10.2) we have

$$\mathbf{d}M\mathbf{v}^T = v_1$$

Thus $\mathbf{d}M$ must be the vector $(1, 0, \ldots, 0)$ of length n. In terms of statistical databases, to compromise the database, which we without loss of generality take to mean computation of the element v_1, we must find a collection of q queries forming a matrix M such that there is some vector $\mathbf{d}$ for which $\mathbf{d}M = (1, 0, \ldots, 0)$. If we put constraints on the queries, which means constraining the rows of M, we may be able to prove that M must have many rows i.e., many queries are necessary, if such a $\mathbf{d}$ exists. In particular, we shall consider two constraints on M.

1. Each row has at least m nonzero elements. That is, queries must each involve at least m values.
2. No two rows have more than k columns in which both have nonzero elements. In database terms, the intersection of the sets of elements involved in two queries has size at most k.

Example 10.8: Let us consider a database of seven elements $v_1, \ldots, v_7$, and use the following five queries.

$$r_1 = v_2 + v_3 + v_4$$
$$r_2 = v_5 + v_6 + v_7$$
$$r_3 = v_1 + v_2 + v_5$$
$$r_4 = v_1 + v_3 + v_6$$
$$r_5 = v_1 + v_4 + v_7$$

Then $v_1 = (r_3 + r_4 + r_5 - r_1 - r_2)/3$. Note that each query involves at least three values, and no two queries have an intersection of size greater than one. That is, $m = 3$, and $k = 1$. In matrix terms the queries compute the matrix-vector

$$
\begin{bmatrix} r_1 \\ r_2 \\ r_3 \\ r_4 \\ r_5 \end{bmatrix} = \begin{bmatrix} 0 & 1 & 1 & 1 & 0 & 0 & 0 \\ 0 & 0 & 0 & 0 & 1 & 1 & 1 \\ 1 & 1 & 0 & 0 & 1 & 0 & 0 \\ 1 & 0 & 1 & 0 & 0 & 1 & 0 \\ 1 & 0 & 0 & 1 & 0 & 0 & 1 \end{bmatrix} \begin{bmatrix} v_1 \\ v_2 \\ v_3 \\ v_4 \\ v_5 \\ v_6 \\ v_7 \end{bmatrix}
$$

Fig. 10.3. Query expressed as matrix-vector product.

product of Fig. 10.3. The vector $\mathbf{d}$ is $(-1/3, -1/3, 1/3, 1/3, 1/3)$. Note that $\mathbf{d}$ times the matrix in Fig. 10.3 is $(1, 0, 0, 0, 0, 0, 0)$. $\square$

We shall now derive upper and lower bounds on the number of queries needed to compromise a database, assuming each query involves at least m elements, and no two queries involve more than k elements in common. We can also assume that p values are already known, and that to compromise the database, we must determine an element not already known.

Theorem 10.1: Suppose we are allowed only to make queries that produce a linear function of at least m elements, and no two queries may involve more than k elements in common. Further suppose that p elements are already known. Then to compute some element not already known, we must make at least $1 + (m - 1 - p)/k$ queries.

Proof: Consider the first query, which produces a linear sum over a set S of at least m elements. Let v_i be a member of S. If v_i is not among the p elements already known, and v_i is not the element computed by the matrix-vector product $\mathbf{d}M$ (using the same notation as previously), then there must be some other query that involves v_i. For we may assume M has the smallest possible number of rows, that is, we make no more queries than necessary to compromise the database. Put another way, we assume the vector $\mathbf{d}$ has no zero components. In this circumstance, if only one query involves v_i, then the product $\mathbf{d}M$ must have a nonzero i^{th} component. Since no query may intersect the set S in more than k places, and altogether, at least $m - p - 1$ members of S must appear in another query, there must be at least $(m - p - 1)/k$ queries in addition to the first, from which the theorem follows. $\square$

Theorem 10.1 has an important consequence. Assuming p, the number of previously known elements, is small compared with m, it takes approximately m/k queries to compromise the database. As m and k are parameters of the protection strategy, we have only to choose them so their ratio is large, say 1000, and we shall be assured that great effort will be required to compromise the database. However, note that a large m and small k may put a burden on the user interested in legitimate statistical information. Also, remembering the last 1000 queries by each user may easily tax the storage capacity of the

$$\begin{bmatrix} 0 & 1 & 1 & 1 & 0 & 0 & 0 \\ 0 & -1 & 0 & 0 & 1 & 1 & 0 \\ 0 & 0 & -1 & 0 & -1 & 0 & 1 \\ 1 & 0 & 0 & -1 & 0 & -1 & -1 \end{bmatrix}$$

Fig. 10.4. A matrix M showing fast compromise.

system, so we question whether limiting the size and intersection of queries is a practical way to proceed in general.

One might wonder if Theorem 10.1 is too pessimistic; perhaps it really takes many more than m/k queries to compromise the database. Unfortunately, this is not the case. Suppose $p = 0, k = 1$, and $n = 1 + m(m+1)/2$. Consider an $(m+1)$ by $(1 + m(m+1)/2)$ matrix M, where the first column has a single 1 and the rest 0's. Each of the remaining columns has two nonzero entries, and no two columns have the same two nonzero rows. This is possible because the number of choices of two rows out of $m+1$ is $m(m+1)/2$. In each of columns 2 through $1 + m(m+1)/2$ there is a single 1 and a single -1. Then the sum of all the rows of M is $(1, 0, 0, \ldots, 0)$, allowing us to compromise the database by computing v_1. Since no two columns are identical, and each column has at most two nonzero entries, it follows that no two rows can be nonzero simultaneously in more than one column. Figure 10.4 shows M for $m = 3$.

By replacing each column but the leftmost by k identical columns, we can generalize the above strategy to compromise a database with $1 + m/k$ queries, which is very close to the lower bound of Theorem 10.1. A proof is left as an exercise.

Perhaps general linear queries allow rapid compromise, but if we restrict ourselves to queries that ask for sums or averages, which is what we would expect a query language to provide, then we can improve on the lower bound of Theorem 10.1. The issue is somewhat in doubt, but we can show that for $k = 1, 2m-1$ queries asking for sums are sufficient to compromise the database. Suppose we have $n = 1 + m(m-1)$. The first query asks for the sum of elements 2 through $m+1$, the second for $m+2$ through $2m+1$, the third for $2m+2$ through $3m+1$, and so on. The last m queries each ask for a sum including the first element; query m also includes $2, m+2, 2m+2, \ldots$, query $m+1$ includes $3, m+3, 2m+3, \ldots$, and so on. The matrix for $m = 3$ was shown in Fig. 10.3. The argument given with that figure generalizes to show that $2m/k - 1$ queries suffice for arbitrary m and k.

Limits on the Structure of Queries

So far we have assumed queries specify arbitrary subsets of the records in the database, with only a lower limit on the size of subsets. We found that compromising a database using such queries is not impossible, but it is time consuming if we limit the overlap of the sets defined by two queries. Perhaps if we did not allow all "big" queries, we could actually guarantee noncompromisability.

One approach that has been studied is to assume that the key for records consists of k bits, and that for each key value, or for almost every key value, a record is actually present. Queries are allowed to specify values for up to s of the bits in a key and retrieve the sum of the data items associated with all records whose key values agree with the query in the s specified bits. For example, if $k = 3$ and $s = 2$, we might specify that bit 1 has value 1 and bit 3 has value 0. Then the result of the query would be the sum of the data in the records with keys 100 and 110.

Note that we are in effect performing a partial match retrieval, as discussed in Section 2.8. As in that section, we are not actually limited to binary key values; we could assume a key consisting of some number of fields, each of which takes values from a particular "small" set of values. Unlike Section 2.8, we are assuming that the result of a query is not the full set of matching records, but rather the sum of the contents of a particular field (the "data" in record) from each of those records.

Example 10.9: Suppose our statistical database consists of U.S. census data, with each record holding data that is the sum of the incomes of all persons whose "characteristics" match the bits of the key value for that record. The key consists of 6 bits representing the state in which the person lives, another 8 bits denoting a locality within the state (perhaps a county or city), 1 bit indicating the sex of the person, 6 bits indicating an occupation (divided arbitrarily into 64 categories), and 5 bits indicating the brand of automobile owned (we assume only one brand of car per person is recorded in the database). Thus

$$k = 6 + 8 + 1 + 6 + 5 = 26$$

As 2^k is about 67 million, each record represents the income of a few individuals, on the average.

We might let $s = 15$, so we could ask in one query for the sum of the incomes of all males living in Washington County, Idaho (which specifies 15 bits), or for the sum of the incomes of all bricklayers owning Plymouths (which specifies 11 bits), but we could not ask for the sum of incomes of bricklayers in Idaho owning Plymouths (which specifies 20 bits). We could, in principle, specify up to 15 bits that included some, but not all, of the bits for a state, some from the occupation, and so on. □

It turns out that in the above model, no collection of legal queries can yield the data of an individual record, provided $s < k$, that is, provided we are not allowed to specify all the bits in a query. In fact we can prove considerably more than that. We cannot compute, from the answers to queries specifying up to s of the k bits of the key, any function involving fewer than 2^{k-s} of the records. The formal statement of the theorem follows.

Theorem 10.2: If queries produce the sum of the "data" in all records whose keys match up to s specified bits, and keys have k bits in all, then no rational function† of the result of such queries can be a function of the data values in more than zero, but fewer than 2^{k-s} of the records.

Proof: The proof is beyond the scope of this book but is found in A. Yao [1979]. □

Corollary: If $s < k$, then no rational function of the results of queries can be the value of the data item in one record; that is, the database cannot be compromised. □

EXERCISES

10.1: Suppose we have a Query-by-Example database consisting of relations

> EMPS(EMP _ NO, NAME, ADDR, SALARY, DEPT _ NO)
> DEPTS(DEPT _ NO, DNAME, MANAGER)

Express the following integrity constraints.
a) No employee earns more than $100,000.
b) No employee in department 72 earns more than $50,000.
c) No employee in the Toy Department ("Toy" is a value for attribute DNAME) earns more than $50,000.
* d) No two departments have the same number. *Hint*: Use the CNT. (count) operator.

** 10.2: Show that every functional and multivalued dependency can be expressed in the QBE constraint language.

10.3: Express in the QBE authorization language the following authorizations, which pertain to the database of Exercise 10.1.
a) Anyone can read the EMPS relation, except for the SALARY attribute.
b) Any employee can read his own salary.
c) The manager of a department can read the salary of any employee in his department.
d) Employee Warbucks can insert and delete EMPS tuples and can modify salaries.

** 10.4: In Fig. 10.5 we see the database of the West Side Mob. Naturally, the members wish to keep their incomes secret, and their database allows only queries asking for the sum of the incomes of m or more mob members. Moreover, no two queries can involve more than k members in common. For what values of m and k is this particular database secure, in the sense that no individual's income can be deduced? *Hint*: The analysis following Theorem 10.1, which implied that the lower bound of that theorem was attainable (i.e., databases were compromisable for all m and k, albeit

---

† That is, a function with addition, subtraction, multiplication, and division for operators.

NAME	BOOKMAKING	SMUGGLING	NUMBERS	INCOME
Ralph the Rat	yes	yes	no	?
"Fingers"	yes	no	yes	?
"Scarface"	no	yes	yes	?
"Gouger"	yes	no	no	?
Sam the Snake	no	no	yes	?
"172039"	yes	yes	yes	?

Fig. 10.5. The West Side Mob database.

slowly), actually assumes the database is sufficiently large. For databases with a small number of individuals, the construction following Theorem 10.1 may not work.

10.5: Suppose we restrict queries of the West Side Mob database to ask for the sum of incomes over categories, where a category is defined by specifying whether a person is or is not engaged in up to two particular activities of the mob. For example, we could ask for the sum of incomes of all persons engaged in smuggling but not numbers. This query would happen to give us the income of Ralph the Rat, so the database is compromisable. Show that using queries constrained as above, we can deduce the income of each member of the mob.

10.6: Why does Exercise 10.5 not contradict Theorem 10.2?

10.7: Prove Lemma 10.1, that if $f(r_1, \ldots, r_q) = v_1$, then we may assume f is linear. *Hint:* Note that

$$\frac{\partial f}{\partial v_i} = \sum_{j=1}^{q} \frac{\partial f}{\partial r_j} \frac{\partial r_j}{\partial v_i}$$

Also, $\frac{\partial r_j}{\partial v_i}$ is the constant c_{ij}, and $\frac{\partial f}{\partial v_i}$ is 1 if $i = 1$ and 0 otherwise.

10.8: Show that Theorem 10.1 is a tight lower bound, even for $k > 1$. *Hint:* Generalize the argument for $k = 1$ given after Theorem 10.1.

10.9: Prove Theorem 10.2.

10.10: We suggested in Section 10.1 that if integrity constraints were expressed as the set inclusion of one relational algebra expression in another, then given a small change to one relation, e.g., the insertion of one tuple, we could derive another, simpler expression that represented all that needs to be checked to verify that the integrity constraint continues to hold. Develop the rules for manipulating expressions in this manner. *Hint:* Think of the problem as one of "formally differentiating" relational algebra expressions.

BIBLIOGRAPHIC NOTES

The books by Hoffman [1977] and DeMillo, Dobkin, Jones, and Lipton [1978] discuss the general problem of security in computer systems. Fernandez, Summers, and Wood [1980] cover security and integrity from the database point of view.

The material in Sections 10.2 and 10.4 on security and integrity in Query-by-Example, is taken from Zloof [1978]. Note that these features are not currently available in the commercial version of QBE described in IBM [1978a]. Similar techniques in connection with the INGRES system, but including the idea of security and integrity checks by adding constraints to the where-clause of each query, are found in Stonebraker and Wong [1974], Stonebraker [1975], and Stonebraker and Rubinstein [1976].

The paper by Fagin [1978] studies and proves correct an algorithm for granting authorizations to a database with the possibility that the right to grant further authorizations can itself be granted. This idea was earlier studied by Griffiths and Wade [1976]. A brief survey of database security techniques is by Mresse [1978], and a more extensive one is by Hsiao, Kerr, and Madnick [1978].

The earliest formulations of the problem of security in statistical databases are in Hoffman and Miller [1970] and Haq [1974, 1975]. Formal study of the problem began with Dobkin, Jones, and Lipton [1979], who proved Theorem 10.1. Their model has been examined further by Reiss [1979] and VanLeeuwen [1979]. Theorem 10.2 is by A. Yao [1979], although Kam and Ullman [1977] had previously proved the theorem for the special case where the rational function is linear.

A variety of strategies for protecting statistical databases have been studied recently. Chin [1978] considers schemes that refuse to answer queries about small sets, and shows that even if values cannot be deduced, the presence of a record in the database can often be confirmed or refuted. DeMillo, Dobkin, and Lipton [1978] consider strategies where the database sometimes deliberately gives a false answer and show that even this mechanism is not secure. Traub, Woźniakowski, and Yemini [1981] develop this idea and show that random perturbations in the data have a probability that often is acceptably low of permitting compromise. Denning, Denning, and Schwartz [1977] consider a database in which there is a partitioning of the keys, with queries forbidden to ask about too many individuals from any one block of the partition.

Generalizing ideas of Schlörer [1975, 1976], Denning, Denning, and Schwartz [1979] show how it is in general possible to construct a "tracker," that is, a query that will obtain information about records satisfying a set of characteristics, even when this set is smaller than the database security system allows. The idea has been studied further by Denning and Schlörer [1980] and Schlörer [1980, 1981].

Surveys of statistical database security and additional references can be found in Yu and Chin [1977], Denning [1978], Beck [1981], Chin and Kossowski [1981], and Chin and Oszyoglu [1981].

11

CONCURRENT OPERATIONS
ON THE DATABASE

Until now, our concept of a database has been one in which programs accessing the database are run one at a time (*serially*). Often this is indeed the case. However, there are also numerous applications in which more than one program, or different executions of the same program, run simultaneously (*concurrently*). An example is an airline reservation system, where many sales agents may be selling tickets and therefore changing lists of passengers and counts of available seats. The canonical problem is that if we are not careful when we allow two or more processes to access the database, we could sell the same seat twice. In the reservations system, two processes that read and change the value of the same object must not be allowed to run concurrently, because they might interact in undesirable ways.

A second example is a statistical database, such as census data, where many people may be querying the database at once. Here, as long as no one is changing the data, we do not really care in what order the processes read data; we can let the operating system schedule simultaneous read requests as it wishes. In this sort of situation, where only reading is being done, we want to allow maximum concurrent operation, so time can be saved. For contrast, in the case of a reservation system, where both reading and writing are in progress, we need restrictions on when two programs may execute concurrently, and we should be willing to trade speed for safety.

In this chapter we shall consider models of concurrent processes as they pertain to database operation. The models are distinguished primarily by the detail in which they portray access to elements of the database. For each model we shall describe a reasonable way to allow those concurrent operations that preserve the integrity of the database while preventing concurrent operations that might, as far as a model of limited detail can tell, destroy its integrity. As a rule, the more detailed the model, the more concurrency we can allow safely.

11.1 BASIC CONCEPTS

A *transaction* is a single execution of a program. This program may be a simple query expressed in one of the query languages of Chapter 6 or an elaborate host language program with embedded calls to a query language. Several independent executions of the same program may be in progress simultaneously; each is a transaction.

Items

We imagine that the database is partitioned into *items,* which are portions of the database that can be *locked.* That is, by locking an item, a transaction can prevent other transactions from accessing the item, until the transaction holding the lock unlocks the item. A part of a DBMS called the *lock manager* assigns and records locks, as well as arbitrating among two or more requests for a lock on the same item.

The nature and size of items are for the system designer to choose. In the relational model of data, for example, we could choose large items, like relations, or small items like individual tuples or even components of tuples. We could pick an intermediate size for items; for example, items could be collections of 100 tuples from some relation. In the network model, an item could be the collection of all records of a single type, or what the DBTG proposal terms a set occurrence, for example.

Choosing large items cuts down on the system overhead due to maintaining locks, since we need less space to store the locks, and we save time because fewer actions regarding locks need to be taken. However, choosing small items allows many transactions to operate in parallel, since transactions are then less likely to want locks on the same items.

At the risk of oversimplifying the conclusions of a number of analyses mentioned in the bibliographic notes, let us suggest that the proper choice for the size of an item is such that the average transaction accesses a few items. Thus if the typical transaction (in a relational system) reads or modifies one tuple, which it finds via an index, it would be appropriate to treat tuples as items. If the typical transaction takes a join of two or more relations, and thereby requires access to all the tuples of these relations, then we would be better off treating whole relations as items.

In what follows, we shall assume that when part of an item is modified, the whole item is modified and receives a value that is unique and unequal to the value that could be obtained by any other modification. We make this assumption not only to simplify the modeling of transactions. In practice, it requires too much work on the part of the system to deduce facts such as that the result of one modification of an item gives that item the same value as it had after some previous modification. Furthermore, if the system is to remember

A in database	5	5	5	5	6	6
T_1:	READ A		$A := A+1$			WRITE A
T_2:		READ A		$A := A+1$	WRITE A	
A in T_1's workspace	5	5	6	6	6	6
A in T_2's workspace		5	5	6	6	

Fig. 11.1. Transactions exhibiting a need to lock item A.

whether part of an item remains unchanged after the item is modified, it may as well divide the item into several smaller items. A consequence of our assumption of the indivisibility of items is that we shall not go wrong if we view items as simple variables as used in common programming languages.

Locks

Example 11.1: To see the need for locking items, let us consider two transactions T_1 and T_2. Each accesses an item A, which we assume has an integer value, and adds one to A. The two transactions are executions of the program P defined as

$$P : \text{READ } A; \ A := A + 1; \ \text{WRITE } A$$

The value of A exists in the database. P reads A into its workspace, adds one to the value in the workspace, and writes the result into the database. In Fig. 11.1 we see the two transactions executing in an interleaved fashion†, and we record the value of A as it appears in the database at each step.

We notice that although two transactions have each added 1 to A, the value of A has only increased by 1. This is a serious problem if A represents seats sold on an airplane flight, for example. □

One solution to the problem represented by Example 11.1 is to provide a lock on A. Before reading A, a transaction T must lock A, which prevents another transaction from accessing A until T is finished with A. Furthermore, the need for T to set a lock on A prevents T from accessing A if some other transaction is already using A. T must wait until the other transaction unlocks A, which it should do only after finishing with A.

Let us now consider programs that interact with the database not only by reading and writing items but by locking and unlocking them. We assume

---

† Note that we do not assume necessarily that two similar steps take the same time, so it is possible that T_2 finishes before T_1, even though both transactions execute the same steps. However, the point of the example is not lost if T_1 writes before T_2.

that a lock must be placed on an item before reading or writing it, and that the operation of locking acts as a synchronization primitive. That is, if a transaction tries to lock an already locked item, it waits until the lock is released by an unlock command, which is executed by the transaction holding the lock. We assume that each program is written to unlock any item it locks, eventually. A schedule of the elementary steps of two or more transactions, such that the above rules regarding locks are obeyed, is termed *legal*.

Example 11.2: The program P of Example 11.1 could be written with locks as

$$P : \text{LOCK } A; \text{ READ } A; A{:=}A + 1; \text{ WRITE } A; \text{ UNLOCK } A$$

Suppose again that T_1 and T_2 are two executions of P. If T_1 begins first, it requests a lock on A. Assuming no other transaction has locked A, the system grants this lock. Now T_1, and only T_1 can access A. If T_2 begins before T_1 finishes, then when T_2 tries to execute LOCK A, the system causes T_2 to wait. Only when T_1 executes UNLOCK A will the system allow T_2 to proceed. As a result, the anomaly indicated in Example 11.1 cannot occur; either T_1 or T_2 executes completely before the other starts, and their combined effect is to add 2 to A. □

Livelock and Deadlock

We have postulated a part of a DBMS that grants and enforces locks on items. Such a system cannot behave capriciously, or certain undesirable phenomena occur. As an instance, we assumed in Example 11.2 that when T_1 released its lock on A, the lock was granted to T_2. What if while T_2 was waiting, a transaction T_3 also requested a lock on A, and T_3 was granted the lock before T_2. Then while T_3 had the lock on A, T_4 requested a lock on A, which was granted after T_3 unlocked A, and so on. Evidently, it is possible that T_2 could wait forever, while some other transaction always had a lock on A, even though there are an unlimited number of times at which T_2 might have been given a chance to lock A.

Such a condition is called *livelock*. It is a problem that occurs potentially in any environment where processes execute concurrently. A variety of solutions have been proposed by designers of operating systems, and we shall not discuss the subject here, as it does not pertain solely to database systems. A simple way to avoid livelock is for the system granting locks to record all requests that are not granted immediately, and when an item A is unlocked, grant a lock on A to the transaction that requested it first, among all those waiting to lock A. This first-come-first-served strategy eliminates livelocks,† and we shall assume from here on that livelock is not a problem.

There is a more serious problem of concurrent processing that can occur if

---

† Although it may cause "deadlock," to be discussed next.

we are not careful. This problem, called "deadlock," can best be illustrated by an example.

Example 11.3: Suppose we have two transactions T_1 and T_2 whose significant actions, as far as concurrent processing is concerned are:

T_1: LOCK A LOCK B UNLOCK A UNLOCK B
T_2: LOCK B LOCK A UNLOCK B UNLOCK A

Presumably T_1 and T_2 do something with A and B, but this is not important here. Suppose T_1 and T_2 begin execution at about the same time. T_1 requests and is granted a lock on A, and T_2 requests and is granted a lock on B. Then T_1 requests a lock on B, and is forced to wait because T_2 has a lock on that item. Similarly, T_2 requests a lock on A and must wait for T_1 to unlock A. Thus neither transaction can proceed; each is waiting for the other to unlock a needed item, so both T_1 and T_2 wait forever. □

A situation in which each member of a set S of two or more transactions is waiting to lock an item currently locked by some other transaction in the set S is called a *deadlock*. Since each transaction in S is waiting, it cannot unlock the item some other transaction in S needs to proceed, so all wait forever. Like livelock, the prevention of deadlock is a subject much studied in the literature of operating systems and concurrent processing in general. Among the approaches to a solution are the following.

1. Require each transaction to request all its locks at once, and let the system grant them all, if possible, or grant none and make the process wait, if one or more are held by another transaction. Notice how this rule would have prevented the deadlock in Example 11.3. The system would grant locks on both A and B to T_1 if it requested first; T_1 would complete, and then T_2 could have both locks.

2. Assign an arbitrary linear ordering to the items, and require all transactions to request locks in this order.

The second approach also prevents deadlock. In Example 11.3, suppose A precedes B in the ordering (there could be other items between A and B in the ordering). Then T_2 would request a lock for A before B and would find A already locked by T_1. T_2 would not yet get to lock B, so a lock on B would be available to T_1 when requested. T_1 would complete, whereupon the locks on A and B would be released. T_2 could then proceed. To see that no deadlocks can occur in general, suppose we have a set S of deadlocked transactions, and each transaction R_i in S is waiting for some other transaction in S to unlock an item A_i. We may assume that each R_j in S holds at least one of the A_i's, else we could remove R_j from S and still have a deadlocked set. Let A_k be the first item among the A_i's in the assumed linear order. Then R_k, waiting for A_k, cannot hold any of the A_i's, which is a contradiction.

Another approach to handling deadlocks is to do nothing to prevent them.

Rather, periodically examine the lock requests and see if there is a deadlock. The algorithm of drawing a *waits-for graph*, whose nodes are transactions and whose arcs $T_1 \rightarrow T_2$ signify that transaction T_1 is waiting to lock an item on which T_2 holds the lock, makes this test easy; every cycle indicates a deadlock, and if there are no cycles, neither are there any deadlocks. If a deadlock is discovered, at least one of the deadlocked transactions must be restarted, and its effects on the database must be cancelled. This process of restart can be complicated if we are not careful about the way transactions write into the database before they complete. The subject is taken up in Section 11.6.

In the future, we shall assume that neither livelocks nor deadlocks will occur when executing transactions.

Serializability

Now we come to a concurrency issue of concern primarily to database system designers, rather than designers of general concurrent systems. By way of introduction, let us review Example 11.1, where two transactions executing a program P each added 1 to A, yet A only increased by 1. Intuitively, we feel this situation is wrong, yet perhaps these transactions did exactly what the writer of P wanted. However, it is doubtful that the programmer had this behavior in mind, because if we run first T_1 and then T_2, we get a different result; 2 is added to A. Since it is always possible that transactions will execute one at a time (serially), it is reasonable to assume that the normal, or intended, result of a transaction is the result we obtain when we execute it with no other transactions executing concurrently. Thus, we shall assume from here on that the concurrent execution of several transactions is correct if and only if its effect is the same as that obtained by running the same transactions serially in some order.

Let us define a *schedule* for a set of transactions to be an order in which the elementary steps of the transactions (lock, read, and so on) are done. The steps of any given transaction must, naturally, appear in the schedule in the same order that they occur in the program of which the transaction is an execution. A schedule is *serial* if all the steps of each transaction occur consecutively. A schedule is *serializable* if its effect is equivalent to that of some serial schedule.

Example 11.4: Let us consider the following two transactions, which might be part of a bookkeeping operation that transfers funds from one account to another.

T_1: READ A; $A := A - 10$; WRITE A; READ B; $B := B + 10$; WRITE B
T_2: READ B; $B := B - 20$; WRITE B; READ C; $C := C + 20$; WRITE C

Clearly, any serial schedule has the property that the sum $A+B+C$ is preserved. In Fig. 11.2(a) we see a serial schedule, and in Fig. 11.2(b) is a serializable, but not serial, schedule. Figure 11.2(c) shows a nonserializable schedule. Note that

T_1	T_2
READ A	
$A := A - 10$	
WRITE A	
READ B	
$B := B + 10$	
WRITE B	
	READ B
	$B := B - 20$
	WRITE B
	READ C
	$C := C + 20$
	WRITE C

(a)

T_1	T_2
READ A	
	READ B
$A := A - 10$	
	$B := B - 20$
WRITE A	
	WRITE B
READ B	
	READ C
$B := B + 10$	
	$C := C + 20$
WRITE B	
	WRITE C

(b)

T_1	T_2
READ A	
$A := A - 10$	
	READ B
WRITE A	
	$B := B - 20$
READ B	
	WRITE B
$B := B + 10$	
	READ C
WRITE B	
	$C := C + 20$
	WRITE C

(c)

Fig. 11.2. Some schedules.

Fig. 11.2(c) causes 10 to be added, rather than subtracted from B as a net effect, since T_1 reads B before T_2 writes the new value of B. It is possible to prevent the schedule of Fig. 11.2(c) from occurring by having all transactions lock B before reading it. $\square$

Recall that we have defined a schedule to be serializable if its effect is equivalent to that of a serial schedule. In general, it is not possible to test whether two schedules have the same effect for all initial values of the items, if arbitrary operations on the items are allowed, and there are an infinity of possible initial values. In practice, we make some simplifying assumptions about what operations do to items. In particular, it is convenient to assume that values cannot be the same unless they are produced by exactly the same sequence of operations. Thus we do not regard $(A+10)-20$ and $(A+20)-30$ as producing the same values. Ignoring algebraic properties of arithmetic causes us to make only "nonfatal" errors, in the sense that we may call a schedule nonserializable, when in fact it produces the same result as a serial schedule, but we shall never say a schedule is serializable when it in fact is not (a "fatal" error). Nonfatal errors may rule out some concurrent operations, and thereby cause the system to run more slowly than it theoretically could. However, these errors never cause an incorrect result to be computed, as a fatal error might. Succeeding sections will use progressively more detailed models that enable us to infer that wider classes of schedules are serializable, and therefore to achieve more concurrency while guaranteeing correctness.

Protocols and Schedules

We have seen that arbitrary transactions can, when executed concurrently, give rise to livelock, deadlock, and nonserializable behavior. To eliminate these problems we have two tools. The first is the *scheduler,* a portion of the database system that arbitrates between conflicting requests. We saw, for example, how a first-come, first-serve scheduler can eliminate livelock. A scheduler can also handle deadlocks and nonserializability by causing one or more transactions to restart, undoing all their actions so far. We shall consider restart of transactions in Section 11.6.

Another approach to handling deadlock and nonserializability is to use one or more protocols, that all transactions must follow. A *protocol,* in its most general sense, is simply a restriction on the sequences of steps that a transaction may perform. For example, the deadlock-avoiding strategy of requesting locks on items in some fixed order is a protocol. Much of what follows in this chapter concerns the development of protocols that guarantee serializability.

11.2 A SIMPLE TRANSACTION MODEL

Let us begin by introducing what is undoubtedly the simplest model of transactions that still enables us to talk about serializability. In this model, a transaction is viewed as a sequence of lock and unlock statements. Each item locked must subsequently be unlocked. Between a step LOCK A and the next UNLOCK A, a transaction is said to *hold a lock on* A. We assume a transaction does not try to lock an item if it currently holds a lock on that item, nor does it try to unlock an item on which it does not currently hold a lock.

We further assume that whenever a transaction locks on item A it changes the value of A, and the value that A has when unlocked is essentially unique, in the sense that if v_1 and v_2 are two values A may have before the LOCK A step, then the values held by A after UNLOCK A are always different in the two cases, provided $v_1 \neq v_2$.

A more formal way to look at the behavior of transactions is to associate with each pair LOCK A and its following UNLOCK A, a unique function f. Note that one transaction may have more than one such pair for a given A, since, although it is not generally a good idea, we may lock and unlock the same item more than once. Let A_0 be the initial value of A before any transactions are executed. *Values* that A may assume are formulas of the form $f_1 f_2 \cdots f_n(A_0)$, where the f_i's are functions associated with LOCK A—UNLOCK A pairs of the various transactions. No distinct values are equal. That is, values are regarded as uninterpreted formulas. This definition of "value" is a rigorous treatment of our informal statement in the previous section that we would assume no algebraic laws regarding the effects of transactions on items.

Example 11.5: In Fig. 11.3 we see three transactions and the functions associated with each LOCK—UNLOCK pair. Fig. 11.4 shows a possible schedule of these transactions and the resulting effect on items A, B, and C. We can observe that this schedule is not serializable. In proof, suppose it were. If T_1

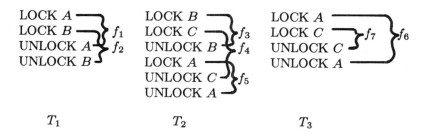

$$T_1 \qquad\qquad\qquad T_2 \qquad\qquad\qquad T_3$$

Fig. 11.3. Three transactions.

precedes T_2, then the final value of B would be $f_3(f_2(B_0))$, not $f_2(f_3(B_0))$. If T_2 precedes T_1, then the final value of A would be $f_6(f_1(f_5(A_0)))$, $f_1(f_6(f_5(A_0)))$, or $f_1(f_5(f_6(A_0)))$, depending on whether the serial order was $T_2T_1T_3$, $T_2T_3T_1$, or $T_3T_2T_1$. As none of these formulas is the actual final value of A in Fig. 11.4, we see that T_2 cannot precede T_1 in an equivalent serial schedule. Since T_2 can neither precede nor follow T_1 in an equivalent serial schedule, so a serial schedule does not exist.

Note how our assumption that functions produce unique values is essential in the proof. For example, if it were possible that $f_3f_2 = f_2f_3$, then we could not rule out the possibility that T_1 precedes T_2. Let us reiterate that our assumption of unique values is not just for mathematical convenience. The work required to enable the database system to examine transactions and detect possibilities such as $f_3f_2 = f_2f_3$, and thereby permit a wider class of schedules to be regarded as serializable, is not worth the effort in general. $\square$

A Serializability Test

If we consider Example 11.5 and the proof that the schedule of Fig. 11.4 is not serializable, we see the key to a serializability test. We examine a schedule with regard to the order in which the various transactions lock a given item. This order must be consistent with the hypothetical equivalent serial schedule of the transactions. If the orders induced by two different items force two transactions to appear in different order, then we have a paradox, since both orders cannot be consistent with one serial schedule. We can express this test as a problem of finding cycles in a directed graph. The method is described formally in the next algorithm.

Algorithm 11.1: Testing Serializability of a Schedule.
Input: A schedule S for a set of transactions $T_1, \ldots, T_k$.
Output: A determination whether S is serializable, and if so, a serial schedule equivalent to S.
Method: Create a directed graph G (called a *precedence* graph), whose nodes correspond to the transactions. To determine the arcs of the graph G, let S be

	Step	A	B	C
(1)	T_1: LOCK A	A_0	B_0	C_0
(2)	T_2: LOCK B	A_0	B_0	C_0
(3)	T_2: LOCK C	A_0	B_0	C_0
(4)	T_2: UNLOCK B	A_0	$f_3(B_0)$	C_0
(5)	T_1: LOCK B	A_0	$f_3(B_0)$	C_0
(6)	T_1: UNLOCK A	$f_1(A_0)$	$f_3(B_0)$	C_0
(7)	T_2: LOCK A	$f_1(A_0)$	$f_3(B_0)$	C_0
(8)	T_2: UNLOCK C	$f_1(A_0)$	$f_3(B_0)$	$f_4(C_0)$
(9)	T_2: UNLOCK A	$f_5(f_1(A_0))$	$f_3(B_0)$	$f_4(C_0)$
(10)	T_3: LOCK A	$f_5(f_1(A_0))$	$f_3(B_0)$	$f_4(C_0)$
(11)	T_3: LOCK C	$f_5(f_1(A_0))$	$f_3(B_0)$	$f_4(C_0)$
(12)	T_1: UNLOCK B	$f_5(f_1(A_0))$	$f_2(f_3(B_0))$	$f_4(C_0)$
(13)	T_3: UNLOCK C	$f_5(f_1(A_0))$	$f_2(f_3(B_0))$	$f_7(f_4(C_0))$
(14)	T_3: UNLOCK A	$f_6(f_5(f_1(A_0)))$	$f_2(f_3(B_0))$	$f_7(f_4(C_0))$

Fig. 11.4. A schedule.

$a_1; a_2; \cdots; a_n$, where each a_i is an action of the form

$$T_j: \text{LOCK } A_m \text{ or } T_j: \text{UNLOCK } A_m$$

T_j indicates the transaction to which the step belongs. If a_i is

$$T_j: \text{UNLOCK } A_m$$

look for the next action a_p following a_i that is of the form T_s: LOCK A_m. If there is one, then draw an arc from T_j to T_s. The intuitive meaning of this arc is that in any serial schedule equivalent to S, T_j must precede T_s.

If G has a cycle, then S is not serializable. If G has no cycles, then find a linear order for the transactions such that T_i precedes T_j whenever there is an arc $T_i \rightarrow T_j$. This can always be done by the process known as *topological sorting,* defined as follows. There must be some node T_i with no entering arcs, else we can prove that G has a cycle. List T_i and remove T_i from G. Then repeat the process on the remaining graph until no nodes remain. The order in which the nodes are listed is a serial order for the transactions. $\square$

Example 11.6: Consider the schedule of Fig. 11.4. The graph G, shown in Fig. 11.5 has nodes for T_1, T_2, and T_3. To find the arcs, we look at each UNLOCK step in Fig. 11.4. For example step (4), T_2: UNLOCK B, is followed by

$$T_1: \text{LOCK } B$$

in this case, the lock occurs at the next step. We therefore draw an arc $T_2 \rightarrow T_1$. As another example, the action at step (8), T_2: UNLOCK C, is followed at step (11) by T_3: LOCK C, and no intervening step locks C. Therefore we draw an

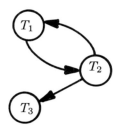

Fig. 11.5. Graph of precedences among transactions.

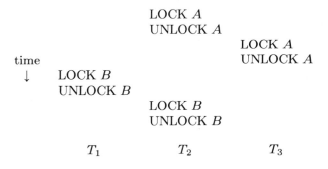

Fig. 11.6. A serializable schedule.

arc from T_2 to T_3. Steps (6) and (7) cause us to place an arc $T_1 \rightarrow T_2$. As there is a cycle, the schedule of Fig. 11.4 is not serializable. □

Example 11.7: In Fig. 11.6 we see a schedule for three transactions, and Fig. 11.7 shows its precedence graph. As there are no cycles, the schedule of Fig. 11.6 is serializable, and Algorithm 11.1 tells us that the serial order is T_1, T_2, T_3. It is interesting to note that in the serial order, T_1 precedes T_3, even though in Fig. 11.6, T_1 did not commence until T_3 had finished. □

Theorem 11.1: Algorithm 11.1 correctly determines if a schedule is serializable.

Proof: Suppose the precedence graph G has no cycles. Consider the sequence of transactions $T_{i_1}, T_{i_2}, \ldots, T_{i_r}$ that in the schedule S lock and unlock item A, in that order. Then in G there are arcs $T_{i_1} \rightarrow T_{i_2} \rightarrow \cdots \rightarrow T_{i_r}$, so the transactions must appear in this order in the constructed serial schedule. As no other transaction locks A, it is easy to check that the value of A after executing S is the same as in the serial schedule constructed by Algorithm 11.1. Since the above holds for any item A, it follows that S is equivalent to the constructed serial schedule, so S is serializable.

Conversely, suppose G has a cycle $T_{j_1} \rightarrow T_{j_2} \rightarrow \cdots \rightarrow T_{j_t} \rightarrow T_{j_1}$. Let there be a serial schedule R equivalent to S, and suppose that in R, T_{j_p} appears first

Fig. 11.7. Precedence graph for Fig. 11.6.

among the transactions in the cycle. Let the arc $T_{j_{p-1}} \to T_{j_p}$ (take j_{p-1} to be j_t if $p = 1$) be in G because of item A. Then in R, since T_{j_p} appears before $T_{j_{p-1}}$, the final formula for A applies a function f associated with some LOCK A—UNLOCK A pair in T_{j_p} before applying some function g associated with a LOCK A—UNLOCK A pair in $T_{j_{p-1}}$. In S, however, $T_{j_{p-1}}$ precedes T_{j_p}, since there is an arc $T_{j_{p-1}} \to T_{j_p}$. Therefore, in S, g is applied before f. Thus the final value of A differs in R and S, in the sense that the two formulas are not the same, and we conclude that R and S are not equivalent. Thus S is equavalent to no serial schedule. $\square$

A Protocol that Guarantees Serializability

We shall give a simple protocol with the property that any collection of transactions obeying the protocol cannot have a legal, nonserializable schedule. Moreover, this protocol is, in a sense to be discussed subsequently, the best that can be formulated. The protocol is, simply, to require that in any transaction, all locks precede all unlocks.† Transactions obeying this protocol are said to be *two-phase;* the first phase is the locking phase and the second the unlocking phase. For example, in Fig. 11.3, T_1 and T_3 are two-phase; T_2 is not.

Theorem 11.2: If S is any schedule of two-phase transactions, then S is serializable.

Proof: Suppose not. Then by Theorem 11.1, the precedence graph G for S has a cycle, $T_{i_1} \to T_{i_2} \to \cdots \to T_{i_p} \to T_{i_1}$. Then some lock by T_{i_2} follows an unlock by T_{i_1}; some lock by T_{i_3} follows an unlock by T_{i_2}, and so on. Finally, some lock by T_{i_1} follows an unlock by T_{i_p}. Therefore, a lock of T_{i_1} follows an unlock of T_{i_1}, contradicting the assumption that T_{i_1} is two-phase. $\square$

Another way to see why two-phase transactions must be serializable is to imagine that a two-phase transaction occurs instantaneously at the moment it obtains the last of its locks. Then the order in which the transactions reach this point must be a serial schedule equivalent to the given schedule. For if in the given schedule, transaction T_1 locks A before T_2 does, then T_1 surely obtains the last of its locks before T_2 does.

We mentioned that the two-phase protocol in is a sense the best that can be done. Precisely, what we can show is that if T_1 is any transaction that is not two phase, then there is some other transaction T_2 with which T_1 could be

---

† To avoid deadlock, the locks could be made according to a fixed linear order of the items. However, we do not deal with deadlock here, and some other method could also be used to avoid deadlock.

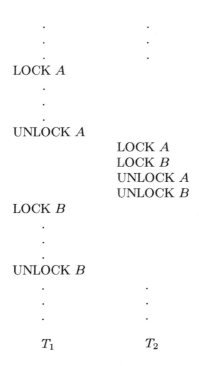

Fig. 11.8. A nonserializable schedule.

run in a nonserializable schedule. Suppose T_1 is not two phase. Then there is some step UNLOCK A of T_1 that precedes a step LOCK B. Let T_2 be:

T_2: LOCK A; LOCK B; UNLOCK A; UNLOCK B

Then the schedule of Fig. 11.8 is easily seen to be nonserializable, since the treatment of A requires that T_1 precede T_2, while the treatment of B requires the opposite.

Note that there are particular collections of transactions, not all two-phase, that yield only serial schedules. We shall consider an important example of such a collection in Section 11.5. However, since it is normal not to know the set of all transactions that could ever be executed concurrently with a given transaction, we are usually forced to require all transactions to be two-phase.

11.3 A MODEL WITH READ- AND WRITE-LOCKS

In Section 11.2 we assumed that every time a transaction locked an item it changed that item. In practice, many times a transaction needs only to obtain the value of the item and is guaranteed not to change that value. If we distinguish between a read-only access and a read-write access, we can develop a more detailed model of transactions that will allow some concurrency forbidden in the model of the previous section.† Let us distinguish two kinds of locks.

1. *Read-locks* (or *shared locks*). A transaction T wishing only to read an item A executes RLOCK A, which prevents any other transaction from writing a new value of A while T is reading A. However, any number of transactions can hold a read-lock on A at the same time.

2. *Write-locks* (or *exclusive locks*). These are locks in the sense of the previous section. A transaction wishing to change the value of item A first obtains a write-lock by executing WLOCK A. When some transaction holds a write-lock on an item, no other transaction can obtain either a read- or write-lock on the item.

Both read- and write-locks are removed by an UNLOCK statement. As in Section 11.2, we assume no transaction tries to unlock an item on which it does not hold a read- or write-lock, and no transaction tries to read-lock an item on which it already holds any lock. Further, a transaction does not attempt to write-lock an item if it already holds a write-lock on that item, but under some circumstances, a write-lock may be issued for an item on which it holds a read-lock. The latter makes sense because a write-lock is more restrictive on the behavior of other transactions than a read-lock.

Two schedules are *equivalent* if

1. they produce the same value for each item, and
2. each read-lock applied by a given transaction occurs in both schedules at times when the item locked has the same value.

A Test for Serializability

As in the previous section, we assume that each time a write-lock is applied to an item, a unique function associated with that lock operates on the value of that item. However, a read-lock on an item does not change the value. Suppose we have a schedule S in which a write-lock is applied to A by transaction T_1, and let f be the function associated with that write-lock. After T_1 unlocks A, let T_2 be one of the (perhaps many) transactions that subsequently read-lock A before any other transaction write-locks it. Then surely T_1 must precede T_2 in any serial schedule equivalent to S. Otherwise, T_2 reads a value of A that does not involve the function f, and no such value is identical to a value that does involve f. Similarly, if T_3 is the next transaction, after T_1, to write-lock A, then T_1 must precede T_3. The argument is essentially that of Theorem 11.1.

Now suppose T_4 is a transaction that read-locks A before T_1 write-locks it. If T_1 appears before T_4 in a serial schedule, then T_4 reads a value of A involving f, while in schedule S, the value read by T_4 does not involve f. Thus T_4 must

† Note that we still do not have write-only locks. The ability of transactions to write an item without reading it first will be seen in the next section to complicate greatly the question of serializability.

precede T_1 in a serial schedule. The only inference we cannot make is that if in S two transactions read-lock the same item A in a particular order, then the transactions should appear in that order in a serial schedule. In fact, just the opposite is true. The relative order of read-locks makes no difference on the values produced by concurrently executing transactions. These observations suggest that an approach similar to that of Section 11.2 will allow us to tell whether a schedule is serializable.

Algorithm 11.2: Serializability test for schedules with read/write-locks.

Input: A schedule S for a set of transactions $T_1, \ldots, T_k$.

Output: A determination whether S is serializable, and if so, an equivalent serial schedule.

Method: We construct a precedence graph G as follows. The nodes correspond to the transactions as before. The arcs are determined by the following rules.

1. Suppose in S, transaction T_i read-locks item A, and T_j is the next transaction (if it exists) to write-lock A. Then place an arc from T_i to T_j.

2. Suppose in S, transaction T_i write-locks A, and T_j is the next transaction (if it exists) to write-lock A. Then draw an arc $T_i \rightarrow T_j$. Further, let T_m be any transaction that read-locks A after T_i unlocks its write-lock, but before T_j write-locks A (if there is no T_j, then T_m is any transaction to read-lock A after T_i unlocks A). Then draw an arc $T_i \rightarrow T_m$.

If G has a cycle, then S is not serializable. If G is acyclic, then any topological sort of G is a serial order for the transactions. □

Example 11.8: In Fig. 11.9 we see a schedule of four transactions, and in Fig. 11.10 is its precedence graph. The first UNLOCK is step (3), where T_3 removes its write-lock from A. Following step (3) are read-locks of A by T_1 and T_2 (steps 4 and 7) and a write-lock of A by T_4 at step (12). Thus T_1, T_2, and T_4 must follow T_3, and we draw arcs from T_3 to each of the other nodes. Notice that there is nothing wrong with both T_1 and T_2 holding read-locks on A after step (7). However, T_4 could not write-lock A until both T_1 and T_2 released their read-locks. As another example, T_4 releases a write-lock on B at step (5), and the next write-lock on B is by T_3, so we draw an arc from T_4 to T_3. We now have a cycle, so the schedule of Fig. 11.9 is not serializable. The complete set of arcs is shown in Fig. 11.11. □

Theorem 11.3: Algorithm 11.2 correctly determines if schedule S is serializable.

Proof: It is straightforward to argue, whenever we draw an arc from T_i to T_j, that in any equivalent serial schedule T_i must precede T_j. Thus if G has a cycle, we may prove as in Theorem 11.1 that no such serial schedule exists. Conversely, suppose G has no cycles. Then an argument like Theorem 11.1 shows that the final value of each item is the same in S as in the serial schedule R that is constructed from the topological sort of G. We must also show that corresponding read-locks on item A obtain the same value in R and S. But this

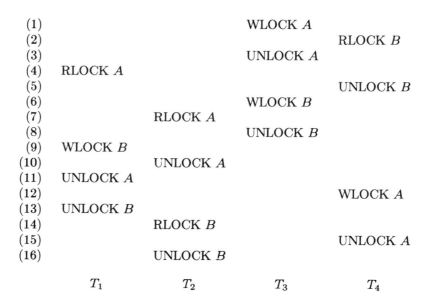

	T_1	T_2	T_3	T_4
(1)			WLOCK A	
(2)				RLOCK B
(3)			UNLOCK A	
(4)	RLOCK A			
(5)				UNLOCK B
(6)			WLOCK B	
(7)		RLOCK A		
(8)			UNLOCK B	
(9)	WLOCK B			
(10)		UNLOCK A		
(11)	UNLOCK A			
(12)				WLOCK A
(13)	UNLOCK B			
(14)		RLOCK B		
(15)				UNLOCK A
(16)		UNLOCK B		

Fig. 11.9. A schedule.

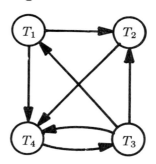

Fig. 11.10. Precedence graph of Fig. 11.9.

proof is easy, since the arcs of G guarantee the write-locks on A that precede the given read-lock must be the same in R and S and that they must occur in the same order. $\square$

The Two-Phase Protocol

As with the model in the previous section, a two-phase protocol, in which all read- and write-locks precede all unlocking steps, is sufficient to guarantee serializability. Moreover, we have the same partial converse, that any transaction in which some UNLOCK precedes a read- or write-lock can be run in a nonserializable way with some other transaction. We leave these results as exercises.

11.4 A READ-ONLY, WRITE-ONLY MODEL

A subtle assumption with profound consequences that was made in Sections 11.2 and 11.3 is that whenever a transaction writes a new value for an item A, then it previously read the value of A, and more importantly, the new value of A depends on the old value. This assumption is built into the definition of "value" in the previous sections. A more realistic model would admit the possibility that a transaction reads a set of items (the *read-set)* and writes a set of items (the *write-set),* with the option that an item A could appear in either one of these sets or both.

For example, any transaction that queries a database but does not alter it has an empty write-set.† In the transaction

READ A; READ B; $C := A + B$; $A := A - 1$; WRITE C; WRITE A

the read-set is $\{A, B\}$ and the write-set is $\{A, C\}$.

Equivalence of Schedules

When we allow write-only access, we must revise our notion of when two schedules are equivalent. One important difference is the following. Suppose, in the model of Section 11.3, that the transaction T_1 wrote a value for item A, and later T_2 wrote a value for A. Then we assumed in Section 11.3 that T_2 write-locked A after T_1 unlocked A, and by implication, T_2 used the value of A written by T_1 in computing a new value, since the function associated with T_2's lock-unlock of A is assumed to produce a distinct new value of A for each old value of A. Therefore, when dealing with serializability, it was taken forgranted that in a serial schedule, T_1 appears before T_2, and, incidentally, that no other transaction T write-locking A appears between T_1 and T_2. One gets the latter condition "for free" in Algorithm 11.2, since that algorithm forced T to appear either before T_1 or after T_2 in the serial schedule, whichever was the case in the given schedule S.

However, if we assume that T_2 has written its value for A without reading A, then the new value of A is independent of the old; it depends only on the values of items actually read by T_2. Thus, if between the times that T_1 and T_2 write their values of A, no transaction reads A, we see that the value written by T_1 "gets lost" and has no effect on the database. As a consequence, in a serial schedule, we need not have T_1 appearing before T_2 (at least as far as A is concerned). In fact, the only requirement on T_1 is that it be done at a time

† Alternatively, if the order in which query answers are produced is important, we could view the output device as an item in the write-set of a query.

when some other transaction T_3 will later write A, and between the times that T_1 and T_3 write A, no transaction reads A.

We can now formulate a new definition of serializability based on the concept that the values written by a transaction are functions only of the values read, and distinct values read produce distinct values written. These conditions are stated informally (and not completely accurately) as follows. If in schedule S, transaction T_2 reads the value of item A written by T_1, then

1. T_1 must precede T_2 in any serial schedule equivalent to S.
2. If T_3 is a transaction that writes A, then in any serial schedule equivalent to S, T_3 may either precede T_1 or follow T_2, but may not appear between T_1 and T_2.

There are also two details needed to make the above definition an accurate one. First, there are "edge effects" involving the reading of an item before any transaction has written it or writing an item that is never rewritten. These rules are best taken care of by postulating the existence of an *initial transaction* T_0 that writes every item, reading none, and a *final transaction* T_f that reads every item, writing none.

The second detail concerns transactions T whose output is "invisible" in the sense that no value T writes has any effect on the value read by T_f. Note that this effect need not be direct, but could result from some transaction T' reading a value written by T, another transaction T'' reading a value written by T', and so on, until we find a transaction in the chain that writes a value read by T_f. Call a transaction with no effect on T_f *useless*. Our second modification of the above rules is to rule out the possibility that T_2, in (1) and (2) above, is a useless transaction.†

Testing for Useless Transactions

It is easy, given a schedule S, to tell which transactions are useless. We create a graph whose nodes are the transactions, including the dummy transaction T_f assumed to exist at the end of S. If T_1 writes a value read by T_2, draw an arc from T_1 to T_2. Then the useless transactions are exactly those with no path to T_f. An example of this algorithm follows the discussion of a serializability test.

A Formal Model

Let us regard transactions as we did in Section 11.3, consisting of a series of steps RLOCK A (read-lock item A), WLOCK A (write-lock item A) and UNLOCK A. As before, we assume transactions do not unlock items on which they do not hold a read-or write lock, and they do not lock items on which they already hold

---

† We cannot simply remove useless transactions from S, since the portion of the system that schedules transactions cannot know that it is scheduling a transaction that will later prove to be useless.

a lock, except that a transaction may write-lock an item on which it holds a read-lock or vice versa. The only substantial difference between this model and the previous one lies in the semantics. Here we assume that when a transaction write-locks an item, it does not read its value (unless it also read-locks it), while previously we implied that a write-lock included reading privileges and in fact included the obligation to read and use the value read.

The Serializability Test

The simple precedence graph test of previous sections does not work here. Recall that there are in the current model two types of constraints on a potential serial schedule equivalent to a given schedule S. *Type 1* constraints are that if T_2 reads a value of A written by T_1 in S, then T_1 must precede T_2 in any serial schedule. This type of constraint can be expressed graphically by an arc from T_1 to T_2. The *type 2* constraints, that any T_3 writing A must appear either before T_1 or after T_2, cannot be expressed by a simple arc. Rather, we have a pair of arcs $T_3 \rightarrow T_1$ and $T_2 \rightarrow T_3$, one of which must be chosen. The schedule S is serializable if and only if after making some choice from each pair, we are left with an acyclic graph.

A collection of nodes, arcs, and pairs of alternative arcs has been termed a *polygraph*. A polygraph is *acyclic* if there is some series of choices of one arc from each pair that results in an acyclic graph in the ordinary sense. The serializability test for the model presently under consideration is to construct a certain polygraph and determine if it is acyclic. Unfortunately, testing a polygraph for acyclicness is a hard problem; it has been shown $\mathcal{NP}$-complete by Papadimitriou, Bernstein, and Rothnie [1977].

Algorithm 11.3: Serializability test for transactions with read-only and write-only locks.

Input: A schedule S for a set of transactions $T_1, T_2, \ldots, T_k$.

Output: A determination whether S is serializable, and if so, an equivalent serial schedule.

Method:

1. Augment S by appending to the beginning a sequence of steps in which a dummy transaction T_0 writes each item appearing in S and appending to the end steps in which dummy transaction T_f reads each such item.

2. Begin the creation of a polygraph P with one node for each transaction, including T_0 and T_f. Temporarily place an arc from T_i to T_j whenever T_j reads an item A that in the augmented S was last written by T_i.

3. Discover the useless transactions. A transaction T is useless if there is no path from T to T_f.

4. For each useless transaction T, remove all arcs entering T.

5. For each remaining arc $T_i \rightarrow T_j$, and for each item A such that T_j reads

the value of A written by T_i, consider each other transaction $T \neq T_0$ that also writes A. If $T_i = T_0$ and $T_j = T_f$, add no arcs. If $T_i = T_0$ but $T_j \neq T_f$, add the arc $T_j \rightarrow T$. If $T_j = T_f$, but $T_i \neq T_0$, add the arc $T \rightarrow T_i$. If $T_i \neq T_0$ and $T_j \neq T_f$, then introduce the arc pair $(T \rightarrow T_i, T_j \rightarrow T)$.

6. Determine whether the resulting polygraph P is acyclic. For this step there is no substantially better method than the exhaustive one. If there are n arc pairs, try all 2^n choices of one arc from each pair to see if the result is an acyclic graph.† If P is acyclic, let G be an acyclic graph formed from P by choosing an arc from each pair. Then any topological sort of G, with T_0 and T_f removed, represents a serial schedule equivalent to S. If P is not acyclic, then no serial schedule equivalent to S exists. □

Example 11.9: Consider the schedule of Fig. 11.11. The arcs constructed by step (2) of Algorithm 11.3 are shown in Fig. 11.12; for clarity, the arcs are labeled with the item or items justifying their presence. In understanding how Fig. 11.12 was created it helps first to observe that the schedule of Fig. 11.11 is legal, in the sense that two transactions do not hold write-locks, or a read-and write-lock simultaneously. Thus, we may assume all reading and writing occurs at the time the lock is obtained, and we may ignore the UNLOCK steps.

Let us consider each read-lock step in turn. The read-locks on A at steps (1) and (2) read the value "written" by the dummy transaction T_0. Thus we draw arcs from T_0 to T_1 and T_2. At step (5) T_3 reads the value of C written by T_1 at step (3), so we have arc $T_1 \rightarrow T_3$. At step (8), T_4 reads what T_1 wrote at step (6), so we have arc $T_1 \rightarrow T_4$, and so on. Finally, at the end, T_f "reads" A, B, C, and D, whose values were last written by T_4, T_4, T_1, and T_2, respectively, explaining the three arcs into T_f.

Now we search for useless transactions, those with no path to T_f in Fig. 11.12; T_3 is the only such transaction. We therefore remove the arc $T_1 \rightarrow T_3$ from Fig. 11.12.

In step (5) of Algorithm 11.3 we consider the arcs or arc pairs needed to prevent interference of one write operation with another. An item like C or D that is written by only one nondummy transaction does not figure into step (5). However, A is written by both T_3 and T_4, as well as dummy transaction T_0. The value written by T_3 is not read by any transaction, so T_4 need not appear in any particular position relative to T_3. The value written by T_4 is "read" by T_f. Therefore, as T_3 cannot appear after T_f, it must appear before T_4. In this case, no arc pair is needed; we simply add to P the arc $T_3 \rightarrow T_4$. The value of A written by T_0 is read by T_1 and T_2. As T_3 and T_4 cannot appear before T_0,

---

† Obviously one can think of some heuristics to make the job somewhat simpler than it appears at first glance. For example, if one of a pair of arcs causes a cycle with existing arcs, we must choose the other of the pair. However, there are cases where neither arc in a pair causes an immediate cycle, yet our choice influences what happens when we try to select arcs from other pairs.

	T_1	T_2	T_3	T_4
(1)			RLOCK A	
(2)	RLOCK A			
(3)	WLOCK C			
(4)	UNLOCK C			
(5)			RLOCK C	
(6)	WLOCK B			
(7)	UNLOCK B			
(8)				RLOCK B
(9)	UNLOCK A			
(10)		UNLOCK A		
(11)			WLOCK A	
(12)				RLOCK C
(13)		WLOCK D		
(14)				UNLOCK B
(15)			UNLOCK C	
(16)		RLOCK B		
(17)			UNLOCK A	
(18)				WLOCK A
(19)		UNLOCK B		
(20)				WLOCK B
(21)				UNLOCK B
(22)		UNLOCK D		
(23)				UNLOCK C
(24)				UNLOCK A

Fig. 11.11. A schedule.

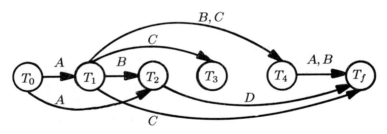

Fig. 11.12. First step in construction of a polygraph.

we place arcs from T_1 and T_2 to T_3 and T_4; again no arc pair is necessary.

Item B is written by T_1 and T_4. The value of B written by T_4 is read only by T_f, so we need arc $T_1 \rightarrow T_4$. The value of B written by T_1 is read by T_2 and T_4. The writing of B by T_4 cannot interfere with the reading of B by T_4. Thus no requirement that "T_4 precedes T_1 or follows T_4" is needed. However,

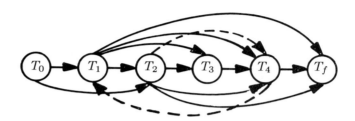

Fig. 11.13. Final polygraph.

T_4 must not be interposed between T_1 and T_2, so we add the arc pair $(T_4{\to}T_1,$ $T_2{\to}T_4)$. The resulting polygraph is shown in Fig. 11.13, with the one arc pair shown dashed. Note that arc $T_1{\to}T_3$, removed in step (4), returns in step (5).

If we choose arc $T_4{\to}T_1$ from the pair we get a cycle. However, choosing $T_2{\to}T_4$ leaves an acyclic graph, from which we can take the serial order T_1, T_2, T_3, T_4. Thus the schedule of Fig. 11.11 is serializable. $\square$

Theorem 11.4: Algorithm 11.3 correctly determines if a schedule is serializable.

Proof: We shall give a brief sketch of the proof. Suppose first that the resulting polygraph is acyclic. That is, there is some choice between arcs in each pair that results in an acyclic graph G. The construction of P in Algorithm 11.3 assures that each nonuseless transaction, including T_f, reads the same copy of each item in S as it does in the serial schedule resulting from a topological sort of G. Thus the corresponding values produced for each item are the same in both schedules.

Conversely, suppose there is a serial schedule S' equivalent to S. Then by the reasoning used in Theorem 11.1, if $T_i{\to}T_j$ is any arc introduced in step (2) and not removed in step (4), T_i must precede T_j in S'. Suppose the arc pair $(T_n{\to}T_i,\ T_j{\to}T_n)$ is introduced in step (5). Then T_n cannot appear between T_i and T_j in S'. Pick arc $T_n{\to}T_i$ from the pair if T_n precedes T_i in S', and pick $T_j{\to}T_n$ otherwise. The linear order implied by S' will be consistent with this choice from arc pairs. Similarly, a single arc added in step (5) must be consistent with this linear order, so we have a way of constructing, based on S', an acyclic graph from polygraph P. $\square$

The Two-phase Protocol, Again

As with the previous models, a two-phase protocol, requiring each transaction to do all locking before any unlocking, is successful in guaranteeing serializability of any legal schedule. To see why, let us suppose S is a legal schedule of transactions obeying the two phase protocol. Suppose $(T_3{\to}T_1,\ T_2{\to}T_3)$ is an arc pair in the polygraph P. Then there is some item A such that T_2 reads the copy of A written by T_1. If in S, T_3 unlocks A before T_1 read-locks A, then select $T_3 \rightarrow T_1$ from the pair. If T_3 write-locks A after T_2 unlocks it, select $T_2 \rightarrow T_3$. No other possibilities exist, since the arc pair was placed in P by Algorithm 11.3.

We now have a graph G constructed from P. Suppose G has a cycle $T_1 \rightarrow T_2 \rightarrow \cdots \rightarrow T_n \rightarrow T_1$. Surely, neither dummy transaction can be part of a cycle. Examination of Algorithm 11.3 and the above rules for constructing G from P indicates that for every arc $T_i \rightarrow T_{i+1}$ (with $T_{n+1} = T_1$) in the cycle, there is an item A_i such that in S, T_i unlocks A_i before T_{i+1} locks A_i. By the two phase protocol, T_{i+1} must unlock A_{i+1} after it locks A_i. Thus T_1 unlocks A_1 before T_{n+1} locks A_n. But T_{n+1} is T_1, and the two-phase protocol forbids T_1 from unlocking A_1 before it locks A_n. We have thus proved the following theorem.

Theorem 11.5: In the model of this section, if transactions obey the two-phase protocol, then any legal schedule is serializable. $\square$

11.5 CONCURRENCY FOR HIERARCHICALLY STRUCTURED ITEMS

There are many instances where the set of items accessed by a transaction can be viewed naturally as a tree or forest. Some examples are:
1. Items are logical records in a database structured according to the hierarchical model.
2. Items are nodes of a B-tree (see Section 2.4).
3. Items of various sizes are defined, with small items nested within larger ones. For example, a relational database could have items at four levels:
    i)   the entire database,
    ii) each relation,
    iii) each block in which the file corresponding to a relation is stored, and
    iv) each tuple.

There are two different policies that could be followed when items are locked. First, a lock on an item could imply a lock on all its descendant items. This policy saves time, as locking many small items can be avoided. For example, in (3) above, a transaction that must read an entire relation can lock the relation as a whole, rather than locking each tuple individually. The second policy is to lock an item without implying anything about a lock on its descendants. For example, if we are searching a B-tree, we shall read a node and select one of its children to read next. We need not lock all descendants at the time we read a node.

These two points of view turn out to yield very different kinds of problems and solutions. It seems that an acceptable protocol for the policy of locking

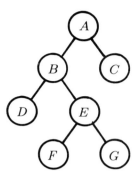

Fig. 11.14. A hierarchy of items.

individual items is easier to explain than a protocol for the policy of locking subtrees, so we shall consider locking individual items first.

A Simple Protocol for Trees of Items

Let us revert to the model of Section 11.2 using only the LOCK and UNLOCK operations.† We assume that locking an item (node of a tree) does not automatically lock any descendants. As in Section 11.2, only one transaction can lock an item at a time. We say a transaction obeys the *tree protocol* if

1. Except for the first item locked (which need not be the root), no item can be locked unless a lock is currently held on its parent.
2. No item is ever locked twice by one transaction.

Observe that a transaction obeying the tree protocol need not be two-phase. For example, it might lock an item A, then lock its child B, unlock A and lock a child C of B. This situation is quite realistic, e.g., in the case that the transaction is performing an insertion into a B-tree. If B is a node of the B-tree that has room for another pointer, then we know that no restructuring of the tree after insertion can involve the parent of B. Thus after examining B we can unlock the parent A, thereby allowing concurrent updates to the B-tree involving descendants of A that are not descendants of B.

Example 11.10: Figure 11.14 shows a tree of items, and Fig. 11.15 is the schedule of three transactions T_1, T_2, and T_3, obeying the tree protocol. Note that T_1 is not two-phase, since it locks C after unlocking B. □

While we shall not give a proof here (see Silberschatz and Kedem [1980]), all legal schedules of transactions that obey the tree protocol are serializable. The algorithm to construct a serial ordering of the transactions begins by creating a node for each transaction. Suppose T_i and T_j are two transactions that lock the same item (at different times, of course). Let FIRST(T) be the item first

---

† The bibliographic notes contain pointers to generalizations of this protocol, where both read- and write-locks are permitted.

	T_1	T_2	T_3
(1)	LOCK A		
(2)	LOCK B		
(3)	LOCK D		
(4)	UNLOCK B		
(5)		LOCK B	
(6)	LOCK C		
(7)			LOCK E
(8)	UNLOCK D		
(9)			LOCK F
(10)	UNLOCK A		
(11)			LOCK G
(12)	UNLOCK C		
(13)			UNLOCK E
(14)		LOCK E	
(15)			UNLOCK F
(16)		UNLOCK B	
(17)			UNLOCK G
(18)		UNLOCK E	

Fig. 11.15. A schedule of transactions obeying the tree protocol.

locked by transaction T. If FIRST(T_i) and FIRST(T_j) are independent (neither is a descendant of the other), then the tree protocol guarantees that T_i and T_j do not lock a node in common, and we need not draw an arc between them. Suppose therefore, without loss of generality, that FIRST(T_i) is an ancestor of FIRST(T_j). If T_i locks FIRST(T_j) before T_j does, then draw arc $T_i \rightarrow T_j$. Otherwise draw an arc $T_j \rightarrow T_i$.

It can be shown that the resulting graph has no cycles, and any topological sort of this graph is a serial order for the transactions. The intuition behind the proof is that at all times, each transaction has a frontier of lowest nodes in the tree on which it holds locks. The tree protocol guarantees that these frontiers do not pass over one another. Thus, if the frontier of T_i begins above the frontier of T_j, it must remain so, and every item locked by both T_i and T_j will be locked by T_j first.

Example 11.11: Let us reconsider the schedule of Fig. 11.15. In this schedule we have FIRST(T_1) = A, FIRST(T_2) = B, and FIRST(T_3) = E. T_1 and T_2 both lock B, and T_1 does so first, so we have arc $T_1 \rightarrow T_2$. Also, T_2 and T_3 each lock E, but T_3 precedes T_2 in doing so. Thus we have arc $T_3 \rightarrow T_2$. The precedence graph for this schedule is shown in Fig. 11.16, and there are two possible serial schedules, T_1, T_3, T_2 and T_3, T_1, T_2. □

Fig. 11.16. Precedence graph for Fig. 11.15.

A Protocol Allowing Locks on Subtrees

We now consider the second kind of hierarchy, a nested structure. It is convenient, when the hierarchy of items includes items that are subsets of other items, as in our earlier example (3) of a hierarchy: database-relations-blocks-tuples, to assume that a lock on an item implies a lock on all its descendants. For example, if a transaction must lock most or all the tuples of a relation, it may as well lock the relation itself. At a cost of possibly excluding some concurrent operations on the relation, the system does far less work locking and unlocking items if we lock the relation as a whole.

However, indiscriminant locking can result in illegal schedules, where two transactions effectively hold a lock on the same item at the same time. For example, suppose transaction T_1 locks E (and therefore, by our new assumptions, F and G) in Fig. 11.14. Then let T_2 lock B, thereby acquiring a conflicting lock on E, F and G. To avoid this conflict, a protocol has been devised in which a transaction cannot place a lock on an item unless it first places a "warning" at all its ancestors. A warning on item A prevents any other transaction from locking A, but it does not prevent it from also placing a warning at A or locking some descendant of A that does not have a warning.

This approach is patterned after that used for concurrency control in System R. What we present here is a simplification of the ideas found in that system. We shall here consider transactions to consist of operations

1. LOCK, which locks an item and all its descendants. No two transactions may hold a lock on an item at the same time.
2. WARN, which places a "warning" on an item. No transaction may lock an item on which some other transaction has placed a warning.
3. UNLOCK, which removes either a lock or a warning or both from an item.
   A transaction obeys the *warning protocol* on a hierarchy of items if
1. It begins by placing a lock or warning at the root.
2. It dos not place a lock or warning on an item unless it holds a warning on its parent.†
3. It does not remove a lock or warning unless it holds no locks or warnings on its children.
4. It obeys the two-phase protocol, in the sense that all unlocks follow all warnings and locks.

---

† Note that there is no need to place a lock on an item if a lock on its parent is already held.

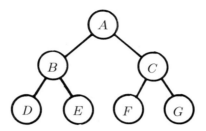

Fig. 11.17. A hierarchy.

Example 11.12: Figure 11.17 shows a hierarchy, and Fig. 11.18 is a schedule of three transactions obeying the warning protocol. Notice, for example that at step (4) T_1 places a warning on B. Therefore T_3 was not able to lock B until T_1 unlocked its warning on B at step (10). However, at steps (1)–(3) all three transactions place warnings on A, which is legal.

The lock of C by T_2 at step (5) implicitly locks C, F, and G. We assume that any or all of these items are changed by T_2 before the lock is removed at step (7). $\square$

Theorem 11.6: Schedules of transactions obeying the warning protocol are serializable.

Proof: Parts (1)–(3) of the warning protocol guarantee that no transaction can place a lock on an item unless it holds warnings on all its ancestors. It follows that at no time can two transactions hold locks on two ancestors of the same item. We can now show that a schedule obeying the warning protocol is equivalent to a schedule using the model of Section 11.2, in which all items are locked explicitly (not implicitly, by locking an ancestor). Given a schedule S satisfying the warning protocol, construct a schedule S' in the model of Section 11.2 as follows.

1. Remove all warning steps, and their matching unlock steps.
2. Replace all locks by locks on the item and all its descendants. Do the same for the corresponding unlocks.

The resulting schedule S' is legal because of parts (1)–(3) of the warning protocol, and its transactions are two-phase because those of S are two-phase, by part (4) of the warning protocol. $\square$

11.6 PROTECTING AGAINST CRASHES

Until now we have assumed that each transaction runs happily to completion. In practice, several things might happen to prevent a transaction from completing.

1. The system could fail from a variety of hardware or software causes. In this case, all active transactions are prevented from completing, and it is even possible that some completed transactions must be "cancelled," because they read values written by transactions that have not yet completed.

	T_1	T_2	T_3
(1)	WARN A		
(2)		WARN A	
(3)			WARN A
(4)	WARN B		
(5)		LOCK C	
(6)	LOCK D		
(7)		UNLOCK C	
(8)	UNLOCK D		
(9)		UNLOCK A	
(10)	UNLOCK B		
(11)			LOCK B
(12)			WARN C
(13)			LOCK F
(14)	UNLOCK A		
(15)			UNLOCK B
(16)			UNLOCK F
(17)			UNLOCK C
(18)			UNLOCK A

Fig. 11.18. A schedule of transactions satisfying the warning protocol.

System crashes cause serious problems, since we must not only find a set of transactions to "cancel" that will bring us back to a consistent state, but we must make sure that some way of reconstructing that state exists.

2. A single transaction could be forced to stop before completion for a variety of reasons. If deadlock detection is done by the system, the transaction could be found to contribute to a deadlock and be selected for cancellation by the system. A bug in the transaction, e.g., a division by zero, could cause an interrupt and cancellation of the transaction. Similarly, the user could cause an interrupt at his terminal for the express purpose of cancelling a transaction.

3. In the next section, we shall discuss "optimistic" concurrency control, where transactions are allowed to run without locking items, and violations of the serializability condition are detected and the offending transaction cancelled.

Backup Copies

It should be evident that we cannot rely on the indefinite preservation of the data in a database. Data in the machine's registers or solid state memory cannot be presumed to survive a power outage, for example. Magnetic devices

such as tapes, disks, or magnetic core memory will usually be preserved even if
the machine has to be shut down, but even this data is vulnerable to physical
problems such as disk "head crashes" or a small child with a large magnet
running amok in the computer room. Further, no data is completely safe from
being obliterated by system software errors.

For these reasons, it is essential that backup copies of the database be made
ally, at least once a day if possible, although enormous databases, for
copying process could take hours, must be copied less frequently.
ce made on tape on disk, should be removed from the vicinity of
in case of fire, for example), and stored in a safe place. For extra
of the most recent copies could be stored in different places.
copy, it is important that the copied data represent a con-
e, the copying utility routine must itself be a transaction
in the database.

store the database to a consistent state that
mber, perhaps a large number, of transactions
of the last backup copy.† For this reason,
place, e.g., on a tape or disk, a history,
he database since the last backup copy
al entries consist of
using the change,

progress of a transaction,
its "commit point."
ent when we consider
to undo them, that
items are large, if
changes only,
we could list
he modified

helps
. There
se, since other
currently with the

is a point during the execution of any transaction at which we regard it as completed. All calculations done by the transaction in its workspace must have been finished, and a copy of the results of the transaction must have been written in a secure place, presumably in the journal. At this time we may regard the transaction as *committed*; if a system crash occurs subsequently, its effects will survive the crash, even though the values produced by the transaction may not yet have appeared in the database itself. The action of committing the transaction must itself be written in the journal, so if we have to recover from a crash by examining the journal, we know which transactions are committe We define the *two-phase commit*† policy as follows.

1. A transaction cannot write into the database until it has committed.
2. A transaction cannot commit until it has recorded all its changes to in the journal.

Note that phase one is the writing of data in the journal and phase writing the same data in the database.

If in addition, transactions follow the two-phase locking prot unlocking occurs after commitment, then we know that no trans read from the database a value written by an uncommitted transac case of a system crash, it is then possible to examine the log and committed transactions that did not have a chance to write their database. If the crash is of a nature that destroys data in the shall have to redo all committed transactions since the last ba made, which is generally far more time consuming. It is not n any transactions that did not reach their commit point before since these have no effect on the database. It would be a g message to the user warning him that his transaction did n able to do so after a crash, it is necessary routinely to enter fact that a particular transaction has begun. Also note th locks to be left on items, either from committed or unco and these must be removed by the recovery routine.

Failure of Individual Transactions

Less serious than a system crash is the failure of a for example, it causes deadlock or is interrupted fo the two-phase commit policy, we know that there provided that no interruption of a transaction If we are following the two-phase protocol, the occur after commitment, so it is not possible t commitment, or that an arithmetic error causes Thus, failed transactions leave no trace on th

† There is no connection between the "two-phase p except that they are both sensible ideas.

that a transaction was cancelled should be placed in the journal, so if restart occurs after a system crash, we know to ignore any journal entries for that transaction.

Transactions That do not Obey the Two-Phase Commit Policy

Let us briefly consider what happens if transactions are not required to reach their commit point before writing into the database. By relaxing this requirement, we may allow transactions to unlock items earlier, and thereby allow other transactions to execute concurrently instead of waiting. However, this potential increase in concurrency is paid for by making recovery after a crash more difficult, as we shall see.

We still assume that each item has its changes entered in the journal before the database itself is actually changed, and we assume transactions obey the two-phase protocol with regard to locking. We also assume a transaction does not commit until it has completed writing into the journal whatever items it changes. Under our new assumptions it is not impossible to recover from system crashes or failures of individual transactions, but it becomes more difficult for two reasons.

1.   A transaction that is uncommitted when the crash occurs must have the changes that it made to the database undone.

2.   A transaction that has read a value written by some transaction that must be undone, must itself be undone. This effect can propagate indefinitely.

Example 11.13: Consider the two transactions of Fig. 11.19. Fundamentally these transactions follow the model of Section 11.2, although to make clear certain details of timing, we have explicitly shown commitment, reads, writes, and the arithmetic done in the workspace of each transaction. The WRITE steps are presumed to write the old and new values in the journal and then in the database. Suppose that after step (14) there is a crash. Since T_1 is the only active transaction, it doesn't matter whether it was a system crash or a failure of T_1, say because division by 0 occurred at step (14).

We must undo T_1 because it is uncommitted. Since it holds a lock on B, that lock must be removed. Then we must restore to A its value prior to step (1). We must also undo T_2, even though it is committed, and in fact completed. If some other transaction T_3 had read A between steps (13) and (14), then T_3 would have to be redone as well, even if T_3 were completed, and so on.

To undo transactions that must be undone, we consider each item C written by one or more of the transactions that must be undone. Examine the journal for the earliest write of C by one of the undone transactions. This journal entry will have the old value of C, which can be placed in the database. Note that since we assume all transactions are two-phase, and we are using the model of Section 11.2, where all items locked are assumed to be read as well as written,

(1)	LOCK A	
(2)	READ A	
(3)	$A := A - 1$	
(4)	WRITE A	
(5)	LOCK B	
(6)	UNLOCK A	
(7)		LOCK A
(8)		READ A
(9)		$A := A * 2$
(10)	READ B	
(11)		WRITE A
(12)		COMMIT
(13)		UNLOCK A
(14)	$B := B/A$	

T_1 T_2

Fig. 11.19. A schedule.

it is not possible that some transaction T, which does not have to be redone, wrote a value for C later than the earliest undone transaction wrote C. We leave as an exercise the correct algorithm for modifying the database to reflect the undoing of transactions when the model of Section 11.4, which permits writing without reading, is used.

In the case of our example in Fig. 11.19, only A was written by the transactions T_1 and T_2 prior to the crash. We find that the earliest write of A by either of these transactions was by T_1 at step (4). The journal entry for step (4) will include the old value of A, the value read at step (2). Replacing A by that value cancels all effects of T_1 and T_2 on the database. $\square$

One might assume that having undone T_1 and T_2 in Example 11.13, it is now possible to redo T_2, since it was committed, simply by examining the journal, rather than by running it again. Such is not the case, since T_2 read the value of A written into the database by T_1, and that value is no longer there. To retrieve that value of A from the journal, without rerunning T_1, might lead to an inconsistency in the database.

11.7 OPTIMISTIC CONCURRENCY CONTROL

Let us briefly consider a method of synchronizing transactions that is radically different from the locking methods discussed in the previous sections. Suppose that we were "optimistic," and executed transactions with no locking at all, reading and writing into the database as we wished. Naturally, if we were executing two transactions such as those of Fig. 11.1, with steps executed in the order shown in that figure, we would have a nonserializable behavior. However, suppose that when we read or wrote into the database, we at least had some way of realizing that we were doing something that might violate serial order, for example, reading a value that had been written by another transaction that belonged after our transaction in the serial order. Then we could abort our transaction and start it over.

This approach is quite efficient, provided that the probability of two transactions conflicting in this way is small. The chance of interaction between two transactions executing at about the same time will be small provided each accesses only a tiny fraction of the database, i.e., the lock granularity is small. If this situation holds, there is substantial benefit in using the "optimistic" approach, as no time will be wasted requesting or waiting for locks. The time wasted redoing transactions that have to be aborted may well be much less than the time spent waiting for locks or undoing deadlocks.

Yet in order to adopt this method, a number of questions must be answered. How do we tell that we are violating serial order? How do we avoid leaving in the database values written by transactions that later abort? When we must abort a transaction, how do we avoid livelock, the situation where the transaction is restarted over and over, but aborts each time? We shall answer these questions in turn.

Timestamps

The key to establishing a serial order and detecting its violations is to have the system generate *timestamps*, which are numbers generated at each clock "tick," where ticks of the computer's internal clock occur with sufficient frequency, say once every microsecond, that two events such as the start of transactions cannot occur at the same "tick." At a special time in the life of every transaction, say when it initiates, or when it issues its first read or write on the database, the transaction is issued its timestamp, which is the current time on the clock. No two transactions can have the same timestamp, and we shall take as our criterion of correctness that transactions should behave as if the order of their timestamps were their serial order as well.

As an aside, one might think that adding one to the clock every microsecond would produce enormous numbers as timestamps. However, the fact is that the number of ticks in a century fits in a 32-bit word, and even 24 bits holds numbers large enough that they would have to repeat only every half year. If we make the reasonable assumption that half a year is long enough for any transaction to complete, no confusion will result if we let timestamps recycle after that amount of time. Even a sixteen bit timestamp is adequate for most purposes.

Now, we must consider how timestamps are used to force those transactions that do not abort to behave as if they were run behave serially. We store

with each item in the database two times, the *read time*, which is the highest
timestamp possessed by any transaction to have read the item, and the *write
time*, which is the highest timestamp possessed by any transaction to have
written the item. By so doing, we can maintain the fiction that each transaction
executes instantaneously, at the time indicated by its timestamp.

We use the timestamps associated with the transactions, and the read and
write times stored with the items, to check that nothing physically impossible
happens. What, we may ask, is not possible?

1. It is not possible that a transaction can read the value of an item if that
    value was not written until after the transaction executed. That is, a
    transaction with a timestamp t_1 cannot read an item with a write time of
    t_2 if $t_2 > t_1$. If such an attempt is made, the transaction must abort and
    be restarted.

2. It is not possible that a transaction can write an item if that item has its
    old value read at a later time. That is, a transaction with timestamp t_1
    cannot write an item with a read time t_2, if $t_2 > t_1$. That transaction
    must abort.

Notice that the other two possible conflicts do not present any problems.
Not surprisingly, two transactions can read the same item at different times,
without any conflict. That is, a transaction with timestamp of t_1 can read an
item with a read time of t_2, even if $t_2 > t_1$. Less obviously, the transaction
with timestamp t_1 need not abort if it tries to write an item with write time t_2,
even if $t_2 > t_1$. We simply do not write the item. The justification is that in
the serial order based on timestamps, the transaction with timestamp t_1 wrote
the item, then the transaction with timestamp t_2 wrote it. However, between
t_1 and t_2, apparently no transaction read the item, or else the read time of
the item would exceed t_1 when the first transaction came to write, and that
transaction would abort by rule (2).

To summarize, the rule for preserving serial order using timestamps, but
no locking, is the following. Suppose we have a transaction with timestamp t
that attempts to perform an operation X on an item with read time t_r and
write time t_w.

a) Perform the operation if X=READ and $t \geq t_w$ or if X=WRITE, $t \geq t_r$,
    and $t \geq t_w$. In the former case, set the read time to t if $t > t_r$, and in the
    latter case, set the write time to t if $t > t_w$.

b) Do nothing if X=WRITE and $t_r \leq t < t_w$.

c) Abort the transaction if X=READ and $t < t_w$ or X=WRITE and $t < t_r$.

Example 11.14: Let us review the transactions of Fig. 11.1. Suppose that T_1
is given timestamp 150 and T_2 has timestamp 160. Also, assume the initial
read and write times of A are both 0. Then A would be given read time 150
when T_1 reads it and 160 at the next step, when it is read by T_2. At the fifth
step, when T_2 writes A, the timestamp, 160, is not less than the read time of

	T_1	T_2	T_3	A	B	C
	200	150	175	RT=0	RT=0	RT=0
				WT=0	WT=0	WT=0
(1)	READ B				RT=200	
(2)		READ A		RT=150		
(3)			READ C			RT=175
(4)	WRITE B				WT=200	
(5)	WRITE A			WT=200		
(6)		WRITE C				
(7)			WRITE A			

Fig. 11.20. Optimistically executing transactions.

A, which is also 160, nor is it less than the write time, which is 0. Thus the write is permitted, and the write time of A is set to 160. When T_1 attempts to write at the last step, its timestamp, 150, is less than the read time of A, so T_1 is aborted, preventing the anomaly illustrated in Fig. 11.1. A similar sequence of events occurs if the timestamp of T_1 is larger than that of T_2. □

Example 11.15: Figure 11.20 illustrates three transactions, with timestamps 200, 150, and 175, operating on three items, A, B, and C, each of which are assumed to have read and write times of 0 initially. The last three columns indicate changes to the read time (RT) and write time (WT) of the items.

At step (6), an attempt to write C is made. However, the transaction doing the writing, T_2, has a timestamp of 150, and the read time of C is then 175. Thus, T_2 cannot perform the write and must be aborted. Then, at step (7), T_3 tries to write A. As T_3 has a timestamp, 175, that is bigger than the read time of A, which is 150, T_3 need not abort. However, the write time of A is 200, so the value of A written by T_3 is not entered into the database, but rather is discarded, no write taking place. □

Commitment of Transactions

The above algorithm will sometimes fail to keep the database in a state that could be reached by the serial execution of transactions, because we have so far failed to account for the possibility that a transaction that aborts may have written something successfully into the database before doing so. To prevent such values written from fouling the database, we must regard the actual write operation as being only phase one of a two-phase commit.

That is, the WRITE action by a transaction does not permanently alter the database. Rather, the value is entered into the log, and the write time of the item tentatively updated, with the old value and write time stored in the log. After performing all its writes, the transaction executes a COMMIT action, whereupon all the values written by the transaction are made permanent.

Between the time the item is written and the time it is committed, no transaction may read the new value, since it is tentative, and a transaction that read it would have to be rolled back if the writer aborts, as discussed in the previous section. We must make any such reading transaction wait for the commitment of the new value or its removal.† If transactions do their writing at the end, just before the commitment, this waiting time will be short. Writes with a higher timestamp may be made, and supercede the tentative write; they are themselves tentative, however. If we keep the old value and write time available in the database, then we may let READ requests with timestamps between the old and new write times read the old value, independent of whether the new value gets committed.

Even with the commitment phase, the optimistic strategy calls for only one step for the READ operation and two for the WRITE operation (write and commit). In comparison, locking with two-phase commitment requires three or four steps per operation: LOCK, READ or WRITE, UNLOCK, COMMIT (if write). Thus, in situations where conflicts and their resulting rollback of transactions was expected not to be common, we might well prefer the optimistic approach.

Restart of Transactions

As we mentioned, the strategy with which we have been dealing does not prevent livelock, a situation where a transaction is aborted repeatedly. While we expect transactions to be aborted rarely, or the whole approach should be abandoned in favor of the locking methods described earlier, we should be aware that the potential for cyclic behavior involving only two transactions exists.

Example 11.16: Suppose we have transaction T_1 that writes B and then reads A, while T_2 writes A and then reads B.‡ If T_1 executes, say with timestamp 100, and T_2 executes with timestamp 110, we might find that T_2 wrote A before T_1 read it. In that case, T_1 would abort, because it cannot read a value with a write time greater than its own timestamp. If we immediately restart T_1, say with timestamp 120, it might write B before T_2 reads it, causing T_2 to abort and restart, say with timestamp 130. Then the second try at T_2 might write A before the second try of T_1 reads A, causing that to abort, and so on. The pattern is illustrated in Fig. 11.21. □

The solution to the problem indicated by Example 11.16 is not easy to find. Probably the simplest approach is to use a random number generator to select a random amount of time that an aborted transaction must wait before

---

† An alternative is to let the reading transaction proceed, but be prepared to roll it back, along with any transactions that read values it writes, as discussed in Section 11.6.

‡ These transactions may read and write other items, so writing before reading need not mean that the transactions are unrealistic.

T_1	T_2	T_1	T_2	A	B
100	110	120	130	RT=0	RT=0
				WT=0	WT=0
(1) WRITE B					WT=100
(2)	WRITE A			WT=110	
(3) READ A					
(4)			WRITE B		WT=120
(5)	READ B				
(6)			WRITE A	WT=130	
(7)		READ A			

Fig. 11.21. Indefinite repetition of two conflicting transactions.

restarting. While, in principle, new transactions could arise forever to cause a given transaction to abort each time it is run, the fact that few transactions conflict makes the probability of having to restart a given transaction k times shrink like c^k, where c is some constant much less than one. Further, the random delay each time a transaction aborts guarantees that the probability that a cyclic behavior like Fig. 11.21 will go on for k cycles shrinks in the same fashion.

EXERCISES

11.1: In Fig. 11.22 we see a schedule of four transactions. Assume that write-locks imply reading, as in Section 11.3. Draw the precedence graph and determine whether the schedule is serializable.

11.2: Repeat Exercise 11.1 under the assumptions of Section 11.4, where a write-lock does not imply that the value is read.

* 11.3: In Fig. 11.23 are two transactions. In how many ways can they be scheduled legally? How many of these schedules are serializable?

11.4: Give an example of why the assumption of Section 11.2, that a unique function can be associated with each time that a transaction locks an item, is too strong. That is, give a schedule of transactions that Algorithm 11.1 says is not serializable, but that actually has the same effect as some serial schedule.

11.5: Prove that if a transaction on a tree of items does not obey the tree protocol, then there is some transaction (that, in fact, does obey the tree protocol) such that the two transactions have a legal schedule that is not serializable.

11.6: Suppose we are using an optimistic concurrency control algorithm. Reinterpret the operations of Fig. 11.22 as if RLOCK were a READ operation, WLOCK were WRITE, and the UNLOCK steps did not exist. Which, if any of the four transactions in Fig. 11.22 abort on the assumption that the

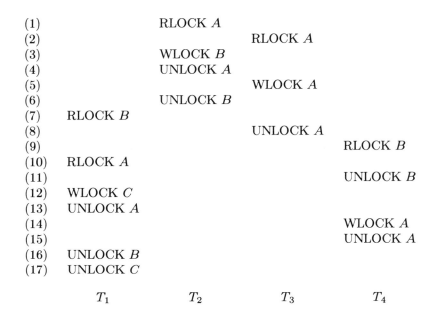

	T_1	T_2	T_3	T_4
(1)		RLOCK A		
(2)			RLOCK A	
(3)		WLOCK B		
(4)		UNLOCK A		
(5)			WLOCK A	
(6)		UNLOCK B		
(7)	RLOCK B			
(8)			UNLOCK A	
(9)				RLOCK B
(10)	RLOCK A			
(11)				UNLOCK B
(12)	WLOCK C			
(13)	UNLOCK A			
(14)				WLOCK A
(15)				UNLOCK A
(16)	UNLOCK B			
(17)	UNLOCK C			

Fig. 11.22. A schedule.

T_1	T_2
LOCK A	LOCK B
LOCK B	UNLOCK B
UNLOCK A	LOCK A
UNLOCK B	UNLOCK A

Fig. 11.23. Two schedules.

timestamps of T_1 through T_4 are respectively

a)   300, 310, 320, and 330.

b)   250, 200, 210, and 275.

In each case, what are the final read and write times of A, B, and C?

* 11.7: Suppose we have three transactions that obey the tree protocol on the hierarchy of Fig. 11.17 in Section 11.5. The first transaction locks A, B, C, and E; the second locks C and F; the third locks B and E. In how many ways can these transactions be scheduled legally?

** 11.8: A generalization of the warning protocol of Section 11.5 allows both read- and write-locks and warnings regarding these locks, with the obvious semantics. There are thus in principle sixteen "states" an item may be given by a transaction, corresponding to the sixteen subsets of two kinds of lock and two kinds of warning. However, some combinations are useless. For example, it is not necessary to place a read-warning and a write-warning on the same item, since a write-warning forbids any action that a read-warning does. In how many different states might a transaction wish to place an item? Give a table indicating which combinations of states can be placed on any item by two different transactions. For example, two transactions can each place a read-warning on an item, but one cannot place a read-lock when the other has a write-warning.

** 11.9: Suppose a set of items forms a directed, acyclic graph *(DAG)*. Show that the following protocol assures serializability.

    i)   The first lock can be on any node.

    ii)   Subsequently, a node n can be locked only if the transaction holds a lock on at least one predecessor of n, and the transaction has locked each predecessor of n at some time in the past.

* 11.10: Show that the following protocol is also safe for DAG's.

    i)   The first lock can be on any node.

    ii)   Subsequently, a transaction can lock a node only if it holds locks on a majority of its predecessors.

BIBLIOGRAPHIC NOTES

The concurrency model of Sections 11.2 and 11.3, the two phase protocol and its necessity for serializability are all from Eswaran et al. [1976]. The model of Section 11.4 (allowing write-only locks) and the polygraph-based serializability test are from Papadimitriou, Bernstein, and Rothnie [1977] and Papadimitriou [1978]. See also Lein and Weinberger [1978] concerning protocols with read- and write-locks and Soisalon-Soininen and Wood [1982] for efficiency of serializability tests.

    The tree protocol for hierarchically structured databases is from Silberschatz and Kedem [1980]. Kedem and Silberschatz [1980] generalize the algorithm to provide for read- and write-locks. Also, Kedem and Silberschatz [1979] explore the limits of what we call the "tree protocol" for use on collections of items structured in more general ways.

    Bayer and Schkolnick [1977], Ellis [1978], and Lehman and Yao [1981] develop algorithms for the special case of concurrent access to B-trees.

    The "warning protocol" is a simplification of ideas (sketched in Exercise 11.7) described in Gray, Putzolo, and Traiger [1976] and Gray [1978]. The latter article also discusses the two-phase commit policy and is a good survey of locking, concurrency, and crash recovery in general. Menasce, Popek, and Muntz [1978] is a careful analysis of a strategy for crash recovery, including what happens when a crash occurs during recovery. Hadzilacos [1982] discusses efficiency of rollback.

Kung and Papadimitriou [1979], Yannakakis, Papadimitriou, and Kung [1979], and Papadimitriou [1981, 1982] develop the theory of how the information one uses in scheduling transactions (e.g., structure like trees of items or assumptions about the effect of operations) influences the protocol one can use to assure serializability. The DAG protocol of Exercise 11.8 is from Yannakakis, Papadimitriou, and Kung [1979], and the protocol of Exercise 11.9 is from Kedem and Silberschatz [1979].

Gray, Lorie, and Putzolo [1975], and Reis and Stonebraker [1977, 1979] discuss the issue of "locking granularity," that is, how large individually lockable items should be.

Korth [1981] examines the different lock modes one can obtain by starting with basic locks, such as read and write, and building new lock modes by union, by warning (as in Section 11.5), and by allowing modes that represent updates of locks from a weak mode (e.g., read) to a more powerful mode (e.g., write).

Bernstein, Goodman, and Lai [1981] discuss how certain nonserializable behaviors can crop up because of subtle differences between real systems and the models we use to represent them, and they suggest certain fixups.

The complexity of *predicate locks*, where the set of items locked is defined by a condition to be satisfied (e.g., lock all tuples with attribute DEPT="Toy") is discussed by Hunt and Rosenkrantz [1979].

Coffman and Denning [1973] is a source for general material on concurrent systems.

12

DISTRIBUTED DATABASE SYSTEMS

Modern database systems are frequently *distributed*, meaning that the data is kept at widely dispersed locations. Several different computers control access to different parts of the data, and several computers are used to interface with users at different locations; these may or may not be the same machines that access the data itself. The various computers are connected by communications links, and it is normal for these links to be relatively low speed, compared with, say, the speed at which a file can be read off of a disk. The consequence of this assumption about communication is that the transfer of data between computers becomes a bottleneck, and most of the issues unique to distributed systems concern ways of dealing with this bottleneck.

In this chapter we shall deal with two general issues. First, there are some special optimization techniques that only become relevant when the database is distributed. The reason we must take a new look at optimization is that often the determinant of response time is not the amount of computation done, as was assumed in Chapter 8, but the amount of data communicated between computers. In the first section we discuss the notion of relation fragments, and we see how algebraic optimization is affected by having the database distributed. Next we consider the "semijoin" operation and see the opportunities it provides for speeding up response. In the third section we consider the System R* algorithm for optimizing distributed queries; it follows the style used in System R for nondistributed databases, by considering exhaustively all possible strategies for query evaluation that can be built from a fixed collection of options.

Finally, we take a look at the problems of concurrency control that present themselves because of distributed systems. For example, if we choose to lock items, we must do so system-wide; that is, each site must agree on what locks are held, and by what transaction. In a distributed database, two transactions at different sites can make much progress toward locking the same item before they discover each other's existence, whereupon one transaction is required to back up. In contrast, a concurrent system at a single site could treat the action of locking an item as an indivisible primitive; either the lock was granted or it wasn't.

Another problem inherent in distributed systems is that the connections between the various computers are limited, and sending a message, such as "lock item X for transaction T" from machine to machine will take substantial time just to set up a communication link, perhaps a few tenths of a second. In addition, a long message will take extra time for transmission.

12.1 FRAGMENTS OF RELATIONS

We shall begin by discussing the way relations can be broken into "fragments," which are then distributed to various places in the distributed database. We take the viewpoint that there are *logical* relations in the database that do not really exist, but that are composed of fragments, principally by the union and natural join operators. Queries and updates are made by the user on the logical relations. There are also *physical* relations that actually exist in the database, and these are fragments of the logical relations.

The purpose of this viewpoint is to adapt algebraic optimization techniques to two levels of operations, the expressions that relate queries to logical relations and the expressions that relate logical relations to physical ones. Before proceeding, we should fix upon the details of the model of a distributed environment that we use.

A Model of a Distributed Database

We shall assume that a distributed database consists of a number of *nodes*, each of which is a computer and a facility for storing data. In general, each node has both a *transaction server* to process queries and updates generated by a user, and a *file server* to handle data access. However, it is possible that one of these two functions is missing at any particular node, and often one computer will act as both the transaction and file server.

As in Chapter 11, we view the database as composed of "items," which are individually lockable pieces of data. We admit the possibility that some items are *duplicated*, in the sense that they appear at two or more nodes. The reason for doing so is that accesses to frequently read items may be sped up if the item is available at the same node that processed the read request. Further, the redundant storage of items makes it less likely that the item will be lost in a crash. The penalty we pay is that more messages must be sent to update or lock a duplicated item than an item that appears only once.

We assume that some or all pairs of nodes are connected by *links*, over which messages can be sent and data transmitted. Based on the technology of the early 1980's, the time to send even a short message between nodes is nontrivial, say 0.1 seconds, and the rate at which data can be transmitted across a link is not too great, perhaps around 10,000 bytes per second or less. The tenth of a second overhead to send a message represents the time for the two processors connected by a link to execute the protocol necessary for one to send a message, assured that the other will receive it and know what to do with it. The shipping rate for data is limited by the speed at which a processor can send or receive data, or the bandwidth of the link (rate at which data can be transmitted across the line) or both.

Fragments

To begin our study of query processing in the distributed environment, we must talk about the difference between the logical view of data that the user may have, and the way the data is actually stored in the database. The distinction between "logical" and "actual" data here is akin to the view/conceptual distinction introduced in Chapter 1, rather than the conceptual/physical distinction, even though we shall often refer to the actual data as "physical." We shall fix our attention, as we usually do, on the relational model. In a sense, the relationship between logical and physical relations that we cover here is a generalization of the correspondence between a single universal relation and the physical relations explored in Chapter 9.

Any relation may be composed of *fragments*. We consider two methods of composing relations.

1. A relation R may be the natural join of several fragments,

   $$R = R_1 \bowtie \cdots \bowtie R_n$$

   If we view R as a table, the R_i's represent certain columns of the table, so we call them *vertical fragments* of R.

2. A relation R may be the union of several fragments, $R = R_1 \cup \cdots \cup R_n$. Here, the table for R has been divided by rows, so we call the R_i's *horizontal fragments*. We do not necessarily assume that the R_i's are disjoint.

Each logical relation of the distributed database is assumed to be composed of fragments (there could be only one), and each fragment might exist at a different node. Alternatively, some fragments might themselves be logical relations, built from fragments, and so on.

Example 12.1: The bank database of Fig. 9.8 is a good candidate to be distributed, since it is natural that each branch would maintain the data that pertained to its own accounts and loans. The benefit in doing so is that customers banking at their usual branch could make transactions without necessarily communicating over a link, thereby saving time, even if only a fraction of a second, but more importantly, limiting the amount of traffic sent over the relatively low capacity links.

Suppose we have logical relations

ACCOUNTS(Br, Ac, Ba)
LOANS(Br, L, Am)
HOLDS(Ac, C)
OWES(L, C)
CUSTOMERS(C, Ad)

We shall assume that the ACCOUNTS and LOANS relations are broken into horizontal fragments, one for each branch, and that in particular, a tuple t with $t[Br] = b$, i.e., an account at branch b, is stored in fragment ACCOUNTS$_b$, which is located in the node at branch b. Similarly, the LOANS relation is composed of horizontal fragments LOANS$_b$ for each branch b, with loans by branch b physically located at b.

The HOLDS and OWES relations are similarly fragmented horizontally into relations HOLDS$_b$ and OWES$_b$ for the accounts and loans made by each branch. The CUSTOMERS relation might well be horizontally fragmented as well, perhaps with the tuple for a customer duplicated if he had accounts or loans at more than one branch, so that address data would be available at any branch likely to need it. However, for the sake of an example, we shall assume that the CUSTOMERS relation is not fragmented at all, but is kept as a physical relation at the main branch.

In the above, it appears that all fragments are horizontal. However, if, for example, we were using a universal relation system, then there would be only one logical relation, the universal one, and the five relations mentioned above would be vertical fragments of the universal relation, in the sense that the universal relation would be taken as the natural join of these five.

Actually, it is not necessary to go to a universal relation to find a use for vertical decomposition. Any time we wish to have a view that is the join of two or more physical relations, we have a vertical decomposition. For example, we might like a view that was the join of HOLDS and CUSTOMERS, with relation scheme $AcCAd$, so addresses would appear with accounts as if in one relation. Then HOLDS and CUSTOMERS would be vertical fragments of this view. These vertical fragments would be distributed over several nodes, since we have assumed that CUSTOMERS is kept at the main branch, while HOLDS is itself distributed among all the branches. Example 12.2 will give another motivation for vertical fragmention; such fragmentation helps when we try to optimize certain queries. $\Box$

Queries Involving Fragments

Let us assume that the user "sees" the logical relations, and he performs queries on the logical relations only. We shall begin from the point we were at in Section 8.2, where we had an algebraic expression representing a query, and we wished to use algebraic manipulation to convert the query into one that could be executed faster. Here, a query is expressed in terms of the logical relations, and the logical relations are expressed in teerms of their fragments, using the operations of union and natural join.

In this manner, we construct an expression whose operands are the physical relations. We can apply the transformations of Section 8.2, chiefly the pushing of selections as far down the expression tree as possible. The order and exact method of implementing the operators of the transformed tree still require careful consideration, and we shall examine the issues in the next two sections.

However, often we can perform a considerable amount of algebraic simplification at this stage. A key observation is that associated with a horizontal fragment is often a *guard* condition that must be satisfied by every tuple in the fragment. For example, the fragment ACCOUNT$_b$ in the banking database of Example 12.1 will have the guard $Br = b$. That is, we know the value of the branch in the fragment at b is b itself. We shall henceforth assume that each logical and physical relation has a guard; it could be the always true condition, which is tantamount to no guard at all.

In general, if a fragment R has guard g, then we can replace any use of R in an expression by $\sigma_g(R)$ without changing the result of the expression. When we pass other selections down the tree, we may find that a selection applied to R conflicts with g. If so, we can eliminate R from the expression entirely.

Example 12.2: We shall reconsider the banking database from Example 12.1. Suppose that there are three branches, which we shall simply designate 1, 2, and 3. The query of concern is to print all the customers who hold an account at branch 1 with a balance greater than \$1,000.

Interestingly, if we use the fragmentation scheme described in Example 12.1, we shall not do very well, because we shall not be able to express the fact that the fragments of HOLDS at branches 2 and 3 contain no tuples for accounts at branch 1. This is because Br is not an attribute of HOLDS, and we therefore cannot express the desired condition with a guard condition. Thus, we might wish to redesign the fragmentation scheme to enable this condition to be expressed.

In our new design, we shall use a logical relation R with scheme $BrAcBaC$. This relation is fragmented horizontally into R_1, R_2, and R_3, with the tuples in R_i having value i in the Br component. Further, each R_i is fragmented vertically into A_i, with relation scheme $BrAcBa$ and H_i with scheme AcC. We may clearly put the guard $Br = i$ on R_i. Thus, in place of R_1 we use $\sigma_{Br=1}(R_1)$, and so on. In terms of physical fragments, we use $\sigma_{Br=1}(A_1 \bowtie H_1)$ for R_1, and of course, we use $R_1 \cup R_2 \cup R_3$ for R in the query $\sigma_{Br=1 \wedge Ba>1000}(R)$. The expression tree for this query in terms of the physical fragments is shown in Fig. 12.1.

The upper selection, $\sigma_{Br=1}$, can be pushed down past the union in Fig. 12.1. As selections should be, it is pushed down every subtree to which it

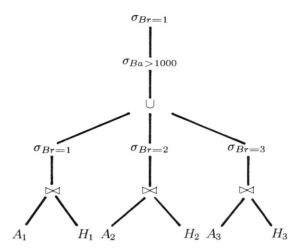

Fig. 12.1. Initial algebraic expression.

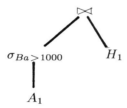

Fig. 12.2. Final expression.

applies. The attribute Br is, naturally, present in all three terms of the union, so the selection is pushed down to each child of the union node in Fig. 12.1. On meeting $\sigma_{Br=2}$ and $\sigma_{Br=3}$ in the second and third subtrees, it combines to get a vacuous condition like $\sigma_{Br=1 \wedge Br=2}$.† We can therefore excise the second and third subtrees, whereupon the union has only one term and can be eliminated.

When we pass the top selection down to the first subtree, it combines with an identical selection to form one instance of the selection $\sigma_{Br=1}$. Since the latter condition is the guard for $A_1 \bowtie H_1$, it is optional, and we can choose to delete it after it has interacted with all other selections. We shall therefore assume that the selection $\sigma_{Br=1}$ is no longer present. The selection $\sigma_{Ba>1000}$ is pushed down to the relation A_1 only, since Ba is not an attribute of H_1. The final tree is shown in Fig. 12.2.

---

† Testing for conditions that are never true is hardly trivial in general. However, in practice, noticing terms of the form $X = a \wedge X = b$, where $a \neq b$, or more generally, $X\ \theta_1\ a \wedge X\ \theta_2\ b$, where both conditions cannot be true simultaneously, is probably sufficient.

In general, we still must consider the order of operations, the use of indices, and many other optimization issues on trees like Fig. 12.2. In this case, however, all the physical relations that remain are at one node, that of branch 1, and the optimization may proceed as in Chapter 8. □

Updates to Logical Relations

Let us now briefly consider how updates to logical relations are performed. To insert a tuple t into logical relation R, we must insert into some fragments of R. We shall define the algorithm recursively, so the insertion of t results in insertions into one or more fragments of R. If these fragments are physical relations, the meaning of insertion is obvious. If they are logical relations, apply the insertion algorithm recursively.

If $R = R_1 \bowtie \cdots \bowtie R_n$, then insert $t[R_i]$ into R_i for each i. If

$$R = R_1 \cup \cdots \cup R_n$$

find one i such that the guard for R_i is satisfied by t, and insert t into R_i. If no such i exists, the insertion is impossible. If we have a choice of i's, we would prefer to insert into a local fragment, that is, one at the same node as the insertion request, to save time sending messages.

Deletion of tuple t from R presents more of a problem. If R is composed of horizontal fragments, then we simply delete t from each of those fragments in which it is present. However, if R is fragmented vertically, we do not know what to do. The problem is essentially that of defining deletions from universal relations in a "correct" way. If we simply delete $t[R_i]$ from R_i for each i, we shall accidently delete from R all tuples s such that $s[R_i] = t[R_i]$ for some i.

A solution used in System R*, which serves the purpose, although it may not be the most efficient solution possible, is to create for each tuple inserted into logical relation R a unique *tuple identifier*. In effect, the relation scheme for R is given another attribute TID that functionally determines all the other attributes. Furthermore, every vertical fragment of R must include TID in its scheme. Thus, when inserting a tuple t into R, the system invents a tuple identifier value for t, and inserts the projections of t with the TID value included, into all the fragments of R.

Now suppose we wish to delete a tuple t from R. We find for each R_i the set S_i of tuples $ab_1 b_2 \cdots b_k$ in R_i, such that a is a TID component, and $b_1, \ldots, b_k$, which are values for the components other than TID, form the projection of t onto R_i. Having obtained the set S_i for each R_i, we take the natural join $S_1 \bowtie \cdots \bowtie S_n$. The result will be zero or more tuples of the form at, where a is a tuple identifier, and t is the tuple we are trying to delete. We now know the tuple identifier or identifiers (if t appeared more than once in R) for t, and we can delete $at[R_i]$ from R_i for each such a and $1 \leq i \leq n$.

12.2 OPTIMIZING TRANSMISSION COST BY SEMIJOINS

We now introduce a surprising way to take joins of relations R and S that are located at different nodes. We assume that we are taking a natural join, throughout this section. However, by imagining that attributes are renamed appropriately, all the methods we discuss apply to arbitrary equijoins. The obvious ways to join are to ship a copy of R to the node of S or to ship a copy of S to the node of R. The cost of doing so is equal to the cost of initiating a message, plus the cost of shipping one of the relations. We shall assume for simplicity that all tuples take the same amount of time to ship, and we shall measure time in units of the time to ship one tuple. Thus, the time to ship a relation equals the size of the relation. Let us use c_0 as the cost of initiating a message in these time units, and suppose that R and S are of sizes r and s, respectively. Then the cost of taking the join in the better of the two obvious ways is $c_0 + min(r, s)$. This formula excludes a term to get the result to a particular node where it is needed, but let us also suppose for simplicity that the result may be computed at any node.

There is another way to save transmission cost, which involves an operation called semijoin. The *semijoin* of relations R and S, written $R \ltimes S$, is $\pi_R(R \bowtie S)$. Note that we are, as usual, taking the name of a relation and its relation scheme to be identical. Also observe that the semijoin is not a symmetric operation. We use $R \rtimes S$ for $\pi_S(R \bowtie S)$, or equivalently, $S \ltimes R$.

Perhaps a better way to view the semijoin $R \ltimes S$ is that we project S onto the set of attributes $R \cap S$ and then delete from R all tuples t such that $t[R \cap S]$ is not in this projection. That is, we remove from R all tuples that are dangling in the sense that they produce no tuples in the join $R \bowtie S$.

The way we take semijoins in a distributed environment reflects the second meaning of this operation. We project S onto $R \cap S$ and ship the projection to the node of R. At the latter node, we perform what is technically a natural join $R \bowtie \pi_{R \cap S}(S)$, to delete the tuples that dangle in R. Suppose that the projections of R and S onto $R \cap S$ have sizes r' and s', respectively. Also suppose that $R \ltimes S$ and $S \ltimes R$ have sizes r'' and s'', respectively. Then we could compute $R \bowtie S$ by the following steps.

1. Ship $\pi_{R \cap S}(S)$ to the node of R.
2. Compute $R \ltimes S$ at the node of R.
3. Ship $R \ltimes S$ to the node of S.
4. Compute $(R \ltimes S) \bowtie S$ at the node of S.

There is a symmetric strategy, where the roles of R and S are reversed above.

Step (1) takes $c_0 + s'$ and step (3) takes $c_0 + r''$, for a total of $2c_0 + s' + r''$. Thus, this strategy or the symmetric strategy will have a lower transmission cost than the straightforward [cost $c_0 + min(r, s)$] way of joining if

$$c_0 + min(s' + r'', r' + s'') < min(r, s)$$

We can be sure that s' and s'' are less than s, and similarly for the r's. Often they are considerably less, and the semijoin method would be preferable, especially if c_0 is small and we are concerned primarily with minimizing transmission cost, rather than minimizing computation at the nodes.

Before proceeding, we should prove that the above steps really compute $R \bowtie S$.

Theorem 12.1: $(R \ltimes S) \bowtie S = R \bowtie S$.

Proof: Since $R \ltimes S = \pi_R(R \bowtie S)$, it follows that $R \ltimes S \subseteq R$. Thus $(R \ltimes S) \bowtie S \subseteq R \bowtie S$. Conversely, suppose t is a tuple in $R \bowtie S$. Then $u = t[R]$ must be in R, and $v = t[S]$ must be in S. It follows that u is in $R \ltimes S$, so t is in $(R \ltimes S) \bowtie S$. Thus $R \bowtie S \subseteq (R \ltimes S) \bowtie S$, proving the theorem. $\square$

Example 12.3: Let $R(A, B) = \{\, 01, 23, 45 \,\}$ and $S(B, C) = \{\, 16, 78 \,\}$. Then $R \ltimes S = \{\, ab \mid ab \text{ is in } R \text{ and } b \text{ is in } \pi_B(S) \,\}$. Since $\pi_B(S) = \{\, 1, 7 \,\}$, ab can only be 01, so $R \ltimes S = \{\, 01 \,\}$. Then $(R \ltimes S) \bowtie S = \{\, 016 \,\} = R \bowtie S$. $\square$

Semijoin Programs

When we must take the join of more than two relations in a distributed database, the number of ways we can take semijoins grows rapidly. In general, there may be some benefit to taking a large number of semijoins, the end result of which is that one or more of the relations have been made as small as possible. It is not hard to see that if we have relations $R_1, \ldots, R_n$, whose natural join we wish to take, then the smallest relation that R_i can become by the use of semijoins is $\pi_{R_i}(R_1 \bowtie \cdots \bowtie R_n)$. We call this relation the *reduction* of R_i (with respect to $R_1, \ldots, R_n$).

Often, all we want in our query is the reduction of one R_i. This is true for the familiar sort of query where we fix a value for one attribute and ask for the associated values of another attribute.

Example 12.4: Let us suppose that the objects of the HVFC database, as portrayed in Fig. 9.1, represent relations, and that we are given the query

>   retrieve (D)
>   where $M = $ "Robin"

That is, print the addresses of the suppliers that supply some item that Robin ordered. We answer this query by taking the join of $R_1 = \sigma_{M=\text{"Robin"}}(MO)$, OI, SIP, and SD. Since we shall project that join onto D, it surely suffices to project it first onto SD by computing the reduction of SD with respect to those four relations.

For example, we might compute $R_2 = OI \ltimes R_1$, then $R_3 = SIP \ltimes R_2$, and finally $R_4 = SD \ltimes R_3$. However, there are other ways too. We might even find it advantageous to reduce R_1 to cut down on the amount of data shipped from it to OI, and so on.† For example, we could compute $R_5 = SIP \bowtie SD$, then $R_6 = OI \bowtie R_5$, $R_7 = R_1 \bowtie R_6$, $R_8 = R_6 \bowtie R_7$, $R_9 = R_5 \bowtie R_8$, and finally compute $SD \bowtie R_9$. □

Each sequence of steps of the form $R := R \bowtie S$, where R and S are given relations, is called a *semijoin program*. Although we invented temporary names in Example 12.4 to hold the new values as we computed them, we can view each step in that example as computing a new value for an existing relation. Thus, the first sequence in Example 12.4 is expressed by the semijoin program

$$OI := OI \bowtie R_1$$
$$SIP := SIP \bowtie OI$$
$$SD := SD \bowtie SIP$$

Of course, we would not actually change the values of existing relations when computing semijoins; rather, temporaries would be used to hold the computed values.

The above program reduces SD, independent of the actual values of the relations R_1, OI, SIP, and SD. Unfortunately, not every set of relations has a semijoin program that reduces one of the relations independent of the current values of the relations, as the next example shows.

Example 12.5: Let our relations be AB, BC, and AC, and for some n, suppose the current values of these relations are $AB = \{ a_1b_1, a_2b_2, \ldots, a_nb_n \}$, $BC = \{ b_1c_1, b_2c_2, \ldots, b_nc_n \}$, and $AC = \{ a_2c_1, a_3c_2, \ldots, a_{n+1}c_n \}$. A moment's reflection tells us that the join of these three relations is empty. However, it is also easy to show by induction on i, that after i steps of any semijoin program, no tuple will be deleted from any of the three relations unless it has a value with subscript i or less, or a subscript $n - i + 1$ or more. For example, a_3c_2 could not be deleted until the second step. In fact, it takes six steps to delete that tuple from AC; the shortest such program is $AB := AB \bowtie AC$; $BC := BC \bowtie AB$; $AC := AC \bowtie BC$; $AB := AB \bowtie AC$; $BC := BC \bowtie AB$; $AC := AC \bowtie BC$.

The conclusion we draw is that no one semijoin program can reduce one of the relations AB, BC, and AC independently of their values. In proof, any such program would have some number of steps, say k. Then letting $n = 2k+2$ above, we conclude that after k steps, the tuple $a_{k+1}b_{k+1}$ remains in AB, so the program did not reduce AB. Similarly, the tuples $b_{k+1}c_{k+1}$ and $a_{k+2}c_{k+1}$ say the same things about BC and AC. □

We recall from Section 9.3 our discussion of cyclic and acyclic hypergraphs. It turns out that acyclicity has something to do with the question of whether a semijoin program to reduce a relation exists. We may view any natural join as a hypergraph, where the nodes are attributes and the edges are the relation

---

† In this case, it is very unlikely to be helpful, because R_1, being the result of a selection, is probably very small, and performing semijoins to reduce it is going to be a waste of time.

schemes in the join.

Theorem 12.2: If a join expression has an acyclic hypergraph, then there is a semijoin program to reduce any relation in the join. Conversely, if the hypergraph is cyclic, then there is at least one relation for which no semijoin program is guaranteed to compute its reduction.

Proof: The converse portion, showing that cyclic hypergraphs do not have semijoin programs reducing each of the relations, is left as a rather difficult exercise generalizing Example 12.5. However, the first part of the theorem can be proved by giving the following algorithm for constructing a semijoin program that computes the reduction of a particular relation R.

The algorithm is defined inductively, starting with joins of a single relation R, for which the empty program suffices, and proceeding to progressively larger sets of relations that have an acyclic hypergraph. Suppose we have an acyclic hypergraph of more than one edge. Then by definition, it has an ear, say edge S. Assume at first that $S \neq R$. As S is an ear, there must be some edge T such that each node in S is either unique to S or is in T. Let us start our semijoin program with the step $T := T \ltimes S$.

By induction, the remaining hypergraph, which must also be acyclic, yields a semijoin program to compute $\pi_R(R_1 \bowtie \cdots \bowtie R_k)$, where $R_1, \ldots, R_k$ are the edges of the remaining hypergraph. Suppose without loss of generality that $T = R_1$. If we precede the constructed program with $R_1 := R_1 \ltimes S$, the resulting program computes $\pi_R((R_1 \ltimes S) \bowtie R_2 \bowtie \cdots \bowtie R_k)$. As S has no attribute in common with any of the R_i's that it does not have in common with $T = R_1$, the above expression is equal to $\pi_R(S \bowtie R_1 \bowtie \cdots \bowtie R_k)$, proving that the constructed semijoin program reduces R.

We now have only to consider the case where $S = R$. In this situation, we inductively construct a semijoin program to reduce T in the remaining hypergraph, and we follow it by the step $R := R \ltimes T$. The resulting program computes $R \ltimes (\pi_T(R_1 \bowtie \cdots \bowtie R_k))$ which, since R has no attribute in common with the R_i's that it does not share with T, is the reduction of R. $\square$

Example 12.6: Figure 9.1 is an acyclic hypergraph as we have often remarked. Suppose we want a semijoin program to reduce OI. We might pick ear BM first, and might begin the program with $MA := MA \ltimes BM$, since MA includes all the nonunique attributes of BM. With the remaining graph, we might then pick ear MA, and add the step $MO := MO \ltimes MA$. Then we might eliminate the ear MO of the remaining graph with the step $OI := OI \ltimes MO$.

We might next pick ear OI. Since this is the target relation, we do not proceed as usual, but rather construct a sequence to reduce the edge SIP in the hypergraph consisting of the two edges SIP and SD. This program is just $SIP := SIP \ltimes SD$. We follow that one-step program by the step $OI := OI \ltimes SIP$ to complete the program, which is

$$MA := MA \bowtie BM$$
$$MO := MO \bowtie MA$$
$$OI := OI \bowtie MO$$
$$SIP := SIP \bowtie SD$$
$$OI := OI \bowtie SIP$$

The above program is only one of many that compute the reduction of OI. $\square$

Chain Queries

Even though we now know how to find a reduction program for any relation in a join of relations whose hypergraph is acyclic, we have not dealt with the question of which, among the various programs, is most efficient. There are two reasons that the selection of a best program is difficult. First, we cannot know in advance how many "dangling" tuples are going to be eliminated by any one step of a semijoin program. This problem cannot be solved, but we can deal with it by making a reasonable model of how the size of a relation shrinks as it is subjected to semijoins.

The second problem is the combinatorial explosion that takes place in the number of possible semijoin programs on n relations, when n gets large. It is important to remember that the number of distinctly different programs is large; it is not the case that "different" programs simply compute the same values in a different order. The reader should review Example 12.4, where we pointed out the possibility that we could even save in the reduction of a relation R by taking the semijoin of R with one of the other relations to reduce the size of the projections being passed around, eventually returning to the site of R itself.

There is, for the case of a general acyclic hypergraph, no better approach known than the strategy of trying all possibilities. However, there is an important special case, typified by Example 12.4, where the hypergraph is a "chain," that is, the edges can be listed in an order $R_1, \ldots, R_n$ such that the only nonempty intersections are between R_i and R_{i+1} for $1 \le i < n$. Further, the relation we wish to reduce is at one end; we may take it to be R_1. Let us call such a reduction a *chain query*.

Our first instinct is that the most efficient way to compute a chain query is to take semijoins from the right end, $R_{n-1} := R_{n-1} \bowtie R_n$; $R_{n-2} := R_{n-2} \bowtie R_n$; $\cdots$; $R_1 := R_1 \bowtie R_2$. That is not always the case, as we shall show by example. To deal with the question of what sequence is best in an given situation, we need to assume the knowledge of some numbers and make a hypothesis about the way relation sizes change when we take semijoins.

We shall assume that for each i, a_i is the size of the projection of R_i onto $R_{i-1} \cap R_i$, that is, the size of the set that would be shipped to the site of R_{i-1} to compute $R_{i-1} \bowtie R_i$. a_1 is not defined. Similarly, b_i is the size of the projection of R_i onto $R_i \cap R_{i+1}$; b_n is not defined. To model the way that the sizes of these projections shrink when semijoins are taken, we shall assume there is a constant d such that when we take the semijoin of R_i with the join of k other relations, the sizes of the projections of R_i become $a_i d^k$ and $b_i d^k$.

Let us define $R_i^{\ell r}$ to be $\pi_{R_i}(R_\ell \bowtie R_{\ell+1} \bowtie \cdots \bowtie R_r)$. That is, $R_i^{\ell r}$ is the semijoin of R_i and the join of all the relations from R_ℓ through R_r. We shall require henceforth that $\ell \leq i \leq r$ in $R_i^{\ell r}$. Note that R_1^{1n} is the value we are asked to compute by the chain query on relations $R_1, \ldots, R_n$. The following lemma says, in essence, that in order for some R_j in a chain query to have been used in reducing some other R_i, we must also have used all R_k's between R_i and R_j in reducing R_i.

Lemma 12.1: If no step of a semijoin program takes the semijoin of relations with disjoint relation schemes, and the program computes a chain query on $R_1, \ldots, R_n$, then each step of the program computes a value $R_i^{\ell r}$ for some i, ℓ, and r.

Proof: The proof is an induction on the number of steps. Each step must take the semijoin of two adjacent relations in the chain, that is, $R_i \ltimes R_{i+1}$ or $R_i \rtimes R_{i+1}$. For the basis, zero steps, the value of each relation R_i is R_i^{ii}.

For the induction, suppose the step is $R_i := R_i \ltimes R_{i+1}$; the symmetric case is similar, of course. The value of R_i before the step is R_i^{jk} for some j and k, and for R_{i+1} the value is expressed as R_{i+1}^{pq}. It is a simple algebraic exercise to check that $R_i^{jk} \ltimes R_{i+1}^{pq} = R_i^{st}$, where $s = min(j, p)$ and $t = max(k, q)$. $\square$

Next we need a lemma that tells us, given our assumptions about the cost of doing a semijoin, all the possibly optimal ways we could compute $R_i^{\ell r}$.

Lemma 12.2: Suppose that for parameters c_0, d, $a_2, \ldots, a_n$, and $b_1, \ldots, b_{n-1}$ as defined above, the cost of taking the semijoin $R_{i-1} \ltimes R_i^{\ell r}$ is $c_0 + a_i d^{r-\ell}$, and the cost of computing $R_i^{\ell r} \rtimes R_{i+1}$ is $c_0 + b_i d^{r-\ell}$. Then in any least-cost semijoin program to compute the chain query on $R_1, \ldots, R_n$, each $R_i^{\ell r}$ that is computed at all, is computed in one of the following ways.

1. Compute the value R_i^{ik} by the step $R_i := R_i \ltimes R_{i+1}$, where R_{i+1} has the current value $R_{i+1}^{i+1,k}$.

2. Compute the value R_i^{ji} by the step $R_i := R_i \ltimes R_{i-1}$, where R_{i-1} has the current value $R_{i-1}^{j,i-1}$.

3. Compute the value of R_i^{jk} by the steps $R_i := R_i \ltimes R_{i-1}$ and $R_i := R_i \ltimes R_{i+1}$, in some order, where at the time these steps are executed, the values of R_{i-1} and R_{i+1} are, respectively, $R_{i-1}^{j,i-1}$ and $R_{i+1}^{i+1,k}$.

4. Compute the value of R_i^{jk} by the step $R_i := R_i \ltimes R_{i-1}$, where the value of R_{i-1} is R_{i-1}^{jk}.

5. Compute the value of R_i^{jk} by the step $R_i := R_i \ltimes R_{i+1}$, where the value

of R_{i+1} is R_{i+1}^{jk}.

Proof: The proof is lengthy and is omitted; see Chiu, Bernstein, and Ho [1981].
$\square$

We can use the above two lemmas to justify that the following algorithm correctly finds a least cost semijoin program for a chain query.

Algorithm 12.1: Optimal Semijoin Program for a Chain Query.

Input: A chain query $\pi_{R_1}(R_1 \bowtie \cdots \bowtie R_n)$.

Output: A semijoin program computing the chain query.

Method: Let c_i^{jk} be the cost of the optimal semijoin program computing R_i^{jk}. Define the *ℓr-family* to be the set of values $\{ R_\ell^{\ell r}, R_{\ell+1}^{\ell r}, \ldots, R_r^{\ell r} \}$. We shall compute $c_i^{\ell r}$ for each member of the ℓr-family together, and we consider families in order of the difference $r - \ell$, so the cost of the ℓr-family is computed after the cost of the jk-family if $k - j < r - \ell$. The rules we use are

a) $c_i^{ii} = 0$ for any i.

b) $c_i^{ik} = min(c_0 + a_{i+1}d^{k-i-1}c_{i+1}^{i+1,k},$
    $\quad c_0 + a_{i+1}d^{k-i}c_{i+1}^{ik})$, for $k > i$.

c) $c_i^{ji} = min(c_0 + b_{i-1}d^{i-j-1}c_{i-1}^{j,i-1},$
    $\quad c_0 + b_{i-1}d^{i-j}c_{i-1}^{ji})$, for $j < i$.

d) $c_i^{jk} = min(c_0 + b_{i-1}d^{k-j}c_{i-1}^{jk},$
    $\quad c_0 + a_{i+1}d^{k-j}c_{i+1}^{jk},$
    $\quad 2c_0 + b_{i-1}d^{i-j-1}c_{i-1}^{j,i-1} + a_{i+1}d^{k-i-1}c_{i+1}^{i+1,k})$, for $j < i < k$.

For example, the three terms in (d) come from cases (4), (5), and (3) of Lemma 12.2, respectively.

It will be observed that when $r > \ell$, the costs for the ℓr-family are defined by the above rules in terms of themselves and the costs of members of previously computed families. It might seem that we have to solve simultaneous equations involving the min operation, which is certainly puzzling. However, observe that each of rules (b), (c), and (d) have one term of the min that involves only previously computed families; these terms come from (1)–(3) in Lemma 12.2.

To compute the costs for the jk-family, let us first choose that term, among those we can evaluate directly for any of the members of the jk-family, that has the smallest value. Say this term yields a value c for c_i^{jk}. Then it is not possible that a less expensive method for computing R_i^{jk} exists. Suppose there were. Then some other member of the jk-family, say R_p^{jk}, would be the first member of that family computed as a subexpression of the computation of R_i^{jk}. But computing R_p^{jk} without the benefit of any other member of the jk-family requires at least c, so no way to compute R_i^{jk} with cost less than c exists.

Having fixed a value for c_i^{jk}, we can find another member of the jk-family that now has the least term among those terms that can be evaluated. We fix its value, and repeat the process until all costs in the jk-family are computed;

then we consider the next family. As this process proceeds, we not only know the cost of computing each R_i^{jk}, but the steps needed to do so, since we select for each R_i^{jk} one of the terms of the appropriate min, and each term comes from a particular semijoin step or steps according to Lemma 12.2.

We finally compute c_1^{1n} and thereby discover a semijoin program that computes R_1^{1n} and has this cost. That program is the output of the algorithm. □

Example 12.7: Suppose we have relations $R_1(A, B)$, $R_2(B, C)$, and $R_3(C, D)$, and we wish to compute R_1^{13}. Let us take $c_0 = 10$, $d = 0.8$, $b_1 = 10$, $a_2 = 50$, $b_2 = 20$, and $a_3 = 1000$.

We shall compute the 12-family first. We have

$$c_1^{12} = min(10 + 50 + c_2^{22},\ 10 + 40 + c_2^{12})$$
$$c_2^{12} = min(10 + 10 + c_1^{11},\ 10 + 8 + c_1^{12})$$

For example, the two 10's in the formula for c_1^{12} represent c_0; the 50 corresponds to a_2, and 40 is $a_2 d$. Since $c_1^{11} = c_2^{22} = 0$, we know the first term of each of the above min's; they are 60 and 20, respectively. The smaller of these must be used, so we know $c_2^{12} = 20$. Then we can evaluate the terms of the first min; we are comparing $10+50$ with $10+40+20$, and prefer the first, telling us that $c_1^{12} = 60$.

Now, let us consider the 23-family. the equations we obtain are

$$c_2^{23} = min(10 + 1000 + c_3^{33},\ 10 + 800 + c_3^{23})$$
$$c_3^{23} = min(10 + 20 + c_2^{22},\ 10 + 16 + c_2^{23})$$

Here we first discover $c_3^{23} = 30$, then use that to compute $c_2^{23} = 840$.

Last, we compute the 13-family, using the equations

$$c_1^{13} = min(10 + 40 + c_2^{23},\ 10 + 32 + c_2^{13})$$
$$c_2^{13} = min(10 + 6.4 + c_1^{13},\ 10 + 640 + c_3^{13},\ 10 + 10 + 10 + 1000 + c_1^{11} + c_3^{33})$$
$$c_3^{13} = min(10 + 16 + c_2^{12},\ 10 + 12.8 + c_2^{23})$$

In this case, we know $c_1^{11} = c_3^{33} = 0$, $c_2^{23} = 840$, and $c_2^{12} = 20$. The smallest evaluatable term is the first term for c_3^{13}, which has the value 46. Then the next smallest term we can evaluate is the middle term of c_2^{13}, which now evaluates to $10+640+46=696$. Finally, we can evaluate $c_1^{13} = 738$, using the second term of the formula for that cost. The latter cost is the one we are after, and we can now construct the desired semijoin program by seeing how it was derived.

We computed c_1^{13} by using c_2^{13}, so the last step of the program will be $R_1 := R_1 \ltimes R_2$. In turn, we computed c_2^{13} using c_3^{13}, so the next to last step is $R_2 := R_2 \ltimes R_3$. c_3^{13} was computed from c_2^{12}, which was computed directly, i.e., it represents the semijoin step $R_2 := R_2 \ltimes R_1$. Thus, the complete program is

$$R_2 := R_2 \bowtie R_1$$
$$R_3 := R_3 \bowtie R_2$$
$$R_2 := R_2 \bowtie R_3$$
$$R_1 := R_1 \bowtie R_2$$

Notice how the most efficient way to reduce R_1 turns out to be to reduce R_3 first, since it is apparently so much larger (because a_3 is so large), and then to reduce R_1 by propagating the reduced R_3's projection towards R_1. $\square$

12.3 THE SYSTEM R* OPTIMIZATION ALGORITHM

System R* is the experimental extension of System R to the distributed environment. Like its parent, it performs optimization in an exhaustive way, confident that the cost of considering many strategies will pay off in lower execution costs for queries, especially for queries that are compiled and used many times.

The optimization algorithm applies to an algebraic query of the kind discussed in Section 12.1, where the expression to be optimized represents the query applied to logical relations, which in turn are expressed in terms of physical relations. The operators assumed to appear in the query are the usual select, project, join, and union, plus a new operator *CHOICE*, which represents the ability of the system to choose any of the identical, replicated copies of a given relation. That is, if relations R_1, R_2 and R_3 are copies of one relation, at different nodes, and S_1 and S_2 are also copies of another relation, then we might express the join of these two relations as

$$CHOICE(R_1, R_2, R_3) \bowtie CHOICE(S_1, S_2)$$

We could, for example, save transmission cost by picking copies of R and S that were at the same node and joining them there.

One modification we shall make to expression trees is to combine nodes having the same associative and commutative binary operator into a single node, provided the nodes being combined form a tree, with no intervening nodes labeled by other operators. The three binary operators, union, join, and choice, are all associative and commutative, so this rule applies to each of them. A tree of nodes labeled by just one of these binary operators we shall call a *cluster*. All the nodes of a cluster will be replaced by a single node, and the children of the nodes in the cluster become children of the new node. The parent of the new node is the parent of the node in the cluster that is an ancestor of all the nodes in the cluster. The result of these operations we call a *compacted* tree.

Example 12.8: The expression tree in Fig. 12.3(a) is replaced by the tree in Fig. 12.3(b). We have combined the two nodes labeled $\cup$, since they form a cluster, and the three nodes labeled $\bowtie$ also happen to be arranged in a tree; thus they are a cluster and are replaced by a single node. $\square$

Let us now enumerate the strategies for evaluation that System R* con-

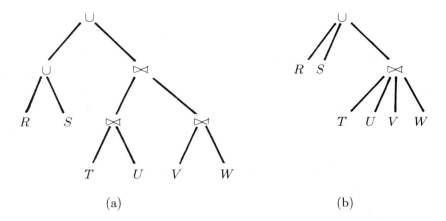

(a)   (b)

Fig. 12.3. Replacement of clusters by single nodes.

siders. We shall assume that each relation is at a single site. If a relation is replicated, then we shall give the replicas different names, and apply the $CHOICE$ operator to the collection of replicas. We assume also that the query asks for a specific expression to be computed at a specific site of the network. The expression is represented as a compacted tree. The algorithm to follow considers all ways to evaluate the nodes of the compacted tree, taking into account

1. the various orders in which an operator like union or join of many relations can be performed as a sequence of binary steps,
2. the various sites at which each node of the tree could have its result computed, and
3. several different ways that the join could be computed.

The Cost Function

When the algorithm considers each of the options listed above, it must evaluate the cost of these methods. The actual cost function used in System R* is quite complex; it takes account of the computation cost at a site as well as the transmission cost. We have had the flavor of the sort of analysis that is used at a single site in Section 8.3, so we shall, for simplicity, take a less detailed cost function that accounts only for the transmission cost. That is, as in the previous section, we shall assume that the cost of sending a message is, in appropriate units, equal to the number of tuples sent, plus a constant c_0.

Join Methods

The options for taking a union of two relations are fairly clear. We can ship one relation to the site of the other, or ship them both to a third site. The costs of these three approaches are obvious, given the cost function above. The options given a $CHOICE$ operator are also clear; the cost is zero for any site at which one of the relations in the choice resides, and otherwise the cost equals the cost of shipping one of the replicas to the desired site. Which replica is shipped doesn't matter, since the cost is the same under our model.

However, with the join of two relations R and S, the scope of options is not so well defined. The algorithm to be described has five options, and two others that can be used when R and S are both at the same site. These options are the following.

1. Ship R to the site of S and compute the join there. The cost is c_0 plus the size of R.
2. Ship S to the site of R and compute the join there. The cost is c_0 plus the size of S.
3. Ship R and S to a third site and compute the join there. The cost is $2c_0$ plus the sum of the sizes of R and S.
4. Run through the tuples of R. For each such tuple t, obtain the matching tuples of S, that is, those tuples u such that $t[R \cap S] = u[R \cap S]$. Ship these tuples to the site of R. The cost of this method equals $T_R(c_0 + T_S/I)$, where T_R and T_S are the number of tuples in R and S, and I is the "image size," the size of the projection of S onto $R \cap S$. That is, T_S/I is the expected number of tuples shipped in response to each request.
5. There is another method similar to (4), in which the roles of R and S are reversed.

We call strategies (1)–(3) *fetches*. Strategies (4) and (5) are referred to as *lookups*.

If R and S are at the same site, there are several other strategies we shall consider.

6. Compute the join at the site of the two relations. and leave it there. Since we charge only for transmission in our simple model, the cost of this action is zero.
7. Compute the join at the site of the two relations and ship the result to another site. The cost is the cost of shipping the result relation. Note that we could also use strategy (3), shipping the unjoined relations to a new site and joining them there. Which is preferable depends on how the size of the join compares with the sum of the sizes of R and S.

The Algorithm for Selecting an Evaluation Strategy

We can now present our simplified version of the System R* algorithm for query evaluation.

Algorithm 12.2: Selecting a Processing Strategy for a Distributed Query.

Input: A query in the form of a compacted tree, with operators select, project, join, union, and choice, and a site at which the result must appear.

Output: A preferred order of application of the operators and sites at which the results of these operations should appear.

Method: The first stage of the algorithm is to generate all the possible evaluation sequences, representing them as ordinary expression trees, with binary operators. We begin by pushing selections and projections as far down the tree as possible, using Algorithm 8.1, with the obvious modification when we encounter a $CHOICE$ operator (push the selection or projection to each child of a node labeled $CHOICE$), and with the techniques of Section 12.1 used to eliminate subtrees whose guard conditions conflict with a selection and to eliminate redundant guard conditions as in Example 12.2.

We proceed up the tree, beginning at the leaves. After visiting a node, we shall have generated for that node a set of expression trees, those that must be considered when finding the least cost application order.

Basis: The basis, a leaf node labeled R, yields a set consisting of the one expression R.

Inductive Step: Let n be a node of the compacted tree. Suppose the children of n, say $c_1, \ldots, c_k$ have each been processed, so we have for each child c_i a set S_i of expressions. If the operator at n is selection or projection, then $k = 1$, and we form the set of expressions for n by applying the same operator as is at n to the root of each expression tree in S_1.

If the operator is $CHOICE$, the set of expressions for n is the union of the S_i's for $1 \leq i \leq k$.

If the operator at n is $\cup$, we consider all unordered binary trees with k leaves. For example, Fig. 12.4(a) shows the three unordered trees with three leaves designated a, b, and c. Since the children of each node are unordered, the first of these could as well have been exhibited as any of the trees in Fig. 12.4(b), where we have shown the two different orders of a and b, and the two different orders of c and the parent of a and b, in all possible combinations.

We may consider only unordered trees, since while the way we group operands of a union may make a difference in the efficiency, the fact that union is a commutative operator guarantees that there can be no difference whether we compute $E_1 \cup E_2$ or $E_2 \cup E_1$. A similar remark holds for the join operator, to be discussed next. We complete construction of the expressions for node n by taking each of the unordered trees, with interior nodes labeled $\cup$, and placing at the leaf for c_i any of the expression trees in S_i, making the replacements for the leaves in all possible ways.

If the label of n is $\bowtie$, we proceed exactly as for a union, except that $\bowtie$ labels the interior nodes of the unordered treee.

Now we must do the second phase of the algorithm, the computation of the best evaluation strategy for each of the expression trees constructed for the

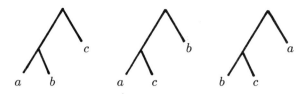

(a) The three unordered binary trees with three leaves.

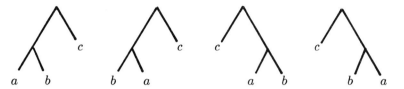

(b) The four ordered trees that are represented by one unordered tree.

Fig. 12.4. Illustration of unordered trees.

root by the first phase. We now have binary trees, and again we work on each tree from the leaves up. At each node, we must compute the cost of evaluating the expression whose root is at that node, with the result left at each of the possible sites. Remember that the exact cost of operations depends not only on the formula for charging for messages shipped, which we take to be c_0 plus the message length, but also on our estimate of the size of relations computed by the subexpressions. We shall assume that such an estimate is available, and later, we shall give an example of one possible way of making the estimate.

Basis: At a leaf node labeled R, the cost of evaluation at the site of R is zero, and the cost of evaluation at any other site is equal to the cost of shipping R, i.e., c_0 plus the number of tuples in R.

Inductive Step: Consider an interior node n. If the label of n is a selection or projection, then that operation can be performed at the same site that the expression rooted at the child of n was computed. Thus, the least cost to compute n at site α equals the cost of computing the child of n at α.

Suppose the label of n is $\cup$. To find the least cost of computing n at site α, we find the minimum over all sites β and γ, of the cost of computing the children of n at β and γ, plus (if $\beta \neq \alpha$) the cost of shipping the first child's result, plus (if $\gamma \neq \alpha$) the cost of shipping the result of the second child.

If the label of n is $\bowtie$, we consider, for each site α, the cost of computing the children of n at some sites β and γ, and using any of the join methods (1)–(7) described prior to Algorithm 12.2 that apply. The least cost method is chosen to evaluate n, of course.

Having computed the cost of evaluating each of the expressions in our set at each of the sites, we find that expression with the lowest cost of evaluation for the desired output site. We must also consider the cost of computing the result at another site and shipping the result to the desired site. Having found the least cost expression, we must find the evaluation method used at each node. The proper evaluation method for a node is the one that assigned the least cost to that node. We can either recompute costs for the winning tree, to see which method is best at each node, or as we evaluate all of the possible trees, we can label each node with the proper method to use. $\square$

Example 12.9: We shall give a simple illustration of the calculations involved in Algorithm 12.2. First, we must settle on a way of estimating the sizes of the results of operations, in particular, the join. We shall assume we know for each relation R and each subset X of the attributes in R's relation scheme, an image size, that is, the expected number of tuples in $\pi_X(R)$. As a special case, we know the expected number of tuples in R itself, since we may let $X = R$.

Suppose R and S are two relations to be joined, and let T_R and T_S be our estimates of the numbers of tuples in these relations. Let the image sizes for the set of attributes $R \cap S$ be I_R and I_S for R and S, respectively. A plausible estimate of the size of $R \bowtie S$ begins by considering the smaller of I_R and I_S; say it is I_R. Then we shall suppose that each member of $\pi_{R \cap S}(R)$ is present in the larger set $\pi_{R \cap S}(S)$. In fact, we shall assume that each tuple in R joins with an average number of tuples from S, that is T_S/I_S tuples. Thus, the size of $R \bowtie S$ is estimated to be $T_R T_S/I_S$, or more generally, considering that either image size could be smaller,

$$\frac{T_R T_S}{max(I_R, I_S)}$$

Suppose that our expression requires us to take the join of three relations $P(A, B)$, $Q(B, C)$, and $R(C, D)$, which are located at three different sites α, β, and γ. As in Fig. 12.4, there are three unordered trees with leaves labeled P, Q, and R, corresponding to the fact that we could take the join of any two of the three relations first. Let us assume the following constants for the problem.

1. $T_P = 10$, $T_Q = 1000$, and $T_R = 100$.
2. The image size I_{PB}, the estimated size of $\pi_B(P)$, is 10.
3. The image size I_{QB} is 20.
4. $I_{QC} = 500$.
5. $I_{RC} = 25$.

We shall first consider that join order in which we join P and Q first, and then join the result to R. If we wish to compute the result at α, we have two choices. We could fetch Q to α, at a cost of $c_0 + T_Q = 10 + 1000 = 1010$. Alternatively, we could examine each of the ten tuples of P and lookup the matching tuples of Q for each of them. The cost of this operation is

$$T_P(c_0 + T_Q/I_{QB}) = 10(10 + 50) = 600$$

Thus, the cost of computing $P \bowtie Q$ at site α is $min(1010, 600) = 600$.

If we wished to evaluate $P \bowtie Q$ at β instead, then there would be the two symmetric strategies, where we do a fetch or a lookup of P. The costs of these operations are respectively $c_0 + T_P = 20$ and $T_Q(c_0 + T_P/I_{PB}) = 11000$. We therefore prefer the fetch operation in this case, with a cost of 20.

Finally, we must evaluate the cost of computing $P \bowtie Q$ at γ. Here we must fetch both relations to γ at a cost of $2c_0 + T_P + T_Q = 1030$. It is worth noting that we could do better by shipping P to β, computing the join there, and shipping the result to γ. However, there is no need to consider this approach now, since when we compute the cost of the complete expression, we shall discover that it is cheaper to evaluate $P \bowtie Q$ at β even if we want the result of that join at γ. On the other hand, if $P \bowtie Q$ were the final expression, and we wanted the result at γ, Algorithm 12.2 would tell us it is cheaper to compute the result at β and ship.

Now we must consider the cost of evaluating the entire expression,

$$(P \bowtie Q) \bowtie R$$

at each of the three sites. To begin, we must obtain our estimate of the size of $P \bowtie Q$. By the formula explained above, this size is

$$T_{PQ} = T_P T_Q / max(I_{PB}, I_{QB}) = 10 * 1000/20 = 500$$

We can also estimate an image size for I_{PQC}, the projection of $P \bowtie Q$ onto C. Each of the 500 C-values appearing in Q is present in $T_Q/I_{QC} = 2$ tuples. As the ratio of I_{PB} to I_{QB} is $1/2$, and we assume every B-value in P is also present in Q, it follows that half the tuples in Q will have a matching B-value in P, and will appear in the join. Thus, of the two tuples with C-value c, the probability is $3/4$ that at least one of them will appear in the join. Thus the image size I_{PQC} will be approximately $\frac{3}{4}I_{QC} = 375$.

Finally, we shall need an estimate for the size of the join of all three relations. By our estimating rule, this number is

$$T_{PQR} = T_{PQ}T_R / max(I_{PQC}, I_{RC}) = 500 * 100/375 = 133$$

Now we must consider for each of the three sites, the best way to compute $(P \bowtie Q) \bowtie R$ at that site. The choices include which site should $P \bowtie Q$ be computed at, and which of the methods (1)–(7) should be used to join $P \bowtie Q$ with R. The options are summarized in Fig. 12.5.

From Fig. 12.5 it is clear that if we want the result at site β, we must compute $P \bowtie Q$ at β (by fetching P to β), then fetching R to β, with a total cost of 130. It seems that if we want the result at α, we should compute $P \bowtie Q$ at β by fetching P, then fetch that result and R to α. However, we must,

site of result	site of $P \bowtie Q$	strategy	cost	cost of $P \bowtie Q$	total cost
α	α	fetch R	$c_0 + T_R = 110$	600	= 710
		lookup R	$T_{PQ}(c_0 + T_R/I_{RC}) = 7000$	600	= 7600
	β	fetch PQ, R	$2c_0 + T_{PQ} + T_R = 620$	20	= 640
	γ	fetch $PQ \bowtie R$	$c_0 + T_{PQR} = 143$	1030	= 1173
		fetch PQ, R	$2c_0 + T_{PQ} + T_R = 620$	1030	= 1650
β	α	fetch PQ, R	$2c_0 + T_{PQ} + T_R = 620$	600	= 1220
	β	fetch R	$c_0 + T_R = 110$	20	= 130
		lookup R	$T_{PQ}(c_0 + T_R/I_{RC}) = 7000$	20	= 7020
	γ	fetch $PQ \bowtie R$	$c_0 + T_{PQR} = 143$	1030	= 1173
		fetch PQ, R	$2c_0 + T_{PQ} + T_R = 620$	1030	= 1650
γ	α	fetch PQ	$c_0 + T_{PQ} = 510$	600	= 1110
		lookup PQ	$T_R(c_0 + T_{PQ}/I_{PQC}) = 1133$	600	= 1733
	β	fetch PQ	$c_0 + T_{PQ} = 510$	20	= 530
		lookup PQ	$T_R(c_0 + T_{PQ}/I_{PQC}) = 1133$	20	= 1153
	γ	none needed	0	1030	= 1030

Fig. 12.5. Strategies for evaluating the join of three relations.

according to Algorithm 12.2, also consider computing the result at another site and shipping the result to α, against the cost of 640 given by Fig. 12.5. In this case, computing the result at β, then shipping it with a cost of $c_0 + T_{PQR} = 143$ has a total cost of 273, which is less than the 640 given by Fig. 12.5 for computation at α. Similarly, the best strategy for computing at γ is to compute at β and ship, with a cost of 273, which compares favorably with the value 530 given in Fig. 12.5.

We are not yet done; we must consider the other two unordered trees, which involve joining P with R first, or Q with R first. The former case is not really a join but a Cartesian product, and we shall rule it out of consideration because of the size of the intermediate result, even though we said we would not consider that cost. The latter strategy, joining Q and R first, will not prove superior to what we have already, since our first step must ship a minimum of 100 tuples, that being the smaller of T_Q and T_R. $\Box$

12.4 DISTRIBUTED CONCURRENCY CONTROL

Now we turn our attention to the second major issue relating to distributed database systems. The task of assuring that transactions behave in a serializable way is made significantly more difficult by the fact that transactions may run at different sites and may access data at many different sites as well. If we use a locking approach to concurrency control, often many more messages are sent concerning locks than are sent to convey data from one place to another. As messages, however short, are expensive, one immediate observation is that a course granularity for locks is appropriate in a distributed environment; that is, the lockable items should be large objects, perhaps even whole relations, so the number of locks taken by a typical transaction will not be large.

A Distributed Concurrency Control Model

Let us review the salient features of the model first introduced in Section 12.1. First, we assume there are a number of nodes, or sites, at which data may be stored and transactions run. There may be multiple copies of any data item, stored at different nodes, and if so, part of the concurrency control problem is to assure that these copies are kept identical. As in Section 11.4, we shall assume that the operations on the database performed by transactions are READ and WRITE, and a transaction may take either a read lock, a write lock, or both, on an item.

We shall assume, as in Chapter 11, that transactions are two-phase. That is, they obtain all their locks on items they need, perform on those items whatever actions they should, and then release the locks. We must interpret locks in such a way that we can view a transaction as occurring at the moment it obtains all its locks, and be sure that a serial order for transactions can be obtained by taking the order in which that moment occurs for each transaction. If we make such an interpretation, then the proofs of serializability will go through exactly as in Chapter 11.

What, then, do we need to assume about read and write locks that they will assure serializability in a distributed environment. First, while no problems occur if many transactions have read locks on the same item, we know violations of serializability can occur if there are two transactions, one having a read lock and one a write lock on the same item at the same time, for then the serial order of transactions based on the order in which transactions obtain their last lock may not be equivalent to the given order. Similarly, no two transactions may hold write locks on the same item at the same time.

When we consider how to define a condition under which a particular item will be deemed to be locked, it becomes clear that the basic locking step is not the direct locking of an item, which is frequently represented by many copies, but rather the locking of a single copy. In the various strategies to be considered, we consider certain combinations of locks on the copies to be locks on the item itself. In some strategies, we can obtain an item lock by interacting with only a subset of the sites that have copies; this situation is desirable, because we want to keep communication to a minimum. We shall now catalog some of the basic methods for distributed locking and compare their advantages and disadvantages.

Write Locks All—Read Locks One

A simple way to achieve the necessary concurrency control is to attach a lock to each copy of each item, and grant or deny locks on these copies to transactions that send RLOCK or WLOCK (read or write lock requests) to the site of the copy. However, we want to view locks as pertaining to items, not copies, and the rule we shall follow for translating locks on copies to locks on items is the following.

1. A transaction is said to have a read lock on item A whenever it has a read lock on any copy of A.

2. A transaction is said to have a write lock on A whenever it has write locks on all the copies of A.

This strategy will be referred to as *write-locks-all*.

At each site, the rules for granting and denying locks on copies are exactly the same as in Chapter 11; we can grant a read lock as long as no other transaction has a write lock on the copy, and we can only grant a write lock if no other transaction has either a read or write lock. The net effect of these rules is that no two transactions can hold a read and write lock on the same item A at the same time. For to hold a write lock on A, one transaction would have to hold write locks at all the copies of A. However, to hold a read lock on A, the other transaction would have to hold a read lock on at least one copy, say A_1. But there is no order in which a read and write lock could be granted for A_1 to two transactions. That is, if the write lock were granted first, the read lock could not be granted until the write lock were released, and similarly if the read lock were granted first. A similar argument tells us that it is not possible for two transactions to hold write locks on A at the same time.

As a special case, if $n = 1$, that is, there is only one copy, then the site of the copy controls locks on the item exactly as if it were the only site in existence.

Let us see how much message traffic is generated by this locking method. Suppose that n nodes have copies of item A. If the site at which the transaction is running does not know how many copies of A exist, or where they are, then we may take n to be the total number of sites.† To execute WLOCK A, the transaction must send messages to all n sites requesting a lock. Then, all n sites will reply, telling the requesting site whether or not it can have the lock. If it can have the lock, then the n sites are eventually sent copies of the new value of the item. The messages with the item's value also include an instruction to unlock A. The messages containing values of items may be considerably longer than the lock messages, since, say, a whole relation may be transmitted. If

---

† It is worth noting that considerable space and effort may be required if each node is to maintain an accurate picture of the entire distributed database, at least to the extent of knowing what items exist throughout the database, and where the copies are. This factor is another reason why items should be large objects.

possible, we should strive to send only the changes to large items, rather than the complete new value.

The net result is that $3n$ messages are sent, although three of these are avoided if the transaction runs at the site of one of the copies. $2n$ of these messages are *short*, which we take to mean that they hold only lock information. The other n are *long*, meaning that they contain item values, either alone or in addition to lock information.

If one or more nodes deny the lock request, then the lock on A is not granted. To avoid deadlocks, the transaction should send messages to any nodes that did grant the lock, telling them to release the lock. Otherwise, two transactions could each hold some write locks on an item and wait indefinitely for the other to release its locks. We shall have more to say in Section 12.6 about avoiding deadlocks of this sort.

To obtain a read lock, we have only to lock one copy, so if we know a node at which a copy of A exists, we can send RLOCK to that site and wait for a reply granting the lock or denying the lock request. If the lock is granted, the value of A will be sent with the message. Thus in the simplest case, where we know a site at which A can be found and the lock request is granted, only two messages are exchanged, one short (the request), and one long (the reply, including the value read). If the request is denied, it probably does not pay to try to get the read lock from another site immediately, since most likely, some transaction has write locked A, and therefore has locks on all the copies. We shall discuss handling these sorts of conflicts in Section 12.6.

The Majority Locking Strategy

Now let us look at another, seemingly rather different strategy for defining locks on items. We shall say that a transaction has a read lock on item A whenever it has a read lock on a majority of the copies of A. The transaction has a write lock on A if it has a write lock on a majority of the copies of A. As before, no two transactions can simultaneously have write locks, or a read and a write lock, on any one copy. We call this strategy the *majority* approach.

To see why this arrangement works, note that two transactions each holding locks on A, whether read or write locks doesn't matter, would each hold locks on a majority of the copies. It follows that there must be at least one copy locked by both transactions. But if either lock is a write lock, then our rule about locking copies is violated. Thus, we conclude that two transactions cannot hold write locks on item A simultaneously, nor can one hold a read lock while the other holds a write lock. They can, of course, hold read locks on an item simultaneously.

To obtain a write lock, a transaction must send requests to at least a majority of the n sites having copies of the item A. In practice, the transaction is better off sending requests to more than the minimum number, $(n+1)/2$, since, for example, one site may not answer, or another transaction may be competing for the lock on A and already have locks on some copies. While a transaction receiving a denial or no response at all from one or more sites could then send the request to additional sites, the delay inherent in such a strategy makes it undesirable unless the chances of a failed node or a competing transaction are very small. We shall, however, take as an estimate of the number of request messages the value $(n + 1)/2$ and use the same value for the number of response messages. Assuming the lock is granted, eventually n messages with a new value of A and a command to unlock A will be sent, for a total of at least $2n + 1$ messages, n of them long, for a write operation.

For a read, we must again send requests to at least $(n + 1)/2$ nodes and receive this number of replies, at least one of which must be a long message including the value that is read. As before, the value need not be transmitted if the transaction runs at the site of one of the copies. We thus estimate the number of messages for a read at $n + 1$, with one of them long. As with the write-locks-all strategy, there are details we defer for later concerning the behavior of transactions when they fail to obtain the lock on the item.

Comparison of Methods

Before proceeding to a variety of other methods for concurrency control, let us compare the write-locks-all and majority methods. The write-locks-all method requires $3n$ messages for a write, n of which are long. In comparison, the majority method uses at least $2n + 1$ messages for a write, perhaps a bit more, but n of them are long. Thus, the majority method has a slight advantage, in that it can do with fewer messages per write, on the average.

However, reads take only two messages under the write-locks-all method, and $n + 1$ under the majority approach. In each case, only one message is long. Thus, if an equal number of read and write locks are requested by typical transactions, there is no advantage to either method, either when counting total messages, or weighting long messages more heavily than short ones. In fact, if $n = 1$, the methods are identical.

On the other hand, if most locks are for reading, the write-locks-all method is clearly preferable, and if write locks dominate, we might prefer the majority method. There is another subtle advantage to the majority approach that only becomes apparent if we
1. frequently have transactions competing for locks on the same item, and
2. arrange that transactions request locks from all sites, or most sites, when desiring to lock an item.

Using the write-locks-all approach, two competing transactions that begin at about the same time are likely each to manage to obtain a lock on at least one copy of the item for which they are competing. This situation causes a deadlock, and while such situations are detectable, they waste time, both real time, since each transaction waits until the deadlock is resolved, and system time, since a procedure for deadlock detection must be run frequently. In comparison, under the majority approach, one of two competing transactions will always succeed in getting the lock on the item, and the other can be made to wait or abort.

A Generalization of the Two Previous Methods

The two strategies we have mentioned are actually just the extreme points in a spectrum of strategies that could be used. The "k-of-n" strategy is to require write locks on at least k out of the n copies of an item A before considering there to be a write lock on the item itself, while a read lock on A is obtained by getting read locks on at least $n - k + 1$ copies of A. This strategy works as long as $k > n/2$. For in that case, no two transactions can write lock A; it would require write locks on $2k$ copies of A, which means, as long as $k > n/2$, that at least one copy is write locked by both transactions, an impossibility. Similarly, a read and write lock on A requires that $k + (n - k + 1) = n + 1$ locks on copies be obtained, and again one copy is locked by both transactions.

It is easy to see that what we referred to as "write-locks-all" is strategy n-of-n, while the majority strategy is $(n+1)/2$-of-n. As k increases, the strategy performs better in situations where reading is done more frequently. On the other hand, the probability that two transactions competing for a lock on the same item will deadlock, by each obtaining enough locks to block the other, goes up as k increases.

Primary Copy Methods

A rather different point of view regarding lock management is to regard the responsibility for locking a particular item A as belonging to one particular site. We shall discuss an approach where one node of the network is given the task of managing locks for all items, in a short while, but in its most general form, the assignment of lock responsibility for item A can be given to any node, and different nodes can be used for different items.

A sensible strategy, for example, is to identify a *primary site* for each item. If the database belongs to a bank, e.g., and the nodes are bank branches, it is natural to consider the primary site for an item that represents an account to be the branch at which the account is held. In that case, since most transactions involving the account would be initiated at its primary site, frequently locks would be obtained with no messages being sent.

There is also a slightly more general strategy than the simple establishment of a primary site for each item. We postulate the existence of *read tokens* and *write tokens*, which are privileges that nodes of the network may obtain for the purpose of accessing items. For an item A, there can be in existence only one write token for A. If there is no write token, then there can be any number of read tokens for A in existence. As expected, if a site has the write token for A, then it can grant a read or write lock on A to a transaction running at that site. A site with a read token for A can grant a read lock on A to a transaction at that site, but cannot grant a write lock. This method will be called the *primary copy token* method.

If a transaction at some site wishes to write lock A, it must arrange that the write token for A be transmitted to its site. If the write token for A is already at the site, it does nothing. Otherwise, it must send messages to all the other sites, asking them to relinquish any read or write tokens on A that they have. From each site α it will receive either a message relinquishing the token, a message saying it has no such token, or a message saying that the token cannot be relinquished because some transaction at α is currently locking A.† If no site sends the third of these messages, then the requesting site assumes it can have the write token, and sends messages to all the other sites to that effect. These messages must again be acknowledged, in case one of the other sites α has given the token to another requesting site in the interrum.

As a possibly better strategy, the first request can serve to "reserve" the token for that site, and until site α hears from the requesting site that that site can have the token, or that it cannot have the token, site α tells any other requesters that the request is denied. However, this approach can lead to repeatedly denied requests for a lock on A from two sites, and some method of avoiding this form of oscillatory behavior must be found; similar problems are discussed in Section 12.6.

In the case that the write token is obtained, a total of $3m$ short messages are exchanged, where m is the total number of nodes in the network. Here, we assume that the "reservation" strategy mentioned above is used, so a second acknowledgement is not needed. If second acknowledgements were used, the total number of messages would be $4m$. As with the previous methods, n long messages are needed to send the new value of A to the sites holding copies of A.

To read A, essentially the same process takes place, except that if the local site has any of the read tokens for A, no messages need to be sent. If no read token is found at the site of the transaction, it must again send messages to all the sites, asking for a read token (and also that that site destroy a write token for A if it has one). The response from each site is either compliance with the request, a message to the effect that it has no token for A, or a message stating that it cannot give such a token, because it has a transaction with a write lock on A. When forced to obtain a read token, the number of messages transmitted is

---

† We should understand that tokens have no physical existence; they even have no electronic existence, at least as far as sending them from node to node is concerned. Rather, each site follows the rules that tell it when it can have a token. The system at each site is responsible for maintaining a record of the tokens it "owns."

$3m$ or $4m$, as with write locks, depending on whether second acknowledgements are needed. One of these messages will have to be long, holding the value to be read, unless a copy of A exists at the site of the transaction.

As a possible improvement on the method of obtaining a read token, if the requesting site knows one or a few sites where a read token is likely to reside, it can send messages only to this subset at first. However, if none of them has a read token, the full set of possible nodes must be sent requests.

Evidently, the primary copy token method uses considerably more messages than the other methods so far. However, its major advantage is that when one site runs most of the transactions that reference a particular item A, then the write token for that item will tend to reside at that site, making locking messages unneeded for most transactions. Thus, a direct comparison with the k-of-n methods is not possible; which is preferable depends on the site distribution of the transactions that lock a particular item.

Similarly, we cannot compare the primary site method directly with the write-locks-all method, since while the former uses smaller numbers of messages on the average, the latter has the advantage when most locks are read locks on copies that are not at the primary site for that item. It appears that the primary site approach is more efficient than the k-of-n methods for $k > 1$. However, there are other considerations that might enter into the picture. For example, the primary site method is vulnerable to a failure at the primary site for an item, as the sites must then detect the failure and send messages to agree on a new primary site. In comparison, k-of-n type strategies can continue locking that item with no interruption.

We can compare primary copy token methods with the primary site approach. In the later method, a write requires two short messages to request and receive a lock from the primary site, then n long messages, as usual, to write the new value. Reading requires a short request message and a long response, granting the request and sending the value. If all transactions referencing A run at the primary site for A, then the two approaches are exactly the same; no messages are sent, except for the obligatory writes to update other copies of A, if any. When other sites do reference A, the primary site method appears to save a considerable number of messages.

However, the token method is somewhat more adaptable to temporary changes in behavior. For example, referring to our imaginary bank database, suppose a customer goes on vacation and starts using a branch different from his usual one. Under the primary site method, each transaction at the new branch would require an exchange of locking messages. However, under the token approach, after the first transaction ran at the new branch, the write token for the account would reside at that branch as long as the customer was on vacation. Provided a copy of the account were furnished to the new branch, so transmission of data in response to a read operation would not be needed by either method, there would be a noticable decrease in the number of messages sent if the primary copy token method were used.

The Central Node Method

The last approach to locking that we shall consider is that in which one particular node of the network is given the responsibility for all locking. This method is almost like the primary site method; the only difference is that the primary site for an item, being the one *central* node, may not be a site that has a copy of the item. Thus, a read lock must be garnered by the following steps

1. Request a read lock from the central node.
2. If not granted, the central node sends a message to the requesting site to that effect. If granted, the central node sends a message to a site with a copy of the item.
3. The site with the copy sends a message with the value to the requesting site.

That is, the central node method often requires an extra, short message to tell some other site to ship the value desired. Similarly, when writing, the site running the transaction must often send an extra message to the central node telling it to release the lock. In the primary site method, this message would be included with the message writing the value, since we assumed the primary site was one of those sites that would receive a new value.

Thus, it seems that the central node approach is almost like the primary site method, but slower. Moreover, while it does not show in our model, which only counts messages without regard for destination, there seems to be the added disadvantage that most of the message traffic is headed to or from one node, thus creating a potential bottleneck. Additionally, this method is especially vulnerable to a crash of the central node.

However, the algorithm has its redeeming features, also in areas not covered by our model. As a case in point, under certain assumptions about loads on the system, there is an advantage to be had by bundling messages to and from the central site. The case for the approach is made by Garcia-Molina [1979].

Summary

The relative merits and demerits of the various approaches are summarized in Fig. 12.6. We use n for the number of copies of an item and m for the total number of nodes. We assume in each case that the lock is granted and we ignore the possible savings that result if we can read or write at the same site as the transaction, thus saving a long message.

12.5 THE OPTIMISTIC APPROACH

The optimistic point of view to concurrency control first mentioned in Section

Method	Short msgs. to write	Long msgs. to write	Short msgs. to read	Long msgs. to read	Comments
write-locks-all	$2n$	n	1	1	good if read dominates
majority	$\geq n+1$	n	$\geq n$	1	avoids some deadlock
primary site	2	n	1	1	efficient; some vulnerability to crash
primary copy token	$0\text{–}4m$	n	$0\text{–}4m$	1	adapts to changes in use pattern
central node	3	n	2	1	vulnerable to crash; efficiencies may result from centralized traffic pattern

Fig. 12.6. Advantages and disadvantages of distributed locking methods.

11.7 can be carried over to distributed databases. In essence, transactions run at any site, and they read and write any copy when they will. Of course, if they write a new value for one copy of an item, they must strive to write the same value into all copies of that item. As in Section 11.7, we need some way of checking that the transaction is not doing something impossible, such as reading a value before it would have been written if the transactions were run in a serial order.

In Section 11.7, we used timestamps and read and write times for items, in order to maintain a behavior that mimicked a serial order. Recall that the hypothetical serial order is one in which a transaction is assumed to run instantaneously at the time given by its timestamp. This approach is still valid in the distributed environment. However, there are three concepts that must be generalized to apply to distributed databases.

First, timestamps were assumed given out by the computer system at large. If there is but one computer, this assumption surely can be satisfied. But what if computers at many sites are assigning timestamps? How do we know they can do so consistently?

Second, when there are many copies of an item, where do we place the read and write times? What if two transactions read two different copies of the same item? Do all copies have to get the same read time?

Third, in Section 11.7 we saw that commitment of transactions was necessary so that other transactions could safely use a value written by another transaction that might have aborted after it wrote the item. How do we generalize the concept of commitment of transactions to a distributed database?

Distributed Timestamps

While not obvious, the most elementary approach to distributed timestamping actually works. That is, we may let the computers at each node of the network keep their own clocks, even though the clocks cannot possibly run in synchronism. To avoid the same timestamp being given to two transactions, we require that the last k bits of the "time" be a sequence that uniquely identifies the node. That is, if there were no more than 256 nodes, we could let $k = 8$ and give each node a distinct eight-bit sequence that it appended to its local clock to form the timestamp.

Even setting aside the theory of relativity, it is not realistic to suppose that all the clocks at all the nodes are in exact synchronism. While minor differences in the clocks at two nodes are of no great consequence, a major difference can be fatal. For example, suppose that at node α, the clock is five hours behind the other clocks in the system. Then, on the assumption that most items are read and written within a five hour period, a transaction initiating at α will receive a timestamp that is less than the read and write times of most items it seeks to access. It is therefore almost sure to abort, and transactions, in effect, cannot run at α.

There is, fortunately, a simple mechanism to prevent gross misalignment of clocks. Let each message sent bear a timestamp, the time at which the message left the sending node, according to the clock of the sender. If a node ever receives a message "from the future," that is, a message with a timestamp greater than its current clock, it simply increments its clock to be greater than the timestamp of the received message. If, say, a node was so inactive that it did not discover that its clock had become five hours slow, then the first time it ran a transaction it would receive a message telling it to abort the transaction it was running. The node would then update its clock and rerun the transaction with a realistic timestamp. We shall thus assume from here on that the creation of timestamps that have global validity is within the capability of a distributed DBMS.

Read and Write Operations

Next, let us consider the steps necessary to read and write items in such a way that the effect on the database is as if each transaction ran instantaneously, at the time given by its timestamp, just as was the case in Section 11.7. As in Section 12.4, we shall consider the elementary step to be an action on a copy of an item, not on the copy itself. However, in the world of optimistic concurrency control, the elementary steps are not locking and unlocking, but examining and setting read and write times on copies.

It turns out that many of the locking methods discussed in the previous section have "optimistic" analogs. We shall discuss only one, the analog of write-locks-all. When reading an item A, we go to any copy of A and check that its write time does not exceed the timestamp of the transaction doing the reading. If the write time is greater than the timestamp, we must abort the transaction. Looking for another copy of A to read is a possible alternative strategy, but it is likely to be futile, and even if it is not, it will surely cause some transaction in the process of writing A to abort.

When writing A, we must write all copies of A, and we must check that for each, the read time is less than the timestamp of the transaction. If the read time of any copy exceeds the timestamp, the transaction must abort. If the read time is less than the timestamp, but the write time exceeds the timestamp, then we do not abort, but neither do we write the item, for reasons discussed in Section 11.7.

It is easy to check that by following these rules, a transaction can never read a value that was created "in the future," nor can a transaction write a value if a value written previously will be read in the future. Thus the method is guaranteed to produce an effect equivalent to a serial order of the transactions.

Commitment of Transactions

Recall from Section 11.7, that when we use an "optimistic" approach to concurrency control, we must be prepared that values written into the database may have to be removed because the transaction that wrote them later aborts. As a consequence, each transaction must commit as its last step, and until it does so, values written must be regarded with suspicion; that is, we must either not permit them to be read, or we must be prepared to roll back transactions that do read them, if the writing transaction aborts.

Since to write an item, all copies must be written, there seems to be no problem if we simply wait for the commit action to be sent to the site of each copy before allowing the copy to be read. There is a subtlely, however, in that commitment is not an atomic operation in the distributed database. While we assume that a transaction cannot fail for any reason after it is ready to commit, the processor on which it is running could fail, perhaps after commit messages were sent to some, but not all, of the copies.

In the case where there is but a single processor, nothing will happen after the processor fails; we shall have the log to figure out what was happening and complete the commitment of the transaction or restart it, as appropriate, as soon as the processor comes up. However, in the distributed case, we want things to proceed as normally as possible while one or more nodes are down. Indeed, this capability is one of the reasons for desiring a distributed system in the first place. Thus, we want to avoid the situation where a node α receives a new value for item A from a transaction running at node β, then β fails and α receives neither a commitment message from β nor a message that the transaction that wrote A aborted and the old value of A should be restored. Until α receives one of these messages, it does not know which value of A to give to other transactions, and therefore all readers of A must wait.†

We shall discuss the general subject of protecting against node failures in the next section, where a reasonable solution to the problems presented here will be discussed.

Locking Vs. Optimistic Concurrency Control

As discussed in Section 11.7 concerning nondistributed databases, the optimistic approach saves some messages, even compared to the best of the methods in Fig. 12.6. A read takes only one short and one long message to request and receive the data, while a write takes n long messages to do the writing (n is the number of sites with copies, as usual), and n short messages to signal that the write is committed.

The other side of the coin is, as usual, that optimistic methods will cause many transactions to abort and restart if there are frequent situations where two transactions are trying to access the same item at the same time. Thus, neither approach can be said to dominate the other.

12.6 MANAGEMENT OF DEADLOCKS AND CRASHES

Distributed databases have considerably more difficulty coping with deadlocks and failures of a node in the network than do nondistributed systems. The difficulty with deadlocks is that they are global phenomena, generally not associated with any particular node. The crash of a single node presents additional problems because we desire more of a distributed system than one that is not. That is, in Section 11.6 we supposed that when the "system" crashed, it was inactive, and our problem was to get it going again in a consistent state. The log was used to help us. In a distributed system, we want life to go on without the failed node as much as possible. In particular, transactions at other sites must run, unless they need an item whose only copy is at the failed node. A description of ways to handle these problems is long and complex, and we shall only touch on the issues here.

Deadlocks

Deadlocks can arise in any of the locking methods discussed in Section 12.4†

---

† Note that a similar problem comes up when locking is used, since a transaction whose node fails after it takes a lock will never unlock, thereby keeping other transactions from referencing the item until the system figures out what is going on.

if we are not careful, and for some methods, they will arise even if we make our best effort to prevent them. Recall from Section 11.1 a simple and elegant method to prevent deadlock. Require each transaction to request locks on items in lexicographic order of the items' names. Then it will not be possible that we have transaction T_1 waiting for item A_1 held by T_2, which is waiting for A_2 held by T_3, and so on, while T_k is waiting for A_k held by T_1. That follows because the fact that T_2 holds a lock on A_1 while it is waiting for A_2 tells us $A_1 < A_2$ in lexicographic order. Similarly, we may conclude $A_2 < A_3 \cdots A_k < A_1$, which implies a cycle in the lexicographic order, an impossibility.

We might naturally assume that the same method, should we wish to employ it, will work for distributed databases as well. For some locking methods, such as central node or the primary site approaches, that is indeed the case. However, for the k-of-n family of methods, there is another source of deadlock, a situation where several transactions have write locks on one or more copies of item A, but none of them has as many as k copies locked. In a sense, the transactions are all waiting for A, so no ordering of the items will help prevent deadlocks.

One technique that is of some use is to require all transactions to request write locks of sites in a particular ordering of the sites. That won't help too much in the majority scheme, since several transactions could leapfrog over each other going down the list of sites, with the result that each of three transactions could still get a lock on a minority of the copies. However, if we use the write-locks-all scheme and require each transaction to lock the copies in order, then we can avoid deadlocks if we also lock items in their lexicographic order.

If we do not use the discipline outlined above, then there will be deadlocks, and the system must be prepared to detect them and deal with them. There are two basic approaches to deadlock detection in a distributed system.

1.   The sites trade information regarding what they know concerning which transactions are waiting for which other transactions to release locks at that site. Putting all this information together gives us a waits-for graph, whose cycles indicate the deadlocks.

2.   Use *timeouts*; that is, abort a transaction that has waited for some particular time, say five seconds, without being granted its requested lock.

The first method, trading information, will only abort transactions when there is truly a deadlock, and it needs to abort only one transaction among those involved in a deadlock. However, it generates a lot of message traffic. Also, to be convinced of deadlock, it may not be sufficient for one site to get messages saying that T_1 is waiting for T_2 at node α, while T_2 is waiting for T_1 at β. It is also necessary to know that these waits occurred simultaneously.

---

† They will not arise if optimistic control is used, and we abort transactions as soon as they cannot perform an action they wish to do. However, these methods can lead to infinite restart of transactions, as discussed in Section 11.7.

For example, it is sufficient to know that T_1 and T_2 are two-phase, and that it is not possible for two transactions to have the same name, even if one is a restarted version of the other. If these reasonable conditions are not satisfied, the only way we can be sure of a deadlock in a situation like the one above is for messages indicating a wait also to tell the interval over which the wait occurred. This interval can refer to a global clock using the trick of Section 12.5 to maintain the clocks of individual nodes in adequate synchronism.

The second approach, timing out, requires less message traffic, only the messages that release locks held by aborted transactions. It is prone, however, to aborting all or many of the transactions in a deadlock, rather than the one that is necessary to break the deadlock. Further, there is a rare, but present risk with the use of timeouts. Suppose that for some reason, many transactions have their lock requests held up, even though there is no deadlock. Then these transactions will time out and abort. Because of the time taken by the system handling the messages that say to unlock items held by the aborted transactions, another large number of transactions times out without there being a deadlock; the aborting of these transactions and the restart of the previously aborted transactions causes further transactions to time out, and the process may repeat indefinitely.

Handling Node Failures

As mentioned, we would like transactions to continue to be processed at live sites when the processors at one or more sites "crash." As in Section 11.6, when nodes may fail, we need a two-phase commit policy for transactions. In fact, that policy is more crucial here than in the single processor case, because not only does two-phase commit assure that we can reconstruct what happened immediately before the site crashed, it protects the nodes that haven't crashed from reading data that does not represent a consistent state. The reason other processors might see an inconsistent state is that a transaction had written some, but not all of its data before its processor crashed.

As a result, we shall hereafter assume that whatever locking method we use, there is a commit message sent to each node at which there resides a value the transaction has written. This assumption adds about n short messages for commitment to the values given for each method in Fig. 12.6. It does not affect the relative advantages of the methods, of course. However, the optimistic approach, which uses a commit step anyway, appears in a better light.

The use of a commit phase, whether with locking or optimistic methods, presents a problem of its own when sites crash. Suppose a transaction T has written some values. The values are not available for other transactions to use until T either commits or aborts, sending a message to the sites of the written values in either case. If T's site crashes after values are written, but before all the sites with written values have received the commit message, then there will be one or more sites that have a value they don't know what to do with; it can neither be read by other transactions nor rolled back.

To handle such cases, the system needs a mechanism for telling when a site has crashed. The usual discovery mechanism is for one site to find that a site to which it has sent a message has failed to acknowledge the message after a normal interval.† The sending site then assumes that the receiving site is down.‡ When one of n sites to which a transaction T has written values discovers that the site of T has crashed, it must communicate with the $n - 1$ other sites to decide what to do. If any one of them has received a message to commit T, then we may assume that T has written all its values and the n sites may all commit T. If none of them have received a commit message, then they must assume that T has not completed; they unlock any locks held by T and roll T back, i.e., they restore the values to what they were before T wrote them. The log at each site can be used to obtain the old values.

Rather than have all n sites talking to all the others, requiring on the order of n^2 messages, we can have the sites commit in a round robin fashion. In this way, fewer messages are sent, although the elapsed time may be greater than if all sites talk directly to one another. The site of T sends the commit message to one site, which passes it to the next, and so on. When the message has gone around twice, that is, $2n + 1$ messages including one return to the site of T, each site will know that T has committed and knows that all the other sites know it. The only important change in our assumptions needed to make this process work is that each of the n sites must know about all the others, or it must be told about the others in the WRITE message from T.

Of course, one of the sites at which T has written may fail while the commit is circulating. If a site tries to pass the message to the failed site, it will detect that, and pass the message to the next site around the chain. If a site fails between the time it receives the message and the time it passes the message on, the message will fail to circulate twice around, and a site having received it once will discover that it did not receive it a second time after a long interval, and will resend the message.

Restarting Nodes

The last issue we must touch upon is what happens when we try to restart a site

---

† It should be pointed out that the process we have viewed as sending a message from one node to the next involves, at the lower levels of the message passing system a sequence of signals between the nodes, including not only the signals that transmit the message but signals acknowledging the receipt of the message. Thus it is not possible for a node to send a message to a failed node without so realizing.

‡ This assumption is another that can lead to occasional chaos, when sites get so busy figuring out other sites are crashed that they cannot acknowledge messages and cause other sites to think they are crashed. The system could conceivably get into a permanent state where everybody thinks everybody else is down.

that has crashed. While we have not stated it explicitly, we may, if we wish, continue to process transactions that involve failed sites, as long as at least one site with the identical data exists. That is, for example, if transaction T tries to write a new value for A at $n \geq 2$ sites, and one of them has failed, the value is simply not written there, and the system proceeds as if the failed site did not exist. The only exception is a transaction that tries to read or write an item whose only copy or copies exist at failed sites. Evidently, such a transaction may not proceed.

When the failed site resumes activity, it must obtain the most recent values for all its items. We shall suggest two general strategies for doing so.

1. When commiting any item, if site α discovers that site β, which also has a copy of the item, is crashed, then α records this fact in its log. When β resumes, it sends a message to each site, which examines its log back to the point it discovered β had crashed, and sends the most recent value it has for all items it holds in common with β. The values of these items must be locked while the restoration of β is in progress, and we must be careful to obtain the most recent value among all the sites with copies. We can tell the most recent values, because all transactions that have committed a value for item A must have done so in the same order at all the sites of A, provided we have a correct locking method. If we are using optimistic concurrency control, the write times of the values determine their order.

2. All copies of all items include a write time, whether or not optimistic concurrency control is in use. When a site β resumes, it sends for the write times of all its items, as recorded in the other sites. These items are temporarily locked at the other sites, and the values of items with a more recent write time than the write time at β have their most recent values sent.

This description merely scratches the surface of the subject of crash management. For example, what happens when a site needed to restore values to a second site has itself crashed, or if a site crashes while another is being restored? The interested reader is encouraged to consult the bibliographic notes for deeper analyses of the subject.

EXERCISES

12.1: Express the following queries about the bank database of Example 12.2, in terms of the fragments given by that example.
a) Print the customers that (possibly jointly) hold account number 123.
b) Print the customers that have accounts at branch 1 and some other branch.

12.2: Optimize the queries of Exercise 12.1 by algebraic manipulation.

12.3: Suppose the beer drinker's database (Exercise 5.6, e.g.) is distributed in such a way that at every brewery, there is a fragment of the SELLS relation for only the beers brewed by that brewery. Also, every bar has a fragment of the FREQUENTS relation with the tuples mentioning that bar. The LIKES relation is at a central site.

a)   What are the guard conditions for each fragment?

b)   Express and optimize the queries of Exercise 5.6 in terms of this distributed database.

12.4: What is the effect on the fragments of Exercise 12.2 of inserting the fact that customer Jones has account number 123 at the Main St. branch, with a balance of $100?

12.5: Let us refer to the maximal object $\mathcal{M}_1$ of Example 9.10 as if its objects were relations. Find a semijoin program to reduce the query

retrieve (Ad)
where $L{=}123$

** 12.6: Prove the converse portion of Theorem 12.2, that for any join expression with a cyclic hypergraph there is some reduction that has no semijoin program guaranteed to perform the reduction.

12.7: Repeat Example 12.7 with the parameters $c_0 = 10$, $d = 0.5$, $b_1 = 100$, $a_2 = 10$, $b_2 = 20$, and $a_3 = 5$.

* 12.8: Suppose Algorithm 12.1 is applied to compute a chain query of length n, and the relevant parameters satisfy $d = 1$, and $a_2 = a_3 = \cdots = a_n = b_1 = \cdots = b_{n-1}$. What semijoin program is found to be optimal?

12.9: Repeat Example 12.9 with the parameters $T_P = T_Q = T_R = 1000$, $I_{PB} = 100$, $I_{QB} = 20$, $I_{QC} = 200$, and $I_{RC} = 50$.

12.10: Suppose we have three nodes, 1, 2, and 3, in our network. Item A has copies at all three nodes, while item B has copies only at 1 and 3. Two transactions, T_1 and T_2 run, starting at the same time, at nodes 1 and 2, respectively. Each transaction consists of the following steps: RLOCK B; WLOCK A; UNLOCK A; UNLOCK B; COMMIT. Suppose that at each time unit, each transaction can send one message to one site, and each site can read one message. When there is a choice of sites to send or receive a message to or from, the system always chooses the lowest numbered site. Simulate the action of the network under the following concurrency rules.

a)   Write-locks-all.

b)   Majority locking.

c)   Primary site, assumed to be node 1 for A and 3 for B.

d)   Primary copy token, with initially sites 2 and 3 holding read tokens for A, and 1 holding the write token for B.

e)   Optimistic concurrency control, assuming the timestamp of T_1 exceeds that of T_2, and both are greater than the initial read and write times for all the copies.

BIBLIOGRAPHIC NOTES

The first systematic study of fragmentation is in Dayal and Bernstein [1978], while Ceri and Pelagatti [1980] and Adiba [1980] developed an algebra of *multirelations* (lists of relations) of which we have only scratched the surface in Section 12.1. The guard condition technique is from Maier and Ullman [1981].

Semijoins were first studied by Bernstein and Chiu [1981], and in the form covered here by Bernstein and Goodman [1981a]. Our development of chain queries is based on Chiu, Bernstein, and Ho [1981]. Theorem 12.2, relating the existence of reduction sequences to hypergraph acyclicity is from Yu and Ozsoyoglu [1979], although a related characterization of join expressions with such reducers was given by Bernstein and Goodman [1981a]. Gouda and Dayal [1981] give an algorithm for producing optimal semijoin sequences.

The System R* algorithm of Section 12.3 is covered by Selinger and Adiba [1980].

The method in Section 12.5 of keeping several clocks synchronized is by Lamport [1978].

For locking strategies, we find the majority approach in Thomas [1975, 1979], while the primary site method is evaluated in Stonebraker [1980], the central node technique in Garcia-Molina [1979], and primary copy token methods in Minoura [1980]. Bernstein and Goodman [1980b] discuss the optimistic approach.

The papers by Rosenkrantz et al. [1978] and Stearns et al. [1976] discuss a form of concurrency control where locks are kept by a central site but may be preempted, that is, taken away from a transaction to which they had been granted and given to a different transaction.

These and other methods and issues are discussed in articles by Rothnie and Goodman [1977], Gray [1978], Bayer et al. [1980], Epstein and Stonebraker [1980], and Bernstein and Goodman [1981b]. An important concept from the latter is that one can divide the problem of concurrency control into two parts: making writes occur in the correct order (*write-write synchronization*) and making reads refer to the correct version of an item (*read-write synchronization*).

A major effort in distributed concurrency control, SDD-1, has been covered in a series of recent papers Bernstein, Goodman, Rothnie, and Papadimitriou [1978], Bernstein and Shipman [1980], Bernstein, Shipman, and Rothnie [1980], Bernstein et al. [1981], and Rothnie, et al. [1980]. See also McLean [1981]. Among the interesting concepts found there is the idea that transactions can be grouped into classes according to their read and write patterns, and different methods of concurrency control applied to members of different classes.

We have already mentioned another major effort in the design of distributed database systems, System R* (Selinger and Adiba [1980]). A third such effort is distributed INGRES, described in Epstein, Stonebraker, and Wong [1978] and

Stonebraker [1979].

The works by Menasce, Popek, and Muntz [1980], Skeen and Stonebraker [1980], and Minoura [1980] contain analyses of the methods for restoring crashed distributed systems.

BIBLIOGRAPHY

Adiba, M. [1980]. "Derived relations: a unified mechanism for views, snapshots, and distributed data," RJ2881, IBM, San Jose, Calif.

Aho, A. V., C. Beeri, and J. D. Ullman [1979]. "The theory of joins in relational databases," *ACM Transactions on Database Systems* **4**:3, pp. 297–314.

Aho, A. V., J. E. Hopcroft, and J. D. Ullman [1974]. *The Design and Analysis of Computer Algorithms*, Addison-Wesley, Reading Mass.

Aho, A. V., J. E. Hopcroft, and J. D. Ullman [1982]. *Introduction to Algorithms and Data Structures*, Addison-Wesley, Reading Mass.

Aho, A. V., B. W. Kernighan, and P. J. Weinberger [1979]. "Awk—a pattern scanning and processing language," *Software Practice and Experience* **9**, pp. 267–279.

Aho, A. V., Y. Sagiv, T. G. Szymanski, and J. D. Ullman [1981]. "Inferring a tree from lowest common ancestors, with an application to the optimization of relational expressions," *SIAM J. Computing* **10**:3, pp. 405–421.

Aho, A. V., Y. Sagiv, and J. D. Ullman [1979a]. "Equivalence of relational expressions," *SIAM J. Computing* **8**:2, pp. 218–246.

Aho, A. V., Y. Sagiv, and J. D. Ullman [1979b]. "Efficient optimization of a class of relational expressions," *ACM Transactions on Database Systems* **4**:4, pp. 435–454.

Aho, A. V. and J. D. Ullman [1979a]. "Optimal partial match retrieval when fields are independently specified," *ACM Transactions on Database Systems* **4**:2, pp. 168–179.

Aho, A. V. and J. D. Ullman [1979b]. "Universality of data retrieval languages," *Proc. Sixth ACM Symposium on Principles of Programming Languages*, pp. 110–120.

ANSI [1975]. "Study group on data base management systems: interim report," *FDT* **7**:2, ACM, New York.

Armstrong, W. W. [1974]. "Dependency structures of data base relationships," *Proc. 1974 IFIP Congress*, pp. 580–583, North Holland, Amsterdam.

Arora, A. K. and C. R. Carlson [1978]. "The information preserving properties of certain relational database transformations," *Proc. International Conference on Very Large Data Bases,* pp. 352–359.

Astrahan, M. M. and D. D. Chamberlin [1975]. "Implementation of a structured English query language," *Comm. ACM* **18**:10, pp. 580–587.

Astrahan, M. M., et al. [1976]. "System R: a relational approach to data management," *ACM Transactions on Database Systems* **1**:2, pp. 97–137.

Atzeni, P. and D. S. Parker [1982]. "Assumptions in relational database theory," *Proc. ACM Symposium on Principles of Database Systems.*

Bachman, C. W. [1969]. "Data structure diagrams," *Data Base* **1**:2, pp. 4–10.

Badal, D. S. [1980]. "The analysis of the effects of concurrency control on distributed database system performance," *Proc. International Conference on Very Large Data Bases,* pp. 376–383.

Bancilhon, F. [1978]. "On the completeness of query languages for relational databases," *Proc. Seventh Symp. on Mathematical Foundations of Computer Science,* Springer-Verlag.

Bayer, R., K. Elhardt, H. Heller, and A Reiser [1980]. "Distributed concurrency control in database systems," *Proc. International Conference on Very Large Data Bases,* pp. 275–284.

Bayer, R. and E. M. McCreight [1972]. "Organization and maintenance of large ordered indices," *Acta Informatica* **1**:3, pp. 173–189.

Bayer, R. and M. Schkolnick [1977]. "Concurrency of operating on B-trees," *Acta Informatica* **9**:1, pp. 1–21.

Beck, L. L. [1978]. "On minimal sets of operations for relational data sublanguages," TR CS-7802, SMU, Dallas.

Beck, L. L. [1980]. "A security mechanism for statistical databases," *ACM Transactions on Database Systems* **5**:3, pp. 316–338.

Beeri, C. [1980]. "On the membership problem for functional and multivalued dependencies," *ACM Transactions on Database Systems* **5**:3, pp. 241–259.

Beeri, C. and P. A. Bernstein [1979]. "Computational problems related to the design of normal form relation schemes," *ACM Transactions on Database Systems* **4**:1, pp. 30–59.

Beeri, C., P. A. Bernstein, and N. Goodman [1978]. "A sophisticate's introduction to database normalization theory," *Proc. International Conference on Very Large Data Bases,* pp. 113–124.

Beeri, C., R. Fagin, and J. H. Howard [1977]. "A complete axiomatization for functional and multivalued dependencies," *ACM SIGMOD International Symposium on Management of Data*, pp. 47–61.

Beeri, C., R. Fagin, D. Maier, and M. Yannakakis [1981]. "On the desirability of acyclic database schemes," RJ3131, IBM, San Jose, Calif.

Beeri, C. and P. Honeyman [1982]. "Preserving functional dependencies," to appear in *SIAM J. Computing*.

Beeri, C., A. O. Mendelzon, Y. Sagiv, and J. D. Ullman [1981]. "Equivalence of relational database schemes," *SIAM J. Computing* **10**:2, pp. 352–370.

Beeri, C. and M. Y. Vardi [1979]. "On the properties of join dependencies," *Proc. of Workshop on Formal Bases for Databases*, Toulouse. Also in Gallaire, Minker, and Nicolas [1980].

Beeri, C. and M. Y. Vardi [1981a]. "The implication problem for data dependencies," *Automata, Languages and Programming* (S. Even and O. Kariv, eds.), pp. 73–85, Springer-Verlag, New York.

Beeri, C. and M. Y. Vardi [1981b]. "Axiomatizaion of tuple and equality generating dependencies," unpublished memorandum, Hebrew Univ., Jerusalem.

Bentley, J. L. [1975]. "Multidimensional binary search trees used for associative searching," *Comm. ACM* **18**:9, pp. 509–517.

Bentley, J. L. and J. H. Friedman [1979]. "Data Structures for range searching," *Computing Surveys* **13**:3, pp. 397–409.

Bentley, J. L. and D. Stanat [1975]. "Analysis of range searches in quad trees," *Information Processing Letters* **3**:6, pp. 170–173.

Bernstein, P. A. [1976]. "Synthesizing third normal form relations from functional dependencies," *ACM Transactions on Database Systems* **1**:4, pp. 277–298.

Bernstein, P. A. and D. W. Chiu [1981]. "Using semijoins to solve relational queries," *J. ACM* **28**:1, pp. 25–40.

Bernstein, P. A. and N. Goodman [1980a]. "What does Boyce-Codd normal form do?" *Proc. International Conference on Very Large Data Bases*, pp. 245–259.

Bernstein, P. A. and N. Goodman [1980b]. "Timestamp-based algorithms for concurrency control in distributed database systems," *Proc. International Conference on Very Large Data Bases*, pp. 285–300.

Bernstein, P. A. and N. Goodman [1981a]. "The power of natural semijoins," *SIAM J. Computing* **10**:4, pp. 751–771.

Bernstein, P. A. and N. Goodman [1981b]. "Concurrency control in distributed database systems," *Computing Surveys* **13**:2, pp. 185–221.

Bernstein, P. A., N. Goodman, and M.-Y. Lai [1981]. "Laying phantoms to rest," TR–03–81, Aiken Computation Lab., Harvard Univ., Cambridge, Mass.

Bernstein, P. A., N. Goodman, J. B. Rothnie, and C. H. Papadimitriou [1978]. "Analysis of serializability of SDD-1: a system of distributed databases (the fully redundant case)," *IEEE Trans. on Software Engineering* **SE4**:3, pp. 154–168.

Bernstein, P. A, N. Goodman, E. Wong, C. L. Reeve, and J. B. Rothnie, Jr. [1981]. "Query processing in a system for distributed databases (SDD-1)," *ACM Transactions on Database Systems* **6**:4, pp. 602–625.

Bernstein, P. A. and D. W. Shipman [1980]. "The correctness of concurrency control mechanisms in a system for distributed databases (SDD-1)," *ACM Transactions on Database Systems* **5**:1, pp. 52–68.

Bernstein, P. A., D. W. Shipman, and J. B. Rothnie, Jr. [1980]. "Concurrency control in a system for distributed databases (SDD-1)," *ACM Transactions on Database Systems* **5**:1, pp. 18–51.

Biskup, J. [1980]. "Inferences of multivalued dependencies in fixed and undetermined universes." *Theoretical Computer Science* **10**:1, pp. 93–106.

Biskup, J., U. Dayal, and P. A. Bernstein [1979]. "Synthesizing independent database schemas," *ACM SIGMOD International Symposium on Management of Data*, pp. 143–152.

Blasgen, M. W. et al. [1981]. "System R: an architechural overview," *IBM Systems J.* **20**:1, pp. 41–62.

Bolour, A. [1979]. "Optimality properties of multiple key hashing functions," *J. ACM* **26**:2, pp. 196–210.

Bolour, A. [1981]. "Optimal retrieval algorithms for small region queries," *SIAM J. Computing* **10**:4, pp. 721–741.

Boyce, R. F., D .D. Chamberlin, W. F. King, and M. M. Hammer [1975]. "Specifying queries as relational expressions: the SQUARE data sublanguage," *Comm. ACM* **18**:11, pp. 621–628.

Burkhard, W. A. [1976]. "Hashing and trie algorithms for partial match retrieval," *ACM Transactions on Database Systems* **1**:2, pp. 175–187.

Burkhard, W. A., M. L. Fredman, and D. J. Kleitman [1981]. "Inherent complexity trade-offs for range query problems," *Theoretical Computer Science* **16**:3, pp. 279–290.

Cardenas, A. F. [1979]. *Data Base Management Systems*, Allyn and Bacon, Boston, Mass.

Carlson, C. R. and R. S. Kaplan [1976]. "A generalized access path model and its application to a relational database system," *ACM SIGMOD International Symposium on Management of Data*, pp. 143–156.

Casanova, M. A., R. Fagin, and C. H. Papadimitriou [1981]. "Inclusion dependencies and their interaction with functional dependencies," *Proc. ACM Symposium on Principles of Database Systems*.

Ceri, S. and G. Pelagatti [1980]. "Correctness of execution strategies of read-only transactions in distributed databases," Rept. 80–16, Inst. di Elettrotecnica Politecnico di Milano.

Chamberlin, D. D., et al. [1976]. "SEQUEL 2: a unified approach to data definition, manipulation, and control," *IBM J. Research and Development* **20**:6, pp. 560–575.

Chamberlin, D. D. et al. [1981a]. "Support for repetitive transactions and ad hoc queries in System R," *ACM Transactions on Database Systems* **6**:1, pp. 70–94.

Chamberlin, D. D. et al. [1981b]. "A history and evaluation of System R," *Comm. ACM* **24**:10, pp. 632–646.

Chandra, A. K. and D. Harel [1980]. "Computable queries for relational database systems," *J. Computer and System Sciences* **21**:2, pp. 156–178.

Chandra, A. K. and D. Harel [1982]. "Horn clauses and the fixpoint query hierarchy," *Proc. ACM Symposium on Principles of Database Systems*.

Chandra, A. K., H. R. Lewis, and J. A. Makowsky [1981]. "Embedded implicational dependencies and their inference problem," *Proc. Thirteenth Annual ACM Symposium on the Theory of Computing*, pp. 342–354.

Chandra, A. K. and P. M. Merlin [1977]. "Optimal implementation of conjunctive queries in relational databases," *Proc. Ninth Annual ACM Symposium on the Theory of Computing*, pp. 77–90.

Chang, C. L. [1980]. "Finding missing joins for incomplete queries in relational databases," RJ2145, IBM, San Jose, Calif.

Chen, P. P. [1976]. "The entity-relationship model: toward a unified view of data," *ACM Transactions on Database Systems* **1**:1, pp. 9–36.

Chen, P. P. (ed.) [1980]. *Proc. Intl. Conf. on the Entity-Relationship Approach to System Analysis and Design*, North Holland, Amsterdam.

Childs, D. L. [1968]. "Feasibility of a set-theoretical data structure—a general structure based on a reconstituted definition of relation," *Proc. 1968 IFIP Congress*, pp. 162–172, North Holland, Amsterdam.

Chin, F. and P. Kossowski [1981]. "The theory of secure policies for inference control by auditing in statistical databases," unpublished memorandum, Dept. of Computer Science, Univ. of Alberta, Edmonton.

Chin, F. Y. [1978]. "Security in statistical databases for queries with small counts," *ACM Transactions on Database Systems* **3**:1, pp. 92–104.

Chin, F. Y. and G. Ozsoyoglu [1981]. "Statistical database design," *ACM Transactions on Database Systems* **6**:1, pp. 113–139.

Chiu, D.-M., P. A. Bernstein, and Y.-C. Ho [1981]. "Optimizing chain queries in a distributed database system," TR–01–81, Harvard Univ. Cambridge, Mass.

Cincom [1978]. *OS TOTAL Reference Manual*, Cincom Systems, Cincinnati, Ohio.

CODASYL [1971]. *CODASYL Data Base Task Group April 71 Report*, ACM, New York.

CODASYL [1978]. *COBOL J. Development*, Materiel Data Management Center, Quebec, Que. Earlier editions appeared in 1973 and 1968.

Codd, E. F. [1970]. "A relational model for large shared data banks," *Comm. ACM* **13**:6, pp. 377–387.

Codd, E. F. [1972a]. "Further normalization of the data base relational model," in *Data Base Systems* (R. Rustin, ed.) Prentice-Hall, Englewood Cliffs, New Jersey.pp. 33–64.

Codd, E. F. [1972b]. "Relational completeness of data base sublanguages," *ibid.* pp. 65–98.

Codd, E. F. [1975]. "Understanding relations," *FDT* **7**:3–4, pp. 23-28, ACM, New York.

Codd, E. F. [1978]. "How about recently," in Shneiderman [1978], pp. 3–28.

Codd, E. F. [1979]. "Extending the data base relational model to capture more meaning," *ACM Transactions on Database Systems* **4**:4, pp. 397–434.

Codd, E. F., R. S. Arnold, J. M. Cadiou, C. L. Chang, and N. Roussopoulos [1978]. "Rendezvous version I: an experimental English language query formulation system for casual users of relational databases," RJ2144, IBM, San Jose, Calif.

Coffman, E. G. and P. J. Denning [1973]. *Operating Systems Theory*, Prentice-Hall, Englewood Cliffs, New Jersey.

Comer, D. [1978]. "The difficulty of optimum index selection," *ACM Transactions on Database Systems* 3:4, pp. 440–445.

Culik, K. II, Th. Ottmann, and D. Wood [1981]. "Dense multiway trees," *ACM Transactions on Database Systems* 6:3, pp. 486–512.

Cullinane [1978]. *IDMS DML Programmer's Reference Guide*, Cullinane Corp., Wellesley, Mass.

Date, C. J. [1981]. *An Introduction to Database Systems*, Addison-Wesley, Reading Mass.

Dayal, U. and P. A. Bernstein [1978]. "The updatability of relational views," *Proc. International Conference on Very Large Data Bases*, pp. 368–377.

Dell'Orco, P., V. N. Spadavecchio, and M. King [1977]. "Using knowledge of a data base world in interpreting natural language queries," *Proc. 1977 IFIP Congress*, pp. 139–144, North Holland, Amsterdam.

Delobel, C. [1978]. "Normalization and hierarchical dependencies in the relational data model," *ACM Transactions on Database Systems* 3:3, pp. 201–222. See also, "Contributions theoretiques a la conception d'un systeme d'informations," doctoral dissertation, Univ. of Grenoble, Oct., 1973.

Delobel, C. and R. C. Casey [1972]. "Decomposition of a database and the theory of Boolean switching functions," *IBM J. Research and Development* 17:5, pp. 370–386.

DeMillo, R. A., D. P. Dobkin, A. K. Jones, and R. J. Lipton [1978]. *Foundations of Secure Computation*, Academic Press, New York.

DeMillo, R. A., D. P. Dobkin, and R. J. Lipton [1978]. "Even databases that lie can be compromised," *IEEE Trans. on Software Engineering* SE4:1, pp. 73–75.

Denning, D. E. [1978]. "A review of research on statistical database security," in DeMillo et al. [1978], pp. 15–26.

Denning, D. E., P. J. Denning, and M. D. Schwartz [1977]. "Securing databases under linear queries," *Proc. 1977 IFIP Congress*, pp. 395–398, North Holland, Amsterdam. Also see *ACM Transactions on Database Systems* 4:2, pp. 156–167.

Denning, D. E., P. J. Denning, and M. D. Schwartz [1979]. "The tracker: a threat to statistical database security," *ACM Transactions on Database Systems* 4:1, pp. 76–96.

Denning, D. E. and J. Schlörer [1980]. "A fast procedure for finding a tracker in a statistical database," *ACM Transactions on Database Systems* **5**:1, pp. 88–102.

Dobkin, D., A. K. Jones, and R. J. Lipton [1979]. "Secure databases: protection against user inference," *ACM Transactions on Database Systems* **4**:1, pp. 97–106.

Douque, B. C. M. and G. M. Nijssen [1976]. *Database Description,* North Holland, Amsterdam.

DTSS [1980]. "DaTaSyS reference manual," DTSS, Inc., Hanover, N. H.

Ellis, C. S. [1978]. "Concurrent search and insertion in 2–3 trees," TR-78–05-01, Dept. of Computer Science, Univ. of Washington, Seattle.

El Masri, R. and G. Wiederhold [1979]. "Data model integration using the structural model," *ACM SIGMOD International Symposium on Management of Data,* pp. 191–202.

Epstein, R. and M. Stonebraker [1980]. "Analysis of distributed database processing strategies," *Proc. International Conference on Very Large Data Bases,* pp. 92–110.

Epstein, R., M. R. Stonebraker, and E. Wong [1978]. "Distributed query processing in a relational database system," *ACM SIGMOD International Symposium on Management of Data,* pp. 169–180.

Eswaran, K. P., J. N. Gray, R. A. Lorie, and I. L. Traiger [1976]. "The notions of consistency and predicate locks in a database system," *Comm. ACM* **19**:11, pp. 624–633.

Fagin, R. [1977]. "Multivalued dependencies and a new normal form for relational databases," *ACM Transactions on Database Systems* **2**:3, pp. 262–278.

Fagin, R. [1978]. "On an authorization mechanism," *ACM Transactions on Database Systems* **3**:3, pp. 310–319.

Fagin, R. [1979]. "Normal forms and relational database operators," *ACM SIGMOD International Symposium on Management of Data,* pp. 153–160.

Fagin, R. [1980]. "Horn clauses and database dependencies," *Proc. Twelfth Annual ACM Symposium on the Theory of Computing,* pp. 123–134.

Fagin, R. [1981a]. "A normal form for relational databases that is based on domains and keys," *ACM Transactions on Database Systems* **6**:3, pp. 387–415.

Fagin, R. [1981b]. "Types of acyclicity for hypergraphs and relational database schemes," RJ3330, IBM, San Jose, Calif.

Fagin, R., A. O. Mendelzon, and J. D. Ullman [1980]. "A simplified universal relation assumption and its properties," RJ2900, IBM, San Jose, Calif.

Fernandez, E. B., R. C. Summers, and C. Wood [1980]. *Database Security and Integrity*, Addison-Wesley, Reading Mass.

Finkel, R. A. and J. L. Bentley [1974]. "Quad trees, a data structure for retrieval on composite keys," *Acta Informatica* **4**:1, pp. 1–9.

Fischer, P. C and D.-M. Tsou [1981]. "Whether a set of multivalued dependencies implies a join dependency is NP-hard," unpublished memorandum, Dept. of Computer Science, Vanderbilt Univ., Nashville, Tenn.

Fredman, M. F. [1982]. "A lower bound on the complexity of orthogonal range queries," to appear in *J. ACM*.

Furtado, A. L. [1978]. "Formal aspects of the relational model," *Information systems* **3**:2, pp. 131–140.

Galil, Z. [1979]. "An almost linear time algorithm for computing a dependency basis in a relational database," RJ2656, IBM, San Jose, Calif.   .

Gallaire, H. and J. Minker [1978]. *Logic and Databases,* Plenum Press, New York.

Gallaire, H., J. Minker, and J.-M. Nicolas [1980]. *Advances in Database Theory,* Vol. I, Plenum Press, New York.

Garcia-Molina, H. [1979]. "Performance comparison of update algorithms for distributed databases," Part I: Tech. Note 143, Part II: Tech. Note 146, Digital Systems Laboratory, Stanford Univ.

Garey, M. R. and D. S. Johnson [1979]. *Computers and Intractability: A Guide to the Theory of NP-Completeness,* Freeman, San Francisco.

Ginsburg, S. and R. Hull [1981]. "Characterizations for functional dependency and Boyce-Codd normal form databases," unpublished memorandum, USC, Los Angeles, Calif.

Ginsburg, S. and S. M. Zaiddan [1981]. "Properties of functional dependency families," to appear in *J. ACM*.

Goodman, N. and O. Shmueli [1980]. "Nonreducible database states for cyclic queries," TR–15–80, Aiken Computation Lab., Harvard Univ., Cambridge, Mass.

Goodman, N. and O. Shmueli [1981a]. "Limitations of the chase," TR–02–81, Aiken Computation Lab., Harvard Univ., Cambridge, Mass.

Goodman, N. and O. Shmueli [1981b]. "Syntactic characterizations of tree database schemas," *Proc. XP/2 Conf.*, State College, Pa.

Gotlieb, C. C. and L. R. Gotlieb [1978]. *Data Types and Structures*, Prentice-Hall, Englewood Cliffs, New Jersey.

Gotlieb, C. C. and F. W. Tompa [1973]. "Choosing a storage schema," *Acta Informatica* **3**:3, pp. 297–319.

Gotlieb, L. R. [1975]. "Computing joins of relations," *ACM SIGMOD International Symposium on Management of Data*, pp. 55–63.

Gouda, M. G. and U. Dayal [1981]. "Optimal semijoin schedules for query processing in local distributed database systems," *ACM SIGMOD International Symposium on Management of Data*, pp. 164–181.

Graham. M. H. [1979]. "On the universal relation," technical report, Univ. of Toronto, Toronto, Ont., Canada.

Gray, J. N. [1978]. "Notes on data base operating systems," RJ2188, IBM, San Jose, Calif.

Gray, J. N., R. A. Lorie, and G. R. Putzolo [1975]. "Granularity of locks in a shared database," *Proc. International Conference on Very Large Data Bases*, pp. 428–451.

Gray, J. N., F. Putzolo, and I. Traiger [1976]. "Granularity of locks and degrees of consistency in a shared data base," in Nijssen [1976].

Greenblatt, D. and J. Waxman [1978]. "A study of three database query languages," in Shneiderman [1978], pp. 77–98.

Griffiths, P. P., M. M. Astrahan, D. D. Chamberlin, R. A. Lorie, and T. G. Price [1979]. "Access path selection in a relational database management system," RJ2429, IBM, San Jose, Calif.

Griffiths, P. P. and B. W. Wade [1976]. "An authorization mechanism for a relational database system," *ACM Transactions on Database Systems* **1**:3, pp. 242–255.

Gudes, E. and S. Tsur [1980]. "Experiments with B-tree reorganization," *ACM SIGMOD International Symposium on Management of Data*, pp. 200–206.

Gurevich, Y. and H. R. Lewis [1982]. "The inference problem for template dependencies," *Proc. ACM Symposium on Principles of Database Systems*.

Hadzilacos, V. [1982]. "An algorithm for minimizing roll back cost," *Proc. ACM Symposium on Principles of Database Systems*.

Hagihara, K., M. Ito, K. Taniguchi, and T. Kasami [1979]. "Decision problems for multivalued dependencies in relational databases," *SIAM J. Computing* **8**:2, pp. 247–264.

Hall, P. A. V. [1976]. "Optimization of a single relational expression in a relational database," *IBM J. Research and Development* **20**:3, pp. 244–257.

Hammer, M. and D. McLeod [1981]. "Database description with SDM: a semantic database model," *ACM Transactions on Database Systems* **6**:3, pp. 351–386.

Haq, M. I. [1974]. "Security in a statistical database," *Proc. Amer. Soc. Inform. Science* **11**:1, pp. 33–39.

Haq, M. I. [1975]. "Insuring individual's privacy from statistical database users," *Proc. 1975 National Computer Conference*, pp. 941–946, AFIPS Press, Montvale, New Jersey.

Heath, I. J. [1971]. "Unacceptable file operations in a relational data base," *ACM SIGFIDET Workshop on Data Description, Access, and Control*, pp. 19–33.

Held, G. and M. Stonebraker [1978]. "B-trees reexamined," *Comm. ACM* **21**:2, pp. 139–143.

Hoffman, L. J. [1977]. *Modern Methods for Computer Security and Privacy*, Prentice-Hall, Englewood Cliffs, New Jersey.

Hoffman, L. J. and W. F. Miller [1970]. "Getting a personal dossier from a statistical data bank," *Datamation* **16**:5, pp. 74–75.

Honeyman, P. [1980]. "Extension joins," *Proc. International Conference on Very Large Data Bases*, pp. 239–244.

Honeyman, P. [1982]. "Testing satisfaction of functional dependencies," to appear in *J. ACM*.

Honeyman, P., R. E. Ladner, and M. Yannakakis [1980]. "Testing the universal instance assumption," *Information Processing Letters* **10**:1, pp. 14–19.

Horowitz, E. and S. Sahni [1976]. *Fundamentals of Data Structures*, Computer Science Press, Rockville, Md.

Hsiao, D. K., D. S. Kerr, and S. E. Madnick [1978]. "Privacy and security of data communications and data bases," *Proc. International Conference on Very Large Data Bases*, pp. 55–67.

Hull, R. [1981]. "Acyclic join dependencies and database projections," unpublished memorandum, USC, Los Angeles, Calif.

Hunt, H. B. III and D. J. Rosenkrantz [1979]. "The complexity of testing predicate locks," *ACM SIGMOD International Symposium on Management of Data*, pp. 127–133.

IBM [1978a]. *Query-by Example terminal Users Guide*, SH20–2078-0, IBM, White Plains, N. Y.

IBM [1978b]. IMS/VS publications, especially GH20–1260 (*General Information*), SH20–9025 (*System/Application Design Guide*), SH20–9026 (*Application Programming Reference Manual*), and SH20–9027 (*Systems Programming Reference Manual*), IBM, White Plains, N. Y.

Jacobs, B. E. [1979]. On queries definable in database structures," TR 757, Dept. of Computer Science, Univ. of Maryland.

Jacobs, B. E. [1980]. "A generalized algebraic data manipulation language and the automatic conversion of its programs," *Proc. XP/1 Conf.*, Stony Brook, N. Y.

Jacobs, B. E. [1982]. "Database logic," to appear in *J. ACM*.

Johnson, D. S. and A. Klug [1982]. "Testing containment of conjunctive queries under functional and inclusion dependencies," *Proc. ACM Symposium on Principles of Database Systems*.

Kambayashi, Y. [1978]. "An efficient algorithm for processing multi-relation queries in relational databases," ER78–01, Dept. of Information Science, Kyoto Univ., Kyoto, Japan.

Kambayashi, Y. [1981]. *Database a Bibliography*, Computer Science Press, Rockville, Md.

Kam, J. B. and J. D. Ullman [1977]. "A model of statistical databases and their security," *ACM Transactions on Database Systems* **2**:1, pp. 1–10.

Kedem, Z. and A. Silberschatz [1979]. "Controlling concurrency using locking protocols." *Proc. Twentieth Annual IEEE Symposium on Foundations of Computer Science*, pp. 274–285.

Kedem, Z. and A. Silberschatz [1980]. "Non-two phase locking protocols with shared and exclusive locks," *Proc. International Conference on Very Large Data Bases*, pp. 309–320.

Keller, A. M. [1981]. "Updates to relational databases through views involving joins," unpublished memorandum, IBM, San Jose, Calif.

Kent, W. [1979]. "Limitations of record-based information models," *ACM Transactions on Database Systems* **4**:1, pp. 107–131.

Kent, W. [1981]. "Consequences of assuming a universal relation," *ACM Trans-*

actions on Database Systems **6**:4, pp. 539–556.

Kerschberg, L., A. Klug, and D. C. Tsichritzis [1977]. "A taxonomy of data models," in *Systems for Large Data Bases* (Lockemann and Neuhold, eds.), North Holland, Amsterdam, pp. 43–64.

Kim, W. [1979]. "Relational database systems," *Computing Surveys* **11**:3, pp. 185–210.

Kim, W. [1981]. "On optimizing an SQL-like nested query," RJ3063, IBM, San Jose, Calif.

Klug, A. [1981]. "Equivalence of relational algebra and relational calculus query languages having aggregate functions," to appear in *J. ACM.*

Klug, A. [1982]. "Inequality tableaux," to appear in *J. ACM.*

Knuth, D. E. [1968]. *The Art of Computer Programming*, Vol. 1, *Fundamental Algorithms*, Addison-Wesley, Reading Mass.

Knuth, D. E. [1973]. *The Art of Computer Programming*, Vol. 3, *Sorting and Searching*, Addison-Wesley, Reading Mass.

Korth, H. [1981]. "Locking protocols: general lock classes and deadlock freedom," Ph. D. thesis, Princeton Univ., Princeton, N. J.

Korth, H. F. and J. D. Ullman [1980]. "System/U: a database system based on the universal relation assumption," *Proc. XP/1 Conf.*

Kuck, S. M. and Y. Sagiv [1982]. "A universal relation database system implemented via the network model," *Proc. ACM Symposium on Principles of Database Systems.*

Kuhns, J. L. [1967]. "Answering questions by computer; a logical study," RM-5428-PR, Rand Corp., Santa Monica, Calif.

Kung, H.-T. and C. H. Papadimitriou [1979]. "An optimality theory of concurrency control for databases," *ACM SIGMOD International Symposium on Management of Data*, pp. 116–126.

Kung, H.-T. and J. T. Robinson [1981]. "On optimistic concurrency control," *ACM Transactions on Database Systems* **6**:2, pp. 213–226.

Lacroix, M. and A. Pirotte [1976]. "Generalized joins," *SIGMOD Record* **8**:3, pp. 14–15.

Lamport, L. [1978]. "Time, clocks, and the ordering of events in a distributed system," *Comm. ACM* **21**:7, pp. 558–565.

Lehman, P. L. and S. B. Yao [1981]. "Efficient locking for concurrent operations on B-trees," *ACM Transactions on Database Systems* **6**:4, pp. 650–670.

Lein, Y. E. [1979]. "Multivalued dependencies with null values in relational databases," *Proc. International Conference on Very Large Data Bases*, pp. 61–66.

Lien, Y. E. [1982]. "On the equivalence of database models," to appear in *J. ACM*.

Lien, Y. E. and P. J. Weinberger [1978]. "Consistency, concurrency and crash recovery," *ACM SIGMOD International Symposium on Management of Data*, pp. 9–14.

Ling, T. W., F. W. Tompa, and T. Kameda [1981]. "An improved third normal form for relational databases," *ACM Transactions on Database Systems* **6**:2, pp. 329–346.

Lipski, W. Jr. [1981]. "On databases with incomplete information," *J. ACM* **28**:1, pp. 41–70.

Liu, L. and A. Demers [1978]. "An efficient algorithm for testing lossless joins in relational databases," TR 78–351, Dept. of Computer Science, Cornell Univ.

Lucchesi, C. L. and S. L. Osborn [1978]. "Candidate keys for relations." *J. Computer and System Sciences* **17**:2, pp. 270–279.

Lueker, G. S. [1978]. "A data structure for orthogonal range queries," *Proc. Nineteenth Annual IEEE Symposium on Foundations of Computer Science*, pp. 28–33.

Lum, V. and H. Ling [1970]. "Multi-attribute retrieval with combined indices," *Comm. ACM* **13**:11, pp. 660–665.

Maier, D. [1980a]. "Discarding the universal instance assumption: preliminary results," *Proc. XP/1 Conf.*

Maier, D. [1980b]. "Minimum covers in the relational database model," *J. ACM* **27**:4, pp. 664–674.

Maier, D. [1982]. *Database Theory*. To appear, Computer Science Press, Rockville, Md.

Maier, D., A. O. Mendelzon, F. Sadri, and J. D. Ullman [1980]. "Adequacy of decompositions in relational databases," *J. Computer and System Sciences* **21**:3, pp. 368–379.

Maier, D., A. O. Mendelzon, and Y. Sagiv [1979]. "Testing implications of data dependencies," *ACM Transactions on Database Systems* **4**:4, pp. 455–469.

Maier, D., Y. Sagiv, and M. Yannakakis [1981]. "On the complexity of testing implications of functional and join dependencies," *J. ACM* **28**:4, pp. 680–695.

Maier, D. and J. D. Ullman [1980]. "Maximal objects and the semantics of universal relation databases," TR–80–016, Dept. of C. S., SUNY, Stony Brook, N. Y.

Maier, D. and J. D. Ullman [1981]. "Fragments of relations: first hack," *Proc. XP/2 Conf.*, State College, Pa.

Maier, D. and J. D. Ullman [1982]. "Connections in acyclic hypergraphs," *Proc. ACM Symposium on Principles of Database Systems.*

Maier, D. and D. S. Warren [1981]. "Specifying connections for a universal relation scheme database," unpublished memorandum, Dept. of CS, SUNY, Stony Brook, N. Y.

Martin, J. [1977]. *Computer Data Base Organization,* Prentice-Hall, Englewood Cliffs, New Jersey.

Maurer, W. D. and T. G. Lewis [1975]. "Hash table methods," *Computing Surveys* **7**:1, pp. 5–20.

McCracken, D. D. [1980]. "A guide to NOMAD for applications development," National CSS, Wilton, Conn.

McLean, G. [1981]. "Comments on SDD-1 concurrency control mechanisms," *ACM Transactions on Database Systems* **6**:2, pp. 347–350.

Menasce, D. A., G. J. Popek, and R. R. Muntz [1980]. "A locking protocol for resource coordination in distributed databases," *ACM Transactions on Database Systems* **5**:2, pp. 103–138.

Mendelzon, A. O. [1979]. "On axiomatizing multivalued dependencies in relational databases," *J. ACM* **26**:1, pp. 37–44.

Mendelzon, A. O. [1981]. "Database states and their tableaux," *Proc. XP/2 Conf.*, State College, Pa.

Mendelzon, A. O. and D. Maier [1979]. "Generalized mutual dependencies and the decomposition of database relations," *Proc. International Conference on Very Large Data Bases,* pp. 75–82.

Minker, J. [1978]. "Search strategy and selection function for an inferential relational system," *ACM Transactions on Database Systems* **3**:1, pp. 1–31.

Minoura, T. [1980]. "Resilient extended true-copy token algorithm for distributed database systems," Ph. D. Thesis, Dept. of EE, Stanford Univ., Stanford, Calif.

Moore, R. C. [1979]. "Handling complex queries in a distributed database," Tech. Note 170, AI, SRI Intl., Menlo park, Calif.

Morris, R. [1968]. "Scatter storage techniques," *Comm. ACM* **11**:1, pp. 38–43.

Mresse, M. [1978]. "Identification and authorization in data base systems," RJ2161, IBM, San Jose, Calif.

MRI [1978]. *System 2000 Reference manual,* MRI Systems Corp., Austin, Tex.

Nicolas, J. M. [1978]. "Mutual dependencies and some results on undecomposable relations," *Proc. International Conference on Very Large Data Bases,* pp. 360–367.

Nijssen, G. M. [1977]. "On the gross architecture for the next generation database management systems," *Proc. 1977 IFIP Congress,* pp. 327–335, North Holland, Amsterdam.

Nijssen, G. M. (ed.) [1976]. *Modeling in Data Base Management Systems,* North Holland, Amsterdam.

Olle, T. W. [1978]. *The Codasyl Approach to Data Base Management,* John Wiley and Sons, New York.

Osborn, S. L. [1977]. "Normal forms for relational databases," Ph. D. Thesis, Univ. of Waterloo.

Osborn, S. L. [1979]. "Towards a universal relation interface," *Proc. International Conference on Very Large Data Bases,* pp. 52–60.

Palermo, F. P. [1974]. "A database search problem," *Information Systems COINS IV* (J. T. Tou, ed.), Plenum Press, N. Y.

Paolini, P. and G. Pelagatti [1977]. "Formal definitions of mappings in a database," *ACM SIGMOD International Symposium on Management of Data,* pp. 40–46.

Papadimitriou, C. H. [1979]. "The serializability of concurrent database updates," *J. ACM* **26**:4, pp. 631–653.

Papadimitriou, C. H. [1981]. "Concurrency control by locking," unpublished memorandum, MIT LCS, Cambridge, Mass.

Papadimitriou, C. H. [1982]. "The power of locking," to appear in *J. ACM.*

Papadimitriou ,C. H., P. A. Bernstein, and J. B. Rothnie [1977]. "Computational problems related to database concurrency control," *Proc. Conf. on Theoretical Computer Science,* Univ. of Waterloo, Waterloo, Ont.

Paredaens, J. [1978]. "On the expressive power of relational algebra," *Inform-*

ation Processing Letters **7**:2, pp. 107–111.

Paredaens, J. [1981]. "A universal formalism to express decompositions, functional dependencies, and other constraints in a relational database," to appear in *TCS*.

Paredaens, J. and D. Jannsens [1980]. "Decompositions of relations: a comprehensive approach," in Gallaire, Minker, and Nicolas [1980].

Pecherer, R. M. [1975]. "Efficient evaluation of expressions in a relational algebra," *Proc. ACM Pacific Conf.*, pp. 44–49.

Perl, Y., A. Itai, and H. Avni [1978]. "Interpolation search—a log log n search," *Comm. ACM* **21**:7, pp. 550–553.

Pirotte, A. [1978]. "High level data base query languages," in Gallaire and Minker [1978], pp. 409–436.

Reis, D. R. and M. R. Stonebraker [1977]. "Effects of locking granularity in a database management system," *ACM Transactions on Database Systems* **2**:3, pp. 233–246.

Reis, D. R. and M. R. Stonebraker [1979]. "Locking granularity revisited," *ACM Transactions on Database Systems* **4**:2, pp. 210–227.

Reiss, S. P. [1979]. "Security in databses: a combinatorial study," *J. ACM* **26**:1, pp. 45–57.

Rissanen, J. [1977]. "Independent components of relations," *ACM Transactions on Database Systems* **2**:4, pp. 317–325.

Rissanen, J. [1979]. "Theory of joins for relational databases—a tutorial survey," *Proc. Seventh Symp. on Mathematical Foundations of C. S.*, Lecture notes in CS, **64**,Springer–Verlag, pp. 537–551.

Rivest, R. L. [1976]. "Partial match retrieval algorithms," *SIAM J. Computing* **5**:1, pp. 19–50.

Roberts, C. S. [1978]. "Partial match retrieval via the method of superimposed codes," unpublished manuscript, Bell Laboratories, Holmdel, N. J.

Rosenberg, A. L. and L. Snyder [1981]. "Time- and space-optimality in B-trees," *ACM Transactions on Database Systems* **6**:1, pp. 174–193.

Rosenkrantz, D. J., R. E. Stearns, and P. M. Lewis II [1978]. "System level concurrency control for distributed data base systems," *ACM Transactions on Database Systems* **3**:2, pp. 178–198.

Rothnie, J. B. Jr. et al. [1980]. "Introduction to a system for distributed databases (SDD-1)," *ACM Transactions on Database Systems* **5**:1, pp. 1–17.

Rothnie, J. B. Jr. and N. Goodman [1977]. "A survey of research and development in distributed database management," *Proc. International Conference on Very Large Data Bases,* pp. 48–62.

Rothnie, J. B. Jr. and T. Lozano [1974]. "Attribute based file organization in a paged memory environment," *Comm. ACM* **17**:2, pp. 63–69.

RSI [1980]. "ORACLE introduction," Relational Software, Inc., Menlo Park, Calif.

Rustin, R. (ed.) [1974]. *Proc. ACM/SIGMOD Conf. on Data Models: Data-Structure-Set vs. Relational,* ACM, New York.

Sadri, F. and J. D. Ullman [1980a]. "A complete axiomatization for a large class of dependencies in relational databases," *Proc. Twelfth Annual ACM Symposium on the Theory of Computing,* pp. 117–122.

Sadri, F. and J. D. Ullman [1980b]. "The interaction between functional dependencies and template dependencies," *ACM SIGMOD International Symposium on Management of Data,* pp. 45–51.

Sagiv, Y. [1981a]. "Can we use the universal instance assumption without using nulls?," *ACM SIGMOD International Symposium on Management of Data,* pp. 108–120.

Sagiv, Y. [1981b]. "A characterization of globally consistent databases and their correct access paths," unpublished memorandum, Univ. of Ill., Urbana, Ill.

Sagiv, Y., C. Delobel, D. S. Parker, and R. Fagin [1981]. "An equivalence between relational database dependencies and a fragment of propositional logic," *J. ACM* **28**:3, pp. 435–453.

Sagiv, Y. and S. Walecka [1982]. "Subset dependencies as an alternative to embedded multivalued dependencies," to appear in *J. ACM.*

Sagiv, Y. and M. Yannakakis [1981]. "Equivalence among relational expressions with the union and difference operators," *J. ACM* **27**:4, pp. 633–655.

Schenk, K. L. and J. R. Pinkert [1977]. "An algorithm for servicing multirelational queries," *ACM SIGMOD International Symposium on Management of Data,* pp. 10–19.

Schkolnick, M. and P. Sorenson [1981]. "The effects of denormalization on database performance," RJ3082, IBM, San Jose, Calif.

Schlörer, J. [1975]. "Identification and retrieval of personal records from a statistical data bank," *Methods of Inform. in Medicine* **14**:1, pp. 7–13.

Schlörer, J. [1976]. "Confidentiality of statistical records: a threat monitoring scheme for on-line dialogue," *Methods of Inform. in Medicine* **15**:1, pp. 36–42.

Schlörer, J. [1980]. "Disclosure from statistical databases: quantitative aspects of trackers," *ACM Transactions on Database Systems* **5**:4, pp. 467–492.

Schlörer, J. [1981]. "Security of statistical databases: multidimensional transformation," *ACM Transactions on Database Systems* **6**:1, pp. 95–112.

Schmid, H. A. and J. R. Swenson [1976]. "On the semantics of the relational model," *ACM SIGMOD International Symposium on Management of Data*, pp. 9–36.

Schmidt, J. W. [1977]. "Some high level language constructs for data of type relation," *ACM Transactions on Database Systems* **2**:3, pp. 247–261.

Sciore, E. [1979]. "Improving semantic specification in the database relational model," *ACM SIGMOD International Symposium on Management of Data*, pp. 170–178.

Sciore, E. [1980]. "The universal instance and database design," Ph. D. thesis, Princeton Univ., Princeton, N. J.

Sciore, E. [1981]. "Real-world MVD's," *ACM SIGMOD International Symposium on Management of Data*, pp. 121–132.

Sciore, E. [1982]. "A complete axiomatization for full join dependencies," to appear in *J. ACM*.

Selinger, P. G. and M. Adiba [1980]. "Access path selection in distributed database management systems," RJ2883, IBM, San Jose, Calif.

Shneiderman, B. (ed.) [1978]. *Database: Improving Usability and responsiveness*, Academic Press, New York.

Sibley, E. (ed.) [1976]. *Computer Surveys* **8**:1, March, 1976.

Silberschatz, A. and Z. Kedem [1980]. "Consistency in hierarchical database systems," *J. ACM* **27**:1, pp. 72–80.

Simpson, J. [1981]. "RELGRAF manual," Relational Sciences, Inc., Redwood City, Calif.

Skeen, D. and M. Stonebraker [1980]. "A formal model of crash recovery in a distributed system," UCB/ERL M80/48, Dept. of EECS, Univ. of California, Berkeley, Calif.

Smith, J. M. and P. Y. Chang [1975]. "Optimizing the performance of a relational algebra database interface," *Comm. ACM* **18**:10, pp. 568–579.

Smith, J. M. and D. C. P. Smith [1977]. "Database abstractions: aggregation and generalization," *ACM Transactions on Database Systems* **2**:2, pp. 105–133.

Snyder, L. [1978]. "On B-trees reexamined," *Comm. ACM* **21**:7, pp. 594.

Software AG [1978]. *ADABAS Introduction,* Software AG of North America, Reston, Va.

Soisalon-Soininen, E. and D. Wood [1982]. "An optimal algorithm for testing safety and detecting deadlocks," *Proc. ACM Symposium on Principles of Database Systems.*

Stearns, R. E., P. M. Lewis II, and D. J. Rosenkrantz [1976]. "Concurrency control for database systems," *Proc. Seventeenth Annual IEEE Symposium on Foundations of Computer Science,* pp. 19–32.

Stonebraker, M. [1975]. "Implementation of integrity constraints and views by query modification," *ACM SIGMOD International Symposium on Management of Data,* pp. 65–78.

Stonebraker, M. [1979]. "Concurrency control and consistency of multiple copies in distributed INGRES," *IEEE Trans. on Software Engineering* **SE-5**:3, pp. 188–194.

Stonebraker, M. [1980]. "Retrospection on a database system," *ACM Transactions on Database Systems* **5**:2, pp. 225–240.

Stonebraker, M. and L. A. Rowe [1977]. "Observations on data manipulation languages and their embedding in general purpose programming languages," TR UCB/ERL M77–53, Univ. of California, Berkeley, July, 1977.

Stonebraker, M. and P. Rubinstein [1976]. "The INGRES protection system," *Proc. ACM National Conf.,* pp. 80–84.

Stonebraker, M. and E. Wong [1974]. "Access control in a relational database management system by query modification," *Proc. ACM National Conf.,* pp. 180–187.

Stonebraker, M., E. Wong, P. Kreps, and G. Held [1976]. "The design and implementation of INGRES," *ACM Transactions on Database Systems* **1**:3, pp. 189–222.

Tanaka, K., Y. Kambayashi, and S. Yajima [1978]. "Properties of embedded multivalued dependencies in relational databases," to appear in *J. IECE,* Japan.

Thomas, R. H. [1975]. "A solution to the update problem for multiple copy databases which use distributed control," Rept. 3340, Bolt Beranek, and Newman, Cambridge, Mass.

Thomas, R. H. [1979]. "A majority consensus approach to concurrency control," *ACM Transactions on Database Systems* **4**:2, pp. 180–219.

Todd, S. J. P. [1976]. "The Peterlee relational test vehicle—a system overview," *IBM Systems J.* **15**:4, pp. 285–308.

Traub, J. F., H. Woźniakowski, and Y. Yemini [1981]. "Statistical security of a statistical database," unpublished memorandum, Dept. of Computer Science, Columbia Univ., New York, N. Y.

Tsichritzis, D. C. and F. H. Lochovsky [1977]. *Data Base Management Systems*, Academic Press, New York.

Tsichritzis, D. C. and F. H. Lochovsky [1982]. *Data Models*, Prentice-Hall, Englewood Cliffs, New Jersey.

Tsichritzis, D. and A. Klug (eds.) [1978]. *The ANSI/X3/SPARC Framework*, AFIPS Press, Montvale, N. J.

Ullman, J. D. [1981]. "A view of directions in relational database theory," *Automata, Languages, and Programming* (S. Even and O. Kariv, eds.), pp. 165–176, Springer-Verlag, New York.

Ullman, J. D. [1982]. "The U. R. strikes back," *Proc. ACM Symposium on Principles of Database Systems.*

Van de Reit, R. P., A. I. Wasserman, M. L. Kersten, and W. de Jonge [1981]. "High-level programming features for improving the efficiency of a relational database system," *ACM Transactions on Database Systems* **6**:3, pp. 464–485.

VanLeeuwen, J. [1979]. "On compromising statistical databases with a few known elements," *Information Processing Letters* **8**:3, pp. 149–153.

Vardi, M. [1982]. "The implication and finite implication problems for typed template dependencies," *Proc. ACM Symposium on Principles of Database Systems.*

Vardi, M. Y. [1980]. "Inferring multivalued dependencies from functional and join dependencies," unpublished memorandum, Weizmann Inst. of Science, Rehovot, Israel.

Vassiliou, Y. [1979]. "Null values in database management—a denotational semantics approach," *ACM SIGMOD International Symposium on Management of Data*, pp. 162–169.

Vassiliou, Y. [1980]. "Functional dependencies and incomplete information," *Proc. International Conference on Very Large Data Bases*, pp. 260–269.

Wiederhold, G. [1977]. *Database Design,* McGraw-Hill, New York.

Wiederhold, G. and R. El Masri [1980]. "The structural model for database design," in Chen [1980].

Willard, D. E. [1978a]. "New data structures for orthogonal range queries," TR–22–78, Aiken Computation Lab., Harvard Univ., Cambridge, Mass.

Willard, D. E. [1978b]. "Predicate-oriented database search algorithms," TR–20–78, Aiken Computation Lab., Harvard Univ., Cambridge, Mass.

Wong, E. and K. Youssefi [1976]. "Decomposition—a strategy for query processing," *ACM Transactions on Database Systems* 1:3, pp. 223–241.

Yannakakis, M. [1981a]. "Algorithms for acyclic database schemes," *Proc. International Conference on Very Large Data Bases,* pp. 82–94.

Yannakakis, M. [1981b]. "Issues of correctness in database concurrency control by locking," *Proc. Thirteenth Annual ACM Symposium on the Theory of Computing,* pp. 363–367.

Yannakakis, M. and C. H. Papadimitriou [1980]. "Algebraic dependencies," *Proc. Twenty-first Annual IEEE Symposium on Foundations of Computer Science,* pp. 328–332.

Yannakakis, M., C. H. Papadimitriou, and H.-T. Kung [1979]. "Locking policies: safety and freedom from deadlock," *Proc. Twentieth Annual IEEE Symposium on Foundations of Computer Science,* pp. 283–287.

Yao, A. C. [1978]. "On random 2–3 trees," *Acta Informatica* 9:2, pp. 159–170.

Yao, A. C. [1979]. "A note on a conjecture of Kam and Ullman concerning statistical databases." To appear in *Inf. Proccessing Letters.*

Yao, A. C. and F. F. Yao [1976]. "The complexity of searching an ordered random table," *Proc. Seventeenth Annual IEEE Symposium on Foundations of Computer Science,* pp. 173–177.

Yao, S. B. [1979]. "Optimization of query evaluation algorithms," *ACM Transactions on Database Systems* 4:2, pp. 133–155.

Yu, C. T. and F. Y. Chin [1977]. "A study on the protection of statistical databases," *ACM SIGMOD International Symposium on Management of Data,* pp. 169–181.

Yu, C. T. and M. Z. Ozsoyoglu [1979]. "An algorithm for tree-query membership of a distributed query," *Proc. IEEE COMPSAC,* pp. 306–312.

Zaniolo, C. [1976]. "Analysis and design of relational schemata for database systems," doctoral dissertation, UCLA, July, 1976.

Zaniolo, C. [1977]. "Relational views in a database system support for queries," *Proc. IEEE COMPSAC 77.*

Zaniolo, C. and M. A. Melkanoff [1981]. "On the design of relational database schemata," *ACM Transactions on Database Systems* **6**:1, pp. 1–47.

Zloof, M. M. [1975]. "Query-by-Example: operations on the transitive closure," IBM RC 5526, Yorktown Hts., N. Y.

Zloof, M. M. [1977]. "Query-by-Example: a data base language," *IBM Systems J.* **16**:4, pp. 324–343.

Zloof, M. M. [1978]. "Security and integrity within the Query-by-Example data base management language," IBM RC 6982, Yorktown Hts., N. Y.

Zook, W., K. Youssefi, N. Whyte, P. Rubinstein, P. Kreps, G. Held, J. Ford, R. Berman, and E. Allman [1977]. *INGRES Reference Manual,* Dept. of EECS, Univ. of California, Berkeley.

INDEX